天津城市文化简史

A Brief History of Tianjin Urban Culture

汉英对照　Chinese-English

刘悦　张畅 ｜ 著

天津社会科学院出版社

图书在版编目（CIP）数据

天津城市文化简史 ：汉英对照 / 刘悦，张畅著.

天津 ：天津社会科学院出版社，2025. 6. -- ISBN 978-
7-5563-1046-3

Ⅰ. K292.1

中国国家版本馆 CIP 数据核字第 2024ZG2912 号

天津城市文化简史

TIANJIN CHENGSHI WENHUA JIANSHI

选题策划：韩　鹏
责任编辑：李思文
责任校对：吴　琼
装帧设计：安　红
出版发行：天津社会科学院出版社
地　　址：天津市南开区迎水道 7 号
邮　　编：300191
电　　话：（022）23360165
印　　刷：北京盛通印刷股份有限公司
开　　本：880×1230　　1/12
印　　张：37
字　　数：750 千字
版　　次：2025 年 6 月第 1 版　　2025 年 6 月第 1 次印刷
定　　价：298.00 元

刘悦，1971 年生于天津，毕业于天津外国语学院、天津大学。天津社会科学发展研究中心主任、研究馆员。主要作品有《比利时在天津的历史遗迹》《胡佛的天梯》《清宫的门缝儿》《近代中国看天津：百项中国第一》《天津的桥》等。另有译著《罗尔夫·盖苓（1884—1952）——辗转于战争与几大洲之间的建筑师》《比利时—中国：昔日之路（1870—1930）》《林大人：清末高官比利时人保禄·林辅臣的生平》《扛龙旗的美国大兵：美国第十五步兵团在中国（1912—1938）》。

Liu Yue, born in Tianjin in 1971, graduated from Tianjin Foreign Languages Institute and Tianjin University. He is now the director and professor of Tianjin Social Science Development Research Center. His main works include: *Belgium's Historical Traces in Tianjin*, *Herbert Hoover's Heavenly Ladder*, *The Door Crack of the Qing Palace*, *Modern China through the Eyes of Tianjin—100 Chinese Firsts*, *The Bridges of Tianjin*, etc. He also has the translations of works: *Rolf Geyling (1884-1952): An Architect between Wars and Continents*, *A Belgian Passage to China (1870-1930)*, *The Belgian Mandarin: Paul Splingaerd*, *The United States 15th Infantry Regiment in China 1912~1938*.

张畅，1973 年生于天津，南开大学社会学学士、硕士，历史学博士，天津大学马克思主义学院副教授。长期从事天津城市史研究以及近代来华外国侨民口述史资料的搜集整理工作。主要作品有《李鸿章的洋顾问：德璀琳与汉纳根》《比利时在天津的历史遗迹》。另有译著《比利时—中国：昔日之路（1870—1930）》等。参与撰写的《近代中国看天津：百项中国第一》一书获 2008 年度天津市社会科学优秀成果二等奖。

Zhang Chang, born in Tianjin in 1973, holds a Bachelor degree and master degree in sociology, and a PhD in history from Nankai University. She is an associate professor in the School of Marxism of Tianjin University. She has been engaged in researching the urban history of Tianjin and collecting and organizing the oral history of foreigners who came to China in modern times. Her main works include: *Li Hongzhang's Foreign Advisors: Gustav Detring and Constantin von Hanneken*, *Belgium's Historical Traces in Tianjin*. Her translations include *A Belgian Passage to China (1870-1930)*, etc. Her co-authored book *Modern China through the Eyes of Tianjin—100 Chinese Firsts* won the second prize of 2008 Tianjin Social Science Excellent Achievements.

所谓城市文化，通俗地讲就是指人们在城市长期的生活过程中，共同创造的物质和精神产品，是城市生活环境、生活方式和生活习俗的总和。其中物质产品包括城市中的居住、宗教、实业建筑、教育文化娱乐设施、道路与交通工具等；精神产品则是指政治、经济、金融、宗教、新闻媒体以及城市居民的生活方式、习俗等。本书就是从空间和时间两个维度，将上述的物质、精神产品做了一个系统的梳理和介绍，给读者全面呈现出天津的近代城市文化、建设成就和发展脉络。

天津是一个既有文化又有历史的城市。相对于我国五千年文明而言，距今只有六百多年的建城历史虽然是非常短暂的，但其中蕴含的文化内涵却异常丰富。天津是我国近代洋务运动、清末新政的策源地，也是第二次鸦片战争、义和团战争期间的重灾区，更是世界上绝无仅有的拥有九国租界的城市。正所谓中国"近代百年历史看天津"，我国近代史中的政治、经济、军事、科教、文化以及城市建设、生活方式等方面的近代化转型与现代化发展，都丰富多彩而又淋漓尽致地反映在天津城市文化之中。

从历史角度看天津城市文化发展，大致可以分为五个时期：1404 年以前为城市产生的萌芽期，天津所在地区出现了聚居的村落，但还没形成城市级规模。1404—1860 年，天津古代城市建设和本土文化的发展期。1404 年 12 月 23 日（明永乐二年十一月二十一日）天津正式筑城。在以后的 450 多年间，三岔河口、老城厢、天后宫、

The so-called urban culture, in simple terms, refers to the material and spiritual products created collectively by people in the long-term process of urban living. It encompasses the sum of urban living environment, lifestyle, and customs. The material products include aspects such as residential, religious, industrial buildings, educational and cultural entertainment facilities, roads, and transportation tools within the city. Spiritual products refer to politics, economy, finance, religion, news media, as well as the lifestyle and customs of urban residents. This book systematically organizes and introduces these material and spiritual products from the dimensions of space and time, presenting readers with a comprehensive view of Tianjin's modern urban culture, construction achievements, and development context.

Tianjin is a city with both cultural and historical significance. Despite its relatively short history of over six hundred years, compared to China's five thousand years of civilization, it is rich in cultural content. Tianjin played a crucial role in China's modern Westernization Movement and late Qing Dynasty reforms. It was also heavily affected during the Second Opium War and the Boxer Rebellion, making it a unique city with concessions from nine different countries. As the saying goes, "To understand China's past hundred years of modern history, look to Tianjin." The city vividly reflects the diverse and thorough transformations in politics, economy, military, education, culture, urban development, and lifestyle during China's modern and contemporary history.

From a historical perspective, the development of Tianjin's urban culture can be broadly divided into five periods. Before 1404: The embryonic period of urban development when the region where Tianjin is located witnessed the emergence of settled villages, although a city-level scale had not yet formed. From 1404 to 1860: The development period of ancient Tianjin urban construction and the development period of local culture. On December 23, 1404 (the twenty-first day of the eleventh month in the second year of

河北大街、大胡同一带成为当时天津人的主要聚集地。1860—1937年，是近代天津快速发展时期，也是近代天津城市文化的成熟期。1860年第二次鸦片战争以后，中英、中法签署《北京条约》，增开天津为商埠。在这个时期天津的城市建设和中心转向租界地，形成九国租界的城市格局。中西文化在此碰撞、交融并积淀而成近代天津城市文化特色。1937—1949年，是近代天津建设停滞时期。七七事变后日军占领天津，寓津的商贾、侨民、名流以及金融、实业、高校等纷纷南渡或西迁，撤离天津，窒碍了天津城市的发展。1945年抗战胜利，尤其1949年之后，天津进入了发展的新时期。

天津近代城市建设和文化发展，孕育出丰富的物质和非物质文化遗产。这些遗产既是城市文化的重要载体，也是城市文化保护的主要对象。1986年，天津被国务院列为以近代史迹为特色的第二批历史文化名城。天津市委、市政府高度重视历史风貌建筑和风貌街区的保护工作。1998年，市政府成立了"天津市保护风貌建筑领导小组"。2003年，"天津市保护风貌建筑办公室"成立，负责历史风貌建筑保护管理。2005年2月，"天津市历史风貌建筑保护委员会"成立。3月，"天津市历史风貌建筑保护专家咨询委员会"成立。7月，天津市人大常委会通过了《天津市历史风貌建筑保护条例》（以下简称《条例》）。按照《条例》的规定，经专家咨询委员会审查，天津市政府于2005—2013年分六批确认了天津历史风貌建筑877幢、126万平方米；2006年3月，国务院批准的天津市城市总体规划的历史文化名城规划中，确定了14片历史文化风貌保护区，大部分历史风貌建筑就坐落在这些历史文化风貌保护区内；2006—2021年，国务院批准命名了五批国家级非物质文化遗产代表性项目名录和扩展项目名录，天津有49项入选。2007—2022年，天津市公布了五批357项市级非遗项目，区级项目更是不胜枚举。纵观之，可以说2005年是天津市文化遗产保护的转折之年，自此以后，天津市对于城市文化遗产保护的意识和力度都得到了很大提升。

the Ming Dynasty Yongle era), Tianjin was officially established as a walled city. Over the next 450 years, areas like Sancha estuary, Old City, Tianhou Temple, Hebei Avenue, and Dahutong area became the main gathering places for the people of Tianjin during that time. From 1860 to 1937: The period of rapid modern development in Tianjin and the maturity of modern urban culture. After the Second Opium War in 1860, the *Convention of Peking* were signed between China and Great Britain, and China and France, leading to the opening of Tianjin as a commercial port. During this period, the city's construction shifted towards the concession areas, forming the urban pattern of nine foreign concessions. Modern Tianjin urban culture characteristics were shaped through the collision, fusion, and accumulation of Chinese and Western cultures during this time. From 1937 to 1949: The period of stagnation in modern Tianjin construction. After the Marco Polo Bridge Incident in 1937, Japanese forces occupied Tianjin. Merchants, expatriates, elites, as well as financial, industrial, and academic institutions migrated south or west, hindering the city's development. After the victory in the War of Resistance Against Japanese Aggression in 1945, especially after 1949, Tianjin entered a new era of development.

Tianjin's modern urban construction and cultural development have given birth to rich tangible and intangible cultural heritage. These heritages serve not only as crucial carriers of urban culture but also as primary objects of urban cultural preservation. In 1986, Tianjin was designated by the State Council as the second batch of historical and cultural cities featuring modern historical sites. The Tianjin Municipal Party Committee and Municipal Government attach great importance to the protection of historical architectural features and streetscapes. In 1998, the municipal government established the "Leadership Group for the Protection of Tianjin Historical and Stylistic Architecture." In 2003, the "Office for the Protection of Tianjin Historical and Stylistic Architecture" was established, responsible for the management of historical architectural features protection. In February 2005, the "Tianjin Historical and Stylistic Architecture Protection Committee" was established, followed by the establishment of the "Tianjin Historical and Stylistic Architecture Protection Specialist Consultative Committee" in March and the approval of the *Regulations on the Protection of Tianjin Historical and Stylistic Architecture* by the Tianjin Municipal People's Congress Standing Committee in July. According to the provisions of the regulations, and after examination by the Specialist Consultative Committee, the Tianjin municipal government confirmed 877 Historical and Stylistic Architectures covering an area of 1.26 million square meters in six batches from 2005 to 2013. In March 2006, as part of the overall urban planning approved by the State Council, 14

文化遗产保护工作离不开学者们对文化遗产的挖掘整理。从事天津历史和文化研究的团队包括天津社会科学发展研究中心（原近代天津博物馆）、天津大学、南开大学、天津师范大学、天津社会科学院、天津博物馆、天津市档案馆等高等院校和科研院所中的专家学者，还有一大批民间志愿者也发挥了重要的作用。张畅老师是我所属意的《中国近代第一所大学——北洋大学（天津大学）历史档案珍藏图录》一书的主要执笔人和文献挖掘者，我曾邀请她到建筑学院授课，同时也了解到她长期深耕于天津城市史研究领域，与我所从事的天津近代城市与建筑等物质文化遗产研究与保护工作具有很大程度的交汇叠合，因此她的新著《天津城市文化简史》邀请我作序，大致就是出自这个原因。正如作者所言，这是一本行文流畅、图文并茂的普及性读物，但也不乏新的叙事角度和观点考证。希望此书对不同类型的读者都能有所裨益，对传播天津城市文化发挥一定的作用。

天津大学建筑学院原院长　宋昆

2024 年 9 月

areas for the protection of historical and cultural landscapes were designated, with most historical and stylistic architectures located within these protected zones. From 2006 to 2021, the State Council approved and named five batches of national-level intangible cultural heritage representative projects list and expansion projects list, with Tianjin having 49 entries. Between 2007 and 2022, Tianjin also announced five batches of 357 municipal-level intangible cultural heritage projects, with numerous district-level projects as well. Looking back, it can be said that the year 2005 was a turning point for cultural heritage preservation in Tianjin. Since then, the city's awareness and efforts toward the preservation of urban cultural heritage have seen significant improvement.

The protection of cultural heritage work relies heavily on scholars' exploration and organization of cultural heritage. Teams engaged in the research of Tianjin's history and culture include experts and scholars from higher education institutions and research institutes such as Tianjin Social Science Development Research Center (former Tianjin Museum of Modern History), Tianjin University, Nankai University, Tianjin Normal University, Tianjin Academy of Social Sciences, Tianjin Museum, and Tianjin Municipal Archives. A large number of grassroots volunteers also play a crucial role. Professor Zhang Chang, who is the main author and document excavator of my favorite book *Collection of Historical Archives of Peiyang University (Tianjin University) - the First University of Modern China*, was invited by me to give a lecture at the School of Architecture. I also found out that she has long been dedicated to the research of Tianjin urban history, which intersects significantly with my work on the research and preservation of material cultural heritage such as modern urban architecture in Tianjin. It is for this reason that she invited me to write a foreword to her new book, *A Brief History of Tianjin Urban Culture*. As the authors mentioned, it's a smooth, well-illustrated, popular read, but not without new narrative perspectives and examinations of viewpoints. I hope this book will be beneficial to different types of readers and contribute to the dissemination of Tianjin urban culture.

Former Dean, School of Architecture, Tianjin University
Song Kun
September 2024

海河夜景。刘悦摄
Nightview of the Hai River. Taken by Liu Yue

第一章　城市的起源与早期历史
Chapter One: The Origin and Early History of Tianjin

第二章　中西碰撞与城市空间的扩张

Chapter Two: Collision between China and the West and the Expansion of Urban Space

第三章　交通、贸易与城市的发展

Chapter Three: Transportation, Trade, and Urban Development

第四章　技术革新与城市的变革

Chapter Four: Technological Innovation and Urban Transformation

第五章　人口、阶层与城市的族群

Chapter Five: Population, Class, and Urban Ethnic Groups

第六章　国际政治与城市里的革命
Chapter Six: International Politics and Revolution in the City

第七章　国际战争与城市的沦陷

Chapter Seven: International Wars and the Fall of the City

第八章　中西合璧的近代天津城市文化

Chapter Eight: The Modern Tianjin Urban Culture with a Fusion of Chinese and Western Elements

1864 年，普魯士畫家坐在天津城墻上繪制的天津東門里附近的城市景觀
In 1864, a Prussian artist sat on the old city wall of Tianjin, depicting the urban scene around the inner East Gate.

大清帝国官兵在天津城外迎接英国使团的船只
The Qing officers and soldiers greeted the British envoy's
ships outside Tianjin City

第 一 章　城市的起源与早期历史

Chapter One: The Origin and Early History of Tianjin

天津的沧海桑田	The Changing Landscape of Tianjin
天津的早期繁荣	Tianjin's Early Prosperity
早期与外界的接触	Early Contacts with the Outside World

城市，在中国历史上占有非常重要的地位。中国古代一直存在相当大的城池，它们一般都是一个政权的首都或者一个区域的行政中心，同时有大量军队驻防，比如长安、洛阳、邯郸、南京等。隋唐以来的城市兴起，则与防卫和贸易有关。中国历朝历代几乎都面临北方少数民族的骚扰和威胁，自秦、汉、三国乃至唐、宋、明等朝代，均在北方屯以重兵，甚至不惜耗费大量人力物力修筑长城和大运河，特别是运河，对中古城市的发展意义重大。隋朝结束了南北朝的长期分裂状态之后，开始兴修大运河，以使军粮北运，运河沿岸的城镇随之发展起来，比如今杭州、扬州、开封、北京等。在近代，两次鸦片战争之后，沿海和沿江的大量小城镇由于重要的地理位置而被迫开放为通商口岸，进而壮大为近代城市，如香港、上海、天津、汉口等。

晚清以来，中国的城市不仅数量逐渐增加，规模也日益扩大。近代的中国城市，不断接受着欧风美雨的侵袭和浸润，成为工业化产生的摇篮、新观念传播的温床、各种新事物发展的试验场。它是如此令人耳目一新，强烈地冲击并改变着以农耕文明为传统的中国社会。快速的工业化、城市化进程，与农村的长期停滞形成了强烈对比，农民不断涌入城市成为新的市民阶层，进而演化出复杂的社会结构和城市体系，一系列变化令人意识到一个崭新时代的到来。到了这个阶段，中国的城市开始迈向了现代化的发展轨道。

天津的沧海桑田

从地质学理论上讲，天津既是一片退海之地，又是黄河、海河等水系所形成的冲积平原。五六千年以前，大海最后一次后退，构

Cities hold a crucial position in the history of China. Ancient China had numerous significant cities, often serving as the capital of a dynasty or as an administrative center for a region. These cities also housed substantial military forces, such as Chang'an, Luoyang, Handan, Nanjing, and others. The rise of cities since the Sui and Tang Dynasties was associated with defense and trade. Throughout Chinese history, various dynasties faced harassment and threats from minority ethnic groups in the north. Starting from the Qin, Han, Three Kingdoms, and continuing to the Tang, Song, Ming Dynasties, considerable military forces were stationed in the northern regions, with extensive human and material resources invested in the construction of the Great Wall and the Grand Canal. Particularly, the Grand Canal played a significant role in the development of medieval cities. Following the end of the Southern and Northern Dynasties' prolonged period of division, the Sui Dynasty initiated the construction of the Grand Canal to facilitate the northward transport of military provisions. As a result, cities along the canal began to flourish, including present-day Hangzhou, Yangzhou, Kaifeng, Beijing, and others. In modern times, after the two Opium Wars, numerous small towns along the coast and rivers were forced to open up as trading ports due to their strategic locations. Subsequently, they expanded into modern cities, examples being Hong Kong, Shanghai, Tianjin (or Tientsin, based on the 'Wade-Giles' transliteration system), Hankou, and others.

Since the late Qing Dynasty, the number and scale of cities in China have been gradually increasing. Modern Chinese cities have been undergoing the influence and infiltration of Western styles and ideas, becoming the cradle of industrialization, the incubator for the dissemination of new concepts, and the experimental ground for the development of various new phenomena. They have brought a refreshing and impactful change to the traditionally agrarian Chinese society. The rapid processes of industrialization and urbanization, in stark contrast to the long stagnation in rural areas, have led to a continuous influx of farmers into cities, forming a new urban citizen class. This, in turn, has evolved into a complex social structure and urban system. A series of

天津贝壳堤与美国路易斯安纳州贝壳堤、南美苏里南贝壳堤并称世界三大古贝壳堤。其中所含贝壳达数十种，按层序分布排列，绵延数十千米。张焘在《津门杂记》中曾说："咸水沽在城东南五十里，该处左近旧有蚌壳满地，深阔无涯，至今不朽，想昔日之海滩即在此无疑也。"〔光绪十年(1884年)印〕。张畅摄于2021年

Tianjin shell ridge, along with the Louisiana shell ridge in the United States and Suriname shell ridge in South America, are known as the world's three ancient shell embankments. They all contain dozens of types of shells, arranged in sequence and extending for tens of kilometers. Zhang Tao wrote in his book *Miscellaneous Notes of Tianjin*: "Xianshuigu Town is located fifty li (1 li equals 500 meters) southeast of the city, where there used to be clamshells covering the deep and boundless ground, of which many can still be seen today. It undoubtedly used to be the location of the beach in the past." [printed in the 10th year (1884) of Emperor Guangxu] Taken by Zhang Chang in 2021

成天津市区的陆地渐渐地从海底露出。来自内陆高原的黄河三次改道由天津入海，带来成千上万吨泥沙，淤积在这片海底。而华北平原上的其他许多河流也纷纷辗转流经这里，在最后东流入海之前，将它们带来的泥沙留下来，贡献于这片土地。一进一退之间，自然地理意义上的天津诞生了。

从大禹治水到天津建城

天津这片土地，从诞生之日起，就形成了其"河海要冲"得天独厚的地理位置，这为它日后的发展奠定了基础。天津的重要性在于它是南北物资集散和军粮转运的重要港口。

传说中，大禹治水成功后，天津地区舟船经黄河入冀州的水运活动就已经开始了。中国古代几位开疆拓土的著名帝王将相为了建立不朽霸业，都在天津留下过他们的印迹。

第一位是秦始皇。公元前215年，秦始皇命蒙恬将军发兵30万

changes have made people realize the advent of a new era. At this stage, Chinese cities have begun to move towards the development trajectory of modernization.

The Changing Landscape of Tianjin

From a geological perspective, Tianjin is both a receding sea area and an alluvial plain formed by water systems such as the Yellow River and the Hai River. Five to six thousand years ago, the sea receded for the last time, gradually exposing the land in the Tianjin urban area from the seabed. The Yellow River, originating from the inland plateau, changed its course three times to flow into the sea at Tianjin, bringing thousands of tons of silt that accumulated on the seabed. Many other rivers from the North China Plain also flowed through this area, depositing the sediment they carried before ultimately flowing eastward into the sea. Between the advances and retreats, the Tianjin we know in terms of natural geography came into existence.

From Da Yu's Flood Control to Tianjin's City Building

Since its birth, the land of Tianjin has formed its unique geographical location as a "river and sea hub", which has laid the foundation for its future development. The importance of Tianjin lies in the fact that it is an important port for the distribution of materials and military supplies between the north and the south.

Legend has it that after Da Yu succeeded in controlling the floods, the water transportation activities of boats from Tianjin area to Jizhou (Hebei Province) via the Yellow River had already begun. Several famous emperors, generals and ministers who opened up new territories in ancient China all left their marks in Tianjin in order to establish immortal hegemony.

The first one is Emperor Qin Shi Huang. In 215 BC, Qin Shi Huang ordered General Meng Tian to send 300,000 troops to the north to attack the Xiongnu, regain the Hetao area south of the Yellow River, and then garrison there. In order to solve the problem of food and wages in the north, Emperor Qin Shi Huang opened up the northern sea route, using Huang county, Chui county, and Langya county in present-day Shandong Province as logistics ports. He mobilized ships to enter the Bohai Sea, enter the ancient Yellow River from Tianjin, and then go up the river to continuously transport grain and grass, to where Meng Tian's army was stationed.

The second one is Emperor Wu of Han Dynasty. In 110 BC, Emperor Wu of the Han Dynasty made his first eastward sea patrol in order to open up a

北击匈奴，收复黄河以南河套地区之后驻军当地。为了解决北方粮饷，秦始皇又开辟北方航路，以今山东省境内的黄县、腄县、琅琊为后勤港，征调船只入渤海，自天津进入古黄河，然后溯河而上，将粮草源源不断地运抵蒙恬大军驻地。

第二位是汉武帝。公元前110年，汉武帝为打通东渡日本的航线，首次东巡海上，由山东东莱海边起航，沿渤海巡行一直到碣石，然后又向东巡察辽西后返回。他派出的船队则继续向东寻找通往日本的水路。之后，汉武帝派军队远征卫氏朝鲜，最终打通渡日航线。为了航线的畅通，他还在今天津区划内的渤海湾西岸设立了四座城池。每座城池相距约50千米，规模近25万平方米。

第三位是曹操。为了统一北方的战争需要，自公元206年开始，曹操征集军民开凿一系列运河，将华北平原上本来自成体系、单独入海的几条河流勾连在一起汇入海河，初步形成了今天呈扇面形的海河水系。这使今天津附近的水路同四面八方连在一起，便利了水运交通，天津地区作为北方航运枢纽的重要地位孕育成形。

第四位是隋炀帝。隋朝统一中国后，为沟通南北、转运军需物资，隋炀帝于公元605年、608年先后开通两条运河，打通今日南至杭州北达北京全长2400多千米的京杭大运河。这样，长江、淮河、黄河、海河四大水系的船舶均可直达今天津，由此转输今北京。

第五位是元世祖忽必烈。忽必烈定今北京为大都，进而统一中国，建立了一个融合欧亚的大帝国。为了满足大都日常的庞大需要，银钱谷米、盐茶丝绢等源源不断地从南方运来。初期只是依靠京杭大运河的河运，之后又增加了由今上海至天津的海运。无论河运、海运，均须汇聚于今天津地区的直沽港再行转运大都。这样，天津地区在沟通南北经济、满足朝廷所需、繁荣首都商业以及转运军需物资方面发挥了极大的作用。

第六位是明成祖朱棣。"天津"这个城市的正式建立，就是由他开始。公元1403年，朱棣将北平改称北京，下令把首都从南京迁到他的"龙兴之地"——北京。美其名曰：天子戍边，即皇帝亲自防卫来自北方蒙古的威胁。公元1406年，朱棣着手筹备北京城的营造工程，直至1420年方告完工；1421年，正式迁都北京。与此同时，

route east to Japan. He set sail from the seaside of Donglai, Shandong, and patrolled along the Bohai Sea to Jieshi. Then he headed east to inspect western Liaoning and returned. The fleet he sent continued eastward to find a waterway to Japan. Afterwards, Emperor Wu sent troops to attack Wiman Joseon by land and water, and finally opened up a route to Japan. In order to smooth the shipping routes, he also established four forts on the west coast of the Bohai Bay within the present-day Tianjin. Each fort is about 50 kilometers apart and covers an area of nearly 250,000 square meters.

The third one is Cao Cao. In order to meet the military needs of unifying the northern regions, starting from the year 206 AD, Cao Cao mobilized both the military and civilians to excavate a series of canals. These canals interconnected several originally independent rivers on the North China Plain, which individually flowed into the sea, directing them into the Hai River. This initiative laid the foundation for the fan-shaped Hai River system seen today. This interconnection of waterways near present-day Tianjin facilitated water transportation, and the strategic position of Tianjin area as a crucial hub for northern navigation began to take shape.

The fourth one is Emperor Yang of Sui Dynasty. After unifying China during the Sui Dynasty, Emperor Yang initiated the construction of two canals in the years 605 and 608 AD, respectively. These canals were intended to connect the north and south and facilitate the transportation of military supplies. They successfully opened up what is known today as the Grand Canal, stretching over 2,400 kilometers from the south in Hangzhou to the north in Beijing. As a result, vessels from the Yangtze River, the Huai River, the Yellow River, and the Hai River systems could all reach present-day Tianjin directly, enabling the transfer of goods to present-day Beijing.

The fifth one is Kublai Khan, the founder of the Yuan Dynasty. Kublai Khan established present-day Beijing as the capital, further unifying China and creating an empire that integrated Europe and Asia. To meet the vast daily needs of the capital, a continuous flow of silver, coins, grain, salt, tea, silk, and other goods were transported from the south. Initially the river transport through the Grand Canal was the main way, later on, maritime transport from present-day Shanghai to Tianjin was also added. Whether by river or sea, all goods had to converge at the Zhigu trading port of present-day Tianjin area before being transported to the capital, Dadu (present-day Beijing). This way, Tianjin area played a significant role in facilitating the communication between the northern and southern economies, meeting the needs of the imperial court, fostering the prosperity of the capital's commerce, and transferring military supplies.

The sixth one is Emperor Chengzu of the Ming Dynasty, Zhu Di. The

公元1404年（永乐二年），朱棣下旨在直沽筑城设卫，并赐名"天津"，这就是天津正式建城的开始。[①]

"天津"名字的由来

关于这个名字的含义，有三种说法。第一种是意为"天子车驾渡河处"：公元1400年，长期驻守北方的燕王朱棣起兵，与自己的侄子建文帝争夺皇位。他率兵由直沽渡河南下，一路势如破竹，直至1402年夺取政权，因此命名"天津"以纪念南下的胜利。第二种是指"通向天子京城的津梁"：从元朝开始，凡是外国使臣去往觐见皇帝的途中，必须在天津等候皇帝的召见，而其他传教士、商人、旅游者等沿水路进出北京时，也须经过天津，"天津"由此得名。第三种说法是，天津之名来源于天上星宿的名字。在《史记》《汉书》《晋书》《隋书》《宋史》等史书的天文志部分都有关于"天津"这个星宿名称的记载，由此清乾隆年间的《天津县志》以此作为天津地名由来的解释。

自1404年起，天津开始修筑土城，至1425年完成。自此，天津成为一个屏障京城、保卫粮仓的卫戍重镇，负责保障北京的物资供应。明朝政府先后设天津左卫、武清卫、天津右卫共三卫，驻兵16800人，兼有屯田守卫之责，管辖海河以南沿南运河至德州以东地区。在1564年以前，天津只设武官，没有文官，这说明了天津早期的城市性质，即保卫首都的军镇。

天津的早期繁荣

有明一代，天津的卫制都保持不变。直到清初的顺治九年（1652年），裁"天津左卫、右卫归并天津卫"。雍正三年（1725年）"改天津卫为州"，隶属于河间府，雍正九年（1731年），天津升州为府，下辖六县一州，即天津县、青县、静海县、南皮县、盐山县、庆云

formal establishment of the city of "Tianjin" began under his reign. In the year 1403 AD, Zhu Di changed the name of Beiping to Beijing and ordered the capital to be moved from Nanjing to his "Dragon Rising" site—Beijing. The official reason was stated as the emperor personally defending against threats from the north, specifically the Mongols. In 1406 AD, Zhu Di initiated the construction of Beijing, a project that continued until 1420 when it was completed. In 1421, the capital was officially moved to Beijing. Concurrently, in the year 1404 (the second year of the Yongle era), Zhu Di ordered the construction of a city and defense system in present-day Tianjin, giving it the name "Tianjin." This marks the official beginning of the establishment of Tianjin as a city.[①]

The Origin of the Name "Tianjin"

There are three theories about the meaning of this name. The first one means "the place where the emperor's chariots cross the river": In 1400, Prince of Yan, Zhu Di, who had been stationed in the north for a long time, raised an army to compete with his nephew Emperor Jianwen for the throne. He led his troops from Zhigu across the river to the south, going all the way with unstoppable momentum until he seized power in 1402, so he named "Tianjin" to commemorate the victory of the southward march. The second theory refers to "the bridge leading to the emperor's capital": starting from the Yuan Dynasty, all foreign envoys on their way to see the emperor had to wait for the emperor's summons in Tianjin. And other missionaries, business men, tourists also had to pass through Tianjin when entering and leaving Beijing by waterway, hence the name "Tianjin". The third theory is that the name of Tianjin comes from the names of the stars in the sky. There are records about the name of the constellation "Tianjin" in the astronomical records of historical books such as *Shiji* (Historical Records), *Hanshu* (History of the Former Han Dynasty), *Jinshu* (History of the Jin Dynasty), *Suishu* (History of the Sui Dynasty) and *Songshi* (History of the Song Dynasty). Therefore, the *Tianjin County Chronicle* written during the Qianlong period of the Qing Dynasty used this as an explanation for the origin of Tianjin's place name.

Starting from 1404, Tianjin began to build rammed earth city walls which were completed in 1425. Since then, Tianjin has become an important garrison town that shields the capital, protects granaries, and is responsible for ensuring Beijing's material supply. The Ming Dynasty government successively established three guards, Tianjin Left Guard, Wuqing Guard and Tianjin Right Guard, with 16,800 troops stationed. They also had the responsibility of farm-

---

① 《明太宗实录》卷三六（五），第0628页。

① *Veritable Records of the Ming Emperor Taizong*, vol.36, p.0628 (5).

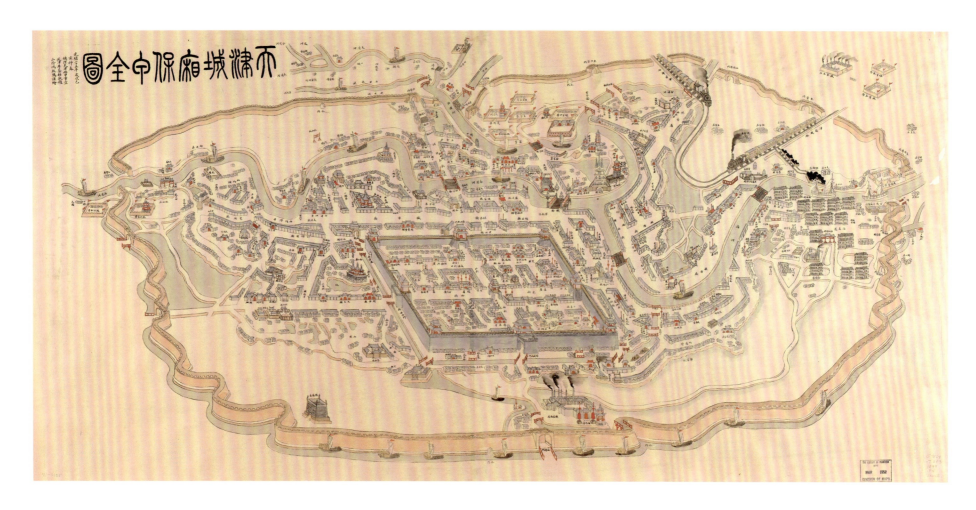

《天津城廂保甲全圖》。本圖大致以北為上方；全圖以俯瞰天津城廂保甲的形式繪制；圖中不注比例，方位亦不甚講究。圖面主要以天津舊城內外為范圍，描繪境內海河、南北大運河沿岸的街巷、建築景觀；另繪出官衙、寺廟、工廠、租界、洋房、橋梁等建築物以及河道分布。環城南、北運河均為京杭運河的北段，為溝通山東、北京的河道，運河中商帆絡繹，凸顯天津之商務繁忙。圖中東北方的津盧鐵路〔天津至北京西郊盧溝橋；光緒二十一年（1895 年）建，兩年后通車。該路段是向英國貸款四十萬英鎊興建，開了借洋債築路的先例〕、津榆鐵路〔在唐胥鐵路的基礎上進行擴展，南至津沽鐵路上的林西鎮，北至山海關（又稱榆關）；光緒十六年（1890 年）動工，二十年（1894 年）春通車，全長 127 千米，后為京奉鐵路的一段；是清朝最早修建的鐵路之一〕刻意放大，而不拘實際比例。全圖反映天津開埠后城市的發展變化，是近代中國城市景觀地圖的代表作。左方落款"光緒二十五年（1899 年）歲次己亥仲春 總理天津保甲事宜延津李蔭梧敬題 山陰馮啟鵾謹繪"

Complete Map of the Community Self-defense System of the Walled City of Tianjin and Its Environs. This map is roughly oriented with the north at the top; the whole map is drawn in the form of a bird's-eye view of Tianjin City; the scale of map is not indicated, and the direction is not very accurate. It mainly covers the interior and exterior of the old Tianjin city, depicting not only the streets, alleys and architectural landscapes along the Hai River and the Northern and Southern Grand Canal; but also the buildings such as government offices, temples, factories, concessions, western-style houses, bridges, and the distribution of waterways. The Northern and Southern Canal around city are both the northern sections of the whole Grand Canal, which connect the rivers of Shandong and Beijing. The canals are filled with merchant sailors, highlighting Tianjin's busy business environment. Tianjin-Marco Polo Bridge Railway in northeast [from Tianjin to Marco Polo Bridge, the western suburbs of Beijing; built in the 21st year of Emperor Guangxu's reign (1895), and opened to traffic two years later. This section of the road was built with a loan of £400,000 from the United Kingdom, setting a precedent for borrowing foreign debt to build railways]. Tianjin-Yuguan Railway [extended on the Tang-Xu Railway, south to Linxi Town on the Tianjin-Tanggu Railway, and north to Shanhaiguan (also known Yuguan); construction began in the 16th year of Emperor Guangxu (1890), and opened to traffic in the spring of the 20th year of Emperor Guangxu (1894); with a total length of 127 kilometers, and later became a section of the Beijing-Fengtian Railway; it was one of the earliest railways built in the Qing Dynasty] was deliberately enlarged without regard to actual proportions. The map reflects the development and changes of Tianjin after its opening as a port, and is a representative work of modern China urban landscape maps. The signature on the left reads "In the 25th year of Emperor Guangxu (1899), during the mid-spring of the year of Ji Hai, inscribed by Li Yinwu from Yanjin County, in charge of self-defense of Tianjin, and drawn by Feng Qihuang from Shanyin County"

清乾隆年间江萱所绘《潞河督运图》描绘了 18 世纪天津三岔河口一带舳舻相衔、两岸商铺林立的繁荣景象。从 1901 年至 1923 年，海河先后进行了 6 次裁弯取直，其中 1918 年第三次的"天主堂裁弯"工程就是针对三岔河口进行的。经过这次裁弯取直，三水交汇之处向北推移，形成了大家今天见到的新三岔河口

Jiang Xuan's *Panoramic Picture of Supervision and Transportation of the Lu River*, painted during the reign of Emperor Qianlong, depicts the prosperous scene of countless boats and shops around Sancha estuary in Tianjin in the 18th century. From 1901 to 1923, the Hai River was straighten six times, of which the third "Catholic Church Cut-Bend" project in 1918 was carried out at Sancha estuary. Afterward, the confluence of the three rivers moved northward, forming the new Sancha estuary that we see today

县及沧州。天津这一建制上的变化主要是其城市经济发展和人口增长所导致的。

财富从何而来？

　　天津的早期繁荣是由于漕运和盐业。它是北方最重要的水路运输枢纽，承担着军粮转运和仓储等物资保障任务。天津原是名副其实的北国水乡，"九河下梢"是对天津自然地理位置最直观的总结。古代汉语里，"九"就是多的意思，并不是固定的数目。因水而兴的天津城，曾经河道纵横、洼淀遍布，随处可见蒲柳纤枝、马莲水草。仲夏时，水光波影，绿草莹莹；冬日里，河面结冰，光洁如镜。子牙河、南运河、北运河三河在三岔河口处交汇，汇聚为华北地区最大的河流——海河，由此一直向东流入大海，成为天津的母亲河。

　　天津的漕粮水运，不仅依靠曹操和隋炀帝下令开挖的运河，在很长一段时间里还依靠沿海海运。北方冬季河水结冰，不利于漕粮的冬季运输；另外，运河水浅，也不利于粮船的大型化。因此，早在秦朝时期，秦始皇就曾经征调粮船从山东的海港入渤海，再经今

ing and guarding and governed the area from the south of the Hai River along the Southern Grand Canal to the east of Dezhou. Before 1564, Tianjin only had military officers and no civilian officials. This illustrates the early nature of Tianjin as a military town to protect the capital.

Tianjin's Early Prosperity

During the Ming Dynasty, the administrative structure of Tianjin's defense system remained unchanged. It was not until the ninth year of the Shunzhi era in the early Qing Dynasty (1652) that the decision was made to merge the "Left Guard" and "Right Guard" of Tianjin into a unified "Tianjin Guard." In the third year of the Yongzheng era (1725), it was further transformed into a "zhou" (a prefecture) under the jurisdiction of Hejian Prefecture. In the ninth year of the Yongzheng era (1731), Tianjin was upgraded to a "fu" (a prefectural capital), overseeing six counties and one prefecture, namely Tianjin County, Qing County, Jinghai County, Nanpi County, Yanshan County, Qingyun County, and Cangzhou. These administrative changes in Tianjin were primarily driven by the city's economic development and population growth.

Where Did Wealth Come From?

The early prosperity of Tianjin was due to the canal transportation

天津的古黄河河道入河为北方的蒙恬大军运输军粮。到了唐宋时期，航海和造船技术又有了极大的进步，居于当时世界领先行列。客观环境和技术进步为国内的漕粮海运奠定了重要基础。因此，在唐代，海运的繁盛与河运的并用使今天津地区的军粮城成为当时重要的海运港湾和军用粮饷的集散地。至元朝统一中国、迁都今北京，今天津的直沽又成为水运枢纽，河运、海运并行。明清两代，一方面疏浚了大运河，河道重新畅通；另一方面，海盗、倭寇横行导致海运衰落，于是天津港的河漕转运再度日益繁盛，人口也不断增加。大的粮商、船户以及各类工匠开始移民天津，他们的商业活动繁荣了天津的商品市场，直沽的漕运也在清代达到了鼎盛时期。

三岔河口曾是天津最早的居民点，是天津城市的发祥地。元朝改直沽寨为海津镇，三岔河口成为海运、漕运的南粮船队的必经之路，运河和海河的船只大多在这里停泊，各种商品在这里装卸，商业贸易也非常繁荣。元代诗人张翥有诗云："晓日三岔口，连檣集万艘"。明朝设卫筑城，将这里选为城址，但天津城里只有负责行政事务的衙署、钟鼓楼、馆驿、同乡会会馆等公共建筑，一些庙宇以及居民住宅。为了满足城市的消费功能，各种进行商品交换的集市、店铺与城市一起壮大，它们不但数量增多，而且规模扩大，以至于狭窄的城区逐渐容纳不下。因此，商店、票号、货栈及专门收税的钞关、盐关等逐渐云集于城外三岔河口一带。

由于商业的繁荣，商店的专业化和等级化也在不断发展。天津的老城厢地区有一些非常有意思的地名，如估衣街、针市街、粮店街、锅店街、布店胡同、肉店、鱼市、菜市等。顾名思义，可知原来那里是专门售卖某一类商品的市场。市场的专门化在世界各主要城市的发展进程中都有所体现。比如，同一时期的法国城市图卢兹（Toulouse）在市区里有小麦市场、葡萄酒商场、皮革商场、皮鞋商场、毛皮商场；16世纪的英格兰城镇往往由当地富商慷慨出资筹建许多名称不一的市集。① 特别要指出的是，当时专门买卖二手衣服的估衣店在不太富裕的市民生活中占有重要地位，所以天津史书上有

① （法）费尔南·布罗代尔著，顾良等译，《十五至十八世纪的物质文明、经济与资本主义》第二卷，生活·读书·新知三联书店，2002年，第11页。

and salt industry. It served as a crucial waterway transportation hub in the northern region, undertaking tasks such as the transport and storage of military provisions. Tianjin was originally a true northern water town, and the phrase "nine rivers converge" is the most straightforward description of its natural geographical location. In ancient Chinese, "nine" simply means many and is not a fixed number. Tianjin, thriving due to its waterways, once had rivers crisscrossing and wetlands everywhere, with willow branches and water plants such as Chinese small iris visible everywhere. In midsummer, the water reflected the sunlight with shimmering waves and lush greenery; in winter, the river surface froze, becoming as clear as a mirror. The Ziya River, Southern Grand Canal, and Northern Grand Canal converged at Sancha estuary, forming the largest river in North China—the Hai River—which then flowed eastward into the sea, serving as the mother river of Tianjin.

The canal transportation of grain in Tianjin relied not only on the canals ordered to be excavated by Cao Cao and Emperor Yang of Sui but also on maritime transport along the coast for a long time. In the northern winter, the river water would freeze, hindering the winter transportation of grain via canals. Additionally, the shallow water in the canals was not conducive to the large-scale operation of grain ships. Therefore, as early as the Qin Dynasty, Qin Shi Huang had requisitioned grain ships from the seaports of Shandong to enter the Bohai Sea and then transport military provisions for the northern army through the ancient Yellow River channel in present-day Tianjin. By the Tang and Song Dynasties, navigation and shipbuilding technologies had made significant progress, placing them at the forefront globally. The objective environment and technological advancements laid an important foundation for domestic grain transportation by sea. In the Tang Dynasty, the prosperity of maritime transport, in conjunction with canal transport, made present-day Tianjin a vital hub for the distribution of military provisions and an important seaport for military supplies. With the unification of China under the Yuan Dynasty and the capital moved to present-day Beijing, present-day Tianjin's Zhigu trading port became a water transport hub, facilitating both river and maritime transportation. During the Ming and Qing Dynasties, while the Grand Canal was dredged to ensure clear waterways, the rampant domestic and Japanese pirates activities led to the decline of maritime transport. Consequently, the river transport and transfer through Tianjin Port flourished again, leading to a continuous increase in population. Prominent grain merchants, shipowners, and various craftsmen began to migrate to Tianjin. Their commercial activities thrived, contributing to the prosperity of Tianjin's commodity market, and the canal transport at Zhigu Port trade reached its peak during the Qing Dynasty.

水西庄。据说是《红楼梦》大观园的原型，著名武侠小说家金庸（原名查良镛）即为水西庄盐商查家后代

Zha Family Garden. It is said to be the prototype of the Grand View Garden in *A Dream of the Red Mansion*, and the famous wuxia novelist Jin Yong (original name Zha Liangyong) is a descendant of the salt merchant Zha family

外国画家所绘三岔河口众多船只"连樯排比"的景象
The scene of numerous boats "together with rows of masts" painted by a foreign painter at Sancha estuary

估衣街
Gu Yi Street

Sancha estuary was once the earliest settlement in Tianjin and the birthplace of the city. During the Yuan Dynasty, the Zhiguzhai was changed to Haijin Town, and Sancha estuary became a necessary route for water transport of southern grain on river or by sea. Boats from the canal and the Hai River mostly docked here, and various goods were loaded and unloaded, making commercial trade exceptionally prosperous. The Yuan poet Zhang Zhu wrote: "At dawn, Sancha estuary gathers a myriad of masts." During the Ming Dynasty, a defensive wall was built, and this location was selected as the site for the city. However, within Tianjin City, only administrative offices, the Bell and Drum Tower, government inns, native place associations, temples, and residential houses existed. To meet the city's consumption needs, various markets and shops for exchanging goods grew with the city, both in number and scale, to the point where the narrow city area could no longer accommodate them. Therefore, shops, exchange shops, warehouses, and dedicated tax and salt offices gradually gathered in the area around Sancha estuary outside the city.

Due to the prosperity of commerce, the specialization and stratification of shops were also constantly evolving. In the old town area of Tianjin, there are some very interesting place names, such as Gu Yi Street, Needle Market Street, Grain Shop Street, Pot Shop Street, Cloth Shop Alley, Meat Shop, Fish Market, Vegetable Market, etc. As the names suggest, it is evident that these were markets specialized in selling certain types of goods. The specialization of markets is reflected in the development of major cities around the world. For instance, during the same period, the French city of Toulouse had markets for wheat, wine, leather, leather shoes, and fur; in the 16th century, English towns often had many markets with various names funded generously by local wealthy merchants.[1] It's particularly worth noting that, at the time, shops specializing in second-hand clothes played an important role in the lives of the less affluent citizens, which is why one of the oldest commercial streets in Tianjin, traceable in historical records, was named Gu Yi Street. In the 4th year of the Daoguang era of the Qing Dynasty (1824), Cui Xu wrote a poem called *Verses of Gu Yi Street*: "Clothes are flipped, half not new, lifting the collar, pulling the lapel, singing sales frequently; summer ramie and winter attire, buy as you wish, not knowing who made them first." The last line inexplicably evokes a sense of melancholy. However, the lives of the lower-class people, whether in China or Europe, were actually quite similar—in 1716, the French city of Lille alone had over 1,000 shops dealing in second-

---

[1]　Fernand Braudel, *Civilisation matérielle, économie et capitalisme, XVe-XVIIIe siècle (Vol.2)*, translated by Gu Liang, et al. SDX Joint Publishing Company, 2002, p.11.

踪迹可循的最古老的商业街之一，就被命名为估衣街。清代崔旭在道光四年（1824 年）写有《估衣街竹枝词》一首："衣裳颠倒半非新，挈领提襟唱卖频；夏葛冬装随意买，不知初制是何人。"最后一句令人莫名生出酸楚之情。不过，当时底层民众的生活，无论中国还是欧洲，其实都是差不多的——1716 年法国里尔（Lille）一地就有 1000 多家估衣店。[1]

伴随各类专门化商店的兴起，各种服务类的特殊商店，如当铺、银号、钱庄、货栈、脚行、镖局等，也应运而生。商人的经营活动最需要的是确保资金和货物运输的安全和便捷。据《天津通志》记载：嘉庆二年（1797 年）山西商人雷履泰在天津经营的日升昌颜料铺，首创汇兑业务，并于道光二年（1822 年）改组为票号，是为中国最早出现的汇兑业。早期金融业的发展，加上港口航道、码头和仓储设施的建设，使天津进入了一个相当长的人口持续增长和经济活动繁盛的阶段。

漕运的发展为天津带来了繁茂的人口和丰富的物资，而盐业则带来了巨大的财富。早在西汉时期，即此时"天津"还没有出现，这里的渔民就已"煮海为盐"，从事食盐的生产。当时的汉王朝在全国 38 个地方设置了盐官，今天津地区就占了两处。此后，今天津地区的盐业生产绵延不绝，至北魏政府开始在这里设立长芦盐运使，专门负责征收盐税。漫长的时间里，河滩上的盐田一望无际，白河两岸处处可见巨大的盐堆。每个盐堆约 6 米见方，7 米高，每一堆约有 500 吨到 1270 吨的盐，绵延两岸达 3 千米之长，足够供应三千万人口一年之用。[2]一座座盐坨给城市的一部分人带来了巨额财富。天津有一些大盐商，他们拥有非常壮观的私人花园，如盐商查家的水西庄，乾隆皇帝来津时就曾住在他家。漕运与盐业成为推动天津向近代城市迈进的两台发动机。

hand clothes.[1]

With the rise of various specialized shops, a range of specialized service shops such as pawnshops, banks, money shops, warehouses, courier stations, and escort agencies also emerged in response. The most crucial aspect of a merchant's business activities was ensuring the safety and convenience of capital and goods transportation. According to the *Tianjin Chorography*, in the 2nd year of the Jiaqing era (1797), Shanxi merchant Lei Lü Tai, who ran the Rishengchang dye shop in Tianjin, pioneered the remittance business. In the 2nd year of the Daoguang era (1822), it was reorganized into a bank, marking the earliest appearance of remittance/exchange business in China. The development of the early financial industry, coupled with the construction of ports, waterways, docks, and storage facilities, ushered Tianjin into a prolonged period of continuous population growth and economic prosperity.

The development of water transportation brought a flourishing population and abundant materials to Tianjin, while the salt industry brought immense wealth. As early as the Western Han dynasty, even before the area was known as "Tianjin," local fishermen were already "boiling the sea for salt," engaging in the production of edible salt. At that time, the Han dynasty set up salt officials in 38 locations nationwide, and present-day Tianjin area accounted for two of them. Since then, salt production in present-day Tianjin area has continued uninterrupted, until the Northern Wei government began to set up a Changlu Salt Commissioner here, specifically responsible for collecting salt tax. Over the long years, the salt fields on the river beaches stretched as far as the eye could see, with huge piles of salt visible on both sides of the Peiho. Each salt pile was about 6 meters square, 7 meters high, with each pile containing about 500 to 1,270 tons of salt, stretching along both banks for 3 kilometers, enough to supply 30 million people for a year.[2] The heaps of salt brought tremendous wealth to a portion of the city's population. Tianjin had some major salt merchants who owned very impressive private gardens, such as Zha Family Garden of the salt merchant Zha family, where Emperor Qianlong stayed during his visit to Tianjin. Grain transportation and the salt industry became the two engines driving Tianjin towards becoming a modern city.

① （法）费尔南·布罗代尔著，顾良等译，《十五至十八世纪的物质文明、经济与资本主义》第二卷，生活·读书·新知三联书店，2002 年，第49—50 页。

② 根据马戛尔尼使团成员司当东记录计算而得。（英）司当东著，叶笃义译，《英使谒见乾隆纪实》，三联书店（香港）有限公司，1994 年，第 229—230 页。

① Fernand Braudel, *Civilisation matérielle, économie et capitalisme, XVe - XVIIIe siècle (Vol.2)*, translated by Gu Liang, et al. SDX Joint Publishing Company, 2002, pp.49-50.

② Calculated based on the records of Staunton, the member of Lord Macartney Mission. George Staunton，*An Authentic Account of an Embassy from the King of Great Britain to the Emperor of China*. Joint Publishing Company (H.K.), 1994, pp.229-230.

广东会馆与新型城市组织

在交通并不发达的时代，相对隔绝于世界各个大小城市的人们，通过各地区小本经营的生产者、运输者和销售者的活动，使大城市的市场供应源源不断。例如，老城附近针市街的定名，是因闽粤商人带来的手工业产品特别是缝衣针销量最大，于是专门售卖缝衣针的店铺集中的地方就取名为针市街。由此可见外地商人对天津城市形成和发展的重要贡献。到清朝中期，天津已形成了若干个大商帮，如浙商、徽商、晋商等，尤其是闽粤一带的商人，影响力更为巨大。

300年前，广东商人就与福建商人结成船队到天津经商。他们勇于冒险，富有开拓意识，世代经商，实力雄厚。他们的商船也是最大的，船头油成红色，上面画有大眼鸡，被称作"红头船"或"大眼鸡船"。每年春天，当季风刮起的时候，他们便满载货物，浩浩荡荡，沿海北上，经渤海湾，顺海河进入天津。《津门保甲图说》中说："及到郡城停泊，连樯排比，以每船五十人计之，舵、水人等约在一万上下。"乾隆年间，清朝严格执行"禁海令"，当时只剩广州一地允许对外贸易。而开辟了通往东方航线的欧洲商人却不远万里踏海而来，往后的80年时间里，往来商船络绎不绝，竟高达5000余艘，贸易额不减反增。闽粤商人将那些洋货以及南方的木料、蔗糖等特产源源不断运往北方，又从北方运回棉花、染色土布、人参、豆类及其他土特产，获利丰厚。①

日久天长，天南地北汇聚于津门的各地客商，为了有一个会商、休息、娱乐的地方，自发组织集资修建了各自的同乡会馆。鸦片战争前天津最主要的几处会馆有：1739年闽粤商人建的"闽粤会馆"，这是天津最早的会馆；1753年江西商人建"江西会馆"；1761年山西商人建了第一所"山西会馆"，1823年山西商人建了第二所会馆，以后又在杨柳青镇建立了第三所山西会馆。这一时期的会馆多设于商业繁华区，虽然数量不多，却已反映出天津的繁荣程度。

第二次鸦片战争后天津被迫开辟为通商口岸，不仅有外省商人，更有许多外国商人络绎而来，进出口贸易大幅增加。中国商人、买

---

① 刘正刚，《清代以来广东人在天津的经济活动》，《中国经济史研究》2002年第3期，第94—103页。

Guangdong Guild Hall and New Urban Organizations

In an era when transportation was not well-developed, people in various large and small cities, relatively isolated from the rest of the world, relied on local small-scale producers, transporters, and sellers to keep the supply in big city markets continuous. For example, the naming of Needle Market Street near the old town was due to the fact that the handmade products brought by merchants from Fujian and Guangdong, especially sewing needles, sold in the largest volumes. Consequently, an area where shops specializing in sewing needles were concentrated was named Needle Market Street. This illustrates the significant contribution of merchants from other regions to the formation and development of the city of Tianjin. By the mid-Qing Dynasty, Tianjin had formed several major merchant groups, such as the Zhejiang, Anhui, and Shanxi merchants, with the influence of merchants from the Fujian and Guangdong regions being particularly immense.

300 years ago, Guangdong merchants formed fleets with Fujian merchants to do business in Tianjin. They were adventurous, entrepreneurial, engaged in trade for generations, and were financially robust. Their merchant ships were the largest, with the bows painted red and adorned with images of large-eyed roosters, earning them the names "Red Head Ships" or "Big Eye Rooster Ships." Every spring, when the monsoon winds began to blow, they would set sail with their cargoes, forming an impressive fleet as they traveled north along the coast, through the Bohai Gulf, and up the Hai River into Tianjin. *The Illustrated History of Defense System in Tianjin* states: "Upon arriving and mooring in the county town, with masts lined up, and counting fifty people per ship, the total number of helmsmen, watermen, etc., was approximately ten thousand." During the Qianlong era, the Qing dynasty strictly enforced the "Maritime Prohibition," leaving Guangzhou as the only port allowed for foreign trade. However, European merchants, who had opened up maritime routes to the East, braved the long journey across the seas. Over the following 80 years, the number of merchant ships coming and going was relentless, reaching over 5,000, with trade volume not decreasing but increasing. Fujian and Guangdong merchants continuously transported foreign goods, southern timber, cane sugar, and other special products to the north. In return, they shipped back cotton, dyed homespun cloth, ginseng, beans, and other local specialties from the north, reaping substantial profits.①

Over time, merchants from various regions who gathered in Tianjin,

---

① Liu Zhenggang, Economic Activities of Cantonese in Tianjin Since the Qing Dynasty, *Researches in Chinese Economic History*, 2002(03), pp.94-103.

广东会馆。刘悦摄于 2024 年
Guangdong Guild Hall. Taken by
Liu Yue in 2024

　　广东会馆规模宏大，建筑面积 1461 平方米，建筑设计上既体现了我国岭南的建筑风格，又融合了北方四合院的特点，是中国罕见的木结构建筑艺术珍品。会馆大门的瓦顶和墙体为青砖灰瓦的厚重北方风格，没有采用南方黛瓦粉墙的做法，与周围建筑相融合而不显突兀。但是进入大门之后，满目岭南风格的设计，令同乡们回家的感觉油然而生。建设会馆的砖瓦木料大多从广东购买，以保证岭南特色的原汁原味。会馆主要由门厅、正房、配房、回廊及戏楼组成，各个厅堂之间都有廊厦相通，使馆内交通风雨无阻。会馆周围还建造了铺房、住房 300 多间，并且在会馆东南面修建了"南园"，栽花种树，设立医药房，供广东同乡休息养病。

　　戏楼是该馆的主要建筑，它利用四合院的天井围成闭合空间，舞台顶部南北向用两根 21 米长的平行枋，东西向用 19 米长的额枋，形成大跨度空间。戏楼最多可容纳六七百人，楼上是包间，楼下是散座。舞台是戏楼的核心，深 10 米，宽 11 米，采用伸出式舞台，即台在前、幕在后，三面敞开，不设角柱，可使舞台三面接触观众，视野更加开阔，并且深入到观众席中，拉近演员与观众的距离，融洽了观众与演员的情感交流，从而创造出最佳的演出氛围。舞台正上方藻井造型外方内圆，斗拱接榫，螺旋向上，据说这种构造可以把声音传到戏园的各个角落。藻井重约 10 吨，采用的是悬臂吊挂式结构。在舞台顶部东西两侧各有一根斜向的钢拉杆，与戏楼顶部的主梁相连，而斜向钢拉杆又被巧妙地隐藏在拱形镂空花罩后面，可谓天衣无缝。同时，舞台顶部有数根纵向钢拉杆和复杂的榫架结构与主梁相连，却被雕刻精美的悬空式垂花门楼所遮盖，从而完成了重量的层层分解。戏台木雕的雕花工艺精美，前台横眉以透雕技法刻成狮子滚绣球图案，两角雕成荷花含苞欲放状的垂花柱，舞台正面镶嵌着巨幅《天官赐福》木雕，天官、童子、猿猴、松柏、云气和四角的蝙蝠，构成活泼、协调的画面。戏楼的门窗也雕有狮、凤、牡丹等传统纹饰。

The Guangdong Guild Hall is a grand architectural complex with a total area of 1,461 square meters. Its design blends the Lingnan architectural style of southern China with the traditional courtyard features of the north, making it a rare masterpiece of wooden architecture in China. The guild hall's main entrance follows the heavy, solid northern style, with gray bricks and tiles, instead of the black tiles and white walls typical of southern China, allowing it to harmonize with the surrounding buildings. However, upon entering the hall, one is immediately immersed in the distinctive Lingnan design, evoking a strong sense of home for fellow countrymen. Most of the bricks, tiles, and wood used in the construction were purchased from Guangdong to ensure the authenticity of the Lingnan style. The guild hall consists of a front hall, main hall, side rooms, corridors, and an opera stage. The various halls are connected by covered walkways, ensuring smooth passage in all weather conditions. Surrounding the hall, over 300 rooms were built for shops and residences, and to the southeast, a "South Garden" was established, featuring flowers, trees, and a medical room for fellow Guangdong natives to rest and recover.

The theatre is the centerpiece of the guild hall. It is enclosed within the courtyard's open-air atrium. The north-south span on top of the stage is supported by two parallel beams, each 21 meters long, while the east-west span uses 19-meter-long architraves, creating a large-span space. The theatre can accommodate six to seven hundred spectators, with private boxes on the upper floor and open seating below. As the core of the theater building, the stage measures 10 meters in depth and 11 meters in width. It is designed as a thrust stage, meaning the stage extends outward, with the performance area in front and the curtain at the back. Open on three sides and free of corner pillars, this design allows actors to be closer to the audience, provides an unobstructed view from multiple angles, enhances emotional interaction, and creates an optimal performance atmosphere. Above the stage, the ceiling features an intricate caisson (coffered ceiling) structure that is square on the outside and circular on the inside, with interlocking brackets spiraling upward. This design is said to help project sound to every corner of the theater. The caisson weighs approximately 10 tons and is suspended using a cantilevered hanging structure. Two diagonal steel tension rods connect the stage roof to the main beam of the theater, cleverly concealed behind an arched openwork floral screen. Additionally, multiple longitudinal steel rods and complex mortise-and-tenon structures connect to the main beam, their weight distribution hidden behind exquisitely carved, suspended flowered eaves. The wooden carvings of the stage are particularly exquisite. The front beam of the stage is decorated with openwork carvings of lions playing with embroidered balls, while the two corners feature hanging lotus bud-shaped carvings. The stage backwall is adorned with a large wood carving of "The Heavenly Official Bestowing Blessings," depicting celestial figures, children, monkeys, pine trees, clouds, and bats in each of the four corners, forming a lively and harmonious composition. The doors and windows of the theater are also intricately carved with traditional motifs, including lions, phoenixes, and peonies.

重南風來

广东会馆戏台。刘悦摄于 2024 年
Stage in Guangdong Guild Hall. Taken by Liu Yue in 2024

民国时期在广东会馆戏台上进行的演讲

Speech given on the stage of Guangdong Guild Hall during the Republic of China period

办与洋行、洋商共同操作着这个大市场，华商与外商之间，国内不同省份及同行业的商人之间，形成了日益激烈的市场竞争，而且来自同一省份的同乡经常从事相近的行业，彼此联合起来无疑有助于其争取商贸中的优势地位，甚至垄断地位。因此，这一时期天津的经济日益得到发展，会馆数量随之大增。

除了原来的闽粤会馆、江西会馆、山西会馆之外，还有由山东济宁府州官商共同出资建的济宁会馆，河南商人集资建的怀庆会馆、中州会馆，安徽籍直隶总督李鸿章倡建的吴楚公所，以及由在津为官的原籍各省官员发起集资兴建的庐阳公所、浙江会馆、江苏会馆、广东会馆、安徽会馆和云贵会馆等。会馆在短短几十年间如雨后春笋般出现，说明天津外地移民数量的增加以及天津作为工商业城市的进一步繁荣发展。[①]

会馆是提供给同乡们的一个联络感情、互通声气、共议商务、休闲娱乐的社会活动场所，所以一般建筑规模较之普通民居为大。财力雄厚的一些大会馆，建筑宏伟，有的甚至还有装修精致的戏楼。例如落成于 1907 年的广东会馆，它位于旧城鼓楼南，是目前天津保存最完整、规模最大的清代会馆建筑（现为天津市戏剧博物馆）。

开埠后，广东人在天津的商号达到 200 多家，广州和香港的买办也随着商船来津。同时一大批广东籍留学生也陆续学成回国，云集于天津，广帮的势力逐渐壮大。1903 年，时任津海关道的旅津广东人、幼年留美的唐绍仪，为了联络乡情，发展巩固广帮势力，联合了几位粤籍大商人，倡议集资筹建广帮会馆。会馆由天津英商怡和洋行买办梁炎卿主办，购置了鼓楼南大街原盐运使署旧址的土地为馆址，计 23 亩，于 1904 年 2 月 12 日动工。1907 年正月十四日落成，取名广东会馆。据民国《天津志略》"会社篇"载："广东会馆地址在城内鼓楼南大街。始于光绪甲辰之秋，成立于丙午之冬。发起者为唐绍仪、陈子珍、梁炎卿、冯商盘诸君。时唐氏任津海关道，捐出巨款，首为之倡。继向同乡劝募。时梁公充任怡和洋行进口船务买办，所有砖瓦木料，多自粤购来。得怡和助以半价运费，所省

---

① 刘莉萍，《社会变迁中的天津会馆》，《聊城大学学报》（社会科学版）2008 年第 4 期，第 14—17 页。

seeking a place for business discussions, rest, and entertainment, spontaneously organized and raised funds to build their respective hometown guild halls. Before the Opium War, the most prominent guild halls in Tianjin included: the "Fujian-Guangdong Guild Hall" built by Fujian and Guangdong merchants in 1739, which was the earliest guild hall in Tianjin; the "Jiangxi Guild Hall" built by Jiangxi merchants in 1753; the first "Shanxi Guild Hall" built by Shanxi merchants in 1761, followed by a second one in 1823, and later, a third Shanxi Guild Hall was established in Yangliuqing Town. Although not numerous, these guild halls, mostly located in bustling commercial areas, already reflected the prosperity of Tianjin during that period.

After the Second Opium War, Tianjin was forced to open up as a commercial port, attracting not only merchants from other provinces but also many foreign traders, significantly increasing import and export trade. Chinese merchants, compradors, foreign firms, and foreign traders jointly operated this vast market. Intense market competition emerged between Chinese and foreign merchants, between merchants from different provinces within the country, and among those in the same industry. Merchants from the same province often engaged in similar trades and banding together undoubtedly helped them gain a competitive edge in commerce, and even achieve a monopolistic position. Consequently, during this period, Tianjin's economy increasingly flourished, and the number of guild halls greatly expanded.

In addition to the original Fujian-Guangdong Guild Hall, Jiangxi Guild Hall, and Shanxi Guild Hall, there were also the Jining Guild Hall, jointly funded by officials and merchants from Shandong's Jining Prefecture; the Huaiqing Guild Hall and Zhongzhou Guild Hall built by Henan merchants; the Wuchu Public Hall initiated by Li Hongzhang, a native of Anhui and Viceroy of Zhili; and the Luyang Public Hall, Zhejiang Guild Hall, Jiangsu Guild Hall, Guangdong Guild Hall, Anhui Guild Hall, and Yunnan-Guizhou Guild Hall, all established by officials from various provinces who served in Tianjin. The rapid emergence of these guild halls in just a few decades highlights the increasing number of migrants to Tianjin and further underscores the city's prosperity and development as a hub of industry and commerce.[①]

Guild halls served as social venues for fellow townsmen to connect, communicate, discuss business, and enjoy leisure activities, which is why they were generally more spacious than ordinary residences. Some of the wealthier

① Liu Liping, Tianjin Guild Halls in the Changing Society, *Journal of Liaocheng University (Social Science Edition)*, 2008(04), pp.14-17.

天津天后宫
Tianjin Tianhou Temple

天后宫大殿
Main Hall of Tianhou Temple

天后宫牌楼
Archways of Tianhou Temple

以上彩色照片由安红摄于 2006 年
Color photos taken by An Hong in 2006

配殿内供奉的各路神仙
Various deities enshrined in the side halls

以上照片由安红摄于 2006 年
Photos taken by An Hong in 2006

娃娃大哥
Clay figurine "Big Brother"

妈祖娘娘从海神变成了"送子观音",这说明了民间信仰的功能性和灵活性。信众有什么需要就立刻满足这种需要,这样信仰才能扎根在人们心中。虽然没有正式宗教的组织性、动员力,但它更具有生机勃勃的活力。

　　谈到"信仰",中国人本来就是奉行"实用主义"的。百姓烧香上供,是为求心愿得偿。林语堂说:中国人得意时信儒教,失意时信道教。一个人总有得意、失意的时候,因此就有了对"儒、释、道"都信的"民间信仰"。天津天后宫里供奉的既有道教的神仙,也有佛教的菩萨,还有本地的神仙,实际上就是这种"实用主义"民间信仰的具体体现。虔诚与否,最主要的还是看"灵"和"不灵"这个"硬指标"。只要是"灵"的神仙,就会引来无数的善男信女。由妈祖到送子娘娘,这是中国民间信仰传承实用主义的最好例证。

of Tianjin.

Originally called Tianfei Palace and later renamed Tianhou Temple, the locals commonly refer to it as Niangniang (Empress) Temple. Having undergone several renovations, the architectural complex faces east towards the Hai River and includes structures like the opera tower, Tianhou Temple Square, flagpole, main gate, archway, front hall, main hall, Fengwei Hall, and left and right auxiliary halls, characteristic of traditional Chinese temple architecture. The opera tower, square, and flagpole, all located outside the main gate of Tianhou Temple, were used for worshiping Mazu. During the Chinese New Year, the square becomes lively with numerous stalls selling window and door decorations, and sometimes the opera tower is also used. Every year on Mazu's birthday (23rd day of the third lunar month), a large-scale folk temple fair is held centered around Tianhou Temple. Boatmen along the river, local believers, and merchants from various places gather, contributing to the prosperity of one of Tianjin's famous commercial streets — Gongnan and Gongbei streets (now Ancient Culture Street).

Mazu worship is one of the traditional folk religious beliefs in China's coastal areas. Mazu culture originated in the Song dynasty, was established in the Yuan, flourished in the Ming, reached its height in the Qing, and continued to prosper in modern times. As a folk religious belief, its emergence was not accidental but due to its positive social functions and roles. In ancient times, when the level of social productivity was low, people had to go to sea to make a living and could not overcome their fear of the roaring waves, so they had to seek help from supernatural powers. The prosperity of a religion or the worship of a deity must rely on the continuous manifestation of miracles to prove its utility.

Distinct from religious buildings in the south and other parts of the world, Tianjin's Tianhou Temple is a "comprehensive" temple that integrates various "useful" folk beliefs. In the main and auxiliary halls, not only Mazu (Tianhou) is worshipped, but also folk Taoist and mythological figures such as Wang Lingguan, Qianli Yan, Shunfeng Er, Jia Shan, and Jia E, as well as Buddhist figures like Jingping Guanyin, Dishui Guanyin, and Duhai Guanyin. To complete all functions, figures like King of Medicine (who blesses patients with health), the Dragon King of the Four Seas (who brings rain), the God of Wealth (who brings fortune), Guan Yu (the embodiment of justice), and Lord of the Southern Dipper (who grants longevity) are also worshipped in various auxiliary halls. Even local folk beliefs in Tianjin, such as Granny Wang, Granny Bai, the Water Carrying Brother, Lord Ma, the Land Deity, the God of Literature, and so on, became very prosperous.

Due to its comprehensive functions, Niangniang Temple has always

早期与外界的接触

由于特殊的地理位置和商业的繁荣，天津很早就与世界结缘。元朝时期，今天津地区是所有进贡国去北京觐见皇帝的必经之路。马可·波罗还在游记中提到过"长芦"。那么，他真的到过天津吗？

马可·波罗到过天津吗？

世界上大概没有一本游记能够像马可·波罗的《马可·波罗游记》那样引发历经几百年的争论，争论的焦点就是：他真的到过中国吗？

 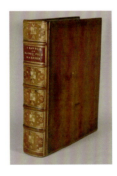

马可·波罗像
Portrait of Marco Polo

《马可·波罗游记》
The Travels of Marco Polo

根据马可·波罗记述，在元帝国生活的 10 多年里，他得到了皇帝的赏识，被任命为官员，最高官至扬州总督；他还曾奉忽必烈之命出使越南、爪哇、苏门答腊等地；他在游记中提到的亚洲城市超过 100 个；他还说看到了喷油的泉（巴库的油田）、可燃烧的石头（煤）、用轻巧的纸张来做货币（钞票）……可是，还是不断有人质疑："如果马可·波罗真到过中国，为什么最重要的事物如长城、茶、筷子、方块汉字、女人缠小脚……全给漏掉了？"不过，这些怀疑改变不了马可·波罗确实到过中国的中外学界正统看法。参加 1793 年英国使团和后来的阿美士德使团的司当东认为，马可·波罗写书时，有可能因笔记不全而漏掉了一些事物；而且，威尼斯的档案馆里保存

been very popular. Not only do boatmen invariably worship and pray here, but farmers from near and far also come to seek blessings and safety. Since they are officially recognized deities, the common people believe that "Mazu" must be omnipotent and powerful. Therefore, people come here to offer incense and prayers, whether they are impoverished or ill, and even those without sons come to pray for a child. Perhaps because of its "effectiveness," the main "business" of Tianjin's Tianhou Temple has evolved into praying for children. Mazu, the sea goddess, has transformed into "Guanyin who bestows children," demonstrating the functionality and flexibility of folk beliefs. Believers' needs are immediately met, rooting the belief deeply in their hearts. Although it lacks the organizational structure and mobilizing power of formal religions, it possesses a vibrant, lively energy.

When it comes to "faith", the Chinese are originally practicing "pragmatism". People burn incense and make offerings in order to fulfill their wishes. Lin Yutang commented: Chinese people believe in Confucianism when they are happy, and in Taoism when they are unhappy. There are always times when a person is happy and unhappy, so there are "folk beliefs" that believe in "Confucianism, Buddhism and Taoism". The Tianhou Temple in Tianjin enshrines Taoist deities, Buddhist Bodhisattvas, and local indigenous deities, which is in fact a concrete embodiment of this "pragmatic" folk belief. Whether they are pious or not, the most important thing is to look at the "hard indicators" of "efficacious" and "not efficacious". As long as the gods and goddesses are "efficacious", they will attract countless devout men and women. This is the best example of the pragmatism inherited from Chinese folk beliefs, from Mazu to the Goddess of Fertility.

Early Contacts with the Outside World

Due to its special geographic location and commercial prosperity, Tianjin has been associated with the world from a very early stage. During the Yuan Dynasty, present-day Tianjin area was the necessary route for all tribute paying countries to go to Beijing for an audience with the emperor. Marco Polo also mentioned "Changlu" in his travels. Did he really visit Tianjin?

Did Marco Polo Ever Visit Tianjin?

Perhaps no travelogue in the world has sparked debates lasting for hundreds of years quite like Marco Polo's *The Travels of Marco Polo*. The focal point of these debates is: Did he really visit China?

According to Marco Polo's accounts, during his more than ten years

的马可·波罗访华路线图显示，他不是通过蒙古人控制的西伯利亚地区到达北京的，而是乘船到印度后沿西藏山脉之南绕道陕西，然后经过山西到达北京的，所以应当没有穿越长城线。[①] 学界还认为，在元代，由西方东迁、旅居在中国的西方人数目是相当多的，总称为"色目人"。作为其中之一，马可·波罗极少与处于被统治地位的汉族人接触，因此不了解上述代表汉文化符号的事物不足为奇。

不管怎样，马可·波罗是世界上第一个将中国介绍给欧洲的人。在他之前，威尼斯人认为他们是地中海乃至整个基督教世界的中心。但这位大旅行家却指出，在东方还有一个更伟大的文明和权力中心。他的游记激发了欧洲人此后几个世纪的东方情结。

马可·波罗笔下的天津（游记中称之为 Cianglu，即长芦），在当时已是一个比较大的富庶城市，以制盐业和渔业为主，是元大都"向南之一大城"。其所产之盐"粒细而色白"，"运贩于附近诸州，因获大利"；"此地产鱼甚众，其味佳，其体巨"。他甚至清楚地记叙说，每条鱼长约 750 公分。[②] 如果马可·波罗没到过天津，他怎么知道得这么详细？！

滞留在天津的利玛窦

蒙古帝国走向衰亡后，中欧之间的交通中断了有两百年的时间。西班牙、葡萄牙人在海上找到新航线之前，中西之间变得彼此隔膜和充满神秘感。在东方，中国的封建社会逐渐发展到它的顶峰，国力强大，罕有其匹，依然是万邦来朝的盛景。之后新航路开辟，欧洲的传教士随商船来到中国，在东西两种文化间架起了一座桥梁。在桥的这一边，16、17 和 18 世纪中国人对欧洲的了解归功于来自欧洲的传教士。他们中的许多人不仅是宗教信仰的传播者，还是科学家、医生、工程师和艺术家。通过与中国学者的密切合作，他们为中国

① （英）司当东著，叶笃义译，《英使谒见乾隆纪实》，三联书店（香港）有限公司，1994 年，第 296—297 页。

② （意）马可·波罗著，冯承钧译，《马可波罗行纪》，上海书店出版社，2006 年，第 300 页。

living in the Yuan Empire, he won the favor of the emperor and was appointed as an official, rising to the highest position of Governor of Yangzhou. He was also sent on diplomatic missions to places like Vietnam, Java, and Sumatra under the command of Kublai Khan. He mentioned over 100 Asian cities in his travelogue; he also spoke of witnessing oil springs (the oil fields of Baku), combustible rocks (coal), and the use of lightweight paper for currency (banknotes)... Yet, there are still constant doubts: "If Marco Polo really visited China, why did he miss mentioning the most important things like the Great Wall, tea, chopsticks, block Chinese characters, and the practice of foot-binding among women...?" However, these doubts do not change the prevailing view among scholars both in China and abroad that Marco Polo indeed visited China. George Staunton, a member of the 1793 British mission and later the Lord Amherst's diplomatic mission, believed that when Marco Polo wrote his book, he might have omitted some details due to incomplete notes. Additionally, the route map of Marco Polo's visit to China preserved in the Archives of Venice indicates that he did not reach Beijing through the Siberian region controlled by the Mongols, but instead took a ship to India and then detoured south of the Tibetan mountains through Shaanxi, then through Shanxi to Beijing, so he would not have crossed the Great Wall line.[①] Scholars also believe that during the Yuan dynasty, there was a considerable number of Westerners who migrated eastward and resided in China, collectively known as "Color-Eyed People" (Semu people). As one of them, Marco Polo had very little contact with the Han Chinese, who were under rule, so it is not surprising that he was unaware of the aforementioned symbols of Han culture.

Regardless, Marco Polo was the first person to introduce China to Europe. Before him, Venetians considered themselves the center of the Mediterranean and even the entire Christian world. But this great traveler pointed out that there was an even greater center of civilization and power in the East. His travelogue ignited an Oriental fascination in Europeans for the centuries that followed.

Marco Polo's depiction of Tianjin (referred to as Cianglu, meaning Changlu, in his travelogue) is of a relatively large and prosperous city of the time, primarily known for its salt industry and fishing, and as a major city "to the south" of the Yuan capital. He described the salt produced there as "fine-grained and white," "transported and sold to nearby states, hence yielding great profit." He also mentioned, "This place produces an abundance of fish,

① George Staunton. *An Authentic Account of an Embassy from the King of Great Britain to the Emperor of China*, translated by Ye Duyi. Joint Publishing Company (H.K.), 1994, pp.296-297.

的科学技术发展作出了一定贡献。在桥的另一头，欧洲人从利玛窦和其他传教士的著作、信件及绘制的地图中增加了对中国的认识，使欧洲人对东方文化充满向往。

最早的"桥梁架设者"当属利玛窦（Matteo Ricci，1552—1610）。他生于意大利马切拉塔城（Macerata），卒于北京，是基督教中国传教事业的创始人。1582年利玛窦和他的同伴启程赴华，途经澳门、广州和南京，于1601年到达北京并定居下来。利玛窦用一生的时间开启了欧洲和中国之间文化交流的大门。

带着西学而来的利玛窦开启了晚明士大夫学习西学的风气。明末清初，一共有150余种的西方书籍被翻译成汉语。利玛窦撰写的《天主实录》以及和徐光启等人翻译的欧几里得《几何原本》等书带给中国许多欧洲的哲学思想和先进的科学知识，许多几何词汇，如点、线、面、平面、曲线、曲面、直角、钝角、锐角、垂线、平行线、对角线、三角形、四边形、多边形、圆、圆心、外切、几何等以及汉语的"星期""欧"就是由他们创造并沿用下来的。

利玛窦是一位科学全才，他还绘制了《坤舆万国全图》，这是中国历史上第一张世界地图，在中国先后被12次刻印。问世后不久，这张世界地图又被介绍到江户时代的日本，使得日本人传统的崇拜中国的"慕夏"观念发生了根本性的变化。这些对日本地理学的发展，亦有重要影响，北极、南极、地中海、日本海等词汇皆出于此地图。

利玛窦（左）与徐光启。出自《中国图说》（1667年荷兰文版）

Matteo Ricci (left) and Xu Guangqi. From *China monumentis qua sacris qua profanis, nec non variis naturae et artis spectaculis, aliarumque rerum memorabilium argumentis illustrata* (Dutch version in 1667)

which are tasty and huge in size." He even distinctly noted that each fish measured about 750 centimeters in length.[1] If Marco Polo had never visited Tianjin, how could he have known such detailed information?!

Matteo Ricci Stranded in Tianjin

After the Mongol Empire waned, transportation between China and Europe was severed for two hundred years. Before the Spanish and Portuguese discovered new maritime routes, China and the West became estranged, each shrouded in a veil of mystery. In the East, China's feudal society steadily ascended to its pinnacle, its national might formidable and rarely matched, maintaining its majestic status as a destination for tribute from numerous nations. Subsequently, with the opening of new sea routes, European missionaries arrived in China aboard merchant ships, constructing a bridge between the two distinct cultures of the East and the West. On this side of the bridge, the Chinese understanding of Europe during the 16th, 17th, and 18th centuries can be attributed to missionaries from Europe. Many of them were not only harbingers of religious faith but also scientists, doctors, engineers, and artists. Through close collaboration with Chinese scholars, they made notable contributions to the development of science and technology in China. At the other end of the bridge, Europeans' knowledge of China was enriched by the writings, letters, and maps of Matteo Ricci and other missionaries, instilling in Europeans a profound fascination with Eastern culture.

The earliest "bridge-builder" between these cultures was undoubtedly Matteo Ricci (1552-1610). Born in the city of Macerata, Italy, and having passed away in Beijing, he is hailed as the pioneer of Christian missionary work in China. In 1582, Ricci and his companions embarked on a journey to China, traveling through Macau, Guangzhou, and Nanjing, before finally arriving and settling in Beijing in 1601. Ricci devoted his life to opening the gates of cultural exchange between Europe and China.

Bringing Western learning with him, Ricci initiated a trend among the late Ming Dynasty literati to study Western knowledge. Between the late Ming and early Qing dynasties, over 150 Western books were translated into Chinese. Works authored by Ricci, such as *Tian Zhu Shi Lu* (The True Meaning of the Lord of Heaven) and translations he collaborated on, like Euclid's *Elements* with Xu Guangqi and others, introduced many European philosophical ideas

---

① Marco Polo. *The Travels of Marco Polo*, translated by Feng Chengjun. Shanghai Bookstore Publishing House, 2006, p.300.

利玛窦在北京的墓
Matteo Ricci's Tomb in Beijing

利玛窦的第一次北京之行适逢明朝援朝抗倭，没有成功。1600 年他第二次启程赴京，原本一路顺风的利玛窦在山东临清遭到天津税监宦官马堂的阻拦，随后被遣往天津，并在那里滞留半年。在津期间，利玛窦先是住在船上，随着冬季的临近，为了避寒，马堂让利玛窦等人带着他们的全部行李搬进一座庙宇，并安排 4 名士兵看守。后来，利玛窦于 1601 年 1 月离开天津，抵达北京，受到了皇帝的召见。①

历经磨难的利玛窦，在北京成功地觐见了皇帝，并且在士大夫阶层中建立起良好的声誉和关系，开启了日后其他传教士进入中国之门。作为传播天主教的第一人，他也开创了日后 200 多年传教士在中国的活动方式：一方面用汉语传播基督教；另一方面用自然科学知识来接近和博取中国人的好感。为了融入当地社会，利玛窦对中国传统习俗保持宽容的态度。他容许中国教徒继续传统的祭天、祭祖和敬孔。他认为，这些只属尊敬祖先的仪式，只要不掺入祈求、崇拜等迷信成分，本质上并没有违反天主教教义。他主张以"天主"称呼天主教的"神"；但他亦认为天主教的"神"早已存在于中国的思想，因为中国传统的"天"和"天帝"本质上与天主教所说的"唯一真神"没有分别。利玛窦本人努力学习汉语，穿戴中国士人服饰。其后来华的传教士，一直遵循他的传教策略和方式，这被称为"利玛窦规矩"。

《荷兰东印度公司出使中国大事记》

传教士不是 17、18 世纪来到东亚的仅有的欧洲人，同时来的还有商人和掠夺者。大约 17 世纪中期，被称为"海上马车夫"的荷兰

---

① 《明神宗实录》卷三五四（一），第 6619 页；卷三五六（一），第 6647—6648 页。

and advanced scientific knowledge to China. Many geometric terms such as point, line, plane, curved line, curved surface, right angle, obtuse angle, acute angle, perpendicular, parallel line, diagonal, triangle, quadrilateral, polygon, circle, center of a circle, tangent, and geometry, as well as the Chinese terms for "week" and "Europe", were coined by them and continue to be used today.

Matteo Ricci was a polymath in science. He also created the *Map of the Myriad Countries of the World*, which is the first world map in Chinese history and was printed 12 times in China. Shortly after its publication, this world map was introduced to Japan during the Edo period, fundamentally changing the traditional Japanese concept of "Muxia" (admiration of China). It also had a significant impact on the development of geography in Japan. Terms such as the Arctic, Antarctic, Mediterranean, and the Sea of Japan all originated from this map.

Matteo Ricci's first journey to Beijing coincided with the Ming Dynasty's military campaign against the Japanese invasions of Korea, and was unsuccessful. In 1600, during his second attempt to travel to the capital, Ricci, who had been proceeding smoothly, encountered obstruction from Ma Tang, an eunuch and tax inspector in Linqing, Shandong. Subsequently, he was sent to Tianjin, where he was detained for half a year. Initially residing on a boat in Tianjin, Ricci, with the approach of winter and to escape the cold, was allowed by Ma Tang to move into a temple with all his belongings, guarded by four soldiers. Later, in January 1601, Ricci left Tianjin for Beijing, where he was granted an audience with the emperor.①

Despite his hardships, Ricci successfully met with the emperor in Beijing and established a favorable reputation and relationships among the scholar-official class, paving the way for other missionaries to enter China. As the pioneer in spreading Catholicism, he also established the approach for missionary activities in China for the next 200 years: on one hand, spreading Christianity in Chinese; on the other hand, approaching and winning the favor of the Chinese people with knowledge of natural sciences. To integrate into the local society, Ricci adopted a tolerant attitude towards traditional Chinese customs. He allowed Chinese converts to continue traditional rituals like worshipping Heaven, ancestors, and Confucius. He believed these rituals were merely about respecting ancestors and, as long as they did not involve superstitious elements like praying or idol worship, they essentially did not contradict Catholic doctrine. He advocated using "Tianzhu" (Lord of Heaven) to refer to the Christian "God"; however, he also believed that the Christian

---

① *Veritable Records of the Ming Emperor Shenzong*, vol.354, p.6619 (6); and vol.356, pp.6647-6648.

人把之前的海上霸主葡萄牙人几乎彻底地赶出了东南亚。他们在世界各地建立殖民地和贸易据点，于1641年占领了马六甲，由此控制了通往南中国海的大门。但是当时进出中国的门户——澳门还掌握在葡萄牙人手中，荷兰人必须通过其他方式打开与中国通商的大门。于是，在清朝早期荷兰东印度贸易公司多次派出使团携带大批贡品到北京，要求与清朝通商，但均未能达成使命。

使团的主要目的虽未达成，但这些使团却对推动欧洲人认识中国做出了重大贡献。第一个荷兰使团的一个成员约翰·纽霍夫（John Nievhoff）在《荷使初访中国记》（中译名）一书中详尽地报道了1655年的中国之行，包括这个国家和她的人民、在北京进行的谈判和礼物的呈送等。其中，他还记述了当时天津的繁荣：

> 同一天（7月5日），我们到达了天津卫的港口，这个地方被认为是中国最著名的沿海城市。当时中国的主要港口有三个：第一个是广东省的主要城市广州；第二个是南京府的镇江县；第三个是位于顺天府东部边缘地区的天津卫，在靠近"沧海"（Sea Cang）的港湾处。该地区的三条河流在天津汇合，那里耸立着坚固的要塞，周围的村庄除了沼泽地以外就是低洼地。天津卫城在距"新镇"约30英里处，也建有25英尺高的坚固的城墙，城墙上布满了守望塔和防御工事。这个地方到处是庙宇，人烟稠密，交易频繁，繁荣的商业景象实为中国其他各地所罕见，这是因为，从中国各地驶往北京的船只必须通过此处，这促进了漕运非同寻常的发展，一艘又一艘的船只接连不断地驶过这个城市。这里也成为各种商品的集散地，因为是自由港，无论进口或出口的货物都不必纳税。三岔河口耸立着要塞，高高的墙上筑有守望塔，这对于保卫这个城市和邻近地区已经是足够了。我们整夜地躺在靠近高墙的船上，准备继续完成到北京的航程。城里的总督和知县们到船上来欢迎我们，并接见了使节。①

---

① （荷）约翰·纽霍夫，《荷兰联邦东印度公司使节哥页和开泽阁下在北京紫禁城晋谒大鞑靼可汗（顺治）》，1669年。转引自（英）雷穆森著，许逸凡等译，《天津租界史（插图本）》，天津人民出版社，2009年，第10—11页。

"God" had already existed in Chinese thought, as the traditional Chinese concepts of "Heaven" and "Heavenly Emperor" fundamentally did not differ from the Christian concept of the "one true God". Ricci himself learned Chinese and wore the attire of Chinese scholars. The missionaries who came to China after him continued to follow his strategy and approach, which came to be known as the "Ricci Method".

Celebrated Account of Two VOC Missions to China

Missionaries were not the only Europeans who came to East Asia in the 17th and 18th centuries; merchants and plunderers arrived as well. Around the mid-17th century, the Dutch, known as the "carriage drivers of the sea," nearly completely ousted the previous maritime dominators, the Portuguese, from Southeast Asia. They established colonies and trading posts around the world, and in 1641, they captured Malacca, thereby controlling the gateway to the South China Sea. However, at that time, the Portuguese still held Macau—the portal to China, so the Dutch had to find other ways to open the doors for trade with China. Consequently, during the early period of Qing Dynasty, the Dutch East India Company sent missions to Beijing, bearing substantial tributes, seeking trade relations with Qing Dynasty, but none succeeded in their mission.

Although the primary objectives of these missions were not achieved, they significantly contributed to advancing Europeans' understanding of China. A member of the first Dutch mission, Johan Nieuhof, gave a detailed account of the 1655 journey to China in his book *An Embassy from the East-India Company of the United Provinces, to the Grand Tartar Cham, Emperor of China*. He covered the country and its people, the negotiations conducted in Beijing, and the presentation of gifts. Among his observations, he also described the prosperity of Tianjin at that time:

> On the same day (July 5), we arrived at the port of Tianjin, which is considered one of China's most renowned coastal cities. At that time, there were three main ports in China: the first was Guangzhou, the principal city of Guangdong Province; the second was Zhenjiang County of Nanjing Prefecture; the third was Tianjin, located on the eastern edge of Shuntian Prefecture, near the harbor of the "Sea Cang." Three rivers converge in this region at Tianjin, where formidable fortresses stand, surrounded by marshlands and low-lying areas. The city of Tianjin, about 30 miles from "Xinzhen," also boasts robust city walls 25 feet high, replete with watchtowers and defensive fortifications. This place is dotted with temples, densely populated, and bustling with frequent trade,

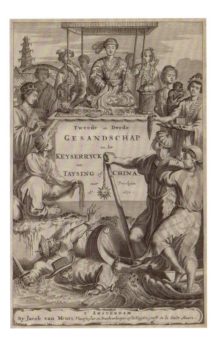

书中所绘 "天津卫"
Tianjin Wei（Garrison）

以上图片为《荷兰东印度公司出使中国大事记》书中插图
Illustrations in the *Celebrated Account of Two VOC Missions to China*

医生达泊尔（Olfert Dapper）于1670年在他的《荷兰东印度公司出使中国大事记》一书中则描述了使团的第二和第三次访华。这两部作品引起了欧洲人对中国的强烈兴趣并被翻译成多种文字。书中的插图描绘了中国的生活景象，其中主要是中国城市和各地风光。尽管这些图片不是很详尽，但是荷兰画家和铜版雕刻家的高超艺术在欧洲刻画了直观的视觉中国形象——一片陌生而又魅力无限、几近世外桃源的土地。

今天在欧洲所能见到巴洛克和洛可可时代无数关于中国人物形象、动植物、建筑、船舶、桥梁、宝塔、风景和水域的艺术作品，都根植于纽霍夫和达泊尔无比美丽的铜版画作品。

马戛尔尼使团与阿美士德使团

在中央集权统治下日益趋向保守的中国，荷兰人并不是唯一吃到闭门羹的外国人。在欧洲，英国凭借日益富强的国力和强大的海军，先后在16、17世纪击败西班牙、荷兰、法国，成为所向无敌的海上霸主。它也将目光投向遥远富庶的东方，继荷兰使团之后，1793年的马戛尔尼（Lord Macartney）使团和1816年的阿美士德（Lord Amherst）使团都曾在天津短暂逗留，然后分别奉诏前往觐见清朝的乾隆皇帝和嘉庆皇帝。可想而知，他们的使命同样没有完成。

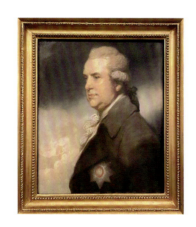

马戛尔尼画像。图片来源：英国驻华大使官邸
Portrait of Lord Macartney. Source: the Residence of the British Ambassador to China

1793年8月11日早晨，马戛尔尼使团到达天津，第二天就沿白河继续前进到通州去了。在短暂的逗留中，使团随行人员记述了官员接待的过程：

presenting a scene of commercial prosperity seldom seen elsewhere in China. This is because ships sailing to Beijing from all over China must pass through here, promoting the remarkable development of grain transportation, with one ship after another continuously passing through the city. It has also become a hub for various goods, being a free port where neither imported nor exported goods are taxed. The fork of the three rivers is dominated by fortresses, and the tall walls are equipped with watchtowers, which are more than sufficient for defending the city and the surrounding area. We lay all night on the boat near the high wall, ready to continue our journey to Beijing. The governor and county magistrate of the city came aboard to welcome us and met with the envoy.[1]

In 1670, Olfert Dapper, in his book *Celebrated Account of Two VOC Missions to China*, described the second and third visits of the mission to China. These two works sparked intense interest in China among Europeans and were translated into various languages. The illustrations in the books depicted scenes of life in China, primarily focusing on Chinese cities and landscapes. Although these images were not very detailed, the exquisite artistry of Dutch painters and copperplate engravers portrayed an intuitive visual image of China in Europe—a land unfamiliar yet infinitely charming, almost a paradisiacal utopia.

Today, countless European artworks from the Baroque and Rococo periods, featuring Chinese characters, flora and fauna, architecture, ships, bridges, pagodas, landscapes, and bodies of water, all have their roots in the incredibly beautiful copperplate prints by Nievhoff and Dapper.

The Lord Macartney Mission and the Lord Amherst's Diplomatic Mission

In an increasingly conservative China under centralized rule, the Dutch were not the only foreigners to face closed doors. In Europe, Britain, bolstered by its growing national strength and formidable navy, successively defeated Spain, the Netherlands, and France in the 16th and 17th centuries, emerging as an unrivaled maritime power. It, too, turned its gaze towards the distant and prosperous East. Following the Dutch missions, the 1793 Lord Macartney Mission and the 1816 Lord Amherst's diplomatic mission both made brief stops in Tianjin before proceeding to seek an audience with the Qing

---

[1] Johan Nieuhof. *An Embassy from the East-India Company of the United Provinces, to the Grand Tartar Cham, Emperor of China*, 1669. Quoted in O. D. Rasmussen. *Tientsin: An Illustrated Outline History*, translated by Xu Yifan, et al. Tianjin People's Publishing House, 2008, pp.10-11.

我们的船队停泊在几乎位于城市中间的总督府前。对面紧靠河边的码头上，为了欢迎我们搭建了一个非常华丽而又宽大的戏台，台上挂着光彩夺目的中国式的装饰和布景，一群演员正表演着各种不同的戏剧和舞蹈，一连几个小时几乎没有间断。河的两岸站满了身着军装的守卫部队，大约长达一英里，队伍中无数镶有垂饰的旗帜迎风招展，时时传来各种乐器演奏军乐的咚咚当当的声音。①

大约在中午时分，马戛尔尼率部下官员及仆从、卫队等全体登岸，直隶总督和钦差大臣在岸边迎接，邀至总督行辕。双方讨论了赴北京的安排之后，英使一行回船。总督大人送上丰盛的筵宴和丝、茶、棉布等礼物，以示友好。之后，天津地方官员也都登船问好、参观，"眉目间颇露惊异之色，盖见所未见，自不得不尔也"。马戛尔尼认为这些地方官员"大都活泼率真，长于言语，工于应酬，而又沉静有毅力"，代表了中国上流社会官员的部分品格。②

两次随团来访的司当东（George Staunton）对天津作了如下评述，第一次他写道：

"天津"二字可以解释为天上境界，据称此地气候适宜，土地肥沃，空气干燥，阳光充足。它位置在两河的汇流，是中国北方几省的商业中心。……这样的地理条件使天津自从中国建成为大一统帝国以来就成为一个交通要地。……虽然在十三世纪天津已是一个大城市了，但天津的老名字叫"天津卫"。按照中国的字义，"卫"只代表一个小的市镇。一个古老市镇延续发展下来，在发展过程中，旧建筑由新建筑所代替，新建筑系在旧建筑的废墟上盖起来的。……天津很多房子是两层的，这同中国其他地方

---

① （英）海伦·罗宾斯，《我们的第一个赴华使节》，1908年。转引自（英）雷穆森著，许逸凡等译，《天津租界史（插图本）》，天津人民出版社，2009年，第11—12页。

② （英）马戛尔尼著，刘半农译，《1793乾隆英使觐见记》，天津人民出版社，2006年，第31—35页。

Dynasty's Qianlong Emperor and Jiaqing Emperor, respectively. As one might surmise, their missions likewise remained unfulfilled.

On the morning of August 11, 1793, the Lord Macartney Mission arrived in Tianjin. The following day, they continued along the Peiho towards Tongzhou. During their brief stay, members of the mission documented the process of being received by officials:

Our fleet docked in front of the Governor's residence, virtually in the center of the city. Opposite, by the riverbank, a very lavish and spacious stage was erected to welcome us. The stage was adorned with dazzling Chinese decorations and backdrops. A troupe of actors was performing a variety of different plays and dances, continuously for several hours with hardly any breaks. Both banks of the river were lined with guards in military uniform, stretching for about a mile. Numerous banners with dangling ornaments fluttered in the wind, and the rhythmic beats of military music from various instruments could be heard constantly.①

Around noon, Lord Macartney, accompanied by his subordinate officers, servants, guards, and the entire entourage, disembarked. The Viceroy of Zhili and the Imperial Commissioner greeted them at the shore and invited them to the Viceroy's temporary office. After discussing the arrangements for their subsequent journey to Beijing, the British delegation returned to their ship. The Viceroy presented a lavish banquet and gifts of silk, tea, and cotton fabric as a gesture of friendship. Subsequently, local officials of Tianjin also boarded the ship to greet and tour around, "displaying a look of surprise and amazement, as they encountered sights they had never seen before". Macartney considered these local officials "generally lively, sincere, articulate, skilled in social interaction, yet calm and resolute," representing certain qualities of the upper-class officials in Chinese society.②

George Staunton, who visited Tianjin twice with the delegation, made the following comments about Tianjin. The first time he wrote:

The word "Tianjin" can be interpreted as the "realm of heaven," indicating a place blessed with favorable climate, fertile land, dry air, and abundant

---

① Helen M. Robbins. *Our First Ambassador to China*, 1908. Quoted in O. D. Rasmussen, *Tientsin: An Illustrated Outline History*, translated by Xu Yifan, et al. Tianjin People's Publishing House, 2008, pp.11-12.

② George Macartney. *An Embassy to China: Being the Journal Kept by Lord Macartney during his Embassy to the Emperor Ch'ien-lung, 1793-1794*, translated by Liu Bannong. Tianjin People's Publishing House, 2005, pp.31-35.

只建一层平房的习惯有所不同。大多数中国人还是喜欢按照各种建筑的原来式样,只建一层。……天津是一个靠海的商埠码头,这可能是建造两层楼房的一个原因。①

1816 年 8 月 12 日,司当东再次随阿美士德使团来华并在天津逗留。尽管这一次他们没有见到皇帝(嘉庆帝)就被驱逐,由大沽口出境,却因此在天津待了两三个星期。这次他写道:

> 我们来到了这座大城市(天津),就发现它增添了许多花园——偶尔也能看到葡萄架——以及一排排秀美、高大的柳树和其他一些树木交杂在一起。我们也发现一些穿着华丽的本地人在河岸策马而行。这儿的房屋看上去比广州附近的房屋更为美观、宽敞。我们也看见几头驴子和一些牡牛……河岸上,人群熙熙攘攘,他们大都穿着很好,举止文雅——比我们在海边上看到的人要整洁、好看得多——他们也确实比广州人高傲。他们不说下流话,也没有任何不满的表示——只是脸上都流露出善意的惊讶和好奇的表情而已。大约下午两点时,我们到达了那不寻常的一排排盐坨的起点,关于这些盐坨的情况,前任使节也提到过。……无数的人群紧紧地挤在成排士兵行列后面的空地上,不仅平地上挤满了人,就是一些盐坨上也站着不少人。这样,在两三英里左右的地带上,几乎形成了一堵连绵不断的人墙,此种景象实为世界各地所罕见。②

盛世繁华下的贫富差距

受马叮·波罗的影响,在西方人的印象中,中国一直是富裕文

---

① (英)司当东著,叶笃义译,《英使谒见乾隆纪实》,三联书店(香港)有限公司,1994 年,第 237—238 页。
② (英)司当东,《英国派往北京的使节》,1824 年个人刊行本。转引自(英)雷穆森著,许逸凡等译,《天津租界史(插图本)》,天津人民出版社,2009 年,第 13 页。

天津附近的炮台。英国画家威廉·亚历山大绘于 1797 年
Fort in Tianjin, drawn by British painter William Alexander in 1797

sunshine. It is situated at the confluence of two rivers and serves as the commercial center for several provinces in northern China... Such geographical advantages have made Tianjin a key transportation hub ever since China was unified into a grand empire... Although Tianjin was already a large city in the 13th century, its old name was "Tianjin Wei." According to Chinese semantics, "Wei" denotes a small market town. An ancient town that continued to develop, where old structures were replaced by new constructions, and new buildings were erected upon the ruins of the old... Many houses in Tianjin are two-storied, differing from the customary practice in other parts of China where single-storied houses prevail. Most Chinese still prefer to build single-storied structures according to the original architectural style. Tianjin, being a port city near the sea, might be one reason for the construction of two-story buildings.①

---

① George Staunton. *An Authentic Account of an Embassy from the King of Great Britain to the Emperor of China*, translated by Ye Duyi. Joint Publishing Company (H.K.), 1994, pp.237-238.

司当东书中所绘为迎接英国使团而搭建的戏台
The stage built to welcome the British mission depicted in Georage Staunton's book

明的象征。传教士关于中国的大量著作促进了欧洲对中华文化的了解，欧洲因此掀起了"中国热"。当时欧洲的思想界普遍将中国视为完美的国度，如法国启蒙运动三杰对中国文化思想都有各自不同的观点。伏尔泰认为，中国是推行开明君主制的成功典范，在他的诸多作品中，尤其是《中国孤儿》（*L'Orphelin de la Chine*）中，他向其他法国人宣传介绍这一遥远而强大的东方古国，将其作为法国学习的榜样。但是另两位启蒙思想家对此表示质疑。孟德斯鸠认为中国只是个毫无美德，人民皆为奴仆的专制国家。在其代表作《论法的精神》（*De l'esprit des lois*）中，他多次提及中国，从方方面面论述了中国的各种弊病，希望诸位同胞能够引以为戒。而卢梭则认为，中国作为一个千年文明古国，离开"纯真自然状态"已久，因而也和堕落了的欧洲文明一样，充满了压迫和不平等，到处是堕落和伪善。他还把清军入关推翻明朝这一历史事件解释为古老的中国因物质文明的进步而变得奢侈和堕落，终于被周边的落后民族所消灭，就如高度文明的古罗马被蛮族日耳曼人所摧毁那样。因此他反对欧洲向中国学习，走中国的道路。

究竟哪一派的观点是正确的呢？前者的观点主要来自在中国长期居住的传教士的观察所得，后者则主要来自外交使节和商人。传教士在传教过程中接触的主要是中国上层知识分子，大都教养良好、品格高尚。而外交官和商人在中国一般只作短暂停留，且因语言不通等原因易与本土居民产生矛盾，因此对中国批评指责的声音较多。对于马戛尔尼使团来说，此行的结果决定了他们对中国的印象是比较负面的。他们显然更赞同后一派的观点，认为清朝只是一个毫无美德的专制国家，盛世繁华的表象之下是广大民众生活在极度贫穷之中。

在马戛尔尼使团和阿美士德使团成员所写的出使记录中，有大量对中国社会民众的细致观察和描述。在一路北上觐见的过程中，他们日常所接触到的主要是中国各地官员、仆役和底层民众。接待他们的官员因人而异，一般地方官员态度恭谨谦虚，仆役们也非常热情真诚，但1793年的钦差则性格刚愎，"处处暴露出忌妒外人、蔑视外人的心理"，"既没有科学常识，又不通达事理"。底层劳

On August 12, 1816, Staunton came to China again with the Lord Amherst's diplomatic mission and stayed in Tianjin. Although this time they were expelled without seeing the emperor (Emperor Jiaqing) and left the country through Taku Forts, they stayed in Tianjin for two or three weeks. This time he wrote:

> Upon arriving at this great city (Tianjin), we found it adorned with numerous gardens—occasionally with grape arbors—and rows of elegant, tall willow trees interspersed with other trees. We also observed some elegantly dressed locals riding horses along the riverbank. The houses here appeared more beautiful and spacious than those near Guangzhou. We also saw a few donkeys and some oxen... On the riverbank, the crowd bustled about, most of them well-dressed and mannerly—much neater and more presentable than those we had seen by the seaside—and indeed, they were haughtier than the people in Guangzhou. They didn't speak crudely, nor showed any dissatisfaction—only their faces expressed a kind surprise and curiosity. Around 2 pm, we reached the beginning of that extraordinary row of salt piles, which the previous envoy had also mentioned... Countless crowds were tightly packed on the open ground behind the rows of soldiers, not just on the flat ground, but also on some of the salt piles. Thus, over an area of about two or three miles, there was practically an unbroken wall of people, a sight rarely seen in the world.[1]

The Gap Between the Rich and the Poor in the Midst of Prosperity

Influenced by Marco Polo, China has long been a symbol of prosperity and civilization in the Western imagination. The extensive works about China by missionaries facilitated Europe's understanding of Chinese culture, sparking a "China craze" in Europe. At that time, the intellectual circles in Europe generally viewed China as a perfect nation, and the leading figures of the French Enlightenment held their own distinct views on Chinese culture and thought. Voltaire saw China as a successful model of enlightened monarchy. In many of his works, especially *L'Orphelin de la Chine*, he promoted this distant and powerful ancient Eastern nation to his fellow Frenchmen as a model for France to learn from. However, the other two Enlightenment thinkers were skeptical. Montesquieu regarded China as a despotic nation devoid of virtue, where people were nothing more than slaves. In his seminal work *De l'esprit*

---

[1] George Staunton. *British Embassy to Pekin*. 1824 (self-publishing). Quoted in O. D. Rasmussen. *Tientsin: An Illustrated Outline History*, translated by Xu Yifan, et al. Tianjin People's Publishing House, 2008, p.13.

动者服务殷勤，体格强健，行动敏捷。他们"外表非常拘谨，这是他们长期处在铁的政权统治之下自然产生出来的。在他们的私下生活中，他们也是非常活泼愉快的，但一见了官，就马上变成另外一个人了。"① 高等官员对于下级官员和仆役态度异常严苛，稍有过错就要行笞责。这种辱人尊严的惩罚让英国人瞠目结舌，"甚骇其所用刑罚之不当"。另一随行人员记录说，"余来中国，几无日不见华官笞责小民"，就好像这是他们每日必有的功课。② 这些现象让英国人认为，清朝完全是一个专制国家，它是依靠高压和暴力才逼迫臣民如此驯服，而这样的国家不值得羡慕。

使团成员无不惊叹于中国人口之多，令人难以想象，如船行在天津运河上他所看到的，连绵不断的围观民众组成的人墙。而且，中国北方的人口还少于南方，越往南行，人口越多。大量人口必然造成激烈的人地矛盾。由于人口过多，供牛羊生活的土地必须用来养活人，中国人不养或很少饲养牛羊，全部土地主要是种植人吃的粮食。所有耕地从不休耕，因此出产不高。"中国的人工非常低廉，只挣仅足糊口的工资。……他们的生活水平还是很低，整天吃素食，很少有肉吃。"③ 与之形成鲜明对照的是，皇帝赏赐使团的食物非常丰盛，根本吃不完。清帝第一次给予的赏赐有"牛二十头、羊一百三十头、猪一百二十头、鸡一百只、鸭一百头、粉一百六十袋、米一百六十袋、满洲面包十四箱、茶叶十箱、小米一箱、红米十箱、白米十箱、南瓜一千个、西瓜一千个、甜瓜三千个以及各种干鲜果品七十六箱，腌制蔬菜四十四箱和新鲜蔬菜四十捆，豌豆荚二十担，蜡烛十箱、陶器三篓。"④ 后面，每天还都会源源不断地供给食物酒水，而整个使团加上水手士兵甚至黑奴，总共也不过700多人。供过于求，

---

① （英）司当东著，叶笃义译，《英使谒见乾隆纪实》，三联书店（香港）有限公司，1994年，第233、227页。

② （英）马戛尔尼著，刘半农译，《1793乾隆英使觐见记》，天津人民出版社，2006年，第37—38页。

③ （英）司当东著，叶笃义译，《英使谒见乾隆纪实》，三联书店（香港）有限公司，1994年，第283页。

④ （英）马戛尔尼著，刘半农译，《1793乾隆英使觐见记》，天津人民出版社，2006年，第16页。

---

des lois, he mentioned China multiple times, discussing its various shortcomings from different aspects, hoping his compatriots would take these as a cautionary tale. Jean-Jacques Rousseau, on the other hand, believed that China, as an ancient civilization, had long departed from the "state of pure nature," and like the fallen civilizations of Europe, was full of oppression and inequality, decadence, and hypocrisy. He also interpreted the historical event of the Qing army's conquest of the Ming Dynasty as ancient China becoming luxurious and corrupt due to the advancement of material civilization, ultimately being vanquished by the surrounding less advanced nations, similar to how the highly civilized ancient Rome was destroyed by the barbaric Germanic tribes. Therefore, he opposed Europe learning from or following the path of China.

Which perspective is correct? The former view mainly comes from the observations of missionaries who resided in China for extended periods, while the latter is primarily from diplomats and merchants. Missionaries, in their process of evangelization, mainly interacted with the Chinese intellectual elite, who were generally well-educated and of noble character. Diplomats and merchants, on the other hand, usually made only brief stays in China and, due to language barriers and other reasons, were prone to conflicts with local residents, leading to more criticisms and complaints about China. For the Lord Macartney Mission, the outcome of their trip determined their rather negative impression of China. They apparently sided more with the latter perspective, viewing the Qing Dynasty as a despotic regime devoid of virtue, with the facade of prosperity masking the widespread poverty among the populace.

The records written by members of the Macartney and Lord Amherst's diplomatic mission contain detailed observations and descriptions of the Chinese society and its people. During their journey northward to seek an audience, their daily interactions were mainly with local officials, servants, and the lower-class populace of various regions. The officials who received them varied in demeanor; local officials were generally respectful and humble, while servants were very enthusiastic and sincere. However, the imperial envoy of 1793 was obstinate and "exhibited a mindset that was jealous of and scornful towards foreigners," "lacking in scientific knowledge and understanding of matters." The laboring class was diligent in service, robust in physique, and agile in movement. They "appeared very restrained on the outside, a natural outcome of living under an iron-fisted regime for a long time. In their private lives, they were very lively and cheerful, but the moment they saw an official, they transformed into someone entirely different."[1] Senior officials

---

① George Staunton. *An Authentic Account of an Embassy from the King of Great Britain to the Emperor of China*, translated by Ye Duyi. Joint Publishing Company (H.K.), 1994, p.233,227.

中国人群聚
Chinese people sitting around and chatting

were exceptionally harsh towards subordinate officials and servants, readily resorting to corporal punishment for even minor offenses. Such degrading punishments left the British astounded, "shocked at the inappropriateness of the punishments used." Another member of the entourage noted, "During my time in China, there has hardly been a day when I haven't seen Chinese officials flogging the common folk," as if it were a daily routine for them.[1] These phenomena led the British to conclude that the Qing Dynasty was utterly despotic, maintaining submissiveness among its subjects through oppression and violence, and that such a state was not worthy of envy.

Members of the mission were astounded by the immense population of China, finding it inconceivable. As they sailed along the Tianjin Canal, they witnessed continuous walls of onlookers. Moreover, the population in the north of China was even less than in the south; the further south they traveled, the more densely populated it became. The vast population inevitably led to intense conflict between people and land. Due to overpopulation, land that could have been used for grazing cattle and sheep was instead utilized to feed people. Consequently, the Chinese raised few or no cattle and sheep, dedicating all land primarily to the cultivation of food crops for human consumption. The land was never left fallow, hence the yield was not high. "Labor in China is incredibly cheap, earning just enough to scrape by... Their standard of living is quite low, subsisting on a vegetarian diet with very little meat."[2] In stark contrast, the food bestowed by the emperor to the mission was excessively abundant and impossible to consume entirely. The first gifts from the Qing emperor included "20 oxen, 130 sheep, 120 pigs, 100 chickens, 100 ducks, 160 bags of flour, 160 bags of rice, 14 boxes of Manchurian bread, 10 boxes of tea leaves, 1 box of millet, 10 boxes of red rice, 10 boxes of white rice, 1,000 pumpkins, 1,000 watermelons, 3,000 melons, and 76 boxes of various dried and fresh fruits, 44 boxes of pickled vegetables, 40 bundles of fresh vegetables, 20 loads of pea pods, 10 boxes of candles, and 3 baskets of pottery."[3] Furthermore, food and drinks were supplied incessantly each day to the entire mission, including sailors, soldiers, and even slaves, totaling just over 700 people. The supply far exceeded the demand, and nearly half was eventually

① George Macartney. *An Embassy to China: Being the Journal Kept by Lord Macartney during his Embassy to the Emperor Ch'ien-lung, 1793-1794*, translated by Liu Bannong. Tianjin People's Publishing House, 2005, pp.37-38.

② George Staunton. *An Authentic Account of an Embassy from the King of Great Britain to the Emperor of China*, translated by Ye Duyi. Joint Publishing Company (H.K.), 1994, p.283.

③ George Macartney. *An Embassy to China: Being the Journal Kept by Lord Macartney during His Embassy to the Emperor Ch'ien-lung, 1793-1794*, translated by Liu Bannong. Tianjin People's Publishing House, 2005, p.16.

乾隆赴热河的行幄御营
Emperor Qianlong's Imperial Camp en route to Jehol

受笞责的中国人
Chinese man being flogged with
a rattan cane as a punishment

最后扔了近一半。很多猪和家禽在路上碰撞而死，于是英国人就将这些已经发臭的动物从船上扔了下去，此时岸上的穷人们就疯了一样跳下海，马上把这些死动物捞起来，洗干净用盐腌好。①

马戛尔尼、司当东等人还注意到，中国社会由于实行"分产制"，所有男性直系后代都有继承权，所以一般"富不过三代"。财富无法积累，"很少有人能坐享其成，而不必再努力从事增产"。而且中国没有英国所谓的中等阶层，他们要么是穷人，要么是富人。从住宅上可以看出贫富之间的巨大差距。"大多数房子都是土墙草顶的草舍，也有很少一些高大的、油漆装饰的房子，可能是富有者的住所。"农民只能住在由晒干的泥巴做的房子里，而当地的地主则住在豪华的庄园里，庄园大门就有三座，庄园之内有好几所房子，

discarded. Many pigs and poultry died during transport due to collisions, and the British threw these already putrid animals overboard. At this point, impoverished locals on the shore frantically dived into the sea, swiftly salvaging these dead animals, washing them clean, and preserving them with salt.①

Macartney, Staunton, and others also noted that due to the practice of "partible inheritance" in Chinese society, where all male direct descendants have inheritance rights, wealth generally "does not last beyond three generations." Wealth cannot accumulate, and "few can enjoy the fruits of their labor without having to strive further for production." Moreover, China lacked what could be termed a middle class in England; individuals were either poor or rich. The vast disparity between the wealthy and the poor was evident from the residences. "Most houses are mud-walled and thatched cottages, though a few are large, painted, and decorated, possibly belonging to the wealthy." Farmers could only live in houses made of sun-dried mud, while local land-

① （英）马戛尔尼著，刘半农译，《1793 乾隆英使觐见记》，天津人民出版社，2006 年，第 16 页。

① George Macartney. *An Embassy to China: Being the Journal Kept by Lord Macartney during His Embassy to the Emperor Ch'ien-lung, 1793-1794*, translated by Liu Bannong. Tianjin People's Publishing House, 2005, p.16.

许多树木，许多羊和马，"非常类似于英国绅士的家庭花园"。城市里的贫富差距可以一目了然地从房屋所用砖瓦的颜色分辨出来，富人的房子用红色的烧过的砖瓦，穷人房子所用的则是土坯，而"天津的房子大半是铅灰砖瓦盖的，少数是红色砖瓦盖的"[①]。

在北京等待皇帝接见的时日，使团成员听当地传教士讲，在堂堂帝都北京，"穷人因为养活不起而弃婴的事经常发生"[②]。步军统领衙门专门准备了一辆大车，用于每天巡视街道，捡拾已死或将死的弃婴，拉到城外义冢掩埋或者直接扔到沟里。北京的传教士就捡走尚有气息的弃婴，救活后在教堂中抚养，待长成后洗礼成为教徒。沿途所见平民百姓的困苦与皇帝的奢侈形成了鲜明对比，对使团的丰厚赏赐并没有得到使团成员的感激，再加上乾隆皇帝断然拒绝了使团的通商要求，更增加了经历了资产阶级革命的马戛尔尼等人的轻视和厌恶。

外交使团历来承担的使命除了表示友好之外，总是离不开充当间谍、搜集情报。马戛尔尼使团和阿美士德使团的首要使命（请求与中国通商）虽然没有达成，但还是得到了关于中国这个古老帝国方方面面的信息，这为他们日后发动殖民侵略战争提供了重要的情报。比如说，因为从未有西方人航行到过大沽口，所以马戛尔尼使团在中国南方请地方官员帮助寻找领航员，最后好不容易才找到两个到过大沽口的人。在向北航行中，这两个人一遇到有风浪的天气或者稍稍看不到海岸就惊慌失措、大呼小叫，让英国人头痛不已。不过，使团由此了解到，中国人的航海水平自宋朝以后大大下降，已丧失了远洋航行的能力，仅仅停留在近海范围，而且中国的海防也几乎不堪一击。在北京，使团卫队的军人还对长城及北京附近的防卫建筑进行了详细的测量，对清军的军事技术做了细致的调查，其精细程度令人惊叹。

马戛尔尼目睹了清朝武力的孱弱，但最让他们震惊的，还是幻

---

① （英）司当东著，叶笃义译，《英使谒见乾隆纪实》，三联书店（香港）有限公司，1994年，第282、221、228—229、237页。

② （英）司当东著，叶笃义译，《英使谒见乾隆纪实》，三联书店（香港）有限公司，1994年，第284页。

lords resided in luxurious estates with three entrance gates, several houses, numerous trees, sheep, and horses, "very much resembling the family gardens of English gentlemen." The wealth gap in cities could be discernibly identified by the color of the bricks and tiles used in houses; the wealthy used red, fired bricks and tiles, while the poor used adobe. "The majority of houses in Tianjin are covered with lead-grey bricks and tiles, with only a few covered in red."[①]

While waiting in Beijing for an audience with the emperor, members of the mission heard from local missionaries that in the illustrious imperial capital, "the abandonment of infants by the poor, unable to feed them, occurred frequently."[②] The infantry commander's office had specially prepared a large cart for patrolling the streets daily, picking up infants who were dead or close to death, taking them outside the city for burial in a charitable cemetery or simply throwing them into a ditch. Missionaries in Beijing would rescue the abandoned infants still breathing, raise them in the church, and, once grown, baptize them into the faith. The dire poverty of the common people seen along the way sharply contrasted with the emperor's extravagance. The generous rewards to the mission did not garner gratitude from its members, and Emperor Qianlong's outright refusal of the mission's trade requests further fueled the contempt and aversion of Macartney and others, who had experienced the bourgeois revolution.

Besides expressing goodwill, diplomatic missions have always involved espionage and intelligence gathering. Although the primary mission of the Macartney and Amherst missions (to request trade with China) was not accomplished, they still obtained a wealth of information about various aspects of this ancient empire, which would later provide crucial intelligence for their colonial wars of aggression. For instance, as no Westerner had ever navigated to the Taku Forts, the Lord Macartney Mission had to request local officials in southern China to help find pilots, eventually managing to find only two who had been to Taku Forts. During the northward voyage, these two would panic, shouting and screaming at the slightest wind or wave or when they lost sight of the shore, causing great distress to the British. However, the mission learned that China's seafaring capabilities had greatly declined since the Song Dynasty, losing the capacity for long-distance ocean voyages and limited to coastal areas, and that China's coastal defenses were almost defenseless. In

---

① George Staunton. *An Authentic Account of an Embassy from the King of Great Britain to the Emperor of China*, translated by Ye Duyi. Joint Publishing Company (H.K.), 1994, p.282,221,237, pp.228-229.

② George Staunton. *An Authentic Account of an Embassy from the King of Great Britain to the Emperor of China*, translated by Ye Duyi. Joint Publishing Company (H.K.), 1994, p.284.

想的破灭。原来，清朝统治下的中国不是马可·波罗说的那样社会繁荣、人民富庶，而是一个采取高压手段的专制国家，底层百姓生活困顿、君主富人奢靡无度、普通人毫无尊严。如果只是武器比英国弱，英国人还不会视清帝国为野蛮国家，如此残忍对待自己国家的百姓，才是真正让马戛尔尼等人鄙夷的一点。随着使团成员的大量笔记陆续出版，中国在欧洲的高大形象彻底坍塌，从一个曾被一些欧洲思想家推崇的文明典范，变成了受殖民主义者调侃鄙夷的野蛮之国，由是埋下了之后一系列欧洲对中国蚕食侵略的祸根。"康乾盛世"后不到短短的五十年，鸦片战争就开始了，清政府不堪一击，从此忍受百年屈辱。

Beijing, soldiers from the mission's guard also conducted detailed measurements of the Great Wall and the defensive structures near Beijing, and meticulously surveyed the Qing army's military technology, astonishing in their thoroughness.

Macartney witnessed the feebleness of Qing military power, but what shocked them most was the shattering of their illusions. Contrary to Marco Polo's descriptions of a thriving society and affluent populace, the China under Qing rule they saw was a despotic state employing oppressive measures, where the common people lived in hardship, the monarch and the wealthy indulged in extreme luxury, and the ordinary citizen lacked dignity. If it were only that China's weaponry was weaker than Britain's, the British would not have regarded the Qing Empire as a barbaric nation. It was the cruel treatment of its own people that truly filled Macartney and others with disdain. As the extensive notes of the mission members were published one after another, China's grand image in Europe completely collapsed. From once being revered as a model of civilization by some European thinkers, it became a subject of mockery and disdain by colonialists, laying the groundwork for a series of European encroachments and invasions of China. Less than fifty years after the so-called "Prosperous Era of Kangxi and Qianlong," the Opium War began. The Qing government crumbled easily, marking the start of a century of humiliation.

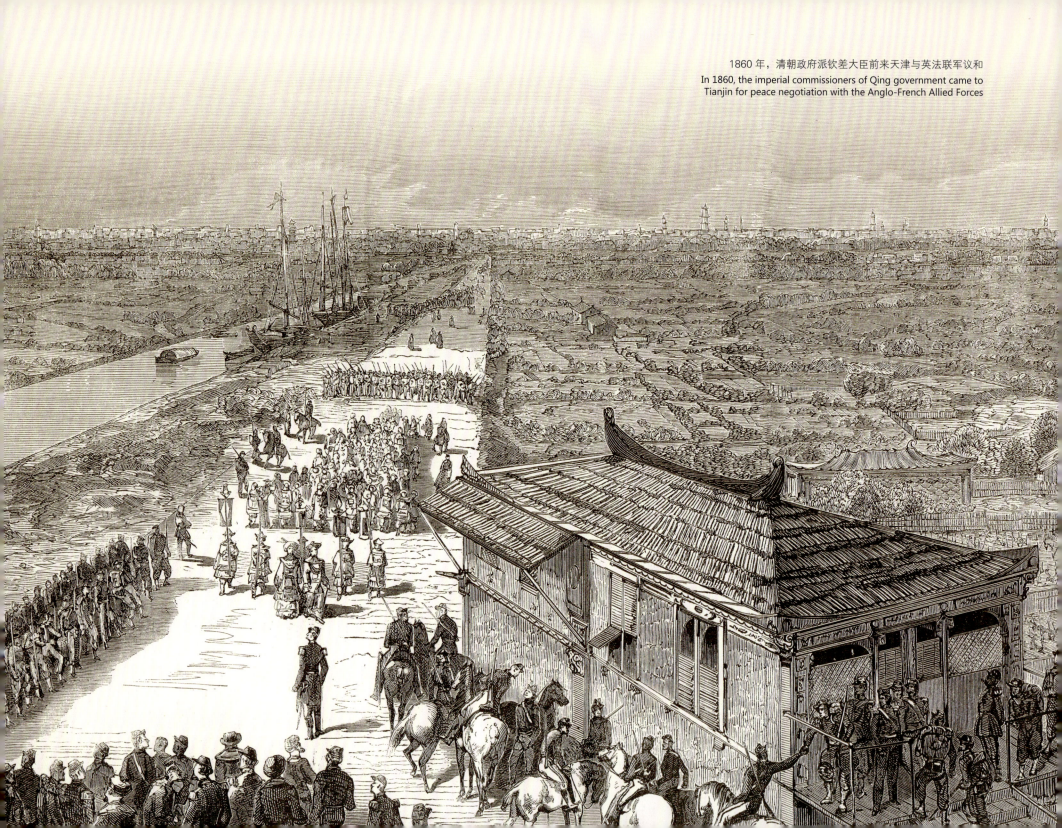

第 二 章　中西碰撞与城市空间的扩张

Chapter Two: Collision between China and the West and the Expansion of Urban Space

第一次鸦片战争与天津

"哥伦比亚麦德林可卡因垄断集团成功地发动一起对美国的军事袭击，迫使美国允许……该垄断组织将毒品出口到美国五个主要城市，不受美国监督并免予征税；美国政府还被迫同意贩卖毒品的官员管理在这些城市活动的所有哥伦比亚人。此外，美国还必须支付战争赔偿1000亿美元——这是哥伦比亚向美国输出可卡因所发动战争的花费。"[①] 这幅场景就是美国一位历史学家在论及鸦片战争时所联想到的一幅场景。然而这样令人看来明显荒谬、不可思议的事件在19世纪的中国确曾发生过，而且不止一次，这就是两次鸦片战争。

战争是各种矛盾冲突到不可调和地步之后的集中爆发。在此之前，让我们回看事情是怎样一步一步地演进成为难以挽回的危机。中国方面，鸦片问题以及由此产生的白银大量外流几乎是唯一的焦点；而在通过新航路扬帆而至的外国商人心目中，除了巨额利润，还有一些比鸦片贸易更重要的问题，这也引起了外国政府及其本国人民的关注。

工业革命与禁海令

在欧亚大陆的西部，15世纪至18世纪，西欧商业资本主义蓬勃发展。为了追求最大利润，一方面资产阶级在全世界奔走，积极发展海外贸易，进行殖民统治，积累了丰富的资本，打开了广阔的海

---

① （美）特拉维斯·黑尼斯三世、弗兰克·萨奈罗著，周辉荣译，《鸦片战争》，生活·读书·新知三联书店，2005年，"序"，第1页。

The First Opium War and Tianjin

"The Colombian Medellin Cocaine Cartel successfully launched a military attack against the United States, forcing the US to allow... it to export drugs to five major US cities without supervision and taxation; the US government was also compelled to agree that Colombian officials involved in drug trafficking would manage all activities of Colombians in these cities. Furthermore, the US had to pay war reparations of $100 billion—this was the cost of the war Colombia waged against the US to export cocaine to America."[①] This scenario is what an American historian associates with when discussing the Opium Wars. However, what seems absurd and unbelievable to modern observers actually happened in 19th-century China, not just once but twice, known as the two Opium Wars.

War is the concentrated outbreak after various contradictions and conflicts have reached an irreconcilable stage. Before that, let's review how things evolved step by step into an irreversible crisis. On the Chinese side, the opium problem and the consequent massive outflow of silver were almost the sole focus; while in the minds of foreign merchants sailing through the new routes, besides enormous profits, there were also some issues more important than the opium trade, which also caught the attention of foreign governments and their people.

The Industrial Revolution and Maritime Prohibition

In the western part of the Eurasian continent, from the 15th to the 18th century, commercial capitalism in Western Europe flourished. In pursuit of maximum profit, on the one hand, the bourgeoisie traveled around the world,

---

① W. Travis Hanes III, Frank Sanello. *The Opium Wars: the Addiction of One Empire and the Corruption of Another*, translated by Zhou Huirong. SDX Joint Publishing Company, 2005, "Preface", p.1.

1805 年的广州十三行，威廉·丹尼尔绘制。图片来源：英国国家航海博物馆
Guangzhou Thirteen Hongs in 1805, drawn by William Daniell. Source: British National Maritime Museum

这片小广场是在广州的洋人唯一可以自由行走的地方，画者不详。图片来源：香港历史博物馆
This small square was the only place in Guangzhou where foreigners were allowed to walk around freely, by an unknown painter. Source: Hong Kong Museum of History

外市场和廉价的原料供应地；另一方面，他们在本国压榨农民，获得了大量廉价劳动力，为提高劳动生产率，大机器生产开始取代工厂手工业，生产力得到突飞猛进的发展，历史上把这一过程称为"工业革命"。孤悬海外的英国因为较少受到外国侵略而拥有更好的外部条件，率先完成了资产阶级革命，也最先开始工业革命。1765 年"珍妮纺织机"的发明揭开了工业革命的序幕。不久，在采煤、冶金等许多工业部门，都陆续有了机器生产。随着机器生产越来越多，1785 年瓦特制成的改良型蒸汽机的投入使用，提供了更加强劲的动力，人类社会由此进入了"蒸汽时代"。

15 世纪到 17 世纪，欧亚大陆的东边，中国经常不断地受到侵略者的攻击侵扰。虽然摧毁了蒙古帝国、建立了明朝，可是明朝统治者还是不得不提防来自北方的骚扰，永乐皇帝朱棣也把首都由南京迁往北京，美其名曰"天子守国门"。由于集中注意力应对北方陆上敌人，中央政府对那些"小"事情——到达中国南方边陲口岸的少数欧洲商船——就只能给予微小的注意，采取对自己麻烦最少的方法来解决，那就是颁布"禁海令"。明朝时期国内所萌生的资本

actively developing overseas trade, establishing colonial rule, accumulating abundant capital, and exploring vast overseas markets and sources of cheap raw materials. On the other hand, they exploited farmers in their own countries to obtain a large amount of cheap labor. To increase labor productivity, large-scale machine production began to replace manual labor in factories, leading to a rapid development of productivity, historically referred to as the "Industrial Revolution." The isolated island nation of Britain, having suffered relatively less foreign aggression, possessed better external conditions and was the first to complete the bourgeois revolution and initiate the Industrial Revolution. The invention of the "Spinning Jenny" in 1765 marked the beginning of the Industrial Revolution. Soon, many industrial sectors such as coal mining and metallurgy began to adopt machine production. With the increasing use of machinery, the introduction of James Watt's improved steam engine in 1785 provided even more powerful driving force, leading human society into the "Steam Age."

From the 15th to the 17th century, in the eastern part of the Eurasian continent, China was frequently subjected to attacks and disturbances by invaders. Despite overthrowing the Mongol Empire and establishing the Ming Dynasty, Ming rulers still had to guard against harassment from the people in the north. Emperor Yongle moved the capital from Nanjing to Beijing, claiming it was to "guard the nation's gates." Due to the central government's focus

主义萌芽过于弱小，更不要说为工业革命提供土壤。明王朝在后期不断被内部的农民起义和新兴的外部挑战者打击，最后被打败，中国再次改朝换代。新的清朝统治者，内心深处始终不安。他们不仅对百姓的反抗一直抱着警惕的态度，而且对不断叩关而来的西方人，因深恐其与百姓联手对付自己，而对其贸易要求也是能拒绝就拒绝，马戛尔尼使团和阿美士德使团因此吃了闭门羹。

即便如此，清朝统治者也不可能完全禁绝对外贸易，特别是它还能带来丰厚的收益。1757年乾隆皇帝下谕，仅留粤海关一口对外通商。清政府指定广州十三家牙行（中介机构，赚差价的中间商）专做对外贸易，称为"十三行"。广州十三行所在区域成为清帝国唯一合法的外贸特区，中国对世界的贸易全部聚集于此。直至鸦片战争为止，这些洋货行垄断中国外贸长达85年。依靠垄断地位，广州十三行给那里的行商们带来了巨额收入。十三行的潘、伍、卢、叶四大行商号称"广州四大富豪"，其家产总和比当时的国库收入还要多，是货真价实的"富可敌国"。

然而，对于那些不远万里踏浪而来、与中国行商打交道的外国商人来说，十三行的设置却不是那么令人愉快了。本身就是依靠垄断本国市场来获取远程贸易高额利润的各国东印度公司，自然不甘心忍受十三行商人的限制和盘剥。首先，所有贸易往来的规则，必须由这些中间商来制定并从中赚取巨大利润，而且外商船只进出广州内河还需缴纳不菲的费用以及各种不定额的关税，实际征收往往是公布税则所核定税率的5—10倍。①不仅如此，对那些在华经商的外国商人，清政府还制定了种种章程，其中有许多限制人身自由的苛刻条件，比如：不允许外国妇女进入商馆；不允许住在行商商馆的外商自由出入；不允许外国人在江中划船娱乐；不允许外国人乘轿，只许徒步行走；贸易季节之后，不允许外国人逗留广州，只能回国或前往澳门。清政府还不允许中国行商借贷或赊欠货物给外国人，不允许外国商人雇用中国籍仆役。这些章程不仅阻碍了商业的发展，也打击了本国的服务业和底层民众的生计。遇有纠纷，外国人也不

---

① （美）马士著，张汇文等译，《中华帝国对外关系史》第一卷，上海书店出版社，2006年，第86—89页。

on dealing with northern land-based enemies, minor issues such as the arrival of a few European merchant ships at southern Chinese border ports received little attention, and the government adopted the least troublesome method to deal with them, issuing the "sea ban." The seeds of capitalist that emerged domestically during the Ming Dynasty were too weak, let alone providing a fertile ground for the Industrial Revolution. In the later period of the Ming Dynasty, constant internal peasant uprisings and attacks from the emerging external challengers weakened the dynasty, leading to its eventual defeat and the transition to a new dynasty in China. The new rulers of the Qing Dynasty, always felt uneasy deep down, holding a vigilant attitude towards the resistance of common people. They also harbored suspicions against Westerners who continuously sought trade, fearing they might join forces with common people against them. As a result, they rejected trade requests, and missions such as the Lord Macartney Mission and the Lord Amherst's diplomatic mission were turned away.

Nevertheless, the Qing rulers could not completely ban foreign trade, especially since it brought lucrative profits. In 1757, Emperor Qianlong decreed to allow foreign trade only through the Guangzhou Customs. The Qing government designated thirteen Guangzhou factories (intermediary agencies, middlemen profiting from price differences) to specialize in foreign trade, referred to as the "Thirteen Hongs". The area where the Thirteen Hongs were located became the sole legal foreign trade zone of the Qing Empire, where China's trade with the world was concentrated. Until the Opium Wars, these foreign commodities factories monopolized China's foreign trade for 85 years. With their monopolistic position, the Thirteen Hongs brought enormous income to the merchants there. The four major merchants of the Thirteen Hongs—Pan, Wu, Lu, and Ye—were known as the "Four Great Wealthy Families of Guangzhou." Their combined wealth exceeded the national treasury's income at the time, making them truly "wealthy enough to rival a nation."

However, for foreign merchants who traveled from afar to deal with Chinese traders, the establishment of the Thirteen Hongs was not so pleasant. The various East India Companies from different countries, which relied on monopolizing their own domestic markets to obtain high profits from long-distance trade, naturally did not want to endure the restrictions and exploitation imposed by the Thirteen Hongs merchants. Firstly, all rules of trade must be formulated by these middlemen, who profited immensely from them. Additionally, foreign ships entering and leaving the inland rivers of Guangzhou had to pay hefty fees and various unpredictable tariffs, often 5-10 times higher

得直接向官府提出申诉请求，必须由行商转呈。[1] 在广州的外国商人被限制在很小的一片区域里，十三行装饰华丽的商馆成为实际上的镀金鸟笼。

不过，外国商人在中国面临的最大问题，其实是赚不到钱。他们在中国购买了大量的茶叶、丝织品，而他们带来的商品，除了钟表等少数奢侈品能卖给中国富人之外，并没有什么市场。不甘心的外国商人们很快找到利润更为丰厚的替代商品——鸦片。最早向中国输入鸦片的是荷兰人和葡萄牙人，后来英国的东印度公司赶走了其他竞争者，把这项获利丰厚的贸易垄断在自己手中。

18世纪印度沦为英国殖民地之后，英国商人从本土把机器大工业生产出来的棉纺织品装船运往印度卖掉，用卖棉纺织品的钱购买在印度种植的鸦片，再运往中国售出。回程中，他们用卖鸦片的钱在中国购买茶叶、丝织品并在印度购买棉花，然后一起装船运回国或销往世界各地。鸦片贸易的存在，使中国、英国和英属殖民地印度之间存在着一种利润丰厚的三角贸易关系，其中鸦片走私成为重要的环节。1834年英国东印度公司对英国贸易的垄断被取消，自由贸易开始，英国商人的鸦片贸易日益高涨，而且被置于英国政府及其军队的直接保护之下。

鸦片贸易使中国的白银储备大量外流。意识到问题严重性的清政府，自1800年开始下令禁止鸦片贸易、禁止在国内种植罂粟。但是走私鸦片的行为却并没有减少，甚至在1821年之后还增长了一倍以上。从中受益的当然不止英国商人，还有贪婪的中国官吏。对于是否坚决对鸦片贸易说不，清政府内部有不同意见，但在1836年，清政府最终下定决心要禁绝鸦片，并严禁银锭出口，以杜绝白银外流。以英商为首的外籍商人一开始心存侥幸，拒不执行，而广东的一些官员对查禁鸦片的命令也三心二意。直到1839年，被誉为"近代中国开眼看世界第一人"的林则徐，在广州缉拿烟贩、销毁鸦片，之后中国参加的第一场近代战争——第一次鸦片战争爆发。

---

① （美）马士著，张汇文等译，《中华帝国对外关系史》第一卷，上海书店出版社，2006年，第76—78页。

than the rates specified in the published tariff schedules.[1] Moreover, the Qing government imposed various regulations on foreign merchants conducting business in China, many of which were stringent conditions restricting personal freedom. For example: foreign women were not allowed to enter the merchants' guildhalls; foreigners staying in the guildhalls were not allowed free access; foreigners were not allowed to row boats for recreation on the river; foreigners were not allowed to ride sedan chairs, and could only walk on foot; after the trading season, foreigners were not allowed to stay in Guangzhou and could only return home or go to Macau. The Qing government also prohibited Chinese traders from lending money or extending credit to foreigners and prohibited foreign merchants from hiring Chinese servants. These regulations not only hindered commercial development but also impacted China's service industry and the livelihoods of the lower classes. In case of disputes, foreigners were not allowed to directly appeal to the government; they had to go through the merchants.[2] Foreign merchants in Guangzhou were confined to a very small area, and the splendidly decorated guildhalls of the Thirteen Hongs became nothing more than gilded cages in reality.

However, the biggest problem foreign merchants faced in China was actually the inability to make profits. They purchased large quantities of tea, silk fabrics, and other goods in China, but the commodities they brought with them, except for a few luxury items such as clocks, had no market except for selling to wealthy Chinese. Dissatisfied with this situation, foreign merchants quickly found a more lucrative alternative—opium. The Dutch and Portuguese were the first to import opium to China, but later the British East India Company drove out other competitors and monopolized this highly profitable trade.

After India became a British colony in the 18th century, British merchants shipped machine-made cotton textiles produced domestically to India for sale. They used the proceeds from selling cotton textiles to purchase opium grown in India, which they then sold in China. On the return journey, they used the money from selling opium to buy tea and silk fabrics in China and cotton in India. These goods were then shipped back to Britain or sold to various parts of the world. The existence of the opium trade created a highly profitable triangular trade relationship between China, Britain, and British colonial India, with opium smuggling being a significant aspect. In 1834, the British East

---

① Hosea Ballou Morse. *The International Relations of the Chinese Empire* (vol.1), translated by Zhang Huiwen, et al. Shanghai Bookstore Publishing House, 2006, pp.86-89.

② Hosea Ballou Morse. *The International Relations of the Chinese Empire* (vol.1), translated by Zhang Huiwen, et al. Shanghai Bookstore Publishing House, 2006, pp.76-78.

白河投书

天津是首都北京的门户，战略位置的重要性不言而喻。1404 年设卫建城伊始，它最主要的职能就是拱卫京师。荷兰使团和马戛尔尼使团都曾坐船来到天津，并在这里短暂逗留，在夜色笼罩下海河静谧的涟漪里，做着打开中国市场大门的美梦。那也是自工业革命开始后中西交流最后的和平时期。

之后，虽然美梦破碎，通商请求遭到乾隆皇帝的拒绝，不过殖民主义时代侵略成性的东印度公司早就做好了两手准备，能让清政府主动打开国门最好，清政府不允的话就诉诸武力。传教士和东印度公司对中国沿海各港口的政治、经济、军事情报的刺探工作早就在进行。通商请求被拒绝后，这种情报搜集就更加目标明确。天津成为殖民者武力压服北京的首要目标。

1831 年 6 月，普鲁士籍传教士郭士腊（Karl F. A. Gutzlaff）搭载一艘福建商人的货船，从泰国曼谷出发前往中国沿海考察，此行终点即为天津。为了方便在中国活动，他给自己取了中国名字"郭士立"，穿上中国服装冒充中国人，随身带着航海图、测绘仪器，混在水手的船舱里，通过聊天了解中国沿海情况。他一路沿海北上，抵达天津后，四处搜集天津城的情报。原本，他还打算潜入北京城，但苦于不会说北方话，只得作罢。第二年，他再受东印度公司聘请，乘坐该公司走私鸦片的"阿美士德号"船到中国沿海航行侦察。他们此行的目的更为明确，即探明中国沿海港口的航道，测绘较为准确的海域图，侦察港口及沿海地带清政府的防务和兵力布置，调查各地出产、商业状况、风土人情以及沿海走私鸦片

穿着中国服饰的郭士腊
Karl F. A. Gutzlaff wearing Chinese clothing

India Company's monopoly on British trade was abolished, and free trade began. British merchants increased their opium trade under the direct protection from the British government and its military.

The opium trade caused a large-scale outflow of silver reserves from China. Recognizing the seriousness of the problem, the Qing government began to issue orders to prohibit opium trade and the cultivation of poppies domestically from 1800 onwards. However, the smuggling of opium did not decrease; in fact, it more than doubled after 1821. Besides British merchants, greedy Chinese officials also benefited from it. There were differing opinions within the Qing government on whether to firmly say no to the opium trade. However, in 1836, the Qing government finally resolved to ban opium and strictly prohibit the export of silver ingots to prevent the outflow of silver. Initially, foreign merchants, led by British traders, were optimistic and refused to comply, and some officials in Guangdong were also ambivalent about enforcing the ban on opium. It wasn't until 1839 when Lin Zexu, hailed as the "first person in modern China to open his eyes to the world," cracked down on opium smuggling and destroyed opium in Guangzhou leading to the first modern war China participated in—the First Opium War.

Lord Palmerston's Letter Delivered at the Peiho ("White River")

Tianjin serves as the gateway to the capital, Beijing, and its strategic importance is self-evident. Since its establishment as a military outpost in 1404, its primary function has been to guard the capital. Both the Dutch and Lord Macartney Missions arrived by ship in Tianjin and briefly stayed here, dreaming of opening the doors to the Chinese market amidst the serene ripples of the Hai River under the cover of nightfall. It was also the last peaceful period of Sino-Western exchanges since the beginning of the Industrial Revolution.

Subsequently, although the dream shattered and their trade requests were rejected by Emperor Qianlong, the East India Company, with its ingrained colonial aggression, had long prepared for both eventualities: it would be best if the Qing government voluntarily opened its doors, but if not, resorting to force was also an option. Missionaries and the East India Company had long been engaged in espionage activities to gather political, economic, and military intelligence on various ports along the Chinese coast. After the trade requests were rejected, this intelligence gathering became even more targeted. Tianjin became the primary target for colonial forces to subdue Beijing through military means.

In June 1831, the Prussian missionary Karl F. A. Gutzlaff boarded a merchant ship from Fujian, departing from Bangkok, Thailand, to conduct a sur-

的可能性等。

　　根据这些情报，1835 年东印度公司向英国外交大臣建议，可以在未来的战争中单独对广州、厦门、上海、天津四座主要沿海港口附近进行封锁，各驻以小型舰队，即可达到封锁中国沿海的目的；尤其是天津，虽然天津的商务不及福建的繁盛，但天津距北京不足五十英里，我们在天津所造成的惊恐大可逼迫清政府早日结束战争。[①] 这便是后来挑起两次鸦片战争时英军入侵大沽口行动计划的原始依据。

　　果不其然，当虎门销烟的烈火熊熊燃起，利益受损的鸦片商们督促英国驻华商务监督义律（Charles Elliot）多次向英国政府呼吁，发出战争叫嚣：封锁白河[②]，威胁天津，压服北京。于是，英国政府制定了武装封锁大沽口、强行向清政府递交照会的战略决策。第一次鸦片战争中，由于林则徐认真备战，英军未能在广州得逞，侵略军遂按照既定方针，留下一部分兵力封锁珠江口，其余北上进犯厦门、定海、宁波，封锁沿海主要港口和长江口后，径直驶向大沽口。

　　1840 年 8 月 7 日，在堂兄弟懿律（George Elliot）与义律（Charles Elliot）二人率领下，由"威里士厘号"（Wellesley）战列舰等八艘军舰组成的英国舰队驶入大沽口海域。尽管"威里士厘号"并不是非常强大的战舰，但对于长期隔绝于世界之外的道光皇帝与驻天津的大臣琦善来说，英军的炮舰确实产生了很大的震慑力。琦善派人到英国船上借交涉之名进行了一番"知己知彼"的调查，发现英国人的船坚炮利远在中国之上。在呈送给道光皇帝的奏折中，他说，英国的汽船"无风无潮，顺水逆水，皆能飞渡"。他们的炮位之下，"设有石磨盘，中具机轴，只需移转磨盘，炮即随其所向"。回想中国的军备，山海关的大炮尚是"前明之物，勉强蒸洗备用"[③]；而天津的防卫更是空虚，大沽口要塞自清朝实行海禁后炮台久已倾圮，

---

① 列岛编，《鸦片战争史论文专集》，生活・读书・新知三联书店，1958 年，第
　　40—41 页。

② 白河即海河。也有一说，白河为北运河，因岸上多有白沙，少生草木，所以叫白河。
　　不过，根据外国地图所标"Peiho"位置，这里应指海河。

③ 转引自蒋廷黻，《中国近代史》，中国华侨出版社，2015 年，第 18 页。

vey along the Chinese coast, with Tianjin as the final destination. To facilitate his activities in China, he adopted the Chinese name "Guo Shili" and dressed in Chinese attire to pass as a local. He carried navigation charts and surveying instruments with him and mingled with sailors in the ship's cabin, gathering information about the coastal regions of China through conversations. Traveling north along the coast, he arrived in Tianjin and gathered intelligence about the city. Initially, he also intended to infiltrate Beijing, but being incapable to speak the northern dialects, he had to abandon the plan. The following year, he was hired by the East India Company again and sailed along the Chinese coast on the smuggling ship "Lord Amherst" to conduct reconnaissance. The purpose of this mission was clearer: to explore the navigational routes of Chinese coastal ports, map more accurate sea charts, survey the Qing government's defense and troop deployments in ports and coastal areas, and investigate local production, commercial conditions, customs, and the potential for coastal opium smuggling, among other objectives.

Based on this intelligence, in 1835, the East India Company proposed to the British Foreign Minister that in future wars, blockades could be enforced individually near the four major coastal ports of Guangzhou, Xiamen, Shanghai, and Tianjin. By stationing small fleets at each port, the objective of blocking the Chinese coast could be achieved. Especially in Tianjin, although Tianjin's business is not as prosperous as that of Fujian, Tianjin is less than fifty miles from Beijing. The terror we cause in Tianjin can force the Qing government to end the war early.[①] This became the original basis for the British invasion plan at the Taku Forts, which later sparked the two Opium Wars.

Sure enough, when the flames of the burning opium at Humen rose, opium traders whose interests were harmed urged Charles Elliot, the British Chief Superintendent of Trade in China, to repeatedly appeal to the British government, calling for war: blockade the Peiho,[②] threaten Tianjin, and subdue Beijing. As a result, the British government formulated a strategic decision to forcibly blockade the Taku Forts and forcibly deliver a memorandum to the Qing government. In the First Opium War, due to Lin Zexu's serious preparations for war, the British army failed to succeed in Guangzhou. Following the established policy, the invading army left a portion of its forces to blockade the Pearl River Estuary, while the rest moved north to attack Xiamen, Dinghai,

① Lie Dao (ed). *Paper Collection on the History of the Opium War.* SDX Joint Publishing Company, 1958, pp.40-41.

② Peiho ("White River") is also known as the Hai River. There is also a saying that Peiho is the Northern Grand Canal, and got its name because there are white sands on the bank while not many grasses and trees. However, according to the location of "Peiho" marked on foreign maps, it should be the Hai River.

大炮要从外地临时调运。最要命的是，天津竟然没有水师军舰。对比敌我双方力量之后，琦善决定屈服，采取"抚夷"策略。本来还有点底气的道光皇帝也没了主意。8 月 30 日，琦善和义律在大沽口的帐篷里进行正式谈判。在琦善的一味妥协之下，懿律闻知清朝下旨查办林则徐，且北方天气渐冷，英国水手中又发生流行疾病，遂答应清朝政府离开大沽口南下继续谈判。至此，在大沽口海域盘踞了近 40 天的英国舰队离开了天津，鸦片战争的形势急转直下。这次事件史称"白河投书"。

白河投书，是外国侵略者第一次武力威胁天津。清政府的妥协证明，在天津动用武力对北京的清政府施加压力的尝试，确实能奏效。一个参加此次行动的英国军官指出，"天津——位于运粮河和白河的交叉点的大商业城市。……我知道，聚集在那里的漕船的火焰，如果需要的话，再加上该城的火焰，就会唤醒皇帝的恐惧感，而我们自己的条件就可以达到。"[1] 在南方的谈判并不顺利，每逢不能满足英国侵略者的要求时，他们就祭出"北上天津"的法宝，压迫清政府屈服，直至 1842 年英军进入南京，签订了中国近代史上第一个不平等条约——《南京条约》。

以鸦片贸易为由而起的战争，在战后缔结的条约中，其实并不是主要关注点。《南京条约》共十三款，其中要求中国：（1）割让香港岛；（2）向英国赔偿鸦片烟价、商欠、军费共 2100 万银元；（3）五口通商，开放广州、福州、厦门、宁波、上海五处为通商口岸，允许英人居住并设派领事；（4）协定关税，英商应纳进出口货税、饷费，中国海关无权自主；（5）废除公行制度，准许英商在华自由贸易等。此外，也规定双方官吏平等往来、释放对方军民以及英国撤军等事宜。

天津的战略地位是如此重要，外国侵略者既欲通过天津进入北京以胁迫清政府，同时又迫切希望打开这个口岸通商，以获得更为广阔的市场。之后，美国和法国也都以"驶往天津白河口""同往天津"等话语相要挟，要求"利益均沾"。而清朝皇帝除了表示愤怒之外，

---

① 中国史学会主编，《鸦片战争》第五册，神州国光社，1954 年，第 89 页。

and Ningbo. After blockading the major coastal ports and the mouth of the Yangtze River, they proceeded directly to the Taku Forts.

On August 7, 1840, under the leadership of cousins George Elliot and Charles Elliot, a British fleet consisting of eight warships, including the battleship "Wellesley," entered the waters of the Taku Forts. Although the Wellesley was not a particularly powerful warship, for Emperor Daoguang and his minister stationed in Tianjin, Qishan, who had long been isolated from the world, the British gunboats indeed exerted significant deterrence. Qishan sent someone to the British gunboats under the pretext of negotiation to conduct a "know thy enemy" investigation and found that the British gunboats were far superior in terms of firepower compared to those of China. In the memorandum submitted to Emperor Daoguang, he said that British steamships "can navigate regardless of wind or tide, with or against the currents." Beneath their gun positions, "there are stone millstones with axles, and just turning the millstone can direct the cannon." Reflecting on China's military capabilities, the cannons at Shanhaiguan Fort were still "relics from the previous Ming dynasty, barely functional after some refurbishment."[1] Moreover, the defense of Tianjin was even more vulnerable, as the Taku Forts had long been dilapidated since the Qing dynasty implemented the sea ban, and the cannons had to be temporarily transported from elsewhere. Most critically, Tianjin surprisingly lacked a navy. After comparing the strengths of both sides, Qishan decided to capitulate and adopt a policy of appeasement towards the British. Emperor Daoguang, who initially had some confidence, lost his resolve. On August 30, Qishan and Charles Elliot conducted formal negotiations in a tent at the Taku Forts. Under Qishan's constant concessions, Elliot learned that the Qing government had issued an order to investigate Lin Zexu, and with the northern weather turning cold and an outbreak of disease among British sailors, he agreed to leave the Taku Forts and head south to continue negotiations at the insistence of the Qing government. Thus, the British fleet, which had been stationed in the waters of the Taku Forts for nearly 40 days, left Tianjin, and the situation of the Opium War took a sharp turn. This incident in history is known as the "Lord Palmerston's Letter Delivered at the Peiho."

The "Lord Palmerston's Letter" marked the first instance of foreign aggressors threatening Tianjin by force. The Qing government's capitulation proved that the attempt to pressure the Qing government in Beijing by using force in Tianjin could indeed be effective. A British officer involved in this action pointed out, "Tianjin—a major commercial city at the intersection of the

---

① Quoted in Jiang Tingfu. *Modern Chinese History*. The Chinese Overseas Publishing House. 2015, p.18.

却没什么有效的措施。1850年6月，英国军舰"雷纳德号"（HMS Reynard）再次投书白河口，皇帝谕旨给大臣说："迩者夷人在天津之行径，实属桀骜侮慢已极，乃竟恬不知耻，径自投函枢臣。爰经叠降谕旨，饬毋庸予以复文，全然等闲视之……"① 声嘶力竭的呵斥除了暴露自己的无能，根本无法阻止外国人来津。天津不仅变成近代列强挟制清政府的命门，而且很快真正成为列强在中国的演兵场。

第二次鸦片战争与天津

《南京条约》仅仅是一个开始

　　鸦片战争虽由鸦片问题而起，实际上是为了解决中国与西方国家的政治经济外交关系。在《南京条约》签订之后，中国又在1844年和美国人签订了《望厦条约》，和法国人签订了《黄埔条约》。这些条约是近代国际关系的主要形式，奠定了中国与列强之间外交和商务关系的原则基础。这一新的条约关系，一方面从形式上给中国带来了近代国际关系的新模式；另一方面在内容上又使中国的主权受到侵害，蒙受着不平等的耻辱。

　　《南京条约》仅仅是一个开始，它带来的问题远比解决的问题多。条约的签订是中国在战败压力之下被迫接受的，所以清政府内部并不打算要认真遵守这些条约。订约之时，清朝君臣打的如意算盘是"暂事羁縻""徐图控驭"。之后，清统治集团内部普遍"拒绝接受这次战争的结局，继续批评这个条约并且敌视条约中的各项规定"，"试图尽量缩小并抗拒它们"。许多人试图运用中国传统的"权术"来与此周旋，"利用解释条约的办法来收回在谈判中失掉的东西"。由于已经领教了英国人的"船坚炮利"，所以他们不敢明里违背条约，只能暗地阻止条约履行，或者以"信守"条约来阻止列强的进一步行动。②

---

① （美）马士著，张汇文等译，《中华帝国对外关系史》第一卷，上海书店出版社，2006年，第435页。

② 李育民，《中国废约史》，中华书局，2005年，第36页。

Grand Canal and the Peiho... I know that the flames of the grain ships gathered there, supplemented if necessary by the flames of the city, will awaken the Emperor's fear, and our own demands can be met."① Negotiations in the south did not proceed smoothly. Whenever the demands of the British aggressors were not met, they would wield the trump card of "heading north to Tianjin" to compel the Qing government to capitulate. This continued until 1842 when British forces entered Nanjing and signed the first unequal treaty in modern Chinese history, the *Treaty of Nanjing*.

The wars sparked by the opium trade did not constitute the primary focus of the treaties concluded after the wars. The *Treaty of Nanjing* comprised thirteen articles, among which China was required to: (1) cede Hong Kong Island; (2) pay Britain a total of 21 million silver dollars as compensation for opium destroyed, debts owed by merchants, and military expenses; (3) open five treaty ports for trade, namely Guangzhou, Fuzhou, Xiamen, Ningbo, and Shanghai, allowing British residence and consulates to be established; (4) implement agreed tariffs, with British merchants paying import and export duties and fees, while China's customs would not have autonomy; (5) abolish the official Canton system and allow British merchants to engage in free trade in China. Additionally, the treaty stipulated matters such as equal exchanges of officials, the release of military personnel and civilians, and the withdrawal of British troops.

The strategic importance of Tianjin is so significant that foreign aggressors both sought to use it as a gateway to pressure the Qing government into Beijing and urgently desired to open this port for trade, to gain access to a broader market. Subsequently, the United States and France also used phrases like "sailing towards the mouth of Tianjin Peiho" and "heading to Tianjin" to threaten, demanding to "share the benefits equally." However, apart from expressing anger, the Qing emperors had little effective recourse. In June 1850, the British warship "HMS Reynard" once again submitted a demand at the mouth of Peiho. The emperor instructed his Ministers, saying, "The recent proceedings of foreigners at Tientsin, in impudently forwarding despatches direct to the Ministers of State, can be looked upon only as contumacious and insulting in the extreme. We have, accordingly, given our commands that no reply be handed to them. But that these documents be passed over in perfect silence..."② Such vehement rebukes not only exposed their own incompetence but also failed to prevent foreigners from coming to Tianjin. Tianjin not only became a gateway

---

① Association of Chinese Historians (ed). *The Opium War* (5). Shen Zhou Guo Guang She, 1954, p.89.

② Hosea Ballou Morse. *The International Relations of the Chinese Empire* (vol.1), translated by Zhang Huiwen, et al. Shanghai Bookstore Publishing House, 2006, p.435.

咸丰皇帝
Emperor Xianfeng

本就是在武力胁迫下签订的条约，不仅清朝君臣不打算认真遵守，西方列强也不想就此收手。英国人总以胜利者的傲慢，试图扩大自己的战果。英国商人从东印度公司垄断的取消到《南京条约》的签订，已经等待了八年多。虽然条约的签订改变了他们过去的卑微地位，然而人性贪婪、得陇望蜀，他们希望获得更多利益，因而屡屡将手伸向条约外的领域，这不免要遭到清政府的抵制。

1854年，英、美、法三国试图修约，扩大在华权益，被清政府拒绝。1856年10月，英国借口"亚罗号事件"，出兵进攻广州，第二次鸦片战争爆发。1857年，法国借口"马神甫事件"加入其中。美国、俄国为了扩大在华权益，决定与英、法两国采取一致行动。1857年12月，广州陷落之后，年轻的咸丰皇帝仍然无视外国人要求，认为南方的战事仅是地方性事件。为了打破清政府的大国迷梦，四个国家决定把战事范围转移到北方。1858年4月，英国公使额尔金（Lord Elgin）、法国公使葛罗（Baron Gros）、美国公使列维廉（William B. Reed）率舰船北上，与先期到达天津大沽口的俄国公使普提雅廷（Count Poutiatine）汇合，这里才是第二次鸦片战争的主战场。

在第二次鸦片战争中，清朝军队与英法联军进行了著名的三次大沽口之战。第一次，英法联军3000余人、舰船26艘于1858年4月攻打大沽口，一支部队登陆，溯河而上，侵入三岔河口，兵临天津城下，迫使清廷签订了城下之盟的《天津条约》。第二次，英法联军2000余人、舰船20余艘于翌年7月再次闯入大沽海口，炮轰炮台，派兵登岸；大沽守军击毁敌船多艘，击杀敌兵数百，敌军不得不狼狈撤出战斗。为了报复清朝，1860年，英法联军25000余人、舰船200余艘第三次攻打大沽口，大沽失守。英法联军长驱直入，

through which modern powers coerced the Qing government but also quickly became the actual battleground for these powers in China.

The Second Opium War and Tianjin

The *Treaty of Nanjing* was just the Beginning

The Opium War, though initiated by the opium issue, was actually aimed at resolving the political, economic, and diplomatic relations between China and Western countries. After the signing of the *Treaty of Nanjing*, China signed the *Treaty of Peace, Amity, and Commerce* with America in 1844 and the *Treaty of Whampoa* with France. These treaties constituted the primary form of modern international relations, laying down the principles for diplomatic and commercial relations between China and the Western powers. This new treaty system, on one hand, formally introduced China to a new model of modern international relations, yet on the other hand, it infringed upon China's sovereignty and subjected it to the indignity of unequal treaties.

The *Treaty of Nanjing* was merely a beginning, bringing about far more problems than it solved. The signing of the treaty was a result of China's concession under the pressure of defeat in war, so the Qing government internally had no intention of earnestly abiding by these treaties. At the time of signing, the Qing rulers and officials were hoping for temporary submission and plotting for future control. Subsequently, within the Qing ruling group all refused to accept the outcome of the war, continued to criticize of the treaty, and kept hostile attitude towards its provisions, attempting to minimize and resist them as much as possible. Many attempted to employ traditional Chinese tactics to maneuver around the situation, "using interpretations of the treaty to regain what was lost in negotiations". Having already experienced the British advantages in naval power and artillery, they dared not openly violate the treaty but instead hindered its implementation covertly or used the "observance" of the treaty to prevent further actions by the Western powers.[1]

The treaty, which was signed under the coercion of force, was not only not intended to be earnestly observed by the Qing rulers and officials, but the Western powers also had no intention of stopping there. With the arrogance of victors, the British constantly sought to expand their gains. From the abolition of the monopoly of the East India Company to the signing of the *Treaty of Nanjing*, British merchants had waited for over eight years. Although the signing of the treaty changed their previous humble status, human greed and

---

① Li Yumin. *The History of China's Abolition of Treaties*. Zhonghua Book Company, 2005, p.36.

僧格林沁（1811—1865），晚清名将，蒙古科尔沁旗贵族，是晚清最能打的武将之一，被清廷称为"国之柱石"，颇得道光、咸丰两帝宠信。咸丰、同治年间，僧格林沁参与对太平天国、英法联军等战争，在历史上留下蒙古骑兵的最后辉煌

Sengge Rinchen (1811-1865), was a famous general in late Qing Dynasty and a nobleman from Horqin Banner of Mongolia. He was one of the most skilled generals and was honored with "the pillar of the state" by the Qing court, being highly favored and trusted by the Emperors Daoguang and Xianfeng. During the reign of Emperors Xianfeng and Tongzhi, Sengge Rinchen participated in the Taiping Rebellion and the Second Opium War, showing the final glory of Mongolian cavalry in history

大沽口北塘炮台。出自《西洋镜：一个英国战地摄影师镜头下的第二次鸦片战争》（台海出版社，2017 年）
Beitang Fort in Taku. From *Western Mirror: The Second Opium War Behind the Lens of a British War Photographer* (Taihai Publishing House, 2017)

占领天津。之后，英法联军击败僧格林沁率领的蒙古骑兵，攻入北京。被圆明园熊熊烈火吓破胆的清政府最终完全接受了英法两国的要求，分别于 10 月 24 日、25 日签订了中英、中法《北京条约》。

之所以会有三次大沽口之战，天津城被占领，以及北京圆明园被焚毁，都是因为围绕《天津条约》的内容，双方产生了严重分歧。

万难接受的《天津条约》

1858 年 5 月 20 日第一次大沽口之战拉开大幕。上午 8 时，联军对清政府发出最后通牒，限定 2 小时内交出大沽口，被拒绝。10 时，英法联军舰队发出作战信号，2 小时后，即 12 时左右，沿河两岸炮台就陷落在联军手里，联军舰队闯进大沽口。在肃清河道之后，英法美俄四国使节搭小火轮于 30 日抵达天津，与清政府代表桂良、花沙纳在海光寺举行谈判。6 月，四国代表分别与清政府代表签订了《天津条约》。

《天津条约》的主要内容为：增开牛庄（今营口）、登州（今烟台）、台湾（今台南）、淡水、潮州（今汕头）、琼州、南京、镇江、汉口、

ambition drove them to seek more benefits, thus repeatedly reaching beyond the confines of the treaty. This inevitably met resistance from the Qing government.

In 1854, the three countries of England, the United States, and France attempted to negotiate treaties to expand their interests in China but were rejected by the Qing government. In October 1856, Britain, citing the "Arrow Incident," launched an attack on Guangzhou, leading to the outbreak of the Second Opium War. In 1857, France joined the conflict citing the "Father Chapdelaine Incident." The United States and Russia, seeking to expand their interests in China, decided to coordinate with Britain and France. After the fall of Guangzhou in December 1857, the young Emperor Xianfeng still disregarded foreign demands, considering the conflict in the south as a local matter. In order to shatter the Qing government's illusion of being a great power, the four nations decided to shift the focus of the conflict to the north. In April 1858, British envoy Lord Elgin, French envoy Baron Gros, and American envoy William B. Reed sailed northward to rendezvous with Russian envoy Count Poutiatine, who had arrived earlier at the Tianjin Taku Forts, which became the main battlefield of the Second Opium War.

In the Second Opium War, the Qing army engaged in the famous three Battles of the Taku Forts with the Anglo-French forces. In the first battle, in April 1858, over 3,000 Anglo-French troops and 26 ships attacked the Taku Forts. A detachment of troops landed and advanced up the river, invading

大沽口地图，可见上方为天津城，河流为白河，即海河，而白河口两侧即为大沽炮台。大沽口是明、清两代的海防要塞。它位于海河的入海口处，东临渤海，地形险要，有京津门户、海陆咽喉之称。大沽炮台最早建于明代，只不过那时是为了防御来自日本倭寇的侵扰。到了清代，英国人的船坚炮利比倭寇的滋扰要厉害得多。第一次鸦片战争中，为防敌军入侵海口，清政府在"白河投书"后亡羊补牢，于1841年、1858年增建大沽南北炮台和北塘炮台，并安置炮位、增加大炮。同时，在河道上只留一条航道，其他地方在水底暗插木桩、装石沉船、堆设障碍以御敌船，这样就构成了大沽要塞防御体系。然而，坚固如此的要塞，也无法阻挡列强一次又一次的侵略

The map of Taku Forts shows Tianjin City at the top, with the river depicted as the Peiho, also known as the Hai River. On both sides of the Peiho estuary lie the Taku Forts. Taku was a crucial coastal defense stronghold during the Ming and Qing dynasties. Located at the mouth of the Hai River, it faces the Bohai Sea to the east and occupies a strategically important position, often referred to as the gateway to Beijing and Tianjin and the vital junction of land and sea. The Taku Forts were first built during the Ming Dynasty to defend against Japanese pirate invasions. However, in the Qing Dynasty, threats from British naval forces, armed with powerful warships and cannons, far exceeded the disturbances caused by the pirates. During the First Opium War, to prevent enemy forces from invading via the sea, the Qing government reinforced the Taku Forts following the "Lord Palmerston's letter delivered at Peiho," making hasty yet necessary preparations. In 1841 and 1858, additional northern and southern forts at Taku, along with the Beitang Fort, were constructed. Gun emplacements were added, and more cannons were installed. At the same time, only a single navigable channel was left in the river, while other areas were reinforced with underwater wooden stakes, sunken stone-filled ships, and other obstacles to block enemy vessels. This formed the Taku Forts defense system. However, despite its strong fortifications, the Taku Forts were ultimately unable to withstand repeated invasions by foreign powers

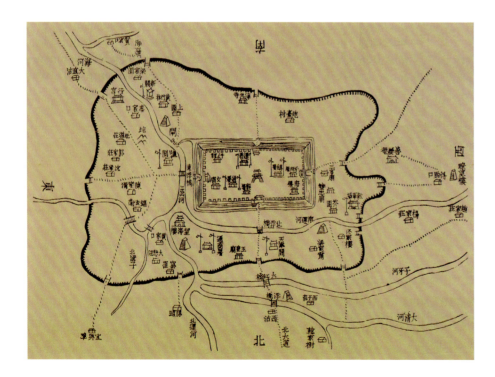

第二次大沽口之战前，清政府任命蒙古亲王僧格林沁为钦差大臣组织大沽和京东防务。僧格林沁立即整顿军队，添设大沽口水师，并在大沽口新建防御设施，严阵以待。不仅如此，他还仅用了18天时间在天津城以南修建了一条长约13英里的高高的土围墙（图中最外面的一圈黑线），以弥补天津在军事防御上的不足。城墙上安装有火炮，并设立了11座营门。此外，城墙的外围还有护城河，后被称为"墙子河"（如今墙子河已经被南京路以及地下呼啸而过的地铁1号线所取代）。不过，这个被英国兵称为"僧格林沁墙"的地方，后来只有阻挡了联军两分钟的时间。一名英国士兵从城壕游了过去，爬过土围墙，打开了大门。其无用程度，大概只有二战中的法国马其顿防线，堪与之相提并论。出自《天津城市历史地图集》（天津古籍出版社，2004年）

Before the Second Battle of Taku Forts, the Qing government appointed the Mongol prince Sengge Rinchen as the imperial commissioner to oversee the defense of Taku and eastern Beijing. Sengge Rinchen immediately reorganized the military, reinforced the Taku naval forces, and constructed new defensive structures at Taku, preparing for the imminent battle. Beyond these preparations, he built a high earthen wall approximately 13 miles (about 21 km) long south of Tianjin in just 18 days to strengthen the city's defenses. This wall, represented by the outermost black line on the map, was equipped with cannons and featured 11 fortified gates. Additionally, a moat surrounded the wall, later known as "Qiangzi River" (which has since been replaced by Nanjing Road and the underground Metro Line 1). However, this fortification, which British soldiers mockingly referred to as the "Sengge Rinchen Wall," ultimately proved ineffective. It held off the allied forces for merely two minutes. A British soldier swam across the moat, climbed over the earthen wall, and opened the gates, rendering the defense useless. In terms of strategic failure, it could be compared to the French Maginot Line in World War II. Source: *Atlas of Historical Maps of Tianjin* (Tianjin Ancient Books Publishing House, 2004)

英法联军。外国画家所绘铜版画
The Anglo-French Allied Forces. Etching by a foreign artist

九江为通商口岸；允许英法人士在内地游历及传教；外国公使常驻北京；扩大领事裁判权；协定关税，修改税则；赔偿英国400万两、法国200万两白银等，并规定第二年在北京换约。

《天津条约》签订后，清政府对条约中的苛刻条款相当不满，咸丰帝认为"万难允准"。对于清朝统治者的心理，作为当事者之一的额尔金伯爵有着这样的看法："在中国政府看来，这些特权的让与等于一种革命，它涉及在帝国传统政策上的某些最宝贵的原则的放弃。因此，这些让与的权利乃是从中国的恐惧中强取来的。"①

那么，中国统治者视为"最宝贵的原则"是什么呢？

对于自居为中原上国的清朝君主们，从来没有接见过一个要求平等而被承认的任何国家的代表，也不愿轻易承认对外关系所需要的任何变更。"中国的政策，一向把它的外交事务，看作纯粹商务性质的，并且把它们的规定和处理委之于在广州的总督，……想与帝国政府发生直接关系是一向不准的。"英国人想要自己的使节常驻北京，"对于这点，中国人提出了他们最坚强的和最长期的反对"。②清政府批准了《天津条约》就意味着承认西方列强国家与中国的平

① 1858年7月12日额尔金伯爵致曼兹柏立勋爵函。转引自（美）马士著，张汇文等译，《中华帝国对外关系史》第一卷，上海书店出版社，2006年，第607页。

② （美）马士著，张汇文等译，《中华帝国对外关系史》第一卷，上海书店出版社，2006年，第608、609页。

Sancha estuary and reaching the outskirts of Tianjin. This forced the Qing court to sign the *Treaties of Tianjin* under duress. In the second battle, in July of the following year, over 2,000 Anglo-French troops and more than 20 ships breached the Taku Forts again, bombarding the forts and sending troops ashore. The defenders of the Taku Forts destroyed many enemy ships and killed hundreds of enemy soldiers, forcing the enemy to retreat in disarray. In retaliation against the Qing, in 1860, over 25,000 Anglo-French troops and more than 200 ships attacked the Taku Forts for the third time, resulting in their capture. The Anglo-French forces advanced and occupied Tianjin. Subsequently, they defeated the Mongolian cavalry led by Sengge Rinchen and marched into Beijing. The Qing government, terrified by the burning of the Old Summer Palace, eventually capitulated to the demands of Britain and France, signing the *Convention of Beijing* with each on October 24th and 25th respectively.

The reason for the three Battles of Taku Forts, the occupation of Tianjin, and the destruction of the Old Summer Palace in Beijing was all due to the serious disagreements between the two sides regarding the contents of the *Treaties of Tianjin*.

The Unacceptable *Treaties of Tianjin*

The First Battle of Taku Forts commenced on May 20th, 1858. At 8 a.m., the allied forces issued a final ultimatum to the Qing government, demanding the surrender of Taku Forts within two hours, which was refused. At 10 a.m., the British and French fleet signaled the start of the attack. About two hours later, around noon, the forts along the riverbanks fell into the hands of the allied forces, and their fleet breached the Taku Forts. After clearing the river channel, envoys from Britain, France, the United States, and Russia arrived in Tianjin on the 30th by small steamers and held negotiations with Qing representatives Gui Liang and Hua Shana at Haiguang Temple. In June, representatives from the four countries individually signed the *Treaties of Tianjin* with Qing representatives.

The main contents of the *Treaties of Tianjin* included: open the additional treaty ports including Niuzhuang (modern-day Yingkou), Dengzhou (modern-day Yantai), Taiwan (modern-day Tainan), Danshui, Chaozhou (modern-day Shantou), Qiongzhou, Nanjing, Zhenjiang, Hankou, and Jiujiang for trade; allow British and French nationals to travel and conduct missionary activities inland; allow the permanent residence of foreign envoys in Beijing; expand the consular jurisdiction; allow the agreed tariffs and modify the customs regulations; indemnification of 4 million taels of silver to Britain, 2

等地位，而这正是让咸丰帝"万难允准"的。所以，翌年，外国公使前来交换批准书的时候，清政府又反悔了。

不仅清政府，英、法等国政府对从《天津条约》获得的权益也并不满足，认为应当借换约的机会再次挑起战争，向清政府索取更多的利益。但是，骄横的英法联军在第二次大沽口之战中惨败，使本来想教训清朝的英法政府相当愤怒。英国内阁连开4次紧急会议，与法国协商，最终一致决定对中国增兵至两万，并把攻入北京作为目标。

北京被占领之后，英法两国如愿以偿分别与清政府签订了《北京条约》，并互换了《天津条约》。中英、中法《北京条约》的主要内容有：承认《天津条约》完全有效；辟天津为商埠；准许外国人在中国招聘人口出洋做苦工；割让广东新安县（今香港界限街以南）的九龙半岛（九龙司）给英国；交还以前没收的天主教堂，法国传教士在内地任意各省租买土地，建筑教堂；赔偿英、法的军费各增加到800万两。《北京条约》最主要的目的就是增辟天津为通商口岸。至此，由马戛尔尼使团开始，西方殖民者梦寐以求将天津开放为商埠的要求终于靠武力得以实现。

城市空间的扩大与天津租界

天津城市空间的扩大与外国租界的划定有直接关系。近代史上，天津曾有九国租界先后存在了85年，这是中国其他城市都没有经历过的。一座城市被迫背负着九个"国中之国"，堪称中国首例乃至世界唯一，那段悲怆历史是天津人也是中国人永远无法忘记的耻辱和负重前行的动力。

九国租界

天津是首都的门户，河海通津的重要地理位置意味着巨大的政治、军事和商业价值。因此在天津被迫开放为通商口岸的当年，英、法、美三国即在靠近天津老城厢的海河西岸开辟了租界。所谓租界，是

million taels to France, and other stipulations, with a provision for a renegotiation in Beijing the following year.

After the signing of the *Treaties of Tianjin*, the Qing government was considerably discontented with its harsh clauses, and Emperor Xianfeng believed it was "extremely difficult to agree to." Regarding the mindset of the Qing rulers, Lord Elgin, as one of the parties involved, had this opinion: "in the eyes of the Chinese government, they amount to a revolution, and involve the surrender of some of the most cherished principles of the traditional policy of the empire. They have been extorted, therefore, from its fears…"[1]

So, what is the "most precious principle" regarded by the rulers of China?

For the Qing Dynasty rulers who considered themselves the central kingdom of the world, they had never received any representatives from any country demanding equality and recognition, nor were they willing to easily acknowledge any changes in their foreign relations. "The Chinese policy had always been to treat its foreign affairs as purely commercial, and to commit their regulation and administration to the provincial authorities at Canton… no direct relations with the Imperial government were ever permitted." The British desired to have their envoys permanently stationed in Beijing, "To this the Chinese offered their strongest and their longest opposition."[2] The approval of the *Treaties of Tianjin* by the Qing government implied recognition of the equal status between Western powers and China, which was precisely what Emperor Xianfeng found "extremely difficult to accept." Therefore, the following year, when foreign ministers came to exchange ratification documents, the Qing government reneged on its agreement.

Not only the Qing government, but also the governments of Britain, France, and other countries were not satisfied with the rights obtained from the *Treaties of Tianjin*. They believed that they should seize the opportunity of renegotiation to provoke war again and demand more benefits from the Qing government. However, the arrogant Anglo-French forces suffered a disastrous defeat in the Second Battle of Taku Forts, leaving the British and French governments, who originally intended to teach a lesson to the Qing Dynasty, quite furious. The British Cabinet held four emergency meetings in a row and consulted with France, ultimately unanimously deciding to increase troops in China to 20,000 and to make the capture of Beijing their objective.

---

① Lord Elgin's letter to Earl of Malmesbury On July 12, 1858. Quoted in Hosea Ballou Morse. *The International Relations of the Chinese Empire* (vol.1), translated by Zhang Huiwen, et al. Shanghai Bookstore Publishing House, 2006, p.607.

② Hosea Ballou Morse. *The International Relations of the Chinese Empire* (vol.1), translated by Zhang Huiwen, et al. Shanghai Bookstore Publishing House, 2006, p.608,609.

指外国人在中国的居留地，自古有之，但都是受中国政府的直接管辖，没有任何特权。而鸦片战争之后，外国人想要开辟的租界，就不满足于仅在各通商口岸建立一小块居留区，而是冲破广州十三行商馆制度，"自由居住，不受限制"甚至享有治外法权的"国中之国"了。

天津租界的设立及其每一次扩张都与近代中国的政治形势紧密相关，都是列强攻占天津的兵刃产物。列强倚仗武器优势推行炮舰政策，其军队每一次入侵天津均以其占领区为既成事实，迫使清政府认可其设立租界。第二次鸦片战争后，英、法、美三国在天津划定了租界。1894 年中日甲午战争以后，德国借口"调停"有"功"，在天津划定了德租界；日本则以"战胜国"的淫威，在天津划定了日租界。1900 年八国联军入侵天津，在天津设有租界的英、法、德、日等国，擅自对租界进行扩张；没有租界的俄、意、奥等国，即以本国军队占领的地盘划定租界；比利时虽未参加八国联军，却也乘机在天津强租了比租界。1902 年，美租界并入英租界，天津形成八国租界并立的局面。这些租界的总面积相当于当时天津老城的八倍多，这在全国设有租界的城市中是独一无二的，天津成为帝国主义瓜分中国的一个缩影。

最早设立的英、法租界选址在天津城南大约 2 英里的一处叫作紫竹林的地段。清政府官员于战败之下而接受天津开放为通商口岸，内心仍然不愿意与非我族类的外国人打交道。租界的划定虽为无奈之举，但是如果能让当时占据天津城的外国人赶紧离开住到城外的租界去，达到"中外界清""华洋分居"的目的，他们也乐见其成。而且依照中国传统城市的建设规划思想，租界所在地并不是理想的建造城市的所在——这里河汊水洼众多、整块平地甚少，且多为河边、海边的盐碱地、泥地，疫病横生。而各国租界却都特意选择在海河边的荒地和沼泽上设立，"这个地区内尽是一些帆船码头、小菜园、土堆，以及渔民、水手等居住的茅屋，而这些破烂不堪的肮脏茅屋彼此之间被一道道狭窄的通潮沟渠隔开，……沼泽四围干燥一些的地方分布着无数座好几代人的坟墓"①。

① （英）雷穆森著，许逸凡等译，《天津租界史（插图本）》，天津人民出版社，2009 年，第 34 页。

After the occupation of Beijing, as desired, Britain and France respectively signed the *Convention of Beijing* with the Qing government and exchanged the *Treaties of Tianjin*. The main contents of the *Convention of Beijing* between China and Britain, and between China and France included: recognize the full validity of the *Treaties of Tianjin*; open Tianjin as a commercial port; allow foreigners to recruit laborers from China for overseas work; cede the Kowloon Peninsula (Kowloon) of Xin'an County, Guangdong Province (south of Boundary Street, Hong Kong today) to Britain; return previously confiscated Catholic churches; allow French missionaries to purchase land and build churches in various provinces of the mainland; increase compensation for British and French military expenses to 8 million taels each. The main purpose of the *Convention of Beijing* was to open Tianjin as a trading port. Thus, starting from the Lord Macartney Mission, the long-desired demand of Western colonialists to open Tianjin as a commercial port was finally achieved through force.

The Expansion of Urban Space and the Tianjin Concessions

The expansion of the urban space in Tianjin was directly related to the demarcation of foreign concessions. In modern history, Tianjin had nine foreign concessions successively existing for 85 years, an experience unparalleled by any other Chinese city. A city burdened with nine "countries within a country" stands as a unique and sorrowful chapter, not only in China but also in the world. This period of tragic history represents a shame and a driving force for both the people of Tianjin and China, an enduring memory that can never be forgotten.

The Nine Foreign Concessions

Tianjin serves as the gateway to the capital, and its strategic location at the confluence of rivers and sea signifies immense political, military, and commercial value. Therefore, in the year Tianjin was forcibly opened as a trading port, the British, French, and American governments established concessions on the west bank of the Hai River, near the old city of Tianjin. The so-called concessions refer to the residential areas for foreigners in China, which have existed since ancient times, but were always under the direct jurisdiction of the Chinese government without any special privileges. However, after the Opium Wars, the concessions sought by foreigners were not limited to small residential areas near each trading port. They aimed to break the Canton system and establish "countries within a country" where they could reside freely

英国人和法国人看中的不是这块地本身，而是它的位置。欧美人重商图利，勘定租界的标准主要看是否交通便利。当时没有火车，以水运为主。南北运河与白河在三岔河口汇合后形成海河，从紫竹林这段开始，水势大增，河道变宽，有利于大型商船的进出和停泊，轮船可以直接驶入并停靠在租界码头，使运输条件更为便利。这里很早便是商货往来水陆交通的要道，而它下游对岸的大直沽更是清代大型漕船转运驳卸和海路商船停泊之所。所以，紫竹林一段的海河航道是漕船、商船、渔船从海上进入三岔河口的必经之路，是扼守天津城的门户。英法两国将这里划为租界，就占据了海河河道最有利的位置。以后其他国家的租界也是沿海河两岸设立，形成了一个从天津城厢东部的繁华区以南，沿着海河向下游延伸的"东西窄而南北长"的租界区，逐渐发展成为天津的航运中心。

英、法、美三国租界建立的初期，由于这一地段地势低洼，需要大量土方填埋地基，花费甚巨，因此一开始旅居天津的外国商人大多不愿住在租界，而是在天津老城内外租地买房。"在1860年到1870年这十年间，大部分新来的外国商人陆续在天津城建起了他们的商号，甚至于那些已在租界建有房屋的，也还在天津城外保留有代理人和仓库。"①1867年天津有洋行17家，其中英商9家、俄商4家、德商2家、美商1家、意商1家，行址多设于天后宫南北的商业街上。然而，1870年天津教案的发生改变了外国侨民的态度。教案中，包括法国领事丰大业在内的20名法国人和俄国人被杀，在租界的侨民中造成了极大的恐慌。事后，他们认为入住租界要比在天津城内外与中国人杂居安全得多，于是纷纷迁入租界租地造屋，因而促进了租界的发展。

天津城区从老城厢向租界的扩展，标志着天津从古代城市向现代城市的跃进。一个近代化的崭新城市把时代的变迁形象清晰地呈现在中国人面前，冲击着他们的视野、洗刷着他们的观念。天津的张焘在他那本著名的《津门杂记》中写道：（租界）"街道宽平，洋房齐整，路旁树木，葱郁成林。行人蚁集蜂屯，货物如山堆垒，

---

① （英）雷穆森著，许逸凡等译，《天津租界史（插图本）》，天津人民出版社，2009年，第37—38页。

without restrictions and even enjoy extraterritoriality.

The establishment and every expansion of the Tianjin Concessions were closely related to the political situation in modern China, all being the result of the armed aggression of the Great Powers in Tianjin. Relying on their military advantage, the Great Powers implemented gunboat diplomacy, with each invasion of Tianjin by their armies regarding their occupation zones as a done deal, forcing the Qing government to recognize the establishment of concessions. After the Second Opium War, Britain, France, and the United States delineated concessions in Tianjin. Following the First Sino-Japanese War in 1894, Germany used the pretext of "mediation" to claim credit and established the German concession in Tianjin; Japan, leveraging its status as a victorious power, delineated the Japanese concession in Tianjin. In 1900, during the invasion of Tianjin by the Eight-Nation Alliance, countries with concessions in Tianjin such as Britain, France, Germany, and Japan unilaterally expanded their concessions; countries without concessions such as Russia, Italy, and Austria delineated concessions in the areas occupied by their own military forces; although Belgium did not participate in the Eight-Nation Alliance, it opportunistically secured a concession in Tianjin. In 1902, the American concession was merged into the British concession, leading to the formation of a situation where the eight nations had concessions side by side in Tianjin. The total area of these concessions was equivalent to more than eight times the size of the old city of Tianjin at that time, which was unparalleled among cities with concessions nationwide, making Tianjin a microcosm of imperialist partitioning of China.

The earliest established British and French concessions were located in an area about 2 miles south of Tianjin City, known as Zizhulin (Purple Bamboo Grove). Despite accepting the opening of Tianjin as a trading port under the defeat of war, Qing government officials still harbored reluctance to interact with foreigners who were not of their own kin. Although the demarcation of concessions was a reluctant move, they were pleased if it could expedite the departure of the foreigners occupying Tianjin City to the concessions outside the city, achieving the goals of "clear separation between Chinese and foreigners" and "Chinese and Western residents living separately." Moreover, according to the traditional urban planning concepts in China, the location of the concessions was not ideal for building cities. This area had many rivers and ponds, with very little flat land, and mostly consisted of saline-alkaline land and mudflats near the rivers and sea, where diseases were rampant. Yet, each country's concession deliberately chose to establish itself on the wasteland and marshes along the Hai River. "This area was full of sailboat docks, small vegetable gardens, mounds of earth, as well as huts inhabited by fishermen,

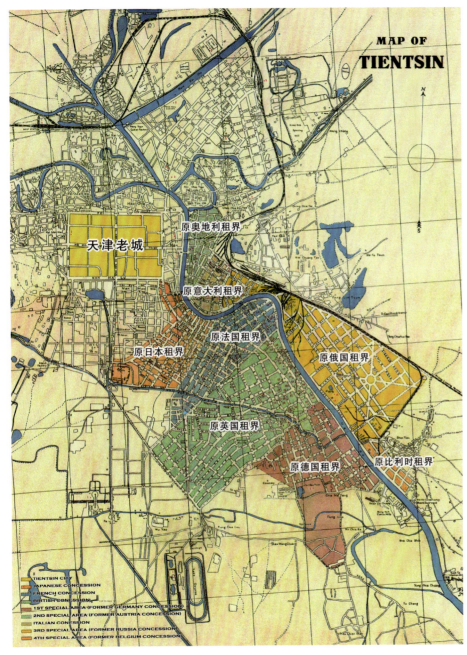

MAP OF
TIENTSIN

天津老城

原奥地利租界

原意大利租界

原法国租界

原日本租界

原俄国租界

原英国租界

原德国租界

原比利时租界

TIENTSIN CITY
JAPANESE CONCESSION
FRENCH CONCESSION
BRITISH CONCESSION
1ST SPECIAL AREA (FORMER GERMANY CONCESSION)
2ND SPECIAL AREA (FORMER AUSTRIA CONCESSION)
ITALIAN CONCESSION
3RD SPECIAL AREA (FORMER RUSSIA CONCESSION)
4TH SPECIAL AREA (FORMER BELGIUM CONCESSION)

天津租界示意图
The map of the foreign concessions in Tianjin

sailors, and others. These dilapidated and filthy huts were separated from each other by narrow tidal channels. ... In the drier areas surrounding the marshes, countless graves from several generations were scattered."[1]

The British and French were not interested in the land itself, but rather its location. Europeans and Americans were profit-oriented, and the main criterion for determining concessions was whether transportation was convenient. At that time, there were no trains, so water transport was predominant. The Grand Canal and the Peiho converged at Sancha estuary to form the Hai River. From the segment of the Zizhulin, the water flow increased significantly, and the river widened, which was conducive to the entry, exit, and berthing of large merchant ships. Steamships could directly sail into and dock at the concession docks, making transportation more convenient. This stretch of the Hai River had long been a vital waterway for the transportation of goods by both land and water. On the opposite bank downstream, Dazhigu was a major hub for the transfer and unloading of large-scale canal boats and the anchorage of sea-going merchant ships in the Qing Dynasty. Therefore, the section of the Hai River at Zizhulin was a vital route for canal boats, merchant ships, and fishing boats to enter Sancha estuary from the sea, serving as the gateway to Tianjin City. By designating this area as concessions, Britain and France occupied the most advantageous position along the Hai River waterway. Subsequently, concessions from other countries were also established along both banks of the Hai River, forming a "narrow from east to west and long from north to south" concession area extending downstream along the Hai River from the bustling area south of the eastern part of Tianjin City, gradually developing into the shipping center of Tianjin.

In the initial stages of the establishment of concessions by Britain, France, and the United States, due to the low-lying terrain of this area, a large amount of earthwork was needed to fill the foundation, resulting in significant expenses. As a result, most of the foreign merchants initially residing in Tianjin were reluctant to live in the concessions, opting instead to rent land and buy houses inside and outside the old city of Tianjin. "During the 10 years from 1860 to 1870, most of the newly arrived foreign merchants continued to operate in Tianjin City. Even those who had built houses in the concessions still worked as managers and warehouses in the suburbs."[2] In 1867, there were 17 foreign firms in Tianjin, including 9 British, 4 Russian, 2 German, 1 American, and 1

---

① O. D. Rasmussen. *Tientsin: An Illustrated Outline History*, translated by Xu Yifan, et al. Tianjin People's Publishing House, 2008, p.34.

② O. D. Rasmussen. *Tientsin: An Illustrated Outline History*, translated by Xu Yifan, et al. Tianjin People's Publishing House, 2008, pp.37-38.

英租界招商局码头
China Merchants Steam Navigation Co.'s dock in the British concession

太古洋行码头，今保定桥和平区一侧
Wharf of Butterfield & Swire, on the west side of
Baoding Bridge, Heping District nowadays

Italian. Many of these firms were located on the commercial streets north and south of the Tianhou Temple. However, the Tianjin Missionary Case of 1870 changed the attitude of foreign residents. In the Missionary Case, 20 French and Russian individuals, including the French Consul Henri Fontanier, were killed, causing great panic among the expatriates in the concessions. Afterwards, they believed that living in the concessions was much safer than cohabiting with the Chinese inside and outside Tianjin City. Consequently, they began to move into the concessions to rent land and build houses, thereby promoting the development of the concessions.

The expansion of Tianjin city from the old city to the concessions marked Tianjin's leap from an ancient city to a modern one. A modernized, brandnew city vividly presented the changes of the times to the Chinese people, impacting their perspectives and refreshing their concepts. Zhang Tao, a native Tianjin resident, wrote in his famous book *Miscellaneous Notes of Tianjin*: "The streets of the concessions are wide and flat, the Western-style houses are neat and orderly, trees line the roads, lush and dense. Pedestrians swarm like ants, goods pile up like mountains, carts, donkeys, sedan chairs, and horses are constantly moving day and night. Electric wires are intertwined like spider webs, street lamps line up like stars, the layout is meticulous, elegant and pleasing to the eye, resembling a miniature version of Shanghai's Bund."[1] The impression gained by the Qing Dynasty elites through immersive experiences was even more profound. In the summer of 1897, Na Tong, then Grand Chancellor and Grand Councillor, along with his friends, arrived in Tianjin for sightseeing by train, which had only been recently opened for travel. For three days, they stayed in Western-style houses in the Zizhulin concession, where they "drank Western wine and dined on Western dishes" in Western restaurants, feeling a unique flavor. During the day, they rode in Western-style carriages to tour the British and French concessions, experiencing smooth roads and fast travel, expanding their horizons and minds. "They also made purchases at the Japanese cotton company and French firms." At night, they toured the French concession, seeing "rows of Western-style buildings, with lights shining brightly, competing with the stars, resembling a Western painting, as if they were in the far west." They went to the theater to watch performances, where they saw gas lamps illuminating the garden and exclaimed, "As bright as daylight, a great spectacle indeed." Upon returning to Beijing, Na Tong summarized in his diary: "This trip lasted only three days, covering over five hundred li, seeing and hearing things never seen or heard before,

---

① Zhang Tao. *Miscellaneous Notes of Tianjin* (vol.2). Tianjin Ancient Books Publishing House,1986, pp.121-122.

车驴轿马，辄夜不休。电线联成蛛网，路灯列若繁星，制甚得法，清雅可观，亦俨如一小沪渎焉。"① 而清朝权贵们由沉浸式体验而获得的观感要更强烈得多。1897年夏季，当朝宰辅、军机大臣那桐与朋友们乘坐一年前刚刚通行不久的火车抵达天津游览。三天里，他们住在紫竹林租界的洋房里，在西餐馆"饮洋酒、餐洋馔"，感觉别具风味；白日，乘西式双马车至英法租界观光，"往来驰骋，道平如砥，车行若飞，眼界胸襟为之一敞"；"至日本棉花公司及法国洋行购买零物"；夜游法租界，但见"洋楼林立，灯火辉映，与星斗争光，俨然一幅洋画，恍如身在太西"；到戏园观戏，见园中煤气灯照明装置，叹道："明如白昼，一大观也"。及至回到北京，那桐在日记中总结："此行仅三日，行程五百余里，见所未见，闻所未闻，诚为壮游。"②

何谓"国中之国"？

历史上的租界，是由外国人治理的中国领土，因其以下特征，被称为"国中之国"。

土地权：外国人取得中国土地权，分为收买、永租、无偿占有等方式。天津英、法、美、德租界为永租；1900年八国联军入侵天津，俄、意、奥租界三国趁机无偿占有；比利时为出银收买。

权力机构：董事会作为租界的权力机构具有立法权、司法权与行政管理权。董事会成员大多是具有经济实力的外国洋行经理、银行家、高级职员等，他们依照西方城市自治的方式来管理租界，同时也要将重大事情，比如租界的管理章程等，向本国领事汇报得到批准。后来增加少数华人董事。

各国在津设立租界后，基本上是按照西方的城市自治制度对租界进行管理。由此，租界成为侨民为维护共同利益、依照西方民主制度、采用地方自治的方式进行管理、处理涉及"公共领域"事务

---

① 张焘，《津门杂记》卷下，天津古籍出版社，1986年，第121—122页。

② 见那桐在光绪二十三年（1897年）八月十七日、十八日、十九日日记。北京市档案馆编，《那桐日记》上册，新华出版社，2006年，第251—252页。

---

truly a magnificent journey."①

What is Meant by "Countries Within a Country"?

Historically, concessions were Chinese territories governed by foreigners and were referred to as "countries within a country" due to the following characteristics.

Land Rights: Foreigners obtained land rights in China through various means such as purchase, perpetual lease, or gratuitous occupation. The concessions of Britain, France, the United States, and Germany in Tianjin were perpetual leases. In 1900, during the invasion of Tianjin by the Eight-Nation Alliance, Russia, Italy, and Austria opportunistically occupied concessions without compensation. Belgium acquired its concession through monetary purchase.

Power Structure: The Board of Directors, as the governing body of the concession, possessed legislative, judicial, and administrative powers. The majority of board members were foreign business managers, bankers, senior officials, etc., who had economic strength. They managed the concessions in accordance with Western urban governance methods and were required to seek approval from their respective consulates for major matters such as the management regulations of the concession. Later, a few Chinese directors were added.

After each country established concessions in Tianjin, they generally managed the concessions according to Western urban governance systems. As a result, the concessions became communities where expatriates maintained common interests, managed affairs according to Western democratic principles, and adopted local self-government. Here, while the "state" played an important role through the consulates and stationed troops, the so-called "public opinion" of concession residents, regardless of nationality, had a greater and more direct influence on general interest issues in daily activities. The highest governing body in the concessions was the Board of Directors, which was elected by taxpayers who had certain assets in the concession area. Its executive agency was the Municipal Council, responsible for daily administrative management under the authorization of the Board of Directors. This fully embodies the characteristics of local self-government of the concession authorities.

Administrative Management Institutions: The management institution

---

① Na Tong's Diary on August 17, 18, and 19 in the 23rd year of the Emperor Guangxu (1897). Beijing Municipal Archives(ed). *The Diary of Na Tong* (Vol.1). Xinhua Publishing House, 2006, pp.251-252.

的社区。在这里，"国家"虽然以领事馆和驻军的形式发挥着重要作用，但是不分国籍的租界居民在涉及一般利益问题上的所谓"公共意见"却在日常活动中发挥着更大、更直接的影响。租界内的最高统治机构是董事会，由具有一定资产的纳税人召开会议选举产生，其执行机构是工部局。工部局在董事会的授权下，负责日常行政管理。这充分体现了各租界当局的地方自治特征。

行政管理机构： 租界的管理机构称为工部局或公议局，即市政厅，对租界内的一切中外居民实行行政管理，中国地方政府甚至不能管理进入租界的中国人。工部局或公议局全面负责租界内的行政、财务、工程、公用事业等各方面的管理工作。

立法制度、司法管辖权： 租界当局拥有立法权，可以设立本国领事法庭、高等法院等、巡捕房（警察局）及监狱，行使司法管辖权。

驻兵权： 租界当局拥有驻兵权，可以在租界内长期驻兵。中国军队不仅不能入驻租界，甚至不能自由地穿越租界。

课税权： 租界内中外居民必须向租界当局交纳各种捐税。除了关税、地税等项捐税以外，中国政府无权向租界内的中外居民征收应该征收的各种国税。

外交权： 各国租界均享有独立的外交权。在中国国内发生战乱或在中国与其他国家发生战争时，租界多成为"中立"地区。各国租界当局凭借其兵力实行"武装中立"。

由于海河两岸地势低洼，到处都是水坑泥地，没有平整的土地。外国侨民想要在英租界或法租界建造房屋，首先必须让承建商买来好多车的土来填平和垫高地基，因此花费甚巨且耗时费力。后来，他们则发明了"吹泥填地"这种就地取材的方式，即"采取围埝筑池的方法，在某一划定的区域四周筑起土埝，其高度高出规划所要求的地平面，中间形成池状，然后向池内泵入海河工程局的戽斗式挖泥船从海河挖掘的河泥"。这些来自海河的淤泥通过埋设在规划好的租界道路下面的管道，用水泵抽送到需要填垫的地区，在池内沉淀，水分经过蒸发和渗透而消失，一块平坦的地基也就出现了。运用这种方法，大片的沼泽以每年 20 万至 25 万土方的速度被填平

of the concession was called the Municipal Council or the Municipal Administration Board, which was equivalent to the municipal hall. It exercised administrative management over all Chinese and foreign residents within the concession, to the extent that even local Chinese governments cannot manage Chinese people entering the concession. The Municipal Council or the Municipal Administration Board was responsible for comprehensive management of administration, finance, engineering, public utilities, and other aspects within the concession area.

Legislative System, Judicial Jurisdiction: The concession authorities had legislative power, enabling them to establish consular courts, higher courts, police stations, and prisons, exercising judicial jurisdiction.

Military Garrison Rights: The concession authorities had the right to station troops, enabling them to have long-term military presence within the concession. Chinese military forces were not only prohibited from entering the concession but also could not freely pass through it.

Taxation Authority: Both Chinese and foreign residents within the concession must pay various taxes to the concession authorities. In addition to customs duties, land taxes, and other taxes, the Chinese government had no authority to levy various national taxes on Chinese and foreign residents within the concession that should be collected.

Diplomatic Authority: Each country's concession enjoyed independent diplomatic authority. During internal conflicts or wars between China and other countries, concessions often became "neutral" areas. The concession authorities of various countries enforced "armed neutrality" based on their military strength.

Due to the low-lying terrain on both banks of the Hai River, there were water pits and mud everywhere, with no flat land available. Foreign residents who wanted to build houses in the British or French concessions had to first purchase large quantities of soil from contractors to fill and raise the foundation, which was costly and time-consuming. Later, they invented the method of "dredging mud to fill land" to use local materials, namely, "using the method of enclosing a pond, building up earthen embankments around a designated area, with the height exceeding the required ground level, forming a pool in the middle, and then pumping the mud dredged from the Hai River by the dredging boats of the Hai-Ho Conservancy Board into the pool." This silt from the Hai River was pumped through pipelines buried under the planned concession roads, to the areas needing filling, settled in the pool, and after evaporation and infiltration, the water disappeared, leaving behind a flat foundation. Using this method, large areas of marshland were filled at a rate of 200,000 to 250,000 cubic meters per year, turning into flat land

变成可以建房的平地。① 天津也终于有了适合建房的土地，地价在十年间就增长到以前的 10 倍。"这些土地很快就被外国商行和投机家认购，刻着多少有些神秘的姓名首字母的界石，如雨后春笋般到处钻了出来。……使那些被葬于地下的居民得以消逝，取而代之的是居住舒适而愉快地生活在世的家庭。"②

20 世纪初，八国联军占领天津后下令拆毁老城城墙，天津八国租界设定，构成今日天津城市面貌的主城区基本形成。由旧城墙上拆下来的砖石被用来铺砌环城道路，侨民还修建了一条由天津旧城西南角经炮台庄，出僧格林沁围墙之海光门，在德租界同大沽路相接的道路，将老城与日、法、英、德四个海河西岸的租界相连。同时新建的还有有轨电车系统，这种价廉快捷的公共交通系统将老城、日、法租界与海河东岸的城区连为一体。畅通的交通网络将老城与租界区混为一体，加上后来的政治局势、商业发展等方面的因素影响，近代天津的城市中心区逐渐转移到华界以外的英法租界的今和平路和解放北路一带。

他乡明月

天津被迫开放后，外国侨民开始大量涌入，他们不仅带来了资本主义生产方式，而且也第一次导入了西方城市自治和市政建设的理念，改变了中国城市的功能和风貌。可以说，近代天津的城市建设源自租界的建设。租界建设的内驱力来自侨民对便利生活的现实需要和对故土的思念，外在因素则是列强之间的角力。来自欧洲、美国和日本的侨民在遥远的异乡试图重建他们的故乡，再造自己熟悉且舒适的生活模式，借以了却思乡之情。同时，在一个八国租界并存的城市，租界就不仅是各国侨民居住和进行商业贸易等活动的环境，也是展示自身实力的国际政治舞台。

① （英）雷穆森著，许逸凡等译，《天津租界史（插图本）》，天津人民出版社，2009 年，第 289 页。

② （英）雷穆森著，许逸凡等译，《天津租界史（插图本）》，天津人民出版社，2009 年，第 51、57 页。

suitable for construction.① Tianjin concessions finally had land suitable for building, and land prices increased tenfold over a decade. "These lands were quickly subscribed to by foreign businesses and speculators, and boundary stones inscribed with somewhat mysterious initials sprouted up everywhere like mushrooms after rain. ... The graves of those buried underground disappeared, replaced by families living comfortably and happily above ground."②

In the early 20th century, after the Eight-Nation Alliance occupied Tianjin and ordered the demolition of the old city walls, the Tianjin Concessions of the Eight-Nation Alliance were established, laying the foundation for the basic formation of today's urban area of Tianjin. Bricks and stones removed from the old city walls were used to pave the roads around the city. The expatriates also built a road connecting the southwest corner of the old city through Paotaizhuang, the Haiguang Gate outside the wall of the Sengge Rinchen, with Taku Road in the German concession, linking the old city with the concessions on the west bank of the Hai River, including the Japanese, French, British, and German concessions. At the same time, a new tram system was also built. This affordable and efficient public transportation system integrated the old city, the Japanese and French concessions, and the urban area on the east bank of the Hai River. The smooth transportation network integrated the old city with the concession areas. Combined with factors such as the subsequent political situation and commercial development, the urban center of modern Tianjin gradually shifted to the areas of today's Heping Road and Jiefang North Road in the British and French concessions outside the Chinese quarters.

The Bright Moon in a Foreign Land

After Tianjin was forced to open up, a large number of foreign expatriates began to pour in. They not only brought with them capitalist modes of production but also introduced for the first time the concept of Western urban autonomy and municipal construction, changing the functions and appearance of Chinese cities. It can be said that the urban construction of modern Tianjin originated from the construction of the concessions. The internal driving force behind the construction of the concessions came from the practical needs of expatriates for a convenient life and their longing for their homeland, while

① O. D. Rasmussen. *Tientsin: An Illustrated Outline History*, translated by Xu Yifan, et al. Tianjin People's Publishing House, 2008, p.289.

② O. D. Rasmussen. *Tientsin: An Illustrated Outline History*, translated by Xu Yifan, et al. Tianjin People's Publishing House, 2008, p.51,57.

在租界设立之初，各国领事馆都对各自租界的社区建设进行了系统的土地规划和市政建设。不过，由于这些租界分属不同国家，他们的规划又存在各自为政的特征。这一点，在天津与上海这样同样拥有多国租界的城市是比较一致的。与大连、青岛等外国独占的新建城市相比，后者的统一性更为现代学者所称赞。

从整体城市布局来看，天津称得上是混乱不堪的。既有老城厢，又有皆沿海河走向而划定、相互毗连的八国租界并立。各国租界发展状况不一。举例来说，海河西岸的租界以居住区和商业区为主，人口密集、商业繁华，各种公用设施齐全；而海河东岸的租界建设相对滞后，俄租界是宽阔的林荫大道、公园和绿化带，比利时租界基本没有开发。各个租界的道路系统自成一体，主要道路沿海河蜿蜒而建，极少有北京、西安等古城那般横平竖直、南北东西纵横的大街；地名更是异彩纷呈，每个租界都以各自国家的地名或者名人的名字来命名，许多贯穿多个租界的道路不同路段有不同的名字，比如一条贯穿法、英、德租界的街道就有三个名字——法租界段称大法国路、英租界段称维多利亚路、德租界段称德皇威廉路（伍德罗·威尔逊路）。初到天津的外地人很难不被搞得晕头转向。

不过，如果从单一的每块租界来看，天津的租界社区规划是相当统一和明晰的。租界设立之初，一般由各国驻天津的领事馆直接管辖，待到侨民增多，各国即把租界里的行政管理权全部或部分移交给本国的侨民。由侨民选举产生的董事会（日租界称为居留民团）对租界进行自治管理。租界作为社区，除了大量的住宅和商业建筑之外，还有许多公共建筑和公用设施以满足社区不同的功能，即社会经济生活功能、社会化功能、社会控制功能、社会参与功能和社会保障功能。例如，在工部局大楼、领事馆、俱乐部、教堂和公墓举行的公共活动可以增强社区的凝聚力、提高社会整合程度，满足社会控制以及社会参与的功能；学校、公共图书馆满足社会化的功能；商店、饭店、菜场、花园等满足社会经济生活功能；医院、兵营则提供社会保障和安全保障。不过，一些投资较大的公用设施则无须重复建设。例如海河西岸租界的自来水都由英租界的"天津自来水有限公司"供给；供电则有四个电厂，即英租界发电厂、法租界电

external factors were the power struggles among the great powers. Expatriates from Europe, the United States, and Japan attempted to rebuild their homeland in a distant land, recreating their familiar and comfortable way of life to alleviate homesickness. At the same time, in a city where eight concessions coexisted, the concessions were not only dwellings for foreign residents to live and engage in commercial activities but also international political stages for showcasing their own strengths.

At the establishment of the concessions, each country's consulate conducted systematic land planning and municipal construction for their respective concession communities. However, due to the fact that these concessions belonged to different countries, their planning exhibited characteristics of each acting independently. This feature is consistent in cities like Tianjin and Shanghai, which also have multi-national concessions. In comparison to newly built cities like Dalian and Qingdao, which were exclusively occupied by foreign powers, the latter's uniformity is more praised by modern scholars.

From the perspective of overall urban layout, Tianjin can be described as chaotic. It had both the old city and the eight foreign concessions, which were delineated along the Hai River and adjacent to each other. The development status of each concession varied. For example, the concessions on the west bank of the Hai River were mainly residential and commercial areas, densely populated, bustling with commerce, and equipped with various public facilities. In contrast, the development of the concessions on the east bank of the Hai River was relatively lagging behind. The Russian concession features broad boulevards, parks, and green belts, while the Belgian concession was largely undeveloped. The road systems of each concession were independent, with main roads winding along the Hai River, unlike the grid-like layout of ancient cities like Beijing and Xi'an. The names of the streets were diverse, with each concession named after its own country or famous individuals. Many roads that traversed multiple concessions had different names for different sections. For example, a road that passed through the French, British, and German concessions had three names: Rue de France in the French concession, Victoria Road in the British concession, and Kaiser Wilhelmstrasse (Woodrow Wilson Street) in the German concession. It's easy for newcomers to Tianjin to get disoriented due to this complexity.

However, if viewed from the perspective of each individual concession, the planning of Tianjin's concession communities was quite unified and clear. At the establishment of the concessions, they were generally directly administered by the consulates of various countries stationed in Tianjin. As the number of expatriates increased, each country transferred all or part of the administrative authority of the concession to its own expatriates. The Board of

法国电灯房
French electric light company

灯房、日租界发电厂和德租界电灯公司。

　　除了各自进行社区规划和建设以外，后来建立的租界往往也会参考先建租界已有的规划而进行相应调整。比如，德租界规划其土地主要用来建设住宅，而不用作商业用途，商店、影院等使用英租界和法租界的相关场所，因而德国人在津开设的银行和洋行都建立在英租界的金融和商业区。大致上，工厂、仓库和码头集中在海河两岸沿河一带，洋行集中在英租界的海大道和中街附近，金融区集中在法租界的大法国路和英租界的维多利亚路，商店、影院、饭店等娱乐休闲场所集中在法租界的杜总领事路和日租界旭街附近。英租界推广界、德租界、意租界兴建的都是比较高档的住宅区，而日本人商业活动和日常生活的主要场所则集中在酷似日本本土的密度较高的日租界社区。由此，各国租界具有既彼此独立又相互融合的特征。

　　在早期的天津各国租界中，由于英国商人和洋行占据优势地位且有良好的规划，所以英租界是所有租界中建设最早和最好的。按照欧洲城市的规划，英租界被一条条笔直宽阔、铺砌整齐的街道划分为一个个矩形街区。租界内的外国居民只要付出一定的租金即可获得土地，建筑自己梦想的房屋（主要依照自己的家乡式样），并缴纳各项捐税给作为侨民自治组织的工部局，诸如道路、路灯、排水、

Directors (referred to as the Japanese Residents' Association in its concession) elected by expatriates autonomously managed the concession. As a community, in addition to a large number of residential and commercial buildings, the concessions also had many public buildings and facilities to meet the diverse functions of the community, including economic life, socialization, social control, social participation, and social security functions. For example, public activities held in the buildings of the Municipal Council, consulates, clubs, churches, and cemeteries can enhance community cohesion and improved social integration, fulfilling the functions of social control and social participation; schools and public libraries fulfilled the functions of socialization; shops, restaurants, markets, gardens, etc., fulfilled the functions of economic life; hospitals and barracks provide social security and safety. However, some larger-scale public facilities did not need to be duplicated. For example, the water supply in the concessions on the west bank of the Hai River was provided by the "Tientsin Water-works Co., Ltd." of the British concession; electricity supply came from four power plants, namely the power plant of the British concession, the electric light company of the French concession, the power plant of the Japanese concession, and the electric light company of the German concession.

In addition to conducting their own community planning and construction, later-established concessions would often refer to the existing plans of previously established concessions and make corresponding adjustments. For example, the German concession planned its land primarily for residential purposes, rather than for commercial use. Shops, cinemas, and other commercial establishments shared the facilities in the British and French concessions. Therefore, German banks and trading firms in Tianjin were established in the financial and commercial districts of the British concession. Generally, factories, warehouses, and docks were concentrated along the banks of the Hai River, foreign trading firms were concentrated near the Taku Road and Victoria Road in the British concession, financial districts were concentrated in the Rue de France in the French concession and Victoria Road in the British concession, while shops, cinemas, restaurants, and other entertainment venues were concentrated near Rue de Chaylard in the French concession and Asahi Road in the Japanese concession. High-end residential areas were developed in the extension area of the British concession, the German concession, and the Italian concession, while Japanese commercial activities and daily life were mainly concentrated in the densely populated Japanese concession community, which closely resembled Japan itself. Thus, the concessions of various countries exhibited characteristics of both independence and integration with each other.

In the early Tianjin concessions, the British concession was the earliest

各种公共建筑设施、娱乐场所等的建设以及社会治安等均由后者负责。1887年在英租界的中心，维多利亚花园落成。同年，天津历史上的第一条碎石子路铺成，随后在租界的道路两旁还种植了树木。1890年天津气灯公司开始为租界提供公共道路照明，从此油气灯逐步取代煤油灯成为更安全的道路照明系统。1890年5月，侨民自行设计的国内各通商口岸中的第一座市政大厅——戈登堂建成，到20世纪20年代，戈登堂正式成为英租界的民政总部。它还长期作为天津旧租界标志性建筑，被印制到明信片上发往世界各地。

从殖民地式建筑风格到"万国建筑博览会"

由于各国租界管理当局严格规定租界内的建筑必须采用外国式样，因此西方近代的建筑风格都曾出现在天津。从早期的殖民地式建筑到复古主义建筑，从折衷主义建筑再到现代主义的摩天大楼，各种建筑风格一应俱全，所以天津租界素有"万国建筑博览会"的美誉。

西洋建筑的出现，猛烈冲击了数千年来形成的中国传统建筑体系。无论在建筑功能和艺术形式上，还是在建筑结构、技术材料及施工工艺上，都产生了深刻的影响。作为通商口岸，当时西方建筑设计中流行的各种建筑思潮、建筑形式，都理所当然地反映到天津近代建筑中来。在日常生活中，它们与本地的自然条件、文化环境、使用者喜好等各种因素融合在一起，使近代天津的建筑以一种特有的方式发展起来，形成了独特的城市风貌。

早期的租界建筑大都带有殖民地的烙印，即一种周边作拱券回廊的一、二层砖木混合结构的房屋形式，是欧洲建筑传入印度、东南亚殖民地后，为适应当地炎热气候而形成的一种建筑风格。但是这种风格显然不太适应中国北方这种四季分明的气候条件，尤其是春季漫天的黄沙和冬季凛冽的寒风。"结果常常是，宽敞的房屋摆满了家具，宜于夏天居住，但一到冬天，却使人一看到就感到寒意"。[①]

---

① （英）雷穆森著，许逸凡等译，《天津租界史（插图本）》，天津人民出版社，2009年，第51页。

and best developed among all concessions due to the dominance of British merchants and trading firms and their excellent planning. According to the planning of European cities, the British concession was divided into rectangular blocks by straight, wide, and neatly paved streets. Foreign residents in the concession could obtain land by paying a certain rent to build their dream houses (mainly according to the style of their hometown), and pay various taxes to the Municipal Council, which served as the organization for immigrant autonomy. The Municipal Council was responsible for the construction of roads, street lamps, drainage systems, various public buildings and facilities, entertainment venues, and social security. In 1887, Victoria Park was completed in the center of the British concession. In the same year, the first macadam road in Tianjin's history was laid, and trees were planted along the roadsides in the concession. In 1890, the Tientsin Gas Company Limited began to provide public road lighting for the concession, gradually replacing kerosene lamps with safer gas lamps. In May 1890, the first municipal hall, Gordon Hall, designed by the immigrants themselves among all the commercial ports in China, was completed. By the 1920s, Gordon Hall had officially become the civil administration headquarters of the British concession. It also served as a landmark of the old Tianjin concessions for a long time and was printed on postcards sent to various parts of the world.

From Colonial-style Architecture to the "World Architecture Expo"

Due to the strict regulations by the management authorities of various concessions, buildings within the concessions had to adopt foreign styles, hence Western modern architectural styles have appeared in Tianjin. From early colonial-style buildings to neoclassical architecture, from eclectic architecture to modernist skyscrapers, various architectural styles were represented, earning Tianjin concessions the reputation of being a "World Architecture Expo".

The emergence of Western architecture profoundly shook the traditional Chinese architectural system that had formed over thousands of years. It had a profound impact on architectural functions, artistic forms, structural designs, technical materials, and construction techniques. As a trading port, various architectural trends and forms prevalent in Western architectural design at that time naturally found their way into modern Tianjin architecture. In daily life, they blended with local natural conditions, cultural environments, and customers preferences, among other factors, giving rise to the development of modern Tianjin architecture in a unique way and forming a distinctive urban landscape.

戈登堂夜景
Night scene of Gordon Hall

法租界内的商业街
Commercial street in the French Concession

这类殖民式风格后来逐渐消失，代之以更加符合本地的气候条件的建筑式样。

随着各国租界的开发建设，租界内的各种功能性建筑，如领事馆、教堂、洋行、银行、工厂、仓库等先后出现，高大漂亮，形式各样。建筑家阿尔多·罗西（Aldo Rossi）尝试从心理学层面引入"相似性"原则，去揭示建筑的永恒性和城市的相似性，从而还原了一种潜藏于人们记忆深处的对场所的群体认知的情感。在对天津的各处租界建设中，都可以看到这种将本国建筑还原到租界的现象。比如各国租界内的教堂、原英租界内的先农大院联排别墅，原德租界的巴伐利亚风格住宅，原法租界内的中心公园，原日租界内的两层小楼，原俄租界建筑的战盔式屋顶，一眼望去即可辨别其本国特色。

不过，租界内最主要的建筑风格以折衷主义为主，通俗说就是"大杂烩"。可以是对各种历史风格的模仿，比如直接地全盘模仿照搬（原新学书院）；也可以是把西洋古典建筑中某些元素符号拿来作为装

Early buildings in the concessions mostly bear the imprint of colonialism, characterized by a one-story or two-story brick-wood mixed structure with surrounding arcades and corridors. This style originated from European architecture introduced to colonies in India and Southeast Asia to adapt to the hot climate. However, this style was not well-suited for the distinct seasonal climate of northern China, especially the spring sandstorms and bitter winter winds. "As a result, spacious houses were often filled with furniture, suitable for summer living, but as soon as winter arrived, they immediately felt chilly."[1] This colonial style gradually disappeared, replaced by architectural styles more suited to the local climate conditions.

With the development and construction of various national concessions, functional buildings such as consulates, churches, foreign firms, banks, factories, warehouses, etc., had successively appeared in the concessions, tall and beautiful, in various forms. Architect Aldo Rossi attempted to introduce the principle of "similarity" from a psychological perspective to reveal the eternity

---

[1] O. D. Rasmussen. *Tientsin: An Illustrated Outline History*, translated by Xu Yifan, et al. Tianjin People's Publishing House, 2008, p.51.

利顺德饭店始建于1863年，1886年改建成三层砖木结构，是当时天津市最高大的建筑，亦是内外装饰最讲究、设备最完善的豪华酒店。主楼沿街而建，突出于主楼之外的半地下室形成整个建筑物的基座和首层的凉台，二层和三层均有长外廊。主楼转角部位有古城堡式的瞭望塔楼。一楼有大堂、餐厅、厨房、台球室、卫生间等，二、三层有高级公寓和客房。半地下室有水泵、锅炉、动力设备、冷库、贮藏以及服务人员用房。饭店里还有天津最早的电梯。

The Astor House Hotel was originally built in 1863 and was rebuilt in 1886 into a three-story brick-and-wood structure. At the time, it was the tallest building in Tianjin and the most elegantly decorated, well-equipped luxury hotel in the city. The main building faced the street, with a semi-basement extending beyond the structure, forming the base of the entire building and a terrace on the first floor. Both the second and third floors featured long exterior corridors. At the corner of the main building stood a castle-like watchtower. The first floor housed a lobby, restaurant, kitchen, billiard room, and restrooms, while the second and third floors contained luxury apartments and guest rooms. The semi-basement accommodated water pumps, boilers, power equipment, cold storage, storerooms, and staff quarters. The hotel also boasted the first elevator ever installed in Tianjin.

殖民地风格的代表性建筑是利顺德饭店。安红摄于 2023 年
The representative building of colonial style is the Astor House Hotel.
Taken by An Hong in 2023

新学书院是英国人赫立德于1902年创办的一所学校。建筑本身仿牛津大学青灰色校园建筑，由中外资深教员任教。书院中学部学制四年，学科内容设有历史、地理、文学、哲学、法律、经济、科学、宗教学、国语和体育等课程和科目。分南北两楼，楼内设施完备，包括礼堂、会议室、机械实验室、化学实验室、理化室、阅览室、体操房、篮球场、饭厅、学生宿舍、淋浴室、博物院等。校长上设董事会，董事们均为社会贤达，如顾维钧、林语堂、张伯苓等。

Tientsin Anglo-Chinese College was founded by British Lavington Hart in 1902. The building itself was designed in the style of Oxford University's gray-blue campus architecture and was staffed by experienced Chinese and foreign teachers. The middle school section of the college had a four-year curriculum, covering subjects such as history, geography, literature, philosophy, law, economics, science, religious study, Chinese and physical education. The school was divided into north and south buildings, both fully equipped with facilities including an auditorium, conference rooms, mechanical and chemical laboratories, a physics and chemistry room, a reading room, a gymnastics hall, a basketball court, a dining hall, student dormitories, showers, and a museum. Above the principal, a board of directors oversaw the academy, consisting of esteemed figures from society, including Gu Weijun, Lin Yutang, and Chang Poling.

新学书院
Tientsin Anglo-Chinese College

吴颂平公馆
The villa of Wu Songping

吴颂平为天津早期四大买办之一吴调卿之长子。1904 年毕业于北洋巡警学堂，捐候补知府衔，后赴美学习军事，回国后任山西教育厅厅长。天津沦陷后，曾任日资大华煤油公司常务董事。此处故居建于 1934 年，占地约 700 平方米，由奥地利建筑师盖苓设计建造。

Wu Songping was the eldest son of Wu Tiaoqing, one of Tianjin's four prominent compradors in the early days. In 1904, he graduated from the Beiyang Police Academy and was granted the honorary title of reserve prefect. He later went to the United States to study military affairs and, upon returning to China, served as the Director of the Shanxi Provincial Department of Education. During the Japanese occupation of Tianjin, he held the position of executive director at the Japanese-funded Dahua Kerosene Company. His former residence was built in 1934, covering an area of approximately 700 square meters. It was designed and constructed by Austrian architect Rolf Geyling.

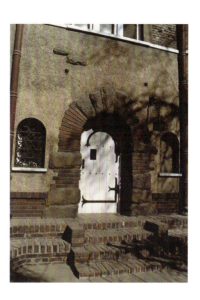

黑白照片由弗兰茨·盖苓提供。彩色照片由航鹰摄于 2003 年
Black and white photos from Franz Geyling. Color photos taken by Hang Ying in 2003

鲍贵卿旧居。航鹰摄于 2006 年
The former residence of Bao Guiqing. Taken by Hang Ying in 2006

李吉甫故居。刘悦摄于 2006 年
The former residence of Li Jifu. Taken by Liu Yue in 2006

鲍贵卿为北洋军高级将领，曾任北洋政府陆军总长、黑龙江督军、吉林督军。在天津有大量房产和土地，并投资实业和银行，集军阀、财阀和大地主于一身。1921 年在津购买并自己设计了两所楼房，占地 7.941 亩，建筑面积 2400 平方米。主楼三层南面大平台有三个亭子，分别为中式、西洋古典式和近代西式，是一座中西合璧、别具一格的建筑。院内还有假山、凉亭、养鱼池、花圃等。所谓"中西合璧"，其实就是"老子有的是钱，老子喜欢的样式都给老子弄上去！"类似的建筑在上海租界也可见到。

Bao Guiqing, a senior general of the Beiyang Army, previously held key positions such as Minister of the Army in the Beiyang Government, as well as Military Governor of Heilongjiang and Jilin. He owned extensive real estate and land in Tianjin and was actively involved in industrial and banking investments, embodying the roles of warlord, financial magnate, and major landlord. In 1921, he purchased a property in Tianjin and personally designed two buildings, covering an area of 7.941 mu (approximately 5,294 square meters), with a total construction area of 2,400 square meters. The main building, a three-story structure, features a spacious southern terrace adorned with three distinct pavilions, each showcasing a different architectural style: traditional Chinese, classical Western, and modern Western. This unique blend of East and West makes the mansion particularly distinctive. The estate also includes artificial rockeries, pavilions, fish ponds, and flower garden. The so-called "fusion of Chinese and Western styles" in architecture was, in essence, a bold display of wealth—Bao spared no expense in incorporating every architectural element he favored. Similar eclectic buildings could be found in the Shanghai concessions as well.

李吉甫是英国仁记洋行买办之子，其父去世后接任天津英商仁记洋行买办。借英租界扩充之机买卖地皮、投机获利，并置有多处房产。此处故居位于和平区花园路 12 号，占地 5429 平方米，由乐利工程司瑞士建筑师陆甫设计，是一座古典主义风格庭院式楼群，建于 1918 年。

Li Jifu was the son of a comprador for the British trading firm William Forbes & Co.. After his father's passing, he succeeded him as the comprador of William Forbes & Co. in Tianjin. Taking advantage of the expansion of the British Concession, he engaged in land transactions and speculative investments, amassing significant wealth and multiple properties. His former residence, located at No.12 Huayuan Road in Heping District, covers an area of 5,429 square meters. Designed by a Swiss architect from Loup & Young, this neoclassical-style courtyard complex was built in 1918.

原俄租界内的教堂
Church in the former Russian Concession

原法租界紫竹林教堂
St. Louis Church

原意租界的新文艺复兴风格建筑
Renaissance Revival architecture in the former Italian Concession

原英租界先农大院联排别墅
Xiannong Courtyard row houses in the former British Concession

原德租界的巴伐利亚风格房子
Bavarian-style houses in the former German Concession

原东莱银行大楼
Former Donglai Bank Building

原汇丰银行
Former HSBC Building

原法租界的中心公园
The Central Park in the former French Concession

原日租界的二层小楼
Two-story buildings in the former Japanese Concession

原日租界建筑
Buildings in the former Japanese Concession

饰，比如古典建筑中常用的宏伟柱子，不管是希腊式的还是罗马式的，都放在银行的外立面加以装饰（原汇丰银行）；还可以是在同一个建筑中集中多种形式，成为众多风格的集仿（原东莱银行大楼）；甚至还可以是中西合璧式的，建筑师完全按照业主的审美和需要来设计（吴颂平公馆）。在建筑学家看来，这种中西合璧的折衷主义建筑形式非常符合通商口岸的"暴发户"们的口味，他们综合所有自己中意的建筑装饰构思于一体，异常繁复、奢华，却对于这些构思的内在联系并不在意。[①] 在历史研究者眼中，折衷主义建筑代表的其实是一种文化变迁：中西合璧的建筑风格，从形式上已经突破了"中学为体，西学为用"的窠臼，走上了兼容并蓄、开拓创新的道路。

消失不见的城墙

城池，是源于古代的军事防御建筑，后来也成了古代城市的代名词。为生命财产安全计，筑城几乎是古代所有国家的传统。不仅中国有城池，东亚的日本、韩国有，欧洲国家也有城堡，功能是一样的。

比较起来，东亚的城郭规模一般比欧洲要大。《礼记·礼运》记载："城郭沟池以为固"。因此，城池包括了城墙和护城河，其中"城"指的是城墙及城墙上的门楼、角楼等，"池"指的是护城河。自明代以来，城池变得特别的高大雄伟。当西方人最初来到中国的时候，他们往往惊叹城墙的高大和城门的雄伟。城墙体现了国家的权力和威严，城池保护了代表皇权的官府衙门和其子民，彰显着一个城市的特殊地位。

1404 年天津设卫筑城，两年后建成。当时，这座"卫城"只不过是土围子罢了。城周长 1626 丈（合 5420 米），东西长 504 丈（合 1680 米），南北长 324 丈（合 1080 米）；城墙高 1.98 丈（合 6.6 米），墙垛高 0.42 丈（合 1.4 米），共高 2.4 丈（合 8 米），是比较典型的中国传统筑城模式。又用了大约 90 年，到 1494 年才砌成砖城墙，

---

① 王受之著，《世界现代建筑史》，中国建筑工业出版社，1999 年，第 9 页。

of architecture and the similarity of cities, thereby representing an emotion hidden deep in people's memories about the collective cognition of a place. In the construction of various concessions in Tianjin, this phenomenon of restoring national architecture to the concessions can be seen. For example, churches in various concessions, the Xiannong Courtyard Row House in the former British concession, Bavarian-style villas in the former German concession, the Central Park in the former French concession, two-story buildings in the former Japanese concession, and Bochka Roof style buildings in the former Russian concession, can all be easily recognized for their national characteristics.

However, the predominant architectural style within the concessions mostly adhered to eclecticism, colloquially termed as a "hodgepodge." This could involve imitation of various historical styles, such as direct and complete replication (as seen in the original Tientsin Anglo-Chinese College); borrowing certain symbols or elements from Western classical architecture as decorative elements, such as grand columns commonly used in classical architecture, regardless of whether they were of Greek or Roman style, being incorporated into the facade of banks (as seen in the original HSBC Building); encompassing multiple styles within the same building, creating a collection of imitations (as seen in the original Donglai Bank Building); or even a fusion of Eastern and Western styles, where architects designed entirely according to the aesthetic preferences and needs of the owner (as seen in the residence of Wu Songping). From the perspective of architectural experts, this form of eclectic architecture, blending Eastern and Western elements, greatly appealed to the taste of the "nouveau riche" merchants in the port cities. They integrated all their favored architectural decorations into one, resulting in intricate and luxurious designs, without much consideration for the intrinsic connections between these ideas.[①] In the eyes of historians, eclecticism in architecture represents a cultural transition: the fusion of Eastern and Western architectural styles, in form, has broken free from the constraints of "Chinese essence as the foundamental structure, Western learning for use," and has embarked on a path of inclusivity, innovation, and exploration.

The Disappeared City Walls

City walls, originating from ancient military defense structures, later became synonymous with ancient cities. Building walls for the security of life and property was a tradition in almost all ancient countries. Not only China

---

① Wang Shouzhi. *A History of Modern Architecture*. China Architecture & Building Press, 1999, p.9.

德国于利希市中心的要塞，建于 16 世纪中期。张畅摄于 2011 年
Fortress in the center of Jülich, Germany, built in the mid-16th century.
Taken by Zhang Chang in 2011

日本大阪城模型。张畅摄于 2013 年
Model of Osaka Castle, Japan. Taken by Zhang Chang in 2013

拥有东、西、南、北四个城门的城楼和四处城角的角楼，城中心修建了鼓楼。（鼓楼是东亚古代城池或传统寺庙中放置大鼓的建筑，一般以"晨钟暮鼓"的方式与钟楼配对建设，即东面修钟楼，西面修鼓楼，两栋建筑以建筑群的中轴线对称，称为钟鼓楼，多用以报时或庆典。）名为鼓楼，实为钟楼，因为天津卫初设之时，只有卫戍京畿、转运漕粮的职责，并不需要按照一个城市的规模来进行规划和建造，所以只有一座鼓楼。

原来的天津鼓楼高三层，砖城木楼，楼基是砖砌的方形城墩台，下宽上窄，四面设拱形穿心门洞，分别与东西南北四个城门相对应。在这座台子上，修建了两层木结构重层歇山顶楼阁。第一层供奉观音大士、天后圣母、关羽、岳飞等。楼的第二层，内悬一口大钟，直径 1.4 米、高 2.3 米，为唐宋制式铁铸大钟，铸工精细、造型古朴。大钟初用以报时，以司晨昏，启闭城门，早晚共敲钟 108 响。清代天津诗人梅小树在鼓楼中撰写了一副抱柱联："高敞快登临，看七十二沽往来帆影；繁华谁唤醒，听一百八杵早晚钟声。"鼓楼

had city walls, but also East Asian countries like Japan and Korea, as well as European countries had castles, serving the same function.

Comparatively, the scale of city walls in East Asia is generally larger than that in Europe. *Li Yun* (Evolution of Ritual), one chapter of *Book of Rites* records: "City walls, moats, and ponds serve as defenses". Therefore, city walls include both the walls themselves and the moats, where "city walls" refer to the walls and structures on the walls such as gates and corner towers, and "moat" refers to the protective waterway. Since the Ming Dynasty, city walls have become particularly tall and majestic. When Westerners first came to China, they often marveled at the height of the city walls and the grandeur of the city gates. City walls embodied the power and dignity of the state, while city defenses protected the government offices representing imperial authority and its subjects, showcasing the special status of a city.

In 1404, Tianjin established a garrison and built a city, which was completed two years later. At that time, this "garrison city" was just a mud embankment. The circumference of the city was 1,626 zhang (about 5,420 meters), with a length from east to west of 504 zhang (about 1,680 meters) and from north to south of 324 zhang (about 1,080 meters); the city wall was 1.98 zhang high (about 6.6 meters), with a battlement height of 0.42 zhang (about 1.4 me-

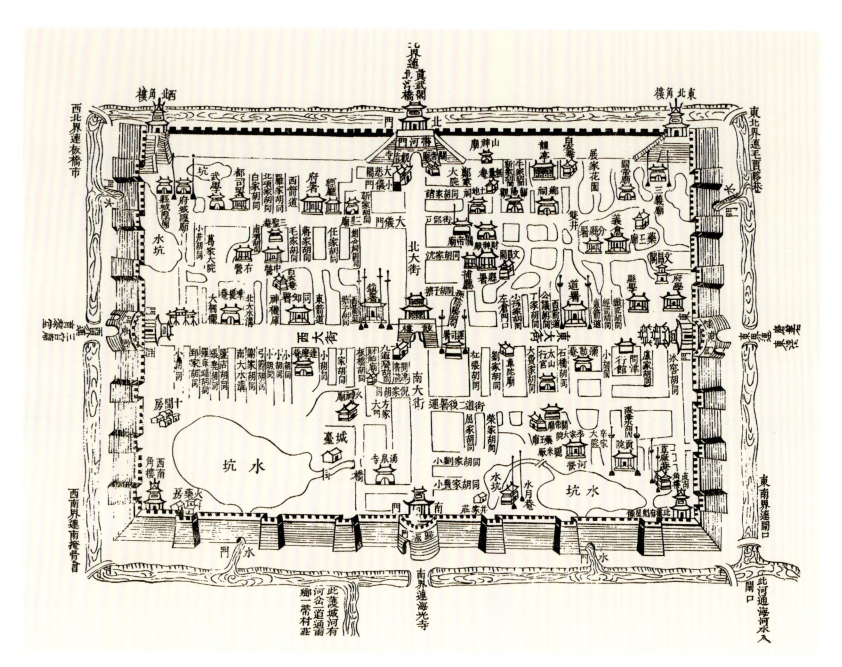

清代天津城内图。出自《天津城市历史地图集》（天津古籍出版社，2004 年）

Map of Tianjin old city during the Qing Dynasty. Source: *Atlas of Historical Maps of Tianjin* (Tianjin Ancient Books Publishing House, 2004)

义和团运动后饱经战火的鼓
楼。摄于 1900 年
The Drum Tower, battered by
the ravages of war after the
Boxer Rebellion. Taken in 1900

重建之后的鼓楼。刘悦摄于 2024 年
The Drum Tower after its reconstruction. Taken by Liu Yue in 2024

荷兰画家描绘的北京紫禁城
The Forbidden City in Beijing as
depicted by a Dutch artist

　　在城墙被拆毁的大规模运动下，很多城市的鼓楼被幸运地保留了下来。天津鼓楼先是为消防队占用，作为瞭望台。1921 年，民国政府重建鼓楼，楼顶大梁上改复绿瓦，较前更为美观。重建后，把鼓楼四个城门的名称"镇东""定南""安西""拱北"，由天津书法家华世奎书写。1952 年鼓楼再遭拆除。2001 年，天津老城厢地区改造，鼓楼重建。一座鼓楼的拆建，是人们对于城市建设理念更迭的真实写照。

　　Amid the large-scale movement of demolishing city walls, many cities were fortunate to have preserved their Drum Towers. The Tianjin Drum Tower was initially repurposed as a watchtower for the fire brigade. In 1921, the Republican government reconstructed the tower, replacing the roof beams with green tiles, making it more aesthetically appealing than before. After the reconstruction, the names of the four city gates—"Zhen Dong" (Pacifying the East), "Ding Nan" (Stabilizing the South), "An Xi" (Securing the West), and "Gong Bei" (Guarding the North)—were written by Tianjin calligrapher Hua Shikui. In 1952, the Drum Tower was once again demolished. In 2001, as part of the redevelopment of Tianjin's Old City, the Drum Tower was rebuilt. The demolition and reconstruction of this landmark reflect the evolving urban planning philosophies over time.

天津老城墙东南角
The Southeast Corner of Tianjin's Old City Wall

因此被称为"天津卫三宗宝，鼓楼、炮台、铃铛阁"之首。

到了近代，城墙越来越被视为阻碍贸易流通和人们出行的历史遗物，尤其是当城门在日落时关闭、拂晓时开启的时候，大批的商人小贩带着他们的商品，聚集在城门口，常常造成严重的交通阻塞。到清末，随着贸易的发展，在大部分通商口岸，比如天津、上海和广州等城市，具有相当规模的商业中心已出现在城墙之外。在这些城市，繁华热闹的外国租界都在城外，华界都在城内，而大多数商业活动也都在城外进行。在天津，帝国主义列强在义和团运动爆发后占领了天津市，并且拆毁了城墙。同样的事情发生在上海、广州，并且波及其他许多城市。旧城墙消失后，取而代之的往往是环城马路和有轨电车。在每一项改造的背后，理由都是相同的：为了促进商贸和方便货物流通，必须拆除造成交通阻塞的旧城门。

旧城墙的拆除虽然是被迫的和令人感到耻辱的，但是也没有让普通民众感到十分不舍。显然，在联军的大炮面前，传统城墙能够

ters), making it a relatively typical model of traditional Chinese city construction. It took about 90 years, until 1494, to rebuild the city wall with bricks. The city had four gates, each with a gatehouse, and corner towers at the four corners. In the center of the city, a drum tower. [A structure in ancient East Asian cities or traditional temples where a large drum is placed was built. Generally, a drum tower (constructed to the west) was paired with a bell tower (constructed to the east) in a manner known as "morning bell and evening drum. The two towers were built symmetrically on the central axis, both of which were used for telling time or celebrations."] However, since Tianjin Garrison was initially established only to guard the capital region and transport grain, and did not require planning and construction according to the scale of a city, there was only one drum tower. It was named the Drum Tower but functioned as a bell tower.

The original Tianjin Drum Tower was three stories high, with a brick base and wooden structure. The base was a square brick pedestal, wider at the bottom and narrower at the top, with arched doorways on all four sides corresponding to the east, west, south, and north gates. On this platform, a two-story wooden structure with double-layered hip roofs was built. The first floor housed statues of Guanyin Bodhisattva, Mazu (Goddess of the Sea), Guan Yu, Yue Fei, and others. In the second floor of the tower, a large bell was hung, with a diameter of 1.4 meters and a height of 2.3 meters. It was a Tang-Song style cast iron bell, finely crafted and of simple design. Initially, the bell was used for timekeeping, tolling 108 times each morning and evening to signal the opening and closing of the city gates. During the Qing Dynasty, Tianjin poet Mei Xiaoshu composed a couplet in the Drum Tower: "Ascend high and spacious to behold, watching the sails' shadows of the seventy-two villages; awakening the bustle, listening to the morning and evening bell chimes of one hundred and eight strokes." Therefore, the Drum Tower was known as the first of the "Three Treasures of Tianjin Garrison: Drum Tower, Fort, and Bell Pavilion."

In modern times, city walls were increasingly seen as historical relics that hindered trade and people's mobility, especially when city gates were closed at sunset and opened at dawn. This led to congestion as large numbers of merchants and vendors gathered at the gates with their goods. By the end of the Qing Dynasty, with the development of trade, significant commercial centers had emerged outside the city walls in most treaty ports such as Tianjin, Shanghai, and Guangzhou. In these cities, bustling foreign concessions were located outside the walls, while the Chinese quarters remained within, and most commercial activities took place outside the walls. In Tianjin, imperialist powers occupied the city after the Boxer Rebellion and demolished the

1900 年 12 月正在拆除的天津老城墙
The Demolition of Tianjin's Old City Wall in December 1900

city walls. Similar events occurred in Shanghai, Guangzhou, and many other cities. After the old city walls disappeared, they were often replaced by ring roads and tram lines. The rationale behind each renovation was the same: to promote trade and facilitate the flow of goods by removing the old city gates that caused traffic congestion.

Although the demolition of the old city walls was forced and shameful, it did not leave the ordinary people feeling deeply regretful. Clearly, traditional city walls were insufficient in providing protection against the cannons of the allied forces. Since they couldn't offer adequate safety and dignity, it was deemed preferable to make way for convenience in transportation and commercial interests. Amidst the horrors of gunfire and bloodshed, people could better understand the profound significance of the concept of "survival of the fittest," introduced by Yan Fu's translation of *Evolution and Ethics*. New values of "progress" emerged, and city walls became symbols of conservatism and isolation that should be eliminated. Of course, city walls remained effective against common bandits, so many small towns and villages retained their walls. Overall, in coastal treaty port cities, the demands for commerce and economic development became paramount for urban residents, overshadowing the sense of security provided by city walls.

After the city walls were dismantled, urban development experienced rapid growth, accompanied by a significant increase in population. Roads were constructed and widened, facilitating commercial flow. Newly laid streets were equipped with drainage ditches and sewers, creating a cleaner urban environment. With wider roads, the phenomenon of indiscriminate defecation disappeared, and police patrols were instituted. In the first half of the 20th century, the rate of urban population growth sharply accelerated, with populations in most cities doubling or even tripling. The growth in urban population was mainly due to rural-to-urban migration, either as a result of seeking refuge and relief or in pursuit of employment opportunities. Therefore, in China, the majority of urban populations are actually composed of immigrants from rural areas.

After a large number of rural residents entered the cities, they began to influence and be influenced by urban life, leading to transformations in the urban landscape. In traditional Chinese rural areas, farmers could only purchase or exchange daily necessities at fixed-time markets, and social interactions were limited. However, in large cities, the convenience of modern transportation and the development of commercial centers allowed urban residents to shop in stores and department stores located in the commercial districts, giving rise to a new consumer culture. Similarly, interactions with strangers in public places such as trams, department stores, or cinemas became a common

提供的保护太微不足道了。既然不能提供应有的安全和威严，那不如为交通方便和商业利益让位。在炮火的腥风血雨中，民众比一般时候更能体会到由严复翻译引进的《天演论》中"优胜劣汰"这一观念的深刻含义，新的"进步"的社会价值观产生，城墙就成为保守闭塞的象征符号，理应被淘汰了。当然，面对普通盗匪，城墙还是有效的，所以，许多小城镇和村庄保留了"城墙"。总的来说，在沿海的通商口岸城市，商业和经济发展成为城市居民的要求，流动性的需求压倒了城墙带来的安全感。

城墙被拆掉之后，城市建设得到快速发展，人口也快速增长。道路被修建和拓宽，有利于商业流通。新铺设的街道还配有排水沟和下水道，实现了城市的清洁环境。道路变宽了，随地便溺的现象消失了，警察巡逻街头。在 20 世纪上半期，城市的人口增长速度急剧加快，大多数城市的人口扩大了一倍到三倍。城市人口的增长主要来自农村人口迁入城市，要么为了逃难以寻求救济，要么为了寻

1906 年 2 月 16 日，中国内地第一条有轨电车线路，由中国和比利时合建的 5.16 千米围城环行线路在天津正式运营

On February 16, 1906, the first tramway line in mainland China, a 5.16-kilometer ring route around the city, jointly constructed by China and Belgium, officially began operations in Tianjin

找就业机会。所以在中国，大多数的城市人口实际上是由农村而来的移民构成的。

大量原农村人口进入城市后，影响着城市的发展，更被城市生活所影响和改造。在中国的传统农村，农民只有在固定时间的集市上，才能购买或者交换一些日常所需物品，人与人之间的交往互动有限。而在大城市里，便利的现代交通和城市商业中心区的形成，使市民可以在位于商业中心区的商店和新式百货公司里购物，一种新的消费文化出现了。同样，在有轨电车上、在百货公司里或者在电影院等公共场所，与陌生人的互动，无疑是一个新的普遍体验，这需要新的社交规则，并由此产生了不同于传统社会生活的公共秩序和城市文化。比如，看电影要排队、观影时不能大声喧哗，这都迥异于在传统的嘈杂戏园听戏的感受。由此可见，作为物质基础的城市空间的拓展和变化，实实在在地改变了作为上层建筑的人们的精神世界。

总之，城墙保护的是古代城市，而城墙被拆除以利交通贸易，则意味着近代城市的崛起。

experience, necessitating new social norms and giving rise to public order and urban culture different from traditional social life. For example, queuing for movies and maintaining silence during screenings were behaviors distinct from the experience of attending noisy traditional theaters. Thus, the expansion and changes in urban spaces as material foundations have significantly altered the spiritual world of urban residents.

In summary, while city walls protected ancient cities, their demolition to facilitate transportation and trade symbolized the rise of modern cities.

有轨电车通过金汤桥进入奥匈租界。摄于 1906 年
The tram passing through the Jintang Bridge and entering
the Austro-Hungrian Concession. Taken in 1906

第 三 章　交通、贸易与城市的发展

Chapter Three: Transportation, Trade, and Urban Development

道路与市内交通工具

交通对一个城市的兴起及其经济社会发展具有十分重要的影响。尤其是在近代，交通技术的发展，早已将世界经济更为紧密地联系在一起，呈现出一个统一的市场——它的商品种类更加丰富、贸易吞吐量更大、交换频率更快。人们的行为习惯因而发生改变。

城市里的交通出行方式往往决定了一个社会的人际交流的方式、频率和范围。城市里的交通主要包含三个方面：一为道路桥梁系统等基础设施；二为交通工具；三为运营系统。以上三者的发展演进亦可视为衡量一个城市发展的重要指标之一，并潜移默化地影响着人们的日常生活。

碎石子路和林荫道

"地当九河津要，路通七省舟车。"天津从几个小渔村发展成为近代大都市，与它地处交通要道密切相关。在天津城外，不仅有运河连接南北，还有若干条通衢大道，向北连通北京，往东直抵大沽口，过海河径奔山海关，向南通往沧州。然而，在19世纪中期，天津市内的交通条件却非常糟糕。本地人习以为常，往往是初到天津的外国人对出行的不便深有所感，由此留下生动细致的描述。

1879年，一位德国侨民初次到访时，形容天津城的道路说："整个天津只有四五条石板铺成的路。其他的五六百条路都是肮脏的淤泥堆积的路。……这些道路大都不过十步宽，非常的狭窄。有时为了躲避马车或者轿子，整个人就会被挤得贴到路边房子的墙上"；

Roads and Urban Transportation Vehicles

Transportation has a significant impact on the rise of a city and its economic and social development. Especially in modern times, the development of transportation technology has already interconnected the world economy more closely, presenting a unified market—with a wider variety of goods, larger trade volumes, and faster exchange rates. As a result, people's behavior patterns have changed.

The modes of transportation in a city often determine the way, frequency, and scope of interpersonal communication in a society. Urban transportation mainly includes three aspects: infrastructure such as roads and bridges, transportation vehicles, and operational systems. The development and evolution of these three aspects can also be seen as important indicators of a city's development and subtly influence people's daily lives.

Gravel Roads and Tree-lined Avenues

"Here at the Nine-River Crossing, roads connect many provinces by boat and carriage." Tianjin's transformation from small fishing villages into a modern metropolis is closely tied to its strategic location as a transportation hub. Outside the city, there were not only canals connecting the north and south, but also several major roads leading north to Beijing, east to Taku Forts, crossing the Hai River to Shanhaiguan, and south to Cangzhou. However, in the mid-19th century, the transportation conditions within Tianjin were very poor. While locals had grown accustomed to it, newly arrived foreigners to Tianjin often felt the inconvenience of travel, leaving behind vivid and detailed descriptions.

In 1879, when a German immigrant visited Tianjin for the first time, he described the city's roads as follows: "The entire Tianjin has only four or five roads paved with flagstones. The other five or six hundred roads are dirty mud piles... These roads are mostly no more than ten paces wide, very

租界区的街道（今建设路与曲阜道交口）。摄于 1914 年
The streets of the concession area (now the intersection of Jianshe Road and Qufu Road). Taken in 1914

清朝末年天津老城街道
Street of the Old City of Tianjin in the late Qing Dynasty

路上不仅有人和车，"路边居民家的猪经常跑到路上，所以有时你不小心还会被猪绊倒"①。不仅没有道路，卫生环境也很恶劣。一位四处旅行经过这里的日本人描述："行走在路上，便会觉得臭气冲鼻，一堆堆污秽的垃圾让你见了眼睛生疾"；城内地基很低，一旦下雨，"路面积水，深处没腰"；夏天，"各处污水沟臭气冲天，热气引发多种流行病，致使丧命无数"。②当然，他们也都承认，并不是只有天津的城市建设状况如此糟糕，当时整个中国乃至世界的城市大都如此。

1887 年侨民在天津铺设了第一条碎石子路。这是在 19 世纪 20 年代才开始在伦敦使用的路面铺设技术，最早只在伦敦特权阶级的生活区使用。碎石路是把小颗粒（5 厘米左右）花岗岩铺在清理过的

narrow. Sometimes, to avoid carriages or sedan chairs, people are squeezed against the walls of the roadside houses." There were not only people and carts on the roads; "Pigs from the houses along the road often run onto the road, so sometimes you accidentally trip over them."[1] Not only were the roads bad, but the sanitation was also terrible. A Japanese traveler passing through here described, "Walking on the road, you will smell a foul stench, piles of filth make your eyes sick." The city's foundation was low, so when it rained, "the road surface is flooded, waist-deep in some places." In summer, "sewage ditches everywhere stank to high heaven, and the heat caused various epidemics, resulting in countless deaths."[2] Of course, they also admitted that it wasn't just Tianjin's urban development that was so bad; at that time, most cities in China and even the world were like this.

In 1887, expatriates in Tianjin laid the first macadam road. This was a

---

① 摘译自康斯坦丁·冯·汉纳根，《1879—1886 发自中国的书信》。转引自张畅、刘悦，《李鸿章的洋顾问：德璀琳与汉纳根》，台北传记文学出版社，2012 年，第 277、278 页。

② （日）曾根俊虎著，范建明译，《北中国纪行：清国漫游志》，中华书局，2007 年，第 6 页。

---

① Selective translation from Constantin von Hanneken, *Briefe aus China: 1879-1886; als deutscher Offizier im Reich der Mitte.* Quoted in Zhang Chang, Liu Yue. *Li Hongzhang's Foreign Consultants: Gustav Detring and Constantin von Hanneken.* Taipei: Biographies Publishing House, 2012, p.277,278.

② Sone Toshitora. *Journey to Northern China: A Record of Roaming in the Qing Dynasty*, translated by Fan Jianming. Zhonghua Book Company, 2007, p.6.

路面上，然后需要十几个工人推动巨大的铁碌或石碌碾平。到 20 世纪初，混合了柏油和木焦油的柏油碎石路出现，提高了碎石路的使用寿命。很快这项铺路技术就传到天津的租界区。1905 年初到天津的一位比利时工程师在日记中写道："欧洲租界非常干净，宽阔的街道铺着柏油。"[1] 侨民还在道路两旁种植树木，成为林荫道，在夏季给马路遮上一片浓荫。并且，因为大部分别墅都带有前院，这些前院使街道变得格外敞亮。行走在这样的街区，有谁不愿意到这样的环境来居住呢？！

受到租界建设的示范影响，天津地方政府下属的工程局也铺设了很多碎石路，大大方便了市民出行。"曾经满处是深沟大洞、充满淤泥和垃圾的水坑，使人恶心和可怕的道路……被垫平、取直、铺筑、加宽，并设置了路灯，使人畜都感到便利。"[2] 1900 年八国联军占领天津后，旧城墙被拆除，在城墙遗址上铺设了环老城的四条碎石马路，加上原有的横穿东西和纵贯南北的两条大道，很大程度上改善了老城的交通状况。老城外，沿海河西岸连接外国租界地的道路也新建成功，沟通了老城和租界，使近代天津城区初见规模。

"骆驼祥子"和洋马车

道路状况的改善使交通工具也得到了更新，最突出的变化是速度和乘坐舒适程度的提高。因为路况问题，原本中国的中间阶层和上流社会人士外出时，只有乘轿子或者乘马车，有急务的话就骑马。1879 年，那位初到天津的德国人，在去直隶总督府拜见李鸿章时，记述道："我们雇了两顶轿子。前面有一个人骑马开道，后面还有一个人保护。每顶轿子都有四个轿夫，另外还有两个人在轿子旁边跟随。总共有十四个人随着我们俩赶往总督府。"[3] 这倒并非为了排

---

① （比）约翰·麦特勒等著，刘悦等译，《比利时—中国：昔日之路（1870—1930）》，社会科学文献出版社，2021 年，第 215 页。

② 转引自（英）雷穆森著，许逸凡等译，《天津租界史（插图本）》，天津人民出版社，2009 年，第 66 页。

③ 张畅、刘悦，《李鸿章的洋顾问：德璀琳与汉纳根》，台北传记文学出版社，2012 年，第 325 页。

road surface paving technology that began to be used in London in the 1820s and was initially only used in the privileged areas of London. A macadam road involves laying small granite particles (about 5 centimeters) on a cleaned road surface, and then requiring a dozen or so workers to push huge iron or stone rollers to flatten it. By the early 20th century, tar-macadam roads mixed with tar and wood tar appeared, extending the life of macadam roads. Soon, this road paving technology spread to the concession areas of Tianjin. In early 1905, a Belgian engineer who arrived in Tianjin wrote in his diary: "The European concession is very clean, with wide streets paved with tar."[1] Immigrants also planted trees along the roads, forming avenues of trees that provided dense shade over the roads in the summer. Additionally, because most villas had front yards, these front yards made the streets particularly bright. Who wouldn't want to live in such an environment walking through such neighborhoods?!

Influenced by the construction of the concessions, the Engineering Bureau under the local government of Tianjin also laid many macadam roads, greatly facilitating the travel of the citizens. "Once full of deep ditches, filled with mud and garbage, disgusting and terrifying roads... have been leveled, straightened, paved, widened, and equipped with street lamps, making it convenient for both people and animals."[2] After the Eight-Nation Alliance occupied Tianjin in 1900, the old city walls were demolished, and four macadam roads were laid around the old city on the site of the city wall remains. Together with the two existing roads running east-west and north-south, the traffic conditions in the old city were greatly improved. Outside the old city, roads connecting the foreign concessions along the west bank of the Hai River were also successfully built, linking the old city and the concessions, thus marking the initial scale of the modern Tianjin urban area.

"Camel Xiangzi" and Foreign Horse Carriage

The improvement of road conditions led to the upgrading of transportation vehicles, with the most prominent changes being the increase in speed and comfort. Due to the poor road conditions, the middle and upper classes in China traditionally traveled by sedan chair or horse-drawn carriage, with horseback riding reserved for urgent matters. In 1879, a German newcomer

---

① Johan J. Mattelaer, et al. *A Belgian Passage to China (1870-1930)*, translated by Liu Yue, et al. Social Sciences Academic Press (China), 2021, p.215.

② Quoted in O. D. Rasmussen. *Tientsin: An Illustrated Outline History*, translated by Xu Yifan, et al. Tianjin People's Publishing House, 2008, p.66.

场，而是这一路行来确实不容易。在天津居住一段时间后，侨民们出行时就跟本地人一样改为骑马，这样不仅更为快捷，且马匹的价格和饲养它们的费用并不昂贵。

由于占用的马路面积大、人力多、速度还慢，传统的轿子开始逐渐消失。从20世纪初只被妇女乘用、轿夫也减为两人，到后来随着妇女越来越被允许"抛头露面"，轿子就被人力车（也叫黄包车或东洋车，橡胶轮胎出现后，天津人称其为"胶皮"）彻底取代了。人力车大约在1882年由日本经上海引进到天津，逐渐占领了北京、天津、上海、汉口等大城市的大街小巷。它比以往的各种车辆更为轻便、价格便宜，于是有些中国的和欧洲的家庭会自行购置这种车辆并雇用车夫，有的则向车行长期租用。车夫多为年轻人，仿佛不知疲倦地奔跑在城市的街头巷尾，即使在夏天也能匀速小跑10千米。[1] 不过，随着人力车数量增加，竞争日益激烈，即使吃苦耐劳如"骆驼祥子"[2] 一般，也只能挣扎在社会底层，"甚或终日街头不得一饱者"[3]。

中国式马车原来为城中富人外出必备，但是一般只有一匹马来牵引，车厢逼仄，仅能稍稍遮风挡雨，并且不像欧洲马车那样装有弹簧，车轴为硬木制成，既慢且颠簸，长途旅行极其辛苦。20世纪初西式马车的使用日渐增多，1906年天津已有西式马车500余辆，洋马800余匹。[4] 这种马车装饰豪华，有大玻璃车窗和两盏车灯、四个轮子（少数两个轮子）和两匹马，且马匹也为重金购买的西洋高头大马而非原来矮小的蒙古马。虽然价格昂贵，但富人们往往在每天中午前包租马车以便下午和晚上出去交游，喜欢炫富的富豪人家甚至自行购买，而特意来津看"西洋景"的外地有钱人也会特意租

---

① （比）约翰·麦特勒等著，刘悦等译，《比利时—中国：昔日之路（1870—1930）》，社会科学文献出版社，2021年，第223页。

② 《骆驼祥子》是老舍的名著，是一部描写城市底层劳动人民悲惨命运的长篇小说，主人公为人力车夫"祥子"，绰号"骆驼祥子"，意为吃苦耐劳。

③ 《直报》1895年2月4日。转引自刘海岩，《空间与社会：近代天津城市的演变》，天津社会科学院出版社，2003年，第68页。

④ 天津市地方史志编修委员会总编辑室编，《二十世纪初的天津概况》，内部发行，1986年，第97—100页。

to Tianjin described his journey to visit Li Hongzhang, the Viceroy of Zhili, saying, "We hired two sedan chairs. There was a man riding ahead to clear the way, and another behind for protection. Each sedan chair was carried by four bearers, and two more men followed beside them. In total, fourteen people accompanied the two of us on our way to the Viceroy's residence."[1] This wasn't done for show; the journey was indeed challenging. After residing in Tianjin for some time, the expatriates switched to horseback riding like the locals for their travels. This method was not only faster but also cost-effective in terms of horse prices and maintenance expenses.

Due to their large road footprint, reliance on manpower, and slow speed, traditional sedan chairs gradually disappeared. From the early 20th century, when they were only used by women and manned by two carriers, to later when women were increasingly allowed to be seen in public, sedan chairs were completely replaced by rickshaws (also called "yellow carriage" or "east-foreign-vehicle" which Tianjin residents referred to as "rubber tires" after the appearance of rubber wheels). Rickshaws were introduced to Tianjin from Japan via Shanghai around 1882 and gradually took over the streets and alleys of major cities such as Beijing, Tianjin, Shanghai, and Hankou. They were lighter and cheaper than previous vehicles, so some Chinese and European families purchased them and hired drivers, while others rented them from rickshaw rental agencies for long periods. The drivers were mostly young men who seemed tireless as they ran through the streets and alleys of the city, even running 10 kilometers at a steady pace in the summer.[2] However, as the number of rickshaws increased, competition intensified, and even hardworking individuals like "Camel Xiangzi"[3] struggled to make ends meet at the bottom of society, "sometimes going hungry all day on the streets."[4]

The Chinese-style horse carriage was originally a necessity for wealthy people to travel outside the city, but typically only one horse was used to pull it. The carriage was cramped, providing only slight protection from wind and rain, and unlike European carriages, it lacked springs. The axles were made of hardwood, making the ride slow and bumpy, and long-distance travel was

---

① Zhang Chang, Liu Yue. *Li Hongzhang's Foreign Consultants: Gustav Detring and Constantin von Hanneken*. Taipei: Biographies Publishing House, 2012, p.325.

② Johan J. Mattelaer, et al. *A Belgian Passage to China (1870-1930)*, translated by Liu Yue, et al. Social Sciences Academic Press (China), 2021, p.223.

③ *Camel Xiangzi (Rickshaw Boy)* is a masterpiece by Lao She, a long novel that depicts the tragic fate of the laborer at the bottom of the society. The protagonist is the rickshaw puller "Xiangzi", nicknamed "Camel Xiangzi", which means hard-working and enduring nature.

④ *Chih Pao*, on February 4, 1895. Quoted in Liu Haiyan. *Space and Society: The Evolution of Modern Tianjin City*. Tianjin Academy of Social Sciences Press, 2003, p.68.

骑马
Horse riding

乘轿
Sedan chair

人力车
Rickshaw

中式马车
Chinese style horse carriages

小车（手推车）
Wheelbarrow

西式马车
Western style horse carriage

民国早期天津街头用来迎亲的西式马车
Western-style carriages used to welcome brides on
the road of Tianjin in the early Republic of China

大车和大车店
Cart and the Inn for carters

图片来源：比利时根特大学档案馆
Source: Archives of Ghent University, Belgium

天津街头的自行车
Bicycles on the road of Tianjin

天津街头的汽车
Car on the road of Tianjin

20 世纪 20 年代天津德国侨民家里的老式汽车
Old-fashioned car of German expatriates in Tianjin in the 1920s

天津街头的电车和人力车
Tram and rickshaws on the road of Tianjin

上一辆享受不一样的乘车体验，时髦的年轻人还会租马车作为迎亲车辆。

原来的中式马车在载运远方旅客或者运输货物时仍然使用，称之为"大车"。这种马车只有两个车轮，为了使马的牵引力或耐久力加强，在马之外会增加两头到三头骡子或驴，运货的话就不需要车厢了，称之为"敞车"。使用这种马车的便利之处在于，在近郊的各处村落或通往陕西、山东、河南及蒙古等地沿途各个驿站或大车店，可以住宿休息并调换骡马。与"大车"相对的是"小车"，有搬运货物的推货小车、运水用的水车、搬运米面等袋装品的布车和卖食品的小车，只有一个车轮，由车夫一人向前方推行，所以又叫手推车。对于狭窄弯曲的老城道路或者崎岖难行的田间小道，这种手推车非常适用。1906 年，天津的大车和小车加起来有近 3000 辆，经营大车运输的有 385 人，大车夫和小车夫加起来有 2000 余人。①

还有一种季节性的交通工具是雪橇。冬季里，天津的各处河道都会结上厚实的冰层，船运暂停，这时河道就变成平坦的街道，雪橇就派上用场。它们通常由两个条状滑行木梁制成，上面铺上一块木板，再加上两个中间坐垫，其上覆着棉垫和山羊皮。乘客坐在山羊皮垫子上，雪橇夫在后面，拿着一端装有铁尖的棍子。车夫推动

extremely arduous. At the beginning of the 20th century, the use of Western-style horse carriages increased. By 1906, there were over 500 Western-style horse carriages and over 800 foreign horses in Tianjin.① These carriages were lavishly decorated, with large glass windows, two carriage lamps, four wheels (some had only two), and two horses. The horses were high-quality Western horses purchased at great expense, rather than the small Mongolian horses used previously. Although expensive, wealthy individuals often hired carriages before noon to socialize in the afternoon and evening. Some affluent families who enjoyed flaunting their wealth even purchased their own carriages. Wealthy visitors from out of town who came specifically to see the "Western scenes" in Tianjin would also rent a carriage to experience a different mode of transportation. Fashionable young people would even rent carriages as wedding vehicles.

The original Chinese-style horse carriage, when transporting travelers from afar or goods, was still in use and referred to as "da che" (literally "big cart"). This type of carriage had only two wheels. To increase the pulling power or endurance of the horse, two to three mules or donkeys were added alongside the horse. When used for transporting goods, there was no carriage, and it was called an "open cart." The convenience of using this type of carriage lay in the fact that at various villages in the suburbs or at relay stations and inns along the routes to Shanxi, Shandong, Henan, and Mongolia, accommodation and rest could be provided, and mules could be exchanged. The "big cart" was in contrast to the "xiao che" ("small cart"). There were hand-pushed

① 天津市地方史志编修委员会总编辑室编，《二十世纪初的天津概况》，内部发行，1986 年，第 98—100 页。

① Editorial Office of the Tianjin Chorography and History Compilation Committee (ed.). *Overview of Tianjin in the Early 20th Century*. Published internally in 1986, pp.97-100.

雪橇后，用棍子撑冰面，速度甚至快过黄包车。

除了西式马车，自行车和汽车也都是纯粹的舶来品。18 世纪末法国人发明了世界上第一辆自行车，19 世纪中后期自行车漂洋过海来到中国。天津的租界里自然也少不了这个新奇玩意儿，不仅有德式、日式、英式等因不同国家生产而制成的不同样式，而且有男车和坤车（女车）之分。男车有横梁，骑乘者须像骑马一样，从车座后跨上跨下；坤车是弯梁，为的是穿旗袍、裙子的女士方便从车座前上下。1886 年，德国工程师卡尔·本茨（Karl Friedrich Benz）发明了世界上第一辆汽车。到 20 世纪二三十年代，汽车开始在天津租界内大量出现，销售汽车的经销商 14 家，而汽车修理厂也有 14 家之多。①

划时代的有轨电车

在近代城市中，真正称得上公共交通方式的，应该是有轨电车。1879 年，使用电力带动轨道车辆的有轨电车由德国工程师西门子（Werner von Siemens）在柏林的博览会上首先展出。此后有轨电车在 20 世纪初的欧洲、美洲、大洋洲和亚洲的一些城市风行一时。对于这种新鲜事物，天津的外国侨民们马上意识到其中商机无限，遂于八国联军占领天津时，成立了天津电车电灯公司（英语：The Tientsin Tramways & Lighting Co., Ltd.，法语：Compagnie de Tramways et d'Eclairage de Tientsin）。天津是第一个建起有轨电车系统的中国城市。这里要强调的是，中国第一条有轨电车路线并非诞生于天津，但是同时拥有多条线路形成城市公共交通系统的却是天津。

1900 年八国联军成立"天津都统衙门"对天津进行城市管理和市政建设。很快就有日本和欧洲侨民分别向"都统衙门"提出申请，要求获得老城与租界间有轨电车的特许经营权。作为一项已经在欧美国家发展起来的公用事业，它虽"钱"景可观，但前期所需投资巨大。最终都统衙门将天津城区部分（但不包括租界）的电车特许经营权授予了有多国财团背景的比利时天津电车电灯公司。1904 年

---

① 《天津行名录》，中国北方告白公司出版，天津印字馆印刷，1928 年，第 204 页。

carts for transporting goods, water carts for carrying water, cloth carts for carrying bagged rice and flour, and small carts for selling food. These carts had only one wheel and were pushed forward by a single cartman, hence they were also called barrows. These barrows were particularly suitable for narrow, winding old city roads or rugged rural paths. In Tianjin in 1906, there were nearly 3,000 big and small carts, with 385 people engaged in big cart transportation and over 2,000 cartmen in total.[①]

Another seasonal means of transportation is the sled. In winter, the various waterways in Tianjin freeze over with thick ice, halting boat traffic. During this time, the waterways become smooth streets, perfect for sleds. They are typically made of two wooden beams for sliding, with a wooden board on top and two middle seats covered with cotton padding and goat skin. Passengers sit on the goat skin cushions while the sled driver stands at the back, holding a stick with an iron tip. After the driver pushes the sled, they use the stick to push against the ice surface, sometimes even faster than a rickshaw.

In addition to Western-style carriages, bicycles and cars are also purely imported goods. At the end of the 18th century, the French invented the world's first bicycle, and in the mid to late 19th century, bicycles crossed the oceans to reach China. Naturally, the concessions in Tianjin were not without this novelty. There were not only German, Japanese, and British styles produced in different countries but also distinctions between men's and women's bicycles. Men's bicycles had a horizontal beam, and riders had to mount and dismount like riding a horse, swinging their leg over the saddle from behind. Women's bicycles had a curved beam for the convenience of ladies wearing cheongsams or skirts to mount and dismount from the front of the saddle. In 1886, German engineer Karl Friedrich Benz invented the world's first car. By the 1920s and 1930s, cars began to appear in large numbers within the concessions in Tianjin, with 14 dealerships selling cars and an equal number of car repair shops.[②]

Groundbreaking Tramways

In modern cities, the true form of public transportation should be the tram. In 1879, the tram powered by electricity was first exhibited at the Berlin Expo by the German engineer Werner von Siemens. Since then, trams

---

① Editorial Office of the Tianjin Chorography and History Compilation Committee (ed.). *Overview of Tianjin in the Early 20th Century*. Published internally in 1986, pp.98-100.

② *North China Hong-List*. Published by the N. C. Advertising Co., printed by the Tientsin Press, 1928, p.204.

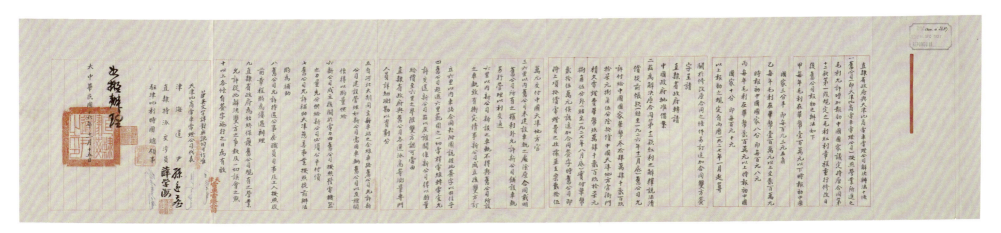

民国时期直隶省政府与比商天津电车电灯公司的合同。图片来源：比利时外交部档案馆
The contract between Zhili Provincial Government and CTET during the Republic of China period.
Source: Archives of the Belgian Ministry of Foreign Affairs

4月26日合同正式签署。合同规定，以天津老城的鼓楼为中心，方圆3千米内的电车、电灯兴建与运行事业，由比公司专权承办，期限50年。

比商天津电车电灯公司的总部设在比利时布鲁塞尔，注册资金为25万法郎，这是当时天津外商中投资最大的企业。天津的公司大楼设在原意租界三马路（今河北区进步道29号）。天津公司有两个部门：管理部和工程部。管理部设有总经理、副经理、秘书、华务主任、会计。工程部员工包括发电厂（300余人）、外线管理部（约60人）、电车部（1200余人）、修理部（150余人）、电灯部（约60人）、电表修理部（40余人），总计1800多人，可谓规模庞大。

电车运行需要直流电，电灯照明需要交流电。为了电力供应，必须保证水源充足，比商天津电车电灯公司先是在前临海河、后凭金钟河的望海楼后金家窑村购买了一块土地，用以修建发电厂。其后，又在海河东浮桥东侧沿河马路处（今河东区）购置楼房一处，作为公司办事处。还在老城西南角的南开中学北侧购买了另一块土地，修建电车的车库及修理厂。所有电车电灯以及一切应需的机件器材，大至发电机、小至螺丝钉，皆由比利时布鲁塞尔买进运抵天津。

1905年开始电车轨道的铺设工程。1906年2月16日沿旧城墙

became popular for a time in some cities in Europe, the Americas, Oceania, and Asia in the early 20th century. Recognizing the business opportunities inherent in this novel technology, foreign residents in Tianjin promptly established the Tientsin Tramways & Lighting Co., Ltd. (Compagnie de Tramways et d'Eclairage de Tientsin, CTET) during the occupation of Tianjin by the Eight-Nation Alliance. Tianjin was the first city in China to establish a tram system. It is important to emphasize that while China's first tram line was not born in Tianjin, it was Tianjin that simultaneously had multiple lines forming an urban public transportation system.

In 1900, the Eight-Nation Alliance established the "Tianjin Provisional Government" to manage the city and undertake municipal construction in Tianjin. Soon, Japanese and European residents separately approached the "Provisional Government" to apply for the franchise rights to operate trams between the old city and the concessions. As a utility already developed in European and American countries, tram operation promised lucrative prospects, but required massive initial investment. Ultimately, the "Provisional Government" granted the tram franchise rights for parts of the Tianjin urban area (excluding the concessions) to the CTET, backed by multinational consortia. The contract was formally signed on April 26, 1904. According to the contract, the tram and lighting construction and operation within a radius of 3 kilometers centered on the Drum Tower of the old city of Tianjin would be exclusively undertaken by the Belgian company, with a term of 50 years.

The headquarters of the CTET was located in Brussels, Belgium, with a

比商天津电车电灯公司厂房，修车厂设备完备，除钢轮外，全部车辆皆可自行制造。厂内共分为：机务段、机工班、电工班、驾车班、铆工班、木工班、钳工班、铁工班、油工班、检车班、洗车班等部门

The factory of CTET was well-equipped, capable of manufacturing all vehicle components except for steel wheels. The facility was divided into multiple departments, including field maintenance, machinists, electricians, drivers, riveters, carpenters, fitters, blacksmiths, painters, inspectors, and vehicle washers

比商天津电车电灯公司员工在厂房前合影
Group photo of the employees of CTET in front of the tram depot

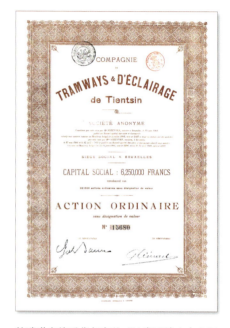

德璀琳家族后代保存的"比商天津电车电灯公司"股票
Stocks issued by CTET by courtesy of the descendant of Gustav Detring

图片来源：比利时根特大学档案馆
Source: Archives of Ghent University, Belgium

遗址马路行驶的第一条环线电车开始试运营，共有 18 辆电车投入低速行驶，第一天共载客约 10000 人。1 个月后，电车通车仪式正式举行，场面非常隆重。1906 年 2 月 28 日《中国时报》对这一事件做了如下报道："在远东地区，其他地方的电车建设工程都比不上天津，也没有哪座城市的电车运营如同这里一般成功。"①

然而，人们对于不了解的新鲜事物的态度，往往融合了好奇、恐惧和抵触等多种心态。即便是火车已经建造通行了若干年，电车还是被视为洪水猛兽，引来了不小的反对声音。其中最主要的阻碍来自人力车夫。人力车处于鼎盛时，在天津登记的"骆驼祥子"有 8800 余人，加上造车者、经营者等相关人员共 10000 余人，占天津当时人口约 3%。②眼看如此众多从业者的生计即将受到影响，从电车公司铺设轨道之始，黄包车协会秘密组织了长达几个月时间的激烈抵制活动。天津商会也向地方政府提出请求，要求禁止修筑。不过天津本地官员不少人为留洋归来者，如唐绍仪、蔡绍基、梁敦彦、梁如浩等人，均为袁世凯网罗任用的留美生，他们指出："电车一项，各国殷盛冲要之区，无不安设，辙迹愈密，商务愈兴，需用人力亦愈广。天津风气早开，绅商多身历外洋，当有真知灼见者。"③在地方政府的坚决支持下，来自人力车夫的抵制逐渐式微。

但困难不止于此，环城路线初始运营时，大多只是吸引乘车取乐的人。最严重的是，有些诋毁者甚至声称电车是苦力和妓女常使用的工具，这使得本地男学生不敢坐电车。电车公司只得采取免费试乘和低廉票价等营销手段吸引乘客。另外不幸的是，1906 年 3 月 3 日，一个 6 岁女孩成为新电车系统的首位受害者。司机辩解说，在事故当天他接到指示说要首次使用电车驱动电机的并联挡位，目的是将环绕老城一周的时间从 45 分钟缩减到 33 分钟。虽经公司协调，这名司机免于被绞刑处死，但仍需要接受竹棍鞭打 50 次的惩罚和 3

① 转引自（比）约翰·麦特勒等著，刘悦等译，《比利时—中国：昔日之路（1870—1930）》，社会科学文献出版社，2021 年，第 163 页。
② 天津市地方史志编修委员会总编辑室编，《二十世纪初的天津概况》，内部发行，1986 年，第 99—100 页。
③ 天津市档案馆等编，《天津商会档案汇编（1903—1911）》（下），天津人民出版社，1989 年，第 2261 页。

registered capital of 250,000 francs, making it the largest foreign investment among Tianjin's foreign businesses at the time. The company's building in Tianjin was situated on Sanma Road in the former Italian Concession (now at No.29 Jinbu Road, Hebei District). The Tianjin company comprised two departments: the Management Department and the Engineering Department. The Management Department included positions such as General Manager, Deputy Manager, Secretary, Chinese Affairs Director, and Accountant. The Engineering Department staff consisted of over 300 employees in the power plant, approximately 60 in the external line management department, over 1,200 in the tram department, over 150 in the repair department, around 60 in the lighting department, and over 40 in the electricity meter repair department, totaling more than 1,800 employees, making it an immensely large operation.

Tram operation requires direct current electricity, while lighting requires alternating current electricity. To supply electricity, sufficient water must be ensured. The CTET first purchased a piece of land in Jinjiayao Village behind Wanghailou Church（Notre Dame des Victoires）, which is adjacent to the Hai River in the front and the Jinzhong River in the back, to build a power plant. Later, the company purchased a building located at the east side of the East Pontoon Bridge on the Hai River (now in Hedong District) as its office. Additionally, they bought another piece of land to the north of Nankai Middle School at the southwest corner of the old city, where they constructed tram depots and repair workshops. All tram and lighting equipment, including everything from generators to screws, were imported from Brussels, Belgium, and shipped to Tianjin.

The tram track laying project began in 1905. On February 16, 1906, the first circular tram line, running along the road built on the ruins of the old city walls, commenced trial operation. Eighteen trams were put into service at low speed, carrying approximately 10,000 passengers on the first day. One month later, a grand opening ceremony for the tram service was held. On February 28, 1906, the *China Times* reported the event as follows: "In the Far East, no other tram construction project compares to that of Tianjin, and no city's tram operation has been as successful as here."①

However, people's attitudes towards unfamiliar novelties often encompass a variety of emotions such as curiosity, fear, and resistance. Even though trains had been in operation for several years, trams were still regarded as formidable threats, eliciting significant opposition. The main obstacle came

① Johan J. Mattelaer, et al. *A Belgian Passage to China (1870-1930)*, translated by Liu Yue, et al. Social Sciences Academic Press (China), 2021, p.163.

年刑期。事故发生后，电车司机士气大受打击。后来，通过重金拉拢警察并向受害者或其亲属提供慷慨赔偿的政策，司机们才得以在发生类似悲剧时免于受到刑罚。

在老城建成环城路线仅仅是迈出的第一步。为了让它成为整座城市名副其实的交通系统，也更加具有商业价值，电车线路需要形成网络，并延伸至繁荣的外国租界内。通过艰难的谈判，先是奥匈帝国、意大利和俄国三国同意有轨电车路线穿过各自租界，最终法国和日本也同意线路经过其租界。[①]为了连通海河东西两岸，天津地方政府与奥租界和意租界还共同出资修建了金汤桥（连接老城与奥租界和意租界），加上此前都统衙门出资修建的万国桥（连接法租界与俄租界内老龙头火车站，今解放桥）。这样，"白牌""红牌""黄牌""蓝牌"四条电车线路全部开通，并且几乎全部为双轨线路，一个覆盖天津市区大部分地域、运营总长13.5公里的城市公交系统终于建成。

市民很快感受到这种交通工具所带来的便捷。两年之后，第一批比利时修建者结束工作离开天津时，"有轨电车运营得已经如火如荼。这导致黄包车价格降低。中国人已经非常熟悉不同颜色的电车目的地标牌，也能够区分不同线路的信号灯。乘客们对各种票价已经了如指掌，票价因距离远近而有所不同。"[②]在那个时代的天津，电车已经成为社会中下层日常生活不可或缺的交通工具。据统计，在天津、上海和北京三大城市，市民每年平均乘坐电车频次分别为：52、38和17。[③]这直接体现了三个城市有轨电车经营发展的状况。据档案记载，到民国初年，比利时电车电灯公司就收回了之前的全部投资。从1916年至1927年的12年，公司共使用130辆电车，年

---

① 英国人认为这项电车计划过于宏大，不愿意参与此项计划。这种态度意味着有轨电车无法扩展到位于英租界以南、与法租界不相邻的德租界。

② 转引自（比）约翰·麦特勒等著，刘悦等译，《比利时—中国：昔日之路（1870—1930）》，社会科学文献出版社，2021年，第165页。

③ H. O. 昆，《上海、天津和北平的电车》，《远东评论》1937年2月号，第58页。转引自刘海岩，《空间与社会：近代天津城市的演变》，天津社会科学院出版社，2003年，第76页。

from the rickshaw pullers. At the height of their prosperity, there were over 8,800 registered rickshaw pullers in Tianjin, along with approximately 10,000 individuals involved in related occupations such as manufacturers and operators, accounting for about 3% of Tianjin's population at that time.[①] Seeing the livelihoods of so many practitioners at stake, from the inception of tram track laying, the Rickshaw Pullers Association secretly organized months-long vigorous resistance activities. The Tientsin Chamber of Commerce also petitioned the local government, requesting a ban on construction. However, many local officials in Tianjin were returnees from studying abroad, such as Tang Shaoyi, Cai Shaoji, Liang Dunyan, and Liang Ruhao, all of whom were American-educated individuals recruited and appointed by Yuan Shikai. They pointed out: "Trams are flourishing in crucial areas of various countries, with increasingly dense tracks and thriving commerce, which in turn requires a wider labor force. Tianjin, with its early openness and many merchants having overseas experiences, should have individuals with true insight."[②] With firm support from the local government, resistance from the rickshaw pullers gradually waned.

However, the difficulties did not end there. When the circular tram route initially began operating, it mostly attracted people taking it just for fun. Most seriously, some detractors even claimed that trams were tools commonly used by laborers and prostitutes, which made local male students afraid to ride the tram. The tram company had to resort to marketing tactics such as offering free trial rides and low fares to attract passengers. Unfortunately, on March 3, 1906, a 6-year-old girl became the first victim of the new tram system. The driver argued that on the day of the accident, he received instruction to use the parallel notches for the tram motor for the first time, with the aim of reducing the time to drive around the old city from 45 minutes to 33 minutes. Although the driver was spared from being executed by hanging through the company's coordination, he still had to endure 50 strokes of bamboo lashes and a three-year prison sentence. The morale of tram drivers was greatly affected after the accident. Later, policies were implemented to avoid punishment for drivers in similar tragedies by offering hefty bribes to the police and providing generous compensation to the victims or their families.

The completion of the circular tram route in the old city was just the first step. In order to make it a truly comprehensive transportation system for the

---

① Editorial Office of the Tianjin Chorography and History Compilation Committee (ed.). *Overview of Tianjin in the Early 20th Century*. Published internally in 1986, pp.99-100.

② Tianjin Archives (ed.). *Compilation of Archives of Tientsin Chamber of Commerce (1903-1911)* (Vol.2). Tianjin People's Publishing House, 1989, p.2261.

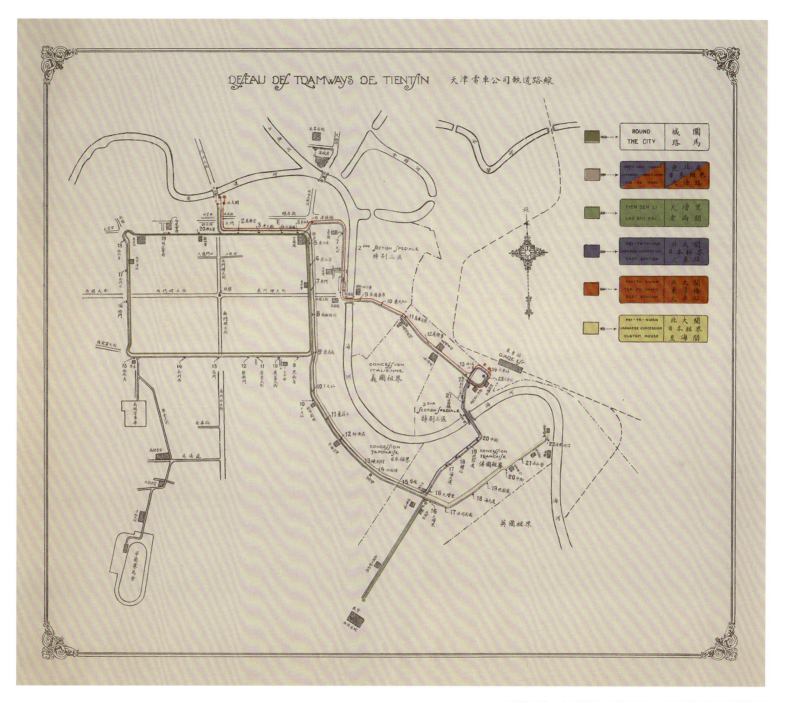

天津有轨电车路线图。图片来源：比利时根特大学档案馆
Tianjin tram route map. Source: Archives of Ghent University, Belgium

比商天津电车电灯公司员工检修电车供电
CTET employees repairing tram power supply lines

为有轨电车线路专门修建的金汤桥。摄于 1906 年
Jintang Bridge was built specifically for tram traffic. Taken in 1906

西开教堂前行驶的有轨电车
A tram running in front of the St. Joseph Cathedral

1906 年 2 月第一条环城线路通车试运营
In February 1906, the city loop tram line circle began the trial operations

图片来源：比利时根特大学档案馆
Source: Archives of Ghent University, Belgium

旭街（今和平路）上行驶的有轨电车，马路上空密如蛛网的有轨电车输电线
Tram running on Asahi Road (now Heping Road), with overhead tram power lines crisscrossing the street like a spider's web

有轨电车通过日租界，电车顶上放置了广告牌
Tram passing through the Japanese Concession, with an advertising sign placed on the top of the tram

运送乘客达 900 万人次。[1] 靠经营电车电灯两项，共获利 25729800 银元，截至 1942 年被日本军队强制接管，共获利至少达五六千万之巨。据说比利时一国的教育经费皆来源于此公司税项。

比商天津电车电灯公司在天津的"美好时代"一直持续到 20 世纪 20 年代。1927 年 1 月 17 日，比利时驻华公使洛恩宣布，比利时愿将天津比租界交还中国，同时比利时财团在天津电车业权也全部交还。1941 年太平洋战争爆发，日本人开始干涉公司行政。1943 年，日方辞退所有比利时员工，并将他们作为敌国侨民送进集中营，用武力强行接收了比商天津电车电灯股份有限公司的产业，后将其归入日本人经营的"天津交通公司"。1945 年，日本投降后，民国政府出面接收。1949 年 1 月 15 日，天津解放，比商天津电车电灯公司更名为"天津市公共汽车公司"。

有轨电车的出现是工业革命后世界城市发展历程中的一个重要里程碑。从城市发展角度来说，电车大大加快了城市的空间扩展和功能分区，将人们的居住区、工作区与商业区区分开来，也促进了天津商业中心由老城厢到和平路一带的转移。从人与社会的现代化角度来说，有轨电车以其便捷和票价低廉，成为最平民化的交通工具。它扩大了人们的活动范围，缩短了路程时间，降低了交通成本，提高了人们的社交欲望和社交频次，提供给人们更多的行动自由。无论是穷苦工人，还是普通学生，或者是晚间去租界享受夜生活的都市男女，他们都是电车的乘客，这实现了某种程度上的平等。在城市的夜晚，"电车载着疲惫的工人从东方（指租界）驶来，东去的电车挤满了'洋气'的城市男女，向灯光之塔下的夜中的白日里（也指租界）去寻乐"[2]。

海河与水上交通运输

天津是一个因水而生的城市，海河水系沟通了河运与海运，在

---

① （比）约翰·麦特勒等著，刘悦等译，《比利时—中国：昔日之路（1870—1930）》，社会科学文献出版社，2021 年，第 171 页。

② 莎蒂，《天津交响乐》，《大公报》1933 年 4 月 22 日。

entire city and enhance its commercial value, tram lines needed to form a network and extend into the thriving foreign concessions. Through difficult negotiations, initially the Austro-Hungarian Empire, Italy, and Russia agreed to allow tram lines to pass through their respective concessions, and eventually France and Japan also agreed to have the lines run through their concessions.[1] To connect both banks of the Hai River, the Tianjin local government, along with the Austrian and Italian concessions, jointly financed the construction of Jintang Bridge (connecting the old city with the Austrian and Italian concessions). This was in addition to the earlier construction of the International Bridge (connecting the French concession with the Russian concession at the Old Dragon Head Station, now Jiefang Bridge), funded by the Provisional Government. As a result, all four tram routes—white, red, yellow, and blue—were opened, and almost all were double-track lines. With a total operational length of 13.5 kilometers, covering most of the Tianjin urban area, the urban public transportation system was finally completed.

Citizens quickly felt the convenience brought by this mode of transportation. Two years later, when the first group of Belgian builders finished their work and left Tianjin, "tram operations were already thriving. This led to a decrease in rickshaw prices. Chinese people had become very familiar with tram destination signs of different colors and could distinguish between signals of different routes. Passengers were well aware of various fare rates, which varied according to distance."[2] In that era, trams had become an indispensable means of transportation for daily life for the lower and middle classes in Tianjin. According to statistics, the average annual tram usage per capita in the three major cities of Tianjin, Shanghai, and Beijing was 52, 38, and 17 times, respectively.[3] This directly reflected the state of tram operation development in these cities. According to records, by the early years of the Republic of China, the CTET had recovered all of its previous investments. Over the 12-year period from 1916 to 1927, the company operated a total of 130 trams, transporting 9 million passengers annually.[4] Through the operation of trams and

---

① The British believed that the tram project was too ambitious and were unwilling to participate in it. This attitude meant that the tram system could not be extended to the German Concession, which was located south of the British Concession and not adjacent to the French Concession.

② Johan J. Mattelaer, et al. *A Belgian Passage to China (1870-1930)*, translated by Liu Yue, et al. Social Sciences Academic Press (China), 2021, p.165.

③ H. O. Kun. Trams in Shanghai, Tianjin, and Beiping. *Far Eastern Review*, February 1937, p.58. Quoted in Liu Haiyan. *Space and Society: The Evolution of Modern Tianjin City*. Tianjin Academy of Social Sciences Press, 2003, p.76.

④ Johan J. Mattelaer, et al. *A Belgian Passage to China (1870-1930)*, translated by Liu Yue, et al. Social Sciences Academic Press (China), 2021, p.171.

古代它连接了中国南北，在近代它连通了中国与世界。因河而兴的天津，地近首都、辐射三北（东北、华北和西北），天然具备宜于贸易发展的优越区位和便利条件。在近代开放为通商口岸后，天津经济发展迅速，成为北方最大的经济中心和国际化港口城市、亚洲最大的原材料出口中心之一。

天津贸易的生命线

海河是中国华北地区最大的河流，但在中国的大江大河中，海河却是最短的。海河干流全长 73 千米，从南北运河与海河相接的三岔河口算起，到大沽口入海，实际直线距离只有不到 50 千米，因此它是沟通天津河海运输的大动脉。铁路修建以后，陆海衔接，它就更加成为天津贸易的生命线。

天津在开埠后很快成为洋货进口大户，按其需求量足可以与原产国直接通商。但是这项在外国商人看来"前途远大"的计划竟至失败，就是因为远航的船舶必须足够大，载货量才更高、航行稳妥且利润更丰，而这样的大船却无法逾越大沽口的拦沙坝和海河的淤泥浅滩。所以，天津的对外贸易仍然不得不以上海作为中转站，然后再以小吨位的驳船运往天津租界码头。以上航运方面的种种不利因素制约了天津对外贸易的发展。情况在 19 世纪末最后几年发展到极其恶劣的程度，1898 年全年没有一艘轮船可以抵达租界河坝，1899 年仅有两艘轮船抵达租界。①

为了发展各国与天津的通商贸易，海河两岸的各国租界当局，竞相整理河道、加宽河面、整修堤岸、填平沼泽、构筑道路和建设仓库，以利于航运发展。八国联军占领天津后，为防止再次发生类似义和团运动事件，使华北一旦有事，大型兵船能停泊在天津租界码头迅速加以援助，联军统帅瓦德西决定将疏浚治理海河的工程纳入都统衙门的管辖范围之内。1901 年海河工程局委员会成立，并开始进行裁弯取直和清理河道的工程。经过整治，由于河道曲折所

---

① 《1892—1901 年津海关十年报告》（一），天津海关译编委员会编译，《津海关史要览》，中国海关出版社，2004 年，第 44 页。

lighting, the company made a profit of 25,729,800 silver dollars, until it was forcibly taken over by the Japanese military in 1942, with profits reaching at least fifty to sixty million. It is said that Belgium's education funds came from taxes generated by this company.

The golden era of the CTET in Tianjin persisted until the 1920s. On January 17, 1927, the Belgian Minister to China, Léon le Maire de Warzee d'Hermalle, announced that Belgium was willing to return the Tianjin Concession to China, and at the same time, all rights of the Belgian consortium in the Tianjin tram business were also relinquished. With the outbreak of the Pacific War in 1941, the Japanese began to interfere in the company's administration. In 1943, the Japanese dismissed all Belgian employees and sent them to concentration camps as citizens of an enemy country, forcibly taking over the assets of the CTET through military action and incorporating them into the "Tianjin Transportation Company" operated by the Japanese. After Japan's surrender in 1945, the Republic of China government took over. On January 15, 1949, Tianjin was liberated, and the CTET was renamed "Tianjin Municipal Bus Company."

The advent of tramways marks a significant milestone in the developmental trajectory of world cities after the Industrial Revolution. From the perspective of urban development, trams greatly accelerated urban spatial expansion and functional zoning, separating residential, work, and commercial areas. They also facilitated the shift of Tianjin's commercial center from the old city to the area around Heping Road. From the standpoint of modernization for individuals and society, trams, with their convenience and low fares, became the most accessible mode of transportation. They expanded people's range of activities, reduced travel time, lowered transportation costs, increased people's desire and frequency of social interaction, and provided them with greater freedom of movement. Whether poor workers, ordinary students, or urban men and women enjoying nightlife in the concessions, they were all tram passengers, achieving a degree of equality to some extent. In the city's evenings, "trams carry weary workers from the east (referring to the concessions), while those heading east are packed with 'stylish' urban men and women, heading to seek pleasure under the tower of light in the night that feels like daytime (also referring to the concessions)."①

The Hai River and Waterborne Transportation

Tianjin is a city born of water, with the Hai River system connecting river

---

① Sadie. Tianjin Symphony. *Ta Kung Pao*, April 22,1933.

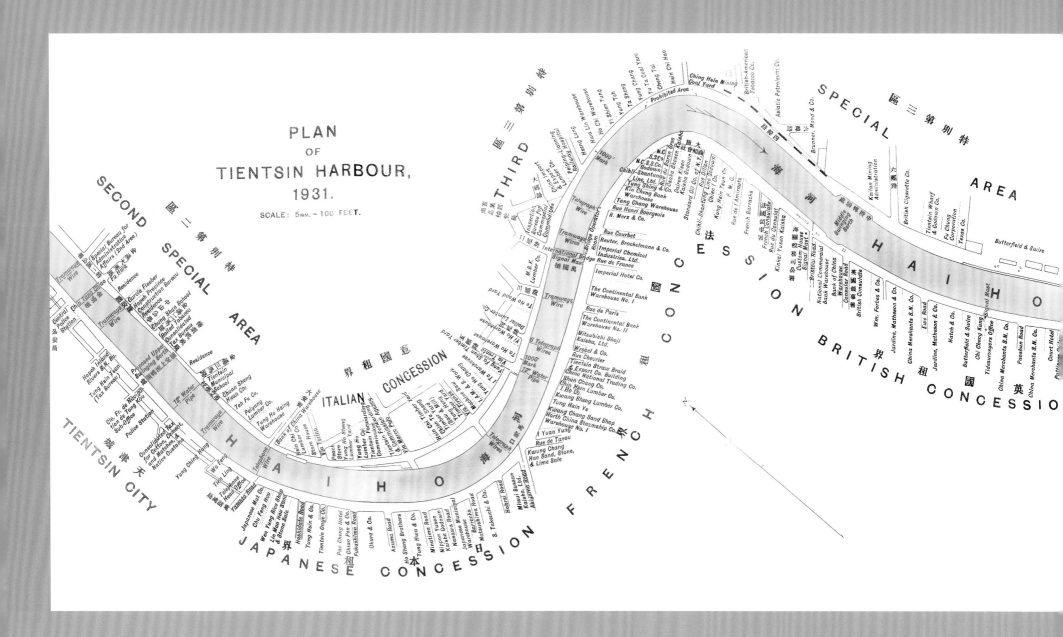

PLAN
OF
TIENTSIN HARBOUR,
1931.

SCALE: 5ᴍᴍ. = 100 FEET.

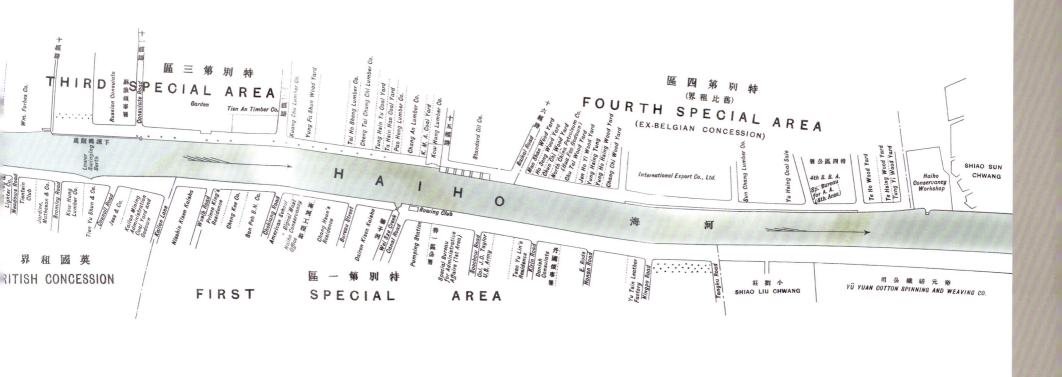

1931 年各租界码头位置示意图。图片来源：法国外交部档案馆
Dock location plan in each concession in 1931. Source: Archives of the French Ministry of Foreign Affairs

怡和洋行码头
Wharf of Jardine, Matheson & Co.

造成的淤沙和航道拥堵问题得到极大改善，进入海河的海轮增加。1902 年秋海轮经七八小时的航程即可畅行至紫竹林码头，1903 年经海河至紫竹林码头的商船计有 333 艘，1904 年有 374 艘。海河航道普遍加宽至 80 米以上，最宽处至 100 米。河道加宽，为大船转头创造了条件。1905 年，到达租界码头最长的轮船——宜昌号，长约 84 米，吃水约 2.93 米。海河整治工程至此获得成功，天津保持住了中国北方最重要港口的地位。

　　码头和仓储设施随着天津对外贸易的发展而日益增多和完善。在 1922 年前已有招商局码头、开滦矿务局码头、日本游船会社码头、美最时洋行码头、亨宝洋行码头、大阪商船会社码头、怡和码头等重要码头。在各码头中，英租界码头的设施和设计是最为完善的。从 1860 年设立英租界后，英国工部局就不断地修筑和改建码头。英租界码头在今天的营口道至开封道段。码头捐办公处就设在怡和码头，此外，还有多处机械房、消防水箱、公共厕所及岸壁起重器，实现了完整的码头功能。当时的英租界码头沿岸，聚集了中英两国

and maritime transportation. In ancient times, it linked the north and south of China, while in modern times, it connected China with the world. Flourishing due to its rivers, Tianjin, located near the capital and radiating towards the three northern regions (northeast, north, and northwest), naturally possesses superior geographical advantages and convenient conditions for trade development. After being opened as a trading port in modern times, Tianjin experienced rapid economic development, becoming the largest economic center in the northern region and one of the largest international port cities, as well as one of Asia's largest centers for exporting raw materials.

The Lifeline of Tianjin's Trade

The Hai River is the largest river in North China, but among China's major rivers, it is the shortest. The main stream of the Hai River is 73 kilometers long. Measured from the confluence of the Grand Canal and the Hai River at Sancha estuary to its mouth at Taku where it flows into the sea, the actual straight-line distance is less than 50 kilometers. Therefore, it serves as the main artery for transportation between the rivers and the sea in Tianjin. After the construction of railways, the connection between land and sea made it even more crucial as the lifeline of Tianjin's trade.

Tianjin quickly became a major importer of foreign goods after its opening, with enough demand to directly trade with the countries of origin. However, this seemingly promising plan failed because ships needed to be large enough for long voyages to carry more cargo, ensure stable navigation, and increase profits. Unfortunately, such large ships couldn't pass through the sandbars at Taku and the silted shallows of the Hai River. Consequently, Tianjin's foreign trade still had to rely on Shanghai as a transit hub before being transported to Tianjin's concessions by smaller barges. Various unfavorable factors in shipping constrained the development of Tianjin's foreign trade. By the late 19th century, the situation had worsened significantly, with not a single ship reaching the concessions' wharf in 1898, and only two ships arriving in 1899.[①]

To promote each countries' trade with Tianjin, the authorities of various concessions along the Hai River raced to dredge the river, widen its channel, repair its banks, fill in swamps, construct roads, and build warehouses to facilitate shipping. After the occupation of Tianjin by the Eight-Nation Alliance, in

---

① *The Ten-year Report of Tianjin Customs from 1892 to 1901*. Quoted in *Overview of the History of Tianjin Customs*, translated and edited by Tianjin Customs Translation and Editing Committee. China Customs Press, 2004, p.44.

最有实力的工商企业和机关，从北至南顺序大致为汇丰银行、英国领事馆、仁记洋行、怡和北栈、怡和洋行、招商北栈、聚立洋行、太古洋行、海关署、招商南栈、永固工程公司、直隶东南教区献县教会（产权）、大阪商船、大沽驳船公司、英国俱乐部、怡和南栈等。而一战前也有许多德商洋行在英国河坝建有货栈码头，如礼和、世昌、瑞记、德华银行等，这些产业战后均被英国大洋行和招商局接收并翻建。如怡和北栈（今台儿庄路"6号院"建筑）原址在一战前是世昌洋行的货栈，其建筑在怡和时期进行了大规模的拆除翻盖，最终形成了著名的"怡和码头"。

充满异国风情的还是危险的海上旅行？

天津的海运分为沿海航线和远洋航线。沿海航线在元代就已发展成熟，主要在运河淤塞时转运漕粮。天津开埠以后，新的沿海航线和远洋航线很快开辟出来，经营海外运输的轮船公司也不断增加。

在西伯利亚铁路修建以前，中国与欧美日国家的往来几乎全部通过海路，船舶是进行国际旅行的唯一交通工具。最初，马戛尔尼使团从英国到中国在海上航行了9个月；之后绕过好望角的航线使航程缩短到4个月；1869年苏伊士运河的通航使得欧洲至中国的航程缩短至两三个月。[①] 蒸汽机船的使用进一步使19世纪70年代欧洲各种商船兵船能够"不畏风浪四十余日抵华"。[②] 20世纪初，前往中国的远洋客运航线主要由法国的法兰西火轮船公司（Messageries Maritimes）、英国的铁行渣华船运公司（P&O）以及德国的北德意志劳埃德船运公司（Norddeutscher Lloyd）三家公司经营，当然还有一些其他船运公司。邮轮从各自国家的港口出发，进入地中海，经苏伊士运河、红海、锡兰（今斯里兰卡）、印度支那（今越南一带）

---

① （美）费正清等编，中国社会科学院历史研究所编译室译，《剑桥中国晚清史.1800—1911》上卷，中国社会科学出版社，1985年，第252页。

② 顾廷龙、戴逸主编，《李鸿章全集》（信函四），安徽教育出版社，2008年，第489页。

order to prevent the recurrence of events similar to the Boxer Rebellion and to ensure quick assistance in case of any trouble in North China, the commander-in-chief of the Alliance, General Alfred von Waldersee, decided to incorporate the dredging and management of the Hai River into the jurisdiction of the Provisional Government. In 1901, the Hai-Ho Conservancy Commission was established, and work began on straightening and clearing the river channel. Through these efforts, the problem of silt accumulation and congested waterways caused by the river's twists and turns was greatly improved, leading to an increase in the number of ships entering the Hai River. By the autumn of 1902, steamers could travel smoothly to the Zizhulin Wharf after seven to eight hours of sailing. In 1903, there were 333 merchant ships that traveled from the Hai River to the Zizhulin Wharf, and in 1904, there were 374. The Hai River channel was generally widened to over 80 meters, with the widest part reaching 100 meters. The wider river channel created conditions for large ships to turn around. In 1905, the longest ship to reach the concessions' wharf was the Yichang, which was about 84 meters long and had a draught of about 2.93 meters. With the success of the Hai River dredging project, Tianjin maintained its position as the most important port in northern China.

The number and quality of docks and storage facilities increased and improved as Tianjin's foreign trade developed. Prior to 1922, important docks included those of the China Merchants Steamship Company, Kailan Mining Administration, Nippon Yusen Kaisha, Melchers & Co., Hamburg-Amerika Linie, Osaka Shosen Kaisha, and Jardine, Matheson & Co.. Among these docks, the facilities and designs of the British Concession's dock were the most advanced. Since the establishment of the British Concession in 1860, the British Municipal Council had continuously constructed and renovated docks. The British Concession's dock was located in the present-day section from Yingkou Road to Kaifeng Road. The Dock and Office were located at the Jardine, Matheson & Co. Wharf, supplemented by numerous machinery rooms, fire water tanks, public toilets, and quayside cranes, fully realizing the functions of the dock. Along the banks of the British Concession's dock at that time, there were gatherings of the most powerful industrial and commercial enterprises and agencies from both China and Britain. Roughly from north to south, they included the Hongkong and Shanghai Banking Corporation, British Consulate, William Forbes & Co., North Warehouse of Jardine, Matheson & Co., Jardine, Matheson & Co., North Warehouse of China Merchants Steamship Company, Hatch, Carter & Co., Butterfield & Swire, Customs Office, South Warehouse of China Merchants Steamship Company, Cook & Anderson, Xian County Church in the Southeast Diocese of Zhili (ownership), Osaka Shosen Kaisha, Taku Tug Boat Co., British Club, and South Warehouse

码头上的吊车
Crane on the wharf

日租界码头
Wharf in the Japanese Concession

海河上大船掉头
A large ship was turning around on the Hai River

海河上大船掉头处（今在营口道海河边）。随着船舶吨位日渐增大，为了更好地让大船转头，在英国河沿的上下游两端各建有一处宽敞锚位用于船舶转头，上游宽敞锚位紧邻英法交界处（今营口道至大同道），下游设在英德交界处（今大光明桥）。刘悦摄于 2024 年

The turning area for large ships on the Hai River (now located along the Hai River near Yingkou Road). As the tonnage of ships gradually increased, spacious anchorages were built at both the upstream and downstream ends along the British Bund to better allow large ships to turn. The upstream anchorage was located near the boundary between the British and French concessions (now from Yingkou Road to Datong Road), while the downstream anchorage was situated at the boundary between the British and German concessions (now near Daguangming Bridge). Taken by Liu Yue in 2024

20 世纪 40 年代海河工程局报告中所附海河淤塞状况照片。图片来源：德国"东亚之友"协会图书馆

A photo attached to the report from the Hai-Ho Conservancy Commission in the 1940s, showing the sedimentation conditions of the Hai River. Source: StuDeo library

海河夜景。刘悦摄于 2024 年
Nightview of the Hai River. Taken by Liu Yue in 2024

到达中国，路程分别用时 33、41 和 44 天。^① 甲午战争后，1896 年日本邮船公司、大阪商船株式会社、日本汽船公司等日本公司在中国相继开辟了多条远洋航线。在中国成立的怡和、太古两家英资公司也开辟了一些远洋航线。中国自己的轮船招商局则开辟了往返于日本的国际客运航线。20 世纪初期，随着天津同欧美各地的直接航线逐渐增加，来往于天津的外国旅客也逐年增多：1890 年，乘坐轮船来津的外国旅客约有 400 多人，离津的则有 300 多人；1899 年，来津外国旅客 1300 人，离津 1100 人。^②

1912 年以后，经营天津与沿海各商埠间的航运公司和航线均明显增加。到日本占领天津以前，天津经营海运的有 21 家轮船公司：规模最大的是英商太古、怡和轮船公司以及中国自己的轮船招商局；其次是中国民营的轮船公司，如北方航业公司、政记轮船分公司、天津航业公司等 12 家；第三类是日商轮船会社，包括大阪、大连、日清等 6 家。航线所达，几乎遍及中国沿海各口岸。最繁忙的航线是天津至上海线和天津至香港及广东线，每周两班；其余航线则无一定班期。

刚开埠时，天津与外国的运输全部以上海为中转站。第一次世界大战中，列强自顾厮杀，无暇东顾，中国民族资本主义获得难得的发展黄金期，甚至本地的洋行生意也未受大的影响。自 1915 年以后，天津逐渐由转口贸易转向直接贸易，经由天津的远洋航线不断增多，进出口船只总数及吨数也不断增长。从 1911 年到 1937 年，20 世纪 10 年代年平均到港船舶 1000 艘，其中外轮占比 80% 以上；20 世纪 20 年代年平均到港 1500 艘，外轮占比 70% 左右；1930—1937 年，年平均到港 2000 艘，而因国际局势动荡，外轮到港数极不稳定。^③

海上航行，特别是远洋航行，虽能体验到众多异域风情，仍然

---

① （比）约翰·麦特勒等著，刘悦等译，《比利时—中国：昔日之路（1870—1930）》，社会科学文献出版社，2021 年，第 182 页。

② 吴弘明编译，《津海关贸易年报（1865~1946）》，天津社会科学院出版社，2006 年，第 161、200 页。

③ 根据天津市地方史志编修委员会编著《天津通志·港口志》第 303 页数据计算而得。

---

of Jardine, Matheson & Co., among others. Before World War I, many German foreign firms also had warehouses and docks built on British embankments, such as Carlowitz & Co., Meyer & Co., Eduard, Arnhold, Karberg & Co., and Deutsch-Asiatische Bank. After the war, these industries were all taken over and rebuilt by British foreign firms and China Merchants Steamship Company. For example, the original site of the North Warehouse of Jardine, Matheson & Co. (now the "No.6 Courtyard" on Taierzhuang Road) was a warehouse of Eduard Meyer & Co., before World War I. The building was extensively demolished and rebuilt during the Jardine, Matheson & Co. period, ultimately forming the famous "Jardine, Matheson & Co. Wharf."

Is Maritime Travel Full of Exotic Charm or Danger?

Tianjin's maritime routes are divided into coastal routes and oceanic routes. Coastal routes had matured as early as the Yuan Dynasty, mainly used for transporting grain when the Grand Canal was silted up. After the opening of Tianjin port, new coastal and oceanic routes were quickly established, and the number of shipping companies engaged in overseas transportation continued to increase.

Before the construction of the Trans-Siberian Railway, almost all exchanges between China and European, American, and Japanese countries were carried out by sea, with ships being the only means of international travel. Initially, the journey from Britain to China by sea took nine months for the Lord Macartney Mission. Later, the route bypassing the Cape of Good Hope shortened the journey to four months. The opening of the Suez Canal in 1869^① further reduced the journey from Europe to China to two or three months.^① The use of steamships further enabled various commercial ships and warships from Europe to "arrive in China after more than forty days against the wind and waves" in the 1870s.^② In the early 20th century, oceanic passenger routes to China were mainly operated by three companies: the French Messageries Maritimes, the British P&O, and the German Norddeutscher Lloyd. Of course, there were also other shipping companies. The cruise ships departed from their respective countries' ports, entered the Mediterranean, passed through the Suez Canal, the Red Sea, Ceylon (now Sri Lanka), French Indochina (now Vietnam area), and arrived in China, with journey times of 33, 41, and 44 days,

---

① John King Fairbank, et al (eds.). *The Cambridge History of China, Late Ch'ing, 1800-1911* (Vol.1), translated by Institute of Ancient History, Chinese Academy of Social Sciences. China Social Sciences Press, 1985, p.252.

② Gu Tinglong, Dai Yi (eds.). *The Collected Works of Li Hongzhang* (Letters 4). Anhui Education Press, 2008, p.489.

是一场真正的冒险。船上生活大多数时候是单调乏味的，有计划在中国长期居住的旅客会在船上学习语言、了解目的地国家的风土民俗，以提前适应自己未来要扮演的角色。在漫长的旅途中，他们时常经历危险，有时是遇上恶劣的天气变化和大洋里的惊涛骇浪，有时是中途停靠上岸时遭遇的意外，还有战争时期的种种危险。20世纪初比利时铁路总局派往天津的工程师弗朗索瓦·内恩斯（Francois Nuyens），于1905年6月24日离开根特，坐火车到法国马赛港，由此出发，经苏伊士运河，过红海，于7月24日抵达香港，一路行来基本上顺风顺水，偶尔上岸会遇到当地人制造的小麻烦。然而从香港到天津的近海航行，却遭遇了很多不测：先是在台风的漩涡中船只剧烈颠簸摇晃，人随之从床头被晃到床尾，并被从打破的酒瓶里挥发出的酒精熏得头晕眼花；然后遭遇了日俄战争中从北方漂来的水雷，幸运的是水雷被船上的机枪击沉且没有爆炸，否则后果不堪设想。

对于经历了海上长达一个多月令人身心疲惫的旅行的来津旅客来说，船舶抵达塘沽港，并不意味着行程的终止。在塘沽港被建成深水港之前，如果是吨位较大的海轮或者遇到海河淤塞加剧的情况，乘客和货物都必须在那里下船，转乘汽艇或运货的驳船。汽艇在潮水很低时，很容易搁浅在大沽口到塘沽市区一段的浅滩上，有时不得不等上几个小时后才能趁潮水上涨而重获自由。然后，旅客们将抵达塘沽火车站，再从那里乘火车最终抵达天津。

提到火车，陆上交通的发展使侨民远行有了更为快速、经济的交通工具。当1903年西伯利亚铁路的一期工程完成后，由欧洲至天津的行程大大缩短。旅客和邮件，由欧洲最远端的伦敦到天津用时22天，柏林及圣彼得堡到津需18天，后来伦敦至天津的邮件又缩短至仅有17日。[1]铁路成为欧洲人往来中国旅行的一个交通选项。比利时电车电灯公司工程师内恩斯在完成天津的全部工作后，于1907年携妻带子搭乘火车经由中东铁路转西伯利亚铁路回到欧洲，这一路除了带着大小行李包换乘火车略显不便之外，相比乘船少了许多

---

① 吴弘明编译，《津海关贸易年报（1865~1946）》，天津社会科学院出版社，2006年，第231、259页。

respectively.[1] After the First Sino-Japanese War, in 1896, Japanese companies such as Nippon Yusen Kaisha, Osaka Shosen Kaisha, and Nippon Steamship Company successively opened multiple oceanic routes in China. The two British companies, Jardine, Matheson & Co. and Butterfield and Swire, established in China, also opened some oceanic routes. China's own shipping company, China Merchants Steamship Company, opened international passenger routes to and from Japan. In the early 20th century, as direct routes between Tianjin and various European and American destinations gradually increased, the number of foreign passengers traveling to and from Tianjin also increased year by year: in 1890, there were about 400 foreign passengers arriving in Tianjin by ship, and over 300 departing. In 1899, there were 1,300 foreign passengers arriving in Tianjin and 1,100 departing.[2]

After 1912, the number of shipping companies and routes operating between Tianjin and various coastal ports increased significantly. Before the Japanese occupation of Tianjin, there were 21 shipping companies operating maritime transport in Tianjin: the largest were the British-owned Butterfield & Swire and Jardine, Matheson & Co., as well as China's own Merchants Steamship Company; followed by privately owned Chinese shipping companies, such as the Northern Steamship Company, the Zhengji Steamship Company, and the Tianjin Steamship Company, among 12 others; and the third category consisted of Japanese Shipping Companies, including Osaka Shosen Kaisha, Dairen Kisen Kabushiki Kaisha, and Nisshin Kisen Kaisha. These routes reached almost all coastal ports in China. The busiest routes were the Tianjin to Shanghai route and the Tianjin to Hong Kong and Guangdong route, with two trips per week, while other routes had no fixed schedules.

When the port was first opened, all transportation between Tianjin and foreign countries went through Shanghai. During the First World War, the great powers were preoccupied with their own conflicts and had no time to spare for China. This allowed for a rare period of development for Chinese national capitalism, and even local foreign businesses were not greatly affected. After 1915, Tianjin gradually shifted from transit trade to direct trade, with an increasing number of ocean-going routes passing through Tianjin, and both the total number and tonnage of import and export ships continued to grow. From 1911 to 1937, the annual average number of ships arriving at the port in the 1910s was 1,000, with foreign ships accounting for over 80%; in the 1920s,

---

① Johan J. Mattelaer, et al. *A Belgian Passage to China (1870-1930)*, translated by Liu Yue, et al. Social Sciences Academic Press (China), 2021, p.182.

② *Tianjin Customs Annual Report of Trade (1865~1946)*, translated and edited by Wu Hongming. Tianjin Academy of Social Sciences Press, 2006, p.161,200.

轮船抵达塘沽
The ship arrived at Tanggu port

塘沽火车站
Tanggu Railway Station

the annual average was 1,500 ships, with foreign ships accounting for around 70%; from 1930 to 1937, the annual average was 2,000 ships, but due to the turbulent international situation, the number of foreign ships arriving at the port was extremely unstable.[①]

Maritime travel, especially ocean travel, despite experiencing numerous exotic cultures, remains a true adventure. Life on board is often monotonous, and passengers planning to live in China for an extended period will use the time onboard to learn the language and understand the customs of the destination country in advance, in order to adapt to their future role. During the long journey, they often face dangers, sometimes encountering adverse weather changes and rough seas in the ocean, sometimes encountering accidents when stopping ashore, and there are various dangers during wartime. In early 20th century, a Belgian engineer named François Nuyens, sent by the Belgian Railway Administration to Tianjin, left Ghent on June 24, 1905, took a train to the port of Marseilles in France, and set off from there, passing through the Suez Canal, the Red Sea, and arriving in Hong Kong on July 24. The journey was mostly smooth, occasionally encountering minor troubles caused by the locals when landing. However, the near-sea voyage from Hong Kong to Tianjin encountered many unexpected events: first, the ship violently rocked in the vortex of a typhoon, causing people to be thrown from the head to the foot of the bed, and dizzy from the alcohol vapor emitted from the broken bottles; then encountered mines drifted from the north during the Russo-Japanese War. Fortunately, the mines were sunk by the machine gun on the ship and did not explode, otherwise the consequences would be unimaginable.

For travelers who have endured a sea journey of over a month, arriving at Tanggu Port does not mean the end of their journey. Before Tanggu Port was developed into a deep-water port, if it was a large-tonnage ocean liner or if the sedimentation in the Hai River worsened, passengers and cargo had to disembark there and transfer to motorboats or freight barges. Motorboats were prone to grounding on the shallows between Taku and Tanggu urban area when the tide was low, sometimes having to wait for hours until the tide rose again to regain freedom. Then, the passengers would arrive at Tanggu Railway Station, from where they would take a train ride to finally reach Tianjin.

Speaking of trains, the development of land transportation provided expatriates with faster and more economical means of travel. When the first phase of the Trans-Siberian Railway was completed in 1903, the journey from

---

① Calculated based on data from the page 303 of *Tianjin Chorography of Port*, compiled by the Tianjin Chorography Compilation Committee.

危险，也节省了很多时间。内恩斯一家的旅程，见证了当时人们旅行方式的不断变化。正是因为有了轮船和铁路等交通工具的不断改进、升级，资本主义才能畅行无阻地进行遍及全球的经济扩张和财富掠夺。

铁路与煤矿

铁路对世界近代史的发展影响巨大。以前只有沿海各地的民众领教过资本主义的"船坚炮利"，而火车这个钢铁巨兽呼啸着将一场技术革命和一个崭新时代迅猛地带到中国人面前，也第一次将中国内陆东西南北与沿海口岸联结在一起，将其混合为一个统一的中国市场，进而与世界资本主义体系联系起来。

中国第一条铁路与开平煤矿

第二次鸦片战争后签订的《天津条约》使英美法俄获得在中国内陆长江流域的通商贸易权，欧美资本主义得以更加靠近原材料产地和商品行销地。预期中贸易量的增长，使列强将铁路引入中国的欲望陡然升腾起来。铁路不仅是近代最重要的交通运输方式，是资本最重要的投资对象，而且其本身就是大宗商品，包括了机车车辆和铁轨等系列工业品①。所以，条约签订后的 1863 年，英国铁路工程师斯蒂芬森（Sir R. M. Stephenson）向中国提出了第一个铁路建设方案，劝清政府修建铁路。他还擅自设计了几条干线：以长江上的重镇汉口为中心，从汉口往西经川、滇到缅甸，从汉口往东到上海，从汉口往南到广州南部；以长江口为另一起点，从镇江往北到天津、北京，从上海到宁波；在南方，从福州到内地。②而在此次条约中获得驻节北京权利的各国"公使们、领事们以及一切有机会跟任何中

---

① 例如，唐胥铁路的塘沽与天津段，其铁轨购自比利时、枕木来自日本、大部分机车则来自英国和美国。

② 中国社会科学院近代史研究所翻译室，《近代来华外国人名辞典》，中国社会科学出版社，1981 年，第 457 页。

Europe to Tianjin was greatly shortened. Passengers and mail from the farthest end of Europe, London, to Tianjin took 22 days, while from Berlin and St. Petersburg to Tianjin, it took 18 days. Later, the mail from London to Tianjin was further reduced to only 17 days.[1] The railway became an option for Europeans traveling to China. After completing all the work in Tianjin, CTET engineer Nuyens, together with his wife and child, took a train via the China Eastern Railway to the Trans-Siberian Railway and returned to Europe in 1907. Apart from the slight inconvenience of carrying luggage and transferring trains along the way, their journey by train was much safer and saved a lot of time compared to traveling by ship. The journey of Nuyens' family witnessed the continuous changes in people's travel methods at that time. It was precisely because of the continuous improvement and upgrading of transportation tools such as ships and railways that capitalism was able to conduct global economic expansion and wealth plundering smoothly and unimpededly.

Railways and Coal Mines

The impact of railways on the development of modern world history is immense. Previously, only people along the coast had experienced the "gunboat diplomacy" of capitalism, but the iron behemoth of the train roared in, swiftly bringing a technological revolution and a new era to the Chinese people. It also, for the first time, connected the eastern, western, southern, and northern inland regions of China to the coastal ports, amalgamating them into a unified Chinese market and subsequently linking it to the world capitalist system.

China's First Railway and the Kaiping Coal Mine

The *Treaties of Tianjin* signed after the Second Opium War granted the British, American, French, and Russian the right to trade in the inland Yangtze River basin of China, allowing European and American capitalism to move closer to raw material sources and markets for goods. Anticipating an increase in trade volume, the desire of the Great Powers to introduce railways into China suddenly surged. Railway was not only the most important mode of modern transportation but also a crucial investment target for capital. Moreover, they were commodities themselves, including locomotives, rolling stock,

---

① *Tianjin Customs Annual Report of Trade (1865~1946)*, translated and edited by Wu Hongming. Tianjin Academy of Social Sciences Press, 2006, p.231, 259.

国官员说上话的外国人，总是利用各种时机赞颂铁路在军事上和经济上的优越性"①。

　　然而这一切努力的效果却适得其反，修筑铁路这项计划披上了令人憎恶的帝国主义侵略色彩，由此引发了中国人对它采取消极抵抗的普遍情绪。甚至于清政府在1877年将一年前怡和洋行在上海与吴淞之间修筑的轻便铁路以近三十万两的代价收回、加以拆毁。清政府之所以不愿兴建铁路，并不仅仅是出于守旧落后的观念，还出于对列强侵略野心的警惕。一些中国官员认识到，铁路的修建与列强入侵和对中国利权的掠夺紧密相连，因此即使是赞同修建铁路的洋务派官员也不得不谨慎从事。1874年李鸿章曾经向掌握实权的开明派恭亲王奕䜣力陈铁路之利。然而，慑于保守派的压力，奕䜣告诉李鸿章，即便"两宫亦不能定此大计"②。

　　尽管如此，螳臂不足以挡车，铁路已成为世界潮流。铁路是资本主义工业的最主要的部门即煤炭和钢铁工业的总结，是世界贸易发展与资产阶级文明的总结和最显著的指标。③中国想要发展近代工业、赶上世界文明发展的脚步，就必须引入铁路、开发煤铁矿，因此中国铁路的创办是作为煤矿生产的重要配套设施而被提出的。1876年在创办开平煤矿时，李鸿章同意唐廷枢为降低煤炭的运输成本秘密修筑一条运煤铁路。但迫于当时情势，只能铺设一条从唐山到胥各庄的一条长11公里的轨道，并且暂时只能用骡马拉车在轨道上运煤。不过唐廷枢深谋远虑地令英国工程师金达（Claude William Kinder）将铁轨设计为国际标准轨幅，而且将轨道通过的桥梁建造得特别坚固，以便火车将来可以在上面行驶。金达还奉命秘密研制了一个火车头，命名为"中国火箭号"，并且这辆机车很快被投入到矿山的日常铁路运输中。1882年"中国火箭号"载着一批官员以每小时13.5千米的速度走完了全程，证实机车确比骡马劲头更大、速

①　（英）雷穆森著，许逸凡等译，《天津租界史（插图本）》，天津人民出版社，2009年，第61页。

②　顾廷龙、戴逸主编，《李鸿章全集》（信函四），安徽教育出版社，2008年，第75页。

③　列宁，《帝国主义是资本主义的最高阶段》，《列宁全集》第27卷，人民出版社，1990年，第326页。

and rails.① Therefore, in 1863, after the treaty was signed, British railway engineer Sir R. M. Stephenson proposed the first railway construction plan to China, urging the Qing government to build railways. He independently designed several main lines: centered around the strategic town of Hankou on the Yangtze River, extending westward through Sichuan and Yunnan to Burma, eastward to Shanghai, and southward to southern Guangzhou; another starting from the mouth of the Yangtze River, extending northward from Zhenjiang to Tianjin and Beijing, and from Shanghai to Ningbo; and in the south, from Fuzhou to the inland regions.② The various countries that gained the right to establish diplomatic missions in Beijing through this treaty "utilized every opportunity to extol the military and economic superiority of railways in conversations with Chinese officials".③

However, all these efforts had the opposite effect. The plan to build railways took on a detestable hue of imperialist aggression, triggering widespread resistance among the Chinese people. Even the Qing government, in 1877, reclaimed and dismantled the light railway built by the Jardine Matheson & Co. between Shanghai and Wusong at a cost of nearly three hundred thousand silver taels, just a year after its construction. The reluctance of the Qing government to develop railways was not only due to conservative and backward views but also stemmed from vigilance against the ambitions of foreign aggressors. Some Chinese officials recognized that the construction of railways was closely linked to the invasion by foreign powers and their plunder of China's interests. Therefore, even officials sympathetic to railway construction, such as those in the Westernization Movement, had to proceed cautiously. In 1874, Li Hongzhang had once emphasized the benefits of railways to the progressive Prince Gong (Yixin). However, under pressure from conservative factions, Yixin informed Li Hongzhang that even "the two dowager empresses could not decide on this grand plan."④

Nevertheless, attempting to stop the progress of railways was futile; railways had become a global trend. Railways are the most important sector

①　For example, the Tanggu and Tianjin sections of the Tang-Xu Railway had tracks purchased from Belgium, ties from Japan, and most of locomotives from the United Kingdom and the United States.

②　Translation Office of the Institute of Modern History, Chinese Academy of Social Sciences. *Dictionary of Foreign Names Coming to China in Modern Times*. China Social Sciences Press, 1981, p.457.

③　O. D. Rasmussen. *Tientsin: An Illustrated Outline History*, translated by Xu Yifan, et al. Tianjin People's Publishing House, 2008, p.61.

④　Gu Tinglong, Dai Yi (eds.). *The Collected Works of Li Hongzhang* (Letters 4). Anhui Education Press, 2008, p.75.

1888 年唐胥铁路通车时李鸿章（前排左四）率幕僚乘车视察
When the Tang-Xu Railway opened in 1888, Li Hongzhang (fourth from the left in the front row) led his staff on a train inspection

度更快。到 1883 年，开平矿务局已拥有三辆客运火车和由"中国火箭"号牵引的 50 辆运煤火车。①

开平煤矿铁路被称为"唐胥铁路"，继续秘密运行达五年之久。1886 年清政府批准在天津组建开平铁路公司，并收购唐胥线。这是中国铁路独立经营的开端。1887 年，李鸿章得到清政府新贵醇亲王奕譞的支持，以加强海防为名，醇亲王向清廷上奏，请求将这条铁路延伸到天津。之后为募集资金，李鸿章指示开平铁路局公开招股白银一百万两，在各地报纸上刊载招商章程。这是中国第一份企业招股章程。有了资金来源之后，铁路修建进展很快，1888 年 8 月，轨道线通到了天津，是为津榆铁路，全长约 55 公里，火车运行时速可达 30 公里。当年海关年度报告指出，铁路的开通，将使之前束缚天津地区经济发展的交通条件大大改善，"有关天津贸易前程似锦之预言，即可认为信而有征矣"，因此"可将 1888 年视为天津编年

---

① 熊性美、阎光华主编，《开滦煤矿矿权史料》，南开大学出版社，2004 年，第 21 页。

of capitalist industry, summarizing the coal and steel industry, and are the epitome and most prominent indicator of the development of world trade and bourgeois civilization.[1] If China wanted to develop modern industry and catch up with the development of world civilization, it had to introduce railways and develop coal and iron mines. Therefore, the establishment of railways in China was proposed as an important supporting facility for coal mining. In 1876, when the Kaiping Mining Bureau was established, Li Hongzhang agreed to Tang Tingshu secretly constructing a railway to transport coal in order to reduce transportation costs. However, due to the situation at the time, only an 11-kilometer-long track was laid from Tangshan to Xugezhuang, and coal could only be transported on the track using mules and horses temporarily. However, Tang Tingshu wisely instructed the British engineer Claude William Kinder to design the railway tracks to international standard gauge and to build the bridges through which the tracks passed especially sturdy, so that trains could eventually run on them. Kinder was also secretly commissioned to develop a locomotive, named the "Rocket of China," which was quickly put into daily railway transport at the mines. In 1882, the "Rocket of China" completed the entire journey with a group of officials at a speed of 13.5 kilometers per hour, proving that the locomotive had greater power and speed than mules and horses. By 1883, the Kaiping Mining Bureau had three passenger trains and 50 coal trains pulled by the "Rocket of China."[2]

The Kaiping Mining Bureau Railway, known as the "Tang-Xu Railway," continued to operate secretly for five years. In 1886, the Qing government approved the establishment of the Kaiping Railway Company in Tianjin and acquired the Tang-Xu line. This marked the beginning of independent operation of railways in China. In 1887, Li Hongzhang got the support of the newly influential Prince Chun (Yixuan), who presented a request to the Qing court to extend the railway to Tianjin under the pretext of strengthening coastal defense. Subsequently, to raise funds, Li Hongzhang instructed the Kaiping Mining Bureau to publicly offer one million taels of silver in shares and published the prospectus in newspapers across the country. This was China's first corporate share offering prospectus. With a source of funding secured, railway construction progressed rapidly. By August 1888, the railway line reached Tianjin, known as the Tianjin-Yuguan Railway, with a total length of about 55 kilometers, and trains could travel at speeds of up to 30 kilometers per hour.

---

① V.I. Lenin. *Imperialism the Highest Stage of Capitalism. V.I. Lenin Selected Works* (Vol.27). People's Publishing House, 1990, p.326.

② Xiong Xingmei, Yan Guanghua (eds.). *Historical Materials on Mining Rights of Kailan Coal Mine*. Nankai University Press, 2004, p.21.

中国火箭号
Rocket of China

史上开纪元之时期"。这一年也被当时在华外国人誉为"中国铁路世纪的正式开始"。[①]

1895 年甲午战争后，中国士民觉醒，奋发图强，发展实业。开平铁路公司于 1896 年被正式命名为中国铁路总公司，总部设在天津，负责以公司形式办理铁路借款及修路事务，后更名为"天津铁路公司"。以天津为总指挥部，先后修成京张铁路、津浦铁路等。天津成为华北地区的重要铁路枢纽，中国铁路总公司也设在天津，管理铁路事务。

1905 年直隶总督袁世凯与会办大臣胡燏棻上奏清政府，获准修建京张铁路，在天津设立京张铁路总局，并任命詹天佑为总工程师，负责从勘测、设计到施工的全部工作。历时四年，于 1909 年 8 月 11 日全部工程竣工，10 月 2 日京张铁路全线通车。在詹天佑的艰苦努力下，京张铁路平均每千米造价仅为 3.45 万两，为当时全国平均造价最低铁路，[②] 同时这也是清朝年间唯一一条由中国人自行设计建造并制定规章的铁路。1908 年 1 月 13 日清政府与英德两国公司签订《天津浦口铁路借款合同》，借款筑路。由于吸取了京汉铁路的经验教训，[③] 中国保留了津浦铁路的几乎全部管理权。1908 年开工典礼在天津举行，四年后，1912 年津浦线全线通车。

有铁路必有车站，天津仅市区内就有三座火车站。1888 年建成天津火车站，又称老龙头车站、东站、老站。1903 年因天津东站前的主要地段被各国列强瓜分为租界，清政府上层官员出入车站极为不便，又建天津北站。1908—1910 年，为津浦铁路所需又建天津西站。由此，天津成为中国第一座拥有铁路"两干线三车站"的城市。

① 吴弘明编译，《津海关贸易年报（1865~1946）》，天津社会科学院出版社，2006 年，第 151 页。

② 北京市地方志编纂委员会，《北京志·市政卷·铁路运输志》，北京出版社，2004 年，第 40、423 页。

③ 京汉铁路是连结华北和华中的铁路。中国投资 1500 万两，其余由比利时辛迪加供给并主管修建。有关营业方面的权利几乎全部为比利时辛迪加所掌握，名义上是中国官营，实际上则是法国和比利时两国的事业。

The Customs Annual Report for that year noted that the opening of the railway would greatly improve the transportation conditions that had previously constrained economic development in the Tianjin area. "Predictions about the bright future of Tianjin's trade seemed to be coming true", indicating that "1888 can be considered the beginning of a new era in Tianjin's history." This year was also hailed by foreigners in China at the time as the "official start of the century of Chinese railways."[①]

After the First Sino-Japanese War in 1895, Chinese intellectuals and civilians became awakened and vigorously pursued industrial development. In 1896, the Kaiping Railway Company was officially renamed as the Chinese Railway Company, headquartered in Tianjin. It was responsible for managing railway loans and construction affairs in the form of a company, later renamed as the "Tianjin Railway Company." With Tianjin as its headquarters, it successively built the Beijing-Zhangjiakou Railway, the Tianjin-Pukou Railway, and others. Tianjin became an important railway hub in North China, with the Chinese Railway Company also headquartered there, managing railway affairs.

In 1905, the Viceroy of Zhili Province, Yuan Shikai, and Minister Hu Yufen, petitioned the Qing government and obtained approval to construct the Beijing-Zhangjiakou Railway. They established the Beijing-Zhangjiakou Railway Administration Bureau in Tianjin and appointed Zhan Tianyou as the chief engineer, responsible for all aspects of surveying, design, and construction. After four years of hard work, the entire project was completed on August 11, 1909, and the Beijing-Zhangjiakou Railway was fully opened on October 2. Thanks to Zhan Tianyou's efforts, the average cost per kilometer of the Beijing-Zhangjiakou Railway was only 34,500 silver taels, the lowest in the country at that time.[②] It was also the only railway built and regulated by Chinese people during the Qing Dynasty. On January 13, 1908, the Qing government signed the *Tianjin-Pukou Railway Loan Contract* with British and German companies to finance its construction. Learning from the lessons of the Beijing-Hankou Railway,[③] China retained almost all management rights

① *Tianjin Customs Annual Report of Trade (1865~1946)*, translated and edited by Wu Hongming. Tianjin Academy of Social Sciences Press, 2006, p.151.

② Beijing Chorography Compilation Committee. *Beijing Chronicles, Municipal Administration, History of Railway Transportation*. Beijing Publishing Group, 2004, p.40, 423.

③ The Beijing-Hankou Railway connects North China and Central China. The Qing government invested 15 million taels, while the remaining funds were provided and managed by the Belgian syndicate. Although it was nominally a state-run Chinese enterprise, in practice, it was a joint venture between France and Belgium, with almost all of the operational rights controlled by the Belgian syndicate.

天津站
Tianjin Railway Station

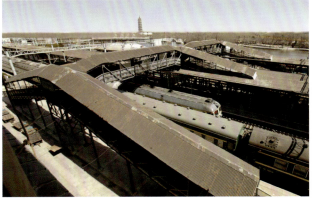

天津北站
Tianjin North Railway Station

天津西站
Tianjin West Railway Station

铁路改变了什么？

从坚决抵制到主动筑路、与列强争夺路权，中国人对于火车这一钢铁巨兽的态度发生了彻底的转变。那么，铁路究竟给中国社会带来了什么、改变了什么呢？

首先，火车改变了远途旅行的方式，扩大了人们的视野，带来社会风气的日趋开放。天津城外原来有一条大道直通北京，骑马寄送邮件，中间有驿站换马，可以在 12 小时内，由海河边的津海关快马加鞭赶到北京的海关总税务司署，但从天津出发的商旅行人则需要两三天才能赶到北京。京津之间火车通行之后，6 个小时即可完成全部旅程。为吸引普通民众乘坐，铁路公司定出了较为适中的票价：头等票三元，二等票减半，对于普通民众来说不是问题。铁路通到天津后不过两年，搭乘旅客在一年内（自 1890 年 12 月至 1891 年 11 月）达到 537000 余人次。[1] 在天津火车东站，"华人近皆在东站票房左右，异常拥挤，火车通到北京，乘车之人数更多，虽乘运货之车犹欣欣

---

[1] 吴弘明编译，《津海关贸易年报（1865~1946）》，天津社会科学院出版社，2006 年，第 167 页。

for the Tianjin-Pukou Railway. The groundbreaking ceremony was held in Tianjin in 1908, and four years later, in 1912, the entire Tianjin-Pukou line was opened.

Where there are railways, there are stations. Tianjin alone had three railway stations within the urban area. Tianjin Railway Station, also known as the Old Dragon Head Station, East Station, or Old Station, was completed in 1888. Due to the main area in front of Tianjin East Station being divided into concessions by foreign powers in 1903, making it inconvenient for senior Qing officials to access the station, Tianjin North Station was built. From 1908 to 1910, Tianjin West Station was built to meet the needs of the Tianjin-Pukou Railway. Thus, Tianjin became the first city in China to have "two main lines and three stations" on its railway network.

What Has the Railway Changed?

From resolute resistance to actively building railways and competing with major powers for railway rights, the attitude of the Chinese people towards the iron giant of the train has undergone a complete transformation. So, what has the railway brought to Chinese society and what has it changed?

Firstly, trains have changed the way people travel long distances, broadening their horizons and leading to a progressively open social atmosphere. Outside Tianjin, there used to be a main road leading directly to Beijing,

《辛丑条约》签订后，1902年慈禧太后自西安回北京，由保定搭乘的皇家特等客车。照片由总工程师沙多的孙子 Jean Jadot 提供
After the signing of the *Boxer Protocol*, in 1902, Empress Dowager Cixi returned to Beijing from Xi'an, traveling by the royal special car from Baoding.
Courtesy of Jean Jadot, the grandson of Belgian Engineer Jean Jadot

然有喜色，盖风气已开，如火车头之喷气然"。[1] 最初修造火车原以战时运兵、平时运货为主要目的，但关内外铁路通行之后，运货与载客所得收入竟不相上下。[2] 就连清朝最高统治者慈禧太后，在《辛丑条约》签订后，于1902年自西安回北京，在保定也坐上了袁世凯特意安排的皇家特等客车，一路舒舒服服地回到北京。由于清皇室每年一次去西陵祭奠祖先要耗费很多时间经费，又下令专门修建了西陵线，作为皇室专用线。可见，物质享受是新鲜事物中最让人乐于接受的。"它没有大炮那么可怕，但比大炮更有力量，它不像思想那么感染人心，但比思想更广泛地走到每一个人的生活里去。"[3]

其次，铁路改变了运输方式和货运的内容，进而改变了水运一家独大的局面，京杭大运河作为昔日"南北生命线"的意义从此不复存在。铁路线正式开始修建不到十年，铁路就占到内地贸易全部货运量近一半（1905—1906年）。[4] 在进口货物方面，工业制造品

where horses were used to send mail, with relay stations along the way for changing horses. One could ride from the Tianjin Customs on the bank of the Hai River to the Customs House in Beijing in just 12 hours, but it took two to three days for travelers and merchants departing from Tianjin to reach Beijing. With trains running between Beijing and Tianjin, the entire journey could now be completed in just 6 hours. To attract ordinary people to travel by train, the railway company set relatively moderate ticket prices: three yuan for first class tickets and half price for second class tickets, which were affordable for ordinary people. Within just two years of the railway reaching Tianjin, the number of passengers exceeded 537,000 within a year (from December 1890 to November 1891).[1] At the Tianjin East Railway Station, "Chinese people were crowded around the ticket office, and when the train arrived in Beijing, there were even more passengers. Even those boarding freight trains were visibly happy, as the trend had opened up, much like the steam from the locomotive."[2] Initially, the construction of trains was mainly for transporting troops during wartime and goods during peacetime, but after the construction of Peking-Mukden Railway (Beijing-Shenyang Railway), the income from freight and passenger transportation became comparable.[3] Even the highest ruler

① 吴弘明编译，《津海关贸易年报（1865~1946）》，天津社会科学院出版社，2006年，第215、245、253页。

② 同上。

③ 陈旭麓，《近代中国社会的新陈代谢》，上海人民出版社，1992年，第218页。

④ 天津市地方史志编修委员会总编辑室编，《二十世纪初的天津概况》，内部发行，1986年，第283页。

① *Tianjin Customs Annual Report of Trade (1865~1946)*, translated and edited by Wu Hongming. Tianjin Academy of Social Sciences Press, 2006, p.167.

② *Tianjin Customs Annual Report of Trade (1865~1946)*, translated and edited by Wu Hongming. Tianjin Academy of Social Sciences Press, 2006, p.215,245,253.

③ Same as above.

1901 年铁轨穿过北京城墙。1896 年 "唐胥铁路" 终于延伸至北京城外的卢沟桥，1897 年铁路进一步延伸至丰台，并与津榆铁路合并，更名为 "关内外铁路"，意为 "连接长城内外的铁路"。义和团运动期间，团民将京津之间的铁路线拆毁，天津站（老龙头火车站）和北京站也被捣毁。1900 年，八国联军占领北京，英国人炸毁一段北京外城墙，终于将铁路修进了城内。这一举动具有巨大的标志性意义，象征着自马戛尔尼使团开始不断叩关而来的西方人终于攻破了清政府统治下的这座封建堡垒。这一年，中国彻底沦为半殖民地半封建社会

In 1901, the railway track passed through the Beijing city wall. In 1896, the "Tang-Xu Railway" was finally extended to the Marco Polo Bridge outside Beijing, and in 1897, the railway was further extended to Fengtai, merging with the Tianjin-Yuguan Railway and renamed the "Guanneiwai Railway," meaning "the railway connecting inside and outside the Shanhaiguan Pass." During the Boxer Rebellion, the Boxers destroyed the railway lines between Beijing and Tianjin, and both Tianjin Station (Old Dragon Head Station) and Beijing Station were also destroyed. In 1900, the Eight-Nation Alliance occupied Beijing, and the British blew up a section of the outer city wall, finally allowing the railway to be extended into the city. This action had enormous symbolic significance, marking the moment when the Western powers, who had been knocking on the door since the Macartney Embassy, finally breached the feudal fortress under the Qing government's rule. This year, China was complete transformation into a semi-colonial, semi-feudal society

火车修进北京城
Railway was built into the Beijing city

以上照片由总工程师沙多的孙子 Jean Jadot 提供
Courtesy of Jean Jadot, the grandson of Belgian Chief Engineer Jean Jadot

空中俯瞰天津东站铁路
An aerial view of Tianjin East Railway Station

军阀占用铁路运兵
Warlords requisitioning the railway for troop transportation

占据大半，其中最主要的是来自日、美、英三国的洋纱洋布从天津港进口，经铁路转运长驱直入北方内陆市场，冲击了传统土纱土布市场，而内地市场对石油、军火、砂糖、面粉、纸张和燃料的需求也增长迅速。在出口货物方面，农产品占据大半，主要是棉花、羊毛、家畜、皮货、猪鬃、果蔬、蚕茧和茶等，制成品只有陶瓷器、药材、丝绸、草帽辫等，入超现象严重。京汉铁路和津浦铁路开通后，日益成为联系南北贸易的新生命线。在铁路强大运力的蚕食之下，内河运输日益萎缩。本就因河沙淤积、干旱水少、冬季结冰等原因而受到严重影响的京杭大运河淮河以北段，渐渐失去了它的航运价值，昔日运河三岔口上"连樯集万艘"的盛景一去不返。

第三，铁路改变了近代中国的经济格局，它唤醒了中国人民的权利意识，进而引发了终结帝制的资产阶级革命。铁路打破了中国传统社会的"小农经济"，将广阔的内陆与东部沿海口岸联结在一起，混合为一个统一的中国市场，使进出口贸易大幅增长，改变了中国的经济格局。清朝末年帝国主义列强对中国铁路和矿山投资开采权的争夺，推动了民众尤其是士绅阶层民族意识和权利意识的觉醒，使民众开始热衷于投资商业企业，振兴民族工业。1878年开平矿务局的股票在天津、上海、武汉、南京、宁波等地销售，引起各地巨

of the Qing Dynasty, Empress Dowager Cixi, after the signing of the *Boxer Protocol*, returned to Beijing from Xi'an in 1902 and was arranged to ride in a specially arranged royal first-class carriage in Baoding by Yuan Shikai, all the way back to Beijing comfortably. Since the Qing imperial family spent a lot of time and money each year on a pilgrimage to Western Royal Tombs to worship their ancestors, a special line was ordered to be built as a dedicated line for the imperial family. It can be seen that material enjoyment is the most readily accepted aspect of new things. "It's not as terrifying as cannons, but it's more powerful than cannons; it doesn't touch people's hearts like thoughts, but it spreads more widely into everyone's lives."[1]

Secondly, the railway has changed the mode of transportation and the goods of freight, thereby altering the dominance of water transport alone, and the significance of the Grand Canal as the former "lifeline between North and South" ceased to exist. Less than ten years after the official start of railway construction, railways accounted for nearly half of the total inland trade freight volume (1905-1906).[2] In terms of imported goods, industrial manufactured goods dominated, with the most significant being yarn and cloth from Japan, the United States, and Britain imported through Tianjin Port, then transported by railway directly into the northern inland markets, which impacted the traditional markets for local yarn and cloth. Meanwhile, the demand in the inland market for petroleum, munitions, sugar, flour, paper, and fuel also grew rapidly. As for exported goods, agricultural products predominated, mainly cotton, wool, livestock, leather goods, hog bristles, fruits, vegetables, silkworm cocoons, and tea, while finished products were limited to ceramics, medicinal herbs, silk, plaited straw, resulting in a severe trade imbalance. With the opening of the Beijing-Hankou and Tianjin-Pukou railways, they increasingly became the new lifeline connecting North and South trade. Under the relentless competition from the robust transport capacity of railways, inland water transportation continued to decline. The section of the Grand Canal in the north of the Huai River, already severely affected by factors such as siltation, low water levels due to drought, and winter ice, gradually lost its navigation value. The once bustling scene of "countless masts gathering at the junction of the canal branches" is gone forever.

Thirdly, the railway changed the economic landscape of modern China, awakening the people's awareness of rights, thus sparking the bourgeois rev-

---

① Chen Xulu. *The Metabolism of Modern Chinese Society*. Shanghai People's Publishing House, 1992, p.218.

② Editorial Office of the Tianjin Chorography and History Compilation Committee (ed.). *Overview of Tianjin in the Early 20th Century*. Published internally in 1986, p.283.

商争相买入，在很短的时间内即募集到巨额资金。甲午战后中国铁路发展大大加快，民间也掀起集股修筑铁路的热潮，直至1911年5月，由于清政府将已归商办的川汉、粤汉铁路收归国有而导致"保路运动"的爆发，进而引发辛亥革命，终结了中国封建王朝几千年的统治。经济基础决定上层建筑。铁路属于基础设施建设，堪称基础的基础。基础变了，清政府岂能不倒？！

最后，不得不提的是，铁路的出现改变了战争的规模和进程，却也为自身的发展带来了阻碍。最早倡议修筑铁路的李鸿章等洋务大臣，提出的理由是军事方面的需要，"如有铁路相通，遇警则朝发夕至，屯一路之兵能抵数路之用"[①]。不过后来，火车的神速没能挽救清王朝的覆亡，却在之后的北洋军阀混战中得到了充分的运用。军阀士兵几乎从来不付车费，司令官更是霸占铁路车辆、货车，有时甚至将整列火车据为己用，影响列车按时运行。战争亦导致铁路时行时断，铁路收入没有任何保障，更不用说修建新的线路了。

洋行与买办

在开放成为通商口岸后，随着交通运输业的发展，天津日益成为北方的经济中心。天津口岸将华北、西北和东北三个地区的市场与国际资本主义市场连结在一起，"华北传统农业生产的商品价值体系开始与代表西方大机器生产的商品价值体系对接"[②]。20世纪30年代初，天津港的进出口总额已占到华北地区的60%，占全国的25%，成为中国北方最大的进出口贸易港、仅次于上海的全国第二大外贸中心。可以说，天津在开埠前仅仅是区域性的经济中心，开埠后则成为世界资本主义市场的一部分，沦为资本主义的原料供应地和产品倾销地，其中各个洋行发挥了巨大作用。

---

① 宓汝成编，《中国近代铁路史资料（1863—1911）》（第一册），中华书局，1963年，第131页。

② 天津市档案馆编，《近代以来天津城市化进程实录》，天津人民出版社，2005年，第96页。

olution that ended the imperial rule. The railway shattered the "small-scale peasant economy" of traditional Chinese society, connecting the vast inland regions with the eastern coastal ports, amalgamating them into a unified Chinese market, leading to a significant increase in import and export trade and altering China's economic structure. The competition among imperialist powers for railway and mining investment and exploitation rights in China at the end of the Qing Dynasty spurred the awakening of national consciousness and rights consciousness, especially among the gentry class, prompting the people to become enthusiastic about investing in commercial enterprises and revitalizing national industries. In 1878, the shares of the Kaiping Mining Bureau were sold in Tianjin, Shanghai, Wuhan, Nanjing, Ningbo, and other places, triggering a rush among local magnates to buy them, resulting in the rapid raising of substantial funds in a short period. After the First Sino-Japanese War, the development of railways in China accelerated significantly, and there was also a fervor among the public to invest in railway construction through stock subscriptions. However, in May 1911, the outbreak of the "Railway Protection Movement" was triggered by the Qing government's nationalization of the Sichuan-Hankou and Guangdong-Hankou railways, leading to the outbreak of the 1911 Revolution and ending the rule of China's feudal dynasties that had lasted for thousands of years. The economic base determines the superstructure. Railways belong to the construction of infrastructure and can be regarded as the foundation of foundations. When the foundation changes, how can the Qing government not collapse?!

Lastly, it must be mentioned that while the emergence of railways changed the scale and course of warfare, it also brought obstacles to its own development. Initially, the advocates for railway construction such as Li Hongzhang, a statesman of the Westernization Movement, cited military needs, stating, "If there is a railway connection, in case of an emergency, troops can be dispatched swiftly, and troops stationed along one route equal to that of several routes."[①] However, later on, the rapid movement of trains failed to save the Qing Dynasty from collapse, but it was extensively utilized during the subsequent Warlord Era conflicts. Warlord soldiers almost never paid for train fares, and commanders often seized railway cars and freight trains, sometimes even taking control of entire train lines, disrupting the trains' punctual operation. Wars also resulted in the intermittent operation of railways, with railway revenues lacking any guarantee, let alone the construction of new lines.

---

① Mi Rucheng (ed.). *Materials on Modern Chinese Railway History (1863-1911)* (Vol.1). Zhonghua Book Company, 1963, p.131.

天津的洋行

所谓洋行，一般是指由外国资本投资在中国设立的贸易公司。后来随着外国资本在华投资办厂日益增多，各种外国人设立的和中外合资的制造业企业，也被称作洋行。

天津成为通商口岸后，外国商人开始在天津设立洋行。1875 年前后已发展到近 30 家，其中包括号称英国"四大洋行"的怡和、太古、仁记、新泰兴洋行和汇丰银行、屈臣氏大药房等 14 家在天津开设的分支机构；俄国的阜通、顺丰（又称萨宝石）等 7 家；德国的世昌、信远、增茂等 6 家；法国的启昌、亨达利；美国的丰昌等。[①] 这些大洋行垄断了天津的进出口贸易，到 1890 年天津洋行仅增加到 47 家。随着帝国主义势力的进一步入侵和天津的城市化进程发展，据海关统计，1906 年天津的洋行总数迅速扩张到 232 家，1926 年则达到 900 余家。1936 年，各国在津总共开设了各类洋行达 982 家，其中日本 689 家、美国 96 家、英国 68 家、德国 43 家、俄国 26 家、法国 22 家、其他国家 38 家。[②] 由此也可以看出，早期是英国的商人在天津的贸易中占优势地位。一战后，德、法、俄等国势力衰竭，美国与日本趁欧洲各国无暇东顾，乘机夺取中国市场，与力图保持原有优势的英国商人，成为在津外国三大势力，而野心勃勃想要吞并中国的日本商人有军界和外交力量做后盾，更是后来者居上。北洋军阀统治时期，日、美、英三国在不同时期各自支持某一派系军阀，它们的洋行在天津租界里的活动正好反映了当时各派军阀势力的此消彼长。所以，尽管天津的洋行经营范围广阔，包括进口洋货、出口中国土产、经营房地产、保险、运输以及电车电灯、自来水等公用事业，但最赚钱的除了鸦片，始终是军火交易。

20 世纪初，天津的各个洋行主要从事进出口贸易。天津洋行对外输出一直主要以毛皮、农副产品为主，进口则从早期的鸦片、军

---

① 天津市政协文史资料研究委员会编，《天津的洋行与买办》，天津人民出版社，1987 年，第 2—3 页。

② 天津市地方史志编修委员会编著，《天津通志·附志·租界》，天津社会科学院出版社，1996 年，第 209 页。

Foreign Firms and Compradors

After opening up as a trading port, with the development of transportation and logistics, Tianjin increasingly became the economic center of the northern region. The Tianjin port connected the markets of North China, Northwest China, and Northeast China with the international capitalist market, where "the commodity value system of traditional agricultural production in North China began to integrate with the commodity value system representing Western large-scale machine production."[①] By the early 1930s, the total import and export volume of Tianjin Port accounted for 60% of that of North China region and 25% of the national total, making it the largest import and export trade port in northern China and the second-largest national foreign trade center after Shanghai. It can be said that Tianjin was merely a regional economic center before the opening of the port, but after opening, it became part of the global capitalist market, serving as a source of raw materials and a market for dumping products, where various foreign firms played a significant role.

Tianjin's Foreign Firms

The term "yang hang" generally refers to trading companies established in China with foreign capital investment. Later, with the increasing investment of foreign capital in setting up factories in China, various manufacturing enterprises established by foreigners or in joint ventures with Chinese entities came to be referred to as "yang hang" as well.

After Tianjin became an open trading port, foreign merchants began establishing trading firms there. By around 1875, there were already nearly 30 such firms, including the so-called "Big Four" British trading firms: Jardine, Matheson & Co., Butterfield & Swire, William Forbes & Co., and Wilson & Co., as well as branches of institutions such as HSBC and Watson's Pharmacy. There were also seven Russian firms including Molchanoff, Pechatnoff & Co. and S. W. Litvinoff & Co., six German firms including Meyer & Co., Eduard, Cordes & Co., A., and Hirsbrunner & Co., French firms like Ouskouli, N. H. A. and Hope Bros & Co, and American firms like Maclay & Co.[②] These major trading firms monopolized Tianjin's import and export trade, with the number of foreign firms in

---

① Tianjin Archives (ed.). *Factual Records of Tianjin's Urbanization since Modern Times*. Tianjin People's Publishing House, 2005, p.96.

② The Culture & History Data Research Committee of the Tianjin Municipal Committee of the Chinese People's Political Consultative Conference (ed.). *Foreign Firms and Compradors in Tianjin*. Tianjin People's Publishing House, 1987, pp.2-3.

原怡和洋行。航鹰摄于 2003 年
Former office building of Jardine, Matheson & Co..
Taken by Hang Ying in 2003

怡和洋行是最著名的一家老牌英资洋行，远东最大的英资财团，清朝时即从事与中国贸易，主要从事鸦片及茶叶的买卖。1832 年 7 月 1 日成立，由两名苏格兰裔英国人威廉·渣甸（William Jardine，1784—1843）及詹姆士·马地臣（James Matheson，1796—1878）在中国广州创办。怡和洋行对香港早年的发展有举足轻重的作用，有"未有香港，先有怡和"之称。也是首家在上海开设的欧洲公司和首家在日本成立的外国公司。1843 年上海怡和洋行成立。1872 年以后怡和洋行放弃对华鸦片贸易，之后怡和的投资业务逐渐多元化，除了贸易外，还在中国大陆及香港投资兴建铁路、船坞、各式工厂、矿务；经营船务、银行等各类业务。

Jardine Matheson is the most famous and longstanding British trading company, the largest British financial conglomerate in the Far East. It engaged in trade with China during the Qing Dynasty, primarily dealing in opium and tea. Founded on July 1, 1832, by two Scottish-born Britons, William Jardine (1784-1843) and James Matheson (1796-1878), it was established in Guangzhou, China. Jardine Matheson played a crucial role in the early development of Hong Kong, earning the reputation "Before Hong Kong, there was Jardine." It was also the first European company to establish a presence in Shanghai and the first foreign company to establish operations in Japan. The Shanghai branch of Jardine Matheson was founded in 1843. After 1872, the company abandoned its opium trade in China, and its investments gradually diversified. In addition to trade, Jardine Matheson invested in the construction of railways, docks, factories, and mines in the Chinese mainland and Hong Kong, while also engaging in shipping, banking, and other business ventures.

明信片上的怡和洋行仓库和码头，今 6 号院创意产业园
Warehouse and wharf of Jardine, Matheson & Co. on postcard. Now No.6 Yard Creative Industrial Park

原仁记洋行。刘悦摄于 2024 年
Former office building of William Forbes & Co..
Taken by Liu Yue in 2024

原仁记洋行。刘悦摄于 2024 年
Former office building of William Forbes & Co..
Taken by Liu Yue in 2024

仁记洋行于鸦片战争前夕在上海成立，天津开埠后即来天津开设分行，行址在英租界河坝路（今台儿庄路），由威廉·傅博斯（William Forbes）等人经营。八国联军侵华期间，该行遭到义和团和清军炮火破坏。后依《辛丑条约》，得到一笔赔偿费，遂在英租界中街 45 号（今解放北路 129—135 号）修建了新行址。该行营业范围极广，进口商品包括轮船、火车、废报纸；出口商品包括古玩玉器、皮毛、头发并代理各项代销业务，以及保险、海陆运输、招募华工等，从中收取佣金。

William Forbes & Co. was established in Shanghai on the eve of the Opium War and opened a branch in Tianjin after the port was opened. The branch was located on Bund Road in the British Concession (now Tai'erzhuang Road) and was managed by William Forbes and others. During the Boxer Rebellion, the company was damaged by artillery fire from the Boxers and the Qing army. Following the *Boxer Protocol*, the company received compensation and rebuilt its office at No.45 Victoria Road in the British Concession (now No.129-135 Jiefang North Road). The company had a wide range of business operations, including the import of goods such as ships, trains, and waste paper; the export of antiques, jade, furs, hair, and acting as an agent for various sales; as well as engaging in insurance, shipping, and recruiting Chinese laborers, earning commissions from these activities.

原新泰兴洋行。刘悦摄于 2024 年
Former office building of Wilson & Co. Taken by Liu Yue in 2024

新泰兴洋行旧址位于和平区解放北路100 号，属于一般保护级别的历史风貌建筑。新泰兴洋行创立于 1876 年，是天津开埠后早期来津的英国"皇家四大行"之一。"皇家四大行"在进入中国的最初都曾参与军火交易和鸦片买卖，后来随着时间的推移，四大行逐渐把主要业务转向了正当行业，怡和、太古两大行在航运、食糖等方面独占鳌头，仁记和新泰兴则主要在土特产品的出口方面大发横财。新泰兴在中国内地设有外庄多处，主营羊毛和农副土特产品，当时基本垄断了中国西北的羊毛生意，另外还逐步接触金融行业，涉足国外保险公司的财险、火险等业务代理。起用熟悉草帽缏业务的中国商人宁星普为经理，新泰兴洋行还投资房地产业，盖有新泰兴大楼。

The former site of Wilson & Co. is located at No.100 Jiefang North Road, Heping District, and is a historically protected building of general significance. Wilson & Co. was founded in 1876 and was one of the early British "Four Royal Trading Houses" to establish a presence in Tianjin after the port was opened. The "Four Royal Houses" were initially involved in arms trading and opium sales when they first entered China. Over time, however, the four companies gradually shifted their focus to legitimate industries. Jardine Matheson and Butterfield Swire dominated in shipping and sugar, while William Forbes & Co. and Wilson & Co. made huge profits from the export of local specialties. Wilson & Co. had multiple branches in inland China, primarily dealing in wool and agricultural by-products. At the time, it effectively monopolized the wool trade in Northwestern China. The company also gradually ventured into the financial sector, acting as an agent for foreign insurance companies in areas like property and fire insurance. Wilson & Co. appointed a Chinese businessman familiar with straw hat business, Ning Xingpu, as its manager. Additionally, Wilson & Co. invested in real estate and built the Wilson & Co. Office Building.

天津太古洋行
Butterfield & Swire in Tianjin

原太古洋行。张畅摄于 2022 年
Former office building of Butterfield & Swire. Taken by Zhang Chang in 2022

太古洋行 1816 年由约翰·施怀雅〔John Swire（1793—1847）〕在英国利物浦创立。1861 年太古集团开始通过代理商与中国进行贸易。太古洋行是近代中国影响力仅次于怡和洋行的商贸机构。太古洋行主营航运业，1867 年组织中国航业公司，1872 年在上海设太古轮船公司，1904 年设天津驳船公司，经营天津—塘沽的浮船拖驳事业，附设船舶修理工厂，成为与怡和轮船公司、旗昌轮船公司并驾齐驱的三大航运公司。除航运业外，太古洋行还涉足其他领域。19 世纪太古的糖厂成为全球规模最大和最先进的糖业基地。

Butterfield & Swire was founded by John Swire (1793-1847) in Liverpool, England in 1816. In 1861, the Swire Group began trading with China through agents. Butterfield & Swire was the second most influential trading organization in modern China after Jardine Matheson & Co., Swire primarily focused on shipping. In 1867, it established China Shipping Company, in 1872, it established Swire Steamship Company in Shanghai. In 1904, it set up the Tianjin Linger Company to operate floating ship towing services between Tianjin and Tanggu, with an attached ship repair factory, becoming one of the three major shipping companies alongside Indo-China S.N. Company and the Shanghai Steamship Navigation Co. In addition to shipping, Swire also ventured into other industries. In the 19th century, Swire's sugar factories became the largest and most advanced sugar production base in the world.

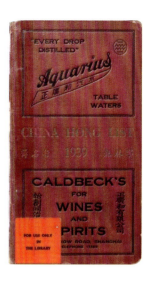

《1919 年中国北方行名录》〔由 The North China Advertising Co.（中国北方广告公司）出版的中国北方商业机构名录，包括天津、北京、哈尔滨、沈阳、营口、秦皇岛和青岛 7 个北方城市〕和《1939 年字林报行名录》〔由 The Offices of the North-China Daily News & Herald Ltd（字林洋行）出版的中国主要港口和城市中所有外国人与重要中国人开办的商行、企业、机构名录。1939 年的名录包括 45 个主要城市和港口〕

North China Hong-List 1919 (a directory of commercial institutions in northern China published by the North China Advertising Co., including seven northern cities: Tianjin, Beijing, Harbin, Shenyang, Yingkou, Qinhuangdao, and Qingdao), and *China Hong-List 1939* (a directory of all trading companies, enterprises, and institutions established by foreigners and important Chinese in major ports and cities of China, which was published by the offices of the North China Daily News & Herald Ltd. This version included 45 major cities and ports)

洋行的数量，往往说明了一个城市的经济社会发展状况。除了各通商口岸的海关数据之外，最能直观体现洋行数量和发展规模乃至经营范围的是当时的一种公开出版物——类似于后来的电话黄页簿——Hong-List（行名簿）。这里的"Hong"，不仅指贸易公司性质的洋行，还包括了工厂、银行、医院、教会、学校、各种批发和零售商店甚至使领馆等机构，统称为 Hong（行）。以《1928 年中国北方行名录》和《1939 年字林报行名录》两本行名录进行比较，1928 年出版的 Hong-List 中包括天津、北京、大连、哈尔滨、青岛等在内的 14 座北方重要城市，1939 年的字林报的行名录则包括天津、上海、广州、汉口、北京等全国 45 个主要城市。粗略统计，天津的洋行数量在北方城市中首屈一指，占到北方城市所有洋行数量的一半左右，北京约占五分之一。放眼全国的话（不包括香港），上海的洋行数量一骑绝尘，占全国首位，达到近 64%；天津居第二位，约占 12%；汉口居第三位，约占 4%；北京居第四位，约占 3.8%。（本文所用统计方法，是将 Hong-List 中各个城市所占篇幅与总篇幅占比进行粗略统计，从这个角度对各个城市的经济体量进行对比。）由此可知，天津是中国北方的经济中心，在全国则居于第二位，仅次于上海

The number of foreign firms often reflects the economic and social development status of a city. In addition to customs data from various treaty ports, one of the most direct ways to gauge the number, scale, and scope of these firms was through publicly published materials—similar to the later telephone directories—such as the Hong-List (business directory). The term "Hong" here refers not only to trading companies (foreign firms) but also includes factories, banks, hospitals, churches, schools, various wholesale and retail stores, and even consulates, all collectively referred to as "Hong" (firms). Comparing the *North China Hong-List 1928* and the *China Hong List 1939* , the 1928 Hong-List included 14 major northern cities such as Tianjin, Beijing, Dalian, Harbin, and Qingdao, while the 1939 directory included 45 major cities nationwide including Tianjin, Shanghai, Guangzhou, Hankou, and Beijing. Rough estimates show that Tianjin had the largest number of foreign firms among northern cities, accounting for roughly half of all foreign firms in northern cities, while Beijing accounted for about one-fifth. Looking at the whole country (excluding Hong Kong), Shanghai's number of foreign firms was far ahead, accounting for nearly 64% nationwide, with Tianjin in second place at approximately 12%, Hankou in third at about 4%, and Beijing in fourth at around 3.8%. (Here roughly calculates the proportion of content of each city to the total length of Hong-List to compare the economic volume of various cities.) Therefore, Tianjin was the economic center of northern China and ranked second nationwide, only after Shanghai

Tianjin increasing to only 47 by 1890. As imperialism further encroached and Tianjin urbanized, according to customs statistics, the total number of foreign firms in Tianjin rapidly expanded to 232 in 1906, reaching over 900 by 1926. In 1936, there were a total of 982 foreign firms of all kinds in Tianjin, including 689 Japanese, 96 American, 68 British, 43 German, 26 Russian, 22 French, and 38 from other countries.[1] It can be seen that early on, British merchants held a dominant position in Tianjin's trade. After World War I, the powers of Germany, France, and Russia declined, and the United States and Japan seized the opportunity to capture the Chinese market while European countries were preoccupied, with the ambitious Japanese businessmen backed by military and diplomatic power, becoming the rising force. During the rule of the Warlords of the Beiyang Army, the three countries, Japan, the United States, and Britain, each supported sone faction of warlords at different times, and the activities of their trading firms in the Tianjin Concessions reflected the rise and fall of the various warlord factions' power. Therefore, although Tianjin's foreign firms had a wide range of operations, including importing foreign goods, exporting Chinese products, managing real estate, insurance, transportation, as well as utilities such as trams, electric lights, and water supply, the most profitable business besides opium was always arms trading.

In the early 20th century, various foreign firms in Tianjin mainly engaged in import and export trade. Tianjin's foreign firms primarily exported fur and agricultural products, while imports gradually expanded from early opium and arms to pharmaceuticals, hardware, glassware, machinery, cotton and woolen goods, sugar, alkali, tobacco and liquor, electrical appliances, cosmetics, and other daily consumer goods. They leveraged their technological ad-

---

[1] *Tianjin Chorography Supplementary: Concession*, compiled by Tianjin Chorography and History Compilation Committee. Tianjin Academy of Social Sciences Press, 1996, p.209.

火开始逐渐增加了药品、日用五金、玻璃、机械、棉毛制品、糖、碱、烟酒、电器、化妆品等日用消费品。他们凭借技术优势和不平等条约所获得的税收优惠政策，向中国市场进行倾销，垄断市场。以下为根据行名录整理的洋行大致分类，括号中为经营此类的洋行数量：

第一是进出口贸易类，包括铁路矿山物资供应（14）、煤炭（10）、烟草（17）、棉花和羊毛（18）、军火（2）、颜料（16）、橡胶（2）、机械设备（28）、纺纱机床（1）、锅炉（6）、精密仪器（6）、文具与办公用品（14）、自行车（3）、汽车（14）、家具（6）、取暖卫生用品供应（16）、旅行用品（8）、食品乳品（2）、葡萄酒与矿泉水（27）、服装衣帽和鞋靴（11）、手表珠宝（8）、眼镜（4）、花边刺绣（10）、皮货（43）等；

第二是建筑类，包括房地产商和仓储公司（25）、施工承包商（37）、建筑师事务所（19）、工程咨询师事务所（4）、建筑材料进口商（10）、水泥厂（5）、砖厂（2）、石棉厂（1）、木材商（3）、装饰木板（1）、玻璃厂（1）、大理石厂（1）等；

第三是制造业工厂，包括地毯制造（12）、制盐（1）、制碱（2）、肥皂（1）、面粉（1）、火柴（3）、家具（6）、墨水（2）、钢琴（2）、印刷（12）、制革（2）、钢铁（1）、打包（6）等；

第四是金融服务类，包括银行（40）、保险寿险代理商（76）、股票证券商（7）、会计师事务所（5）、火灾鉴定公司（2）等；

第五是交通运输业和公共服务业，包括轮船公司（58）、驳船公司（2）、船运和货运代理公司（14）、石油公司（13）、电厂（27）、水厂（2）等；

第六是本地生活服务类，包括律师（11）、公证人（1）、拍卖师（3）、广告代理（1）、汽车修理厂（14）、百货零售（22）、旅馆饭店（11）、照相（2）、影剧院（8）、菜市场（2）、面包烘焙（5）、乳品店（3）、干洗店（3）、制冰厂（4）、金银首饰加工（11）、殡葬服务（1）、刻字师（5）等；

第七是医疗和文化教育类，包括医院（18）、诊所（34）、牙医（13）、兽医（2）、药店（13）、报纸（11）、学校（54）、商会（8）等。

其中值得注意的有几点：

vantages and tax incentives obtained through unequal treaties to dump goods into the Chinese market and monopolize it. Below is a rough classification of foreign firms based on directories, with the number of firms engaged in each type in parentheses:

The first category is import and export trade, including supplies for railway and mining (14), coal (10), tobacco (17), cotton and wool (18), arms (2), pigments (16), rubber (2), machinery and equipment (28), spinning and weaving machinery (1), boilers (6), precision instruments (6), stationery and office supplies (14), bicycles (3), automobiles (14), furniture (6), supplies for heating and sanitation (16), travel supplies (8), food and dairy products (2), wine and mineral water (27), clothing, hats, and shoes (11), watches and jewelry (8), eyeglasses (4), lace and embroidery (10), and leather goods (43), etc.

The second category is construction, including real estate developers and warehouse companies (25), construction contractors (37), architectural firms (19), engineering consulting firms (4), importers of building materials (10), cement factories (5), brick factories (2), asbestos factories (1), timber merchants (3), decorative wood panels (1), glass factories (1), marble factories (1), etc.

The third category is manufacturing factories, including carpet (12), salt (1), alkali (2), soap (1), flour (1), matches (3), furniture (6), ink (2), pianos (2), printing (12), leather (2), steel (1), packaging (6), etc.

The fourth category is financial services, including banks (40), insurance and life insurance agents (76), stock brokerage firms (7), accounting firms (5), fire assessment companies (2), etc.

The fifth category is transportation and public services, including shipping companies (58), barge companies (2), shipping and freight forwarding agencies (14), oil companies (13), power plants (27), waterworks (2), etc.

The sixth category is local life services, including lawyers (11), notaries (1), auctioneers (3), advertising agencies (1), auto repair shops (14), general retail (22), hotels and restaurants (11), photography studios (2), cinemas (8), markets (2), bakeries (5), dairy shops (3), dry cleaners (3), ice factories (4), gold and silver jewelry processing (11), funeral services (1), engravers (5), etc.

The seventh category is medical and cultural education, including hospitals (18), clinics (34), dentists (13), veterinarians (2), pharmacies (13), newspapers (11), schools (54), chambers of commerce (8), etc.

Several points are worth noting:

Firstly, although Tianjin's foreign firms primarily engaged in import and export trade, starting from the 1870s, as global capitalism transitioned towards monopoly capitalism, there was a shift towards direct investment and establishing factories. Thus, foreign firms were no longer just synonymous with trading companies. Those involved in manufacturing and processing for

首先，虽然天津洋行主要经营的是进出口贸易，但从19世纪70年代开始，世界资本主义向垄断资本主义过渡，开始资本输出直接投资设厂，所以洋行不再仅仅是贸易公司的代名词，那些从事生产加工然后对外出口的制造业企业也称自己为"洋行"。天津原有的近代工业在1900年的八国联军侵华战争中几乎全部遭到破坏，经过20世纪初期的重建，迅速得到恢复。特别是第一次世界大战中，由于各交战国家无暇东顾，无法满足中国的市场需求，而且少了外来的竞争，在中国的国内外资本家正好可以发展工业生产填补中国乃至世界市场的空白。20世纪一二十年代，无论是民族工业还是外资工业都欣欣向荣地发展起来，到七七事变前，天津已经形成比较完整的工业体系，并发展到前所未有的高度，工业投资总额仅低于上海，居全国第二位。

其次，作为工商企业发展辅助的银行、保险公司等金融服务业，几乎是与商贸洋行同时来到天津的，并且发展的速度快、数量多。1928年的《天津行名录》里，有中外银行共40家（不包括银号），有76家商行代理了190余家中外保险公司，而同期的各种商行总数不过900余家。商业资本与金融资本交织在一起，共同垄断了在华的商业利益，是近代中国遭受的另一种形式的侵略。

最后，天津洋行的经营内容是与时俱进的。随着各国租界社区建设的繁荣发展，本地人口与外国侨民人口日益增长，洋行不仅在数量上成倍增长，而且所从事的经营范围也不断扩张，几乎涵盖了人们生产生活中的各个方面。早期进口的洋货主要是钟表、仪器、火器等，这些奇技淫巧和火炮兵器带来的震撼吸引了上流社会的兴趣，是各洋行经营的重要货品。汽车、汽油等在欧美发明后不久很快被引进到中国。洋行不仅为天津城中上阶层市民提供了完善而舒适的生活，而且推动了天津的城市化进程，使城市社区成为中外居民共同的家园。

洋行里的中国人

洋行里的中国人，最重要的就是买办。20世纪20年代以前，洋

export also referred to themselves as "yang hang." Tianjin's original modern industry was nearly destroyed during the Eight-Nation Alliance's invasion of China in 1900. However, it swiftly recovered during the reconstruction efforts of the early 20th century. Particularly during World War I, due to the preoccupation of warring nations, they were unable to meet China's market demands. This scarcity of competition allowed both domestic and foreign capitalists to develop industrial production to fill the gap in the Chinese and even global markets. In the 1910s and 1920s, both domestic and foreign industries flourished, and by the outbreak of the Marco Polo Bridge Incident in 1937, Tianjin had developed a relatively complete industrial system, reaching unprecedented heights. The total industrial investment was only lower than that of Shanghai, ranking second nationwide.

Secondly, the financial services sector, such as banks and insurance companies, which served as auxiliary to the development of industrial and commercial enterprises, arrived in Tianjin almost concurrently with trading foreign firms, and they developed rapidly and in large numbers. In the *Tientsin Hong-List 1928*, there were a total of 40 domestic and foreign banks (excluding private banks), with 76 trading firms representing over 190 domestic and foreign insurance companies. Meanwhile, the total number of various trading firms during the same period was just over 900. Commercial capital and financial capital intertwined, jointly monopolizing commercial interests in China, representing another form of aggression suffered by modern China.

Lastly, the operations of Tianjin's foreign firms kept pace with the times. With the flourishing development of various countries' concession communities, the local population and the population of foreign residents continued to grow. The number of foreign firms not only increased exponentially but also expanded their scope of operations, covering almost every aspect of people's production and life. In the early days, imported foreign goods mainly included clocks, instruments, firearms, and so on. These novelties and the shock brought by cannons and firearms attracted the interest of the upper-class society and became important commodities for various foreign firms. Shortly after inventions like automobiles and gasoline emerged in Europe and America, they were quickly introduced to China. Foreign firms not only provided a sophisticated and comfortable lifestyle for the upper-middle class citizens in Tianjin but also propelled the urbanization process of Tianjin, making the urban community a common home for both Chinese and foreign residents.

The Chinese in the Foreign Firms

Within the foreign firms, the most important role for Chinese individuals

行一般都是通过买办进行商品贸易买卖，他们协助将产品销往内地，从内地购买羊毛、茶叶、生丝等原材料。可以说，买办是进出口贸易的中间人或金融活动的经纪人，是外国商业资本在中国进行渗透和扩张的必不可少的工具。随着外国资本主义对华经济侵略日益加深，到20世纪20年代，买办的职责不断扩大，其贸易中间人的地位越来越重要。但是随着外资在华直接投资设厂，降低成本的需要最终使买办制度走向消亡，经理人和高级职员逐渐取代买办。

鸦片战争之后，《南京条约》的签订虽然为外国资本进入中国扫清了制度障碍，外国商人终于摆脱十三行中国商人的垄断可以自由经商了，然而他们仍旧面临语言不通、国情不熟、货币及度量衡制度混乱、市场信息不灵等诸多难题。而买办则拥有相对全面的信息，可以充分利用自身的地缘、业缘和血缘关系建立起复杂的商业网络，为外商从事将产品销往内地、从内地购买原材料的进出口贸易或者作为金融活动的帮手。当然，内地的中国商人、农民与外国人做生意，遇到的麻烦也是同样的。这种文化类别和经济发展上的差异和差距所造成的中西交流障碍，就成为买办广阔的活动空间和利润空间。

通常情况下，洋行给买办一个商品的价格和标准，买办按照这个价格买进或者卖出。这个价格是洋行在计算好自己预期的利润之后给出的。不管买办从中得到多少佣金或者其他好处，只要洋行预期的利润能够达到就可以了。所以买办是外国洋行的实际供货人，有时还负责按照出口商要求安排好一切出口业务。洋行只对商品的种类、质量和价格感兴趣，对买办与中国商人之间的关系、买办的花销和得到的利润则漠不关心。这种体制对洋行来说避免了许多不确定的因素，确保了利润的稳定性和连续性；而且，依靠买办做业务简化了外国商人的职责，省下来大把的时间和精力可以花在"打网球、乘马、游猎、赛马等竞技游戏"[1]。

当世界资本主义开始过渡到垄断资本主义阶段，资本输出成为资本主义向全球扩张的另一种主要手段。中国在这一时期成为一个诱人的场所。首先，当资本主义在西方国家得到一定发展后，利润

---

① 天津市地方史志编修委员会总编辑室编，《二十世纪初的天津概况》，内部发行，1986年，第253页。

was that of compradors. Before the 1920s, foreign firms generally conducted their commodity trading through compradors. They assisted in selling products to the interior regions and purchasing raw materials such as wool, tea, and raw silk from the interior. It can be said that compradors acted as intermediaries in import-export trade or as brokers in financial activities, serving as indispensable tools for the penetration and expansion of foreign commercial capital in China. As economic aggression by foreign capitalism deepened in China, the responsibilities of compradors expanded, and their role as intermediaries in trade became increasingly significant by the 1920s. However, as the need to lower costs drove foreign capital to invest directly in factories in China, the comprador system eventually became obsolete, and managers and senior staff gradually replaced compradors.

After the Opium War, although the signing of the *Treaty of Nanjing* cleared institutional barriers for foreign capital to enter China, and foreign merchants finally broke free from the monopoly of the Thirteen Hongs' Chinese merchants and could conduct business freely, they still faced many challenges such as language barriers, unfamiliarity with local customs, confusion in currency and measurement systems, and lack of market information. Compradors, on the other hand, had relatively comprehensive information and could leverage their geographical, professional, and kinship connections to establish complex commercial networks, assisting foreign merchants in conducting import-export trade of products to and from the interior or acting as assistants in financial activities. Of course, doing business for Chinese merchants and farmers in the interior with foreigners faced similar troubles. The barriers to communication between China and the West caused by the differences and gaps in cultural categories and economic development became vast spaces for activities and profit for compradors.

Typically, foreign firms provide compradors with a price and standard for a commodity, and the compradors buy or sell according to this price. This price is set by the foreign firm after calculating their expected profit. Regardless of how much commission or other benefits the compradors receive, as long as the expected profit of the foreign firm is met, it is acceptable. Thus, compradors are the actual suppliers for foreign firms, sometimes also responsible for arranging all export business as requested by the exporters. Foreign firms are only interested in the type, quality, and price of the commodities, indifferent to the relationship between compradors and Chinese merchants, the expenses of the compradors, and the profits they receive. This system helps foreign firms avoid many uncertainties, ensuring the stability and continuity of profits. Moreover, relying on compradors simplifies the responsibilities of foreign merchants, saving them plenty of time and energy that can be spent

率开始下降，资本过剩，资本家必然将眼光转向能够为自己带来更大利润、资本少的地方进行投资，特别是经济不发达地区。中国廉价的劳动力、地价和原料以及较少的竞争使资本家更有可能获得高额利润，因此吸引力巨大。已经来到中国的各国商人常常向本国商人宣传说中国原料富、工资低、利润厚，号召他们到中国来经营企业。[①]其次，19世纪30至50年代，在最早进行工业化的英国，反对工业资本家压迫工人的运动开始显现成果，通过了一系列立法保护工人利益。例如，1847年英国通过10小时工作日提案，1850年和1853年又通过两项工厂立法，限制纺织工厂每天最多开工12小时等。之后，其他工业化国家也相继出台了保护工人利益的法律。对资本家来说，本国工人阶级的觉醒、工人运动的崛起和对工人保护的立法使得中国没有法律保护的劳动力市场变得更为诱人。第三，中国不仅拥有廉价的原料市场和劳动力市场，更拥有广阔的消费市场。这是外国商人从开辟新航路和进行工业革命之后就一直急于打开的市场。第四，近代中国半殖民地半封建的地位，有它优于完全殖民地（如印度）的好处：侨民在通商口岸和租界投资办厂，既可充分享受不平等条约所规定的对侨民的种种优惠政策（主要是关税上的自由和领事裁判权），同时，又可逃避英国本土和殖民地的税收，不受法律约束，尤其不受英国本土和殖民地的税法和工厂法的约束。因为租界里的工部局（相当于市议会）是由侨民自治，并不完全听命于本国政府。这就是中国的通商口岸被称作"资本家的乐园"的由来。

　　基于以上优越条件的考虑，外国在华设立企业大大增多。除了采矿工业和进出口商附设的小工场以及日本工厂以外，1895年以前，外商在华仅设立了10余家工厂。但从那以后到1936年，不计日本占领下的东北，各国在华设立各种类型的工厂不下820多家，其中大部分是在20世纪20年代和20世纪30年代设立的。从1902年到1914年，外国在华资本增加了近一半；从1914年到1930年，增加

on "playing tennis, riding horses, hunting, and participating in horse races, and other competitive games."[①]

As world capitalism transitioned into the stage of monopoly capitalism, capital export became another major means of capitalist expansion globally. China became an enticing destination during this period. Firstly, as capitalism developed in Western countries and profit rates began to decline, leading to surplus capital, capitalists inevitably turned their attention to investing in places where they could achieve greater profits with less capital, especially in economically underdeveloped regions. China's cheap labor, land prices, raw materials, and relatively low competition made it more likely for capitalists to obtain high profits, thus making it highly attractive. Foreign merchants already in China often promoted to their compatriots back home that China was rich in raw materials, had low wages, and offered substantial profits, encouraging them to come and do business in China.[②] Secondly, in the 1830s to 1850s in Britain, the first industralized nation, movements against the exploitation of workers by industrial capitalists began to show results. A series of legislation protecting worker interests was passed. For example, in 1847, Britain passed a proposal for a 10-hour workday, and in 1850 and 1853, two factory laws were passed to limit textile factories to a maximum of 12 hours of work per day. Subsequently, other industrialized countries also enacted laws to protect worker interests. For capitalists, the awakening of the working class, the rise of labor movements, and the legislation protecting workers in their own countries made the unprotected labor market in China even more attractive. Thirdly, China not only had a cheap raw material market and labor market but also had a vast consumer market. This was a market that foreign merchants had been eager to tap into since the opening of new trade routes and the Industrial Revolution. Fourthly, the semi-feudal and semi-colonial status of modern China had advantages over fully colonial territories like India: migrants could invest in factories in treaty ports and concessions, enjoying various preferential policies stipulated in unequal treaties (mainly tariff freedom and consular jurisdiction). They could also evade taxes in Britain and the colonies, escaping legal constraints, especially those of British domestic law and factory law. This was because the Municipal Council in the concessions was autonomous, not entirely subject to the control of the home government. This is how China's treaty

①　《北华捷报》，1879年上卷，第45页。转引自黄逸平编，《中国近代经济史论文选集（二）》，上海师范大学历史系，1979年，第671页。

①　Editorial Office of the Tianjin Chorography and History Compilation Committee (ed.). *Overview of Tianjin in the Early 20th Century*. Published internally in 1986, p.253.

②　*North-China Herald*, 1879 (vol.1), p.45. Quoted in Huang Yiping (ed.). *Selected Works of Chinese Modern Economic History (II)*. History Department of Shanghai Normal University, 1979, p.671.

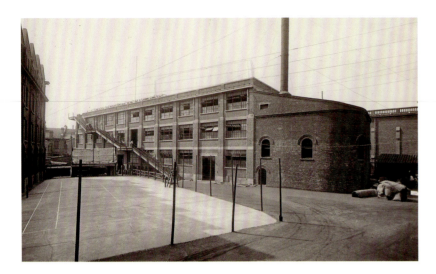

美古绅厂房
A. & M. Karagheusian factory in Tianjin

工人编织地毯
Workers weaving carpets

工人修剪地毯
Workers trimming carpets

美古绅的纺毛机器
Spinning machine of A. & M. Karagheusian

工人清洗地毯
Workers washing carpets

了一半以上；从 1930 年到 1936 年，增加了近 23%。①

不过随着工厂的设立，买办制度的弊端也逐渐暴露出来。以当时中国乃至世界最大的地毯生产厂天津美古绅洋行为例，美古绅洋行大约设立于 20 世纪 20 年代，其前身为达绅洋行，创办者为波斯籍（今伊朗）亚美尼亚人。他们因逃避奥斯曼土耳其政府于 1915 年至 1917 年发动对亚美尼亚人的种族屠杀而来到天津。美古绅洋行建立起大规模机器纺毛厂的时间大约在 1927 年，正值一次大战结束不久。由于战争，原本国际市场上的主要地毯生产国土耳其、伊朗出口受阻，天津大小地毯生产厂家乘机设立，出口量锐增。从 20 世纪 20 年代开始，天津地毯出口额逐年增长：20 世纪 20 年代到 20 世纪 30 年代，常年保持在约 400 万海关两；1941 年太平洋战争爆发，美古绅等英美地毯厂作为"敌产"被日本没收之前，出口额更达到最高峰的 821 万海关两，是天津对外出口的大宗商品。② 天津地毯 90% 出口国外，销往美国的地毯占天津出口总量的 66%。③

美古绅洋行在津开办地毯厂的鼎盛期，仅天津的工厂即拥有织机 1250 架，工人 6350 人，地毯生产能力达 120 万平方尺。④ 它不仅生产地毯，还经营机器洗毛、纺纱。其羊毛清洗部门年产能约为 27216 担，粗纺毛纱产能约为 11340 担，染毛产能约为 7258 担。⑤ 加工的羊毛、毛纱等，除供应本公司外，还供应国内其他地毯厂，并远销美国。因此，美古绅洋行对羊毛的需求量极大。由于特殊的地理位置和优越的交通条件，天津港成为三北地区羊毛出口的最大口岸。据海关统计，从天津出口的三北羊毛年均出口量 1885—1894 年为 76907 担；1895—1904 年增至 149998 担；1905—1920 年达 250000 担；1920—

① 以上数据摘自吴承明《帝国主义在旧中国资本的扩张》。转引自黄逸平编，《中国近代经济史论文选集（二）》，上海师范大学历史系，1979 年，第 754—756 页。

② 姚洪卓主编，《近代天津对外贸易（1861~1948 年）》，天津社会科学院出版社，1993 年，第 154 页。

③ 《1929 年津海关贸易报告》。吴弘明编译，《津海关贸易年报（1865~1946）》，天津社会科学院出版社，2006 年，第 486 页。

④ 据沙巴斯编写的小册子《中国地毯行业》中数据。

⑤ 同上。

ports came to be known as the "capitalists' paradise."

Considering the superior conditions mentioned above, the number of foreign enterprises established in China increased significantly. Prior to 1895, apart from mining industries and small workshops attached to import-export merchants and Japanese factories, foreigners had only established over 10 factories in China. However, from then until 1936, excluding the Northeast under Japanese occupation, various types of factories set up by various countries in China numbered no fewer than 820, with the majority established in the 1920s and 1930s. From 1902 to 1914, foreign capital in China increased by nearly half; from 1914 to 1930, it increased by more than half; and from 1930 to 1936, it increased by nearly 23%.①

However, with the establishment of factories, the drawbacks of the comprador system gradually became apparent. Taking the example of the Tianjin A. & M. Karagheusian, which was the largest carpet production factory in China and even the world at that time, it was established around the 1920s, founded by a Persian (Iran today) Armenian. They came to Tianjin to escape the Ottoman Turkish government's genocide against Armenians between 1915 and 1917. The large-scale machine spinning wool factory of the A. & M. Karagheusian was established around 1927, shortly after the end of World War I. Due to the war, the major carpet-producing countries on the international market, Turkey and Iran, faced export restrictions, prompting Tianjin's carpet manufacturers to set up factories and increase exports. From the 1920s onwards, Tianjin's carpet exports grew annually: from the 1920s to the 1930s, it consistently remained at around 4 million customs taels per year; by 1941, with the outbreak of the Pacific War and the confiscation of A. & M. Karagheusian and other British and American carpet factories as "enemy property" by Japan, exports reached a peak of 8.21 million customs taels, making carpets the major export commodity of Tianjin.② 90% of Tianjin's carpets were exported overseas, with carpets sold to the United States accounting for 66% of Tianjin's total exports.③

During the heyday of the A. & M. Karagheusian's carpet factory in Tianjin, the factory alone had 1,250 looms and employed 6,350 workers, with a

① Data from Wu Chengming. *Imperialism's Capital Expansion in Old China*. Quoted in Huang Yiping (ed.). *Selected Works of Chinese Modern Economic History (II)*. History Department of Shanghai Normal University, 1979, pp.754-756.

② Yao Hongzhuo (ed.). *Foreign Trade of Modern Tianjin (1861-1948)*. Tianjin Academy of Social Sciences Press, 1993, p.154.

③ *Tianjin Customs Trade Report in 1929*, translated and edited by Wu Hongming. *Tianjin Customs Annual Report of Trade (1865~1946)*. Tianjin Academy of Social Sciences Press, 2006, p.486.

1935 年为 256804 担。[1] 美古绅在天津设厂，自然是为了就地取材，方便快捷地获取最廉价、最充足的原材料。

然而，买办制度下，买办只关心自己的佣金，不愿意操心羊毛的质量。在买办的经营下，所有运往海港的羊毛，不是未清洗的，就是在天津经过清洗后损失 50%~60% 的重量，而且每包货物至少掺杂 50% 的次等羊毛。从内地运往天津每担羊毛运费是 30 元（鹰洋），算起来就有 18 元钱白白浪费掉了。[2] 出口的羊毛，如果掺杂泥沙和次等羊毛，会大大降低价格；而作为地毯的原料，无疑又会提高羊毛处理的成本。而且，买办常常通过囤积羊毛而抬高价格。这些因素对美古绅这样的羊毛出口商和大型地毯生产商来说，都是刀刀致命的。因此，美古绅洋行为了获得稳定、廉价且优质的羊毛，同时将管理成本降到最低，进而得到高额利润回报，是不可能与买办结成利益同盟的。

随着外国资本主义对中国商品输出和原材料的掠夺的需要日益增高、中外贸易量不断上涨、中外交流日益增多，进入垄断阶段的外商已不甘心再让买办分一杯羹了。他们要求直接与中国内地商人做生意，从而直接占有和垄断原材料和市场。因此，买办制度必然走向衰落。

20 世纪初，高级职员制和代理人制逐渐取代了原先的买办制度。高级职员制：买办只领薪金，取消或部分取消佣金，代之以销售提成。代理人制：买办不再固定受雇于某一行，洋行与华商订立经销、包销、代销合同。但这些变化主要是在部分日、美、德企业，英、法的许多老企业照旧。到了日本全面侵华时期，特别是太平洋战争爆发后，欧美籍外商相继歇业或产业被没收，日商不再雇用买办。近代买办制度终于消失了，而原来的部分买办转型成为真正的商人，自己直接做生意了。

---

① 天津海关译编委员会编译，《津海关史要览》，中国海关出版社，2004 年，第 104—136 页。

② 摘译自俄国商人维亚锡金 1934 年写给沙巴斯的一封信。

carpet production capacity of 1.2 million square feet.[1] In addition to carpet production, it also operated machinery for wool washing and spinning. Its wool cleaning department had an annual capacity of approximately 27,216 dan (1 dan equals 50 kilograms), coarse wool yarn production capacity of about 11,340 dan, and dyeing capacity of around 7,258 dan.[2] Processed wool and yarn, besides supplying the company itself, were also provided to other carpet factories domestically and exported to the United States. Therefore, the demand for wool by A. & M. Karagheusian was immense. Due to its special geographical location and excellent transportation conditions, Tianjin Port became the largest port for wool exports in the Three Northern Regions. According to customs statistics, the annual average export volume of wool from the Three Northern Regions through Tianjin was 76,907 dan from 1885 to 1894, increased to 149,998 dan from 1895 to 1904, reached 250,000 dan from 1905 to 1920, and was 256,804 dan from 1920 to 1935.[3] The establishment of the A. & M. Karagheusian factory in Tianjin was naturally for sourcing materials locally, facilitating the acquisition of the cheapest and most abundant raw materials conveniently and quickly.

However, under the system of compradors, the compradors only cared about their own commissions and were unwilling to concern themselves with the quality of the wool. Under the management of compradors, all wool transported to the seaport was either unwashed or had lost 50% to 60% of its weight after washing in Tianjin, and each batch of goods was at least adulterated with 50% inferior wool. The freight cost for transporting wool from the interior to Tianjin was 30 yuan (1 yuan equals to one Mexican dollar) per dan, which amounted to wasting 18 yuan for nothing.[4] For exported wool, if it was mixed with mud and inferior wool, it would significantly reduce the price. As raw material for carpets, it would undoubtedly increase the cost of wool processing. Moreover, the compradors often raised prices by hoarding wool. These factors were fatal for wool exporters and large carpet manufacturers like A. & M. Karagheusian. Therefore, it was impossible for A. & M. Karagheusian to form an alliance of interests with the compradors in order to obtain stable, inexpensive, and high-quality wool, while minimizing management costs and obtaining high profits in return.

As the need for foreign capitalist plunder of Chinese exports and raw

---

① Data from *The Chinese Carpet Industry* by H. Shabas.

② Same as above.

③ *Overview of the History of Tianjin Customs*, translated and edited by Tianjin Customs Translation and Editing Committee. China Customs Press, 2004, pp.104-136.

④ Translated from the letter of Russian Businessman S. Viazigin to H. Shabas in 1934.

银行与华尔街

银行保险业属于第三产业，是为商业和工业发展提供服务的。在资本主义由商品输出发展到资本输出的阶段，外资银行更是充当了列强进行经济侵略的急先锋。天津的外国银行紧随洋行而来，比邻而建，生意上相互扶持，建筑上相映生辉。近代银行业的兴起为天津迅速成为新兴的商贸和工业城市提供了强大助力，再加上20世纪初不断崛起的华商银行，它们与早期繁盛的银号业一起，构筑了天津作为中国北方工商业和金融中心的雄厚基础。

银行与赔款、外债、借款

19世纪末20世纪初，随着列强不断扩大在华势力，各国银行纷纷来津设立分行。20世纪初期，天津的中街上一座座恢宏壮观的建筑拔地而起。其中，最早的一批是英国的汇丰银行、麦加利银行，沙俄的华俄道胜银行，德国的德华银行，法国的东方汇理银行和中法实业银行，日本的横滨正金银行和朝鲜银行，比利时的华比银行，美国的花旗银行等。

这些外国银行大都为殖民地银行。所谓殖民地银行，是殖民主义时代英国、法国、比利时、葡萄牙、荷兰等老牌资本主义国家，专门为扶植殖民贸易而在其殖民地或海外设立的银行，其主要职能是办理国际贸易中商业汇票的承兑、外汇业务和提供对外贸易信贷，甚至发行铸造殖民地的当地货币、承揽政府借款等，从而达到控制海外贸易和对殖民地经济进行资本输出的目的。

各国海外银行的一般性特点，是具有程度不一的政府支持。比如麦加利银行（今为渣打银行）是1853年由维多利亚女皇特许设立的银行，主营业务是为在当时其殖民地印度、澳大利亚、中国香港、新加坡、南非等地的各种贸易提供资金帮助，后来将业务延伸至中国内地。法国东方汇理银行成立于1875年，总部位于法国巴黎，主要帮助法国政府管理在东南亚的殖民地的资产，并发行货币。1889年该行业务重心由印度支那转移至中国，此后从1900年至1941年，

materials increased, the volume of Sino-foreign trade continued to rise, and exchanges between China and foreign countries became more frequent, foreign capitalists entering the monopoly stage were no longer willing to let the compradors have a share. They demanded to do business directly with Chinese mainland merchants, thus directly occupying and monopolizing raw materials and markets. Therefore, the comprador system inevitably declined.

At the beginning of the 20th century, the system of senior executives and agents gradually replaced the original comprador system. The system of senior executives: compradors only received salaries, and commissions were canceled or partially canceled, replaced by sales commissions. The system of agents: compradors were no longer fixedly employed by a certain firm, and foreign firms concluded distribution, underwriting, and agency contracts with Chinese merchants. However, these changes mainly occurred in some Japanese, American, and German enterprises, while many old enterprises in Britain and France remained unchanged. By the time of Japan's Comprehensive Invasion of China, especially after the outbreak of the Pacific War, many European and American foreign-owned businesses closed down or had their industries confiscated, and Japanese businesses no longer employed compradors. The modern comprador system finally disappeared, and some of the original compradors transformed into genuine merchants, doing business directly on their own.

Banks and Wall Street

The banking insurance industry belongs to the tertiary sector, providing services for the development of commerce and industry. In the stage where capitalism transitions from commodity exports to capital exports, foreign banks have played a leading role in the economic aggression of the great powers. Foreign banks in Tianjin followed closely behind the foreign trading firms, neighboring each other, mutually supporting each other in business, and shining together architecturally. The rise of the modern banking industry provided strong support for Tianjin's rapid emergence as a new commercial and industrial city. Coupled with the emergence of Chinese owned banks in the early 20th century, along with the earlier flourishing Qianzhuang (local independent Chinese banks in the early modern period), they laid a solid foundation for Tianjin to become the commercial, industrial, and financial center of northern China.

Banks and Indemnities, Foreign Debts, Loans

In the late 19th and early 20th centuries, as the great powers continued to

该行代表法国政府处理庚子赔款以及法中之间的国际贸易结算和信贷。1912 年新成立的中华民国政府财政拮据，遂由东方汇理银行提出合资成立中法实业银行（后改组为中法工商银行），借此输入资本，法国亦将退还中国庚款余额用于该行运营。1889 年成立的德华银行总部设在柏林，属德国海外银行系统，是德国资本在华活动的中心机构，参与借款给中国的活动，支持铁路、码头工厂、开矿的建设，其在中国的势力不亚于英国汇丰等银行。1880 年成立的横滨正金银行亦具有半官方性质，享受日本政府的特殊优惠和保护。成立于 1895 年的华俄道胜银行，干脆就是中俄两国政府出资（法国也有出资，但支配权在俄国手中）的合资银行，甚至享有在中国北方代收关税、盐税、经营铁路建筑、发行货币等各项特权。

清朝末年，清政府连连在战争中败给列强，不得不割地赔款，导致外债激增。1895 年后，为支付甲午赔款，清政府举借了俄法借款、英德借款和英德续借款等大借款。1900 年《辛丑条约》签订后，清政府因无力偿还赔款，遂将赔款直接、间接转成外债，占这一阶段外债的三分之一以上；同时，列强为达到瓜分中国的目的，竞相向中国提供建筑铁路之类的借款，也占当时债务的三分之一。在数十家外资银行中，汇丰银行是在近代中国影响力最大的，它不仅垄断国际汇兑控制中国对外贸易，而且为中国政府募集外债，甚至自己投资和经营铁路、矿山或者各种垄断企业，早已超出了普通贸易银行的经营范围，成为英帝国主义对中国进行资本输出的急先锋。

汇丰银行于 1865 年 3 月在香港成立，开始设立的目的是为与中国进行贸易的公司提供更有效率的融资服务，其股东几乎全部为以中国为其主要基地的通商口岸各大洋行的老板。1865 年，银行开始营业，同年在上海设立分行。之后主要在广州、汉口、福州等南方口岸设立分支机构。1880 年汇丰银行准备拓展北方业务，1882 年在天津开设代办处（这也是天津首家外资银行）。它在天津的客户首先就是津海关。当时直隶总督李鸿章的同乡吴调卿被派到天津任汇丰银行天津分行的首任买办（后他担任此职 25 年）。借由同乡关系，李鸿章创办北洋水师所需的海防经费由津海关直接存入汇丰银行天津代办处，之后再从汇丰银行支取费用。同时汇丰银行还搭上了海

expand their influence in China, banks from various countries set up branches in Tianjin. In the early 20th century, magnificent buildings emerged one after another on Tianjin's Victoria Road. Among the earliest were Hongkong and Shanghai Banking Corp. (HSBC) from Britain, Chartered Bank of India, Australia & China, Russo-Asiatic Bank (Русско-Китайский банк) from Russia, Deutsch-Asiatische Bank from Germany, Banque de l'Indo-chine and Banque Industrielle de Chine from France, Yokohama Specie Bank, Ltd. and Bank of Chosen from Japan, Belgian Bank, and National City Bank of New York from the United States.

These foreign banks were mostly colonial banks. Colonial banks, in the era of colonialism, were banks established by old capitalist countries such as Britain, France, Belgium, Portugal, and the Netherlands specifically to support colonial trade in their colonies or overseas. Their main functions were to handle commercial bills of exchange, foreign exchange transactions, trade credits in international trade, and even issue local currencies in colonies, undertake government loans, etc., in order to control overseas trade and carry out capital export to colonial economies.

The general characteristics of overseas banks of various countries were that they had varying degrees of government support. For example, Chartered Bank of India, Australia & China (now Standard Chartered Bank), which was established in 1853 by Queen Victoria's charter, primarily provided financial assistance to various trades in its colonies such as India, Australia, Hong Kong, Singapore, South Africa, and later extended its operations to China's mainland. The French Banque de l'Indo-chine, established in 1875 with headquarters in Paris, primarily helped the French government manage assets in its colonies in Southeast Asia and issued currency. From 1889, the focus of its operations shifted from Indochina to China. From 1900 to 1941, the bank represented the French government in handling the Boxer Indemnity and international trade settlements and credits between France and China. In 1912 when the newly established government of the Republic of China faced financial difficulties, it proposed the establishment of Banque Industrielle de Chine (later reorganized as the Banque Franco-Chinoise pour le Commerce et l'Industrie) as a joint venture to import capital. France also used the return of Boxer Indemnity for the operation of the bank. Deutsch-Asiatische Bank, established in 1889 with headquarters in Berlin, was the center of German capital activities in China, participating in lending activities to China, supporting the construction of railways, docks, factories, and mines. Its influence in China was no less than that of British banks like HSBC. Yokohama Specie Bank, established in 1880, also had a semi-official nature and enjoyed special privileges and protection from the Japanese government. Russo-Asiatic Bank,

关总税务司英国人赫德（Robert Hart）的关系，借由他的关照游说，汇丰得到清政府的信任。1884年赫德在汇丰银行开立账户，将海关各种经营类款项都存入该账户。赫德甚至向清政府建议，汇丰银行理应成为中国的"政府银行"，由它来经理中国所有的借款事务。[①]在赫德主持海关的后期，就连解入国库的海关税收也开始部分地由海关官银号转存汇丰银行。要知道，当时海关关税占清政府财政收入的四分之一。汇丰银行在天津开业，标志其在中国所有外资银行对华进行金融侵略的竞争中力拔头筹。

此后，从1874年到1890年，清政府共借外债26笔，总额4136万两，汇丰银行一家贷了17笔，金额2897万两，占70.04%。1894年后，西方列强把借款优先权的争夺作为瓜分中国的主要手段，而汇丰银行在承贷的外国银行中独占鳌头，并在每一笔对华贷款中，附加苛刻的条件，如"英德续借款"合同中规定，中国海关总税务司职位在借款偿清前一直由英国人担任。辛亥革命之后，列强以保障债权为借口，夺取了关税支配权，中国关税归汇丰、德华、华俄道胜三家银行存储保管，但汇总和收支拨解的总枢纽为汇丰银行上海分行。1913年的"善后大借款"是以中国全部盐税收入为担保，所有盐税收入都必须解入汇丰等五家外国银行存储。至此，两大中央税收的存管权都被汇丰等外资银行攫取，汇丰银行成了事实上的中央银行。

"东方华尔街"

20世纪初，天津的中国银行也开始发展起来，而且中外银行差不多都开设在毗邻海河的中街（今名解放北路）。因为各大银行云集，这两条路今日被称为"东方华尔街"或"金融街"，直至中华人民共和国成立很长一段时间，这里都是天津的金融中心。

各外国银行除了前面所述具有代表本国经济利权的借款、赔款等特殊业务之外，主营方向还是作为各国对华贸易机构的汇兑银行，

[①] 1878年1月3日赫德致金登干第411号函件。陈霞飞主编，《中国海关密档——赫德、金登干函电汇编（1874—1907）》第二卷，中华书局，1990年，第1—2页。

established in 1895, was a joint venture bank funded by the governments of China and Russia (with French participation, but under Russian control), with various privileges such as collecting customs duties and salt taxes in northern China, operating railway construction, issuing currency, etc.

In the late Qing Dynasty, the Qing government repeatedly lost to the great powers in wars and had to cede territory and pay indemnities, leading to a sharp increase in foreign debts. After 1895, to pay the indemnities for the First Sino-Japanese War, the Qing government borrowed large loans such as the Russo-French Loan, Anglo-German Loan, and Anglo-German Extension Loan. After the signing of the *Boxer Protocol* in 1900, as the Qing government was unable to repay the indemnities, the indemnities were directly or indirectly converted into foreign debts, accounting for more than one-third of the foreign debts during this period. At the same time, in order to achieve the goal of partitioning China, the great powers competed to provide loans for building railways and other projects, also accounting for one-third of the debt at that time. Among dozens of foreign banks, HSBC had the greatest influence in modern China. It not only monopolized international exchanges to controll the China's foreign trade but also raised foreign loans for the Chinese government and even invested in and operated railways, mines, or various monopolistic enterprises, which had already exceeded the scope of ordinary trading banks and become the vanguard of British imperialism for capital export to China.

HSBC was established in Hong Kong in March 1865 with the initial purpose of providing more efficient financing services to companies trading with China. Its shareholders were almost exclusively the owners of major foreign trading firms based in China's main port cities. It began operations in 1865 and opened a branch in Shanghai the same year. Afterwards, it mainly established branches in southern ports such as Guangzhou, Hankou, and Fuzhou. In 1880, HSBC prepared to expand its business in the north, and in 1882, it opened an agency in Tianjin (also the first foreign bank in Tianjin). Its first clients in Tianjin were the Tianjin Customs. At that time, Wu Tiaoqing, a fellow townsperson of Li Hongzhang, the Viceroy of Zhili Province, was appointed as the first comprador of HSBC's Tianjin branch (he served in this position for 25 years). Leveraging their hometown relationship, Li Hongzhang arranged for the maritime defense funds needed for the Beiyang Fleet to be directly deposited into HSBC's Tianjin branch by the Tianjin Customs, and then withdrawn from HSBC. At the same time, HSBC also benefited from the relationship with Sir. Robert Hart, the British Commissioner of Customs, who persuaded the Qing government to trust HSBC. In 1884, Hart opened an account at HSBC and deposited various operational funds from the customs into the account. Hart even suggested to the Qing government that HSBC should

汇丰银行于 1865 年 3 月在香港成立。汇丰银行的发起人，都来自于当时在对华贸易中占据统治地位的英国洋行或英裔印度洋行，还有挪威、德国和美国洋行。1882 年在天津开设代办处，为天津最早、最大的外资银行。首任买办为吴调卿，为天津四大买办之首。刘悦摄于 2024 年

HSBC was founded in March 1865 in Hong Kong. Its founders came from British trading firms and British-Indian firms that dominated trade with China at the time, as well as Norwegian, German, and American trading houses. In 1882, HSBC established an agency in Tianjin, making it the earliest and largest foreign bank in the city. Its first comprador was Wu Tiaoqing, who was recognized as the foremost of Tianjin's four major compradors. Taken by Liu Yue in 2024

汇丰银行（今中国银行）内景。刘悦摄于 2024 年
Interior of HSBC (now Bank of China). Taken by Liu Yue in 2024

华俄道胜银行 1895 年成立，资本
来自法、俄、大清帝国三国，总部
在圣彼得堡。1896 年设立天津分
行。享有在华发放贷款、发行货币、
税收、经营、筑路、开矿等特权。
1917 年十月革命后，总行和 85 处
分行被苏维埃政府收归国有，即改
以巴黎分行为总行，但实力受到严
重削弱。1926 年 9 月 25 日因巴
黎总行外汇投机失败而清理停业。
刘悦摄于 2024 年

The Russo-Asiatic Bank was founded
in 1895 with capital from France,
Russia, and the Qing Empire, with
its headquarters in St. Petersburg.
In 1896, it established a branch in
Tianjin, enjoying privileges in China
such as issuing loans, currency, tax
collection, business operations, road
construction, and mining. After the
October Revolution in 1917, the bank's
headquarters and 85 branches were
nationalized by the Soviet government,
and its Paris branch was restructured
as the new headquarters. However,
its financial strength was significantly
weakened. On September 25, 1926,
the bank was liquidated and ceased
operations due to the failure of foreign
exchange speculation by the Paris
headquarters. Taken by Liu Yue in 2024

东方汇理银行于 1888 年将业务扩展到中国，1907 年在天津法租界大法国路开设天津分行。1949 年中华人民共和国成立后，上海东方汇理银行被中华人民共和国政府批准为外汇业务"指定银行"。后由于外商企业撤出上海，业务清淡，1955 年向中国政府提出申请，被批准停业清算。刘悦摄于 2024 年

Banque de l'Indochine expanded its business to China in 1888 and established its Tianjin branch on Rue de France in the French Concession in 1907. After the founding of the People's Republic of China in 1949, its Shanghai branch was designated by the Chinese government as an authorized foreign exchange bank. However, as foreign enterprises withdrew from Shanghai and business declined, the bank applied for closure in 1955 and was approved for liquidation. Taken by Liu Yue in 2024

华比银行于 1902 年成立，总部设在布鲁塞尔。华比银行的母公司是由国王利奥波德二世担任董事长的比利时通用公司。天津分行成立于 1906 年。除经营存款、汇兑等一般银行业务外，更专注于承揽大宗长期贷款。清政府历次所借由比利时承建铁路的贷款，如京汉铁路、陇海铁路，均由该行经理。1908 年华比银行在天津开始发行纸币，还于 1921 年修建了银行大楼。中华人民共和国成立后，华比银行曾被批准为经营外汇的指定银行，后于 1956 年停业清算

Sino-Belgian Bank was established in 1902, with its headquarters in Brussels. Its parent company, Société Générale de Belgique, was chaired by King Leopold II. The Tianjin branch was founded in 1906. In addition to general banking operations such as deposits and remittances, the bank specialized in handling large-scale, long-term loans. It managed loans taken by the Qing government for railway projects constructed by Belgium, including the Beijing-Hankou Railway and the Lanzhou-Lianyungang Railway. In 1908, Sino-Belgian Bank began issuing banknotes in Tianjin and constructed its bank building in 1921. After the founding of the People's Republic of China, it was initially designated as an authorized foreign exchange bank but ceased operations and was liquidated in 1956

德华银行于 1889 年在柏林成立，董事会也设在柏林，其在中国的势力不亚于英国汇丰等银行。一战结束后，1922 年德华银行曾经在天津大沽路复业，但实力已不可与以前同日而语。1936 年 7 月迁至法租界中街。1945 年由中国银行天津分行接收清算。张畅摄于 2022 年

Deutsch-Asiatische Bank was established in Berlin in 1889, with its board of directors also based in Berlin. Its influence in China was comparable to that of British banks such as HSBC. After the end of the First World War, the bank resumed operations on Taku Road in Tianjin in 1922, though its strength was no longer what it had been before. In July 1936, it relocated to Zhongjie in the French Concession. In 1945, it was taken over and liquidated by the Tianjin branch of the Bank of China. Taken by Zhang Chang in 2022

花旗银行，主要前身是1812年成立的"纽约城市银行"，总部设在华尔街，是美国第一家成立国际部的银行。1902年开始向海外扩张，同年在上海和香港开设分行（这时花旗在美国不可跨州开展业务，却跨国开设分行）。1916年在天津设立分行。张畅摄于2022年

Citibank, primarily originating from the "City Bank of New York," was established in 1812 and headquartered on Wall Street. It was the first U.S. bank to establish an international department. In 1902, Citibank began its overseas expansion, opening branches in Shanghai and Hong Kong—at a time when it was prohibited from operating across state lines within the United States but was permitted to establish international branches. In 1916, the bank further expanded by opening a branch in Tianjin. In 1916, a branch was established in Tianjin

横滨正金银行为东京银行前身，1880年成立于横滨，1899年在天津设立分行。20世纪初天津的日本洋行数达到60家、侨民人口达到近两千人，在所有外国洋行和侨民中所占比例最高，横滨正金银行的设立主要是为本国洋行和侨民提供汇兑业务。航鹰摄于2006年

Yokohama Specie Bank, the predecessor of the Bank of Tokyo, was established in Yokohama in 1880 and opened a branch in Tianjin in 1899. By the early 20th century, the number of Japanese trading firms in Tianjin had reached 60, and the Japanese expatriate population had grown to nearly 2,000, making them the largest foreign community in the city. The establishment of Yokohama Specie Bank primarily aimed to provide remittance and exchange services for Japanese trading firms and expatriates. Taken by Hang Ying in 2006

麦加利银行，为渣打银行前身，是维多利亚女皇特许设立的银行。1853年成立于伦敦，1858年在上海成立分行。早期的渣打银行在中国的银行业务主要经营外汇、兑换外国币券及旅行支票、吸收存款、活存透支、发放贷款、国内汇兑等项。1895年，渣打银行天津分行成立。刘悦摄于2024年

Chartered Bank of India, Australia & China, the predecessor of Standard Chartered Bank, was a bank chartered by Queen Victoria. It was established in London in 1853 and opened a branch in Shanghai in 1858. In its early years in China, Standard Chartered Bank primarily engaged in foreign exchange transactions, currency exchange for foreign banknotes and travelers' checks, deposit-taking, overdraft facilities, lending, and domestic remittance services. In 1895, the bank expanded its presence by establishing a branch in Tianjin. Taken by Liu Yue in 2024

中法工商银行初名中法实业银行，是20世纪上半叶的中法合资银行。前身中法实业银行是第一家中外合资银行，1913年7月开业，在法国注册，总行设在巴黎，1919年在天津开设分行，在中国经营发行纸币、借款等业务。在第一次世界大战期间，该行遭受重大损失，亏损严重，到1921年7月2日停业。1925年，中法实业银行改组为中法工商银行。中法工商银行天津分行于1925年开业，1948年歇业。刘悦摄于2024年

The Sino-French Industrial and Commercial Bank, originally named the Sino-French Industrial Bank, was a Sino-French joint venture bank in the first half of the 20th century. Its predecessor, the Sino-French Industrial Bank, was the first joint venture bank between China and a foreign country. Established in July 1913, it was registered in France with its headquarters in Paris. In 1919, the bank opened a branch in Tianjin, engaging in banknote issuance, lending, and other financial operations in China. During World War I, the bank suffered significant losses and severe financial difficulties, leading to its closure on July 2, 1921. In 1925, it was reorganized as the Sino-French Industrial and Commercial Bank. The Tianjin branch of the newly restructured bank reopened in 1925 but ceased operations in 1948. Taken by Liu Yue in 2024

become the "government bank" of China and manage all of China's borrowing affairs.[①] In the later period of Hart's tenure at the Customs, even some of the customs duties paid into the national treasury were partially transferred from the Customs official silver depository to HSBC. It's worth noting that at that time, customs duties accounted for one-quarter of the Qing government's fiscal revenue. The opening of HSBC in Tianjin marked its leading position in the financial aggression competition among all foreign banks in China.

Subsequently, from 1874 to 1890, the Qing government borrowed loans from abroad for a total of 26 times, amounting to 41.36 million taels. HSBC alone lent 17 times, amounting to 28.97 million taels, accounting for 70.04%. After 1894, Western powers made the competition for the priority of borrowing a major means of dividing China. HSBC took the lead among the foreign banks that lent to China and attached stringent conditions to each loan to China. For example, in the "Anglo-German Extension Loan" contract, it was stipulated that the position of Commissioner of Customs in China would be held by a British national until the loan was repaid. After the 1911 Revolution, the great powers seized control of the customs under the pretext of protecting their loan rights. The Chinese customs duties were stored and managed by HSBC, Deutsch-Asiatische Bank, and Russo-Asiatic Bank, but the total collection and disbursement hub was the Shanghai branch of HSBC. The "Reorganization Loan" of 1913 was secured by all of China's salt tax revenues, which had to be deposited into five foreign banks including HSBC. At this point, the custody of the two major central tax revenues was taken over by foreign banks such as HSBC, making HSBC the de facto central bank.

"Oriental Wall Street"

In the early 20th century, Chinese banks in Tianjin also began to develop, and both Chinese and foreign banks were almost all located on Victoria Road (now called Jiefang North Road) adjacent to the Hai River. Because major banks were concentrated here, these two streets are now known as "Oriental Wall Street" or "Financial Street." For a long time after the founding of the People's Republic of China, this area remained the financial center of Tianjin.

Apart from the special operations representing the economic interests of their respective countries such as loans and indemnities as mentioned earlier, foreign banks mainly functioned as exchange banks for trade with China, en-

东方华尔街
Oriental Wall Street

① The No.411 letter of Robert Hart to James Duncan Campbell on January 3, 1878. Chen Xiafei (ed.). *Chinese Customs Confidential Files - Compilation of Letters and Telegrams by Robert Hart and James Duncan Campbell (1874-1907)*. Vol.2. Zhong Hua Book Company, 1995, pp.1-2.

经营汇兑业务。为此，它们在世界各地主要商贸城市和港口都设有分行、代理机构或交易所，成为本国对外贸易的有力帮手。同时，在各通商口岸，为了服务本国侨民，它们也兼营普通银行业务，如储蓄、贷款、贴现、金银买卖等。而早期的中国银行，大都脱胎于传统的银号，沿袭传统方法经营，且均为官办、半官半民或官吏们合资而办，虽然能得到官方保护，但保密性不够。而外国银行是不允许中国政府查账的，这样存在外国银行的存款就能被隐蔽起来，不被当权者没收。因此自民国初年以来，特别是北洋军阀混战最激烈的时候，为了躲避战乱，迁居到天津租界居住的清朝遗老遗少、北洋军阀、政客们都喜欢把大笔现钞存在外国银行，因此这个时代也是租界最繁荣的时代。外国银行同其本国的洋行紧密相联，它们彼此互为股东、交换董事，例如汇丰银行和怡和洋行等老牌英国洋行血肉相连，因此那些存入外国银行的钱款又被放贷给其洋行，更是支持了外国工商业者在天津的商业发展。

外国银行通过本行的买办，与中国人打交道，从中国封建地主、军阀、官僚、政客们身上吸收了巨额资金。银行为了揽储，纷纷在中街上建起壮观的银行建筑。各大银行之所以集中在一起，不光是为了彼此在业务联系和资金上的互通有无，也是因为要"同台竞技"！前文所述，各国银行都有程度不同的政府背景，因此在这里的银行不仅代表了各自背后的财团实力，也是各国在华利益的事实上的代表。中街上的银行建筑，外形宏大雄伟，内部富丽堂皇，建筑质量非常高，在近代天津城市的公共建筑中十分突出。这当中既有国家之间的国力竞争，也有银行之间资本雄厚与否的财力竞争。总之，就是要让已有的和潜在的客户觉得这家银行实力非凡，从而放心地把钱交给自己打理。一直保留到现在的这些银行建筑，实际上大都建于20世纪20年代近代天津经济最为繁荣的时期。对比上海外滩的恢宏建筑，后者虽体量更大，但一般建于20世纪30年代，比天津晚了近10年。由此可见，当时各大银行天津分行和上海分行的资金状况和来源的差异。

为了保证建筑质量，这些银行进行项目建设时，对各大建筑设计所和承建商广发"英雄帖"进行招标，重金礼聘中标者，然后大

gaging in exchange operations. To this end, they established branches, agencies, or exchanges in major commercial cities and ports around the world, becoming powerful assistants to their countries' foreign trade. Meanwhile, at various treaty ports, to serve their nationals, they also conducted ordinary banking business such as savings, loans, discounting, and buying and selling of gold and silver. Early Chinese banks mostly evolved from traditional money shops, operating in traditional ways, and were state-run, semi-state-run, or run jointly by officials and civilians. Although they enjoyed official protection, their confidentiality was insufficient. Foreign banks, on the other hand, were not subject to Chinese government audits, so deposits in foreign banks could be concealed and not confiscated by the authorities. Since the early years of the Republic of China, especially during the most intense periods of warlords era, to avoid turmoil, Qing dynasty remnants, warlords, and politicians who moved to live in the Tianjin Concessions preferred to keep large sums of cash in foreign banks. Therefore, this era was also the most prosperous time for the concessions. Foreign banks were closely linked to their home country's trading companies, with mutual shareholding and exchange of directors. For example, HSBC and Jardine, Matheson & Co., Ltd., among other well-established British trading companies, were closely connected. Therefore, the money deposited in foreign banks was lent to their trading companies, further supporting the commercial development of foreign businessmen in Tianjin.

Foreign banks, through their compradors, dealt with Chinese feudal landlords, warlords, bureaucrats, and politicians, absorbing huge sums of money from them. In order to attract deposits, banks erected magnificent bank buildings on Victoria Road. The concentration of major banks here was not only for business contacts and financial transactions among themselves but also for "competitive display"! As mentioned earlier, foreign banks all had varying degrees of government backing, so the banks here not only represented the financial strength behind them but also represented the interests of various countries in China. The bank buildings on Victoria Road were grand and magnificent in appearance, splendid and luxurious inside, and of very high architectural quality, standing out among the modern public buildings in Tianjin. Among them, there were both competition between nations and competition between banks in terms of financial strength. In short, the goal was to make existing and potential customers feel that the bank was exceptionally strong, so they could confidently entrust their money to it. Most of these bank buildings that have been preserved to this day were actually built during the heyday of Tianjin's modern economy in the 1920s. Compared to the grand buildings on the Bund in Shanghai, the latter, although larger in scale, were generally built in the 1930s, nearly 10 years later than those in Tianjin. This

量进口贵重的建筑石材和其他高级装修材料。因此银行的建筑设计经典、建筑质量很高，历经百年风雨，无论是洪灾地震，还是战争洗礼，屹立至今。在建筑风格的选择上，银行不仅要炫耀财富，还要体现出稳健可靠的经营手段，所以倾向于比较传统保守的风格。表现出来就是：外立面装饰性的古希腊古罗马各种样式的柱子、拱门和穹顶，内部装饰则金碧辉煌，大理石或黑白相间的马赛克地面，高大的穹顶下是五彩缤纷的彩色玻璃和低调奢华的吊灯。这些繁复、奢华的形式，目的无他，就是为了显示它们的财富和权力之巨大。

银行聚集的金融街上，其实不止有壮观恢宏的中外银行，还有洋行、领事馆、工部局、公议局、俱乐部等风格不一、各具形态的商业、公共建筑，因此这条中文名为"中街"①的街道是英法两国租界的核心区域，不仅是经济中心，也是政治中心。英、法两国租界在天津划定最早、建设最好、人口众多，临近街区既有外国侨民居住，也迁入了许多非富即贵的中国居民。这条街的繁荣，反映出天津作为工商业和港口城市财富、人口和经济实力的集中，也反映出天津作为中国北方经济和政治中心的特定地位随着这条街的建设完成而形成。

indicates the differences in the financial conditions and sources between the Tianjin branches and the Shanghai branches of major banks at that time.

To ensure the quality of construction, these banks, during project development, widely issued invitations for bids to major architectural design firms and contractors, offering substantial rewards to the winning bidders, and then imported a large quantity of expensive building stones and other high-quality decoration materials. Therefore, the architectural designs of the banks are classic, with high-quality construction. They have stood the test of time for centuries, enduring floods, earthquakes, and the ravages of war, standing tall to this day. In the selection of architectural styles, banks not only aim to flaunt wealth but also to reflect reliable and prudent business practices, thus tending toward more traditional and conservative styles. This is manifested in decorative elements such as ornamental columns, arches, and domes in various styles of ancient Greek and Roman architecture on the facade, while the interior decorations are magnificent, featuring marble or black-and-white mosaic floors, colorful stained glass and understated luxurious chandeliers beneath tall domes. These elaborate and luxurious forms serve no other purpose than to showcase the immense wealth and power they possess.

On the Financial Street where banks are clustered, there are not only magnificent Chinese and foreign banks but also various styles of public buildings such as foreign firms, consulates, municipal councils, clubs, etc. Therefore, this street, named "Zhongjie"① in Chinese, is the core area of the British and French concessions, serving not only as an economic center but also a political one. The British and French concessions in Tianjin were the earliest demarcated, best constructed, and most populous. The adjacent neighborhoods were inhabited by both foreign expatriates and many affluent Chinese residents. The prosperity of this street reflects Tianjin's concentration of wealth, population, and economic strength as an industrial and port city. It also reflects Tianjin's specific status as the economic and political center of northern China, which emerged with the completion of this street's construction.

---

① 中街在英租界段名为维多利亚路，法租界段名为大法国路。后德租界划定之后，修筑威廉路（一战后改称威尔逊路）与中街相接。中华人民共和国成立后，中街改名为解放北路，威廉路改名为解放南路。

① Zhongjie was known as Victoria Road in the British Concession, Rue de France in the French Concession. After the delineation of the German Concession, Kaiser Wilhelmstrasse (renamed Woodrow Wilson Street after the First World War) was built to connect with Zhongjie. After the founding of the People's Republic of China, Zhongjie was renamed Jiefang North Road and Kaiser Wilhelmstrasse was renamed Jiefang South Road.

第 四 章　技术革新与城市的变革

Chapter Four: Technological Innovation and Urban Transformation

洋务运动是一项系统工程	The Westernization Movement is a Systematic Project
培育人才与设立学堂	Cultivating Talents and Establishing Schools
实业家与民族工业	Industrialists and National Industry

洋务运动是一项系统工程

近代城市发展处于一个产生了大量技术进步的时代，这些技术进步是财富积累和社会开放的结果。技术方面的爆炸性发展，不仅推动了城市工商业的发展，也引发了城市自身组织结构的演进。

北方的洋务中心

鸦片战争结束了中国"与世隔绝"的状态，中国同西方的接触日益频繁。一部分先进的中国知识分子开始睁开眼睛看世界。林则徐、魏源提出了向西方学习、"师夷长技以制夷"的观点。第二次鸦片战争后，先后增开了11个通商口岸，帝国主义势力由此开始深入中国内陆。面对此"数千年来未有之变局"，如何抵御那些"数千年来未有之强敌"？清朝统治阶层打出了"自强"的旗帜，着手办理各项所谓洋务，自此开始了中国第一次对内改革、对外开放、引进西方先进科学技术的现代化尝试。在这场改革中，居于领导地位的，在中央是负责一切对外事务的"总理各国事务衙门"，在地方则是一批思想较为开放的实权派督抚大臣，其中李鸿章办理"洋务"数量最多、时间最长。而天津作为其驻在地，成为洋务运动的策源地。

1870年李鸿章来津，任直隶总督兼北洋通商大臣，并被授予钦差大臣关防。凡是华北地区范围内的洋务、海防、海关，涉及全国范围的给外国人颁发内地通行护照外交以及轮船招商局和各煤铁矿招商局、铺设电报等事务均归北洋大臣全权负责管理。这样，李鸿章一身兼二任，避免了职权分散和互相掣肘的情况。而直隶总督府

The Westernization Movement is a Systematic Project

Modern urban development is in an era of significant technological advancement, which is the result of wealth accumulation and social openness. The explosive development in technology not only drives the development of urban industry and commerce but also triggers the evolution of urban organizational structures.

The Center of the Westernization Movement in the North

The Opium War ended China's "isolation" from the world, leading to increasingly frequent contacts with the West. Some progressive Chinese intellectuals began to open their eyes to the world. Lin Zexu and Wei Yuan put forward the viewpoint of learning from the West and "to use western science and technology to counter imperialist encroachment." After the Second Opium War, eleven new treaty ports were opened successively, and imperialist influences began to penetrate inland China. Faced with this "unprecedented change" and how to resist those "unprecedented powerful enemies" for thousands of years, the ruling class of the Qing Dynasty raised the banner of "self-strengthening" and began to carry out various so-called "Westernization" efforts. Thus began China's first attempt at internal reform, external opening, and the introduction of advanced Western science and technology in modern times. In this reform, the leading position was held by the "Office for the General Management of Affairs Concerning the Various Countries (Ministry of Foreign Affairs)," responsible for all foreign affairs at the central level, and by a group of relatively open-minded powerful governors in the regions, among whom Li Hongzhang handled the most and for the longest time in "Westernization." Tianjin, as his seat, became the birthplace of the Westernization Movement.

In 1870, Li Hongzhang arrived in Tianjin and was appointed as the Viceroy of Zhili Province and concurrently as the Minister of Beiyang,

北洋机器局西局
Tianjin Arsenal West Bureau

直隶总督衙门。图片来源：比利时根特大学档案馆
Viceroy's Office of Zhili Province. Source: Archives of Ghent University, Belgium

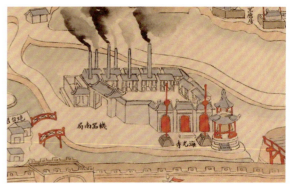

《天津城厢保甲全图》中的北洋机器局（西局，又称"南局"）
Tianjin Arsenal West Bureau (or South Bureau) in *Complete Map of the Community Self-defense System of the Walled City of Tianjin and Its Environs*

所在的天津，自然成为北方的洋务中心。

洋务运动由军工业开始，然后逐渐扩展到民用工业。之所以遵循这样的发展次序，是由于李鸿章以镇压太平天国运动起家，培养了一支富有战斗力并且效忠于他本人的武装力量——淮军。在与外国雇佣军并肩作战对付太平军的过程中，李鸿章见识了西方洋枪洋炮和军舰的厉害。此后，在洋务运动中，为了武装自己的军队、扩充个人实力，李鸿章开始大力发展近代军工企业，并大量向国外购买军火，用国外的先进军事技术武装淮军，使其成为清朝战斗力最强、装备最好、最精锐的一支武装力量，后来更一手创建了在当时世界海军中吨位排名第四的北洋水师。

1870 年，李鸿章抵津后，即继续他在南方业已展开的洋务活动。先是接办天津（北洋）机器局（分为东局和西局），经过先后 5 次扩充，使其成为包括机器制造、基本化学、金属冶炼、铸造、热加工、船舶修造等门类齐全、产量巨大的北方规模最大的工业企业（当然，此时北方其他地区的工业基础基本为零）。机器东局的火药年产量达 100 万磅，西局制造子弹年产 400 万颗。据外国记者报道，东局火药厂是"以最新式的机器制造最新式的火药"，"将成为世界上最大最好的火药厂"[①]。除生产军火之外，天津机器局还具备一定的

① 《北华捷报》1887 年 10 月 27 日。

and was granted the title of Imperial Commissioner in charge of military defense. All matters related to foreign affairs, coastal defense, customs within the jurisdiction of North China, issuing internal passports to foreigners nationwide, consular affairs, the China Merchants Steamship Company, various coal and iron mines commercial bureaus, telegraph construction, etc., fell under the full authority of the Minister of Beiyang. In this way, Li Hongzhang held dual positions, avoiding the situation of dispersed powers and mutual constraints. Tianjin, where the Viceroy's office of Zhili Province was located, naturally became the center of the Westernization Movement in the north.

The Westernization Movement began with military industry and gradually expanded to civilian industry. The reason for following this sequence of development is due to Li Hongzhang's background in suppressing the Taiping Rebellion, where he cultivated a highly combat-effective and loyal armed force under his command, known as the Huai Army. Through fighting alongside foreign mercenaries against the Taiping forces, Li Hongzhang witnessed the effectiveness of Western firearms, cannons, and warships. Subsequently, in the Westernization Movement, to arm his own army and enhance his personal power, Li Hongzhang began vigorously developing modern military industries and extensively purchasing weapons from abroad. He armed the Huai Army with advanced foreign military technology, making it the strongest, best-equipped, and most elite armed force of the Qing Dynasty. Later, he also played a pivotal role in establishing the Beiyang Fleet, which ranked fourth in terms of tonnage in the world's navies at that time.

In 1870, after Li Hongzhang arrived in Tianjin, he continued his

研发能力。如，它曾试制一艘机械挖泥船，还曾制造出一艘可以在水底行驶的"水底机船"，这是有史可考的我国自行制造的第一艘潜水艇。[1]

1875 年清政府命令李鸿章督办北洋海防，开始筹建北洋海军。天津海防有水无师。当第二次鸦片战争中"威里士厘"号停泊在大沽口外的拦江沙水域时，天津守军却无法派战舰出海迎敌。1879 年李鸿章在天津设立海军营务处，负责主持筹建海军事宜。至 1880 年北洋海军已初具规模，拥有从英国、德国购买的各类舰船 25 艘，并雇用英国和德国的军官来训练海军。为了使日益庞大的北洋海军的舰船能够就近修理，1880 年李鸿章于大沽海口选购民地 110 亩，建起一座船坞，命名为"北洋水师大沽船坞"，也称海神庙船坞。它是我国北方最早的船舶修造厂和重要的军火基地。因李鸿章坐镇天津，北洋海军的指挥总部及各附属机构均设在天津，如海军营务处（相当于后来的海军总参谋部和总后勤部）、海防支应局、海军储药施医总医院等。

在兴办军事工业的过程中，李鸿章及其身边洋务派官僚开始认识到洋务事业是一项系统工程，打一场现代化战争不仅需要军工，而且需要采矿、冶炼、铁路、航运、电讯等多方面的配合。这些若没有相当的财富基础不可能实现，仅仅依靠农耕文明的税收远远无法满足需要。欧美国家的工业革命更让洋务派认识到举办实业以"求富"的重要性。所以，洋务运动从 19 世纪 70 年代开始转向民用工业，着手兴办各项企业，天津从此在近代成为一座得风气之先、引领现代文明潮流的城市。

---

[1] 《益文录》1880 年 6 月 20 日记载了试制过程："现于津厂后面缭以周垣，开工设造，雇用工匠十余人""均设严禁，不准窥视"。同年《益文录》10 月 30 日记载了演示情况："兹已造成，盖驶行水底机船也。式如橄榄，入水半游水面，上有水标及吸气机，可于水底暗送水雷，置于敌船之下，其水标缩水一尺，船即入水一尺。中秋节下水试行，灵捷异常，颇为合用。因为河水不甚深，水标仍浮出水面尺许，若涉大洋，能令水面一无所见，而布置无不如志，洵摧敌之利器也。"海军司令部《近代中国海军》编辑部编著的《近代中国海军》（海潮出版社 1994 年出版）一书认定为中国最早研制的潜水艇。

Westernization activities, which had already begun in the south. First, he took over the Tianjin (Beiyang) Arsenal Bureau (divided into East and West bureaus), which, after five expansions, became the largest industrial enterprise in the north, including a complete range of categories such as machinery manufacturing, basic chemistry, metallurgy, casting, heat treatment, and shipbuilding, with huge output (of course, at this time, the industrial base in other parts of the north was basically non-existent). The annual production of gunpowder at the East Bureau reached one million pounds, while the West Bureau produced four million bullets per year. According to foreign journalists, the gunpowder factory at the East Bureau was "manufacturing the latest gunpowder with the latest machinery" and "would become the largest and best gunpowder factory in the world."[1] In addition to producing munitions, the Tianjin Arsenal Bureau also had certain research and development capabilities. For example, it once attempted to manufacture a mechanical dredger and also produced a "submarine boat" capable of traveling underwater, which is the first recorded domestically made submarine in China.[2]

In 1875, the Qing government ordered Li Hongzhang to supervise the defense of the Beiyang and began to establish the Beiyang Fleet. The defense of Tianjin was guarded by water but not by troops. When the HMS Wellesley was anchored in the shallow waters outside Taku Forts during the Second Opium War, the Tianjin garrison could not send warships to sea to meet the enemy. In 1879, Li Hongzhang established the Naval Administrative Office in Tianjin, responsible for overseeing the construction of the navy. By 1880, the Beiyang Fleet had begun to take shape, with 25 ships of various types

---

[1] *North-China Herald* on October 27, 1887.

[2] The *Yi Wen Lu* recorded the experimental manufacturing process on June 20, 1880, stating: "A perimeter wall has been erected at the rear of the Tianjin Arsenal, where work has commenced. More than ten craftsmen have been employed." It also noted strict security measures: "All access is strictly prohibited, and no one is allowed to observe." Later, on October 30, 1880, *Yi Wen Lu* documented the demonstration: "The vessel has now been completed; it is essentially a submersible watercraft. Shaped like an olive, it partially floats on the water's surface. It is equipped with a water marker and an air intake mechanism, allowing it to secretly deploy underwater mines beneath enemy ships. The marker submerges in direct proportion to the vessel's descent—if the marker sinks one foot, the vessel descends by the same amount. It was tested in the water during the Mid-Autumn Festival, exhibiting remarkable agility and practical effectiveness. Since the river was not very deep, the marker remained about a foot above the surface. However, in the open sea, it could become completely invisible while functioning precisely as intended. It is truly a formidable weapon against the enemy." The book *Modern Chinese Navy*, published by Haichao Press in 1994 and compiled by the PLA Naval Command Headquarters *Modern Chinese Navy* Editorial Department, identifies this as the earliest known attempt at developing a submarine in China.

明信片上的北洋机器局（东局）
Tianjin Arsenal East Bureau on the postcard

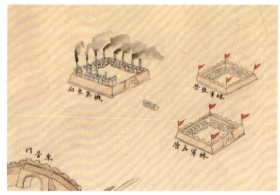
《天津城厢保甲全图》中的北洋机器东局
Tianjin Arsenal East Bureau in *Complete Map of the Community Self-defense System of the Walled City of Tianjin and Its Environs*

1880 年建成的北洋水师大沽造船厂。图片来源：北京故宫博物院
Taku shipyard of Beiyang Fleet built in 1880. Source: The Palace Museum in Beijing

邮政、电报和电话

　　蒸汽机、煤、铁和钢是促成工业革命技术加速发展的四项主要因素，洋务派发展工业亦从引入铁路和开发矿山开始，这在前面一章中的"中国第一条铁路与开平煤矿"已经提及。与技术创新、市场拓展相辅相成密不可分的，还有通信技术的不断发展。在现代信息技术发展成熟之前，邮政在近代工商业发展中占有极其重要的地位，信息畅通才能使物流畅通，全球化市场因而形成。

　　中国自古即有驿站，负责传递官方文书，但并不用于民间信件传递。明朝随着商业发展，才有了专门为商民寄递信件的民办信局，然而并不能完全满足人们需要。近代中国被迫开放通商口岸后，外国侨民大批涌入，他们之间以及他们同各自国家的通信联络，既不能通过中国官方的驿站也不能通过民间的信局，于是纷纷自行设立邮政机关，各自为政，这无疑侵犯了中国的主权。1867 年开始，海关内部设海关书信馆，通过外国邮轮和轮船招商局寄递各处通商口岸海关之间以及使馆的往来邮件，逐渐形成海关内部的邮政体系和章程制度。1878 年在总理衙门和李鸿章的支持下，决定先以天津为中心在北京、天津、烟台、牛庄（今营口）、上海五处海关试办邮

purchased from Britain and Germany, and British and German officers hired to train the navy. In order for the increasingly large Beiyang Fleet's ships to be repaired nearby, Li Hongzhang purchased 110 mu (1 mu equals 666.67 square meters) of land at Taku in 1880 and built a dock, named the "Taku Shipyard of Beiyang Fleet," also known as the Temple of Sea Goddess Shipyard. It was the earliest shipyard and important military base in northern China. As Li Hongzhang was stationed in Tianjin, the headquarters of the Beiyang Fleet and its affiliated institutions were all located in Tianjin, such as the Naval Administration Office (equivalent to the later Naval General Staff Headquarters and General Logistics Department), the Coastal Defense Supply Bureau, and the Naval General Hospital.

In the process of developing military industry, Li Hongzhang and the Westernization bureaucrats around him began to realize that the Westernization cause was a systematic project. To fight a modern war, cooperation in mining, smelting, railways, shipping, telecommunications, and other areas was needed, which could not be achieved without a considerable financial foundation. Relying solely on tax revenue from agricultural civilization was far from enough to meet the needs. The Industrial Revolution in Europe and America further made the Westernization bureaucrats realize the importance of conducting industry to "seek wealth." Therefore, starting from the 1870s, the Westernization Movement shifted towards civilian industries and began to establish various enterprises. Tianjin thus became a city that led the trend of modern civilization in modern times.

大龙邮票。该套邮票有一分银、三分银、五分银三种面值，由上海海关造册处设计和印制，于1878年7月在天津正式发行。邮票是由一个国家或地区的邮政机关发行，作为交寄邮件的缴费标志。它也是一个国家或地区主权的象征，因此中国印制发行邮票意义重大

The Large Dragon Stamps were issued in three denominations: 1 Candareen, 3 Candareens, and 5 Candareens. Designed and printed by the Shanghai Customs Statistical Department, they were officially released in Tianjin in July 1878. Postage stamps, issued by a nation's or region's postal authority, serve as proof of postage payment. They also symbolize national or regional sovereignty, making the issuance of China's first postage stamps a momentous event in the country's history

政。天津的海关书信馆率先对中外公众开放。为解决邮资付费问题，津海关还发行了中国第一套邮票——大龙邮票。

海关书信馆于1878年3月23日对公众开放，收寄一般民众邮件，不论中文或外文，一律照收。海关书信馆设在英租界，起初主要仍为外侨所使用，中国人还不习惯，"民间用之者尚鲜"。后通过大昌洋行在北京、牛庄、天津、烟台和上海开办邮务代理机构，命名为华洋书信馆，收到的邮件由海关连同海关邮件通过轮船或信差免费运送。

在李鸿章的支持下，华洋书信馆的信件委托轮船招商局和太古轮船公司的船只免费代运，甚至北洋水师各军舰亦协助在天津和牛庄之间托带邮件。陆上邮路则有三条：一条是京津陆上邮路，每日由天津和北京发送邮件各一次；北方冬季封冻期间，则开辟了天津—山海关—牛庄和牛庄—小平岛—烟台两条陆上邮路，以便往来于天津和上海之间的信差交换邮件。

在海关书信馆对公众开放一年零三个月后，海关邮政初见成效。仅津海关书信馆即收到来自北京、牛庄、烟台、上海和镇江的邮件

Post, Telegraph, and Telephone

Steam engines, coal, iron, and steel were the four main factors that accelerated technological development during the Industrial Revolution. The industrial development under the Westernization Movement also began with the introduction of railways and the development of mines, as mentioned in the previous chapter "China's First Railway and the Kaiping Coal Mine." Inseparable from technological innovation and market expansion is the continuous development of communication technology. Before the maturity of modern information technology, postal services played an extremely important role in the development of modern industry and commerce. Smooth communication is essential for smooth logistics, thus leading to the formation of a globalized market.

China has had postal stations since ancient times, responsible for transmitting official documents, but they were not used for delivering private correspondence. It wasn't until the Ming Dynasty, with the development of commerce, that privately operated post offices dedicated to delivering letters for merchants and civilians emerged. However, they couldn't fully meet people's needs. After China was forced to open its ports to foreign trade in modern times, a large number of foreign immigrants poured in. They needed to communicate with each other and with their respective countries, but they couldn't rely on China's official postal stations or private post offices. Consequently, they began establishing their own postal agencies, each acting independently, which undoubtedly infringed on China's sovereignty. Starting from 1867, within the customs, the Customs Postal Office was established to handle the exchange of mail between the customs and embassies of various commercial ports through foreign mail steamers and the China Merchants Steamship Company, gradually forming an internal postal system and regulatory framework within the customs. With the support of the Ministry of Foreign Affairs and Li Hongzhang in 1878, it was decided to first establish postal services in Beijing, Tianjin, Yantai, Niuzhuang (present-day Yingkou), and Shanghai, centered in Tianjin. The Customs Postal Office in Tianjin was the first to be opened to the public, and to address the issue of postage payment, Tianjin Customs issued China's first set of stamps—the Large Dragon Postage stamps.

The Customs Postal Office opened to the public on March 23, 1878, accepting and sending ordinary mail from both Chinese and foreign sources without discrimination. Located in the British concession, the Customs Postal Office was initially mainly used by foreigners, as Chinese people were not yet accustomed to it, and "few in the private sector used it." Later, through

海关书信馆，后改为中国大清邮政总局。图片来源：比利时外交部档案馆
The Customs Postal Service was later reorganized into The Great Qing Imperial Post Office. Source: Archives of the Belgian Ministry of Foreign Affairs

共 1028 袋（每袋约重 3 市斤），发寄以上各地邮件共 1396 袋。津海关售出邮票 418.39 两（关平银），各地总共售出邮票 1986.67 两。[1]试办期间没有发生过任何丢失邮件的事故。海关书信馆对公众开放一年零九个月之后，因津海关的出色表现，总税务司将负责邮政推广的总办事处暂设在天津，还要求各关对于邮递业务要尽力予以推广。之后 1879 年，又有新建的四条陆上邮路在冬季开放：天津—北京线、天津—牛庄线、天津—镇江线和齐河—烟台线。到 20 世纪初，中国邮政体系已基本建立起来。

中国近代邮政事业的创办符合时代发展的需要。它不仅方便了

the establishment of postal agencies by the Nile, Rheims & Co. in Beijing, Niuzhuang, Tianjin, Yantai, and Shanghai, collectively named as the Sino-Foreign Postal Office, the received mail was transported free of charge by the Customs along with Customs mail via ships or messengers.

With the support of Li Hongzhang, the Sino-Foreign Postal Office entrusted the ships of the China Merchants Steamship Company and the China Navigation Co., Ltd. to transport mail free of charge, and even the various warships of the Beiyang Fleet assisted in carrying mail between Tianjin and Niuzhuang. There were three overland postal routes: one was the Beijing-Tianjin overland postal route, with mail sent from Tianjin and Beijing once daily; during the winter freeze in the north, two overland postal routes were opened: Tianjin-Shanhaiguan-Niuzhuang and Niuzhuang-Xiaopingdao-Yantai, facilitating the exchange of mail between Tianjin and Shanghai via messengers.

After one year and three months of opening to the public, the Customs Postal Office began to show results. The Tianjin Customs Postal Office alone received a total of 1,028 bags of mail (each bag weighing about 3 jin) from Beijing, Niuzhuang, Yantai, Shanghai, and Zhenjiang, and sent a total of 1,396 bags of mail to these places. The Tianjin Customs sold postal stamps worth 418.39 taels (customs silver), while a total of 1,986.67 taels were sold across various locations.[1] During the trial period, there were no incidents of lost mail. After one year and nine months of opening to the public, due to the excellent performance of Tianjin Customs, the General Customs Office responsible for postal promotion was temporarily stationed in Tianjin by the Chief Customs Commissioner, who also required all customs offices to make efforts to promote postal services. In 1879, four new overland postal routes were opened in winter: Tianjin-Beijing, Tianjin-Niuzhuang, Tianjin-Zhenjiang, and Qihe-Yantai. By the early 20th century, the postal system in China was essentially established.

The establishment of modern postal services in China was in line with the needs of the times. It not only facilitated domestic communication within China but also enhanced China's exchange of information with the world, marking another significant step towards modernization by adopting advanced Western systems. Moreover, after the establishment and expansion of the Chinese postal service, similar to the customs, it became an important source of revenue for the Qing government. However, it cannot be denied that with the development of the postal service, foreign powers further infiltrated

① 中国近代经济史资料丛刊编辑委员会主编，《中国海关与邮政》，中华书局，1983 年，第 10—15 页。

① Editorial Committee of the Series of Modern Chinese Economic Historical Data (ed.). *China Customs and Postal Service*. Zhonghua Book Company, 1983, pp.10-15.

中国国内的通信往来，而且增强了中国与世界的信息往来，是中国引进西方先进制度走向现代化的又一项重大进步。而且，中国邮政创办并发展壮大后，同海关一样，成为清政府财政收入的一项重要来源。然而，不可回避的是，随着邮政事业的发展，外国势力进一步渗透进而控制了清政府的财政。而且，在创办海关邮政的过程中，外国人控制下的海关一方面极力打压中国的民办信局、争夺它们的业务，另一方面却努力与外国的客局进行密切合作，这充分暴露了海关作为外国势力在华代言人的本来面目。

除了邮政之外，随着电力的应用，电报电话也开始在中国得到应用。1839 年首条真正投入营运的电报线路出现在英国。1866 年跨大西洋电缆铺设成功，几年后海底电缆通到香港和日本。李鸿章等洋务派官员深知通信对于商务发展和国防安全的重要性。特别是当他升任直隶总督兼北洋大臣、移驻天津后，日常需要处理大量军事、外交等事务，书信往来频繁，而驿递迟缓，容易贻误时机。李鸿章筹办北洋水师时，早期曾通过赫德等人购买英国船舰，其间也必得通过德璀琳和赫德向欧洲发电报联系，甚至与清政府驻外使节进行通讯往来时，也须经海关的转达，几乎毫无国家机密可言。因此，

用电话谈生意的外国商人。摄于 20 世纪初
Foreign merchant used telephone as a communication tool for business. Taken in the early 20th century

and controlled the finances of the Qing government. Additionally, in the process of establishing the customs postal service, foreign-controlled customs offices vigorously suppressed Chinese private postal agencies, competing for their business, while also actively cooperating with foreign agencies. This fully exposed the true nature of the customs as spokespersons for foreign interests in China.

In addition to postal services, with the application of electricity, telegraph and telephone began to be used in China. The first operational telegraph line appeared in Britain in 1839. In 1866, the transatlantic cable was successfully laid, and a few years later, submarine cables reached Hong Kong and Japan. Li Hongzhang and other members of the Westernization Movement were well aware of the importance of communication for both commercial development and national defense. Particularly, when Li Hongzhang was appointed as the Viceroy of Zhili Province and the Minister of Beiyang, and moved to Tianjin, he had to handle a large number of military, diplomatic, and other affairs on a daily basis, with frequent correspondence. However, the postal service was slow, leading to delays and missed opportunities. During the establishment of the Beiyang Fleet, Li Hongzhang initially purchased British ships through intermediaries like Robert Hart, and had to communicate with Europe through intermediaries like Gustav Detring and Robert Hart, and even when communicating with Qing government officials stationed abroad, the messages had to be relayed

总督衙门门口的电话线。摄于 20 世纪初
The telephone line at the entrance of the Viceroy's Office. Taken in the early 20th century

李鸿章深刻认识到建设中国自己的电报线路的必要性。1877年，他尝试在自己的总督衙门至天津机器局之间架设电报线，并收发电报成功。1879年这条电报线延伸至大沽炮台和北塘兵营，成为中国第一条军用电报线。1880年，清政府终于批准上海、镇江、南京与天津之间架设电报线，并同意海底电缆在上海登陆。李鸿章在天津成立中国电报总局，派盛宣怀为总办，指挥全国各地架设电报线的工作。由天津到上海的电报线路，于1881年12月24日建成开通并正式对外营业，此为中国民用电报通讯之肇始。至1895年，十数年间，中国境内业已建立起四通八达的电报网。

电报事业开创后，电话的发展就顺理成章了。电话传入中国时，被称作"德律风"，是英文名"telephone"的译音。如电报的创设一样，李鸿章先是在自己的行辖做试验。1884年，李鸿章在天津总督衙门架设了至津海关、北塘、大沽以及保定等处的电话线。这是近代中国人自行架设的最早的长途电话线。据当时的报纸报道说："德律风（即电话）之设，虽数百里不殊面谈。事为李傅相闻知，亦饬匠竖杆设线，就督辕接至津海新关等处，文报传递，诸形便捷。"① 为了使电话能为天津的贸易发展服务，主办此事的电报局将电话线接到天津各个洋行。除电话设备由这些洋行自行购备之外，它们还将每年支付一定费用，这样一来，电报局每年也有一笔可观的收入。

很多保守的中国人本来很讨厌在他们的田地里架设电线，他们认为架设电线会损坏土地的元气，而落在坟地的电线杆的影子会玷污祖先之灵。义和团运动期间，电报电话线路与铁路轨道被团民全部破坏，很大程度上阻碍了八国联军的侵犯行动。义和团运动之后，少了很多掣肘的时任直隶总督兼电政大臣袁世凯，立即下令架设天津至北京的长途电话线，翌年竣工，天津电话局亦正式成立，从电报局中分离出来，这是中国自办长途电话之开端。不久，连接北京与天津的两条复线式长途电话线也架设成功。由于业务发展顺利，天津电话局还从外国人手中收回了电话业务，此后，电话业务的主权一直掌握在自己手中。

---

① 王述祖、航鹰编著，《近代中国看天津：百项中国第一》，天津人民出版社，2007年，第81—82页。

through the customs, disclosing national secrets. Therefore, Li Hongzhang deeply recognized the necessity of building China's own telegraph lines. In 1877, he attempted to install a telegraph line between his Viceroy's office and the Tianjin Arsenal Bureau, and successfully sent and received telegraphs. In 1879, this telegraph line was extended to the Taku Forts and the Beitang Barracks, becoming China's first military telegraph line. In 1880, the Qing government finally approved the construction of telegraph lines between Shanghai, Zhenjiang, Nanjing, and Tianjin, and agreed to land submarine cables in Shanghai. Li Hongzhang established the General Bureau of Telegraph Services in Tianjin, appointing Sheng Xuanhuai as the director-general, overseeing the construction of telegraph lines across the country. The telegraph line from Tianjin to Shanghai was completed and opened for external business on December 24, 1881, marking the beginning of civilian telegraph communication in China. By 1895, within a decade, a comprehensive telegraph network had been established throughout China.

After the establishment of the telegraph industry, the development of the telephone naturally followed suit. When the telephone was introduced to China, it was referred to as "delvfeng," a transliteration of the English word "telephone". Just like the establishment of the telegraph, Li Hongzhang first conducted experiments in his own residence. In 1884, Li Hongzhang installed telephone lines from his Viceroy's office in Tianjin to places such as the Tianjin Customs, Beitang, Taku, and Baoding. These were the earliest long-distance telephone lines set up by modern Chinese people. According to newspaper reports at the time: "With the establishment of the telephone, communication over hundreds of miles is as easy as a face-to-face conversation. Upon hearing about this, Li Hongzhang instructed craftsmen to set up poles and lines, connecting the Viceroy's office to the Tianjin Customs and other places, facilitating the transmission of documents and messages."[1] In order to serve the trade development of Tianjin, the Telegraph Office, which organized this initiative, connected the telephone lines to various foreign firms in Tianjin. In addition to purchasing their own telephone equipment, these foreign firms also paid a certain fee annually. As a result, the Telegraph Office also had a substantial income each year.

Many conservative Chinese initially disliked the installation of electric wires in their fields, believing it would damage the vitality of the land, and the shadows of electric poles falling on graves would defile the spirits of ancestors. During the Boxer Rebellion, telegraph and telephone lines, along with railway

---

[1] *Modern China through the Eyes of Tianjin: 100 Firsts*, compiled by Wang Shuzu, Hang Ying. Tianjin People's Publishing House, 2007, pp.81-82.

培育人才与设立学堂

李鸿章在架设电报线的同时，即于 1880 年奏请朝廷批准，在天津创办北洋电报学堂，由此近代洋务教育肇始于天津。天津近代教育发展经历了三个阶段：第一阶段是洋务教育时期，初创各种专门学堂，其集大成者是北洋大学堂的创办；第二阶段是"新政"时期，这一时期建立起从基础教育、精英教育到职业技术培训的比较完备的近代教育体系；第三阶段是受五四新文化运动影响的民国时期，教育进一步迈向现代化，教育救国的思想深入人心。

洋务学堂与中国第一所大学

中国的各级人才教育和选拔，基本上来自传承千年的科举考试，所教所学皆为被奉为封建统治圭臬的八股文章和所谓经世学问，对于工业革命性质的各项洋务基本上一窍不通，师承无门。所以李鸿章、张之洞这样的洋务派大臣，在身边组建了庞大的幕府，聘用了许多外国人帮助与列强打交道，同时充当其了解西方世界的有用知识的洋顾问。然而那些不远万里来到中国的外国人，在为中国雇主服务的同时，除了获得丰厚回报之外，还充当了各自国家在华利益的代言人。因此，为了能确保"权自我操"，李鸿章等人一直注意培养中国自己的各类实用型人才，以便在将来替代洋人洋匠，并收回利权。而"自强之道，以作育人才为本；求才之道，尤宜以设立学堂为先"，所以开设学堂以培育人才是洋务运动其中一项重要内容，也是李鸿章、盛宣怀乃至袁世凯等洋务派官员多年来从事洋务活动得出的经验总结。

李鸿章作为直隶总督在天津 25 年间，开办了一系列洋务学堂。从 1876 年至 1894 年，李鸿章奏请朝廷批准，先后在天津创办了附设于天津机器局东局的电气水雷学堂、北洋电报学堂、北洋水师学堂、北洋水师轮机学堂（又称水师驾驶学堂）、北洋武备学堂、北洋西医学堂。这些学校均教学正规、授课严谨，在后来的 20 年间培育出大批人才。例如，北洋电报学堂通过大北公司聘请两个丹麦人为教习，

tracks, were all destroyed by Boxers, greatly impeding the actions of the Eight-Nation Alliance. After the Boxer Rebellion, Yuan Shikai, who served as the Viceroy of Zhili and Minister of Posts and Communication, immediately ordered the construction of a long-distance telephone line from Tianjin to Beijing. It was completed the following year, and the Tianjin Telephone Office was formally established, separated from the Telegraph Office, marking the beginning of China's self-operated long-distance telephone system. Soon after, two double-track long-distance telephone lines connecting Beijing and Tianjin were also successfully installed. With the smooth development of operations, the Tianjin Telephone Office also regained control of the telephone business from foreigners. Since then, the sovereignty of the telephone business has remained in Chinese hands.

Cultivating Talents and Establishing Schools

While establishing telegraph lines, Li Hongzhang petitioned the Qing court in 1880 to establish the Beiyang Telegraph School in Tianjin, marking the beginning of modern Western-style education in Tianjin. The development of modern education in Tianjin went through three stages: the first stage was during the era of Westernization, when various specialized schools were established, with the culmination being the founding of Peiyang University; the second stage was during the "New Policies" period, during which a relatively complete modern education system was established, covering basic education, elite education, and vocational training; the third stage was during the Republic of China era influenced by the May Fourth Movement, during which education further moved towards modernization, and the idea of education saving the nation became deeply rooted in people's minds.

The Westernization Schools and China's First University

The talent education and selection system in China at all levels were primarily based on the millennia-old imperial examination system. The education and learning revolved around the Eight-Legged Essay, revered as the epitome of feudal rule, and the so-called practical knowledge for governance. They were utterly ignorant of the industrial revolution and the nature of various Western reforms, lacking any apprenticeship opportunities. Therefore, prominent figures like Li Hongzhang and Zhang Zhidong, advocates of the Westernization Movement, established large bureaucracies around them, employing numerous foreigners to handle dealings with foreign powers and serve as useful consultants to understand the Western

明信片上的北洋大学第一处校址
The first campus of Peiyang University on the postcard

北洋水师学生习用测仪器图。摄于 19 世纪 80 年代
Beiyang Naval Academy students learning to use measuring
instruments. Taken in 1880s

北洋水师学生习练上桅图。摄于 19 世纪
80 年代
Beiyang Naval Academy students practicing
climbing mast. Taken in 1880s

北洋水师驾驶专业学生伏案图。摄于 19 世纪 80 年代
Beiyang Naval Academy students in navigation major at the desks.
Taken in 1880s

北洋水师学生操枪图
Beiyang Naval Academy students holding guns

图片来源：北京故宫博物院
Source: The Palace Museum in Beijing

招募学生学习电报技术，共培育出 300 余名毕业生，他们成为中国电信事业的先驱者。由留英归来的严复任总教习的北洋水师学堂，为北洋海军培养了大批新式实用型军官人才，张伯苓、黎元洪、郑汝成、王劭廉、温世霖等均为该校毕业生。令人惋惜的是，1900 年义和团运动期间这些学校被迫停办。而当时北洋武备学堂更是在八国联军入侵天津时，有留校的 90 余名学员顽强抵抗，最后全部壮烈牺牲。

洋务教育的顶峰是北洋大学堂的创办。李鸿章及其身边幕僚推动洋务事业多年，逐渐认识到，能够使中国走向富强的绝不是只掌握发电报或者驾驶舰船的一般技术人员，而是受到系统教育的高级复合型人才，也就是受过高等教育的大学毕业生。这不仅是洋务运动的需要，也是世界潮流发展趋势。因此，洋务教育不应当是急功近利的，而应当从储备人才和国家发展的长远立场出发。甲午战败，举国皆呼"自强"，洋务官员以此为契机指出，日本"援照西法，广开学堂书院，不特陆军海军将弁取材于学堂，即外部出使诸员及制造开矿等工，亦皆取材于学堂"①。1895 年，盛宣怀禀时任直隶总督北洋大臣的王文韶为创办西学学堂事进折光绪皇帝，拟请设立大学堂，以资造就人才。以往阻碍大学堂设置的种种阻碍（尤其是经费问题）此时亦不复存在，中国近代第一所大学——天津北洋西学学堂（即北洋大学）正式创立。

从 1895 年北洋大学开办至 1947 年于抗战胜利后再次复校，已有理、工两学院，分设数学、物理、化学、地质和建筑、土木、水利、采矿、冶金、机械、航空、电机、化工、纺织 14 个系，并恢复和建立了土木工程、水利工程、采矿工程、冶金工程和化学工程 5 个研究所，成为全国学术重镇，推动了近代科学技术的创造革新。

学堂不仅育才，亦为学术研究重镇。1889 年天津武备学堂在其院内（位于大直沽）升起中国第一只载人气球，引起全国轰动。当时，上海《点石斋画报》特别以图文并茂的报道，记载了这一科学技术

---

① 中国第一历史档案馆、天津大学，《中国近代第一所大学——北洋大学（天津大学）历史档案珍藏图录》，天津大学出版社，2005 年，第 6 页。

world. However, these foreigners who traveled thousands of miles to China, while serving their Chinese employers and receiving handsome rewards, also acted as advocates for their respective countries' interests in China. Hence, to ensure "self-control," figures like Li Hongzhang constantly focused on cultivating various practical talents of their own, intending to eventually replace foreign experts and reclaim their own interests. Thus, "the path to self-strengthening lies in nurturing talents, and the way to seek talent particularly lies in establishing schools first." Therefore, setting up schools to cultivate talents was an essential aspect of the Westernization Movement, reflecting the accumulated experience of figures like Li Hongzhang, Sheng Xuanhuai, and even Yuan Shikai, who had been engaged in Westernization activities for many years.

During his 25 years as the Zhili Viceroy in Tianjin, Li Hongzhang established a series of Westernization schools. From 1876 to 1894, Li Hongzhang petitioned the imperial court for approval and successively established several schools in Tianjin, including the Electrical and Torpedo School affiliated with the Tianjin Arsenal East Bureau, the Beiyang Telegraph School, the Beiyang Naval Academy, the Beiyang Naval Engineering Academy (or Navigation Academy), the Beiyang Military Academy, and the Beiyang Western Medicine School. These schools all provided formal education with rigorous teaching methods and nurtured a large number of talents over the next 20 years. For example, the Beiyang Telegraph School, with the assistance of two Danes hired by the Great Northern Telegraph Company, recruited students to learn telegraph technology, graduating over 300 pioneers in China's telecommunications industry. The Beiyang Naval Academy, led by Yan Fu, who had returned from studying in the United Kingdom, trained a large number of new practical naval officers for the Beiyang Navy, including graduates such as Chang Poling, Li Yuanhong, Zheng Rucheng, Wang Shaolian, and Wen Shilin. Unfortunately, during the Boxer Rebellion in 1900, these schools were forced to close. During the invasion of Tianjin by the Eight-Nation Alliance, around more than 90 students who remained at the Beiyang Military Academy valiantly resisted and ultimately sacrificed their lives.

The pinnacle of Westernization education was the establishment of the Peiyang University. Li Hongzhang and his entourage had been promoting the Westernization Movement for many years, gradually realizing that what could truly lead China to prosperity was not just individuals proficient in telegraphy or ship navigation, but rather highly educated, advanced professionals who received systematic education—university graduates. This was not only the need of the Westernization Movement but also the trend of global development. Therefore, Westernization education should not seek

新闻。该画报刊登了一幅纪实绘画:一只硕大的气球冉冉升起,球体缆于巨索,索下悬挂藤篮。篮内坐有两人,一人仰首观察空中情况,一人俯首挥动令旗和地面联络。武备学堂校舍阳台上坐着两位清朝官员和两位洋人。院子里有众多观众,官民相杂,众人皆翘首以望。这只载人气球是中国科学家华蘅芳督工自制的。勇敢地乘上气球升空的两个人,是北洋水师著名将领丁汝昌和刘步蟾。

1909 年中国第一个研究地理的学术团体——"中国地学会"在天津创办,得到了全国地学界响应。1910 年中国地理学会首任会长张相文与其同人们在天津创办了中国第一家地理学术期刊《地学杂志》。该杂志的诞生,使中国的地理学从传统的纯经验描述,迈向了探讨地理事物和现象的因果关系及其发展规律的科学进程,奠定了中国近代地理学的研究基础。1932 年,由北洋工学院^①院长李书田发起,在天津开始筹建中国第一个水工试验所,1934 年 6 月在今河北区黄纬路南侧河北工学院内奠基,1935 年 11 月建成。我国有史以来第一个水利试验机构"中国第一水工试验所"诞生,闻名国内外的天津大学水利工程科学,即是在此基础上发展起来的。

中国近代第一所大学——北洋大学

北洋大学在中国第一次完全引进了近代西方的大学制度,以美国哈佛、耶鲁和康奈尔等大学为蓝本进行专业设置、课程安排和学制规划。分为头等学堂(本科四年)和二等学堂(预科四年)。任课教授除了中文为我国著名学者外,其他学科皆为聘自海外知名大学的学者。初创法律、土木、矿冶、机械四科,均为国家现代化建设所亟须科目。

北洋初设时,法科为四大学门之一,后于 1917 年并入北京大学。"此一变动,影响北洋非细,论者惜之。"北洋法科开办二十余年中,培养了大批民国时期的重要人物,如王宠惠、王正

---

① 1917 年,国民政府教育部对北洋大学与北京大学进行科系调整,北洋大学改为专办工科,法科移并北京大学。从此,北洋大学进入专办工科时代,称"北洋工学院"。1945 年抗战胜利,教育部正式下令恢复北洋大学。

---

immediate gains but rather start from the long-term perspective of talent reserves and national development. After the defeat in the First Sino-Japanese War, the whole country called for "self-strengthening," and Westernization officials took this opportunity to point out, Japan, "emulating the West, widely establishes schools and academies. Not only do they draw military and naval officers from these institutions, but also staff for external missions and various industrial sectors such as mining and manufacturing."[1] In 1895, Sheng Xuanhuai reported to the Viceroy of Zhili and the Beiyang Minister, Wang Wenshao, proposing the establishment of a Western-style school to cultivate talents. Wang Wenshao presented this memorial to Emperor Guangxu. Many obstacles that had previously hindered the establishment of universities (especially financial issues) no longer existed at this time. The first modern university in China, Tianjin Peiyang Western Study School (Peiyang University), was officially founded.

From the establishment of Peiyang University in 1895 until its reopening in 1947 after the victory in the War of Resistance Against Japan, it had faculties of science and engineering, with 14 departments including mathematics, physics, chemistry, geology, architecture, civil engineering, hydraulic engineering, mining, metallurgy, machinery, aviation, electrical engineering, chemical engineering, and textile. It also restored and established five institutes including civil engineering, hydraulic engineering, mining engineering, metallurgical engineering, and chemical engineering. It became a national academic center, driving innovation and advancement in modern science and technology.

The school not only nurtured talents but also became a hub for academic research. In 1889, within the premises of the Tianjin Military School (located in Dazhigu), the first manned balloon in China ascended, causing a sensation nationwide. At that time, the Shanghai *Dianshizhai Pictorial* specially reported on this scientific and technological news with vivid illustrations and descriptions. The magazine published a realistic painting: a large balloon rising steadily, tethered to a huge rope with a basket hanging below. Inside the basket sat two people, one looking up to observe the situation in the sky, while the other looked down, waving a flag and communicating with the ground. On the balcony of the Military School building sat two Qing Dynasty officials and two foreigners. In the courtyard, there were numerous spectators, both officials and civilians, all eagerly watching. This manned balloon was

---

① The First Historical Archives of China, Tianjin University. *Collection of Historical Archives of Peiyang University (Tianjin University) - the First University of Modern China*. Tianjin University Press, 2005, p.6.

中国第一所大学——北洋大学。图片来源：天津大学档案馆

The first university in modern China - Peiyang University. Source: Tianjin University Archives

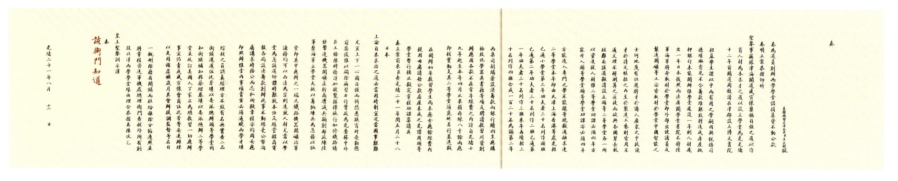

1895 年《津海关道盛宣怀禀明创办西学学堂事》奏折，光绪皇帝朱批："该衙门知道"

In 1895, the memorial titled *Tianjin Customs Taotai Sheng Xuanhuai's Petition on the Establishment of a Western Studies School* was submitted. Emperor Guangxu's imperial rescript bore the remark: "The office is informed"

廷、金问泗、赵天麟等人，为维护国家主权、完善民国法律制度以及发展各项公益事业等作出了积极的贡献。

我国早期从事水利工作的人大都从北洋大学土木和水利系毕业。近代以来基于治理华北水系、黄河下游和淮河流域灾害的需要，相继成立治理机构，北洋大学毕业生在其中发挥了重大作用，如李书田、徐世大、张含英、李荣梦等人，曾分别担任黄河水利委员会副主任、华北水利委员会总工程师、海河工程局局长、钱塘江工程局总工程师、长江水利科学研究院副总工程师等职。李书田还在北洋大学成立了中国第一水工试验所。

北洋大学机械系不仅在国内高校中创建最早，而且师资、设

built by the Chinese scientist Hua Hengfang. The two brave individuals who ascended in the balloon were the famous naval commanders of the Beiyang Fleet, Ding Ruchang and Liu Buchan.

In 1909, China's first academic group studying geography, the "Chinese Geographical Society", was founded in Tianjin and received a welcoming response from the geoscience community across the country. In 1910, Zhang Xiangwen, the first president of the Chinese Geographical Society, along with his colleagues, founded China's first geographical academic journal, *Geographical Journal*, in Tianjin. The birth of this journal marked a transition in Chinese geography from traditional empirical description to scientific exploration the causal relationships and development laws of geographical phenomena, laying the research foundation for modern geography in China. In 1932, initiated by Li Shutian, the president of Peiyang

北洋大学团城。安红摄于 2006 年
Tuancheng Building of Peiyang University. Taken by An Hong in 2006

Engineering College[①], the construction of China's first hydraulic laboratory began in Tianjin. In June 1934, the foundation was laid in the southern part of Huangwei Road, Hebei Provincial Technological Institute, in present-day Hebei District. It was completed in November 1935. The establishment of the first hydraulic laboratory in China, known as the "First Hydraulic Laboratory of China," laid the foundation for the development of hydraulic engineering science at Peiyang University, which became renowned both domestically and internationally.

The First University of Modern China—Peiyang University

Peiyang University introduced the modern Western university system into China for the first time, modeling its professional settings, curriculum arrangements, and academic planning after prestigious American universities such as Harvard, Yale, and Cornell. It was divided into a first-class school (four-year undergraduate program) and a second-class school (four-year preparatory program). Apart from Chinese scholars who were renowned in China, professors in other disciplines were recruited from well-known overseas universities. Initially, the university established four departments: Law, Civil Engineering, Mining and Metallurgy, and Mechanical Engineering, all of which were urgently needed subjects for the country's modernization efforts.

When Peiyang University was initially established, the Department of Law was one of its four major departments. However, it was later merged into Peking University in 1917. "This change had a significant impact on Peiyang, which was regretted by many." Over the twenty-plus years of its existence, the Department of Law at Peiyang University nurtured a large number of important figures during the Republic of China era, such as Wang Chonghui, Wang Zhengting, Jin Wensi, Zhao Tianlin, among others, who made significant contributions to safeguarding national sovereignty, improving the legal system of the Republic of China, and developing various public welfare initiatives.

Most of the early practitioners in hydraulic engineering in our country graduated from the Department of Civil Engineering and Hydraulic Engineering at Peiyang University. Since modern times, various governance institutions have been established based on the needs of managing the water systems in North

备实力雄厚。因此，1935 年北洋大学被民国教育部选中成立中国第一个航空系。成立不久，即制造出中国第一台飞机发动机。北洋大学航空系还培养出我国"两弹一星"元勋吴自良。

北洋大学最初设置的四个学门中以矿冶最为著称。许多校友在国内矿冶界和铁道工程方面卓有贡献。如创建中国第一座炼锑厂之王宠佑、铁路名宿刘景山、勘察到世界上储量最大菱镁矿的王正黼、北京大学工科教务长温宗禹、上海钢铁厂厂长周志宏等人。北洋大学矿冶系还为我国石油工业的发展培养了大批人才。矿冶系亦为后来北京地质学院、钢铁学院等校的前身。

新政与天津近代教育体系的建立

1900 年八国联军入侵，胁迫清政府签订了丧权辱国的《辛丑条约》。在民族危机如此深重的局势下，清政府为保住自己的阶级统治，于 1902 年宣布实行"新政"并推行了一系列新措施，内容之一就是改革科举制度。1905 年直隶总督袁世凯等以科举"阻碍学堂，妨碍人才"为由，强烈奏请立刻停科举，以广学堂。同年，清政府接受

[①] In 1917, the Ministry of Education of the National Government restructured academic programs between Peiyang University and Peking University, designating Peiyang University as a specialized engineering institution while transferring its law department to Peking University. From that point forward, Peiyang University entered an era of exclusive engineering education and was renamed "National Peiyang Technical College". After the victory in the War of Resistance Against Japan in 1945, the Ministry of Education officially ordered the restoration of Peiyang University.

天津初级师范学堂学生合影。摄于 20 世纪初。图片来源：北京故宫博物院
Photo of students from Tianjin Junior Normal School. Taken in early 20th century.
Source: The Palace Museum in Beijing

了袁世凯等人的吁请，正式下令停止科举，推广学堂。并于 1906 年设立了学部，负责教学教务、修建工程、职官、留学、财经等事务。至此，从隋文帝杨坚创始，前后沿用近一千三百年的科举制度终于寿终正寝。

　　在庚子大乱后，创巨痛深的天津士绅与地方政府一道，痛定思痛，共谋创办地方学堂、开启民智，一时掀起兴学高潮。不仅各种小学堂、中学堂、女学等如雨后春笋般创立起来，各种专业学堂、师范学堂乃至私立大学亦皆创办。"新政"期间，天津先后创办了中国历史上第一所警察学校——"天津警务学堂"，中国第一所中医学校——天津私立中国医学传习所，中国第一所法政专科大学——北洋法政学堂（中国共产党的创始人之一李大钊是该校首届毕业生），中国第一所女子师范学校——北洋女师学堂（无产阶级革命家邓颖超同志是其中佼佼者），中国第一所公立护士学校——北洋女子医学校，中国第一所培养音乐、体育教师的专科学校——天津音乐体操传习

China, the lower reaches of the Yellow River, and the Huai River basin. Graduates from Peiyang University have played significant roles in these institutions, such as Li Shutian, Xu Shida, Zhang Hanying, Li Rongmeng, who have respectively served as the Deputy Director of the Yellow River Conservancy Commission, the Chief Engineer of the North China Conservancy Commission, the Director of the Hai-Ho Conservancy Commission, Chief Engineer of the Qiantang River Engineering Bureau, and Deputy Chief Engineer of the Yangtze River Institute of Water Resources. Li Shutian also established the first Hydraulic Engineering Laboratory in China at Peiyang University.

The Mechanical Engineering Department of Peiyang University was not only established earliest among domestic universities but also had strong faculty and equipment capabilities. Therefore, in 1935, Peiyang University was selected by the Ministry of Education of the Republic of China to establish the first Aeronautical Engineering Department in China. Shortly after its establishment, it manufactured the first aircraft engine in China. The Aeronautical Engineering Department of Peiyang University also trained Wu Ziliang, a pioneer in China's "Two Bombs, One Satellite" project.

Among the four departments initially established at Peiyang University, the Mining and Metallurgy department was the most renowned. Many alumni have made significant contributions to the domestic mining and metallurgy industry and railway engineering. For instance, Wang Chongyou, who established China's first antimony smelter; Liu Jingshan, a railway expert; Wang Zhengfu, who discovered the world's largest reserves of magnesite; Wen Zongyu, the academic dean of the engineering department at Peking University; and Zhou Zhihong, the director of the Shanghai First Iron & Steel Plant. The Mining and Metallurgy department of Peiyang University also nurtured a large number of talents for the development of China's petroleum industry. Additionally, the Mining and Metallurgy department served as the precursor to later institutions such as the Beijing College of Geology and the Beijing Institute of Iron and Steel Technology.

New Policies and the Establishment of Modern Educational System in Tianjin

In 1900, the Eight-Nation Alliance invaded China and coerced the Qing government into signing the humiliating *Boxer Protocol*. In the face of such a profound national crisis, the Qing government, in order to preserve its own class rule, announced the implementation of the "New Policies" in 1902 and enacted a series of new measures, one of which was the reform of the imperial examination system. In 1905, Viceroy of Zhili, Yuan Shikai, and others strongly

天津公立女学堂教习学生合影。摄于 20 世纪初
Teachers and students of Tianjin Public Women's School.
Taken in early 20th century

天津官立两等小学堂学生合影。摄于 20 世纪初
Students of Tianjin Public Complete Primary School. Taken in early 20th century

图片来源：北京故宫博物院
Source: The Palace Museum in Beijing

所，中国第一所水产学校——直隶水产讲习所，以及第一套包含综合性大学、中学、女中、小学系列学校的私立教育体系——南开系列学校（后于抗战期间改为公立学校）。

"新政"时期的近代教育不仅重视基础教育（中小学）、专业教育（专科学校）和精英教育（大学），亦传承了洋务教育的务实传统，举办了各种职业技术培训学校，为天津民族工商业的发展培养各方面、多层次的人才。1903 年天津知府受袁世凯委托创办了"直隶高等工艺学堂"，学堂设化学、机器、化工、绘图等科目，聘英、日教员授课，培养能进行技术培训、操作并能在工业上有所发明创造的专业技师。袁世凯还下令在津设立教养局、习艺所、实习工场，在天津监狱附设游民习艺所，专门收容并教授没有生活来源的贫困者和流民产业技能，学习织布、织带、铁工、搓绳、印刷等项技艺。这样做不仅为底层民众提供求生技能、维护了社会秩序，并且为工厂企业提供了具备一定技能的劳动力，客观上推动了天津工业的发展。举例来说，教养局专设织布、地毯、染色三科，招收官费工徒

urged the immediate cessation of the imperial examinations on the grounds that they "hindered education and talent development," advocating instead for the expansion of modern schools. That same year, the Qing government accepted their plea and officially ordered the cessation of the imperial examinations, promoting modern education. In 1906, a Ministry of Education was established to oversee educational affairs, construction projects, civil service appointments, overseas studies, finance, and other matters. Thus, the imperial examination system, which had been in use for nearly 1,300 years since its inception by Emperor Yang of Sui, finally came to an end.

After the chaos of the Boxer Rebellion, deeply affected Tianjin gentry and local government came together, learning from their lessons, and jointly planned to establish local schools to promote enlightenment, sparking a wave of educational fervor. Not only were various elementary schools, secondary schools, and girls' schools established rapidly like mushrooms after rain, but also various professional schools, normal schools, and even private universities were founded. During the period of the "New Policies," Tianjin successively established the first police school in Chinese history—the Tianjin Police School, the first traditional Chinese medicine school in China—the Tianjin Private Chinese Medical School, the first law and

100 名在两年内学习。这些学徒聪明勤奋，"仅仅在两年的短时期内，各项科目都达到了熟练的技术工人的程度"①。毕业学徒大部分作为地方上的技术员，从事织布、染色、地毯、织造等工业。作为中国最大的羊毛出口港，第一次世界大战期间至 1929 年，天津的地毯工人已达到 10000 多人，②地毯也成为天津对外出口的大宗商品。

据《天津县新志》统计，新政时期（1900—1911 年），天津县范围内，有大学校 1 所、高等学堂 3 所、中学堂 7 所、男小学堂 89 所、女学堂 23 所、其他各类学堂 24 所、外国人创办的学堂 6 所、蒙养院 3 所，共计 156 所。据《天津政俗沿革记》记载，截至辛亥革命前，民办小学堂和初等小学堂已达 67 所，公立小学堂及初等小学堂 11 所，民办女子小学堂 5 所，此外有民办艺徒学堂、商务半夜学堂、广育半夜学堂、民办半日学堂等。③这些学堂学校的创设使近代天津教育形成多种办学形式和多类型、多层次的教育体系。

民国时期教育与民族工业发展

1912 年民国建立之后，孙中山为首的临时政府在对政治、经济、社会等方面进行变革的同时，也对教育进行了改革，设教育部，任命蔡元培为首任教育总长。蔡元培对当时的教育制度进行了革命性的变革，颁行了一系列改革教育的法令，先后颁布了 1912 年制定的"壬子学制"和 1913 年制定的"癸丑学制"。通过这些改革措施，推进天津教育摆脱封建桎梏，逐渐走向近代化。

这一时期，天津新建包括小学、中学和大学在内的学校 20 余所。在教育内容上，废止了读经讲经课，彻底废除了束缚思想和科技进步的封建教育；在学制上，缩短了学业年限，加快了人才培养速度。鉴于天津教育在北方的重要地位，1915 年在天津成立了全国教育联

---

① 天津市地方史志编修委员会总编辑室编，《二十世纪初的天津概况》，内部发行，1986 年，第 256 页。

② 《1929 年天津海关贸易报告》。吴弘明编译，《津海关贸易年报（1865~1946）》，天津社会科学院出版社，2006 年，第 478—489 页。

③ 张大民主编，《天津近代教育史》，天津人民出版社，1993 年，第 135 页。

political science university in China—the Beiyang School of Law and Politics (one of the founders of the Communist Party of China, Li Dazhao, was the first graduate of this school), the first women's normal school in China—the Beiyang Women's Normal School (comrade Deng Yingchao, a proletarian revolutionary, was one of its outstanding graduates), the first public nursing school in China—the Beiyang Women's Medical School, the first specialized school for training music and physical education teachers in China—the Tianjin Music and Gymnastics Institute, the first fisheries school in China—the Zhili Aquaculture Institute, and the first private educational system comprising comprehensive universities, secondary schools, girls' schools, and primary schools—the Nankai series of schools (later converted to public schools during the War of Resistance against Japan).

During the period of the "New Policies," modern education not only emphasized basic education (primary and secondary schools), professional education (technical schools), and elite education (universities), but also inherited the practical tradition of Westernization education. Various vocational and technical training schools were established to cultivate talents of various levels and backgrounds for the development of Tianjin's national industry and commerce. In 1903, at the request of Yuan Shikai, the Tianjin Prefect established the "Zhili Higher School of Technology," which offered subjects such as chemistry, machinery, chemical engineering, and drawing, with English and Japanese instructors teaching, aiming to train professional technicians capable of conducting technical training, operations, and making inventions and innovations in industry. Yuan Shikai also ordered the establishment of educational bureaus, vocational schools, and practical workshops in Tianjin. A vocational school was set up adjacent to the Tianjin prison specifically for homeless people and refugees to teach them industry skills such as weaving, knitting, ironwork, and rope-making. This not only provided survival skills for the lower class and maintained social order but also provided skilled labor for factories and enterprises, objectively promoting the development of Tianjin's industry. For example, the educational bureau specifically offered weaving, carpet-making, and dyeing courses, admitting 100 apprentices whose tuition fee was paid by the government to study within two years. These apprentices were diligent and intelligent, and "within just two years, they had reached the level of skilled workers in various subjects."[1] Most of the graduates worked as technicians in local industries such as weaving, dyeing, carpet-making, and textile manufacturing. As China's

---

[1] Editorial Office of the Tianjin Chorography and History Compilation Committee (ed.). *Overview of Tianjin in the Early 20th Century*. Published internally in 1986, p.256.

合会，并召开了第一次会议。会议中总结了已经在天津推行的一些新教育思想，准备向全国推广。例如，在全国推行曾以天津为试点的义务教育；在大中小学教育内容中增加军事训练课，培养国民尚武精神和军事素质等。

天津亦为近代社会教育的发祥地。天津近代社会教育从洋务运动开始发展，一直延续到新文化运动时期。洋务运动及新政时期的主力是洋务派官员如李鸿章、袁世凯等，而后来的中坚力量则变为地方士绅，如严修、林墨青、卢木斋和张伯苓等。他们广泛动员社会力量，不仅为贫苦家庭学生和民众开办了许多小学堂、半日学堂和夜校等教以知识和技能，而且创办了报纸进行社会道德教育，推行白话文和拼音字母，还相继创办图书馆、博物馆、体育场等社会教育场所等，使民国初年的社会教育取得可观成效，并为后来的平民教育运动打下基础。

平民教育是社会教育的组成部分。新文化运动时期，南开学校、直隶第一女子师范学校、北洋法政专门学校等，成为天津新文化运动的传播中心。这些学校相继出版了许多进步刊物，宣传了民主、科学的新思想，有力反击了尊孔复辟的逆流。李大钊、陈独秀、胡适、陶孟和、李石曾等一大批在新文化运动中熠熠生辉的倡导者和引领者，纷纷来到天津宣讲新思想，大大开拓了青年学生的思想和文化视野。在他们的影响下，很多知识青年走向社会，参与到平民教育活动中去。

平民教育运动领导者认为，中国社会当时的主要问题为贫、愚、弱、私，针对此四大病症，主张以文艺教育救愚、生计教育救贫、公民教育治私、卫生教育救弱。又因这四者具有连带性，所以这四大教育任何一方面的解决办法，都必须和其他方面取得密切联系，任何一方面的成绩都必须依赖其他方面的协助。他们还认为实施平民教育，必须深切了解人民的心理和需要。南开大学的校长张伯苓强调教育要为社会谋进步、要适应社会之需要，首先要使学生了解社会真正情况。早在 1916 年南开教师就结合课堂教学带领学生深入天津社会开展社会调查。后来几经改革，这种形式的社会调查形成了制度。1921 年暑期，张伯苓要求学生将进行社会调查作为暑期作

largest wool export port, from the First World War until 1929, the number of carpet workers in Tianjin had exceeded 10,000,[1] and carpets had become a major commodity for Tianjin's foreign exports.

According to the statistics from the *New Chronicle of Tianjin County*, during the period of the New Policies (1900-1911), within the jurisdiction of Tianjin County, there were a total of 156 educational institutions, including 1 university, 3 advanced schools, 7 secondary schools, 89 boys' primary schools, 23 girls' schools, 24 various other types of schools, 6 schools established by foreigners, and 3 nurseries. According to the *Records of Tianjin's Political and Social Evolution*, before the 1911 Revolution, there were already 67 private elementary schools, 11 public elementary schools, and 5 private girls' elementary schools. Additionally, there were private apprentice schools, commercial night schools, general education night schools, and private half-day schools.[2] The establishment of these schools and educational institutions in Tianjin during the modern era led to the formation of various forms of education and a multi-layered educational system.

The Development of the Education and National Industry During the Republic of China Era

After the establishment of the Republic of China in 1912, the provisional government led by Sun Yat-sen initiated reforms in various aspects such as politics, economy, and society. Simultaneously, education underwent significant changes with the establishment of the Ministry of Education and the appointment of Cai Yuanpei as the first Minister of Education. Cai Yuanpei initiated revolutionary reforms to the education system at that time, issuing a series of laws aimed at reforming education, including the "Renzi Education System" enacted in 1912 and the "Guichou Education System" enacted in 1913. Through these reform measures, Tianjin's education system was gradually liberated from feudal constraints and moved towards modernization.

During this period, Tianjin established approximately 20 new schools, including primary, secondary, and tertiary institutions. In terms of educational content, the recitation of classics and Confucian lectures were abolished, completely eliminating the feudal education that constrained

---

[1] *Tianjin Customs Trade Report in 1929*, translated and edited by Wu Hongming. *Tianjin Customs Annual Report of Trade (1865~1946)*. Tianjin Academy of Social Sciences Press, 2006, pp.478-489.

[2] Zhang Damin (ed.). *History of Modern Education in Tianjin*. Tianjin People's Publishing House, 1993, p.135.

严修与张伯苓（右）
Yan Xiu and Chang Poling
(right)

业的一项重要内容。1926 年张伯苓将"社会视察"作为高中必修课之一，到工商企业、司法、教育、交通、救济、新闻、卫生等机关去参观，然后进行座谈讨论，写出调查报告。之后，他还进一步完善了南开学校教育教学中加强社会调查工作的目的和组织的改革。五四运动中，天津各高校大学生成立天津学生联合会，组织成立了许多支演讲小分队，走上街头、深入厂矿，向广大群众宣讲时事，推动了全市人民的爱国斗争，实现了罢工、罢课、罢市，形成了强大的社会压力，使北洋政府最终不得不罢免了曹汝霖、陆宗舆、章宗祥，并拒绝在《巴黎和约》上签字。可以说，这一时期，天津教育方面的最大亮点是开展平民教育运动。

社会是一个不可分割的整体，社会进步是农业、人口、教育、对外贸易、工业技术、金融信贷等各个部门相互依赖、相互解放的结果。民国初年民族工业的发展，是中国社会精英试图重走欧美日工业化老路的尝试。这个过程需要社会各个方面的彻底变革，包括经济、社会、政治、文化从结构到体制的彻底改变。而生产力的诸要素中，人（即劳动者）是最活跃的能动的要素。因为科学技术是由人发现和发明的，科学技术只有被人在生产中加以运用，才能转化为现实的生产力。所以，教育的改革是社会变革的重要基础和前提。

中华民国成立之后，天津的工业企业与社会教育的发展是相辅相成的。民族工业的发展提供了教育发展所需的经济基础，也对教育发展提出了要求，即要求后者为其培养与之相适应的科学技术人

thinking and hindered scientific and technological progress. In terms of school system, the duration of study was shortened, accelerating the pace of talent cultivation. Recognizing the significant role of Tianjin in northern education, the National Education Association was established in Tianjin in 1915, and its first conference was convened. During the conference, some new educational ideas that had been implemented in Tianjin were summarized, ready for nationwide promotion. For example, compulsory education, which had been piloted in Tianjin, was promoted nationwide; military training courses were added to the curriculum of primary, secondary, and tertiary education to foster national martial spirit and military quality.

Tianjin is also considered the birthplace of modern social education. Modern social education in Tianjin began with the Westernization Movement and continued into the New Culture Movement period. During the Westernization Movement and the New Policies period, the main force was comprised of advocates of Westernization such as Li Hongzhang and Yuan Shikai. Later, the backbone of the movement shifted to local gentry such as Yan Xiu, Lin Moqing, Lu Muzhai, and Chang Poling. They mobilized social forces extensively, not only establishing numerous elementary schools, half-day schools, and evening schools for poor students and the general public to impart knowledge and skills but also founding newspapers for social and moral education, promoting vernacular Chinese and phonetic alphabets. Furthermore, they successively established libraries, museums, sports grounds, and other social education facilities, achieving remarkable results in the social education of the early years of the Republic of China and laying the foundation for later movements advocating education for the common people.

Mass education is an integral part of social education. During the New Culture Movement period, schools like Nankai School, the First Women's Normal School of Zhili Province, and the Beiyang School of Law and Politics became the dissemination centers of the New Culture Movement in Tianjin. These schools successively published many progressive publications, promoting new democratic and scientific ideas, effectively countering the reactionary trend of reverting to Confucianism. A large number of advocates and leaders who shone brightly in the New Culture Movement, such as Li Dazhao, Chen Duxiu, Hu Shi, Tao Menghe, and Li Shizeng, came to Tianjin to preach the new ideas, greatly broadening the intellectual and cultural horizons of young students. Under their influence, many intellectuals ventured into society and became involved in grassroots educational activities.

The leaders of the grassroots education movement believed that the main problems in Chinese society at that time were poverty, ignorance, weakness, and selfishness. To address these four major ailments, they advocated using

才，既包括具有相当科学文化知识的高级人才，也包括具备一定生产技能和组织性纪律性的普通劳工。而天津近代教育体系的建立与完善，特别是社会教育的成就，为天津发展民族工业、民族经济，进而成为北方经济中心奠定了重要基础。

实业家与民族工业

古代天津的发展依赖漕运和盐业，而民族工业的发展则有力推动了近代天津的经济增长，为之后的一系列社会结构的演进夯实了基础。

从官督商办、官商合办到民族工业

天津的工业家和民族工业不是凭空而生的，他们经历了从清末洋务运动、"新政"到中华民国时期的奖励实业发展，亲身体验了西方资本主义的物质文明，在追求利润的过程中发展出强烈的民族自尊心和社会责任感，坚强地在帝国主义列强的经济侵略中挣扎图存。

在近代成为通商口岸后，西方资本主义在天津开辟租界、开设洋行。一船船欧美工业产品涌入天津口岸的同时，有关工业革命的各项新技术也都借由洋行引入。比如开矿所需的巷道、通风系统、抽水泵、提升装置，运输所需的船舶和修理厂、铁路的铁轨和机车，打造枪炮的机床和锅炉等。一旦引入这些能产生极高利润的新技术，就需要创办一系列规模庞大的近代工业，所需厂房高大宽敞、工人人数众多。毫无疑问，建厂投资需要巨额资金，不仅固定资产投资巨大，流动资金亦大，动辄以几十万乃至百万两白银计。很多情况下，流动资本方面的困难更大于固定资本方面，因此大型工厂经常出现银根短缺状况。

在资金短缺的情况下，1877 年李鸿章为筹办开平矿务局，批准总办唐廷枢拟定的招股章程十二条，集资 80 万两白银。1878 年 10 月 2 日，开平煤矿正式开凿第一眼钻井。几个月内，井架、厂房、绞车房、工棚、供技术员居住的房子及办公用房等平地而起，招募

literary and artistic education to alleviate ignorance, livelihood education to alleviate poverty, civic education to counter selfishness, and health education to alleviate weakness. Because these four issues were interconnected, they believed that any solution to one aspect of education must be closely linked to others, and achievements in any aspect must rely on assistance from other areas. They also believed that to implement grassroots education, it was necessary to deeply understand the psychology and needs of the people. Chang Poling, the president of Nankai University, emphasized that education should promote progress in society and should adapt to the needs of society. He believed that students must first understand the true situation of society. As early as 1916, a teacher at Nankai had led students to conduct in-depth social investigations in Tianjin society as part of his classroom teaching. Later, after several reforms, this form of social investigation became institutionalized. In the summer of 1921, Chang Poling required students to conduct social investigations as an important part of their summer assignments. In 1926, Chang Poling made "social investigation" one of the compulsory courses in high school, where students visited industrial and commercial enterprises, judicial, educational, transportation, relief, news, health agencies, and then held discussions and wrote investigation reports. Later, he further improved the purpose and organization of social investigation work in Nankai School's education and teaching reforms. During the May Fourth Movement, students from various universities in Tianjin established the Tianjin Student Union and organized many speech teams to take to the streets and visit factories and mines, spreading current events to the masses, promoting the patriotic struggle of the entire city, initiating strikes, class boycotts, and market boycotts, creating significant social pressure, and ultimately forcing the Beiyang government to dismiss Cao Rulin, Lu Zongyu, and Zhang Zongxiang, and refusing to sign the *Treaty of Versailles*. It can be said that during this period, the greatest highlight of education in Tianjin was the grassroots education movement.

Society is an inseparable whole, and social progress is the result of the interdependence and liberation of various sectors such as agriculture, population, education, foreign trade, industrial technology, and financial credit. In the early years of the Republic of China, the development of national industry was an attempt by China's social elites to follow the path of industrialization taken by Europe, America, and Japan. This process required thorough changes in all aspects of society, including the economy, society, politics, and culture, from structural to systemic changes. Among the various factors of productivity, humans (or laborers) are the most active and dynamic. This is because science and technology are discovered and

盛宣怀
Sheng Xuanhuai

唐廷枢
Tang Tingshu

invented by people, and scientific and technological advancements can only be transformed into real productivity when applied by people in production. Therefore, educational reform is an important foundation and prerequisite for social change.

After the establishment of the Republic of China, the development of industrial enterprises and social education in Tianjin complemented each other. The development of national industry provided the economic foundation necessary for the development of education and also made demands on education, requiring it to cultivate scientific and technological talents adapted to it. This included not only senior talents with considerable scientific and cultural knowledge but also ordinary laborers with certain production skills and organizational discipline. The establishment and improvement of Tianjin's modern education system, especially the achievements in social education, laid an important foundation for the development of national industry and economy in Tianjin, thereby becoming a key pillar of the northern economic center.

Industrialists and National Industry

The development of ancient Tianjin relied on canal transportation and salt industry, while the development of national industry strongly propelled the economic growth of modern Tianjin, laying a solid foundation for the subsequent evolution of a series of social structures.

From Government Supervision and Merchant Operation, to Government-business Cooperation, and then to National Industry

The industrialists and national industries in Tianjin did not emerge out of thin air. They experienced the promotion of industrial development from the late Qing Dynasty's Westernization Movement, the "New Policies", to the period of the Republic of China. They personally experienced the material civilization of Western capitalism and, in the pursuit of profit, developed a strong sense of national pride and social responsibility. They struggled tenaciously to survive in the face of economic aggression from imperialist powers.

After becoming a trading port in modern times, Western capitalism opened concessions and established foreign firms in Tianjin. While ships filled with industrial products from Europe and America poured into the Tianjin port, various new technologies related to the Industrial Revolution were also

工人 3000 人。后开平矿务局历年扩充设备、建设运煤铁路、购买运输煤轮、修建专用码头和堆栈等，先后共集资约 160 万两白银。到 19 世纪末，总资产已近白银 600 万两。这种投资规模，无论是政府还是单独的商人个体都无力承担，所以只能通过集资入股、官督商办的方式来兴办企业。"官督商办"企业是一种由商人出资认股、政府派官员管理的商业组织方式，但官督商办企业的政策决定权大都掌握在由政府委任的洋务派官员手中。这类企业中的总办、会办、帮办、提调等职位的官员成分大于商人成分，虽有唐廷枢、盛宣怀、张謇、周学熙等出色人物，但更多人则根本不懂企业经营、贪腐无能，把企业办成了官僚衙门，而商民"虽经入股，不啻路人"，无权过问企业经营情况。这类企业由于经营不善，最终大多改为官商合办，或直接变成商办。

天津早期的官办企业主要是李鸿章创办的两个机器局，制造军火、铸造硬币以及制造小批量的硫酸等，还有就是官督商办的开平煤矿和曾任英商天津汇丰银行买办的吴懋鼎自筹资本创办的一家机器纺绒厂。这些企业基本在八国联军入侵天津期间被全部摧毁或者盗卖。袁世凯接任直隶总督后，奖励工业发展，任命周学熙担任工艺总办，设立教养局、实习工场、考工厂、教育品陈列馆以及高等工业学堂等，奠定了近代天津工业发展的基础。与此同时，一批民营企业也发展起来，从事简单机械制造及修理、制革、清洗羊毛、制作服装鞋帽、制造纸烟、制作玻璃、肥皂以及规模较小的地毯厂等。这些工厂一般有工人几十到一百多人，资金有几万到十几万两，而一名熟练的缝纫工月工资只在 3 元以内（学徒 3 年内供给饭费和 50 分津贴）。①

辛亥革命推翻了清王朝的统治，建立了中华民国临时政府，颁布了若干新的政策法令，如《临时约法》规定，"人民有保有财产及营业之自由"。北洋军阀掌政后，资本主义的发展已成大势所趋，1914 年颁布了民国以来第一个保护民族工商业者的法令，同年又以天津造币厂铸造的"袁大头"来统一新币制，为资本主义发展提供便利条件。接下来，第一次世界大战爆发，战争进行的这一时期可

---

① 天津市地方史志编修委员会总编辑室编，《二十世纪初的天津概况》，内部发行，1986 年，第 260—265 页。

introduced through these foreign firms. For example, tunnels, ventilation systems, pumps for water extraction, lifting devices needed for mining, ships and repair yards required for transportation, railway tracks and locomotives, machine tools, and boilers for manufacturing firearms, among others. Once these highly profitable new technologies were introduced, it was necessary to establish a series of large-scale modern industries, requiring spacious and tall factory buildings and a large number of workers. Undoubtedly, setting up such factories required huge investments, not only in fixed assets but also in working capital, often amounting to hundreds of thousands or even millions of silver taels. In many cases, the difficulties in terms of working capital were greater than those in fixed capital, hence large factories often faced shortages of funds.

In the situation of fund shortage, in 1877, Li Hongzhang approved the twelve articles of the prospectus drafted by the general manager Tang Tingshu for the establishment of the Kaiping Mining Bureau, raising 800,000 taels of silver through stock subscription. On October 2, 1878, the Kaiping coal mine officially started drilling its first borehole. Within a few months, structures such as well frames, workshops, winch rooms, sheds, houses for technical personnel, and office buildings emerged on level ground, recruiting 3,000 workers. Later, the Kaiping Mining Bureau expanded its equipment year by year, built coal transportation railways, purchased coal transport ships, and constructed dedicated wharves and warehouses, raising a total of about 1.6 million taels of silver. By the end of the 19th century, the total assets were close to 6 million taels of silver. Such investment scale was beyond the capacity of both the government and individual merchants, so the only way to establish such an enterprise was through joint stock financing and government-supervised commercial operations. "Government-supervised commercial operation" was a form of business organization in which merchants invested and subscribed shares, while government officials were appointed to manage the business. However, the decision-making power of government-supervised commercial operations mostly rested in the hands of the officials appointed by the government, who were followers of the Westernization Movement. Officials in positions such as general manager, executive manager, assistant manager, and supervisor in these enterprises were more prevalent than merchants. Although there were outstanding figures like Tang Tingshu, Sheng Xuanhuai, Zhang Jian, and Zhou Xuexi, many were incompetent and corrupt, turning the enterprises into bureaucratic offices. Despite merchants having invested, they were no more than bystanders, with no authority to inquire about the operation of the enterprise. Due to poor management, most of these enterprises eventually became joint ventures between officials and merchants

展示天津工业工艺品的劝业会场
Quanye Exhibition Center for showcasing industrial products in Tianjin

俗称"袁大头"的银元
Silver coin with the head of Yuan Shikai,
called "Yuan Da Tou"

以说是中国民族资本主义发展的"黄金时期"。几个主要帝国主义国家卷入重新瓜分世界的战争中，外国资本主义势力相对减弱，洋货输入额明显下降，为中国民族工业发展提供了机会。天津作为一个重要的工业城市亦是如此，如开战前后进入天津港的洋船吨位，英国由 1912 年的 916005 吨减至 1918 年 555972 吨，美国由 1912 年的 45606 吨减至 1918 年的 10390 吨。[①] 它们空下来的市场即被本土民族工业所占领。据 1912—1920 年在北洋政府工商部注册的天津的工厂数字说明，万元以上的工厂达 23 家，资本总额达 12115000 元，

or were directly turned into purely commercial operations.

In the early days of Tianjin, the main state-run enterprises were two arsenal bureaus founded by Li Hongzhang, which manufactured military weapons, minted coins, and produced small batches of sulfuric acid. Additionally, there was the Kaiping coal mine, operated under government supervision, and a machinery spinning mill established by Wu Maoding, who previously served as a purchasing agent for the British-owned Hongkong and Shanghai Banking Corporation Tianjin Branch, using his own capital. These enterprises were either completely destroyed or looted during the invasion of Tianjin by the Eight-Nation Alliance. After Yuan Shikai succeeded as the Viceroy of Zhili, he incentivized industrial development by appointing Zhou Xuexi as the head of industrial affairs. Institutions such as training bureaus, apprenticeship workshops, examination factories, educational product exhibitions, and advanced industrial schools were established, laying the foundation for the modern industrial development of Tianjin. Meanwhile, a number of private enterprises also emerged, engaging in activities such as simple machinery manufacturing and repair, tanning, wool cleaning, garment and footwear production, cigarette manufacturing, glassmaking, soap production, and carpet-weaving. These factories generally employed tens to over a hundred workers, with capital ranging from tens of thousands to several hundred thousand taels of silver. Skilled seamstresses earned less than 3 yuan per month (apprentices were provided with food expenses and a subsidy of 50 cents per month for the first three years of training).[①]

The 1911 Revolution overthrew the rule of the Qing Dynasty and established the Provisional Government of the Republic of China, which promulgated several new policies and laws. For instance, the *Provisional Constitution of the Republic of China* stipulated, "The people have the freedom of property and business." After the Beiyang Warlords took power, the development of capitalism became an unstoppable trend. In 1914, the first law protecting national industrial and commercial interests since the founding of the Republic was enacted. In the same year, the "Yuan Da Tou" (Yuan Shikai's portrait) coins minted by the Beiyang Mint were introduced to unify the new currency system, providing favorable conditions for capitalist development. Subsequently, the outbreak of World War I marked a "golden period" for the development of Chinese national capitalism. During the war, several major imperialist powers were engaged in carving up the world again, leading to a relative weakening of foreign capitalist influences and a

---

① 《1912—1921 年津海关十年报告》（三）。天津海关译编委员会编译，《津海关史要览》，中国海关出版社，2004 年，第 108 页。

① Editorial Office of the Tianjin Chorography and History Compilation Committee (ed.). *Overview of Tianjin in the Early 20th Century*. Published internally in 1986, pp.260-265.

坐落在天津法租界内的美古绅地毯公司（右下角）
A. & M. Karagheusian Carpet Company in the French Concession
in Tianjin (in the lower right corner)

主要行业包括纺织、面粉、化学、制革等，其中较为突出的是：居全国第二位的棉纺织工业和居全国前列的面粉工业。而精盐纯碱的研制和生产，更填补了我国化学工业的一个空白，打破了列强的垄断。

欧战虽令列强无暇东顾，但此时的国内政局也并不稳定，从1916 年 6 月袁世凯去世、北洋军阀分裂，到 1926 年 7 月国共合作、国民革命军北伐，再到 1929 年国民政府宣布统一全国。十余年的分裂与争战状态，出乎意料地没有对天津的工业发展造成破坏性影响。究其原因，主要是军阀打仗要购买军火、发放兵饷，所以他们必须将聚敛的财富变为资本进行再投资，以使"财源广进"。天津是北洋军阀争夺的地盘，租界是各派军阀势力盘踞的地方。他们开始只投资于房地产、金融、当铺、粮店等。由于看到欧战后工厂企业利润大大超过其他行业，这些大小军阀便纷纷投资工业。如1916—1922 年建立的华新、裕元、恒源、北洋、裕大、宝成六大纱厂中，除北洋、宝成外，都有军阀投资。资料显示，1914—1925 年

noticeable decrease in the importation of foreign goods, thereby providing an opportunity for the development of Chinese national industry. Tianjin, as an important industrial city, experienced similar trends. For example, the tonnage of foreign ships entering Tianjin Port after the outbreak of the war decreased significantly: from 916,005 tons for Britain in 1912 to 555,972 tons in 1918, and from 45,606 tons for the United States in 1912 to 10,390 tons in 1918.[①] The market left vacant by them was occupied by domestic national industries. According to the data of factories registered under the Ministry of Industry and Commerce of the Beiyang Government in Tianjin from 1912 to 1920, there were 23 factories with a capital exceeding ten thousand yuan, with a total capital of 12,115,000 yuan. The main industries included textiles, flour milling, chemicals, and leather processing. Notably, Tianjin ranked second in the nation in cotton textile industry and was at the forefront in the flour milling industry. Moreover, the research and production of refined salt and soda ash filled a gap in China's chemical industry, breaking the monopoly of foreign powers.

Although the European War preoccupied the Great Powers, the domestic political situation during this time was also far from stable. From the death of Yuan Shikai and the subsequent fragmentation of the Beiyang Warlords in June 1916, to the cooperation between the Nationalists and the Communists and the Northern Expedition of the National Revolutionary Army in July 1926, and then to the announcement of the Nationalist Government's unification of the country in 1929, more than a decade of division and conflict unexpectedly did not have a destructive impact on the industrial development of Tianjin. The main reason for this was that warlords needed to purchase arms and pay soldiers' salaries, so they had to turn their accumulated wealth into capital for reinvestment to ensure a steady flow of income. Tianjin was a battleground for the Beiyang Warlords, and the concessions were where various warlord factions were entrenched. Initially, they only invested in real estate, finance, pawnshops, and grain shops. However, witnessing the significant profits of industrial enterprises after the European War, these warlords began to invest in industry. For instance, among the six major textile mills established between 1916 and 1922—Hua Xin, Yu Yuan, Heng Yuan, Beiyang, Yu Da, and Bao Cheng—except for Beiyang and Bao Cheng, all had investments from warlords. Data shows that from 1914 to 1925, Tianjin saw the establishment of 26 new factories with a total capital of 29.26 million yuan. Among them,

① *The Ten-year Report of Tianjin Customs from 1912 to 1921*. Quoted in *Overview of the History of Tianjin Customs*, translated and edited by Tianjin Customs Translation and Editing Committee. China Customs Press, 2004, p.108.

东亚毛纺厂的"抵羊牌"毛线是国货精品、国际知名品牌
"Diyang" woolen yarn of Oriental Wool Manufacturers Company was a high-quality domestic product and an internationally renowned brand

天津东亚毛纺厂
Oriental Wool Manufacturers Company

天津新建 26 家工厂，资本总额 2926 万元，其中有 11 家工厂、资本总额 1572 万元属于军阀投资，分别占建厂数的 42.2%，投资总额的 53.7%。如 1918 年开业的裕元纱厂实际上就是安福系军阀官僚所办，该厂董事会的主要成员有：时任国务总理段祺瑞、安徽督军倪嗣冲、陆军次长徐树铮、外交总长曹汝霖、交通总长朱启钤、众院议长王揖唐、督理奉天军务段芝贵和安福议员王郅隆等。全部股本 200 万元，仅倪嗣冲一人就占有 110 万元。[①] 天津的工厂企业成了军阀政客们敛财的工具，他们自然不愿破坏天津平安的投资环境，也不敢骚扰外国势力盘踞的租界。

随着城市经济发展和城市化进程，天津的市民阶层力量也随之壮大起来，支持和推动近代一次又一次的反帝爱国民主运动，促进了民族工业的发展。1905 年因美国提出排华法案，遭到爱国工商界抵制，包括天津在内的全国 20 多个大城市市民、学生、工商业者抵制美货；抵制活动持续约一年多，在此期间，美国对中国的贸易量减少 40%，中国的工业生产量也相应提高。1915 年日本向袁世凯提出灭亡中国的"二十一条"，天津人民又与全国人民一起掀起抵制

11 factories with a total capital of 15.72 million yuan were invested by warlords, accounting for 42.2% of the number of factories and 53.7% of the total investment. For example, the Yu Yuan textile mill, established in 1918, was actually operated by officials affiliated with the Anfu Clique of warlords. The main members of the Board of Directors included the then Prime Minister Duan Qirui, Anhui Governor Ni Sichong, Army Vice Minister Xu Shuzheng, Foreign Minister Cao Rulin, Transportation Minister Zhu Qiqian, Speaker of the House of Representatives Wang Yitang, Military Affairs Commissioner for Fengtian (now Shenyang) Duan Zhigui, and Anfu Clique member Wang Zhilong. The total capital was 2 million yuan, with Ni Sichong alone holding 1.1 million yuan.[①] The factories in Tianjin became tools for warlords and politicians to accumulate wealth. Naturally, they were unwilling to disrupt the investment environment of Tianjin's stability or provoke the concessions occupied by foreign powers.

With the development of urban economy and urbanization, the strength of the citizenry in Tianjin has also grown, supporting and propelling one patriotic democratic movement after another in modern times, which has promoted the development of national industry. In 1905, due to the United States proposing the Chinese Exclusion Act, it faced resistance from patriotic

---

① 来新夏，《天津早期民族近代工业发展简况及黄金时期资本来源的特点》，天津市政协文史资料未刊稿。

---

① Lai Xinxia. *A Brief Introduction to the Development of Early National Modern Industry in Tianjin and the Characteristics of Capital Sources during the Golden Age*. Unpublished drafts of the cultural and historical data of the Tianjin Municipal Committee of the Chinese People's Political Consultative Conference.

日货运动。1916年天津人民反对法国侵占老西开，做出"抵制法货"的决定，同时提出"爱用国货"的号召，既开辟和扩大了国货的国内市场，也鼓舞了民族资本家办工业的积极性。

北方商业巨子周学熙与其北方工业集团

说到天津乃至整个华北地区的工业发展，不得不提的一个重要人物就是中国近代著名实业家——周学熙。他最为人熟知的身份虽然是实业家、资本家，但其实他最初的身份是官员。周学熙和他的父亲周馥是由李鸿章创立、袁世凯继承的北洋集团的重要成员。

封建社会，父亲是家庭中最重要的角色。周学熙的父亲对其影响极大。周馥是李鸿章所有幕友中追随其时间最长的。他从1861年开始服务于李鸿章，终其一生都对幕主忠心耿耿，并在建立电报局、北洋水师学堂、北洋武备学堂及其他工作中给予李鸿章宝贵的帮助。李鸿章死后，他官至山东巡抚、四川总督和两广总督等。可以说，周馥是一个非常有能力的人，虽没有取得过任何科举功名，却受过大约十年的正规学校教育，且实际工作能力强。周馥在李鸿章幕府服务期间，一直对那些虽然拿着中国俸禄却巧取豪夺、侵害中国利权的洋顾问非常痛恨，甚至经常与对方拍着桌子对骂。他的爱国主义精神和高尚品质赢得了李鸿章身边其他正直的外国人的敬重：北洋大学的掌校人丁家立称周馥是一位"著名的儒家学者"；而津海关税务司庆丕（Paul King）则评价他是"伟大的人"。[①]

周学熙幼承庭训，从父亲那里所接受的都是"师夷长技以制夷""自强""求富"的思想，并且耳濡目染皆为具体运作方式方法而非空谈大道理。父亲的人脉关系和政治地位，还为科举失利的周学熙铺就了另一条事业发展道路。他先是于1897年进入开平矿务局，负责在上海推销煤炭；翌年升任开平矿务局会办，后又升任总办。八国联军入侵时，开平矿务局矿权被盗卖给英国商人，周学熙看破阴谋，不顾威胁，拒绝在卖矿契约上签字，并愤而辞去总办职务，

① 张畅、刘悦，《李鸿章的洋顾问：德璀琳与汉纳根》，台北传记文学出版社，2012年，第63—64页。

industrial and commercial circles. Citizens, students, and businesspeople from over 20 major cities nationwide, including Tianjin, boycotted American goods. The boycott lasted for more than a year, during which time US trade with China decreased by 40%, and China's industrial production correspondingly increased. In 1915, when Japan presented the "Twenty-One Demands" aimed at the subjugation of China to Yuan Shikai, the people of Tianjin joined the nationwide movement to boycott Japanese goods. In 1916, the people of Tianjin opposed the French occupation of the Laoxikai area and decided to boycott French goods while also advocating for the use of domestic goods. This not only opened up and expanded the domestic market for domestic products but also inspired the enthusiasm of nationalist capitalists to establish industries.

The Northern Business Tycoon Zhou Xuexi and His Northern Industrial Group

When it comes to the industrial development of Tianjin and even the entire North China region, one cannot ignore an important figure, namely the renowned industrialist of modern China—Zhou Xuexi. While he is best known as an industrialist and capitalist, his initial identity was actually that of a government official. Zhou Xuexi, along with his father Zhou Fu, was an important member of the Beiyang Group established by Li Hongzhang and inherited by Yuan Shikai.

In feudal society, the father was the most important figure in the family. Zhou Xuexi's father had a significant influence on him. Zhou Fu was among the longest-serving associates of Li Hongzhang among all his close aides. He began his service with Li Hongzhang in 1861 and remained loyal to his master throughout his life, providing valuable assistance to Li Hongzhang in establishing the Telegraph Office, the Beiyang Naval Academy, the Beiyang Military Academy, and other endeavors. After Li Hongzhang's death, Zhou Fu held positions such as Governor of Shandong, Governor of Sichuan, and Viceroy of Liangguang. It can be said that Zhou Fu was a highly capable individual. Although he never achieved any success in the imperial examinations, he received about ten years of formal schooling and demonstrated strong practical skills. During his service in Li Hongzhang's administration, Zhou Fu harbored deep resentment towards foreign advisors who, despite receiving Chinese salaries, engaged in exploitation and infringed upon China's interests. He often engaged in heated arguments with them, even slamming his hand on the table. His patriotism and noble qualities earned him the respect of other upright foreigners around Li Hongzhang.

北洋实业巨子周学熙（1866—1947）
Zhou Xuexi (1866-1947), an industrial tycoon of Beiyang group

义和团运动后周学熙奉命恢复重建的"北洋银元局"（即户部造币总厂）示意图。图片来源：北京故宫博物院
Diagram of the "Beiyang Mint" (also known as the Central Mint of the Ministry of Revenue) that Zhou Xuexi was ordered to restore and rebuild after the Boxer Rebellion. Source: The Palace Museum in Beijing

天津户部造币总厂。摄于 1909—1911 年。图片来源：北京故宫博物院
Central Mint of the Ministry of Revenue. Taken around 1909-1911. Source: The Palace Museum in Beijing

天津户部造币总厂的马力蒸汽机。摄于 1909—1911 年。图片来源：北京故宫博物院
Steam engine of Central Mint of the Ministry of Revenue. Taken around 1909-1911.
Source: The Palace Museum in Beijing

表现了一个正直的中国人的民族气节。此后，与周馥曾同为李鸿章幕僚、关系密切的袁世凯担任山东巡抚后，即将周学熙带到济南，推荐其任山东大学堂的校长。办学过程中，周学熙采取中外结合的教育方法，取得了实效。李鸿章去世后，袁世凯接任直隶总督兼北洋大臣，接手了前任的班底和发展的实业思想。周学熙跟随来津，成为袁世凯在直隶实行新政最为得力的助手。从此，他以天津为基地，开始创办北洋实业。

八国联军占领天津期间，天津经济遭受巨大损失，大批银钱被抢走，当务之急就是造币。袁世凯当即委派周学熙为北洋银元局总办，尽快恢复造币厂，铸出铜元。周学熙临危受命，仅用 73 天就重建了造币厂，铸出铜元 150 万枚，一举满足了市场流通的需要，稳定了社会秩序，同时也获得了巨大的利润。袁世凯认为他是不可多得的人才，遂将北洋一切工商业发展事宜都交给他主持，使其能充分发

Charles D. Tenney, the head of Peiyang University, referred to Zhou Fu as a "renowned Confucian scholar," while Paul King, the Commissioner of Tianjin Customs, praised him as a "great man."[1]

Zhou Xuexi received early upbringing and education, inheriting from his father the ideas of "learning from the West to counter the foreigners," "self-strengthening," and "seeking wealth." What he saw and heard were not merely abstract principles but practical methodologies. His father's social connections and political status also paved another path for Zhou Xuexi's career after his failure in the imperial examinations. In 1897, he first entered the Kaiping Mining Bureau, responsible for promoting coal sales in Shanghai. The following year, he was promoted to become an associate of the Kaiping Mining Bureau, and later became its director. During the invasion of the Eight-Nation Alliance, the mining rights of the Kaiping Mining Bureau were illegally sold to British merchants. Zhou Xuexi saw through the conspiracy, refused to sign the sale contract despite threats, and resigned from his position as director, demonstrating the integrity and national spirit of a righteous Chinese. Later, when Yuan Shikai, who had close ties with Zhou Fu and had served as Li Hongzhang's aide, was appointed as the Governor of Shandong, he brought Zhou Xuexi to Jinan and recommended him as the principal of Shandong University. During his tenure, Zhou Xuexi adopted an educational approach that combined Chinese and Western methods, which proved to be effective. After Li Hongzhang's death, Yuan Shikai succeeded him as the Viceroy of Zhili and concurrently as the Minister of Beiyang, inheriting the team and industrial development ideas from his predecessor. Zhou Xuexi followed him to Tianjin and became Yuan Shikai's most trusted assistant in implementing the New Policies in Zhili. From then on, he established the Beiyang industries with Tianjin as its base.

During the occupation of Tianjin by the Eight-Nation Alliance, the Tianjin economy suffered immense losses, with a large amount of silver being looted. The urgent task at hand was to mint coins. Yuan Shikai immediately appointed Zhou Xuexi as the director of the Beiyang Mint to quickly restore the mint and mintage of copper coins. Zhou Xuexi accepted the mission in a time of crisis and rebuilt the mint in just 73 days, minting 1.5 million copper coins. This move not only met the market's circulation needs and stabilized social order but also generated significant profits. Yuan Shikai regarded him as an invaluable talent and entrusted him with all matters related to industrial and commercial development in Beiyang, allowing him to fully leverage his

---

①　Zhang Chang, Liu Yue. *Li Hongzhang's Foreign Consultants: Gustav Detring and Constantin von Hanneken*. Taipei: Biographies Publishing House, 2012, pp.63-64.

挥所长。

为了推进实业发展，1903年周学熙专程赴日本考察。40多天里，马不停蹄，连续考察了几十个不同行业和不同规模的厂矿、商业、金融财政部门，以及几十所不同类型的学校。这次考察使他对如何兴办洋务有了更加全面系统的认识和规划。回国后，他积极向袁世凯倡议，成立了负责领导整个直隶地区实业发展的直隶工艺总局，并自荐任总办。他从上任开始，就有计划地筹集资金兴工办学。从1903年到1908年的5年里，他先后筹集了几百万两白银扶持官办和民办企业，先后创建商品陈列所、植物园、天津铁工厂、天津造币厂。同时，还创办了直隶高等工艺学堂，分设化学、机器、绘图三科，并要求所有学员都学习英语和日语，毕业生要达到日本中等工业学校毕业的同等学力，进一步通过考试，授予举人资格。此外，他还招募英国、美国和日本有真才实学的技术专家，以重金聘为教习；选择优秀学员派往日本留学，这些人后来都成为北洋实业的骨干力量。

周学熙时时不忘收回被帝国主义盗取的开平煤矿矿权，将其视作自己的使命责任。他先是于1906年收回了唐山水泥厂，改名为"启新洋灰公司"，迅速恢复了生产。这是当时全国唯一一家水泥厂。由于产品优质，很快被全国重大建筑工程所采用，如津浦铁路上的淮河铁路桥、黄河大桥，京汉铁路上的洛河铁桥，北宁铁路上的渭水铁桥，青岛、烟台、厦门、威海等地的海坝、码头，以及北京图书馆、辅仁大学、燕京大学、大陆银行、交通银行、上海邮政总局等当时的有名建筑，都是用马牌水泥建造的，这些建筑大部分至今仍然完好无损。1907年他又建立起"滦州煤矿有限公司"，以制约开平煤矿。滦州煤矿安装使用了最新采掘机器，并在袁世凯的支持下，在各矿之间建成了专用铁路，安装了电话，产量猛增，又因为所产煤炭质量比开平煤好，在市场上大受欢迎，对开平煤矿形成了很大的威胁。

1909年新任直隶总督陈夔龙再次决定要收回开平煤矿的主权，任命周学熙主持这项工作。经过与英国外交部和英国公司长达半年的交涉，双方终于达成协议：英国把开平煤矿交还中国，中国付给

expertise.

In order to promote industrial development, Zhou Xuexi made a special trip to Japan for inspection in 1903. In over 40 days, he tirelessly visited dozens of different industries and mines, commercial, financial, and fiscal departments, as well as various types of schools. This inspection provided him with a more comprehensive and systematic understanding and planning of how to promote modernization. Upon his return, he actively proposed to Yuan Shikai the establishment of the Zhili Industrial Bureau responsible for leading the industrial development of the entire Zhili region and volunteered to serve as its director. From the beginning of his tenure, he systematically raised funds to promote industrial development and education. Over the five years from 1903 to 1908, he raised several million taels of silver to support both government-run and privately operated enterprises, establishing Quangong Exhibition Center, Botanical Gardens, Tianjin Ironworks, and the Tianjin Central Mint of the Ministry of Revenue. Additionally, he founded the Zhili Higher School of Technology, offering courses in chemistry, machinery, and drawing, and required all students to study English and Japanese. Graduates were expected to attain the same level of competency as graduates of Japanese secondary industrial schools and, upon further examination, would be granted the status of "Juren" (a scholarly title in imperial China). Furthermore, he recruited skilled technical experts from Britain, the United States, and Japan at great expense as instructors and selected outstanding students to study in Japan, many of whom later became the backbone of Beiyang industries.

Zhou Xuexi constantly sought to reclaim the mining rights of the Kaiping Coal Mine stolen by imperialists, viewing it as his mission and responsibility. In 1906, he first reclaimed the Tangshan Cement Factory, renaming it "Chee Hsin Cement Co.", and quickly restored production. At that time, it was the only cement factory in China. Due to its high-quality products, it was quickly adopted for major national construction projects, such as the Huai River Railway Bridge and the Yellow River Bridge on the Tianjin-Pukou Railway, the Luo River Bridge on the Beijing-Hankou Railway, the Weishui Bridge on the Beijing-Harbin Railway, as well as dams and docks in Qingdao, Yantai, Xiamen, Weihai, and other places, as well as famous buildings at the time such as the Beijing Library, Fu Jen Catholic University, Yenching University, Continental Bank, Bank of Communications, and the Shanghai General Post Office, all of which were constructed using cement with the trademark of "Horse Brand", most of which remain intact to this day. In 1907, he established the "Luanzhou Mining Company" to restrain the Kaiping coal mine. The Luanzhou coal mine installed the latest mining machinery and, with the

英商 178 万英镑。眼看大功告成，政局变化，新上台的摄政王载沣拒绝由大清银行发行债券给付英商，而滦州煤矿无力承担，致使收回开平煤矿的事再次功败垂成。之后在与开平煤矿进行市场竞争的过程中，因资本不足以抗衡有国际财团为背景的开平矿务局，最终因时局动荡、股东压力而使周学熙"以滦收开"的目的未能达成，反而损失了滦州煤矿的利权。为此，他深感内疚，饮恨辞职。

民国初年，袁世凯当总统时任用周学熙为财务总长。袁世凯为了稳定政权、充裕国库，而要求周学熙与英法德美四国银行团签订善后大借款。周学熙办理借款的本意是谋求国家建设和裁兵，却被袁世凯利用，成为重启战端的经费。此次借款亦成为周学熙一生之耻。

1916 年 4 月，周学熙终于脱离政界，开始全力施展自己的商业才能。1918 年，他出任华新纺织公司总理，先后创办华新所属的天津、青岛、唐山、卫辉四家纱厂，执华北棉纺织业牛耳。1919 年为方便募集企业所需的资金流，将工业资本与金融资本融合起来，创办中国实业银行。1922 年与比利时商人合办耀华玻璃公司。1924 年再成立实业总汇处，任理事长，管理所属各企业。一个以天津为基地，

中国实业银行天津总行大楼。刘悦摄于 2024 年
Tianjin head office of China Industrial Bank. Taken by Liu Yue in 2024

support of Yuan Shikai, built dedicated railways between mines, installed telephones, and experienced a sharp increase in production. Because the quality of coal was better than that of the Kaiping coal mine, it was highly popular in the market, posing a significant threat to the Kaiping coal mine.

In 1909, the newly appointed Viceroy of Zhili, Chen Kuilong, once again decided to reclaim sovereignty over the Kaiping coal mine and appointed Zhou Xuexi to oversee this task. After six months of negotiations with the British Ministry of Foreign Affairs and British companies, an agreement was finally reached: Britain would return the Kaiping coal mine to China, and China would pay the British £1.78 million. Just as success seemed imminent, there was a political change. The newly appointed Regent, Zai Feng, refused to allow the Ta-Ching Government Bank to issue bonds to pay the British, and the Luanzhou coal mine was unable to bear the burden, resulting in the failure of the effort to reclaim the Kaiping coal mine once again. Subsequently, during the process of competing with the Kaiping coal mine in the market, due to insufficient capital to compete with the Kaiping Mining Bureau backed by an international consortium, Zhou Xuexi ultimately failed to achieve his goal of "reclaiming Kaiping with Luanzhou" due to the turbulent situation and pressure from shareholders. Instead, he lost the rights to the Luanzhou coal mine. Deeply remorseful, he resigned in bitterness.

In the early years of the Republic of China, when Yuan Shikai served as president, he appointed Zhou Xuexi as the Minister of Finance. Yuan Shikai, in order to stabilize his regime and fill the national treasury, demanded that Zhou Xuexi sign a large loan agreement with banking consortia from Britain, France, Germany, and the United States. Zhou Xuexi's intention in handling the loan was to seek funds for national development and disarmament, but he was exploited by Yuan Shikai, who used the funds to restart military conflicts. This loan became a lifelong disgrace for Zhou Xuexi.

In April 1916, Zhou Xuexi finally withdrew from politics and began to fully utilize his commercial talents. In 1918, he became the general manager of Huaxin Textile Company, successively establishing four yarn factories in Tianjin, Qingdao, Tangshan, and Weihui under Huaxin, dominating the cotton textile industry in North China. In 1919, to facilitate the raising of funds needed for the enterprise, he merged industrial capital with financial capital and founded the China Industrial Bank. In 1922, he co-founded Yaohua Glass Company with Belgian businessmen. In 1924, he established the Industrial Syndicate, serving as its chairman, managing its affiliated enterprises. Under the leadership of Zhou Xuexi, a business conglomerate based in Tianjin emerged, including large-scale enterprises in cement, ceramics, textiles, mining, and glass manufacturing, with its own bank and currency issuance,

包括水泥、陶瓷、纺织、矿业、玻璃制造等大型企业，拥有自己的银行和货币发行，掌控公路、铁路和内河航运主动权的周氏企业集团崛起，周学熙从此站在北方实业的巅峰。他与南方实业家张謇齐名，有"南张北周"之说。

纵观周学熙一生，他无疑是一位爱国者，始终致力于发展民族工业，收回被外国资本主义侵占的经济利益。他曾经为了与外国商人特别是日本商人争夺水泥市场而展开价格战并最终取胜；也曾为"以滦收开"而与英商控制下的开平煤矿不惜血本进行竞争，终不敌清政府昏聩和对方资本雄厚。尽管如此，周学熙却不是一位狭隘的民族主义者，而是从实际出发，该与外商合作则合作，该引进外国技术则引进。在受命创办"京师自来水公司"时，国内还没有生产自来水器材的厂家，所有的设备材料都要进口。周学熙采取向洋商招标的办法，精心筛选、反复比较，使中标的外国公司不得不精打细算，多快好省地完成施工，造福当地民众达半个多世纪。1922年，他又与比利时人共同出资，建立了近代中国第一家中外合办企业——耀华玻璃公司。所以说，周学熙是一位务实的讲求经济效益的实业家，而不是空谈误国、盲目排外的梦想家。

一介书生范旭东奠基中国化工业

范旭东（1883—1945）
Fan Xudong (1883-1945)

范旭东是天津民族工业发展的后起之秀，是中国重化学工业的奠基人、化工实业家，被称作"中国民族化学工业之父"。

范旭东出身寒微，6岁丧父，母亲靠为人浆洗衣物和做针线将他抚养长大。后随维新派的兄长逃亡，赴日本求学。1910年范旭东毕业于京都帝国大学化学系，毕业留校任教。不久后回国，于1914年在天津塘沽创办久大精盐公司。1917年，他创建永利碱厂。当时，中国的日用消费品尤其是日化产品市场，全部被外国产品占领，这些商品被称作"洋面""洋

controlling the initiative of highways, railways, and inland waterway transportation. From then on, Zhou Xuexi stood at the peak of northern industry. He was renowned alongside Zhang Jian, a southern industrialist, leading to the saying "Zhang of the South, Zhou of the North."

Looking back on Zhou Xuexi's life, he was undoubtedly a patriot, and was devoted to developing national industry and reclaiming economic interests occupied by foreign capitalism. He once engaged in a price war with foreign businessmen, especially Japanese businessmen, to compete for the cement market and ultimately emerged victorious. He also competed fiercely, at great expense, against the British-controlled Kaiping coal mine in the hope of reclaiming it under the slogan "reclaim Kaiping with Luanzhou," but ultimately succumbed to the blindness of the Qing government and the formidable capital of the opposing party. Nevertheless, Zhou Xuexi was not a narrow-minded nationalist but rather a pragmatic individual who cooperated with foreign businessmen when necessary and introduced foreign technology when appropriate. When tasked with establishing the "Peking Water Works," there were no domestic manufacturers of water supply equipment, and all equipment materials had to be imported. Zhou Xuexi adopted the method of inviting tenders from foreign merchants, carefully selecting and comparing bids, forcing the winning foreign companies to carefully calculate costs and efficiently complete construction, benefiting the local people for more than half a century. In 1922, he again jointly invested with Belgians to establish the first Sino-foreign joint venture in modern China, the Yaohua Glass Company. Therefore, Zhou Xuexi was a pragmatic industrialist who prioritized economic efficiency over empty dreams of nationalism and blind exclusion.

Fan Xudong, a Scholar Who Laid the Foundation for China's Chemical Industry

Fan Xudong is a rising star in the development of Tianjin's national industry, a pioneer in China's heavy chemical industry, and an industrialist in the chemical industry. He is known as the "Father of China's National Chemical Industry."

Fan Xudong came from humble origins. His father passed away when he was six years old, and his mother supported him by washing clothes and doing needlework. Later, he followed his brother, who was associated with the reformist movement, to escape and study in Japan. In 1910, Fan Xudong graduated from the Department of Chemistry at Kyoto Imperial University and stayed on to teach after graduation. Shortly afterward, he returned to China and founded Chiuta Refined Salt Company in Tanggu, Tianjin, in 1914.

布""洋火""洋盐""洋油（煤油）"，由此可见一斑。民族企业的创办具有收复失地、夺回商业利益的重大意义，同时也面临着实力雄厚的外国公司的激烈竞争。

旧毡帽朋友今天上镇来，原来有很多的计划的。洋肥皂用完了，须得买十块八块回去。洋火也要带几匣。洋油向挑着担子到村里去的小贩买，十个铜板只有这么一小瓢，太吃亏了；如果几家人家合买一听分来用，就便宜得多。陈列在橱窗里的花花绿绿的洋布听说只要八分半一尺，女人早已眼红了好久，今天枭米就嚷着要一同出来，自己几尺，阿大几尺，阿二几尺，都有了预算。

——摘自叶圣陶《多收了三五斗》

范旭东所面临的是更加险恶的国内外商业环境。范旭东创办公司时，股本只有 5 万元，公司就设在塘沽渔村，开办仅一年即研制出纯度达到 90% 以上的精盐，商标名为"海王星"，象征海盐结晶。久大精盐立即招致外国盐商的围剿，日本商人在报纸上散布"海王星"

20 世纪 20 年代黄海社及久大精盐厂远景
Distant view of Yellow Sea Chemical Industry Research Society and Chiuta Refined Salt Company in 1920s

In 1917, he established the Yungli Alkali Manufacturing Corporation. At that time, China's daily consumer goods market, especially the market for daily chemical products, was entirely dominated by foreign products. These goods were referred to as "yang mian" (foreign flour), "yang bu" (foreign cloth), "yang huo" (foreign matches), "yang yan" (foreign salt), and "yang you" (foreign oil, kerosene), illustrating the extent of foreign dominance. The founding of national enterprises had significant implications for reclaiming lost ground and reclaiming commercial interests, but it also faced fierce competition from powerful foreign companies.

An old friend in the felt hat comes to town today with many plans. He has run out of foreign soap and need to buy ten or eight pieces to take back. He also needs to bring a few boxes of foreign matches. Buying foreign oil from the peddlers who carry it to the village on their shoulders costs ten copper coins for just this little bit; it's too expensive. If several households pool together to buy a tin and share it, it's much cheaper. The colorful foreign cloth displayed in the shop window is said to be only eight and a half cents per foot. The women have been envious for a long time, and today they're clamoring to come out together. They've budgeted for a few feet for themselves, a few feet for the eldest son, and a few feet for the second son.

— Excerpt from Ye Shengtao's *Collecting Three or Five More Dou*

Fan Xudong faced an even more perilous domestic and international business environment. When he founded his company, with a capital of only 50,000 yuan, it was located in a fishing village in Tanggu. Within just one year of operation, they managed to develop refined salt with a purity exceeding 90%, branded as "Neptune," symbolizing crystallized sea salt. However, Chiuta Refined Salt Company immediately faced encirclement from foreign salt merchants, with Japanese businessmen spreading rumors in newspapers that "Neptune" was poisonous. In China, for hundreds of years, the buying and selling of traditional table salt had been monopolized by government-authorized salt merchants, forming a vast interest group. As a result, Chiuta Refined Salt Company was unable to be sold in markets south of the Yangtze River for a long time. Fan Xudong broke through the blockade with high-quality products and competitive prices. After expanding the new factory in 1919, the annual output reached 62,500 tons, making it the earliest, largest, and best refined salt production base in China.

After achieving a breakthrough in refined salt, Fan Xudong challenged the alkali-manufacturing industry. Alkali is one of the important chemical

侯德榜(1890—1974),中国化工专家。"侯氏联合制碱法"的发明者,著有《制碱》。与永利碱业创始人范旭东同为中国近代民族化学工业的先驱。北洋大学兼职教授
Hou Debang (1890-1974), a Chinese chemical expert, invented Hou's Process and had written the book *Alkali Production*. He and Fan Xudong, the founder of Yungli Alkali Manufacturing Corporation, were pioneers of national chemical industry in modern China. He was also an adjunct professor at Peiyang University

有毒的谣言。在国内,几百年来中国传统的食盐买卖皆由政府授权盐商垄断,他们形成了一个庞大的利益集团。因此,久大精盐长时间无法销售到长江以南的市场。范旭东凭借优质的产品和优惠的价格突破重围,1919 年扩建新厂后,年产量达到 62500 吨,成为我国最早、最大、最好的精盐生产基地。

在精盐上取得突破后,范旭东又挑战制碱业。碱是重要的化工原料之一,主要用途是轻工、建材、化学工业等领域,约占 2/3;其次是冶金、纺织、石油、国防、医药及其他工业。制作玻璃、炼钢炼锑、印染布料、制革、合成洗涤剂,乃至生产味精、制作面食糕点,都离不开碱。当时,只有西方国家掌握专利技术,形成垄断。第一次世界大战造成远洋运输困难,垄断中国纯碱市场的英国卜内门公司趁机抬价惜售,使许多民族织染厂生产陷于停顿。

范旭东团结了一批国内青年科学家,形成了一个真正意义的科学攻关团队,其中包括苏州东吴大学化学硕士陈调甫、上海大效机器厂的厂长兼总工程师王小徐、东京高等工业学校电气化学专业毕业生李烛尘和美国哥伦比亚大学化学博士侯德榜。他们于 1917 年筹备,翌年正式在塘沽成立永利制碱公司。他们在范旭东家里搭建实验室,进行了 3 个多月的反复实验,终于打通了工艺流程,造出 9 公斤合格的纯碱。1924 年永利投入 200 万元进行批量生产,结果失败,制出的碱为劣质碱。为彻底解决制碱技术问题,范旭东决定派侯德榜等技术人

raw materials, mainly used in light industry, building materials, chemical industry, and other fields, accounting for about 2/3 of its usage. It is also used in metallurgy, textiles, petroleum, national defense, medicine, and other industries. The production of glass, steel refining, printing and dyeing fabrics, tanning, synthetic detergents, as well as the production of monosodium glutamate, and making noodles and pastries, all rely on alkali. At that time, only Western countries held patented technology, forming a monopoly. The difficulties in long-distance transportation caused by the First World War led to price hikes and limited sales by the British Brunner, Mond and Company, which monopolized the Chinese soda ash market, causing many domestic textile and dyeing factories to halt production.

Fan Xudong united a group of young domestic scientists, forming a truly meaningful scientific research team, including Chen Tiaofu, a chemistry master from Soochow University in Suzhou, Wang Xiaoxu, the director and chief engineer of Shanghai Da Xiao Machinery Factory, Li Zhuchen, a graduate in electrochemical engineering from Tokyo Higher Technical School, and Hou Debang, a chemistry Ph.D. from Columbia University in the United States. They began preparations in 1917 and formally established the Yungli Alkali Manufacturing Corporation in Tanggu the following year. They set up a laboratory at Fan Xudong's home and conducted over three months of repeated experiments, finally mastering the process and producing 9 kilograms of qualified soda ash. In 1924, Yungli invested 2 million yuan for mass production, but the result was a failure, producing inferior quality alkali. To thoroughly solve the problem of alkali production technology, Fan Xudong decided to send technical personnel including Hou Debang to the United States for study and purchase of new equipment. In June 1926, the first domestically produced soda ash in China, branded as "Red Triangle" soda ash, went into production. In August, "Red Triangle" soda ash won the Gold Award at the Philadelphia World Expo, ranking at the world's leading level.

Due to the Japanese occupation of the Northeastern provinces and the precarious situation in North China, Fan Xudong and others evacuated from the northern region. In 1934, they established the Yungli Chemical Industry Company Nanjing Ammonia Factory. In 1937, they produced China's first batch of ammonium sulfate products, marking a new page in the history of China's chemical fertilizer industry. It was compared to DuPont Company of the United States by the Chinese people and dubbed as the "largest plant in the Far East." With the progression of the Anti-Japanese war, Fan Xudong pioneered the establishment of a new wartime chemical base in southwestern Sichuan. In 1943, his chief engineer, Hou Debang, invented the world-famous "Hou's Process" there. Just after the victory of the Anti-Japanese war, Fan

员赴美考察学习，并采购新式设备。1926年6月，中国第一代自制纯碱——"红三角"牌纯碱投产。8月，"红三角"牌纯碱获美国费城万国博览会金奖，居于世界领先水平。

因日本侵占东三省，华北形势危急，范旭东等撤离北方，于1934年在南京创办永利化学工业公司南京锭厂，1937年生产出中国第一批硫酸铵产品，这是中国化肥工业史上崭新的一页，国人把它和美国杜邦公司相媲美，称它为"远东第一大厂"。随着抗战情势，范旭东又率先在川西南开辟出新的战时化工基地，1943年在这里，他的总工程师侯德榜发明了世界著名的"侯氏联合制碱法"。抗战刚刚胜利，长期呕心沥血的范旭东因病去世。

范旭东与周学熙是最具典型性的近代实业家。他们均以天津为创业基地，利用这里的天时地利人和，与西方列强支持下拥有资金和技术优势的外国商人进行商战，抗击西方的经济侵略。与受传统文化熏陶、官商一体、拥有更多政府和民间资本支持的周学熙相比，范旭东是承前启后的一代新型民族工业家，他在海外接受现代教育，毅然归国，用技术而不是资本打败了西方，赢得了世界的尊重。

范旭东在创办工厂的过程中，也十分热衷于学术活动和教育事业。他的身边吸引聚集了一大批年轻科学家，在久大研究室的基础上，创办了"黄海化学工业研究社"，第一任社长是毕业于美国哈佛大学的化学博士孙学悟。"黄海社"不断招聘国内外化学家到社工作，先后成立了化工原理、应用化学、发酵化学、海洋化学等研究室。该社研究成果丰硕，并培养出大批化工人才，与"永利制碱""久大精盐"一起，并称为"永久黄"团体，这是近代中国第一个大型私营化工生产和研究组织。范旭东还曾担任中国自然科学社理事达30余年，受国民政府中央研究院的聘请担任评议员达10余年，被推选为中华化学工业会副会长、中国化学会副理事长。他继兄长范源濂之后担任过中华书局董事，对出版事业提出了许多有益的建议。他还是天津南开大学和湖南私立隐储女校的校董，给南开大学化学系和经济研究所捐赠过奖学金，以鼓励优秀学生。

范旭东经营企业奉行以人为中心的管理哲学，最早注意到要"维持培养同仁的人情友谊"。永利先后兴建起了工人食堂、宿舍、职

Xudong, who had dedicated himself to the cause for a long time, passed away due to illness.

Fan Xudong and Zhou Xuexi are the most typical modern industrialists. Both of them chose Tianjin as their entrepreneurial base, taking advantage of the favorable geographical location and resources, and engaging in commercial battles against foreign businessmen who had financial and technological advantages under the support of Western powers, thus resisting Western economic aggression. Compared with Zhou Xuexi, who was influenced by traditional culture, belonged to the integrated bureaucracy and business class, and had more support from both the government and private capital, Fan Xudong represented a new generation of nationalist industrialists. He received modern education overseas, returned home resolutely, defeated the West with technology rather than capital, and won respect worldwide.

In the process of establishing factories, Fan Xudong was also deeply involved in academic activities and educational endeavors. He attracted a large number of young scientists around him. Based on the Chiuta research laboratory, he founded the "Yellow Sea Chemical Industry Research Society," with Dr. Sun Xuewu, a chemistry Ph.D. graduate from Harvard University, as its first president. The "Yellow Sea Society" continuously recruited chemists from domestic and foreign sources to work in the society and established research laboratories for chemical principles, applied chemistry, fermentation chemistry, and marine chemistry. The society's research results were fruitful, and it trained a large number of chemical talents. Together with "Yungli Alkali Manufacturing Corporation" and "Chiuta Refined Salt Company," it formed the "Yong-Jiu-Huang" group, which was the first large-scale private chemical production and research organization in modern China. Fan Xudong also served as a director of the Natural Science Society of China for over 30 years, was appointed as an evaluator by the Academia Sinica of the National Government for more than 10 years, and was elected as the vice chairman

"黄海化学工业研究社"章程
Charter of Yellow Sea Chemical Industry Research Society

工消费合作社、运动场、图书室、附属医院、幼稚园、明星小学校等。1925年，永利开始实行职工三班工作制，成为中国企业界最早实行每日八小时工作制的工厂。所以范旭东不是单纯追求利润的实业家，而是一位具有社会责任感和现代企业经营理念的新型企业家。

范旭东一贯自称书生，从不把自己看作商人。他曾经说："我总觉得中国受病已久，它的存亡关键，决不在敌国外患的有无，完全是握在全国智（知）识分子手里，智（知）识分子教它兴就兴，

of the China Institute of Chemical Industry and vice director of the Chinese Chemical Society. He succeeded his elder brother Fan Yuanlian as a director of the Zhonghua Book Company, where he made many beneficial suggestions for the publishing industry. He also served as a director of Nankai University in Tianjin and Hunan Private Yinchu Girls' School, donating scholarships to the Chemistry Department of Nankai University and the Economic Research Institute to encourage outstanding students.

Fan Xudong practiced a people-centered management philosophy in his business operations, being among the first to recognize the importance

天津塘沽永利碱厂。图片来源：永利化工公司
Yungli Alkali Manufacturing Corporation in Tanggu, Tianjin. Source: Yungli Chemical Company

永利碱厂万国博览会金奖证书
Gold Award of the World Expo won by Yungli Alkali Manufacturing Corporation

教它亡就亡。"他是中国化学工业的开创者。

工业发展，改变了天津的经济结构和城市面貌，拉大了天津与周边城市的等级差距。在技术的加持下，天津逐渐成为华北地区的中心城市，不断吸纳周边地区的人口和财富。这种在历史上占统治地位的城市的更替，深刻说明了决定城市地位的统治武器的改变及其价值：航运、贸易、技术、工业、信贷以及政治权力等。在接下来的章节中我们将继续加以阐释。

of "maintaining and cultivating the friendship among colleagues". Yungli successively established workers' canteens, dormitories, employees' consumer cooperatives, sports fields, libraries, affiliated hospitals, kindergartens, and primary schools. In 1925, it began implementing a three-shift system for workers, becoming one of the earliest factories in China to adopt the eight-hour workday. Therefore, Fan Xudong was not merely a profit-driven industrialist but a new type of entrepreneur with a sense of social responsibility and modern business management concepts.

Fan Xudong consistently referred to himself as a scholar and never saw himself as a businessman. He once said, "I always feel that China has been sick for a long time. The key to its survival or demise does not lie in the existence of foreign enemies, but entirely in the hands of the nation's intellectuals. It is the intellectuals who can lead it to prosperity or downfall." He was the pioneer of China's chemical industry.

The development of industry has changed Tianjin's economic structure and urban landscape, widening the gap in status between Tianjin and surrounding cities. With the support of technology, Tianjin has gradually become the central city in the North China region, continuously attracting population and wealth from surrounding areas. This succession of cities dominating throughout history profoundly illustrates the changes and value of the dominant weapons determining urban status: shipping, trade, technology, industry, credit, and political power, among others. We will continue to elaborate on this in the following chapters.

第 五 章　人口、阶层与城市的族群

Chapter Five: Population, Class, and Urban Ethnic Groups

工业化、城市化与人口流动　　Industrialization, Urbanization, and Population Mobility

城市与城市病　　　　　　　Cities and Urban Diseases

工业化、城市化与人口流动

　　城市是工业文明的集大成者，人类社会生活所散发出来的一道道光束聚集成一个巨大的光源，吸引着人们从四面八方汇聚于此。它也像一个黑洞，无情吞噬着一个个被它的绚丽光芒吸引来的追随者。它是"冒险家的乐园"，也是滋生贫困、疾病、犯罪、社会危机、族群冲突的"歹土"。成功者不会告老还乡，失败者也回不去梦里田园，这就是近代化中单向的城市化进程。

近代市民阶层的产生

　　新技术（机械化生产）和新能源（煤炭）的使用为工业发展奠定了物质基础，大规模生产成为可能；萧条的农村为新兴工业组织提供了源源不绝的劳动力；合股公司、科层制管理和分工协作，大大提高了生产效率；城市汇集各种资源所产生的聚集效应开始显现，在与乡村的竞争中优势尽显。物质基础和上层建筑均已粗具规模，建设完备的租界社区展示了舒适的城市生活的消费属性。于是，人们一切行为的动机都简化为追求金钱上的成功。无论是新兴的工业家和银行家，还是巧取豪夺的投机分子，各色人等一窝蜂地涌入天津这样的通商口岸城市，寻找发财致富或勉强糊口的路径，由此形成持续不断的移民潮。

　　刚刚对外开放为通商口岸时，1860 年的天津有人口约 30 万，1872 年约有人口 40 万，1896 年人口则达到 60 万，人口增长的速度几乎是一年增加 1 万人。进入 20 世纪，随着民族工商业的发展和城

Industrialization, Urbanization, and Population Mobility

City is the culmination of industrial civilization, where beams of light emitted by human social life converge into a vast source of light, attracting people from all directions. It is also like a black hole, mercilessly devouring followers drawn to it by its dazzling light. It is both "the adventurer's paradise" and the "pernicious land" that breeds poverty, disease, crime, social crises, and ethnic conflicts. Successful individuals do not return to their hometowns, and those who fail cannot return to the idyllic countryside in their dreams. This is the one-way process of urbanization in modernization.

The Emergence of Modern Urban Middle Class

The use of new technology (mechanized production) and new energy sources (coal) laid the material foundation for industrial development, making mass production possible. The depressed countryside provided a steady stream of labor for emerging industrial organizations. Joint-stock companies, hierarchical management, and division of labor greatly improved production efficiency. The aggregation effect of various resources in cities began to emerge, demonstrating advantages in competition with rural areas. Both the material foundation and the superstructure had taken shape, and the well-constructed concession communities showcased the consumption attributes of comfortable urban life. Consequently, the motivation behind all actions simplified to the pursuit of monetary success. Whether emerging industrialists and bankers or speculative adventurers, people of all kinds flocked to port cities like Tianjin, seeking paths to wealth or merely to make ends meet, resulting in a continuous influx of immigrants.

When Tianjin opened up as a trading port to foreign countries in 1860, it had a population of about 300,000. By 1872, the population had increased to around 400,000, and by 1896, it reached 600,000, with an annual growth rate of nearly 10,000 people. In the 20th century, with the development of

市化进程，更有大量人口从周边地区涌入天津，人口规模不断扩大。1925 年天津市人口数量超过 100 万，跨入特大城市行列，1928 年跃升至 136 万余人，到 1948 年底发展到 190 多万人。据原天津市日伪警察局于 1937 年对市区约 107 万中国人的籍贯的统计分析，天津本地人口占 41.6%，外省籍人口占 58.4%。外省籍中，以邻近的河北省籍为最多，占 41.9%；其次是山东籍，占 10.1%；第三是北京籍，占 2.2%；河南、山西籍占 1.8%。1947 年国民党警察局再次进行统计表明，天津市 168 万市民当中，来自河北省的人口占第一位，共 78 万；天津本地籍占第二位，68 万；第三位是山东人，15 万；其余几万人来自全国各省市，甚至包括西康、青海和新疆等边远省份。[1] 其实，天津本就是移民城市，本地籍贯的人口往往也并非真正的天津籍，上溯几代大都是来自其他省份然后改变籍贯。

出于各种原因来到天津的外乡人，进入大城市之后，往往如小溪汇入大海，溅起一些水花后，融为一个整体，逐渐构成了一个新的社会阶层，即市民阶层。这是一个不同于传统社会中与"官"相对立的"民"的新阶层，由拥有权力、财富、社会声望各不相同、却都居住于同一城市环境的居民所构成。市民所从事的职业各不相同，他们中既有人口占比最大的产业工人、职员、服务业人员等，也有民族资本家、新型商人、工程师、律师、医生、大学教授、报人等拥有更多社会资源的社会精英。

市民阶层具有几个显著的特征：首先，经济上，市民阶层是经济领域的发展在社会结构变迁上的体现，是资本主义经济发展的产物，同时其活动又推动了资本主义经济的发展。其次，政治上，市民阶层是一种特殊的维护社会秩序的政治力量。虽然在这个阶层内部有大大小小的利益集团，但当面对共同的敌人时，他们也能结成短暂的同盟，联合起来反对共同的敌人，并向掌权者反映自己的政治诉求，寄希望于通过制定政策来维护自己的利益。第三，思想上，市民阶层推崇民主、自由、公平、法治，他们所萌发的权利意识推动了近代民族意识的觉醒和争取独立自主的民族解放运动的发展。

---

[1] 天津市档案馆编，《近代以来天津城市化进程实录》，天津人民出版社，2005 年，第 629、630 页。

national industry and commerce and the urbanization process, a large number of people flocked to Tianjin from surrounding areas, leading to continuous expansion of the population. In 1925, the population of Tianjin exceeded one million, making it a metropolis. By 1928, the population had risen to over 1.36 million, and by the end of 1948, it had grown to over 1.9 million. According to a statistical analysis conducted by the original Tianjin Japanese police station in 1937 on the origins of about 1.07 million Chinese people in the urban area, 41.6% were locals of Tianjin, while 58.4% were from other provinces. Among the non-local population, those from neighboring Hebei Province accounted for the majority at 41.9%, followed by Shandong Province at 10.1%, Beijing at 2.2%, and Henan and Shanxi at 1.8% each. A census conducted by the Nationalist police bureau in 1947 showed that among the 1.68 million residents of Tianjin, 780,000 were from Hebei Province, ranking first, followed by 680,000 locals of Tianjin, and 150,000 from Shandong. The rest came from various provinces and cities nationwide, including remote provinces such as Xikang (eastern Tibet and western Sichuan), Qinghai, and Xinjiang.[1] In fact, Tianjin has always been a city of immigrants, and even the local population often does not have genuine Tianjin ancestry. Many of them originally came from other provinces and changed their place of origin over several generations.

For various reasons, outsiders who come to Tianjin often blend into the city like streams merging into the sea. After splashing some water, they gradually become part of a new social class, namely the urban citizenry. This is a new class distinct from the traditional social division between "officials" and "commoners." It consists of residents with varying degrees of power, wealth, and social status, all living in the same urban environment. The occupations of urban citizens vary widely, including industrial workers, clerks, service industry workers, as well as ethnic capitalists, new businessmen, engineers, lawyers, doctors, university professors, journalists, and other social elites who possess more social resources.

The urban citizenry has several notable characteristics: Firstly, economically, the urban citizenry embodies the development of the economy in the social structure transition and is a product of capitalist economic development. At the same time, their activities also drive the development of capitalist economy. Secondly, politically, the urban citizenry is a special political force that upholds social order. Although there are various interest groups within this class, they can form temporary alliances when facing common enemies. They unite to oppose common enemies and reflect their

---

[1] Tianjin Archives (ed.). *Factual Records of Tianjin's Urbanization since Modern Times*. Tianjin People's Publishing House, 2005, p.629,630.

第四，市民阶层具有开放性、包容性的特质，它们突破了地域、血缘、家族等的限制，成为一个新的有机整体。第五，由于薄有资产、生活安逸，市民阶层中的许多人也容易产生保守的观念性格和耽于物质享受的弱点。

商人和商会

　　商业是一项古老的行业。对商业的基本定义，指提供顾客所需的商品和服务的一种行为。即使在自给自足的自然经济环境下，仍然需要各式各样的交换以互通有无。近代在工业资本与金融资本结合之下，商业的形式变得更加丰富。饭店的老板、售卖胭脂的货摊、广东会馆的南货商、洋行里的买办、纺纱厂的股东，都属于经营不同行当、但均以盈利为目的的商人。近代，天津商人的出身构成有了很大的变化，其社会地位也有了极大的提升。传统社会里，商人属于"士农工商"中的末流，尽管曾有约等于拥有特许经营权的类似"东印度公司"那样的十三行商人，但他们几乎没有任何政治地位，只能通过姻亲故旧的关系来为自己代言。近代的大商人则有所不同，背靠各种政治势力保护，其话语权伴随经济权力而大大提升。

　　一名商人总是与一些顾客、供货人、借款人、债权人相联系，因而有其相对固定的地盘。铁路开通之前，近代天津商人倚仗海河流域的水运便利，其经商范围囊括几乎整个中国北部，包括河北、河南、山东、山西、甘肃、陕西、吉林、辽宁以及内外蒙古地区。商人们将天津口岸进口的西方工业品销往那些区域，再收购当地的土产运往天津港输出到海外。铁路开通之后，沿线的港口城市逐渐成为天津的有力竞争者，如京汉铁路终点的汉口、胶州铁路通抵的青岛、由唐胥铁路而发展起来的秦皇岛以及京奉铁路和南满铁路所联结的沈阳和大连。天津的商业地盘虽然受到这些港口的侵夺，但也因为京张铁路、正太铁路的开通，而将商业版图扩展到恰克图和山西，由此蒙古和俄罗斯的茶叶、皮货以及山西的煤炭在天津取得了进出口的通道，愈发促进了天津贸易和商业的显著发展。

　　由于天津商人所从事的交易内容以土货、煤炭等大宗商品为主，

political demands to the ruling authorities, hoping to safeguard their interests by formulating policies. Thirdly, ideologically, the urban citizenry advocates democracy, freedom, fairness, and the rule of law. The consciousness of rights that they develop propels the awakening of modern national consciousness and the development of movements for national liberation and independence. Fourthly, the urban citizenry possesses openness and inclusiveness. They transcend limitations such as territory, blood relations, and family, becoming a new organic whole. Fifthly, due to their modest wealth and comfortable lifestyles, many in the urban citizenry tend to develop conservative attitudes and a penchant for material indulgence.

Merchants and Trade Associations

Commerce is an ancient industry. The basic definition of commerce refers to the act of providing goods and services needed by customers. Even in a self-sufficient natural economy, various exchanges are still required to meet different needs. In modern times, under the combination of industrial capital and financial capital, the forms of commerce have become more diverse. Whether it's an owner of a restaurant, a stall selling cosmetics, a merchant dealing in Southern goods in a Guangdong Guild Hall, a comprador in a foreign firm, or a shareholder in a spinning mill, they all belong to different trades but share the common goal of profit-making. In modern times, there have been significant changes in the backgrounds of Tianjin merchants, leading to a substantial improvement in their social status. In traditional society, merchants were considered the lowest among the "scholars, farmers, artisans, and merchants," despite some powerful merchant groups like the Thirteen Hongs that operated with quasi-monopoly rights. However, they had little political influence and could only advocate for themselves through personal connections and relationships. Modern-era wealthy merchants, on the other hand, enjoyed the protection of various political forces, and their influence and power greatly increased along with their economic status.

A merchant is always connected to some customers, suppliers, borrowers, and creditors, thus having a relatively fixed area of operation. Before the opening of railways, modern Tianjin merchants relied on the convenience of water transport in the Hai River Basin. Their business scope covered almost the entire northern China, including Hebei, Henan, Shandong, Shanxi, Gansu, Shaanxi, Jilin, Liaoning, as well as the Inner and Outer Mongolia regions. Merchants sold Western industrial products imported through the Tianjin port to those areas, and then purchased local products to be transported to Tianjin port for export overseas. After the opening of railways, port cities

天津各饭馆的赊账单
Credit bills from various restaurants in Tianjin

因此交易的季节性强且货物数量和交易所需资金数额极大，这也导致华北地区的商业主要是延期付款，极少使用现金交易。不仅顾客在本地的饭店、果品店、鱼肉店、蔬菜店等的消费可以赊欠（即延期支付，一般一个季度一结清），其他交易更是如此。外国商人对中国商人的延期付款的时长一般是 2 到 5 个月，一家洋行赊欠给中国商人的账款甚至能达到百万两白银之巨。在这种情况下，华北地区的商人，同业之间必须互相依赖、互相帮助，因而他们非常重视体面、信用和承诺，往往一诺千金，口头的约定即可进行成千上万的巨额交易，而不需要频繁地交换契约、合同以及担保等。①

当然这种信用关系不是随随便便就可以建立起来的，常常需要经年交易的考验，所以地缘关系和业缘关系非常重要，同乡和同业之间关系紧密，并排斥外来者。那些初来乍到的外省籍商人只能依靠同乡关系进行买卖。比如汇丰银行之所以成为近代中国最有影响力的银行，离不开其买办吴调卿与直隶总督李鸿章的同乡情谊，后者同意将北洋水师和津海关的经费存放于汇丰银行。后来李鸿章主

along the railway lines gradually became powerful competitors to Tianjin, such as Hankou, the terminus of the Beijing-Hankou Railway, Qingdao, connected by the Qingdao-Jinan Railway, Qinhuangdao, developed from the Tang-Xu Railway, and Shenyang and Dalian connected by the Beijing-Fengtian Railway and the South Manchuria Railway. Although Tianjin's commercial territory was encroached upon by these ports, the opening of the Beijing-Zhangjiakou Railway and the Zhengding-Taiyuan Railway expanded the commercial territory to Kyakhta and Shanxi. As a result, channels for the import and export of Mongolian and Russian tea, fur, and Shanxi coal were established in Tianjin, further promoting the significant development of trade and commerce in Tianjin.

Since Tianjin merchants mainly deal in bulk commodities such as local products and coal, trading is highly seasonal and involves large quantities of goods and significant amounts of capital. This also results in commercial transactions in the North China region being mainly on credit, with very little cash transactions. Not only can customers in local restaurants, fruit shops, fish markets, vegetable stores, etc., buy on credit (meaning payment is deferred, generally settled every quarter), but this also applies to other transactions. Foreign merchants typically allow Chinese merchants a credit period of 2 to 5 months, and the accounts owed by a foreign firm to Chinese merchants can even amount to a million taels of silver. In this situation, merchants in the North China region must rely on and help each other within the industry. Therefore, they place great importance on dignity, creditworthiness, and commitment. Often, a verbal agreement is sufficient to conduct transactions worth hundreds or even thousands of taels of silver without the need for frequent exchanges of contracts, agreements, or guarantees.①

Of course, such credit relationships are not established casually; they often require years of testing through transactions. Therefore, geographical and professional relationships are crucial, and there is a close-knit bond among people from the same hometown and in the same trade, while outsiders are often excluded. Those newcomers from other provinces can only rely on relationships with fellow provincials for their business dealings. For example, the reason why HSBC became the most influential bank in modern China was largely due to the hometown friendship between its comprador Wu Tiaoqing and the Viceroy of Zhili, Li Hongzhang. The latter agreed to deposit the funds for the Beiyang Fleet and Tianjin Customs in HSBC. Later, when Li Hongzhang was in charge of building the Tianjin-Yuguan Railway

---

① 天津市地方史志编修委员会总编辑室编，《二十世纪初的天津概况》，内部发行，1986 年，第 245—252 页。

① Editorial Office of the Tianjin Chorography and History Compilation Committee (ed.). *Overview of Tianjin in the Early 20th Century*. Published internally in 1986, pp.245-252.

持修筑津榆铁路等，也曾多次通过吴调卿获得汇丰银行贷款，吴本人则被李鸿章任命为"关内外铁路总办"。

虽然李鸿章任职直隶总督兼北洋大臣长达 25 年，但内忧外患之下，他对天津本地商人的影响力却不大。一方面出于天津籍商人顽固保守的风气，另一方面也是看透清政府所谓"官督商办"企业经营的重重弊端，他们对投资于李鸿章的洋务企业反应冷淡。1887 年开平铁路公司改组为中国铁路公司后，扩大招股 100 万两，却应者寥寥。由于政府实力弱小不足以在列强面前提供保护，也由于对政府官员的不信任，天津本地商人养成了独立自治的风气，成立了各个会馆（同乡出身者的俱乐部）、公所（同业者的商业会议所）等组织相互扶助和救济。后来更在外国商会的影响下，成立了自己的商会。

天津最早的商会组织是 1887 年成立的洋商总会。初创时有 15 家来自不同国家的洋行，以及我国的大清银行。1904 年，为了鼓励工商业发展、对抗外商势力、维护利权，天津商务总会在清政府开明官员的支持下诞生。自 1905 年到清王朝灭亡，商会总共有 30 名总理、协理和会董，初创时约有 61 家商号。民国成立之后，商会组织呈现了蓬勃发展的态势，从 1912 年至 1922 年，天津商会的会董人数从 32 人增加到 70 人，会员数增加到 1362 个。[①]1928 年天津有华商总会、美国商会、英国商会、法国商会、洋商总会、德国商会、意大利商会、日本商会等八大商会组织，天津商会（即华商总会）成为与其他国家商会实力相当的社会团体。

在清末最后的十年，天津商会在维持市面、振兴实业、兴办教育、调解纠纷等方面都踊跃支持，直接参与了政府推进的各项现代化改革活动，与地方政府之间形成了一种良好的互动合作关系。商会最主要的作用在于维护市场秩序、稳定金融市场。民国成立以后，从 1916 年到 1937 年天津所经历的九起不同程度的金融危机中，为维持一个稳定的金融环境，天津商会的商人们扮演了维持人的角色以确保货币价值，即便代价高昂——"此类监护（维持）行为成本

---

① 数据来源："1912—1922 年间天津商会概况一览表"。宋美云，《近代天津商会》，天津社会科学院出版社，2002 年，第 76 页。

and others, he repeatedly obtained loans from HSBC through Wu Tiaoqing. Wu himself was appointed by Li Hongzhang as the "Director-General of Beijing-Shenyang Railway".

Although Li Hongzhang served as Viceroy of Zhili and Minister of Beiyang for 25 years, his influence on local Tianjin merchants was not significant due to internal and external challenges. On one hand, this was due to the stubbornly conservative nature of Tianjin-born merchants. On the other hand, it was due to their insight into the many drawbacks of the Qing government's "official supervision of business operations". They showed little interest in investing in Li Hongzhang's Westernization enterprises. When the Kaiping Railway Company was reorganized into the Chinese Railway Company in 1887 and expanded its shares by 1 million taels of silver, the response was lukewarm. Due to the government's weak strength, which was insufficient to provide protection against foreign powers, and due to their lack of trust in government officials, local Tianjin merchants developed an independent and autonomous spirit. They established various guild halls (clubs for those from the same hometown) and commercial organizations (business meeting places for those in the same trade) to support and assist each other. Later, under the influence of foreign chambers of commerce, they formed their own chamber of commerce.

The earliest commercial organization in Tianjin was the Foreign Merchants Association established in 1887. At its inception, it comprised 15 foreign firms from different countries and the Imperial Bank of China. In 1904, to encourage industrial and commercial development, counteract foreign influence, and safeguard interests, the Tientsin Chamber of Commerce was born with the support of enlightened officials of the Qing government. From 1905 until the downfall of the Qing Dynasty, the chamber had a total of 30 directors, deputy directors, and board members, with approximately 61 firms at its inception. After the founding of the Republic of China, the chamber experienced vigorous development. From 1912 to 1922, the number of directors increased from 32 to 70, with membership reaching 1,362.[①] By 1928, Tianjin boasted eight major commercial organizations: the Chinese Chamber of Commerce, the American Chamber of Commerce, the British Chamber of Commerce, the French Chamber of Commerce, the Foreign Merchants Association, the German Chamber of Commerce, the Italian Chamber of Commerce, and the Japanese Chamber of Commerce. The Tientsin Chamber of Commerce (also known as the Chinese Chamber of Commerce) became a

---

① Source: "Overview of Tianjin Chamber of Commerce from 1912 to 1922". Song Meiyun. *Modern Tianjin Chamber of Commerce*. Tianjin Academy of Social Sciences Press, 2002, p.76.

高昂，常常要吞没精英自有的资源"①。曾长期任天津银行公会会长（主席、理事长）、天津市商会执委、常委的中国银行天津分行行长、近代著名银行家卞白眉，就是一位享有相当威望和影响力的银行家。1921 年 11 月 15 日，北京中国银行、交通银行突然发生挤兑风潮，起因是当年北洋政府两次借垫警饷 480 万元，公债基金又借垫 700 万元，以及原不兑现钞券调换的存单陆续到期。消息传来，天津中国银行也立即发生挤兑风潮，不得不自 17 日起限制每人只能兑换 10 元。卞白眉立即采取应急措施：通知各代理银行补足六成现金准备；商请上海分行运津现洋 150 万元；与天津磨坊公会商妥预存现洋 5 万元，并通知全市 1300 多家米面铺，收到中国银行钞券，保证兑现。同时，由银行公会电北洋政府国务院饬令天津海关照收中、交两行钞券，海关税务司并允将六厘公债基金提前拨来备用；又催收盐余款 10 余万元。至 12 月 1 日取消了限额兑换的规定，一场 10 余天的兑现风潮就这样迅速平息了。类似"扶大厦之将倾，挽狂澜于既倒"之类的事情，卞白眉在其一生的金融活动中还做过多次，包括支援民族棉纱布业渡过难关、开办中国自己的外汇业务、发放农业贷款扶助农民、调解军阀勒索银行事件等，并在天津沦陷后拒绝与日伪合作，保持了民族气节。他在近代纷繁复杂的国际国内政治经济环境中，对国家尤其是天津金融事业和民族工商业的发展作出了杰出贡献。由此可见，商人在近代社会发挥了政府无法或者不愿发挥的许多功能，已成为地方经济社会发展中的中流砥柱。

在近代中国慈善公益事业发展的进程中，商会发挥了重要作用。近代天津灾害频仍，水灾约 4 年发生一次，②使大量市民受灾。而当周围省份发生灾情时，灾民也都会背井离乡逃难到天津寻找生路。因此，每当天津及其周边发生自然灾害时，商会即组织粮商进行大规模粮食平粜活动，平抑粮价，同时开设粥厂赈济灾民。例如，1908 年的水灾后，商会在各界劝募，共收到赈灾款 13000 余大洋，

1939 年水灾后，灾民向北四行（即盐业银行、金城银行、中南银行和大陆银行的合称）与中国航空公司组织的水灾临时救济船乞讨
After the 1939 flood, the disaster victims begging for food from a temporary relief boat which was organized by the Four Northern Banks (including Yien Yieh Commercial Bank, Kincheng Bank, China & South Sea Bank, and Continental Bank) and China Airlines

social organization of comparable strength to other national chambers.

In the last decade of the Qing Dynasty, Tianjin's Chamber of Commerce actively supported various modernization reform activities promoted by the government, such as maintaining market order, revitalizing industries, promoting education, and mediating disputes. This led to a good interactive cooperation relationship between the Chamber of Commerce and the local government. The main role of the Chamber of Commerce was to maintain market order and stabilize the financial market. After the establishment of the Republic of China, Tianjin experienced nine financial crises of varying degrees from 1916 to 1937. In order to maintain a stable financial environment, Tianjin's merchants played a role in ensuring currency value, even at a high cost. "The cost of such behavior is high, devouring their own resources of merchants." [1] Bian Baimei, a well-respected and influential banker of modern times, who served as the chairman (president, chairman of the board of directors) of the Tianjin Banking Association, executive committee member and standing committee member of the Tientsin Chamber of Commerce, and the branch manager of the Bank of China in Tianjin, played a significant role. On November 15, 1921, a run on banks suddenly occurred in Beijing, affecting the Bank of China and the Bank of Communications, due to the government

①　（美）史瀚波著，池桢译，《乱世中的信任：民国时期天津的货币、银行及国家－社会关系》，上海辞书出版社，2016 年，导论，第 6 页。

②　王素香、李丽敏，《解放前天津历年水灾概况》，《天津档案史料》1966 年创刊号，第 68 页。

①　Brett Sheehan. *Trust in Troubled Times: Money, Banks, and State - Society Relations in Republican Tianjin*, translated by Chi Zhen. Shanghai Lexicographical Publishing House, Introduction, 2016, p.6.

购买粮食 3773 石 6 斗，挨家挨户发给灾民。[1] 平常年间，商会也重视抚恤贫民，重视将慈善与实业教育相结合，教育贫民和灾民自食其力。

随着商人们越来越多地承担起社会责任，他们的话语权也不断增加。1915 年的老西开事件中，天津市民在商会的资金支持和组织动员下，进行了长达 4 个月的罢工罢市，体现了强大的组织动员能力和强烈的爱国主义情怀。几年后的 1919 年五四运动中，也是商会与天津织布工人联合会、天津电车工人联合会相继组织了罢市和罢工，有力地支持了学生们的罢课和抵制日货活动，从而形成了近代整个民族的反帝爱国运动，并取得了部分胜利。

北洋军阀、政客和清朝遗老遗少

北洋军是清末民初最有战斗力的军事集团，其核心领导是袁世凯，领导层中还包括冯国璋、段祺瑞、徐世昌等人，他们在晚清十年的政治变革中发挥了重要作用。特别是后三人在袁世凯称帝时，都直接或间接地表示反对；在与南方革命党和军阀对峙时，也坚持在民主共和制的框架下解决问题。袁世凯死后，因冯国璋、段祺瑞实力相当，却又政见不合，加上张作霖崛起于关外，北洋军阀开始分裂为皖系、直系和奉系三大势力。这三大势力凭借手里的兵力和地盘，争权夺利，军阀之间的斗争非常激烈，都想一统天下。在 1916 年袁世凯去世到 1928 年张作霖被日本关东军炸死这一段时间里，北洋政府的更迭速度非常快，出现了在北京轮番执政的局面：1916—1920 年是皖系执政，1920—1924 年是直系，1924—1928 年是奉系。

尽管政见不合、利益纠葛，然而这些军阀们却有一个共同点，就是在失败下野后，都跑到天津租界里当寓公。

第一个下野的是北洋军阀中皖系首领段祺瑞。1920 年直皖发生战争，最后段祺瑞的皖系战败，心灰意冷的他选择通电下野，跑到

---

footnote left
[1] 宋美云，《近代天津商会》，天津社会科学院出版社，2002 年，第 357 页。

borrowing 4.8 million yuan twice for police expenses and an additional 7 million yuan for the public debt fund, as well as the non-redemption of the notes. Upon hearing this news, a run on the Bank of China in Tianjin also occurred immediately, forcing the bank to limit withdrawals to 10 yuan per person starting from the 17th. Bian Baimei immediately took emergency measures: instructing all agent banks to replenish 60% of their cash reserves; requesting the Shanghai branch to send 1.5 million yuan in silver dollars to Tianjin; negotiating with the Tianjin Millers' Guild to pre-deposit 50,000 yuan in silver dollars and notifying over 1,300 rice and flour shops in the city that they would be able to exchange Bank of China notes as guaranteed. At the same time, the Banking Association telegraphed the Beiyang government's State Council to order Tianjin Customs to accept the Bank of China and Bank of Communications notes, and the Customs Commissioner agreed to allocate the public debt fund with the monthly interest of 0.6% in advance. Additionally, more than 100,000 yuan in surplus salt payments were collected. The limit on withdrawals was lifted by December 1, and the panic was quickly calmed down after more than ten days. Similar to "supporting a tilting building, and calming a raging wave before it collapses," Bian Baimei did similar things many times in his lifetime of financial activities, including supporting the national cotton textile industry through difficult times, establishing China's own foreign exchange business, issuing agricultural loans to assist farmers, mediating incidents of warlords extorting banks, and refusing to cooperate with the Japanese puppet government after Tianjin fell, maintaining national integrity. In the complex international and domestic political and economic environment of modern times, he made outstanding contributions to the development of the country, especially in Tianjin's financial and national industrial and commercial sectors. This shows that in modern society, merchants have performed many functions that the government cannot or is unwilling to perform, and have become the mainstay of local economic and social development.

In the process of the development of charity and public welfare in modern China, chambers of commerce played an important role. In modern Tianjin, disasters occurred frequently, with floods happening approximately once every four years,[1] causing a large number of citizens to suffer. When disasters struck neighboring provinces, refugees would also flock to Tianjin in search of refuge. Therefore, whenever natural disasters occurred in Tianjin and its surrounding areas, chambers of commerce would organize grain

---

[1] Wang Suxiang, Li Limin. Overview of Floods in Tianjin Before Liberation. *Tianjin Archives of Historical Materials*, first issue, 1966, p.68.

1912 年 3 月 10 日，袁世凯在北京原清政府外务部公署宣誓就任临时大总统后，与北洋将领合影
On March 10, 1912, Yuan Shikai took the oath of office as the provisional president at the former Ministry of Foreign Affairs of the Qing Dynasty in Beijing and posed for a photograph with Beiyang generals

天津的租界里做寓公。继他之后，大大小小的北洋军阀及其幕僚下野后，都搬到天津居住，知名的就有北洋政府的五大总统、十位总理，以及倪嗣冲、孙传芳、王占元等大大小小的军阀。那么，为什么军阀首领会在失败后选择来天津呢？

首先，天津距离北京近。京津之间，一个电报、一通电话之后，火车运行只需 6 小时，比朝发夕至还快。因此对于北洋政府来说，台前是北京，幕后就是天津。这里信息灵通，不仅与国内各方势力可以方便地交流意见，而且还有各国在津设立的领事馆，便于对外联络以获得外国势力支持。因此，就连末代皇帝溥仪被冯玉祥逐出紫禁城后，也来到天津躲避并伺机复辟。表面闲居的军阀们时刻关注着北京的动向，准备一有机会就东山再起。

其次，天津租界有安全保障。根据《辛丑条约》规定，列强可以在天津租界里驻兵，维持租界秩序，保护侨民安全。与北京频繁的政权更迭相比，天津因为有外国势力庇护，相对来说比较安全。军阀混战时期，各路军阀的队伍多次进入天津，但是在外国军队的警戒下，都没有开进租界里。因此，天津的社会秩序相对稳定。

第三，天津是北洋军阀发源地。北洋军阀的前身是北洋新军，

merchants to conduct large-scale grain relief activities, stabilizing grain prices, and simultaneously establish porridge cooking house to provide relief to the victims. For example, after the flood in 1908, the Chamber of Commerce raised relief funds from various sectors, totaling more than 13,000 silver dollars, purchased 3,773 dan and 6 dou of grain, and distributed them to the victims door-to-door.[1] During normal times, the Chamber of Commerce also paid attention to providing relief to the poor, emphasizing the integration of charity with industrial education, and educating the poor and disaster victims to become self-reliant.

As businessmen increasingly assume social responsibilities, their influence continues to grow. In the Laoxikai Incident of 1915, Tianjin citizens, with the financial support and organizational mobilization of the Chamber of Commerce, carried out a four-month-long strike and boycott, demonstrating strong organizational mobilization capabilities and a deep sense of patriotism. Several years later, during the May Fourth Movement in 1919, the Chamber of Commerce, along with the Tianjin Weaving Workers' Union and the Tianjin Tram Workers' Union, organized strikes and boycotts, effectively supporting students' class boycotts and the boycott of Japanese goods, thus contributing to the broader anti-imperialist and patriotic movement of the modern nation and achieving partial victories.

Beiyang Warlords, Politicians, and Remnants of the Qing Dynasty

The Beiyang Army was the most powerful military group in the late Qing and early Republic of China period, with its core leadership consisting of Yuan Shikai, along with figures such as Feng Guozhang, Duan Qirui, and Xu Shichang, who played important roles in the political changes of the late Qing dynasty. In particular, the latter three expressed direct or indirect opposition when Yuan Shikai declared himself emperor. During the confrontation with the southern revolutionary party and warlords, they insisted on resolving issues within the framework of a democratic republic. After Yuan Shikai's death, due to the comparable strength of Feng Guozhang and Duan Qirui, but with differing political views, and with Zhang Zuolin's rise in Manchuria, the Beiyang warlords began to split into three major factions: the Anhui Clique, the Zhili Clique, and the Fengtian Clique. These three factions, relying on their military forces and territories, competed for power and profit, resulting in intense struggles among warlords, each aiming to unify the country.

① Song Meiyun. *Modern Tianjin Chamber of Commerce*. Tianjin Academy of Social Sciences Press, 2002, p.357.

这支部队最开始的时候就是袁世凯在天津的小站组建训练的。从天津小站走出来的民国总统有五位，总理有九位。当年的小兵虽然成了风靡一时的人物，但在小站时，他们都是老同事、老同学、老同乡。因为有这样的交情，在后来下野后，只要缴械，一般都会得到善待。而且这些军阀，对于天津非常有感情，他们告老不还乡，而是回到津宅养老。

第四，天津的工商业繁荣。洋务运动发展实业时，天津的很多重要工商企业为官督商办或有政府背景。军阀们虽然下野，但是军人、政客和官商相互熟识，便于他们来津做寓公时将手里的钱投资于天津的房地产和工商业，或者把钱存到中外银行里，以钱生钱。这样，天津的许多企业和银行就成为军阀的"钱袋子"，为他们日后东山再起募集资金或作养老金。

第五，天津的生活环境优越。作为开放已久的港口城市和移民城市，天津得风气之先，不同的文化在这里交流，城市化工业化程度乃至娱乐业发展都居于全国前列，生活舒适便利，不用出远门，就可以看到不同的风景、获得不同的享受。即使他们争权失败，日子依然可以过得逍遥自在。

出于以上原因，无论是天津籍出身的还是其他省籍的北洋军阀都纷纷在下野后来天津买房置产、投资实业，因此天津有众多的军阀加财阀。如直系军阀的"长江三督"①在天津均广置房产、投资实业。"长江三督"之首李纯，天津人，在任期间横征暴敛，在津京两地广置房地产，是当时天津最大的房产主之一，另投资于工商金融实业。"长江三督"之二陈光远，亦为天津人，1922年来津做寓公，购置大量房地产，并开设银号与当铺多座，通过亲家龚心湛②在北洋企业中大量投资，购买了启新洋灰公司、开滦煤矿、华新纱厂、耀华玻璃厂、中原公司等企业的股票，为津门巨富。"长江三督"

---

① 袁世凯死后，直系军阀江苏督军冯国璋、江西督军李纯、湖北督军王占元结成联盟。后因冯国璋代理总统，李纯调任江苏督军，陈光远接任江西督军，与王占元仍称"长江三督"。

② 龚心湛曾任民国时期安徽省省长、财政总长、代理国务总理，后致力于兴办实业，曾任启新洋灰公司总经理、董事长多年。

From the death of Yuan Shikai in 1916 to the assassination of Zhang Zuolin by the Japanese Kwantung Army in 1928, the turnover rate of the Beiyang government was very high, with different factions taking turns to govern in Beijing: the Anhui Clique from 1916 to 1920, the Zhili Clique from 1920 to 1924, and the Fengtian Clique from 1924 to 1928.

Despite their differing political views and conflicting interests, these warlords all had one thing in common: after their failures and downfall, they all sought refuge in the concessions of Tianjin.

The first to fall from power was Duan Qirui, the leader of the Anhui Clique among the Beiyang warlords. In 1920, the Zhili-Anhui War broke out, and eventually Duan Qirui's Anhui Clique was defeated. Disheartened, he chose to resign by sending a telegram and then sought refuge in the concessions of Tianjin, becoming a resident there. Following him, various warlords and their staff, both big and small, from the Beiyang regime also moved to Tianjin after their downfall. Among them were the five presidents and ten prime ministers of the Beiyang government, as well as figures like Ni Sichong, Sun Chuanfang, and Wang Zhanyuan. So, why did warlord leaders choose Tianjin after their failures?

Firstly, Tianjin is close to Beijing. Between the two cities, with just a telegram or a phone call, a train journey takes only six hours, faster than the saying "leave in the morning and arrive in the evening." Therefore, for the Beiyang government, Beijing is the front stage, and Tianjin is the backstage. Information flows smoothly here, facilitating easy communication with various domestic forces. Additionally, there are consulates of various countries established in Tianjin, making it convenient for external contacts to garner support from foreign powers. Consequently, even the last emperor, Puyi, expelled from the Forbidden City by Feng Yuxiang, sought refuge in Tianjin, biding his time for a potential restoration. The warlords, ostensibly living leisurely, constantly monitored the situation in Beijing, preparing to make a comeback at the first opportunity.

Secondly, the Tianjin Concessions provides security guarantees. According to the *Boxer Protocol*, foreign powers shall be allowed to station troops in the Tianjin Concessions to maintain order and protect the safety of the expatriate community. Compared to the frequent changes of regime in Beijing, Tianjin was relatively safer due to the protection offered by foreign powers. During the period of warlord conflicts, various warlord forces repeatedly entered Tianjin, but they were prevented from entering the Concessions by the vigilance of foreign troops. Therefore, the social order in Tianjin is relatively stable.

Thirdly, Tianjin is the birthplace of the Beiyang Warlords. The precursor

之三王占元 1922 年下野，在天津有房产三千多间出租，并投资纺织、面粉、银行、电力、煤矿等企业，在中国、交通、盐业、金城等银行均有股份。皖系军阀、奉系军阀的主要人物也均在天津拥有众多房产和投资等。

学者齐锡生分析，北洋军阀是建立在"个人关系的结合""自身利益的考虑"和"意识形态上的联系"三个层面关系上的复杂群体。军人的个人联系包括血缘和婚姻这两个主要联系，次要联系包括师生关系、老同事、老同学或老同乡。自身利益主要体现在拥有的地盘（意味着所能盘剥到的财富收入）、军队和政治上的地位。而对于最后一点，并不是所有军阀（特别是受教育程度低）都有自觉的"意识形态"。只有少数领袖类人物才有明确的政治主张，如张勋、吴佩孚、陈炯明、李宗仁、冯玉祥以及阎锡山，都是有互不相同的意识形态或政治纲领的人。[1]综合三种因素去分析军阀之间的关系网络，那将是非常复杂的。不过考虑到北洋军阀所处的时代背景，清末民初的大多数军阀都是受传统教育成长起来的，除了军事技能受教于外国军事教官之外，其他文化基础难免还是传统儒家思想的三纲五常，即如张作霖那样出身草莽的军人，也要接受正统社会规范的约束。因此，军人之间"个人关系的结合"是形成军阀派系的最首要的基础，也是最显而易见的、清楚明晰的联系。

举例来说，倪嗣冲曾与段祺瑞、段芝贵等都是袁世凯的得力部下，也同为安徽人，后来成为皖系军阀的核心人物，这是建立在同乡和同事基础之上的个人关系。直皖战争失败后，倪嗣冲下野来到天津定居，广泛投资于银行、纱厂、面粉厂、油漆公司等，还在英、日租界广置房地产，时有资产价值银洋八千万元之多，是天津商界的重量级人物。他的儿女亲家有大总统徐世昌堂弟徐世章、天津"八大家"中的李家和韩家、安徽同乡望族、清军将领聂士成家族等；徐世昌—徐世章家族的姻亲有曾任内阁总理的朱启钤家、原山东巡抚冯汝骙家、原镇安上将军张锡銮家、晚清文豪郑东府家、八大家之一卞家；朱启钤家的姻亲又有张作霖、段祺瑞、曾任陆军总长的

___

[1] （美）齐锡生著，杨云若、萧延中译，《中国的军阀政治（1916—1928）》，中国人民大学出版社，2010 年，第 31—62 页。

of the Beiyang Warlords was the Beiyang New Army, which was initially organized and trained by Yuan Shikai at Xiaozhan in Tianjin. Five presidents and nine prime ministers of the Republic of China emerged from this Xiaozhan. Although these former soldiers became prominent figures later on, during their time at Xiaozhan, they were just old colleagues, classmates, and fellow townsfolk. Because of these relationships, after their downfall, as long as they surrendered their weapons, they generally received good treatment. Moreover, these warlords had strong emotional ties to Tianjin. Instead of retiring to their hometowns, they chose to spend their retirement years in Tianjin.

Fourthly, Tianjin's industrial and commercial prosperity played a role. During the Westernization Movement when industrialization was promoted, many significant industrial and commercial enterprises in Tianjin were either government-controlled or had government backgrounds. Although the warlords fell from power, military personnel, politicians, and officials were familiar with each other, facilitating their investment in Tianjin's real estate and industrial and commercial enterprises or depositing money in domestic and foreign banks when they settled in Tianjin. This enabled them to generate income from their investments. Consequently, many enterprises and banks in Tianjin became the "financial resources" of the warlords, providing them with funds for their resurgence or retirement pensions in the future.

Fifthly, Tianjin offers a superior living environment. As a long-established open port city and immigrant city, Tianjin has been at the forefront of cultural exchange, urbanization, industrialization, and even the development of the entertainment industry. Life here is comfortable and convenient. Without traveling far, one can enjoy different scenery and experiences. Even if they failed in their power struggles, they could still live carefree lives.

For the reasons mentioned above, whether they were natives of Tianjin or from other provinces, the Beiyang warlords all rushed to Tianjin after their downfall to buy houses, invest in properties, and engage in business. Therefore, Tianjin has numerous warlords turned tycoons. For example, the "Three Governors of the Yangtze River"[1] from the Zhili Clique all owned extensive real estate and invested in various industries in Tianjin. The first of the "Three Governors of the Yangtze River," Li Chun, a Tianjin native, engaged in rampant extortion during his tenure and acquired vast real estate

___

[1] After the death of Yuan Shikai, among the Zhili Clique of Warlords, Jiangsu Governor Feng Guozhang, Jiangxi Governor Li Chun, and Hubei Governor Wang Zhanyuan formed an alliance. Later, due to Feng Guozhang assuming the role of acting president and Li Chun being reassigned to the governorship of Jiangsu, Chen Guangyuan took over as the Governor of Jiangxi. Li Chun and Chen Guangyuan, along with Wang Zhanyuan, were still referred to as the "Three Governors of the Yangtze River."

海河边上的袁氏宅邸。航鹰摄于 2003 年
Yuan Shikai family's residence on the bank of the Hai River. Taken by Hang Ying in 2003

袁世凯（1859—1916），河南项城人。中华民国第一任大总统，北洋军阀领袖。袁世凯去世后，他的 17 个儿子和 15 个女儿大都迁来天津隐居，婚嫁对象也大都为清末重臣、北洋军阀或天津本地富商的子女。其中六子袁克桓曾任启新洋灰公司总经理，还参与创办了江南水泥厂（南京）、华新南辰溪水泥厂、北京琉璃水泥厂等企业，为北方著名的实业家

Yuan Shikai (1859-1916), originally from Xiangcheng, Henan Province, was the first President of the Republic of China and a prominent leader of the Beiyang warlord faction. After his death, most of his 17 sons and 15 daughters moved to Tianjin, where they lived in seclusion. Their marriage partners were mostly descendants of high-ranking officials from the late Qing Dynasty, Beiyang warlords, or wealthy local businessmen in Tianjin. Among them, his sixth son, Yuan Kehuan, served as the General Manager of Chee Hsin Cement Company and was also involved in founding several key enterprises, including Jiangnan Cement Factory (Nanjing), Huaxin South Chenxi Cement Factory, and Beijing Liuli Cement Factory. He became a well-known industrialist in northern China

黎元洪（1864—1928），湖北黄陂人。中华民国第一任副总统、第二任大总统。下台后定居天津。在津期间，热心发展实业，先后投资煤矿、盐碱、钢铁、纺织、烟酒、食品、制药、林场、银行、证券、信托、保险、邮电等各种企业 70 多个。在天津有两处房产，现已不存

Li Yuanhong (1864-1928), a native of Huangpi, Hubei Province, was the first Vice President and the second President of the Republic of China. After stepping down from office, he settled in Tianjin. During his time there, he actively promoted industrial development, investing in over 70 enterprises across various sectors, including coal mining, salt and alkali, steel, textiles, tobacco and alcohol, food, pharmaceuticals, forestry, banking, securities, trust, insurance, and postal services. Li owned two properties in Tianjin, both of which no longer exist today

徐世昌（1855—1939），直隶天津人。1918 年被国会选为第四任民国大总统。退出政界后在天津过隐逸生活，投资于银行业，亦在英租界有大量房产自住和出租

Xu Shichang (1855-1939), a native of Tianjin, was elected as the fourth President of the Republic of China by the National Assembly in 1918. After retiring from politics, he lived a secluded life in Tianjin, where he invested in the banking industry. He also owned a significant amount of real estate in the British concession, both for personal residence and rental purposes

徐世昌旧居（新华南路 255 号）。张畅摄于 2022 年
The former residence of Xu Shichang (No.255 Xinhua South Road). Taken by Zhang Chang in 2022

倪嗣冲（1868—1924），安徽阜阳人。皖系军阀实权人物。袁世凯心腹，民国初年独霸安徽。1920年直皖大战失败后，隐居于天津，投资银行、纱厂、面粉厂、油漆公司等，还在英租界、日租界及河东、河西等区广置房地产，当时资产价值银洋八千万元之多

Ni Sichong (1868-1924), originally from Fuyang, Anhui, was a powerful military figure in the Anhui Clique warlords. A close confidant of Yuan Shikai, he dominated Anhui in the early years of the Republic of China. After his defeat in the 1920 Zhili-Anhui War, Ni lived in seclusion in Tianjin. There, he invested in various industries, including banking, textile mills, flour factories, and paint companies. He also acquired substantial real estate in the British Concession, the Japanese Concession, and various districts such as Hedong and Hexi. At the time, his assets were valued at a staggering 80 million silver dollars

段祺瑞（1865—1936），安徽合肥人。皖系军阀首领。1916年至1920年为北洋政府实际掌权者。曾四任总理，四任陆军总长，一任参谋总长，一任国家元首。在位期间，反对帝制、总统制，提倡责任内阁制，主张武力统一中国。下野后隐居天津。后拒绝与日本人往来，避居上海，1936年病逝

Duan Qirui (1865-1936), a native of Hefei, Anhui Province, was the leader of the Anhui Clique warlords. From 1916 to 1920, he was the de facto ruler of the Beiyang government. He held the position of Prime Minister four times, served as the Minister of the Army four times, was Chief of Staff once, and held the office of head of state once. During his tenure, he opposed the monarchy and the presidential system, advocated for a responsible cabinet system, and supported the use of military force to unify China. After stepping down, Duan lived in seclusion in Tianjin, later refused to engage with the Japanese and moved to Shanghai, where he passed away in 1936 due to illness

倪嗣冲旧居（南京路88号）。安红摄于2023年
The former residence of Ni Sichong (No.88 Nanjing Road). Taken by An Hong in 2023

段祺瑞旧居（鞍山道38号）
The former residence of Duan Qirui (No.38 Anshan Road)

段祺瑞旧居内景
Interior view of the former residence of Duan Qirui

以上彩色照片由张威摄于2022年
Color photos taken by Zhang Wei in 2022

吴光新等；八大家又是津门巨富，与袁世凯家族、曹锟家族、陈光远家族、杨以德家族、丁宏荃家族、雍剑秋家族、胡寿田家族等都有直接间接的姻亲关系。①

除了北洋军阀将领下野后寓居于天津，那些依附于各派系军阀的官僚政客也大多在天津拥有房产，甚至定居于此。中华民国首任总理唐绍仪，留美幼童出身，回国后曾任清政府天津海关道兼北洋大学督办。历经清朝、北洋政府、民国、日伪、新中国五个历史时期的近代政治家、实业家朱启钤，在袁世凯任总统时任国务总理，1916 年遭通缉后逃到天津英租界，参与经营中兴煤矿和中兴轮船公司。颜惠庆是北洋政府老牌政客和外交家，曾经组阁，后隐居英租界，专心从事金融和慈善活动，曾任天津大陆银行董事长和南开大学董事长。另一位著名近代外交家顾维钧在天津的住宅为奉系军阀张学良所赠。1919 年代理国务总理的龚心湛辞任下台后住在英租界，先后担任大陆银行、中孚银行董事、耀华玻璃公司总董、开滦矿务局董事、启新洋灰公司总经理、董事长等。北洋政府最后一位总理潘复在东北易帜中正式下野，移居天津英租界。

天津距北京近，又是外国租界最多的繁华大城市。不仅北洋军阀及政客失势或暂时失权后避往天津的各个租界居住，清帝逊位后，那些清朝贵胄重臣也纷纷逃往天津。地位最显赫的莫过于逊帝溥仪，先后居住于日租界的张园和静园。其他遗老遗少如载沣、载振、载涛，以及满汉臣僚那桐、荣庆、李准，等等。这些贵族权臣在天津继续享受优越的物质生活，也大都生财有道。比如末代庆王载振，在天津远离政治，投资商业，曾参与创办当时天津最大的商场——劝业场，其中西合璧的显赫王府坐落于英租界剑桥道上。

来到天津的军阀们自然不会老老实实在家里做寓公，他们把天津当作阴谋的巢穴。比如，北洋军阀时期，主张武力压服南方的皖系军阀段祺瑞、徐树铮为进一步反击主张和平统一南北方的直系冯国璋及长江三督（江西督军陈光远、江苏督军李纯、湖北督军王占元），在天津举行重要会议。徐树铮受段祺瑞的派遣，北到奉天（今

---

① 李良玉、吴修申主编，《倪嗣冲与北洋军阀》，黄山书社，2012 年，第 153—156 页。

in Tianjin and Beijing. He was one of the largest property owners in Tianjin at the time, and he also invested in industrial, commercial, and financial sectors. The second of the "Three Governors of the Yangtze River," Chen Guangyuan, also from Tianjin, came to Tianjin in 1922 and purchased large amounts of real estate. He opened multiple pawnshops and banks, invested heavily through his relative Gong Xinzhan① in various Beiyang enterprises, and bought shares in companies such as Chee Hsin Cement Company, Kailan Coal Mine, Huaxin Textile Company, Yaohua Glass Company, and Chungyuen Company, becoming one of the wealthiest individuals in Tianjin. The third of the "Three Governors of the Yangtze River," Wang Zhanyuan, who stepped down in 1922, owned over three thousand rental properties in Tianjin. He also invested in textile, flour, banking, electricity, and coal mining enterprises, and held shares in banks such as Bank of China, Bank of Communications, Yien Yieh Commercial Bank, and Kincheng Banking Corporation. Similarly, the principal figures of the Anhui and Fengtian Clique also owned numerous properties and investments in Tianjin.

Scholar Qi Xisheng analyzed that the Beiyang warlords were a complex group built on three levels of relationships: "the combination of personal relationships," "relationships based of self-interest," and "ideological connections." Personal connections among military personnel include primary links such as blood relations and marriage, as well as secondary links like teacher-student relationships, former colleagues, classmates, or fellow townsmen. Self-interest is primarily manifested in the possession of territory (which implies the wealth that can be extracted), military power, and political status. However, not all warlords, especially those with low levels of education, have a conscious "ideology." Only a few leaders have clear political ideas, such as Zhang Xun, Wu Peifu, Chen Jiongming, Li Zongren, Feng Yuxiang, and Yan Xishan, who all have different ideologies or political agendas.② Analyzing the network of relationships between warlords based on these three factors would be very complex. However, considering the historical context in which the Beiyang warlords operated, most of them grew up under traditional education. Besides receiving military training from foreign military advisors, their cultural foundation was inevitably rooted in traditional Confucian ethics. Even military figures like Zhang Zuolin, who

---

① Gong Xinzhan served as the Governor of Anhui Province, Minister of Finance, and Acting Premier of the Republic of China. Later, he dedicated himself to industrial development and served as the General Manager and Chairman of the Chee Hsin Cement Company for many years.

② Qi Xisheng. *Warlord Politics in China 1916-1928*, translated by Yang Yunruo, Xiao Tingzhong. China Renmin University Press, 2010, pp.31-62.

曹锟（1862—1938），直隶天津人。1919 年被拥为直系军阀首领。1923 年贿选而被选举为第五任中华民国大总统。下野后回到天津，他的现金大都存于外国银行，同时买下多处房产。其中"曹家花园"占地面积 200 余市亩，是一座包括廊庑、亭池、岛榭的豪华园林别墅

Cao Kun (1862-1938), a native of Tianjin, was appointed as the leader of the Zhili Clique in 1919. In 1923, he was elected as the fifth President of the Republic of China through bribery in election. After falling out of the power, he returned to Tianjin and deposited most of his money in foreign banks, while purchasing many properties. The Cao Family Garden covers an area of over 200 mu and is a luxurious garden villa that has corridors, pavilions, pool, rockery and lake

曹锟旧居一（南海路 2 号）。安红摄于 2024 年
One of the former residences of Cao Kun (No.2 Nanhai Road).
Taken by An Hong in 2024

曹锟旧居二（民主道 27—29 号）。刘悦摄于 2024 年
Another residence of Cao Kun (No.27-29 Minzhu Road).
Taken by Liu Yue in 2024

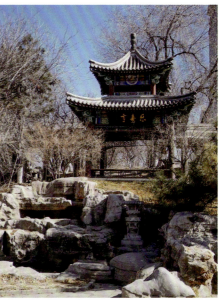

曹家花园（黄纬路 60 号拥军花园）。张畅摄于 2023 年
Cao Family Garden (No.60 Huangwei Road, Yongjun Garden).
Taken by Zhang Chang in 2023

爱新觉罗·溥仪（1906—1967），清朝末代皇帝。1908 年登基，辛亥革命后被迫退位。1917 年军阀张勋曾拥其复辟帝制 12 天。1924 年冯玉祥发动北京政变，废除其大清皇帝称号，迁出皇宫。次年前往天津居住。九一八事变之后被日本人偷送到东北做了伪满洲国傀儡皇帝，年号康德（1934—1945）。1945 年日本投降后，被苏军逮捕。1950 年移交中国，被监禁于抚顺。1959 年大赦释放，后成为全国政协委员。1967 年病逝于北京。著有自传《我的前半生》

Aisin Gioro Puyi (1906-1967), the last Emperor of the Qing Dynasty, ascended to the throne in 1908 and was forced to abdicate following the 1911 Revolution. In 1917, warlord Zhang Xun briefly restored him to the throne for 12 days. In 1924, Feng Yuxiang led a coup in Beijing, abolishing his title as the Emperor of the Qing Dynasty and removing him from the Imperial Palace. The following year, he moved to Tianjin. After the September 18th Incident in 1931, he was secretly brought to Manchuria by the Japanese and became the puppet emperor of the Japanese-controlled Manchukuo, taking the reign name Kangde (1934-1945). After Japan's surrender in 1945, he was captured by the Soviet Army and in 1950 was handed over to China, where he was imprisoned in Fushun. In 1959, he was released under amnesty and later became a member of the Chinese People's Political Consultative Conference. He passed away in 1967 in Beijing. He authored his autobiography, *From Emperor to Citizen*

张园，清代湖北提督兼驻武昌新建陆军第八镇统制张彪旧居。1924 年孙中山二次护法后北上在此小住。1925 年溥仪初到天津时居住于此，后移居静园。溥仪离津后，张彪之子将张园卖与日本人并辟为日本警备司令部。建于 1915 年，位于旧日租界宫岛街（今鞍山道 59 号）。刘悦摄于 2003 年

Zhang Garden was the former residence of Zhang Biao, the Governor of Hubei Province during the Qing Dynasty and the Commander of the newly established Eighth Army Division in Wuchang. After Sun Yat-sen's second Constitutional Protection Movement in 1924, he briefly stayed here during his northern expedition. In 1925, Puyi, the last emperor, resided in Zhang Garden upon his arrival in Tianjin, before moving to Jing Garden. After Puyi left Tianjin, Zhang Biao's son sold Zhang Garden to the Japanese, who then transformed it into the Japanese Garrison Headquarters. Built in 1915, the residence was located on the former Japanese Concession's Miyajima Road (now No.59, Anshan Road). Taken by Liu Yue in 2003

静园，清朝末代皇帝溥仪在天津的故居。建于 1921 年，位于旧日租界宫岛街（今鞍山道 70 号）。占地面积约为 3360 平方米，建筑面积约 1900 平方米，园内主要建筑为两幢砖木结构的二层西式小楼，主楼为西班牙和日本合璧式样。安红摄于 2010 年

Jing Garden, the former residence of Puyi, the last emperor of the Qing Dynasty, in Tianjin, was built in 1921. It is located on the former Japanese Concession's Miyajima Road (now No.70, Anshan Road). The estate covers an area of approximately 3,360 square meters, with a building area of about 1,900 square meters. The main structures in the garden are two two-story brick and wood Western-style villas. The main building features a fusion of Spanish and Japanese architectural styles. Taken by An Hong in 2010

冯国璋（1859—1919），直隶河间人。直系军阀首领。1916 年被选为总统。在天津、北京有大量房产，又在直隶夹山、遵化、兴隆有 3 座金矿，在南京、北京、天津有 10 座钱庄和银号，并在中华汇业银行和"北四行"均有大量股票和存款

Feng Guozhang (1859-1919), originally from Hejian, Zhili, was a prominent leader of the Zhili clique. He was elected as President in 1916. Feng owned a large amount of real estate in both Tianjin and Beijing. Additionally, he held three gold mines in Jiashan, Zunhua, and Xinglong in Zhili, as well as ten banks and money shops in Nanjing, Beijing, and Tianjin. He also owned significant stocks and deposits in Exchange Bank of China and the "Four Northern Banks"

张学良（1901—2001），辽宁鞍山人，奉系军阀首领张作霖长子，中国近代著名爱国将领。"皇姑屯事件"后，继任为东北保安军总司令，拒绝日本人的拉拢，坚持"东北易帜"，促成祖国统一。后任中华民国陆海空军副司令，陆军一级上将。1936 与杨虎城将军一起发动西安事变，促成国共二次合作，结成抗日民族统一战线。后遭蒋介石父子长期软禁。2001 年 10 月 14 日病逝于檀香山

Zhang Xueliang (1901-2001), a native of Anshan, Liaoning Province, was the eldest son of Zhang Zuolin, the warlord leader of the Fengtian Clique. He was a prominent patriotic general in modern China. After the Huanggutun Incident, Zhang succeeded his father as the Commander-in-Chief of the Northeast Security Army. He resisted Japanese persuasion and upheld the "Northeast Flag Replacement" policy, advocating for the reunification of China. Later, he served as the Deputy Commander of the Army, Navy, and Air Force of the Republic of China and became a first-class general in the Army. In 1936, Zhang, alongside General Yang Hucheng, initiated the Xi'an Incident, which promoted the second cooperation between the Kuomintang and the Communist Party, leading to the formation of the Anti-Japanese National United Front. Following this, Zhang was placed under long-term house arrest by Chiang Kai-shek and his son. Zhang Xueliang passed away on October 14, 2001, in Honolulu

冯国璋旧居（民主道 50—54 号）。航鹰摄于 2010 年
The former residence of Feng Guozhang (No.50-54 Minzhu Road).
Taken by Hang Ying in 2010

张学良旧居（赤峰道 78 号）。安红摄于 2023 年
The former residence of Zhang Xueliang (No.78 Chifeng Road).
Taken by An Hong in 2023

载振（1876—1947），清朝宗室，末代庆亲王。1902 年曾代表清朝廷赴英参加英国国王爱德华七世加冕礼。1903 年赴日本考察第五届劝业博览会。回国后积极参与新政。1906 年任新成立的农工商部大臣。1907 年因歌妓杨翠喜案辞职。辛亥革命后一度避居上海，后返回北京。1924 年迁入天津庆王府，从事工商投资活动，参与创办劝业商场。1947 年病逝于天津

Zai Zhen (1876-1947), a member of the Qing imperial family, was the last Prince of Qing. In 1902, he represented the Qing court at the coronation of King Edward VII of the United Kingdom. In 1903, he traveled to Japan to visit the Fifth Industrial Exposition. Upon returning to China, he actively participated in the reforms of the late Qing Dynasty. In 1906, he was appointed as the Minister of the newly established Ministry of Agriculture and Commerce. He resigned in 1907 due to Yang Cuixi incident involving a courtesan. After the 1911 Revolution, he briefly lived in Shanghai before returning to Beijing. In 1924, he moved to Tianjin to reside at the Prince Qing's Mansion, where he became involved in industrial and commercial investments, including helping to establish the Quanye Bazaar. He passed away in Tianjin in 1947

庆王府（重庆道 55 号）。安红摄于 2023 年
Prince Qing's Mansion (No.55 Chongqing Road). Taken by An Hong in 2023

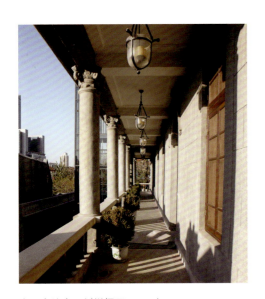

庆王府外廊。刘悦摄于 2011 年
The veranda of Prince Qing's Mansion. Taken by Liu Yue in 2011

庆王府大门前十七级半台阶。航鹰摄于 2007 年
Seventeen and a half steps in front of the entrance of Prince Qing's Mansion. Taken by Hang Ying in 2007

庆王府花园。刘悦摄于 2011 年
The garden of the Prince Qing's Mansion. Taken by Liu Yue in 2011

庆王府天锡厅。刘悦摄于 2024 年
Tianxi Hall of Prince Qing's Mansion. Taken by Liu Yue in 2024

章瑞庭故居（花园路9号）。建于1922年，为二层、局部三层，带地下室，混合结构的建筑。据建筑设计师盖苓之子介绍，此楼曾用于东北军高级将领聚会。刘悦摄于2003年

The former residence of Zhang Ruiting (No.9, Huayuan Road) was built in 1922. It is a two-story building with a partial third floor and a basement, constructed using a mixed structure. According to the architect's son, Franz Geyling, the building was used as a gathering place for senior commanders of the Northeast Army. Taken by Liu Yue in 2003

came from humble origins, had to adhere to orthodox social norms. Therefore, the "combination of personal relationships" among military personnel is the most fundamental basis for the formation of warlord factions, and it is the most obvious and clear connection.

For example, Ni Sichong, who had served as a trusted subordinate of Yuan Shikai along with Duan Qirui, Duan Zhigui, and others, all hailing from Anhui, later became a core figure of the Anhui Clique warlords. This was based on personal relationships established on the basis of being fellow townsfolk and colleagues. After the failure of the Zhili-Anhui War, Ni Sichong retreated to Tianjin and settled there, extensively investing in banks, textile mills, flour mills, paint companies, and more. He also owned extensive real estate in the British and Japanese concessions, with assets valued at up to eighty million silver dollars, making him a heavyweight figure in the Tianjin business community. His children were in-laws with President Xu Shichang's cousin Xu Shizhang, the Li and Han families among Tianjin's "Eight Great Families," Anhui gentry, the family of Qing military general Nie Shicheng, and others. The Xu Shichang-Xu Shizhang family's relatives included the family of Zhu Qiqian, a former prime minister, the family of Feng Ruji, a former governor of Shandong, the family of General Zhang Xiluan, the family of late Qing literary figure Zheng Dongfu, and the Bian family, one of the "Eight Great Families." The in-laws of Zhu Qiqian's family included Zhang Zuolin, Duan Qirui, Wu Guangxin, former Minister of War, and others. The "Eight Great Families" were also wealthy in Tianjin, with direct or indirect marital relations with the Yuan Shikai family, the Cao Kun family, the Chen Guangyuan family, the Yang Yide family, the Ding Hongquan family, the Yong Jianqiu family, and the Hu Shoutian family, among others.[1]

In addition to the warlords of the Beiyang Army settling in Tianjin after retiring, many bureaucratic politicians who were affiliated with various warlord factions also owned properties in Tianjin, and some even settled there. Tang Shaoyi, the first Premier of the Republic of China, studied abroad in the United States and served as Customs Taotai of Tianjin and concurrently as the supervisor of Peiyang University for the Qing government after returning to China. Zhu Qiqian, a modern politician and industrialist who experienced the five historical periods of the Qing Dynasty, the Beiyang government, the Republic of China, the Japanese puppet regime, and the People's Republic of China, served as the Prime Minister under Yuan Shikai's presidency and went into hiding in the Tianjin British Concession in 1916 after being wanted,

①　Li Liangyu, Wu Xiushen (eds.). *Ni Sichong and the Northern Warlords*. Huangshan Publishing House, 2012, pp.153-156.

苦力
Chinese laborers

沈阳），南到蚌埠，与张作霖、倪嗣冲等军阀联络，并且把曹锟也拉到了主战阵线来。1917 年 12 月 2 日，即接替段祺瑞的王士珍内阁在北京成立的第三天，天津热闹起来了。直隶督军曹锟、山东督军张怀芝以及山西、奉天、福建、安徽、浙江、陕西、黑龙江、上海、察哈尔、绥远、热河等省区督军、都统、护军使代表云集天津。最后一致商定出兵湖南作战，史称"天津会议"。由此可见天津在清末民初时的重要政治职能，这是它与上海、汉口、青岛、大连等近代崛起的其他城市显著不同的地方。

产业工人和服务业人员

尽管人们甚至是史学家的目光常常被帝王将相、军阀富商、战争史诗所吸引，人们喜闻乐见的也是城市的高楼大厦、灯红酒绿和都市传说，但敏锐的观察者指出，在近代，无论东方还是西方，"工厂和贫民窟就是这种新兴城镇里两个主要的构成成分"①。在粉尘污染、机器声轰隆的工厂车间和阴暗低矮、垃圾遍地的贫民窟里苦苦挣扎的工人，以及奔波在冽冽寒风或炎炎酷日下、勉强挣得一日三餐的贩夫走卒、底层服务业人员，他们才是构成金字塔形城市结构

① （美）刘易斯·芒福德著，宋俊岭等译，《城市文化》，中国建筑工业出版社，2009 年，第 186 页。

where he participated in the management of the Zhongxing Coal Mine and the Zhongxing Steamship Company. Yan Huiqing, a veteran politician and diplomat of the Beiyang government, once formed a cabinet but later retired to the British Concession in Tianjin, dedicating himself to finance and charitable activities. He served as the chairman of the Continental Bank of Tianjin and the chairman of Nankai University. Another renowned modern diplomat, Gu Weijun, was gifted a residence in Tianjin by the warlord of the Fengtian Clique, Zhang Xueliang. Gong Xinzhan, who acted as acting Prime Minister in 1919, lived in the British Concession after resigning and held various positions such as director and chairman of the Continental Bank, director of Chung Foo Union Bank, general manager and chairman of the Yaohua Glass Company, director of the Kailan Mining Administration, and general manager and chairman of the Chee Hsin Cement Company. Pan Fu, the last Premier of the Beiyang government, officially retired during the Northeast Flag Replacement and moved to the Tianjin British Concession.

Tianjin is close to Beijing and is the bustling metropolis with the most foreign concessions. After the decline or temporary loss of power of the Beiyang warlords and politicians, they sought refuge in various concessions in Tianjin. After the abdication of the Qing emperor, those aristocrats and high-ranking officials of the Qing Dynasty also fled to Tianjin. The most prominent figure among them was the abdicated emperor, Puyi, who resided successively in the Japanese concession of Zhang Garden and Jing Garden. Other remnants of the Qing Dynasty, such as Zaifeng, Zaizhen, Zaitao, as well as Manchu and Han officials like Na Tong, Rong Qing, and Li Zhun, also sought refuge in Tianjin. These noble and influential figures continued to enjoy superior material lifestyles in Tianjin and most of them were adept at making money. For example, the last Prince Qing, Zaizhen, stayed away from politics in Tianjin and invested in commerce. He was involved in establishing the largest shopping mall in Tianjin at the time, the "Quanye Bazaar". The prominent Prince Qing's Mansion, which was an epitome of the fusion of Eastern and Western architectural styles, was located on Cambrige Road in the British Concession.

Upon arriving in Tianjin, the warlords naturally wouldn't just sit idly at home. They regarded Tianjin as a nest for their conspiracies. For instance, during the Beiyang warlord era, the Anhui Clique warlord Duan Qirui and Xu Shuzheng, who advocated using force to subdue the southern regions, in order to oppose the Zhili Clique warlord Feng Guozhang, as well as the "Three Governors of the Yangtze River" warlords (Chen Guangyuan of Jiangxi, Li Chun of Jiangsu, and Wang Zhanyuan of Hubei) who advocated for peaceful reunification of the north and south, held important meetings

中庞大基座的阶层。

　　近代对外开放以后，天津作为聚集了工业、商业和金融业的大城市，无疑为那些寻找生计的人带来了希望。从洋务运动创办各工厂企业之后，产业工人作为一种职业开始出现，为大量农村破产农民提供了养家糊口的机会。据不完全统计，至 1894 年天津近代工业和交通运输业的工人已达 5000 人以上。民族工商业逐渐发展壮大之后，提供了更多的就业机会。仅 1915 年到 1922 年建立的六大纱厂就雇用了 11500 多名工人，到 1922 年天津产业工人已有十余万。[①]1931 年，天津的民族工业中有工人约 56000 名，其中六大纱厂有工人 15580 名；卷烟厂有 4 家，工人 4180 名；规模较大的面粉厂有 6 家，工人 920 名；地毯厂上百家，有工人 11568 名；化学工业有 4 家工厂，工人 1007 名；洋灰厂 1 家，工人 5000 名；火柴厂 5 家，工人 13750 名；盐厂 2 家，工人 722 名。[②]1949 年年底的统计数字，天津有产业工人 13 万名，商业服务业从业人员有 71043 名，合计 201043 人。[③]

　　天津的工人主要来自周边地区的破产农民、因水旱饥荒或军阀混战而逃离故土的灾民。如前文所述，天津在开埠后不久就成为洋货进口大户，来自海外的洋纱洋布、洋米洋面从天津港进口，经铁路转运长驱直入北方内陆市场，冲击了传统社会的自然经济，从而使天津所辐射的三北地区大批农民收入减少进而破产。从 1906 年至 1928 年的 20 多年间，华北灾荒频仍，凋敝的社会经济更加难以负担水利设施的修建维护，致使洪涝、干旱、蝗灾接踵而至，常常瞬间摧毁农民数年甚至数代的劳作积累。这 20 年还是北洋军阀之间为争夺兵源、财源和权力而大打出手征战不休的年代，军阀军队军纪涣散、残忍好杀，所到之处社会生产受到极大影响，使很多农民不得不携家带口逃往天津、上海等沿海大城市。这样，这些破产农民、灾民和难民便成了工业发展所需的重要因素——群集于港口和铁路沿线

①　天津市档案馆编，《近代以来天津城市化进程实录》，天津人民出版社，2005 年，第 631 页。

②　据《1922 年至 1931 年十年间天津工业发展状况》计算。天津市档案馆编，《近代以来天津城市化进程实录》，天津人民出版社，2005 年，第 218—223 页。

③　天津市档案馆编，《近代以来天津城市化进程实录》，天津人民出版社，2005 年，第 232—236 页。

in Tianjin. Xu Shuzheng, dispatched by Duan Qirui, traveled northward to Fengtian (now Shenyang) and southward to Bengbu, contacting warlords such as Zhang ZuoLin and Ni Sichong, and even pulling Cao Kun into the main battlefront. On December 2, 1917, just three days after the establishment of the Wang Shizhen Cabinet in Beijing, succeeding Duan Qirui, Tianjin became lively. Warlords from provinces and regions such as Zhili, Shandong, Shanxi, Fengtian, Fujian, Anhui, Zhejiang, Shaanxi, Heilongjiang, Shanghai, Chahar, Suiyuan, and Rehe, along with representatives of military governors such as Cao Kun and Zhang Huaizhi, gathered in Tianjin. They unanimously agreed to launch a military campaign in Hunan, known as the "Tianjin Conference". This illustrates Tianjin's significant political function during the late Qing and early Republic periods, which sets it apart from other modern emerging cities like Shanghai, Hankou, Qingdao, and Dalian.

Industrial Workers and Service Industry Personnel

Although the attention of people, even historians, is often drawn to emperors and generals, warlords and tycoons, and epic tales of war, what people enjoy seeing and hearing about are the towering skyscrapers, the bustling nightlife, and urban legends of cities. However, keen observers point out that in modern times, whether in the East or West, "factories and slums are the two main components of these emerging towns".[①] It is the workers struggling in the dusty, noisy factory workshops and the impoverished struggling in the dark, litter-strewn slums who make up the vast base of the pyramid-shaped urban structure. These are the laborers, barely making ends meet, toiling in the bitter cold or scorching heat, and the lower-class service workers hustling to earn their daily bread, who constitute the massive base of the urban pyramid structure.

Since the modern era of opening up to the outside world, Tianjin, as a major city gathering industry, commerce, and finance, undoubtedly brought hope to those seeking livelihoods. With the establishment of various industrial enterprises during the Westernization Movement, industrial workers began to emerge as a profession, providing opportunities for many bankrupt farmers from rural areas to make a living. According to incomplete statistics, by 1894, the number of modern industrial and transportation workers in Tianjin had exceeded 5,000. After the gradual development and growth of national industry and commerce, more employment opportunities were provided. Just

①　Lewis Mumford. *The Culture of Cities*, translated by Song Junling. China Architecture & Building Press, 2009, p.186.

在外国侨民家里当保姆的中国妇女
A Chinese woman working as amah in foreign
expatriates' home

外国洋行里工作的"苦力"
The "coolies" working in foreign firms

城市的大量人口，即廉价劳动力。而零落衰败的农村从此成为回不去的故土。

在城市找工作，一般有几个途径。首先就是投亲靠友。传统社会的地缘和血缘关系是维系社会秩序的首要纽带，找工作尤其是找一份各方面待遇都不错的工作，就得有人介绍并充当保人。乡亲父老知根知底，自然是最合适且义不容辞的中介人。其次是投入帮派组织。帮派具有地域性。帮派首领也要吃饭养家，他们往往自己就是工头，负责帮助工厂主招纳工人。工头是资本家与工人之间的中介。天津地区最大的帮会组织是由漕运而来的漕帮，民国后改称青帮，是清初以来流行最广、影响最深远的民间秘密结社之一。很多人为了找工作而加入青帮，实际上并不参加帮派活动。第三种就是加入脚行。天津河道、码头众多，需要靠人力搬运装卸，甚至为河船拉纤。后来火车逐渐替代内河航运后，货物装卸依然需靠人力。因此脚行成为那些没有任何社会关系、唯有出卖体力的青壮年劳力寻找工作的途径。那些青年被称作"苦力"。

工人们的劳动条件大都十分恶劣，收入极其低微，生活普遍贫困。工业化早期的天津工厂大都设备落后，70% 的工厂主要是手工操作，生产效率低、工人劳动时间长、劳动强度大。1920 年的调查显示，无论是三条石的小铁厂，还是成立已久的正式国家大厂——天津造币总厂，工人们不仅没有固定假日，而且经常每天加班劳动

between 1915 and 1922, six major textile mills established employed more than 11,500 workers, and by 1922, Tianjin had over 100,000 industrial workers.[1] In 1931, there were about 56,000 workers in Tianjin's national industry, including 15,580 workers in the six major textile mills; 4,180 workers in the 4 cigarette factories; 920 workers in the 6 large-scale flour mills; 11,568 workers in the over a hundred carpet factories; 1,007 workers in the 4 chemical factories; 5,000 workers in the 1 cement factory; 13,750 workers in the 5 match factories; and 722 workers in the 2 salt factories.[2] By the end of 1949, Tianjin had 130,000 industrial workers and 71,043 personnel engaged in commercial and service industries, totaling 201,043 people.[3]

The workers in Tianjin mainly came from bankrupt farmers in the surrounding areas and refugees who fled their homes due to water shortages, droughts, famines, or warlord conflicts. As mentioned earlier, shortly after its opening, Tianjin became a major importer of foreign goods. Imported Western textiles, rice, and flour entered Tianjin Port and were transported by railway to the northern inland markets, undermining the traditional natural economy and causing significant reductions in the income of many farmers in the Three North regions radiated by Tianjin, leading to bankruptcies. Over the twenty-plus years from 1906 to 1928, famines frequently struck North

[1] Tianjin Archives (ed.). *Factual Records of Tianjin's Urbanization since Modern Times*. Tianjin People's Publishing House, 2005, p.631.

[2] Calculated based on *Industrial Development in Tianjin during the Ten Years from 1922 to 1931*. Tianjin Archives (ed.). *Factual Records of Tianjin's Urbanization since Modern Times*. Tianjin People's Publishing House, 2005, pp.218-223.

[3] Tianjin Archives (ed.). *Factual Records of Tianjin's Urbanization since Modern Times*. Tianjin People's Publishing House, 2005, pp.232-236.

至 13、14 个小时。他们整日在厂工作，没有时间休息，也没有"工人补习学校"，无法学习提高劳动技能，精神萎靡不振，日趋烦闷。[1] 据 1933 年当局在天津 1200 个工厂所做的调查，约有 3/4 的工厂，其工人劳动时间在 11 个小时以上。相比之下，他们的收入却极其微薄。20 世纪二三十年代，工人工资按技术岗位来划分，能操作机器的工匠每月 30 元，普通工人每月只有 10 元，小型工厂的工人最低则只有 7 元。[2] 家庭服务业者在职业人口中所占的比重不大，但却是底层妇女从事的主要职业，工作条件稍好，但报酬一样很低。1905 年天津的外国人家里佣人的每月工资如下：伙计或女佣 9—12 元，苦力 7 元，厨师 10—16 元，阿妈（保姆）5—10 元，马夫 15 元（包括喂马的饲料）。[3] 1923 年北洋大学雇用的一位美国教师在写给他太太的信中提到，他们在天津的家中将雇用一位会做西餐的厨师、一名仆人（No.1 boy）、一个苦力（负责打扫卫生和洗衣）和一位阿妈（女仆兼保姆）。四个仆人的佣金加起来才只有 45 墨西哥元（即银元），而食品的费用每月还要 75 墨西哥元。[4]

入城农民很多都是举家搬迁，"今日农民的离村，已非个人的而是家族的，至少是直系亲属，已非一时的，而为永久的"[5]。此种特征在民国以后尤为凸显。1929 年，南开大学经济学院对天津市织布业工人的籍贯进行了调查，在调查的 867 名工人中，天津本市籍贯仅有 39 人，占总数的 4.5%，其余大都来自河北各县及其他外省的农民，"细察外来工人之身世，则多半出自农家，其趋驰津市，无非为谋生计焉"。这些入城的农民多为城市的开拓者和定居者，

① 杨赓陶，《天津造币总厂底层工人状况》。李文海主编，《民国时期社会调查丛编（二编）城市（劳工）生活卷（下）》，福建教育出版社，2014 年，第 113—116 页。

② 《1922 年至 1931 年十年间天津工业发展状况》（1931 年 12 月 31 日）。天津市档案馆编，《近代以来天津城市化进程实录》，天津人民出版社，2005 年，第 218—223 页。

③ （比）约翰·麦特勒等著，刘悦等译，《比利时—中国：昔日之路（1870—1930）》，社会科学文献出版社，2021 年，第 201 页。

④ 张畅，《近代西方侨民来华原因剖析》，《天津师范大学学报（社会科学版）》，2007 年第 5 期，第 53—58 页。

⑤ 蔡斌咸，《从农村破产中挤出来的人力车夫问题》，《东方杂志》第 32 卷第 16 号，1935 年 8 月 16 日，第 37 页。

China, exacerbating the already impoverished social economy, making it increasingly difficult to afford the construction and maintenance of water conservancy facilities. Consequently, floods, droughts, and locust plagues frequently occurred, often instantly destroying the labor accumulations of farmers spanning several years or even generations. During this period, warlords in the Beiyang government constantly fought each other for military resources, financial sources, and power. Their armies were undisciplined and brutal, severely impacting social production wherever they went, forcing many farmers to flee to coastal cities such as Tianjin and Shanghai with their families. Consequently, these bankrupt farmers, refugees, and displaced persons became crucial factors needed for industrial development—a large population gathering around ports and railway cities, providing cheap labor. The scattered and declining rural areas thus became irretrievable homelands.

There are generally several ways to find a job in the city. The first is to rely on personal connections. In traditional society, geographical and blood relations are the primary bonds maintaining social order. When it comes to finding a job, especially a well-paying one, one needs someone to introduce them and act as a guarantor. Local acquaintances who know the ins and outs naturally serve as the most suitable and obligatory intermediaries. The second is to join gang organizations. Gangs are often regional. Gang leaders also need to feed their families, and they often act as foremen themselves, responsible for helping factory owners recruit workers. Foremen serve as intermediaries between capitalists and workers. One of the largest gang organizations in the Tianjin area is the Cao Bang, which originated from canal transport and was later renamed Qing Bang during the Republic of China era. It was one of the most widely spread and influential secret societies among the people since the early Qing Dynasty. Many people joined the Qing Bang to find work, but in reality, they did not participate in gang activities. The third method is to become a laborer. Tianjin has many rivers and docks, requiring manual labor for loading and unloading goods, and even towing river boats. Even after trains gradually replaced river transportation, manual labor was still needed for loading and unloading goods. Therefore, becoming a laborer became a way for young adults without any social connections to find work by selling their physical strength. These young people are called "coolies."

The working conditions for workers were generally very harsh, with extremely low incomes and widespread poverty. In the early stages of industrialization, most factories in Tianjin had outdated equipment, with 70% of them relying mainly on manual operations, resulting in low productivity, long working hours, and high labor intensity for workers. A survey in 1920 revealed that whether it was a small ironworks in the Santiaoshi area or a well-

"此辈居留天津有年，在津成立家室者，亦所在多有"①。一般工人家庭子女较多，有收入者不过1—2口，养家糊口并非易事。即使当时的天津物价并不算高，但是工人们的饭碗里却鲜少能见到肉丝，他们只能吃着几乎没有一丝油水的饭菜。吃饭尚且艰难，其他穿衣、住房等自然更加鄙陋。

工人们因地缘、祖籍、性别、受教育程度、技艺才能不同而存在差异，因此他们并非一个可以用少数特征加以概括的整体。但随着劳工队伍的壮大，他们的力量越来越难以被忽视。第一次世界大战中，北洋政府宣布加入协约国一方作战，派出14万来自山东、河北等地的劳工"以工代兵"奔赴欧洲战场。当时国内外报刊都对华工为欧战作出的杰出贡献进行了报道。不仅北洋政府，还有广大社会精英，都对劳工表达了尊重和认可。1918年11月16日，在天安门前举行的庆祝协约国获胜的演讲大会上，蔡元培喊出了"劳工神圣"的口号。一战中，中国民族资本主义得到难得的黄金发展，工人阶级队伍也迅速壮大。他们开展了为改善劳动条件和增加工资待遇的反抗活动，显示了强大的影响力，这之后才有五四运动时期无产阶级作为一支独立的政治力量登上政治舞台，持续影响中国未来政治。

高级职员、教师、记者和医生

因洋务运动兴办教育，近代接受西方现代基础教育、职业教育、高等教育乃至留学教育的城市人口越来越多。与此同时，在天津、上海这样的沿海开放城市里，有越来越多的洋行、银行、工厂以及市政管理、文化教育和社会服务机构设立，从而造就了大批买办阶层和城市职员阶层。他们一般受过良好教育，具有较高的文化知识和专业技能，在洋行、银行等工商企业担任职员，在政府、军队和警察部门任公务员，在中小学任教师。其中的高级知识分子，如自行开业的律师、医生、工程师等自由职业者和大学里的教授们，更是收入高、社会声望也高的社会精英阶层。

---

① 方显廷，《天津织布工业》，南开大学经济学院，1931年，第77页。

established state-owned factory like the Tianjin Central Mint, workers not only lacked fixed holidays but also frequently worked overtime for 13 to 14 hours a day. They worked all day in the factories, with no time for rest, and without "workers' supplementary schools," they were unable to learn and improve their labor skills, leading to spiritual lethargy and increasing boredom.① According to a survey conducted by the authorities in 1933 of 1,200 factories in Tianjin, about three-quarters of them had workers laboring for more than 11 hours a day. In contrast, their incomes were extremely meager. In the 1920s and 1930s, worker wages were divided according to technical positions, with artisans operating machines earning 30 yuan per month, ordinary workers earning only 10 yuan per month, and workers in small factories earning as little as 7 yuan per month.② While the proportion of household service workers in the working population was not large, it was the main occupation for lower-class women. Although the working conditions were slightly better, the remuneration was still very low. In 1905, the monthly wages for domestic servants in foreign households in Tianjin were as follows: butlers or maidservants earned 9 to 12 yuan, coolies earned 7 yuan, chefs earned 10 to 16 yuan, nannies (babysitters) earned 5 to 10 yuan, and stable boys earned 15 yuan (including horse feed).③ In 1923, an American teacher employed by Peiyang University mentioned in a letter to his wife that they would hire a chef who could cook Western food, a No.1 boy, a coolie (responsible for cleaning and laundry), and a nanny (maid and babysitter) in their home in Tianjin. The combined wages for the four servants amounted to only 45 Mexican dollars (silver dollars), while the monthly food expenses were 75 Mexican dollars.④

Many rural migrants moving into the city bring their entire families with them. "Today, when farmers leave their villages, it is no longer an individual decision but a family one, involving at least immediate relatives, and it is no longer temporary but permanent."⑤ This characteristic became particularly

---

① Yang Gengtao. *The Status of Bottom-Level Workers at Tianjin Central Mint of the Ministry of Revenue*. Li Wenhai (ed.). *Compilation of Social Surveys during the Republic of China: Urban (Labor) Life Volume (Part 2)*. Fujian Education Press, 2014, pp.113-116.

② *The Industrial Development Status of Tianjin from 1922 to 1931* (December 31, 1931). Tianjin Archives (ed.). *Factual Records of Tianjin's Urbanization since Modern Times*. Tianjin People's Publishing House, 2005, pp.218-223.

③ Johan J. Mattelaer, et al. *A Belgian Passage to China (1870-1930)*, translated by Liu Yue, et al. Social Sciences Academic Press (China), 2021, p.201.

④ Zhang Chang. *An Analysis of the Reasons for Western Expatriates Coming to China in Modern Times*. Journal of Tianjin Normal University (Social Science Edition), 2007(5), pp. 53-58.

⑤ Cai Binxian. The Issue of Rickshaw Pullers Who Are Turned from Bankrupted Peasants. *The Eastern Miscellany* (Vol.32, No.16), August 16, 1935, p.37.

民国时期的学者和地方管理者关注社会改造。他们通过进行社会调查研究，对劳工的劳动和生活状况都进行了详细的调查统计，[①]但是对于经济状况相对较好的职员阶层则远没有那么关注，又或是社会学家们本就属于中间阶层，"不识庐山真面目，只缘身在此山中"。职员的具体数量很难进行统计，首先是当时的人口调查是按照所属行业来划分和统计，而不是按照其具体的职位，而同一企业中各个职位的收入状况和社会等级相距较大。当然，还有一个因素就是，职员阶层的流动性比较大，自由职业者更不具有"组织性"，而且常常兼职，所以难以统计，只能估算。根据天津市公安局档案科 1936—1947 年的人口统计材料（不包括租界），[②]公务员约在 10000—20000 人，自由职业者在 10000—15000 人，[③]但其中并未包含在工矿企业、商业和交通运输业中任职的职员人数。如果将这个人数大致估算为 5000 人的话，[④]职员阶层人数总和约为 25000—40000 人。据 1950 年天津市人民政府对 1949 年以前外资工商业的调查统计，在 259 家外资企业中工作的有中国籍职员 12387 人。[⑤]把所有中外资工商业和自由职业者都加在一起，天津市包括职员、公务员、自由职业者在内的所有从业者人数应在 35000—55000 人。按照阶层划分的一般原则，一个家庭的成员（主要包括父母、祖父母和未成年子女）都属于主要收入者所属阶层。1947 年天津市每户平均人口为 5 口人，[⑥]那么这个城市的中间阶层就有 17 万—34 万人之多，

---

① 如 20 世纪 30 年代的《天津市面粉业调查报告》《天津市纺纱业调查报告》《南大校工生活调查》等。

② 中间缺 1939—1941 年和 1945 年材料。李竞能主编，《天津人口史》，南开大学出版社，1990 年，第 249 页。

③ 自由职业者中包括幼稚园、中小学和专科以上教职员。1939 年，小学和幼稚园的教职员共有 2028 人，师范学校、中学和职业学校的教职员总数为 596 名，1949 年，粗略统计专科以上院校教职员有约 900 人。天津市档案馆编，《近代以来天津城市化进程实录》，天津人民出版社，2005 年，第 646—658、667—674 页。

④ 1922 年《天津指南》所记录律师就达 500 多人，医院 42 家、报社 23 家，估计当时这样的自由职业者有 5000—8000 人。

⑤ 《天津外资工商业户名册》。天津市档案馆编，《近代以来天津城市化进程实录》，天津人民出版社，2005 年，第 303—356 页。

⑥ 李竞能主编，《天津人口史》，南开大学出版社，1990 年，第 255 页。

prominent after the Republic of China era. In 1929, the Economics School of Nankai University conducted a survey of the origins of textile workers in Tianjin. Among the 867 workers surveyed, only 39 were native to Tianjin, accounting for 4.5% of the total. The majority came from various counties in Hebei Province and other provinces, "upon closer examination, most of the migrant workers come from farming families, and their migration to Tianjin is simply to seek a livelihood." These rural migrants are often the pioneers and settlers of the city. "Those who have resided in Tianjin for years and established families here are quite common."[①] Generally, workers' families have many children, with only 1-2 earners per household, making it difficult to support the family. Even though the cost of living in Tianjin at that time was not considered high, workers rarely had meat in their meals, and they could only eat meals that were almost devoid of any oil. Eating was difficult enough, and other aspects such as clothing and housing were naturally even more impoverished.

Workers differ due to factors such as geographical origins, ancestral backgrounds, gender, education levels, and skill sets, so they are not a homogeneous group that can be summarized by a few characteristics. However, with the growth of the labor force, their power has become increasingly difficult to ignore. During the First World War, the Beiyang government declared joining the Allies and dispatched 140,000 laborers from Shandong, Hebei, and other regions to the European battlefield under the "Going into the War with Chinese Laborers" program. At that time, both domestic and foreign newspapers reported on the outstanding contributions made by Chinese laborers to the European war. Not only the Beiyang government but also the broader social elites expressed respect and recognition for the laborers. On November 16, 1918, during a celebratory speech in front of Tiananmen Square to mark the victory of the Allies, Cai Yuanpei shouted the slogan "Labor is Sacred". During the First World War, Chinese national capitalism experienced rare golden development, and the working class quickly grew in size. They engaged in resistance activities to improve labor conditions and increase wages, demonstrating significant influence. It was after this period that during the May Fourth Movement, the proletariat emerged as an independent political force, stepping onto the political stage and continuously influencing the future politics of China.

Senior Staff, Teachers, Journalists, and Doctors

Due to the Westernization Movement, there was an increasing population

---

① Fang Xianting. *Tianjin Textile Industry*. School of Economics, Nankai University, 1931, p.77.

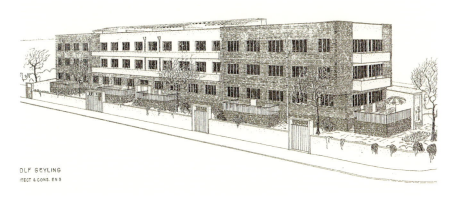

民园大楼图纸。由奥地利籍设计师盖苓之子弗兰茨提供

The drawing of Minyuan Apartment Building. Courtesy of Franz Geyling, son of Austrian architect Rolf Geyling

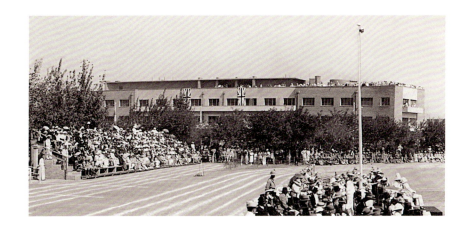

民园大楼（重庆道66—68号）。出租给职员家庭居住的高级公寓，由奥地利建筑师盖苓设计建造

The Minyuan Apartment Building (No.66-68, Chongqing Road) was a high-end apartment complex rented to clerk class families for residential purposes. It was designed and built by Austrian architect Rolf Geyling

香港大楼（睦南道2—4号）。出租给职员家庭居住的高级公寓，由奥地利建筑师盖苓设计建造

The Herakles Apartment Building (No.2-4, Munan Road) was a high-end apartment complex rented to employee families for residential purposes. It was designed and built by Austrian architect Rolf Geyling

剑桥大楼（重庆道24号）。出租给职员家庭居住的高级公寓，由奥地利建筑师盖苓设计建造

The Cambridge Apartment Building (No.24, Chongqing Road) was a high-end apartment complex rented to employee families for residential purposes. It was designed and built by Austrian architect Rolf Geyling

约占当时天津市总人口的 10%~18%。

职员的薪资标准根据职务、年资和受教育程度而有很大差别。在 20 世纪二三十年代，一般来说，店铺里的职员薪水较低，薪资最高的掌柜（相当于部门经理）也只有月薪 8—10 元银洋，[①] 洋行中的工资要高许多，高级职员月薪 30 元。公务员的薪水，税务局监督（局长）的月薪是 600 元，会办是 300 元；卫生局的科长为 30 元，普通书记员月薪只有 8 元。海关、邮局和铁路的职员，薪水不是最高，但属于"铁饭碗"，要求的学历至少是中学毕业，会英文。[②] 高校的教职工是新兴职业群体的代表。民国时期，教师的待遇是中间阶层中比较高的，特别是抗战全面爆发之前，教师的待遇稳定而有保障。1927 年《大学教员薪俸表》中规定的教授月薪 400—600 元，副教授260—400 元，讲师 160—260 元，助教 100—160 元。教授最高月薪600 元，与国民政府部长基本持平。在 20 世纪 30 年代初，大中小学教师的平均月薪分别为 220 元、70 元、30 元。民国时北洋大学的薪金标准，老教授的底薪是 600 元，著名教授是 560 元左右，职员80—300 元。[③] 不过，需要注意的是，1935 年国民党政府进行币制改革，1 银元约等于 2 法币。随着抗战和解放战争，法币就越来越贬值了，以上月薪应为银元。

那么以这样的薪资收入，能达到什么样的生活水平呢？20 世纪二三十年代到全面抗战开始之前的物价比较稳定。上海的物价较高，一块银元可以买 150 余只鸡蛋，一枚铜元可以买一根油条和一张大饼或者坐一段有轨电车，大饭店的一桌丰盛酒席约在 10 元，一身长

---

① 银洋每个用白银 7 钱 3 分铸成，银质最标准的是墨西哥铸成的，上面有一只鹰的图案，所以又称为"鹰洋"。鹰洋在晚清时已普遍流行，清政府在光绪年间铸造了多种银元，因图案是一条龙，称为"龙洋"。民国初年，袁世凯执政时期，又铸造了有袁世凯头像的"袁大头"。以上三种银元在同一时期等价使用。民国初年，一块银元大约可以兑换 128 枚铜元，20 世纪二三十年代兑换价超过 180 枚铜元。1935 年 11 月 3 日，南京国民政府财政部颁布《法币政策实施法》及《兑换法币办法》，其中规定中央银行、中国银行、交通银行 3 家银行发行的货币为法币，概以法币为限，禁止白银流通。

② 陈存仁，《银元时代生活史》，广西师范大学出版社，2007 年，第 8、42、54、88、93、198 页。

③ 天津国立北洋大学（天津大学）。天津市档案馆编，《近代以来天津城市化进程实录》，天津人民出版社，2005 年，第 639—642 页。

in modern cities who received Western-style basic education, vocational education, higher education, and even education abroad. At the same time, in coastal open cities like Tianjin and Shanghai, there was a growing number of foreign firms, banks, factories, as well as municipal administration, cultural education, and social service institutions, thus creating a large number of comprador and urban clerical classes. They generally received good education, possessed high cultural knowledge and professional skills, worked as clerks in foreign firms, banks, and other commercial enterprises, served as civil servants in government, military, and police departments, and taught in primary and secondary schools. Among them, senior intellectuals, such as self-employed lawyers, doctors, engineers, and professors in universities, were the elite class with high incomes and social prestige.

During the Republic of China era, scholars and local administrators focused on social transformation. They conducted detailed investigations and statistics on the labor and living conditions of workers through social surveys.[①] However, comparatively little attention was paid to the relatively well-off clerical class, or perhaps sociologists themselves belonged to the middle class, and they could not "see the true face of the mountain because they were in it." It was difficult to accurately count the specific number of clerical workers. Firstly, population surveys at that time were conducted based on industries rather than specific positions, and the income and social status of various positions within the same enterprise varied greatly. Additionally, the clerical class had high mobility, and self-employed professionals lacked "organizational" characteristics and often worked part-time, making them challenging to count and only estimations were possible. According to population statistics from the Tianjin Public Security Bureau's archives from 1936 to 1947 (excluding concessions),[②] there were approximately 10,000 to 20,000 civil servants and 10,000 to 15,000 self-employed professionals.[③] However, this did not include the number of clerical workers in industrial and mining enterprises, commerce, and transportation. If this number is

---

① Such as *The Survey Report of Tianjin Flour Industry*, *The Survey Report of Tianjin Textile Industry*, and *The Survey of School Worker Life of Nankai University* in 1930s.

② Lack of materials from 1939-1941 and 1945. Li Jingneng (ed.). *Population History of Tianjin*. Nankai University Press, 1990, p.249.

③ Among freelancers, this includes teachers from kindergartens, primary schools, and higher education institutions. In 1939, the total number of teachers in elementary schools and kindergartens was 2,028, while the total number of teachers in normal schools, secondary schools, and vocational schools was 596. By 1949, rough statistics showed that the number of faculty members in colleges and universities was approximately 900. Tianjin Archives (ed.). *Factual Records of Tianjin's Urbanization since Modern Times*. Tianjin People's Publishing House, 2005, pp.646-658,667-674.

津南里（重庆道与新华路交口）。中南银行为职工建设的集合式公寓，由奥地利建筑师盖苓设计建造

Jinnanli Apartment Building (at the intersection of Chongqing Road and Xinhua Road). It was built by China & South Sea Bank for its employees, designed and built by Austrian architect Rolf Geyling

袍马褂要 10 元左右，一件绣花的高级旗袍大约要 20 元，一处独立的住房月租约 10 元，一座华界占地 1 亩的楼房售价约 2.5 万元，一辆小型轿车车价为 1100 元，司机的月薪为 20 元。北方的物价便宜很多，一个四合院的租金每月约为 30 多元，但房间也有 20 多间。平均每个月的食品消费支出也就在十几元左右，天津的鸡蛋大约只要 1 分钱，一只鸡只要 5 角钱，请客花上十几块钱便可摆上一桌很讲究的有海参、鱼翅的宴席。① 粗略计算一下，一个普通职员租房住，一日三餐，供养一个 7—8 人的大家庭，可以达到温饱。而若想过上有房（租独立住房一栋）有车（黄包车）有保姆的更加体面的生活，

① 陈存仁，《银元时代生活史》，广西师范大学出版社，2007 年，第 25、81、90、195 页。

roughly estimated to be 5,000 people,[1] the total number of clerical workers would be between 25,000 and 40,000. According to a survey conducted by the Tianjin Municipal People's Government in 1950 on foreign-funded industries and commerce before 1949, there were 12,387 Chinese clerical workers employed by 259 foreign-funded enterprises.[2] Combining all workers at the Chinese and foreign-funded industries and commerce with self-employed professionals, the total number of workers in Tianjin, including clerical workers, civil servants, and self-employed professionals, should be between 35,000 and 55,000. According to the general principle of class division, members of a household (mainly including parents, grandparents, and minor children) belong to the same class as the primary income earners. In 1947, the average household size in Tianjin was 5 people.[3] Therefore, the middle class in this city comprised as many as 170,000 to 340,000 people, accounting for approximately 10% to 18% of the total population of Tianjin at that time.

The salary standards for clerical workers varied greatly depending on their positions, seniority, and level of education. In the 1920s and 1930s, generally speaking, clerks in shops received lower salaries, with the highest-paid managers (equivalent to department managers) earning only 8 to 10 silver dollars (yuan)[4] per month. The salaries in foreign firms were much higher, with senior clerical workers earning 30 yuan per month. For civil servants, the salary varied significantly. The monthly salary for the director (supervisor) of the Tax Bureau was 600 yuan, while the assistant director received 300 yuan; the head of a department in the Health Bureau received

① In 1922, the *Tianjin Guide Book* recorded there were over 500 lawyers, 42 hospitals, and 23 newspapers. It could be estimated that there were around 5,000-8,000 freelancers at that time.

② *List of Foreign Industrial and Commercial Businessmen*. Tianjin Archives (ed.). *Factual Records of Tianjin's Urbanization since Modern Times*. Tianjin People's Publishing House, 2005, pp.303-356.

③ Li Jingneng (ed.). *Population History of Tianjin*. Nankai University Press, 1990, p.255.

④ Each silver dollar, known as "Yin Yang," was minted with 7 taels and 3 fen of silver. The most standard silver was that minted in Mexico, which featured an eagle design, thus it was also referred to as the "Eagle Dollar." The Eagle Dollar became widely circulated during the late Qing Dynasty, and during the Guangxu period, the Qing government minted various silver coins, with a dragon motif, called the "Dragon Dollar." In the early years of the Republic of China, during Yuan Shikai's rule, another type of silver coin, known as the "Yuan Shikai Dollar" or "Yuan Big Head," was minted featuring his portrait. These three types of silver dollars were used interchangeably during the same period. In the early years of the Republic, one silver dollar could be exchanged for approximately 128 copper coins. By the 1920s and 1930s, this exchange rate had increased to over 180 copper coins per silver dollar. On November 3, 1935, the National Government in Nanjing issued the *Legal Currency Policy Implementation Law* and *Regulations on the Exchange of Legal Currency*, which stipulated that the currency issued by the Central Bank, Bank of China, and the Bank of Communications would be the official currency. Legal tender was to be limited to this currency, and the circulation of silver coins was prohibited.

月薪要在 100 元以上。月薪 200—400 元的高级大学教职员们可以经常去大店铺定做材质上乘的衣服，冬天有皮袄、貂皮大衣，夏天有丝绸。教授、医生等高级知识分子们常常还有很高雅但很费钱的爱好，比如收藏古董、古书、古钱币，郊游，打桥牌和打猎。

近代天津的中间阶层中，有一个非常有社会影响力的群体，那就是新闻媒体人，当时称为"报人"。晚清时期外国人开始在租界创办报刊，20 世纪二三十年代是天津报业发展鼎盛时期，当时最有名的是创办于 1902 年的《大公报》、1915 年的《益世报》和 1926 年的《北洋画报》，其他还有几十份大报小报，所涌现的报人何止百人，如《大公报》的英敛之、萧乾、范长江，《益世报》的罗隆基、唐梦幻，《新民意报》的马千里，在各报连载小说的刘云若、宫白羽，为报纸画漫画的赵望云、高龙生，写天津民俗掌故的戴愚庵等。他们不仅是用笔谋生的知识分子，而且是为实现启发民智、移风易俗、救国图强的理想而奋斗的启蒙者，是中国新闻事业的先驱。他们在移风易俗方面提出很多主张，如反对妇女缠足，反对早婚、纳妾，反对吸食鸦片，批评重男轻女思想，主张破除封建迷信，批判官场恶习等。他们的收入居于中间阶层的中间，也能经常出入西餐厅、戏院、影院等时髦消费场所。

天津的社会精英中还有一个非常令人瞩目的群体，那就是中西名医们。洋务运动中，西方医学的发展包括医院和医生的培养是其中的重要内容。西医自 1840 年以前已有传入中国，但是影响力有限。在天津，西医得到了直隶总督李鸿章的认可，1881 年由官方在天津创办北洋施医局、北洋海军医学堂，1902 年袁世凯办北洋医学堂，1912 年北洋政府公布医学校条例。近现代医学事业的发展、国人对西医的认可和接受，使医生这个行业逐渐成为新兴的城市精英阶层。特别是 1941 年 12 月 28 日太平洋战争爆发，日军接管了协和医学院和附属医院，原来在协和的医师们出于爱国之心，纷纷离去，有不少人来到天津继续行医。这些医生来到天津，使天津医疗水平大大提高。

在职员阶层中最上层的是医生，独立开业的医生月赚约 40 元，在药铺坐诊的中医大夫约 20 元，做到有名的大医生，比如被聘作工

30 yuan, while ordinary clerks earned only 8 yuan per month. Employees of customs, post offices, and railways had relatively high job security, although their salaries were not the highest. They were required to have at least a high school diploma and proficiency in English.[1] Faculty members at universities represented an emerging professional group. During the Republic of China era, teachers enjoyed relatively high treatment in the middle class, especially before the outbreak of the full-scale war with Japan, when their treatment was stable and guaranteed. According to the *University Faculty Salary Scale* in 1927, the monthly salary for professors was 400-600 yuan, associate professors 260-400 yuan, lecturers 160-260 yuan, and teaching assistants 100-160 yuan. The highest monthly salary for professors was 600 yuan, which was roughly equivalent to that of a minister in the Nationalist government. In the early 1930s, the average monthly salaries for teachers in primary, secondary, and tertiary schools were 220 yuan, 70 yuan, and 30 yuan, respectively. At Peiyang University during the Republic of China era, the basic salary for senior professors was 600 yuan, while renowned professors received around 560 yuan, and clerical workers earned between 80 and 300 yuan.[2] However, it is worth noting that in 1935, the Nationalist government carried out currency reform, with 1 silver dollar being approximately equal to 2 Legal Currency. With the progression of the Anti-Japanese War and the Chinese Civil War, the Legal Currency depreciated more and more, so the above-mentioned salaries should be in silver dollars.

With such income, what kind of living standards could be achieved? In the 1920s and 1930s, before the full-scale outbreak of the Anti-Japanese War, prices were relatively stable. Prices in Shanghai were relatively high: one yuan could buy more than 150 eggs, one copper coin could buy a youtiao (fried dough stick) and a large pancake, or a tram ride. A lavish banquet in a high-end restaurant cost about 10 yuan, while a long gown or a maqwa (a type of jacket) cost around 10 yuan. A high-quality embroidered cheongsam (traditional Chinese dress) cost approximately 20 yuan. The monthly rent for an independent house was around 10 yuan, and a mansion occupying 1 mu of land in the foreign concession areas was priced at about 25,000 yuan. The price of a small car was 1,100 yuan, with the driver's monthly salary being 20 yuan. Prices were much cheaper in the north: the monthly rent for a siheyuan

---

[1] Chen Cunren. *Life History of the Silver Age*. Guangxi Normal University Press, 2007, pp.8, 42, 54, 88, 93, 198.

[2] National Peiyang University (Tianjin University). Tianjin Archives (ed.). *Factual Records of Tianjin's Urbanization since Modern Times*. Tianjin People's Publishing House, 2005, pp.639-642.

厂的长聘医生或者富商的家庭医生，年金都能有 300 元以上，而且是可以兼做几家的，所以年收入达到千元以上也并不在少数。许多医生被请到患者家中出诊，甚至要用金条做报酬。医生拥有了丰厚的收入，可以租住在天津最高级、环境最好的住宅区——原英租界五大道，有的甚至在这里置办了房产。他们结邻而居，构成了一个星光熠熠的名医群体。据不完全统计，五大道的中西名医故居有 40 所之多。

(traditional courtyard house) was around 30 yuan, although it might have over 20 rooms. Average monthly food expenses were only around ten yuan. In Tianjin, an egg cost only 1 cent, and a chicken cost 50 cents. Hosting a refined banquet with delicacies like sea cucumber and shark fin could cost just over ten dollars.[1] Roughly estimating, an ordinary clerk could afford housing, three meals a day, and support a large family of 7 to 8 people, ensuring basic needs were met. However, for a more decent life with a rented independent house, a rickshaw, and a nanny, a monthly salary of over 100 yuan was required. University professors earning between 200 and 400 yuan per month could often afford tailor-made clothes from upscale stores, including fur coats in winter and silk garments in summer. Professors, doctors, and other high-level intellectuals often indulged in expensive hobbies such as collecting antiques, old books, and coins, as well as going on outings, playing bridge, and hunting.

In the middle class of modern Tianjin, there was a highly influential group, known as the "journalists" at the time. During the late Qing Dynasty, foreigners began to establish newspapers and periodicals in the concessions. The 1920s and 1930s were the heyday of Tianjin's newspaper industry, with the most famous being *Ta Kung Pao* founded in 1902, *Social Welfare* in 1915, and *Beiyang Pictorial News* in 1926. There were also dozens of other major and minor newspapers, with numerous notable journalists emerging, including Ying Lianzhi, Xiao Qian, and Fan Changjiang from *Ta Kung Pao*, Luo Longji and Tang Menghuan from *Social Welfare*, and Ma Qianli from *Xin Min Yi Pao*. Writers like Liu Yunruo and Gong Baiyu serialized novels, while artists like Zhao Wangyun and Gao Longsheng drew cartoons, and Dai Yu'an wrote about Tianjin folklore and anecdotes. They were not only intellectuals who earned a living by writing but also enlighteners who strove to enlighten the people, change customs, and strengthen the nation. They were pioneers of China's journalism. They put forward many propositions to change customs, such as opposing foot-binding for women, early marriage, concubinage, opium smoking, criticizing the patriarchal mindset, advocating the elimination of feudal superstitions, and criticizing corrupt practices in the bureaucracy. Their income was in the middle of the middle class, allowing them to frequent fashionable places like Western restaurants, theaters, and cinemas.

In Tianjin's social elite, there was another remarkable group, namely the Chinese and Western doctors. The development of Western medicine,

---

[1]　Chen Cunren. *Life History of the Silver Age*. Guangxi Normal University Press, 2007, p.25, 81, 90, 195.

原天和医院（睦南道 122 号）
The former Tianhe Hospital (No.122 Munan Road)

京城有协和医院闻名海内外，津门亦有天和医院无人不晓。"天和"一词寓含"天津的协和"之意。天和医院，从院长、董事会成员到主要医护骨干，几乎都是原"协和"的人。1942 年，从"协和"来天津的张纪正大夫联合方先之、柯应夔、邓家栋等人发起筹建了天和医院。以马场道原西湖饭店旧址作院舍，又得到津门社会各界人士支持，帮助购置或借用办公家具、医疗器械等，以解燃眉之急。经过数月筹备，医院改建完工并完成注册，于 1942 年 7 月 1 日正式开业，名为"天津市私立天和医院"。医院设内科、外科、骨科、妇产科等，共有病床 100 张。由骨科方先之、胸科张纪正、妇产科柯应夔任院长，轮流主持医院院务，并分别在科室应诊。

The Peking Union Medical College Hospital (Xiehe) in the capital is renowned both at home and abroad, and similarly, Tianhe Hospital in Tianjin is widely recognized. The name "Tianhe" signifies "Tianjin's Union Medical College Hospital." Its president, board members, and key medical staff were almost all former members of Union Hospital. In 1942, Dr. Zhang Jizheng, who had moved to Tianjin from Union Hospital, collaborated with Dr. Fang Xianzhi, Dr. Ke Yingkui, Dr. Deng Jiadong, and others to establish Tianhe Hospital. They selected the former site of the West Lake Hotel on Race Course Road as the hospital's location. With support from various sectors of Tianjin society, they managed to acquire or borrow office furniture, medical equipment, and other essential supplies to facilitate the hospital's launch. After several months of preparation, the hospital completed renovations and registration, officially opening on July 1, 1942, under the name "Tianjin Private Tianhe Hospital." It housed departments of internal medicine, surgery, orthopedics, and obstetrics & gynecology, with a total of 100 beds. Dr. Fang Xianzhi (Orthopedics), Dr. Zhang Jizheng (Thoracic Surgery), and Dr. Ke Yingkui (Obstetrics & Gynecology) served as hospital directors, taking turns managing hospital affairs while continuing to practice in their respective fields.

卞万年
Bian Wannian

恩光医院首任院长卞万年早年就读于天津新学书院。著名银行家卞白眉之四子。1931 年毕业于北平协和医学院，后留校任教，擅长内科、心脏科。1942 年，北京协和医学院被日本侵略军占领，医院被迫关闭。率先来津的内科医生卞万年和外科医生方先之回北京，把极有实力的眼科医生林景奎、牙科医生关颂凯、小儿科医生王志宜、外科医生金显宅、耳鼻喉科医生林必锦、妇产科医生林崧、泌尿科医生施锡恩、皮肤科医生卞学鉴等人召来，每人五千块钱，集资接办了陈善理的恩光医院。

卞万年旧居（云南路 57 号）
The former residence of Bian Wannian (No.57 Yunnan Road)

Bian Wannian, the first director of Sunnyside Hospital, studied at Tianjin Anglo-Chinese College in his early years. He was the fourth son of the renowned banker Bian Baimei. After graduating from Peking Union Medical College in 1931, he remained as a faculty member, specializing in internal medicine and cardiology. In 1942, after the Japanese occupation of Beijing Union Medical College forced the hospital to close, Bian Wannian and orthopedic surgeon Fang Xianzhi were among the first to relocate to Tianjin. They later returned to Beijing and assembled a group of highly skilled medical professionals, including ophthalmologist Lin Jingkui, dentist Guan Songkai, pediatrician Wang Zhiyi, surgeon Jin Xianzhai, otolaryngologist Lin Bijin, obstetrician-gynecologist Lin Song, urologist Shi Xi'en, and dermatologist Bian Xuejian. Each contributed 5,000 yuan to collectively take over and run Sunnyside Hospital, originally established by Chen Shanli.

恩光医院原址（今成都道与河北路口），医院建筑已不存
The former site of Sunnyside Hospital (at the intersection of Chengdu Road and Hebei Road today). It no longer exits

方先之
Fang Xianzhi

中国现代骨科先驱方先之旧居（睦南道 109 号）
Former Residence of Pioneer in Modern Orthopedics Fang Xianzhi (No.109 Munan Road)

方先之（1906—1968），中国现代骨科先驱，天津骨科医院创始人，被誉为"骨圣"。太平洋战争爆发后，与北京协和医院一批著名医生来到天津，创建天和医院。1950 年抗美援朝战争爆发，方先之首批赴朝鲜前线救治伤员。1953 年卫生部委托方先之在天津创办了骨科医师进修班，到他去世时，一共培训了 15 期，每期 40 人，这些学员如今分布在全国各地医院，为我国骨科医学权威。

Fang Xianzhi (1906-1968) was a pioneer in modern Chinese orthopedics and the founder of Tianjin Orthopedic Hospital, earning the title "Sage of Orthopedics." After the outbreak of the Pacific War, he and a group of renowned doctors from Peking Union Medical College Hospital came to Tianjin to establish Tianhe Hospital. In 1950, during the War to Resist U.S. Aggression and Aid Korea, Fang Xianzhi was among the first to travel to the Korean front lines to treat wounded soldiers. In 1953, the Ministry of Health entrusted him with establishing an orthopedic physician training program in Tianjin. By the time of his passing, he had trained 15 cohorts, each with 40 physicians. Today, his students are spread across hospitals throughout China, forming the backbone of the country's orthopedic expertise.

金显宅
Jin Xianzhai

肿瘤外科专家金显宅旧居（睦南道 69 号）
Former Residence of Surgical Oncologist Jin Xianzhai (No.69 Munan Road)

金显宅（1904—1990），肿瘤外科专家，出生于朝鲜汉城（今韩国首尔），早年毕业于北京协和医学院，获得美国医学博士学位。中华人民共和国成立以后，受国家委托建立了中国肿瘤医学，是中国在此专业上的开山鼻祖。曾任天津市人民医院院长，创办天津市肿瘤医院。

Jin Xianzhai (1904-1990) was a renowned surgical oncologist. Born in Seoul, Korea, he graduated from Peking Union Medical College and later earned a Doctor of Medicine degree in the United States. After the founding of the People's Republic of China, he was entrusted by the government to establish the field of medical oncology in China, making him a pioneer in the discipline. He served as the president of Tianjin People's Hospital and founded the Tianjin Medical University Cancer Institute & Hospital.

朱宪彝
Zhu Xianyi

朱宪彝故居（成都道 100 号）
Former Residence of Zhu Xianyi (No.100 Chengdu Road)

朱宪彝（1903—1984），天津人，我国临床内分泌学的创始人和奠基人之一，也是杰出的医学教育家，天津医学院（现天津医科大学）的创建人。中华人民共和国成立后，历任天津医学院院长，天津市内分泌研究所所长，河北医学科学院院长，中华医学会常务理事，中华内科学会主任委员，中华内分泌学会主任委员，卫生部科学技术委员会委员等职。

Zhu Xianyi (1903-1984), born in Tianjin, was one of the founding pioneers of clinical endocrinology in China and a distinguished medical educator. He was also the founder of Tianjin Medical College (now Tianjin Medical University). After the establishment of the People's Republic of China, he held several key positions, including President of Tianjin Medical College, Director of Tianjin Endocrine Research Institute, President of Hebei Academy of Medical Sciences, Executive Director of the Chinese Medical Association, Chairman of the Chinese Internal Medicine Society, Chairman of the Chinese Endocrine Society, and a member of the Science and Technology Committee of the Ministry of Health.

赵以成
Zhao Yicheng

中国神经外科之父赵以成旧居（常德道 69 号）
Former Residence of Zhao Yicheng, the father of
Chinese Neurosurgery (No.69 Changde Road)

　　赵以成（1908—1974），中国神经外科之父。1953 年，他总结制定了干羊膜的制作过程及防止脑术后黏连的临床应用，为中国的脑神经外科作出了巨大贡献，当时中国只有两名神经外科专家，赵以成是其中一人。

　　Zhao Yicheng (1908-1974) is regarded as the father of neurosurgery in China. In 1953, he developed the method for preparing dry amniotic membrane and its clinical application in preventing postoperative adhesions, making a significant contribution to the field of neurosurgery in China. At that time, Zhao Yicheng was one of only two neurosurgery specialists in the country.

范权
Fan Quan

范权旧居（常德道 24 号）
Former Residence of Fan Quan (No.24
Changde Road)

　　范权（1907—1989），儿科专家，毕生致力于儿科事业，在儿科医疗、科研、教学工作中，特别是在水盐代谢及液体疗法研究中作出积极贡献，创范氏输液法。在儿科人才培养、医院营养方面也积累了丰富经验，是中国儿科事业的奠基人之一。他亦是天津市儿童医院首任院长。

　　Fan Quan (1907-1989) was a pediatric expert who dedicated his entire life to the field. He made significant contributions to pediatric medical treatment, research, and education, particularly in the study of water and salt metabolism and fluid therapy. He also developed the Fan's intravenous infusion method. Additionally, he accumulated extensive experience in pediatric talent cultivation and hospital nutrition, becoming one of the pioneers of pediatric medicine in China. He served as the first director of Tianjin Children's Hospital.

施锡恩
Shi Xi'en

施锡恩旧居（睦南道 75 号）
Former Residence of Shi Xi'en (No.75 Munan Road)

　　施锡恩（1904—1990），著名泌尿外科专家、医学教育家，中国泌尿外科创始人之一。1941 年太平洋战争爆发后，施锡恩与北京协和医院的众多名医一同来到天津，他先是落脚在恩光医院，后建立了天和医院，1956 年天和医院更名为"天津市第一中心医院"，施锡恩被评定为一级教授。

　　Shi Xi'en (1904-1990) was a renowned urologist and medical educator, and one of the founding figures of urology in China. After the outbreak of the Pacific War in 1941, he came to Tianjin along with many prominent doctors from Peking Union Medical College Hospital. He initially worked at Sunnyside Hospital before founding Tianhe Hospital. In 1956, Tianhe Hospital was renamed "Tianjin First Central Hospital," and Shi Xi'en was honored with the title of first-class professor.

林崧
Lin Song

妇产科专家林崧旧居（睦南道 67 号）
Former Residence of Lin Song, an expert in gynaecology and
obstetrics (No.67 Munan Road)

　　林崧（1905—1999），著名妇产科医生。中华人民共和国成立以后，林崧在新组建的天津第一中心医院任妇产科主任，还受聘于水阁医院，指导临床医疗，在他的带领下，天津的妇产科医学得到了空前的发展，培养了大批妇产科医生。

　　Lin Song (1905-1999) was a renowned obstetrician and gynecologist. After the establishment of the People's Republic of China, Lin Song served as the director of obstetrics and gynecology at the newly established Tianjin First Central Hospital. He was also appointed by Shuigao Hospital to guide clinical practices. Under his leadership, obstetrics and gynecology in Tianjin experienced unprecedented development, and he trained a large number of obstetricians and gynecologists.

"直把他乡作故乡"的外国侨民

在近代，有许多外国侨民生活在天津的各国租界，他们的到来促进了天津贸易的繁荣和租界的发展。需要说明的是，侨民是指那些近代到中国居住并保留本国国籍或无国籍的外国人，不包括列强在华的驻军。他们中的绝大多数一开始只是普通工薪阶层，为了一份不错的薪水，不远万里来到中国工作和生活。后来，他们有的发财离开了，有的留下了，把这里当作自己的家乡，精心维护，繁衍生息。他们也是这个城市的重要组成部分，在这里留下了他们深深的足迹。

"在开始的头一两年，贸易量颇大，商人大发其财，例如某商人从 1861 年起，以一年 5000 元的速度积聚了大笔财产，刚刚带着这笔财产退隐了。"[①] 这种事例很容易被到处传扬，吸引越来越多的人来刚刚对外开放的天津寻找发财致富的机会。"几乎每个来中国的人都认为在这里可以快速致富"[②]，因此租界中总是不缺少做着发财梦来中国淘金的外国侨民。

天津开埠时，只有不多的外国商人和两三个基督教（新教）传教士住在天津老城的内外。1861 年，天津总计有 28 位侨民。他们当中包括：第一个到天津传教的美籍新教传教士柏亨利（Rev. Henry Blodget）以及其他 5 位传教士和他们的夫人，英国驻津副领事，第一任津海关税务司，还有其他在津开办洋行或洋行的雇员们。[③]1866年，据英国领事统计，包括商人、传教士及外交官在内，共有 112 人，其中英国 58 人、美国 14 人、德国 13 人、俄国 13 人、法国 10 人、意大利 2 人、瑞士 1 人、丹麦 1 人。1879 年天津口岸的侨民人口增加至 262 人，其中有成年男性 123 人、女性 58 人、儿童 81 人。1890 年，侨民人口大幅增长，有 612 人在各领事馆登记。1898 年日本在津划

---

① （英）雷穆森著，许逸凡等译，《天津租界史（插图本）》，天津人民出版社，2009 年，第 41 页。

② 1879 年 12 月 23 日汉纳根致其父母的信函。（德）康斯坦丁·冯·汉纳根，《1879—1886 发自中国的书信》，布劳出版社，1998 年，第 38—40 页。

③ （英）雷穆森著，许逸凡等译，《天津租界史（插图本）》，天津人民出版社，2009 年，第 36—37 页。

including the establishment of hospitals and the training of doctors, was an important part of the Westernization Movement. Western medicine had been introduced to China before 1840, but its influence was limited. In Tianjin, Western medicine gained recognition from Li Hongzhang, the Viceroy of Zhili Province. In 1881, the Beiyang Medical Bureau and the Beiyang Naval Medical School were established in Tianjin by the government. In 1902, Yuan Shikai established the Beiyang Military Medical School, and in 1912, the Beiyang government promulgated regulations for medical schools. The development of modern medical industry, the recognition, and acceptance of Western medicine by the Chinese people gradually made the profession of doctors become an emerging urban elite class. Especially on December 28, 1941, when the Pacific War broke out and the Japanese army took over the Peking Union Medical College (PUMC) and its affiliated hospitals, many physicians who had been working at PUMC left out of patriotism. Many of them came to Tianjin to continue their medical practice. The arrival of these doctors significantly improved the medical standards in Tianjin.

Among the upper echelons of the employee class, doctors stand at the top. Independent practitioners earned around 40 yuan per month, while traditional Chinese medicine practitioners who practiced in pharmacies earned approximately over 20 yuan. Renowned doctors, such as those employed as permanent doctors in factories or as family physicians for wealthy merchants, could earn an annual income of over 300 yuan, and they could also work for multiple establishments, so it was not uncommon for their annual income to exceed a thousand yuan. Many doctors were invited to make house calls, and sometimes they were even compensated with gold bars. With their substantial income, doctors could afford to rent residences in Tianjin's most exclusive and well-appointed residential areas—the former British Concession on the Five Avenues. Some even purchased properties in this area. Living in close proximity to each other, they formed a brilliant constellation of distinguished physicians. According to incomplete statistics, there are as many as 40 former residences of renowned Chinese and Western doctors on the Five Great Avenues.

Foreign Expatriates Who "Regard a Foreign Land as Their Homeland"

In modern times, many foreign expatriates lived in the various foreign concessions in Tianjin, and their arrival promoted the prosperity of Tianjin's trade and the development of the concessions. It should be noted that expatriates refer to those foreigners who resided in China in modern times

侨民在俱乐部庆祝节日。约摄于 20 世纪二三十年代
Foreign expatriates celebrating festival in club. Taken around
1920s and 1930s

天津的外国女侨民。摄于 1911 年
Foreign female expatriates in Tianjin. Taken in 1911

图片来源：德国"东亚之友"协会
Source: StuDeo

定租界以后，日本在津侨民人数飞速增长，1901 即增至 1210 人。[1] 1906 年，根据海关统计，居住在天津的外国人口达到 6341 人。[2] 民国时期，20 世纪 20 年代天津有外国人 1 万人左右，1937 年外籍人口增长到 26437 人。日本全面侵华后，日籍人口激增。二战结束前，天津的外国人口达到 10 万多人。随着战后对日本侨民的遣送，天津市外侨人口下降到 4624 人。到中华人民共和国成立，天津市外侨总计 3550 人，涉及 35 个国家和无国籍者。[3] 从外国侨民的国籍和数量来看，近代天津确实可以称得上是一个国际化程度很高的大都市。

从职业分布来看，近代来华的侨民中，以商人为最多，其次是外交官和医生、建筑师等专业技术人员以及传教士，还有就是手工业者、工人、小贩等较低职业从业者。男性中大多数人受雇于跨国公司在华机构或本国及中国政府或军队，而女性来华主要是因为结

while retaining their nationality or statelessness, excluding the troops stationed in China by the colonial powers. The vast majority of them were initially just ordinary wage earners who came to China from afar to work and live for a decent salary. Later, some of them made fortunes and left, while others stayed behind, treating this place as their hometown, carefully maintaining it and multiplying. They are also an important part of this city, leaving behind their deep footprints here.

"In the first year or two, the volume of trade was quite large, and merchants made a fortune. For example, a certain merchant, starting from 1861, accumulated a large sum of wealth at a rate of 5000 yuan per year and just retired with this fortune."[1] Such examples were easily spread everywhere, attracting more and more people to Tianjin, which had just opened up to the outside world, in search of opportunities to get rich. "Almost everyone who comes to China believes that they can get rich quickly here,"[2] so there was never a shortage of foreign expatriates in the concessions dreaming of striking it rich in China.

① 吴弘明编译，《津海关贸易年报（1865~1946）》，天津社会科学院出版社，2006 年，第 24、110、162、209 页。

② 天津市地方史志编修委员会总编辑室编，《二十世纪初的天津概况》，内部发行，1986 年，第 18 页。

③ 李竞能主编，《天津人口史》，南开大学出版社，1990 年，附录三，第 307—314 页。

① O. D. Rasmussen. *Tientsin: An Illustrated Outline History*, translated by Xu Yifan, et al. Tianjin People's Publishing House, 2008, p.41.

② Letter from von Hanneken to his parents on December 23, 1879. *Constantin von Hanneken: Briefe aus China: 1879-1886; als deutscher Offizier im Reich der Mitte*, Böhlau Verlag GmbH & Cie, 1998, pp.38-40.

李鸿章
Li Hongzhang

德璀琳
Gustav Detring

婚。总的来说，近代来华侨民早期以商人为主，后期随着租界的发展，各种专业技术人才陆续出现并日益增多。这体现了帝国主义对中国政治经济侵略程度的日益加深。

外国侨民通过其在华活动参与和影响了中国的现代化进程，刺激和促进了中国社会在许多方面的变革，这使他们成为近代中西文化交流的桥梁与纽带。例如，长期担任津海关税务司（即海关关长）的德国人德璀琳（Gustav Detring），他不仅在中国海关任职近 40 年，而且是晚清最有权势的大臣之一——李鸿章的私人顾问，因此德璀琳是在天津甚至在中国近代史上都有重要影响的外国人。

在《烟台条约》的谈判过程中，德璀琳得到参与谈判的李鸿章的青睐，成为深受其信任和倚仗的私人顾问。自 1876 年开始，他几乎参与了李鸿章的各项洋务活动，涉及经济、政治、军事、外交、文化等各个方面。特别是，他积极参与了李鸿章创建北洋水师和修筑大沽船坞、炮台等军事活动，还以李鸿章的私人密使的身份参与中英鸦片贸易谈判、中法和谈和中日和谈等秘密外交活动。德璀琳被认为是一个能对李鸿章产生重要影响的洋顾问。

近代天津的发展首要的是来自贸易，而海关在这方面发挥了很大的作用。1861 年天津开埠不久，赫德创办了津海关。1877 年 9 月德璀琳开始任职津海关税务司。从此，他把家安在天津，也把根扎在了这里。德璀琳任职津海关税务司 22 年，由于李鸿章的要求，他没有像海关的其他税务司那样在海关的各个港口循环任职，成为赫德手下唯一不能随意调动的

At the time when Tianjin opened as a treaty port, there were only a few foreign merchants and two or three Protestant missionaries living inside and outside the old city of Tianjin. In 1861, there were a total of 28 expatriates in Tianjin. Among them were the first American Protestant missionary to arrive in Tianjin, Rev. Henry Blodget, along with five other missionaries and their wives, the British vice-consul in Tianjin, the first commissioner of the Tianjin Customs, and other employees of foreign firms or trading houses in Tianjin.[①] In 1866, according to British consular statistics, including merchants, missionaries, and diplomats, there were a total of 112 people, including 58 British, 14 Americans, 13 Germans, 13 Russians, 10 French, 2 Italians, 1 Swiss, and 1 Dane. By 1879, the expatriate population in Tianjin's port had increased to 262 people, including 123 adult males, 58 females, and 81 children. In 1890, the expatriate population saw a significant increase, with 612 people registered at various consulates. After Japan established its concession in Tianjin in 1898, the number of Japanese expatriates in Tianjin rapidly increased to 1,210 by 1901.[②] In 1906, according to customs statistics, the foreign population residing in Tianjin reached 6,341.[③] During the Republic of China era, in the 1920s, there were around 10,000 foreigners in Tianjin, and by 1937, the number of foreign nationals had increased to 26,437. After Japan's comprehensive invasion of China, the Japanese population surged. Before the end of the Second World War, the foreign population in Tianjin exceeded 100,000. With the repatriation of Japanese expatriates after the war, the number of foreign expatriates in Tianjin dropped to 4,624. By the establishment of the People's Republic of China, Tianjin's expatriate population totaled 3,550, representing 35 countries and stateless individuals.[④] Judging from the nationality and quantity of foreign expatriates, modern Tianjin can indeed be considered a highly internationalized metropolis.

In terms of occupational distribution, among the modern expatriates who came to China, merchants were the most numerous, followed by diplomats, doctors, architects, and other professional technical personnel, as well as missionaries. There were also artisans, workers, peddlers, and other lower-level occupational practitioners. Most men were employed by multinational

① O. D. Rasmussen. *Tientsin: An Illustrated Outline History*, translated by Xu Yifan, et al. Tianjin People's Publishing House, 2008, pp. 36-37.

② *Tianjin Customs Annual Report of Trade (1865~1946)*, translated and edited by Wu Hong-ming. Tianjin Academy of Social Sciences Press, 2006, p.24,110,162,209.

③ Editorial Office of the Tianjin Chorography and History Compilation Committee (ed.). *Overview of Tianjin in the Early 20th Century*. Published internally in 1986, p.18.

④ Li Jingneng (ed.). *Population History of Tianjin*. Nankai University Press, 1990, pp.307-314.

人。在德璀琳的海关任内，不仅天津的贸易进出口量大幅增长，而且以保护商人利益、促进贸易发展为目的的天津洋商总会（Tientsin Chamber of Commerce）也于1887年成立。直到第一次世界大战前，它是代表天津外国商人利益的唯一团体。海河是天津贸易的生命线，德璀琳利用自身地位，敦促直隶总督和天津洋商总会制定措施挽救海河航运，在1901年成立并长期担任海河工程局的委员，主持裁弯取直、炸除全部沉船以清理河道、建造码头等工程，确保了天津北方第一大港口地位。

由于长期担任津海关税务司，并且与总督李鸿章大人有"深厚而持久的友谊"，德璀琳成为天津租界的侨民领袖，对天津租界的发展，进而对近代天津的城市化进程发挥了极其重要的作用。在租界的外国人圈内，他被称作"古斯塔夫大王"。在他的建议和影响下，天津英租界得以几次扩张。他还被多次选举为英租界工部局董事长。在市政建设方面，他整治海河、清淤疏浚，排干海河两岸沼泽、填埋地基；修建了天津第一条碎石子街道，建造了中国第一座市政大厦并修建了维多利亚花园，使英租界成为天津各国租界中最大和建设最好的一个。在文化教育方面，他向李鸿章建议开办一所西式大学，并从海关拨款创建博文书院（未实际开办）；还与他人一起创办了天津第一家英文报纸《中国时报》、中文报纸《时报》，并开办了天津第一家印刷厂天津印刷公司。在娱乐方面，他创建了天津赛马会，修筑了世界一流的跑马场。所以说德璀琳对近代天津城市发展所起的作用不容小觑。

来华侨民中除了德璀琳这样的大人物，也有许多只是为了给家人创造更好生活而不远万里来到天津的普通人。1905年比商天津电车电灯公司为在天津修建和运营有轨电车线路与发电厂，招募了许多比利时工程师和技术人员。年仅27岁的弗朗索瓦·内恩斯由于技术和组织能力出色而被聘用，被派往天津担任维修车间和仓库经理，为期三年。任期里，他指导中国工人，一起建造厂房、安装发电机和其他设备、组装车辆，同时还要监管诸如安排宿舍、设置储藏柜等各种行政工作。在中外员工的共同努力下，仅用了两年时间，第一条有轨电车线路就正式通车。到1908年内恩斯结束任期回国时，

companies in China, their own countries, or the Chinese government or military, while women mainly came to China for marriage. Overall, in the early stages of modern expatriates coming to China, merchants predominated. Later, with the development of concessions, various professional and technical talents gradually emerged and increased. This reflects the increasing depth of imperialism's penetration into China's political and economic spheres.

Foreign expatriates participated in and influenced China's modernization process through their activities in China, stimulating and promoting changes in many aspects of Chinese society. This made them the bridge and link in the cultural exchange between China and the West in modern times. For example, Gustav Detring, a German who served as the Commissioner of Tianjin Customs for a long time, not only worked in the Chinese Customs for nearly 40 years, but also served as a personal advisor to Li Hongzhang, one of the most influential ministers in the late Qing Dynasty. Therefore, Detring was a foreigner of significant influence in Tianjin and even in modern Chinese history.

During the negotiations of the *Treaty of Yantai* (Chefoo), Gustav Detring gained the favor of Li Hongzhang, who was involved in the negotiations, and became his trusted and relied-upon personal advisor. Starting from 1876, he was involved in almost all of Li Hongzhang's Westernization activities, covering various aspects including economy, politics, military, diplomacy, and culture. In particular, he actively participated in Li Hongzhang's initiatives such as the establishment of the Beiyang Fleet, the construction of the Taku shipyard, forts, and other military activities. He also engaged in secret diplomatic activities such as the negotiations on the opium trade with Britain, the negotiations with France, and the negotiations with Japan, acting as Li Hongzhang's personal envoy. Detring was considered as a Western advisor who could exert significant influence on Li Hongzhang.

The primary driver of modern Tianjin's development was trade, and the customs played a significant role in this aspect. Shortly after the opening of Tianjin in 1861, Robert Hart established the Tianjin Customs. In September 1877, Gustav Detring began his tenure as the Commissioner of Tianjin Customs. From then on, he made Tianjin his home and rooted himself here. Detring served as the Commissioner of Tianjin Customs for 22 years. At the request of Li Hongzhang, he did not rotate like other customs commissioners among the various ports of the customs, making him the only person under Hart who could not be easily transferred. During Detring's tenure at the customs, not only did Tianjin's trade volume increase significantly, but also the Foreign Merchants Association, with the aim of protecting the interests of merchants and promoting trade development, came into being in 1887. Until the eve of the First World War, it was the only organization representing

李鸿章亲笔题写的匾额
The plaque inscribed by Li Hongzhang

津海新关办公楼
Tianjin Customs office building

有轨电车已经运营得如火如荼。

弗朗索瓦·内恩斯是一个工作非常认真、同时又非常眷恋家庭的人。他接受这样一份极具冒险性和挑战性的工作，大概出于两个方面的原因，且后者占比最重：一是受到父亲青年时期海外探险经历的影响，渴望到海外旅行生活增长见闻；二是这份工作的薪资待遇非常优厚，可以为家庭提供很好的生活条件。根据他与电车公司的合同规定，他在比利时的工资是每月 200 法郎，[①] 而自他抵达天津的那一天起，他的工资就变为 600 法郎（216 银元），并在大约一年后涨到 700 法郎（252 银元），即年薪 8400 法郎。此外，他每月还

---

① 19 世纪末 20 世纪初各国货币币值大约是：1 英镑 =5 美元 =9 银元 =25 法郎 =10 卢布 =7 日元。

the interests of foreign merchants in Tianjin. The Hai River was the lifeline of Tianjin's trade, and Detring, leveraging his position, urged the Viceroy of Zhili and the Foreign Merchants Association to take measures to salvage the Hai River shipping. In 1901, he established and served as a member of the Hai-Ho Conservancy Commission for a long time, overseeing projects such as straightening bends, removing sunken ships to clear the river channel, and building docks, ensuring Tianjin's position as the largest northern port.

Due to his long tenure as the Commissioner of Tianjin Customs and his "deep and lasting friendship" with Governor Li Hongzhang, Gustav Detring became a leader among the foreign residents in the Tianjin Concessions, playing an extremely important role in the development of the Tianjin Concessions and consequently in the urbanization process of modern Tianjin. Within the foreign community of the concessions, he was known as "The Great Gustav." Under his advice and influence, the Tianjin British Concession expanded several times. He was also elected multiple times as the Chairman of the British Municipal Council. In terms of urban development, he undertook projects such as the cleansing and dredging of the Hai River, draining the marshes along the banks of the river, and filling landfills; he constructed Tianjin's first macadamized street, built China's first municipal building, and established Victoria Park, making the British Concession the largest and best-built among all the concessions in Tianjin. In the realm of culture and education, he suggested to Li Hongzhang the establishment of a Western-style university and allocated funds from the customs to create the Bowen College (which was not realized); he also co-founded Tianjin's first English newspaper, *The China Times*, and its Chinese counterpart, the *The Eastern Times*, and established Tianjin's first printing press, the Tientsin Printing Company. In terms of entertainment, he founded the Tientsin Race Club and constructed a world-class racecourse. Therefore, Detring's role in the urban development of modern Tianjin cannot be underestimated.

Among the overseas residents who came to Tianjin, besides prominent figures like Gustav Detring, there were also many ordinary people who traveled a long way to Tianjin just to create a better life for their families. In 1905, the Belgian company, Compagnie de Tramways et d'Eclairage de Tientsin (CTET), was contracted to build and operate tramway lines and power plants in Tianjin. They recruited many Belgian engineers and technicians. François Nuyens, a talented young man of 27, was hired for his excellent technical and organizational skills. He was sent to Tianjin to serve as the manager of the maintenance workshop and warehouse for a three-year term. During his tenure, he supervised Chinese workers in constructing factory buildings, installing generators and other equipment, assembling

可得到 40 鹰洋（银元）的住宿补贴，直至公司为他提供住处。公司还为他报销本人及其家属的旅费，共计 5600 法郎。① 这个待遇当时无论在比利时还是中国都是很有吸引力的。同一时期，英国工人的年薪在 40—80 英镑，② 比利时工人的工资水平可以参照这个数字，为 700—2000 法郎。不过，初到天津的内恩斯不得不为此忍受孤独，当他收到妻子和孩子的照片时，"见到孩子天真可爱的样子，眼泪不禁夺眶而出，他全然不知与父亲相聚多么遥远，但这一切都是为了保证他未来能过上幸福生活。"③

在那个时代，初到中国的绝大多数外国人都难以避免带着殖民者的观点和优越感，内恩斯也不例外。但在工程实施过程中，中国工人以他们的勤劳质朴最终纠正了外来者的傲慢与偏见，双方因共同完成一个个"不可能的任务"而结下深厚情谊。合同到期时内恩斯一家即将离开天津，内恩斯最后一次巡视库房，然后去车间与中国工人告别。他在日记中记下了工人和电车司机们为他送别的场景：

1908年6月14日

早上 6 点 15 分左右，库房经理傅金榜前来接我。他请我去大门口，迎接即将来送礼物的职员。我走到大门口时，听到远处传来了中国音乐的声音，一群人向我们走来。一看到我，就有人点燃了一连串的鞭炮。噪声太大，什么都听不见了。这群人走到跟前，先是几个小男孩拿着大铜盘或铜钹，不停地敲着。接下来是一些举着旗子与罗盖伞的人，其后跟着吹喇叭的乐手，和我拜访袁世凯时见到的一模一样。紧随其后，有人举着两面非常好看的黄色丝旗，上面绣着黑丝绒汉字，其间还有一把官员专用的丝质罗伞。这些都是电车售票员们赠送给我的礼物，他们走在职员队伍的前列。所有人都穿着 1 号制服。正、副主管穿着他

---

① （比）约翰·麦特勒等著，刘悦等译，《比利时—中国：昔日之路（1870—1930）》，社会科学文献出版社，2021 年，第 148 页。

② （英）罗德里克·弗劳德，《1700 年以来英国经济史：劳动市场演变》，剑桥大学出版社，1994 年，第 119 页。

③ （比）约翰·麦特勒等著，刘悦等译，《比利时—中国：昔日之路（1870—1930）》，社会科学文献出版社，2021 年，第 193 页。

vehicles, and overseeing administrative tasks such as arranging dormitories and setting up storage cabinets. With the joint efforts of Chinese and foreign employees, the first tramway line was officially inaugurated in just two years. By the time Nuyens completed his term and returned home in 1908, the tramway system was operating vigorously.

François Nuyens was a person who worked very diligently and was deeply attached to his family. He accepted such a highly adventurous and challenging job probably for two main reasons, with the latter being predominant: first, he was influenced by his father's overseas exploration experiences in youth and desired to travel abroad to broaden his horizons; second, the salary and benefits of this job were very generous, which could provide a good living condition for his family. According to his contract with the tramway company, his monthly salary in Belgium was 200 francs,① but from the day he arrived in Tianjin, his salary increased to 600 francs (equivalent to 216 silver dollars), and about a year later, it rose to 700 francs (252 silver dollars), making his annual salary 8,400 francs. Additionally, he received a monthly accommodation allowance of 40 silver dollars until the company provided him with accommodation. The company also reimbursed his travel expenses and those of his family, totaling 5,600 francs.② This compensation package was very attractive both in Belgium and China at that time. During the same period, the annual salary of British workers was around £40-£80,③ and the wage level of Belgian workers could be inferred from this figure, approximately 700-2,000 francs. However, upon arriving in Tianjin, Nuyens had to endure loneliness. When he received photos of his wife and children, "When I received this letter, tears came to my eyes, seeing my sweet innocent child, who had no idea how far away his father was from him, and all to ensure his future happiness."④

In that era, the vast majority of foreigners who arrived in China for the first time found it difficult to avoid carrying colonialist perspectives and a sense of superiority, and Nuyens was no exception. However, during the implementation of the project, Chinese workers, with their diligence and

---

① At the end of the 19th century and the beginning of the 20th century, the approximate value of various currencies was as follows: 1 British pound = 5 US dollars = 9 silver dollars = 25 French francs = 10 rubles = 7 Japanese yen.

② Johan J. Mattelaer, et al. *A Belgian Passage to China (1870-1930)*, translated by Liu Yue, et al. Social Sciences Academic Press (China), 2021, p.148.

③ Roderick Floud: *Labour Market Evolution, The Economic History of Britain Since 1700*. Cambridge University Press,1994, p.119.

④ Johan J. Mattelaer, et al. *A Belgian Passage to China (1870-1930)*, translated by Liu Yue, et al. Social Sciences Academic Press (China), 2021, p.193.

们最好的西装、戴着最漂亮的配饰,他们走在队伍最前面,向我敬礼。从我身边经过时,他们一边向右朝我的方向转头,一边继续直挺挺地向前迈步。他们的态度与着装堪比阅兵一般整齐。士兵们也不可能比他们表现得更好。售票员后面跟着一顶装潢精美的镀金轿子,至少有 8 人抬着。上面摆放着一块硕大的匾,盖着红绸,绣着漂亮的黑丝绒汉字。后面还有两名苦力扛着两块小匾,也都盖着红绸,绣着黑字。队伍最后跟着白班与夜班的所有工人,主管走在前面。他们脸上都露着喜悦。……

以下是匾、罗伞和旗帜上所写内容:

大匾:同甘共苦
    他在华工作期间,对工人关怀备至。

罗伞:永谋慈悲
    他始终对职员呵护有加,就像细心浇灌花朵一般。

旗帜:第一面旗:情义如山
        他是职员们如山般的坚强后盾。

    第二面旗:同沾雨露
        他如雨露般滋润万物。

1908年7月18日

现在 10 点半了,我也该离开了。有轨电车已经就位,所有检票员、办公室职员、工人,以及中央办公室和库房的欧洲人在院子里站成了几排。除了车间工人,其他人都陪着我们去火车站。首席驾驶员亲自驾驶,他不想将电车交给别人掌管。为了这个场合,他特意穿着最干净的制服。工人们都来和我握手。……

电车开动时,工人们挥舞着他们的草帽或制服帽以示告别。电车开出了一段距离后,许多人仍在挥舞致意。有人在入口处燃放鞭炮,并且轨道上每隔 200 或 300 米就有一个苦力拿着一根绑着鞭炮的长棍。电车开近时,他就会点燃鞭炮,然后追着我们跑。这也是我们最后一次路过天津的中国老城。①

---

① (比)约翰·麦特勒等著,刘悦等译,《比利时—中国:昔日之路(1870—1930)》,社会科学文献出版社,2021 年,第 220—222、172 页。

simplicity, ultimately corrected the arrogance and prejudice of the outsiders, and both sides forged a deep friendship through the completion of one "impossible task" after another. As the contract expired and the Nuyens family was about to leave Tianjin, Nuyens made a final tour of the warehouse and then went to the workshop to bid farewell to the Chinese workers. He recorded in his diary the scenes of the workers and tram drivers bidding him farewell:

June 14, 1908

    At around 6:15 a.m., François Fou King Pang, my warehouse manager, came to pick me up. He invited me to go to the large entrance gate, in order to welcome the staff who were coming to present the gifts. When I arrived at the gate, I heard Chinese music in the distance, as the procession approached. Strings of firecrackers were lit when I appeared. The noise was so intense that you could not hear anything else. Then the procession arrived. First, there were little boys with large copper discs or cymbals, which they constantly kept banging. Next, came the carriers of flags and parasols, followed by musicians with their trumpets, the same as I had seen when we visited Yuan Che-Kaï. They were followed by the carriers of two very nice yellow silk flags with black velvet letters and a red mandarin silk umbrella. These were the gifts of the tram conductors, who headed the procession of my staff. All had put on their n° 1-uniforms. The chief and vice-chief, wearing their best suits and decorations, were marching ahead of them and greeted me with a military salute. As they passed me, the men turned their heads to the right in my direction, while continuing to march stiffly. Their attitude and dress were as orderly as those of a military parade. Soldiers could not have done it any better. After the conductors came a nice gold-plated and decorated sedan chair, carried by at least eight men. On it was positioned a large tablet, covered in red silk and with beautiful embroidery in black velvet Chinese letters. Behind this, there were two coolies carrying two small tablets, also covered in red silk with black letters. They were followed by all the workers of both the day and the night shifts, preceded by their superiors. One could read joy on their faces.

Here is the translation of what was written on the tablets, umbrella and flags:
Large tablet: T'onchanGwie Kon:
He has been good for the workmen, when carrying out his international task
Umbrella: Young MouTseiP'é:
He always took good care of them, like he would have watered his plants.
Flags:
1st flag: Tson Y Jou San:
He gave them support as strong as a mountain.
2nd flag: T'onTchaan Yu Lou:
All have been nourished by his rain and his dew.

内恩斯（居中揽儿童而坐者）告别照片。图片来源：比利时根特大学档案馆
Photo of François Nuyens (sitting in the middle with a child) before returning home.
Source: Archives of Ghent University, Belgium

在过去的研究中，一般称这些随帝国主义侵略而来华工作生活的外国人为"淘金者"或"冒险家"。然而，近代侨民来华的这个时代，既是带给中华民族耻辱的时代，也是近代中国由闭关自守、故步自封走向厉行自强、对外开放，并由传统农业社会向现代工业社会转变的时代。虽然他们来华的目的并不是帮助中国走向富国强民道路，但侨民通过其在华活动参与和影响了中国的现代化进程，刺激和促进了中国社会在许多方面的变革，这使他们成为近代中西文化交流的桥梁与纽带。

城市与城市病

资本主义快速发展的时代同时也是问题猛增的时代。这些问题包括贫困、犯罪、传统社会解体、环境危机、阶级矛盾冲突等。近代中国的工业化和城市化进程长期滞后，城市其实并未为那么多人口的到来做好充分的准备。不过，相比于经济凋敝、灾害频发、秩

July 18, 1908

It was now half past ten and time to leave. The tram car was already in place and all the inspectors, office staff and workers were lined up in the courtyard, as well as all the Europeans from the central office and the depot. With the exception of the workshop workers, they all accompanied us to the railway station. The first chief conductor was driving us there; he didn't want to leave anyone else in charge of the tram car. For the occasion, he was wearing his cleanest suit. The workmen were all shaking my hand.

When the tram car drove away, the workers waved with their hats or caps. Many kept waving even when the tram car was already some distance away. Fire crackers were lit at the entrance gate and every 200 or 300 meters along the track there was a coolie carrying fire crackers tied to a stick. As soon as the tram car approached, he lit the firecrackers and ran after us. And so it was that we crossed the Chinese quarter of the city for the final time. [1]

In previous studies, these foreigners who came to work and live in China as a result of imperialist aggression are generally referred to as "fortune seekers" or "adventurers." However, the era of modern immigrants coming to China was not only a period of shame for the Chinese nation but also an era in which China transitioned from isolation and self-seclusion to vigorous self-improvement and opening-up to the outside world, and from a traditional agrarian society to a modern industrial society. Although their purpose in coming to China was not to help China become prosperous and strong, immigrants contributed to and influenced China's modernization process through their activities in China, stimulating and promoting changes in many aspects of Chinese society. This made them bridges and links for the cultural exchange between the East and the West in modern times.

Cities and Urban Diseases

The era of rapid capitalist development is also an era of rapidly increasing problems. These problems include poverty, crime, the disintegration of traditional society, environmental crises, and conflicts of class contradictions. The industrialization and urbanization process in modern China lagged behind for a long time, and cities were actually not adequately prepared for the arrival of so many people. However, compared to the economic stagnation, frequent disasters, and disorder in the countryside, cities still

---

① Johan J. Mattelaer, et al. *A Belgian Passage to China (1870-1930)*, translated by Liu Yue, et al. Social Sciences Academic Press (China), 2021, pp.220-222, p.172.

序混乱的乡村，城市仍然是为许多人提供庇护所和谋生手段的地方。

贫民窟与卫生、犯罪问题

天津开埠后的早期，城市中有大量贫民窟。那些匆匆涌入的外乡人，亟须安身立脚的居所。因此，住房建设开展得很匆忙，几乎来不及进行规划和认真思考，就拆掉了原来的建筑物又忙着盖新的了，或者根本就把建筑建在一片坟地、烂泥潭和大大小小的水坑之间。贫民的居处十分简陋，多数是土房，即以土坯砌墙身，无立柱，把房檩的两端直接搭在土坯山墙上，檩上平铺柳条笆和芦席、秫秸席（天津称炕席），上面再抹上混有麦秸的黄泥。黄泥干后即可防雨水。但若遇到雨水就难免将那层外壳冲走了，所以每年夏天到来之前，人们都要在房顶上重新抹一层黄泥。土房中那种立有木棍之构架、再用秫秸篱笆做墙身内层、外面抹泥的，称之"篱笆灯"，是最简陋的建法。1917 年及 1939 年天津大水后，从四乡逃入的灾民很多，为了节省材料，他们匆匆用竹片撅成半圆形，两端埋入地面，上铺破旧席片，席片上再抹黄泥，形成低矮、狭小、如同动物的"窝"一样的居处，天津人称其为"窝铺"。不管怎样，新来的移民，男女老幼，都饥不择食地住进"新居"，权且住进去就是了。大规模的因陋就简、将就凑合的勉强之下，"临时代用建筑"层出不穷。天津当时著名的成片贫民窟，有环老城厢之外地区的万德庄、沧德庄，英德租界以南的谦德庄等。事实上，对于中国庞大的人口来说，城市住宅始终都是非常紧缺的，这些贫民窟直到改革开放之后重启城市化进程才得到根本改造。

恶劣的居住条件造成恶劣的卫生条件。贫民窟里的土房排列紧密，光线的摄入和空气的流通都很不充分，阴暗潮湿的环境很容易成为蝎子、臭虫、白蛉、跳蚤等各种毒虫的潜伏地，或者滋生传染性病毒细菌。[①] 贫民窟里没有上下水管道，也没有排水设施和供水系统。事实上，义和团运动之前，只有租界区有上下水。1900 年之后，

---

① 天津市地方史志编修委员会总编辑室编，《二十世纪初的天津概况》，内部发行，1986 年，第 329 页。

Slums and Issues of Sanitation and Crime

provided shelter and livelihoods for many people.

In the early days after the opening of Tianjin, there were large numbers of slums in the city. The influx of outsiders urgently needed a place to settle down. Therefore, housing construction proceeded hastily, almost without planning or careful consideration. The original buildings were torn down and new ones were hurriedly built, sometimes even constructed amidst graveyards, muddy swamps, and various sizes of water pits. The dwellings of the poor were extremely rudimentary, mostly made of earth, with walls built of adobe without pillars, and the ends of the rafters were directly placed on the adobe walls. Willow twigs, reed mats, and millet straw mats (called "kangxi" in Tianjin) were laid flat on the rafters, and then coated with yellow mud mixed with wheat straw. The yellow mud, once dried, could prevent rainwater. However, when it rained, the outer shell layer was inevitably washed away, so every summer before the rainy season arrived, people had to reapply a layer of yellow mud on the roof. Among these earth houses, the most rudimentary construction method was called "fence lamp", which had a framework of wooden poles, inner walls made of millet straw fences, and outer walls coated with mud. After the great floods in Tianjin in 1917 and 1939, many refugees fled into the city from the surrounding areas. In order to save materials, they hastily made semi-circular structures with bamboo strips buried into the ground at both ends, covered with old mat pieces, and then coated with yellow mud on top, forming low, narrow dwellings resembling animal "nests". These were called "nest beds" by the people of Tianjin. However, regardless of the conditions, newcomers, men, women, and children, all moved into these "new homes" as a temporary solution. Under the circumstances of large-scale makeshift construction due to scarcity and makeshift arrangements, "temporary emergency buildings" emerged in abundance. Famous slum areas in Tianjin at that time included Wandezhuang and Cangdezhuang outside the old city, and Qiandezhuang south of the British and German concessions. In fact, for China's large population, urban housing was always in extremely short supply, and these slums were fundamentally transformed only after the resumption of urbanization processes following the reform and opening up.

The poor living conditions result in poor sanitation conditions. The adobe houses in the slums are densely packed, with inadequate light intake

一位德国侨民汉纳根（Constantin von Hanneken）承接了天津老城厢地区的地下排水系统工程，自来水厂也建立起来，但这一切都是贫民窟没有的。天津地区的土壤污染严重，数百年来的垃圾、人畜排泄物无人处理，尸体随处掩埋（主要在天津老城的西方和北方，那里相对地势高些），从不火葬，导致地下水随之被污染。天津地下水位高，居民饮用水主要来自随处开掘的水井和海河水，水质极差，居民饮水前需先进行沉淀和过滤。好在中国人向来不喝生水，都是煮沸之后饮用，这就在一定程度上降低了由不洁水源导致染上肠道疾病的风险。

在天津的传染病当中，占大多数的仍是肠道疾病等，尤其是在夏季。致病原因主要是食用腐烂食品，即保存不当或由苍蝇传播导致细菌滋生的食品。人在食用腐烂食品后，就很容易患上霍乱、伤寒、副型伤寒、痢疾等疾病。尽管当时地方当局利用报纸、传单等对食品卫生安全进行了广泛宣传，但有害健康的食品却始终无法绝迹。当然，这并不是因为人们没有卫生观念，"每个人都是愿讲卫生的……作小生意的贫人"其实也知道腐坏食品的危害，但"为了本钱的关系"[1]，也只能置卫生于不顾。那些一锅煮的污秽不堪的杂畜肉，以及走街串巷叫卖的腐败劣质食物，"市民亦贪贱购买之"[2]。其余疾病中的皮肤病（包括湿疹、癣、疥、寄生性匐行疹等）、呼吸器官疾病（肺结核、支气管炎及咽喉疾病等）、沙眼和性病，也都主要是公共环境差所导致的个人卫生条件差而致病。[3]

1900 年八国联军占领天津成立临时政府之时，适逢医学史上的一个重要时期，即细菌病理学的霸权地位日渐稳固，美日科学家发现细菌是导致许多传染性疾病的根源，由此改变了疾病预防的理念和卫生管理的方式。临时政府用刺刀逼迫本地人接受"卫生"的新观念——平整乱葬坟地，将染病尸体集中焚烧，把垃圾运到城外，

and airflow, creating a dark and damp environment that easily becomes a breeding ground for various poisonous insects such as scorpions, bedbugs, sandflies, fleas, and the proliferation of infectious viruses and bacteria.[1] There are no sewage pipes, drainage facilities, or water supply systems in the slums. In fact, prior to the Boxer Rebellion, only the concession areas had sewage systems. After 1900, a German immigrant named Constantin von Hanneken undertook the underground drainage system project in the old city area of Tianjin, and a waterworks was also established, but none of this existed in the slums. Soil pollution was severe in the Tianjin area, with garbage and human and animal waste accumulating for centuries without proper disposal. Bodies were buried everywhere (mainly in the western and northern parts of the old city of Tianjin, where the terrain is relatively higher), without cremation, leading to groundwater contamination. The groundwater level in Tianjin is high, and residents mainly rely on water wells and the Hai River for drinking water, which is of extremely poor quality. Residents need to settle and filter the water before drinking. Fortunately, the Chinese people have never drunk untreated water, always boiling it before consumption, which to some extent reduces the risk of contracting intestinal diseases caused by contaminated water sources.

Among the infectious diseases in Tianjin, the majority are still intestinal diseases, especially in the summer. The main cause of illness is the consumption of rotten food, either improperly preserved or contaminated by bacteria spread by flies. After consuming rotten food, people are prone to diseases such as cholera, typhoid fever, paratyphoid fever, and dysentery. Although local authorities extensively promoted food hygiene and safety through newspapers, leaflets, and other means, harmful food could not be eradicated. Of course, this is not because people lack hygiene awareness. Even "every person who conducts small business and is poor" understands the dangers of spoiled food, but due to "financial considerations,"[2] they have to disregard hygiene. Those filthy mixed meats cooked in one pot, as well as the rotton and inferior quality food sold in the streets, were also purchased by the citizens due to their greed for cheap prices.[3] Other diseases such as

---

① 琴，《卫生与贫民》，载《天津午报》，1929 年 1 月 22 日。转引自朱慧颖，《天津公共卫生建设研究：1900~1937》，天津古籍出版社，2015 年，第 117 页。

② 李根古，《市民与市政》，载《益世报》，1928 年 1 月 1 日。转引自朱慧颖，《天津公共卫生建设研究：1900~1937》，天津古籍出版社，2015 年，第 117 页。

③ 天津市地方史志编修委员会总编辑室编，《二十世纪初的天津概况》，内部发行，1986 年，第 324—326 页。

① Editorial Office of the Tianjin Chorography and History Compilation Committee (ed.). *Overview of Tianjin in the Early 20th Century*. Published internally in 1986, p.329.

② Qin. Health and Poor People. *Tianjin Noon Newspaper*, January 22, 1929. Quoted in Zhu Huiying. *A Study of Public Health in Tianjin: 1900~1937*. Tianjin Ancient Books Publishing House, 2015, p.117.

③ Li Gengu. Citizen and Municipal Administration. *Social Welfare*, January 1, 1928. Quoted in Zhu Huiying. *A Study of Public Health in Tianjin: 1900~1937*. Tianjin Ancient Books Publishing House, 2015, p.117.

建造公共厕所，要求人们不得随地便溺等。袁世凯收回天津主权后，接受了临时政府的卫生政策，并成立了一个"天津卫生总局"对市民进行公共卫生教育，还设立北洋防疫处，对出入境人员进行防疫，有效维护了当时中国的防疫主权。

尽管如此，城市仍然是充满生机、令人向往的。随着港口贸易的增长，大量洋货涌入，这虽然冲击了传统的农业手工业，但却带来了充足的粮食供应。此外，还有一个因素也发挥了作用，就是生产肥皂的工厂增加，机械化生产降低了改善个人卫生条件的成本。20世纪初，天津有5家肥皂工厂，[1]民国时期肥皂厂增加到12家。[2]随着机械设备的改善，肥皂产量也从几百箱增加到几十万箱，并主要供应本地市场。第一次世界大战期间，天津商人开始投资面粉业，至1930年，本地已有面粉厂6家，加工华北和东北地区生产的麦子，年产量达到近20万吨。[3]以八口之家，每月200斤口粮计算，这些面粉厂的产量足以养活一个城市的人口，再加上进口面粉，天津及其周边地区的粮食供应基本都能保障。充足的粮食供应减少了大规模饥荒的危险，提高了人口抵抗疾病的能力，加上个人以及公共卫生条件的改善，这几项重要因素的共同作用，虽然对生活条件优越的中上层市民影响不大，但却使贫困人口的生存概率大大提高。

贫穷不仅是"卫生"的敌人，更是导致犯罪的直接原因。恩格斯在其著作《英国工人阶级状况》中指出："当无产者穷到完全不能满足最迫切的生活需要，穷到要饭和饿肚子的时候，蔑视一切社会秩序的倾向就愈来愈增长了"，而"蔑视社会秩序最明显最极端的表现就是犯罪"。[4]自给自足的自然经济在工业化大生产之下被打破，农村经济破产，被战争、灾荒等逼入城市的农民一无所长又穷

---

① 天津市地方史志编修委员会总编辑室编，《二十世纪初的天津概况》，内部发行，1986年，第264页。

② 天津市档案馆编，《近代以来天津城市化进程实录》，天津人民出版社，2005年，第223页。

③ 根据《1922年至1931年十年间天津工业发展状况》中面粉业统计数据计算。天津市档案馆编，《近代以来天津城市化进程实录》，天津人民出版社，2005年，第220页。

④ 《马克思恩格斯全集》（第2卷），人民出版社，1957年，第400、416页。

skin diseases (including eczema, ringworm, scabies, and parasitic creeping eruption), respiratory diseases (such as tuberculosis, bronchitis, and throat diseases), trachoma, and sexually transmitted diseases were also mainly caused by poor personal hygiene conditions due to poor public environmental conditions.[1]

At the time when the Eight-Nation Alliance occupied Tianjin and established a provisional government in 1900, it coincided with an important period in medical history, namely the increasing dominance of bacteriology. American and Japanese scientists discovered that bacteria were the root cause of many infectious diseases, thereby changing the concept of disease prevention and the methods of public health management. The provisional government used bayonets to force the local people to accept the new concept of "hygiene"—leveling disorderly graves, cremating infected corpses, transporting garbage outside the city, building public toilets, and prohibiting people from urinating anywhere. After Yuan Shikai regained sovereignty over Tianjin, he accepted the provisional government's health policies and established a "Tianjin Health Bureau" to provide public health education to citizens. He also established the Beiyang Quarantine Office to quarantine incoming and outgoing personnel, effectively safeguarding China's sovereignty over epidemic prevention at that time.

Nevertheless, the city remained vibrant and desirable. With the growth of port trade, a large quantity of foreign goods poured in. Although this impacted traditional agriculture and handicrafts, it brought about an abundant food supply. Additionally, another factor came into play: the increase in soap production factories, where mechanized production reduced the cost of improving personal hygiene. In the early 20th century, Tianjin had five soap factories,[2] which increased to twelve during the Republic of China period.[3] With improvements in machinery, soap production increased from a few hundred boxes to several hundred thousand boxes, primarily supplying the local market. During World War I, Tianjin merchants began investing in the flour industry. By 1930, there were six local flour mills processing wheat from North and Northeast China, with an annual output of nearly 200,000

---

① Editorial Office of the Tianjin Chorography and History Compilation Committee (ed.). *Overview of Tianjin in the Early 20th Century*. Published internally in 1986, pp.324-326.

② Editorial Office of the Tianjin Chorography and History Compilation Committee (ed.). *Overview of Tianjin in the Early 20th Century*. Published internally in 1986, p.264.

③ Tianjin Archives (ed.). *Factual Records of Tianjin's Urbanization since Modern Times*. Tianjin People's Publishing House, 2005, p.223.

途末路，"男盗女娼"几乎是他们的唯一出路。根据我国著名犯罪学家严景耀做过的犯罪调查，20世纪的二三十年代"贪污和偷窃罪大幅度增加，诈骗犯的增加也相当明显"。这种状况到南京国民政府时期达到了顶点。①

小偷和妓女是两项最古老的职业。由于女性在体力上的天生劣势，加上封建社会长期以来"男尊女卑"的毒害思想，在妓院卖身的妓女（不是暗娼）相比于小偷，是合法的。民国时期天津妓院最多时有650户，妓女3100余人。一、二等妓院开在租界，二、三、四等妓院主要集中在南市、侯家后和北开这些商业繁荣区，四、五等妓院由于条件简陋而被称作"窑子"，一般开在贫民窟。无论是几等妓院的娼妓，"生活所迫"都是女性为娼最主要的原因，妓女文化程度为"文盲"的占绝大多数，籍贯上本市与外埠基本各占一半。妓院一般都是单一老板经营，规模越大雇用的伙计和打手越多，看管妓女、负责安全。经营娼业虽然利润丰厚，但"皮肉生意"的名声并不好听，风险也大，三教九流的客人都有，所以妓院老板并没有什么政治势力，跟帮派团伙的关系其实并没有想象的那么密切。一、二等妓院的嫖客主要是商人与小贩，四、五等妓院的嫖客则主要是工人、车夫、船夫还有劳苦群众。娼妓业虽然是合法生意，妓女一般也能得到总收入的40%~60%，但是根本上，娼妓业仍然是建立在对底层妇女的剥削之上。因此，1950年之后，天津市政府即着手取缔娼妓业，对从业者进行改造。②

相比于娼妓业，赌博和走私贩毒的利润更高。尤其是后者，当然风险也更高，因此不是少数几个人就可以经营的，其背后均有帮会力量，属于有组织犯罪。当时整个华北、东北和西北范围的毒品走私枢纽是北京、天津，由军阀和帮会把持。清末民初，革命党为了加强革命力量，不仅与以漕帮为前身的青帮相勾结，而且直接参加了洪门，因此民国时期的青帮、洪门大都与军政商界紧密勾连。就连"民国四公子"之一的袁世凯次子袁克文，也曾加入青帮，成

---

① 严景耀，《中国的犯罪问题与社会变迁的关系》，北京大学出版社，1986年，第17页。

② 江沛、项宝生，《20世纪中叶天津娼业构成及其改造问题论述》。江沛、王先明主编，《近代华北区域社会史研究》，天津古籍出版社，2005年，第84—123页。

---

tons.① Considering a family of eight with a monthly ration of 200 jin (1 jin equals 500g) of grain, the output of these flour mills was sufficient to feed the population of a city. Coupled with imported flour, the food supply in Tianjin and its surrounding areas could be largely guaranteed. Adequate food supply reduced the risk of widespread famine, improved the population's resilience to diseases, and, combined with improvements in personal and public hygiene conditions, significantly increased the survival chances of the impoverished population, although it had little impact on the lifestyle of the affluent middle and upper classes.

Poverty is not only the enemy of "sanitation" but also the direct cause of crime. Engels pointed out in his work *The Condition of the Working Class in England*: "When the proletariat is so poor that it cannot satisfy its most urgent life needs, when it is reduced to begging and starving, the tendency to disregard all social order grows stronger and stronger," and "the most obvious and extreme manifestation of disregarding social order is crime."② The self-sufficient natural economy was shattered under industrial mass production, rural economies collapsed, and farmers driven into cities by war, famine, and other factors found themselves with no skills and no way out. "Male thieves and female prostitutes" were almost their only way out. According to a crime survey conducted by the famous Chinese criminologist Yan Jingyao, in the 1920s and 1930s, "embezzlement and theft crimes increased significantly, and there was also a considerable increase in fraudsters." This situation reached its peak during the period of the National Government in Nanjing.③

Thieves and prostitutes are two of the oldest professions. Due to the natural physical disadvantage of women, coupled with the long-standing feudal society's poisonous ideology of "male superiority and female inferiority," prostitutes (not brothel keepers) who sell themselves in brothels are considered legal compared to thieves. During the Republic of China period, Tianjin had the most brothels, with up to 650 establishments and over 3,100 prostitutes. First and second-class brothels were located in the concessions, while third, fourth, and fifth-class brothels were mainly concentrated in the commercial districts of Nanshi, Houjiahou, and Beikai. Fourth and fifth-class brothels, due to their simple conditions, were known as

---

① Calculated based on the statistical data of the flour industry on *The Industrial Development Status of Tianjin from 1922 to 1931*. Tianjin Archives (ed.). *Factual Records of Tianjin's Urbanization since Modern Times*. Tianjin People's Publishing House, 2005, p.220.

② *Karl Marx, Frederick Engels: Collected Works* (Vol.2). People's Publishing House, 1957, p.400,416.

③ Yan Jingyao. *The Relationship between Crime and Social Changes in China*. Peking University Press, 1986, p.17.

为当时青帮辈分最高的大佬——青帮津北堂堂主。不过天津的帮会扎根于脚行，与上海的"流氓大亨"不同，脚行头子们几乎都是胸无点墨的粗人、地头蛇，专干些上不得台面的肮脏勾当。

贫穷是开出"恶之花"的土壤，而新旧交存、多元异质的城市社会则是滋生犯罪的外部环境。在近代，本就处于由传统农业社会向现代工业社会转型的天津，社会道德败坏，社会动荡失序。在此基础上，又加之主权被侵犯而造成华界与八国租界并立的局面，天津社会形成多元独立而又彼此异质的文化、意识、法律及行政司法范围，社会管控存在很多间隙，这就为帮派横行、犯罪滋生提供了空间环境。袁克文去世后，天津最有名的青帮头子就是袁文会。袁文会原是把持日租界码头运输的脚行头子。抗战时期，他投靠日本人做汉奸，不仅开设赌场、烟馆、走私贩毒，而且专门压榨曲艺艺人。1938 年马三立从沈阳翔云阁茶社回到天津，在南市"东兴市场"和刘宝瑞等一起演出。南市正是袁文会的地盘儿，凡不是"青帮""认家礼"的都备受欺辱。马三立拒绝认青帮的师父，只得再次远走他乡。1940 年，再次没了"饭辙"的马三立又回到了天津"东兴市场"演出。当时，袁文会凭借自己的势力，请来了最当红的曲艺艺人，生意自然火爆，但赚来的钱都被他拿走。有一次，马三立提出要离开，袁文会的手下对他说："你不在这儿干，哪儿也干不了，出了这个门，天津卫你就甭想待了！"有一位艺人王剑云因问了问拖欠数月的包银什么时候给，就被袁文会的爪牙毒打一顿，开除出社，出门时分文未给，后因无钱救治含恨而亡。[1]

灾害与灾民、救灾

近代的天津灾害频仍，水灾、旱灾、兵灾、疫情、地震……既有自然灾害，也有人为灾害。有灾害就有灾民，突发的灾难是对原有社会秩序的突然打破，如果不能对灾民进行及时救济，就会对社会的正常秩序造成影响。无论是从维护社会秩序、保持社会有效运

---

① 《艺海浮萍——相声泰斗马三立（一）》，天津档案方志网。https://www.tjdag.gov.cn/zh_tjdag/jytj/jgsl/jgfq/details/1594032502517.html

"Yaozi" and were generally located in slums. Regardless of the class of brothel, "economic necessity" was the main reason women entered prostitution. The majority of prostitutes were illiterate, and roughly half were from the city while the other half were from outside areas. Brothels were generally operated by a single owner, with larger establishments employing more assistants and bouncers to oversee the prostitutes and ensure security. Although operating a brothel was profitable, the reputation of the "flesh trade" was unsavory and risky, attracting clients from all walks of life. Therefore, brothel owners did not wield much political power, and their ties to gang organizations were not as close as imagined. The clientele of first and second-class brothels were mainly merchants and peddlers, while those of fourth and fifth-class brothels were primarily workers, carters, boatmen, and other laboring masses. Although prostitution was a legal business and prostitutes generally received 40% to 60% of the total income, fundamentally, the sex trade still exploited women at the lower strata of society. Therefore, after 1950, the Tianjin municipal government began to crack down on the sex trade and rehabilitate those involved.[1]

Compared to the prostitution industry, gambling and smuggling drugs offer higher profits. Especially the latter, because the risks are also higher, it is not something that can be operated by just a few individuals. Behind it, there are organized crime syndicates involved, making it organized crime. During that time, the entire northern, northeastern, and northwestern regions of China had drug smuggling hubs in Beijing and Tianjin, controlled by warlords and criminal syndicates. In the late Qing Dynasty and early Republic of China, in order to strengthen revolutionary forces, the revolutionary party not only collaborated with the Qing Gang, which evolved from the Cao Gang, but also directly participated in the Hongmen. Therefore, during the Republic of China period, the Qing Gang and Hongmen were closely associated with the military, government, and business circles. Even Yuan Kewen, one of the "Four Princes of the Republic of China" and the son of Yuan Shikai, once joined the Qing Gang and became the top leader of the Qing Gang in Tianjin—the head of the Qing Gang's Jinbei Hall. However, the gangs in Tianjin were rooted in the lower strata of society, unlike the "gangsters" in Shanghai. The leaders of these gangs were mostly illiterate rough men and local bullies, specializing in dirty dealings that were not brought to light.

Poverty is the soil from which the "flower of evil" blooms, while the

---

① Jiang Pei, Xiang Baosheng. *Discussions on the Composition and Transformation of Prostitution in Tianjin in the Mid-20th Century*. Jiang Pei, Wang Xianming (eds.). *Research on the Social History of Modern North China*. Tianjin Ancient Books Publishing House, 2005, pp.84-123.

转出发，还是站在人道主义立场上，应对突发紧急事件都是城市的管理者和社会组织需要承担的重要职能。

对近代天津人民来说，影响最大、印象最深的就是水灾。天津人一般不说发洪水，而是说闹大水。一个"闹"字，是对天津的水患最精准的描述。所谓"闹"，就是搅扰、就是不得安静，甚至有戏耍的成分，当然也有短暂的意思。20世纪的前几十年，每到夏秋之季，关于水的讨论就热闹起来，扰动得天津人心神不宁，海河上游的哪个省下了一场雨，都会让天津人担心几日。也许哪一天早晨，就突然看到海河水上涨了许多，能看到"乌央乌央"的河水。今年闹不闹大水，是天津人经常挂在嘴边的话题。不单是闹大水，之后伴随而来的还有闹饥荒、闹瘟疫。

天津地处华北平原，地势低洼。子牙河、大清河、永定河、南运河、北运河、白河、浑河、涞河等九大河流以及众多支流等在天津汇聚成海河，形成一个宽度不大、泄水能力小的扇形水系。九是最大的个位数，"九河"其实是很多条河的意思。众多河流给天津带来丰沛的水源，也带来水患灾难，再加上华北平原西起太行山、北依燕山，这两座山脉的地形地势，本就为锋面雨的形成创造了有利条件，容易造成暴雨，进而引发洪水。因此，当天津及周边地区进入夏季雨季时，洪水来势凶猛且宣泄不畅，极易引起海河地区洪水泛滥。历史上，天津曾经多次发生过水灾。其中，近代最严重的就是1890年、1917年和1939年发生过的三次大水灾。

1890年5月，连续九天降雨，使海河西岸的英法租界一片汪洋。金钢桥附近的水势"澎湃奔腾，诚有高屋建瓴之势，一往莫御，直穿各街道而过，致倒塌房屋数百椽，居民多有葬于断础颓垣之下"。三岔河口处"惊涛骇浪，……漫溢城南"[①]。

1917年7月下旬直至入秋，华北地区普降暴雨，海河流域数十条河流相继漫水或决堤破防，京汉、京奉、津浦铁路中断，受灾范围遍及直隶全境，其中以天津、保定两地受灾最为严重。据1918年2月22日《申报》记载：1917年的特大洪灾，与河道年久失修有关。

---

① 吴弘明编译，《津海关贸易年报（1865~1946）》，天津社会科学院出版社，2006年，第157—158页。

coexistence of old and new, diverse and heterogeneous urban societies is the external environment that breeds crime. In modern times, Tianjin, which was already transitioning from a traditional agricultural society to a modern industrial society, experienced social moral decay and turmoil. On this basis, coupled with the infringement of sovereignty resulting in the coexistence of the Chinese old city and the Eight-Nation Concessions, Tianjin's society formed a diverse, independent, and heterogeneous culture, consciousness, legislation, and administrative jurisdiction. There were many gaps in social control, providing space for gangs to flourish and crime to breed. After Yuan Kewen's death, the most famous leader of the Qing Gang in Tianjin was Yuan Wenhui. Yuan Wenhui originally controlled the transportation at the Japanese concession wharf. During the Anti-Japanese War, he collaborated with the Japanese as a traitor, not only operating gambling dens, opium dens, and smuggling drugs but also exploiting folk artists. In 1938, Ma Sanli returned to Tianjin from Xiangyun Pavilion Tea House in Shenyang and performed in the Dongxing Market in the Nanshi District with Liu Baorui and others. The Nanshi District was Yuan Wenhui's territory, and anyone who did not show allegiance to the Qing Gang was subjected to humiliation. Ma Sanli refused to acknowledge the Qing Gang as his master and had to leave again. In 1940, Ma Sanli, who was once again without a source of income, returned to perform at the Dongxing Market in Tianjin. At that time, Yuan Wenhui, using his influence, invited the most popular folk artists, and business naturally boomed, but all the money earned was taken by him. Once, when Ma Sanli requested to leave, Yuan Wenhui's henchmen told him, "If you don't work here, you won't be able to work anywhere else. Once you leave this place, you can forget about staying in Tianjin!" Another artist, Wang Jianyun, was beaten by Yuan Wenhui's lackeys and expelled from the troupe just for asking when he would be paid the wages owed to him for several months. Yuan Wenhui did not give him a single penny when he left, and Wang Jianyun later died with resentment due to lack of money for medical treatment.[①]

Disasters, Victims, and Disaster Relief

In modern Tianjin, disasters occurred frequently, including floods, droughts, wars, epidemics, earthquakes, and both natural and man-made disasters. With disasters come displaced people or disaster victims. Sudden

---

① *Ups and Downs in the Art - Ma Sanli, the Grand Master of Crosstalk (Part 1)*. Tianjin Archives and Local Chronicles Network. https://www.tjdag.gov.cn/zh_tjdag/jytj/jgsl/jgfq/details/1594032502517.html

1917 年大水街景
Flooded streets in 1917

"查京畿各河二十余年未经修治，堤防尽行残缺。此次水患，五大河及数十余小河同时并涨，泛滥横流，淹及一百余县，面积之广，所有堤埝无不破坏。人民被灾之后，救死不赡，焉有余力以筹修浚。" 河道之所以失修是因为自 1916 年袁世凯死后，北方进入一个军阀混战、群雄割据的乱世，京津地区更是争权夺势的北洋各派将领的角斗场，加之 1917 年张勋忙着复辟清朝，第一次世界大战爆发，各国租界当局也彼此纷扰不断。在混乱的政治环境下，维护堤坝这样的民生大计自然无人问津。水灾使得天津一大半区域被淹没在洪水之中，许多百姓的房屋因为是土垒的，或被洪水冲毁或被洪水浸泡坍塌，整个城市百姓流离，四民辍业。《申报》报道说，"天津灾情之重为历来所未有，就全境而论，被灾者约占五分之四，灾民约有八十余万人。""查水之始至也系在夜半，顷刻之间平地水深数尺，居民或睡梦未觉，或病体难支，或值产妇临盆，或将婴儿遗落，老者艰于步履，壮者恋其财产，致被淹毙者实已有二三百人，而其逃生者亦皆不及着衣，率以被褥蔽体，衣履完全者甚属有限。"[1]

1939 年的天津大水发生在 8 月至 10 月。这场水灾的规模和危害程度远超 1917 年水灾，造成当时天津市区 80% 的地区被洪水所淹，超过 10 万间房屋被冲毁，65 万天津及其周边居民成为灾民。天津大部分地区被洪水浸泡长达一个半月，陆路交通和工商业濒临瘫痪，

---

① 《申报》1918 年 2 月 22 日。

catastrophes disrupt the existing social order, and if timely relief is not provided to the victims, it can have an impact on the normal functioning of society. Whether from the perspective of maintaining social order, ensuring the effective operation of society, or from a humanitarian standpoint, responding to emergencies is an important function that urban administrators and social organizations need to undertake.

For the people of modern Tianjin, the most significant and memorable impact was the frequent occurrence of floods. Tianjin residents typically don't say "flood," but rather "nào dàshuǐ," which translates to "big water" or "great water." The word "nào" used here perfectly describes Tianjin's water disasters. The "nào" implies disturbance, unrest, and even a sense of playfulness, though it also suggests a temporary nature. In the first few decades of the 20th century, discussions about water would heat up every summer and autumn, unsettling the minds of Tianjin residents. Whenever a province upstream of the Hai River received rainfall, Tianjin residents would worry for several days. Perhaps one morning, they would suddenly see the Hai River rising significantly, its waters churning. Whether there would be major flooding this year was a topic frequently discussed by Tianjin residents. Alongside the floods, there were also periods of famine and epidemic outbreaks.

Tianjin is located in the North China Plain, characterized by low-lying terrain. Nine major rivers including the Ziya River, Daqing River, Yongding River, South Canal, North Canal, Peiho, Hun River, and Lai River, along with numerous tributaries, converge in Tianjin to form the Hai River, creating a fan-shaped water system with a small drainage capacity and not very wide. Nine is the largest single digit, and "nine rivers" actually means many rivers. The numerous rivers provide Tianjin with abundant water sources but also bring water-related disasters. Moreover, the geographical features of the Taihang

1917 年大水后商会为灾民修建的临时居所
The temporary shelters built by the Chamber of Commerce
for refugees after the 1917 flood

1917 年天津南开中学被淹
The flooded Tianjin Nankai Middle School in 1917

Mountains to the west and the Yan Mountains to the north of the North China Plain create favorable conditions for the formation of frontal rainfall, which easily leads to heavy rain and subsequently triggers floods. Therefore, when Tianjin and its surrounding areas enter the summer rainy season, floods often occur with great ferocity and poor drainage, which can easily lead to flooding in the Hai River area. Historically, Tianjin has experienced frequent water disasters. Among them, the most severe in modern times were the three major floods that occurred in 1890, 1917, and 1939.

In May 1890, continuous rainfall for nine days resulted in flooding on the western bank of the Hai River in the British and French concessions. Near the Jingang Bridge, the water surged and roared with such force that it seemed to "have the momentum of a towering building, unstoppable and passing straight through the streets, causing the collapse of hundreds of houses and burying many residents beneath the ruins." At Sancha estuary, there were "shocking waves and raging torrents, overflowing to the south of the city."[①]

In late July 1917 until the onset of autumn, torrential rains fell across the North China region, causing numerous rivers in the Hai River basin to overflow or breach their banks successively. The Beijing-Hankou, Beijing-Fengtian, and Tianjin-Pukou railways were interrupted, and the disaster area extended throughout the entire province of Zhili, with Tianjin and Baoding being the hardest hit. According to a report in the *The Shun Pao* on February 22, 1918, the catastrophic flood of 1917 was related to the long-term disrepair of the river channels. "Inspecting the rivers in the Beijing area, they had not been repaired for more than twenty years, and the embankments were all damaged. In this flood, the five major rivers and dozens of small rivers simultaneously rose and overflowed, inundating more than one hundred counties. The affected area was vast, and all embankments were destroyed. After the people were affected by the disaster, there was no surplus energy to raise funds for repairs and dredging." The reason for the disrepair of the river channels was due to the chaotic warlord conflicts and power struggles following Yuan Shikai's death in 1916. The Beijing-Tianjin region was a battleground for various Beiyang factions competing for power. In addition, in 1917, Zhang Xun was busy restoring the Qing Dynasty, and the outbreak of World War I caused constant turmoil among the authorities of various foreign concessions. In such a chaotic political environment, there was naturally no one concerned about maintaining the embankments, a major project for the livelihood of the people. The floods submerged more than half

---

① *Tianjin Customs Annual Report of Trade (1865~1946)*, translated and edited by Wu Hongming. Tianjin Academy of Social Sciences Press, 2006, pp.157-158.

1939 年大水中的日租界街景
The flooded streets in the Japanese concession in the 1939

1939 年水灾时的街边贫民
Poor people on the street in the 1939 flood

水灾造成直接经济损失约 6 亿元法币。洪水退后，霍乱、伤寒和痢疾等疫病肆虐天津。当时天津正处于被日军侵略占领时期，水灾除了自然原因之外，还由于日本军方为削弱华北的抗日武装力量，在部分地区采取决堤放水的行动，这也加剧了水灾的严重程度。据报纸报道："冀中冀南之日军，因图水淹隐存于高粱中之游击队，竟将所有之河堤破坏。"① 水火无情，害人终害己。当洪水进入天津市区后，包括海河沿岸、特别是地势低洼的天津英租界、法租界和日租界等地区亦成为重灾区。尽管在水灾前期，天津市政当局开始全面抢护市内堤坝，步步为营，但此时围堤之外烟波浩渺、各河水势盈盈，各种补救措施终属无功，最终陈塘庄大围堤、海光寺小围堤破坝，全市被淹。

1890 年水灾之后，当时的主要救灾力量是教会。"为予以救助，天津本地及相邻城邑无不捐款并转与邻地之传教士，彼等为纾民瘼而建有无与匹敌之勋劳。"② 其后开平矿务局及政府开始增援。1917

① 《申报》1939 年 11 月 2 日。

② 《1892—1901 年津海关十年报告》（一）。天津海关译编委员会编译，《津海关史要览》，中国海关出版社，2004 年，第 53 页。

of Tianjin's area, and many people's houses, being made of mud, were either washed away or collapsed due to being soaked by floodwaters. The entire city's population was displaced, and economic activities were disrupted. The *The Shun Pao* report stated, "The severity of the Tianjin disaster has never been seen before. Regarding the entire area, the affected people of about 800,000 accounted for four-fifths. The flooding began at midnight, and within moments the water was several feet deep on flat ground. Residents were either asleep, in poor health, in labor, abandoning their babies, or struggling to walk. Some were drowned, with two to three hundred deaths, and those who survived did not even have time to dress properly, covering themselves with blankets. Those with intact clothing were very few."[1]

The Tianjin flood of 1939 occurred between August and October. The scale and severity of this flood far exceeded that of the 1917 flood, with 80% of the Tianjin urban area inundated by floodwaters. Over 100,000 houses were destroyed, and 650,000 Tianjin residents and those in surrounding areas became refugees. Much of Tianjin remained submerged for a month and a half, with land transportation and commercial activities on the verge of paralysis. The flood caused direct economic losses estimated at around 600 million legal currency. After the waters receded, diseases such as cholera, typhoid, and dysentery ravaged Tianjin. At that time, Tianjin was under

[1] *The Shun Pao*, February 22, 1918.

年的天津特大水灾中，天津的商人自发成立"天津华北华洋义赈会"负责救济工作。他们组织义卖活动，募集救灾资金，为灾民搭建临时安置房，收容无家可归者达 5 万人。义赈会对灾民每月提供粮食，发放衣物被褥，以小额贷款扶助实业，以提供就业机会，还"建立少女收容所，饥民学校，兴办适于妇女之实业"。① 种种举措，致使奸商无法哄抬物价，避免了灾民沦为乞丐和娼妓。1939 年的水灾规模空前，天津商会通过各个慈善团体，如黄卍字会、黄十字会、红十字会等慈善组织，开展救灾活动，发起收容、赈济、防疫、施水、施粮、劝募、捐启、筑堤、排水、清淤、消毒、隔离、粪便处理、掩埋尸体等行动，并设立粥棚暖厂、统一调配物资、平粜廉卖、控制物价、处理房租纠纷，尽量减小水灾损失、抑制市场动荡，还组织义务募捐、发起水灾纪念与标记水位标志以及撰写灾后文学等诸多举动。以上种种说明，在 20 世纪的二三十年代的社会生产力基础上，天津已经具有了相当高的城市社会管理水平和市民自治能力。

除了救灾，天津本地有关机构还开展了积极的减灾防灾、治理海河的活动，不过由于战乱频仍、财政紧张，海河整治工程以及周边河流水利工程并不能得到持续的关注。早在天津被迫开埠之后不久，由外国人控制的天津海关就曾要求天津地方政府疏浚治理海河。但清政府因惧怕外国兵舰借由海河和运河直抵北京，一直推拒。直到义和团运动之后，天津由八国联军临时政府——都统衙门共管，1901 年 3 月，都统衙门下令开始进行海河整治的首期工程，工程费用约 25 万两白银由都统衙门承担，并成立海河工程局负责海河工程。② 这一工程主要是裁弯取直，并拓宽了流经各租界的河段。此后，1904 年 8 月内地连降暴雨，海河水位大涨，由于裁弯取直的功效，洪水得以迅速排入大海，天津未遭洪水淹没。③ 民国时期，由于战火纷飞，经济建设受到严重影响，水利工程建设大多处于停滞状态，

---

① 《1912—1921 年津海关十年报告》（三）。天津海关译编委员会编译，《津海关史要览》，中国海关出版社，2004 年，第 128 页。

② 1901 年 3 月 15 日第 119 次会议。刘海岩等编，《八国联军占领实录：天津临时政府会议纪要》，天津社会科学院出版社，2004 年，第 217 页。

③ 《1892—1901 年津海关十年报告》（一）。天津海关译编委员会编译，《津海关史要览》，中国海关出版社，2004 年，第 49—50 页。

Japanese occupation, and besides natural factors, the severity of the flood was exacerbated by actions taken by the Japanese military to weaken anti-Japanese armed forces in North China, including breaching dikes in some areas to release water. According to newspaper reports, "The Japanese troops in central and southern Hebei, to drown out guerrillas hidden in sorghum fields, destroyed all the river embankments."[1] Water and fire are merciless, harming others ultimately harms oneself. When the floodwaters entered the Tianjin urban area, including along the Hai River and especially in low-lying areas such as the Tianjin British Concession, French Concession, and Japanese Concession, these areas also became heavily affected. Despite comprehensive efforts by the Tianjin municipal authorities to protect the city's embankments prior to the flood, the vastness of the waters outside the embankments and the failure of various remedial measures ultimately led to the breach of the Chentangzhuang and Haiguang Temple embankments, resulting in the flooding of the entire city.

After the flood in 1890, the main relief efforts were carried out by the church. "To provide assistance, donations were made from Tianjin and neighboring cities and transferred to missionaries in neighboring areas, who made unparalleled contributions to alleviating the suffering of the people."[2] Later, the Kaiping Mining Bureau and the government began to provide assistance. During the massive flood in Tianjin in 1917, local merchants spontaneously formed the "Tianjin North China and Foreign Charity Relief Association" to handle relief work. They organized charity sales, raised relief funds, built temporary shelters for the victims, and accommodated up to 50,000 homeless individuals. The Relief Association provided monthly food rations, distributed clothing and bedding, provided small loans to support industries, created employment opportunities, and established shelters for young women, famine relief schools, and women's industries.[3] These measures prevented profiteers from inflating prices and prevented the victims from falling into beggary or prostitution. The unprecedented scale of the flood in 1939 led the Tientsin Chamber of Commerce, through various charitable organizations such as the Yellow Swastika Society, the Yellow Cross, and the Red Cross, to carry out relief activities. They initiated

---

① *The Shun Pao*, November 2, 1939.

② *The Ten-year Report of Tianjin Customs* from 1892 to 1901. Quoted in *Overview of the History of Tianjin Customs*, translated and edited by Tianjin Customs Translation and Editing Committee. China Customs Press, 2004, p.53.

③ *The Ten-year Report of Tianjin Customs* from 1912 to 1921. Quoted in *Overview of the History of Tianjin Customs*, translated and edited by Tianjin Customs Translation and Editing Committee. China Customs Press, 2004, p.128.

1939 年天津被淹场景俯瞰
The 1939 Tianjin flood scene from an aerial view

1939 年水灾中救护队劝说坚守在倾斜屋顶上的难民撤离情景
The scene of a rescue team persuading refugees, who were taking shelter on the slanted rooftops, to evacuate during the 1939 flood

1939 年大水中翘望救生船的小女孩（地点大约为今桂林路与睦南道交口附近）
The little girl anxiously awaiting the lifeboat during the 1939 flood (approximately near the intersection of Guilin Road and Munan Road today)

1939 年大水中的日租界旭街
Asahi Road in the Japanese Concession during the 1939 flood

actions such as sheltering, relief distribution, epidemic prevention, water and grain distribution, fundraising, donation collection, embankment construction, drainage, dredging, disinfection, isolation, waste disposal, and burial of bodies. They also established soup kitchens and warming stations, coordinated material distribution, controlled prices, settled rent disputes, minimized flood losses, suppressed market volatility, organized voluntary donations, initiated flood memorials, erected water level markers, and engaged in post-flood literature writing. All of these actions demonstrate that, based on the social productive forces of the 1920s and 1930s, Tianjin had achieved a relatively high level of urban social management and citizen self-governance capabilities.

In addition to disaster relief, local institutions in Tianjin have also carried out active disaster prevention and mitigation activities and governance of the Hai River. However, due to frequent wars and financial constraints, the Hai River improvement project and surrounding river water conservancy projects have not received sustained attention. Shortly after Tianjin was forcibly opened to foreign trade, the Tianjin Customs, controlled by foreigners, requested the local government of Tianjin to dredge and manage the Hai River. However, the Qing government, fearing that foreign warships could use the Hai River and canals to reach Beijing, continuously refused. It was

1939 年大水中的日租界日本公会堂
The public hall in the Japanese Concession during the 1939 flood

1939 年被淹的中原百货公司
The flooded Chungyuen Department Store in 1939

1939 年大水中的英租界英国文法学校
Tientsin Grammar school in the British Concession during the 1939 flood

not until after the Boxer Rebellion, when Tianjin was jointly administered by the provisional government of the Eight-Nation Alliance, that the first phase of the Hai River improvement project started in March 1901. The project cost approximately 250,000 taels of silver, borne by the provisional government, and the Hai-Ho Conservancy Commission was established to oversee the project.[1] This project mainly involved straightening and widening the river sections flowing through various concessions. Subsequently, in August 1904, heavy rain fell in the hinterland, causing the water level of the Hai River to rise significantly. Due to the effectiveness of the straightening efforts, the floodwaters were quickly discharged into the sea, preventing Tianjin from being submerged by floods.[2] During the Republic of China era, due to the ongoing wars, economic development was severely affected, and water conservancy projects were mostly stagnant, or even severely damaged. Particularly in the Hai River basin under Japanese aggression, existing

[1] The 119th meeting on March 15, 1901. Liu Haiyan, et al (eds.). *Record of the Eight Nation Alliance's Occupation - Minutes of the Tianjin Provisional Government Meeting.* Tianjin Academy of Social Sciences Press, 2004, p.217.

[2] *The Ten-year Report of Tianjin Customs* from 1892 to 1901. Quoted in *Overview of the History of Tianjin Customs,* translated and edited by Tianjin Customs Translation and Editing Committee. China Customs Press, 2004, pp.49-50.

甚至遭到严重破坏。特别是日本侵略下的海河流域更是深受其害，不但既定的建设计划受到严重干扰，甚至原有的水利工程也因为战争而遭到毁灭性破坏。即使在这样艰难的情况下，抗日战争前国民政府仍然在海河流域建设了许多水利工程。1918 年 3 月成立顺直水利委员会，负责海河、黄河流域水利行政工作；1928 年 9 月改名为华北水利委员会，管理华北地区的水利工程。1934 年华北水利委员会联合长江、黄河、淮河、陕西等九家水利机构和科研院所，1935 年 11 月在北洋大学建成中国第一水工试验所，至 1937 年 6 月，先后开展了官厅水库坝下消力试验、卢沟桥溢流坝消能消力试验等五项试验。

中国人历来"安土重迁"，如果不是生存不下去，人们是极少愿意离开故土的。天津是一个由各方移民汇聚而成的城市，近代民族工业发展和城市建设为人们提供了大量的就业机会和生存条件，是城市人口增长的物质基础和前提条件，而战争、灾害则是造成华北地区人口向天津市区涌入的另两个重要因素。天津是灾民最愿意选择的避难地。1928 年 5 月《益世报》记者写道："本埠各街巷近来乞丐异常众多，彼此往来，终日络绎不绝。此项乞丐，多操直南及山东等处口音，闻系直鲁难民。"[1] 1935 年天津市救济院收容的 249 名灾民中，有河北籍 133 人、山东籍 60 人，共占比 77.5%。[2] 从 1840 年人口不足 20 万，至 1947 年发展成为拥有近 172 万人口的大都市，[3] 天津不仅是充满野心欲望的冒险家所向往的遍地黄金的乐土，也是为那些失去家园一无所有的贫苦者提供庇护和希望的新生之地。

construction plans were severely disrupted, and existing water conservancy projects were even destroyed due to war. Even in such difficult circumstances, the Nationalist government before the War of Resistance Against Japan still built many water conservancy projects in the Hai River basin. In March 1918, the Shunzhi Water Conservancy Committee was established, responsible for the administrative work of water conservancy in the Hai River and Yellow River basins. In September 1928, it was renamed the North China Water Conservancy Committee, responsible for managing water conservancy projects in North China. In 1934, the North China Water Conservancy Committee, together with nine other water conservancy institutions and research institutes such as the Yangtze River, Yellow River, Huai River, and Shaanxi, jointly established China's first Hydraulics Laboratory at Peiyang University in November 1935. By June 1937, they had conducted five experiments including the dissipation of energy below the Guanting Reservoir dam and the dissipation of energy at the Marco Polo Bridge overflow dam.

Chinese people have always had a strong attachment to their native land, and they are rarely willing to leave their homeland unless they cannot survive there. Tianjin is a city formed by immigrants from all directions. In modern times, the development of national industry and urban construction has provided a large number of employment opportunities and living conditions for people. This serves as the material basis and prerequisite for urban population growth. Wars and disasters are two other important factors leading to the influx of people from northern China into the Tianjin urban area. Tianjin is the preferred refuge for refugees. In May 1928, a reporter from the *Social Welfare* wrote: "There are unusually many beggars in the streets and lanes of this place recently. They are associated with each other, and there is a constant stream of them all day long. These beggars mostly speak with accents from South Zhili, Shandong and other places, and it is heard that they are refugees from Shandong."[1] In 1935, among the 249 refugees accommodated by the Tianjin Alms-house, there were 133 from Hebei and 60 from Shandong, accounting for a total of 77.5%.[2] From a population of less than 200,000 in 1840 to a metropolis with a population of 1.72 million in 1946,[3] Tianjin has not only been a land of golden opportunities coveted by ambitious adventurers but also a new land of refuge and hope for the destitute who have lost their homes.

① 《益世报》1928 年 5 月 2 日。
② 《益世报》1935 年 6 月 17 日。
③ 李竞能主编，《天津人口史》，南开大学出版社，1990 年，第 82 页。

① *Social Welfare*, May 2, 1928.
② *Social Welfare*, June 17, 1935.
③ Li Jingneng (ed.). *Population History of Tianjin*. Nankai University Press, 1990, p.82.

第 六 章　国际政治与城市里的革命

Chapter Six: International Politics and Revolution in the City

作为前奏的天津教案

第一次鸦片战争后，传教士开始在各地传教。在华传教士不仅享有传教、建造教堂的权利，还享有治外法权，而信教的中国民众也因"宽容条款"①享有特权。因此，许多地痞流氓也混入教会，横行乡里。这为后来各地发生民教纠纷及引起教案埋下严重隐患。第二次鸦片战争后，《天津条约》中规定，法国宣教士可以在内地任意各省租买土地，建筑教堂。此后教案发生的次数逐渐增多，19世纪70年代至90年代更为频繁，成为近代教案发生的高潮时期。某种意义上，其后爆发的义和团运动是这些教案发生的顶峰和总汇合。天津教案是19世纪70年代规模最大的教案，且由于其发生于北京近畿的天津，影响更大。

天津人眼中的育婴堂杀婴事件和曾国藩的调查结果

1870年端午前后，天津法国天主教仁慈堂收养的中国幼孩突然大批死亡，先后达三四十人，葬于河东荒野，有的"两尸三尸共一棺"。因趁夜草草埋葬，导致尸体暴露，鹰啄狗刨，"胸腹皆烂，肠肚外露"，惨不忍睹。②由此民心疑惑，每天都有人到坟地去看，谣言渐起。恰好当时在天津地区又发生了好几起拐骗儿童的案件，更引起民心浮

---

① 所谓"宽容条款"，是指1844年中法《黄埔条约》签订过程中，时任两广总督的耆英向朝廷请求"兴善避恶是天主教的宗旨"，"要一视同仁，中外臣民，凡是慕道并入天主教，而没有借天主教以作恶以获利的教徒，免受所有的罪责"。

② 《曾文正公奏稿》第二十九卷，传忠书局，光绪二年刊本，第38页。

"The Tianjin Missionary Case" as a Prelude

After the First Opium War, missionaries began proselytizing in various regions. Missionaries in China not only had the right to preach and build churches but also enjoyed extraterritoriality, while the Chinese populace who converted to Christianity also enjoyed privileges due to the "Toleration of Christianity"① clause. Consequently, many hooligans infiltrated the church and wreaked havoc in the countryside. This laid the serious groundwork for later disputes between missionaries and locals, sparking what became known as "missionary incidents." After the Second Opium War, the *Treaties of Tianjin* stipulated French missionaries shall be allowed to lease land and build churches in various inland provinces at their discretion. Subsequently, the frequency of missionary incidents increased gradually, peaking during the 1870s to 1890s, marking the climax of modern missionary incidents. In a sense, the subsequent eruption of the Boxer Rebellion represented the pinnacle and culmination of these incidents. The Tianjin Missionary Case in the 1870s was the largest in scale during that period and, due to its occurrence near Beijing in Tianjin, had a greater impact.

The Infant Killing Incident in the Eyes of Tianjin Residents and the Investigation Results by Zeng Guofan

Around the time of the Dragon Boat Festival in 1870, a large number of Chinese infants adopted by the Tianjin French Catholic Sisters of Mercy suddenly died, reaching a total of thirty to forty, and were buried in the

---

① The so-called "Tolerance Clause" refers to a provision during the negotiation of the Sino-French *Treaty of Whampoa* in 1844. At that time, Qiying, the Governor-General of Liangguang, petitioned the imperial court, stating that "promoting good and avoiding evil is the fundamental principle of Catholicism" and that "all subjects, both Chinese and foreign, should be treated equally." He requested that those who embraced Catholicism out of genuine faith—without using it as a pretext for wrongdoing or personal gain—be exempt from any form of punishment.

动和社会不安。民众既怀疑法国教堂借口治病虐杀儿童，也怀疑迷拐幼童之事与教堂有关，但始终拿不出确凿的证据。不久，天津民众拿获了三名涉嫌拐卖儿童的犯人，其中一人是天主教徒，被天主堂经三口通商大臣崇厚要去。一时间天津人民群情激愤，大街小巷出现了许多反洋教的揭帖。天津道府官员迫于民众压力，只好将另外两名拐犯迅速审结正法，并宣称崇厚要去之人并非拐犯，以解众疑。"自此人心稍安，浮议渐息，而百姓仍疑拐犯系天主堂指使，县官不敢深究，且以河东前葬幼孩多棺，终觉怀疑莫释。"①

又过了几天，民众抓获一名叫武兰珍的拐犯。他供称有教徒将其引诱到教堂，交给他迷药，让他到外面去拐骗人到教堂来，每拐来一个人，教堂就给五块银元。他还说，引诱他的教徒叫"王三"，并供称："王三系天津口音，脸上有白麻。有天津人开药店教民王三，且面上果有白麻。则迷药之得自王三，似非虚捏。"②因为武兰珍言之凿凿，于是不仅天津"城乡四境早已哄传天主堂真有用药迷人之事"③，负责地方行政和司法的天津道台、知府和知县也都认为教会和修女有罪，但因事关教堂和洋人，必须请示负责管理外交事务的钦差大臣崇厚。崇厚亦以为面对汹涌的民情不能不理，不得不亲自去见法国驻天津领事丰大业（Henri Victor Fontanier），请其协助向教会调查。双方商定于6月21日上午由天津地方官员带犯人赴教堂指认门径。结果，堂内里的情况与供情不符。天津地方官感到此案已无法再查下去，遂与崇厚"议以不了了之，即可完案"，"拟即出示晓谕，并将武兰珍先行正法"④。

官员们离开后，民众与教会中人发生争斗。因法国天主堂和领事馆离三口通商衙门很近，丰大业即带领秘书西蒙"各执利刃洋枪"，一同去找崇厚。他们脚踹仪门而入，一见崇厚就放了一枪。崇厚赶紧逃向内室，丰大业随即将屋内器具砸毁。见众巡捕将丰大业劝住，崇厚硬着头皮又出来。丰大业一见他又放一枪，大声质问道："尔

---

① 《张光藻密禀》，《湘乡曾氏文献》第7册，台湾学生书局，1965年，第4518—4519页。

② 《湘乡曾氏文献》第7册，台湾学生书局，1965年，第4479页。

③ 《曾文正公奏稿》第二十九卷，传忠书局，光绪二年刊本，第38页。

④ 《湘乡曾氏文献》第7册，台湾学生书局，1965年，第4467—4468页。

---

desolate wasteland east of the river. Some were buried together, sharing a single coffin. Due to the hurried burial at night, the bodies were exposed, subjected to pecking by birds and digging by dogs. "Their chests and abdomens were rotten, with intestines and stomachs exposed," presenting a scene too gruesome to bear.① This led to doubts among the people, with individuals visiting the gravesite daily, and rumors gradually spread. Coincidentally, several cases of child abduction and kidnapping occurred in the Tianjin area at the same time, further fueling public anxiety and social unrest. The populace suspected that the French church, under the pretext of treating illness, was killing children, and also suspected that child abduction cases were related to the church, but no concrete evidence could be produced. Shortly thereafter, the Tianjin residents apprehended three suspects involved in child trafficking, one of whom was a Catholic, and was handed over to the Catholic Church via Chonghou, Superintendent of Trade for the Three Treaty Ports. At this, the people of Tianjin were inflamed, and many anti-foreign church posters appeared in the streets and alleys. Faced with pressure from the public, the Tianjin officials swiftly tried and punished the other two kidnappers, while declaring that the Catholic suspect was not involved in the abductions, in an attempt to allay suspicions. "Although people's hearts were somewhat calmed and rumors gradually subsided, the suspicion that the kidnappers were instigated by the Catholic church persisted. The county officials dared not investigate further, and the numerous coffins of buried infants in the east of the river continued to fuel suspicion."②

A few days later, the populace apprehended a kidnapper named Wu Lanzhen. He confessed that a believer lured him to the church, gave him drugs, and instructed him to lure people to the church. For every person he brought, the church paid him five silver dollars. He also mentioned that the believer who lured him was named "Wang San" and described him as "having a Tianjin accent and a pockmarked face. Since there were Tianjin residents who ran pharmacies and fit this description, it seemed likely that the drugs came from Wang San and not from fabrication."③ Because Wu Lanzhen's account seemed credible, rumors had spread throughout Tianjin that the church indeed used drugs to lure people.④ Tianjin officials responsible for

---

① *Chronicles of Managing Foreign Affairs (Chouban Yiwu Shimo)*, Tongzhi Reign, Vol.76, p.33.

② *Zhang Guangzao's Secret Memorial. Zeng's Documents from Xiangxiang County*. Vol.7. Taiwan Student Books Press, 1965, pp.4518-4519.

③ *Zeng's Documents from Xiangxiang County*. Vol.7. Taiwan Student Books Press, 1965, p.4479.

④ *Zeng Wenzheng's Memorials*. Vol.29. Chuanzhong Book Company. Edition in the second year of Emperor Guangxu, p.38.

百姓在天主堂门外滋闹，因何不亲往弹压？我定与尔不依。"[1]

那时，聚集在三口通商大臣衙门前的民众们听到衙门里的枪声，以为官府已与法国人开仗，遂鸣锣召集来更多的人前往救援。听到消息的人们如潮水般从四面八方向这里涌来，满面怒容，手执刀枪。崇厚怕乱中出事，劝丰大业不要此时出去。丰大业更怒，口称："尔怕百姓，我不怕尔中国百姓。"之后他怒气冲冲手持刀枪，"竟飞奔出署"。[2]衙门外的民众执刀怒视，犹未动手，且纷纷后移，给丰大业让出通道。丰大业行至浮桥，与天津知县刘杰迎面相遇。丰大业怒火更盛，突然向刘杰开枪，打伤跟班高升。于是，人们的愤怒再也无法忍耐，如火山爆发般迸发出来，一齐动手将丰大业、西蒙群殴而死。[3]随即激动的民众奔往天主堂和仁慈堂，将修女们杀死，将教堂拆毁焚烧。

事后查明，这场针对法国人的暴乱，被打死的包括法国修女 10 名、神父 2 名（其中一名神父是中国人）、丰大业和西蒙两人、两对法国夫妇以及被教堂和育婴堂所雇用的三四十名中国人，还有一对恰好骑马路过的俄国夫妇和一名俄国商人，共计外国人 20 名。按照国籍来算，此次教案共打死 13 名法国人、3 名俄国人、2 名比利时人、1 名意大利人和 1 名爱尔兰人。此外，还涉及美国、英国、西班牙等国的财产损失。[4]因此，法国、英国、美国、比利时、俄国、普鲁士、西班牙等七国列舰天津海口，对中国进行军事威胁。七国公使以法国为首向总理衙门强烈抗议，并发出最后通牒，要求惩办肇事者，赔偿损失。这就是有名的天津教案。

清政府极为紧张，一面通令各地督抚弹压民众，防止类似事件发生；一面命正在病假中的直隶总督曾国藩立刻销假，到天津查办此案。曾国藩带病应命，派人赴津调查，令地方官详禀事件经过及

① 《湘乡曾氏文献》第 7 册，台湾学生书局，1965 年，第 4469—4470 页。
② 王守恂，《天津政俗沿革记》（卷一六）。天津市地方史志编修委员会编著，《天津通志·旧志点校卷》，南开大学出版社，2001 年，第 80 页。
③ 《筹办夷务始末》同治朝，卷七二，第 23—24 页。
④ （英）雷穆森著，许逸凡等译，《天津租界史（插图本）》，天津人民出版社，2009 年，第 46—47 页。

local administration and judiciary, including the Tianjin Taotai, prefect, and county magistrate, believed that the church and nuns were guilty. However, due to the involvement of the church and foreigners, they had to consult the Imperial Commissioner Chonghou, who was responsible for managing diplomatic affairs. Chonghou believed that they could not ignore the surging public sentiment and had to personally meet with Henri Victor Fontanier, the French consul in Tianjin, to seek his assistance in investigating the church. Both parties agreed that on the morning of June 21st, Tianjin local officials would bring the suspect to the church for identification. The situation inside the church did not match the confession. Tianjin local officials felt that the case could no longer be pursued, so they discussed with Chonghou and agreed that it could be concluded as inconclusive. They planned to issue a notice to this effect and proceed with the trial of Wu Lanzhen.[1]

After the officials left, a confrontation erupted between the populace and members of the church. Since the French Catholic Church and consulate were close to the office of the Imperial Commissioner Chonghou, Henri Victor Fontanier led his secretary Simon, each armed with a sharp weapon and a foreign gun, to find Chonghou. They kicked open the ceremonial gate and barged in, firing a shot as soon as they saw Chonghou. Chonghou quickly fled to the inner room, and Fontanier immediately began smashing the furniture. When the constables persuaded Fontanier to stop, Chonghou reluctantly came out. Fontanier fired another shot when he saw Chonghou and loudly questioned, "Why didn't you personally suppress the chaos outside the church? I will not tolerate this!"[2]

At that moment, when the crowd gathered outside the office of the Imperial Commissioner heard the sound of gunfire from within, they thought that the officials had clashed with the French. They sounded gongs to summon more people for reinforcements. Upon hearing the news, people rushed here from all directions like a tide, their faces filled with anger, wielding knives and guns. Chonghou, fearing chaos, advised Fontanier not to go out at this time. Fontanier, even more furious, retorted, "You fear the people, but I do not fear the people of China." Then, in a fit of rage, he grabbed his weapons and "rushed out of the office."[3] The people outside the gate glared angrily with

① *Zeng's Documents from Xiangxiang County*. Vol.7. Taiwan Student Books Press, 1965, pp.4467-4468.
② *Zeng's Documents from Xiangxiang County*. Vol.7. Taiwan Student Books Press, 1965, pp.4469-4470.
③ Wang Shouxun. *The Evolution of Politics and Customs in Tianjin* (Vol.16). *Tianjin Chorography · The Revised Edition of the Old Chronicles*, compiled by Tianjin Chorography and History Compilation Committee (ed.). Nankai University Press, 2001, p.80.

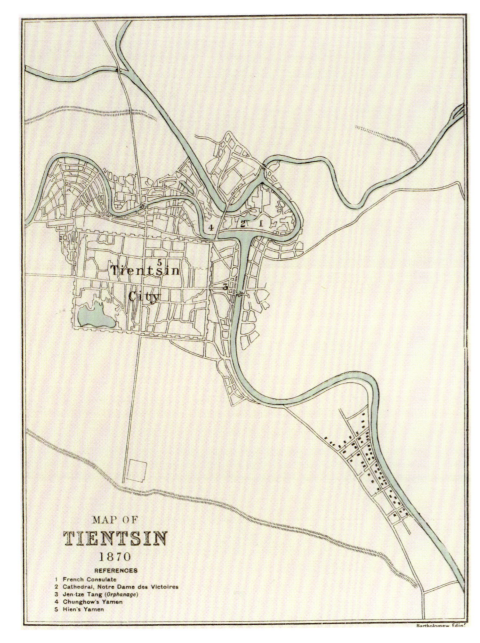

1870 年的天津地图（图中标示 1 为法国领事馆，2 为望海楼教堂，3 为育婴堂，4 为崇厚衙署，5 为县衙）。出自《地图中的近代天津城市》（天津大学出版社，2018）

The map of Tianjin in 1870 (No.1 is the French Consulate, No.2 is the Wanghailou Church, No.3 is the Orphanage, No.4 is the Chonghou's Yamen, and No.5 is the Tianjin County Magistrate's Yamen). Source: *Modern Tianjin City in the Map* (Tianjin University Press, 2018)

their knives but did not yet move. Instead, they stepped back, making way for Fontanier. Fontanier reached the floating bridge and encountered Tianjin Magistrate Liu Jie face to face. Enraged even further, Fontanier suddenly shot at Liu Jie, injuring Liu's attendant Gao Sheng. At this point, the people's anger could no longer be contained. Like a volcano erupting, they erupted in unison, beating Fontanier and Simon to death.[1] Immediately, the agitated crowd rushed to the Catholic Church and the Church of Sisters of Mercy, killing the nuns and demolishing and burning down the churches.

After investigation, it was found that the casualties in this riot against the French included ten French nuns, two priests (one of whom was Chinese), Fontanier and Simon, two French couples, and thirty to forty Chinese employees hired by the church and the orphanage. There was also a Russian couple and a Russian merchant who happened to be passing by on horseback, totaling twenty foreigners. According to nationality, there were thirteen French, three Russians, two Belgians, one Italian, and one Irish killed in this incident. Additionally, there were property losses involving the United States, the United Kingdom, Spain, and other countries.[2] Consequently, France, the United Kingdom, the United States, Belgium, Russia, Prussia, Spain, and seven other countries sent warships to Tianjin Port, threatening China militarily. The ministers of the seven countries, led by France, lodged strong protests with the Ministry of Foreign Affairs and issued an ultimatum demanding the punishment of the perpetrators and compensation for the losses. This is known as the Tianjin Missionary Case.

The Qing government was extremely nervous. On the one hand, it ordered the governors in various regions to suppress the masses and prevent similar incidents from happening again. On the other hand, it ordered Zeng Guofan, the Viceroy of Zhili who was on sick leave, to immediately end his sick leave and proceed to Tianjin to handle the case. Despite his illness, Zeng Guofan complied with the order and dispatched personnel to Tianjin to investigate, instructing local officials to provide detailed reports on the incident and their proposed actions. Soon, Zeng Guofan received two confidential letters, one from Zhou Jiaxun, the Tianjin Governor-General, and one from Zhang Guangzao, the Tianjin Prefect. Based on this information, Zeng Guofan compiled a report on the Tianjin Missionary Case and submitted it to the central government. In the report, Zeng Guofan placed the blame

---

[1] *The Beginning and End of the Westernization Movement.* During the period of Emperor Tongzhi, Vol.72, pp.23-24.

[2] O. D. Rasmussen. *Tientsin: An Illustrated Outline History,* translated by Xu Yifan, et al. Tianjin People's Publishing House, 2008, pp.46-47.

处理意见。很快，曾国藩收到天津道周家勋密函一件、天津知府张光藻密禀一件。据此，曾国藩就天津教案写了一份调查报告，密报给中央政府。在报告中，曾国藩认为教案责任在中国人身上。后清政府将天津知府和知县革职充军，处死祸首黑社会组织水火会16人，充军25人，赔款修建教堂，并派崇厚赴法国道歉。恰在此时，普法战争爆发，崇厚到法国并未受到苛责。

外国侨民视野下的天津大屠杀

1870年6月21日，天津英国领事馆的一位助理发出了一封紧急书信，信中说："法国领事馆、仁慈堂的育婴堂、法国的大会堂全在焚烧中。法国领事和所有修女以及另外几名法国人全被害死。我仓促地由一个特别信差发送这封信件。"[①] 这封信6月27日到达上海，7月4日到达香港，7月25日到达伦敦。这是欧洲收到的最早的关于天津屠杀事件的报道。

与曾国藩就事论事的调查结果和看法不同，外国侨民，尤其是一些学者，面对如此惨案，有比较深刻的自省。他们分析事件的起因时提到，首先，在第二次鸦片战争中，天津被英法联军占领了两年多的时间，期间，法国军队和官员的行为恶劣，在这里"留下了仇恨的种子"。其次，那座被烧毁的"圣母得胜堂"（Cathedral Notre Dames des Victories）的所在地，过去是皇帝的行宫和神圣的庙宇，所以中国人当然对此"深为愤恨"。第三，教会的仁慈堂修女向来有在城市里收养孤儿或弃儿的慈善传统，但是没有中国人将儿童交给她们照看，于是修女们就为每一个送儿童到孤儿院的人颁发奖金，这种奖金的负面效果就是"奖励"了诱拐儿童行为的发生。第四，由于中国人常常把濒死的儿童交给神父或者修女，后者为他们受洗以使他们能上天堂，而那些儿童往往在受洗后不久就死亡，教会以草率的掩埋方式处理，这些给中国人留下了恐怖的印象——拐骗、神秘受洗仪式、挖去眼睛和心脏。以上这些都使天津

---

① （美）马士著，张汇文等译，《中华帝国对外关系史》（第二卷），上海书店出版社，2006年，第252页。

---

for the incident on the Chinese people. The Qing government subsequently dismissed and exiled the Tianjin Prefect and County Magistrate, executed 16 members of the mafia organization Fire and Water Society as the chief offenders, exiled 25 others, compensated for the construction of the church, and sent Chonghou to France to apologize. Coincidentally, the Franco-Prussian War broke out at this time, and Chonghou did not face harsh criticism when he arrived in France.

The Tianjin Missionary Case as Seen by Foreign Expatriates

On June 21, 1870, an assistant at the British Consulate in Tianjin sent an urgent letter stating: "The French consulate, the [orphanage of the] Sisters of Mercy, the French cathedral are all burning. The French consul and all the sisters, as well as several other Frenchmen, are all killed. I despatch this in haste by a special courier."[①] This letter arrived in Shanghai on June 27, Hong Kong on July 4, and London on July 25. It was the earliest report of the Tianjin Incident received in Europe.

Unlike the investigation results and views of Zeng Guofan, foreign expatriates, especially some scholars, have a deeper introspection in the face of such a tragedy. When analyzing the causes of the event, they mentioned several factors. Firstly, during the Second Opium War, Tianjin was occupied by the British and French allied forces for more than two years. During this time, the behavior of the French army and officials was atrocious, leaving "seeds of hatred" here. Secondly, the location of the burnt "Cathedral Notre Dames des Victories" was previously the imperial palace and sacred temples, so Chinese people naturally felt "deeply resentful" about it. Thirdly, the nuns of the Sisters of Mercy had a charitable tradition of adopting orphans or abandoned children in the city, but since no Chinese people entrusted children to them for care, the nuns awarded bonuses to anyone who brought children to the orphanage. The negative effect of these bonuses was that they "rewarded" the occurrence of child abduction behavior. Fourthly, since Chinese people often entrusted dying children to priests or nuns, the latter baptized them to ensure their entry into heaven. However, these children often died shortly after baptism, and the church hastily buried them, leaving a terrifying impression on the Chinese—kidnapping, mysterious baptismal rituals, and the removal of eyes and hearts. All of these factors plunged the

---

① Hosea Ballou Morse. *The International Relations of the Chinese Empire* (vol.2), translated by Zhang Huiwen, et al. Shanghai Bookstore Publishing House, 2006, p.252.

望海楼教堂。1897 年，望海楼天主堂在空置了 20 多年后重建，1900 年又在庚子之乱中第二次被烧毁。1903 年用庚子赔款第二次重建

Wanghailou Church (Notre Dame des Victoires). In 1897, the Cathedral was reconstructed after being vacant for more than 20 years. In 1900, it was burned down for the second time during the Boxer Rebellion. In 1903, it was rebuilt again with the Boxer Indemnity

人陷于一种对教会恐惧和仇恨的疯狂状态中。[1]

这种谣言不仅传遍底层民众，那些上层社会的士绅们也相信了。在屠杀事件发生前的几个星期中，修女们无论走到什么地方，人们都纷纷避开她们。使事态恶化的是，6 月初，有三四十名儿童死于流行病，成群的中国人天天闯入教堂小墓地，强行从坟墓中掘出病死孩童的尸体。在接下来的审讯中，谣传代替了证据，舆论把持了权力，各项指控都被宣称证实。当崇厚与法国领事丰大业进行会商时，府衙外面的双方民众开始发生互殴，会谈破裂。于是，"半个世纪的种族憎恶，十年来国家间的怨恨，反基督教情绪的滋长，一部分基于宗教偏见，一部分基于猜疑，一部分基于轻信，所有这一切聚

---

① （美）马士著，张汇文等译，《中华帝国对外关系史》（第二卷），上海书店出版社，2006 年，第 255—256 页。

people of Tianjin into a frenzy of fear and hatred towards the church.[1]

This kind of rumor not only spread among the lower classes, but also believed by the upper-class gentry. In the weeks leading up to the incident, wherever the nuns went, people avoided them. What exacerbated the situation was that in early June, thirty or forty children died of an epidemic. Groups of Chinese people invaded the church cemetery every day, forcibly digging out the bodies of the deceased children from the graves. During the subsequent interrogations, rumors replaced evidence, public opinion controlled power, and all accusations were declared confirmed. When Chonghou met with the French Consul, Henri Victor Fontanier, outside the government office for consultation, the two sides of the populace began to fight each other, causing the negotiations to collapse. Thus, "A half-century of racial antipathy; a decade of national hatred; the gathering growth of anti-Christian feeling, based partly on religious bigotry, partly on superstition, partly on credulity; all these were brought to a common focus, and the growing disorder culminated in three hours of murder, arson and plunder," as described by foreign scholars.[2]

The anger of the people and the fire at the church should have been extinguished by a heavy rainstorm later that evening and did not spread to the concessions and other foreign settlements. However, to appease the frightened expatriates, the British Consul in Tianjin, W. H. Lay, organized a "volunteer corps" for self-defense. Foreigners in China, mainly merchants but also including missionaries and pastors, were generally shocked and called for retaliation. At the same time, those who understood the truth and could objectively assess the situation, such as John A. T. Meadows, the then American Consul in Tianjin and chairman of the Municipal Council board, in his report on the Tianjin Incident for the *North China Daily News*, criticized the nuns for "bringing it upon themselves."[3] Some also pointed out that the main character involved, Henri Victor Fontanier, was "impetuous" and "contrary," and that the incident's occurrence and escalation were "overexcited by the presence of a danger which he had neither foreseen nor tried to avert."[4] However, in the atmosphere of the time, such objective comments not only failed to reassure the terrified foreign expatriates but also aroused

---

① Hosea Ballou Morse. *The International Relations of the Chinese Empire* (vol.2), translated by Zhang Huiwen, et al. Shanghai Bookstore Publishing House, 2006, pp.255-256.

② Hosea Ballou Morse. *The International Relations of the Chinese Empire* (vol.2), translated by Zhang Huiwen, et al. Shanghai Bookstore Publishing House, 2006, pp.260-261.

③ O. D. Rasmussen. *Tientsin: An Illustrated Outline History*, translated by Xu Yifan, et al. Tianjin People's Publishing House, 2008, p.47.

④ Hosea Ballou Morse. *The International Relations of the Chinese Empire* (vol.2), translated by Zhang Huiwen, et al. Shanghai Bookstore Publishing House, 2006, p.265.

合成一个共同的焦点，不断加剧的骚动最终酿成三个小时的杀人、放火和抢劫"，外国学者如是说。①

民众的怒火和教堂的大火应当是被当天傍晚的一场倾盆大雨浇灭的，并没有延烧到租界和其他外国侨民生活区域。但是为了安抚惶恐不安的侨民，英国驻津领事李蔚海（W. H. Lay）组织了"义勇队"准备自卫。在华的外国人，主要是商人，也包括传教士和牧师，普遍感到震惊，呼吁报复。与此同时，了解事实真相并能客观看待的人，比如时任美国驻津领事和租界工部局董事长的密妥士（John A. T. Meadows），在为《字林西报》撰写的关于此次屠杀的报道中，指责修女们是"咎由自取"②。还有人指出，事变主要当事人丰大业的性格"急躁""乖戾"，事件的发生发展"由于他既未预见到又未企图去扭转的一种危险的出现，而更加激化"③。不过，在当时的气氛下，这种客观的言论不但安抚不了被吓破胆的外国侨民，反而引起了强烈的反感，密妥士"由于显著的缺乏同情心而被迫辞职"。④

当然，在华外国人对清政府官员的批评是更严厉的。他们指责清廷上层保守派官员对相对开明官员的批评和掣肘；他们更加谴责天津的地方官员听信谣言，断定修女们有罪，放任此次事变的发生，酿成悲剧，所以要求惩办包括崇厚在内的当地官员。驻北京的外国公使们认为，天津教案虽然是针对法国人发生的，但几乎引起了所有在华外国人的不满和恐惧，此次事件的爆发"使所有的外国利益和所有的外国人生命都陷于危险的境地"。他们在得到来自天津的确实消息后，立即向总理衙门发出一项集体照会，断言"事件证明了在华的外国人并不是到处受到地方当局充分保护的"，要求中国

---

① （美）马士著，张汇文等译，《中华帝国对外关系史》（第二卷），上海书店出版社，2006年，第260—261页。

② （英）雷穆森著，许逸凡等译，《天津租界史（插图本）》，天津人民出版社，2009年，第47页。

③ （美）马士著，张汇文等译，《中华帝国对外关系史》（第二卷），上海书店出版社，2006年，第265页。

④ （英）雷穆森著，许逸凡等译，《天津租界史（插图本）》，天津人民出版社，2009年，第47页。

strong resentment, leading Meadows to resign "due to a conspicuous lack of sympathy."①

Of course, the criticism of Qing government officials by foreigners in China was even harsher. They accused the conservative officials in the Qing court of criticizing and obstructing relatively enlightened officials. They further condemned the local officials in Tianjin for believing rumors, concluding that the nuns were guilty, allowing the incident to occur, and causing the tragedy. Therefore, they demanded punishment for local officials, including Chonghou. Foreign ministers stationed in Beijing believed that although the Tianjin Incident targeted the French, it had almost aroused dissatisfaction and fear among all foreigners in China. The outbreak of this incident "placed all foreign interests and all foreign lives in a dangerous situation." Upon receiving confirmed information from Tianjin, they immediately issued a collective note to the Office for the General Management of Affairs Concerning the Various Countries, asserting that "events prove that foreigners are not everywhere sufficiently protected by the local authorities in China." They demanded that the Chinese government must punish those responsible and ensure the safety of foreign citizens in China.②

A few hours before the Missionary Case, William Hyde Lay, the British consul in Tianjin who sensed the impending danger, sent a telegram to the British Legation in Beijing, requesting the dispatch of warships to Tianjin to intimidate the Chinese. Several foreign gunboats arrived at the mouth of the Hai River near Tianjin eight days later, threatening the Qing government to thoroughly investigate the matter and punish the criminals. Lay also requested, "Do not dispatch French warships until a large number of troops are ready." He feared that "a French gunboat with a few crew members" would become "the fuse that sets the whole city on fire." Once the French attacked, the British and the British Concession would also be at risk, "and the attack would inevitably fail." He emphasized repeatedly that if there were retaliation, "sufficient forces must be assembled at certain locations."③

However, because investigations after the incident showed that the

---

① O. D. Rasmussen. *Tientsin: An Illustrated Outline History*, translated by Xu Yifan, et al. Tianjin People's Publishing House, 2008, p.47.

② Hosea Ballou Morse. *The International Relations of the Chinese Empire* (vol.2), translated by Zhang Huiwen, et al. Shanghai Bookstore Publishing House, 2006, p.267.

③ Annex 17. Letter from Acting Consul William Hyde Lay to Sir. Thomas Wade (Tianjin, June 25, 1870). The First Historical Archives of China and the History Department of Fujian Normal University (eds.). *Selected Translation of British Parliament Documents: The Missionary Case in Late Qing, Sixth Volume*. Zhonghua Book Company, 2006, pp.361-362.

政府必须惩治他们的罪行并保证在华外国公民的安全。①

教案发生前的几个小时，预感到危险临近的英国驻津领事李蔚海向英国驻北京公使馆发出电文，要求派遣兵舰来津威吓中国人。几艘外国炮艇于 8 天后驶抵天津大沽口外，威胁清政府彻查此事并惩办罪犯。李蔚海还要求，"在大量兵力未准备妥当之前，切不要调派法国舰只来"。他唯恐"一艘法国炮舰带着少数几个兵员"将成为"引起全城皆兵的导火线"，一旦法国人进行攻击，英国人和英租界也将受到连带危险，"而且攻击也必然遭到失败"。他再三强调，倘若报复，"则必须在某些地点集结足够的兵力"。②

不过，因为教案发生后的调查显示，当时天津人的怒火只是针对法国人，所以英国和美国为首的西方国家并不打算就此与中国开战。英国公使威妥玛（Thomas Francis Wade）在写给英国外交大臣克拉伦登伯爵（4th Earl of Clarendon）的报告中指出，"看问题要看两面"。他引用了教案发生前一位法国天主教"权威人士"和教案发生后的两位不同国籍的天主教徒的说法——"仁慈堂的育婴堂大有可能成为整个教会团体遭殃惹祸的根源"和"广州慈善会的育婴堂一年内收纳了 700 名婴儿，全部都死光了"——以此说明法国人并不是清白无辜的。他还指出，中国人无论是否受过教育，都相信拐卖人口的贩子能用药品麻醉受害人，且相信人类器官可以入药；此外，中国人还深信，"罪孽深重者必遭天诛地灭的报应，如干旱，洪水，瘟疫，战争和地震等"；教案发生后就大雨倾盆使中国人确信"天神因已达到降罪于法国人的目的，而感到高兴"。他还认为，没有证据证明教案的发生是天津地方官员所煽动和准许的，反倒是法国领事丰大业的"麻木不仁"使他没有察觉到教案之前"最少三四个星期"在天津人民心中激荡的愤怒情绪，没有及时采取适当行动避免激化矛盾。当然，作为一名外交官，威妥玛认为，根本的解决办

被烧毁的望海楼教堂
The burnt-down Wanghailou Church

被烧毁的仁慈堂
The burnt-down Church of Sisters of Mercy

---

① （美）马士著，张汇文等译，《中华帝国对外关系史》（第二卷），上海书店出版社，2006 年，第 267 页。

② "附件 17 李蔚海代理领事致威妥玛先生文"（天津，1870 年 6 月 25 日）。中国第一历史档案馆、福建师范大学历史系编，《清末教案·第六册，英国议会文件选译》，中华书局，2006 年，第 361—362 页。

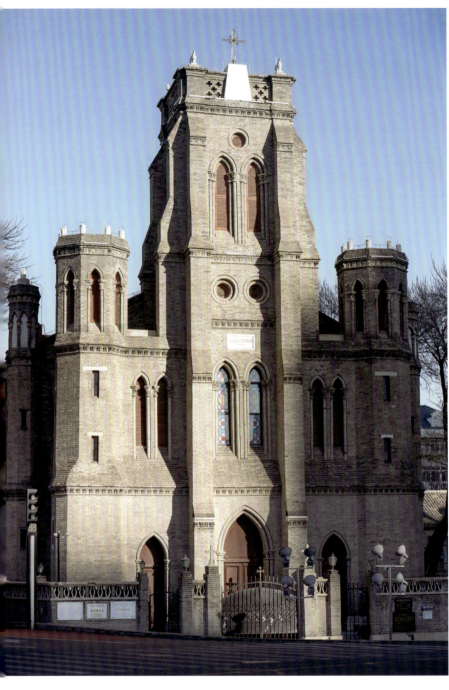

望海楼教堂今景。刘悦摄于 2024 年
Wanghailou Church today. Taken by Liu Yue in 2024

anger of the people of Tianjin at the time was only directed towards the French, Western countries led by Britain and the United States did not intend to go to war with China over this. Thomas Francis Wade, the British envoy, pointed out in his report to the British Foreign Minister, the 4th Earl of Clarendon, that "one must consider both sides of the issue." He cited the views of a French Catholic "authority" before the incident and two different nationalities of Catholics after the incident—"the Orphanage of the Sisters of Mercy is likely to become the source of disaster for the entire church group" and "the Orphanage of the Guangzhou Charity Association took in 700 babies in a year, all of whom died"—to illustrate that the French were not blameless. He also pointed out that regardless of whether they were educated or not, Chinese people believed that traffickers who kidnapped people could use drugs to anesthetize victims and believed that human organs could be used as medicine; furthermore, Chinese people deeply believed that "those who commit serious sins will receive divine punishment, such as droughts, floods, epidemics, wars, and earthquakes"; after the incident, heavy rain made the Chinese believe "the heavens had already achieved their purpose of punishing the French, and they felt happy." He also believed that there was no evidence to prove that the incident was incited and permitted by local officials in Tianjin, but it was the "indifference" of the French Consul, Fontanier, that made him unaware of the anger brewing among the people of Tianjin for "at least three or four weeks" before the incident and fail to take timely action to prevent the escalation of contradictions. Of course, as a diplomat, Wade believed that the fundamental solution lay in the Qing government's recognition of the equal rights of foreigners in China, inspiring the people, and eliminating the psychological barriers of dislike and distrust towards foreigners by both the people and the authorities.[1]

In the end, under pressure from the great powers, around 20 Chinese were beheaded, over 25 were sentenced to penal servitude, the church was compensated with 210,000 taels of silver, and a total of 460,000 taels of silver were paid in compensation to the victims (not everyone received the same amount of compensation). In the imperial decree of July 23rd, it was stated, based on the joint investigation results of Chonghou and the Viceroy of Zhili, Zeng Guofan, that all accusations of kidnapping and mutilation against the Sisters of Mercy were completely refuted, declaring

---

[1] Annex 35. Letter from Sir. Thomas Wade to Count Clarendon (Excerpt) (Beijing, July 16, 1870). The First Historical Archives of China and the History Department of Fujian Normal University (eds.). *Selected Translation of British Parliament Documents: The Missionary Case in Late Qing, Sixth Volume*. Zhonghua Book Company, 2006, pp.415-420.

法在于，清政府能够承认外国人在中国的平等权利，启发民智，消除人民和当局不喜欢、不信任洋人的心理。①

最终，迫于列强的压力，20 名左右的中国罪犯被斩首，超过 25 人被充军，赔偿教会损失 21 万两，遇害者的赔款数共计 46 万两（不是每个人都获得同样多的赔款）。7 月 23 日的皇帝谕旨中指出，根据崇厚和直隶总督曾国藩的联合调查结果，完全洗刷了对仁慈堂拐骗和剜目剖心的指控，声明天津民众是受了其他各地仇教揭帖的误导。之后遇难者遗体被葬于天津，法国和英国代办、法国和英国海军司令、崇厚以及新任道台、知府和知县等出席了葬礼仪式。被免于处罚的崇厚带着道歉的照会前往法国，但是由于法国正与德国交战（普法战争），找不到一个可以呈递照会的负责官员。最后梯也尔（Adolphe Thiers）总统接见了他。

用今天的文化交流视角来看，天津教案无疑是晚清中西文化交流融合过程中出现的一次冲突。基督教作为一种外来文化，与中国本土的思想、信仰、风俗习惯互不相容。传教士把深入群众的佛教和道教说成邪教，引起民众反感；教堂散布在城乡各处，干涉当地人迎神祭祖仪节，经常与民间发生摩擦。民众的反抗亦得到部分士绅的支持，初期不少的冲突便是直接由地方官绅所发动。作为儒家代表的士绅阶层对于异质文化大多持排斥态度，他们固守传统文化反对基督信仰。他们以孔庙、书院等作为集结地，支持民众的反教仇教行为，甚至挑动教徒与非教徒的纠纷，引起两者争斗。再加上少数奉教者依仗教会势力，肆意横行乡里，更激起群众对传教士的仇恨。这种仇恨不会仅因为一次教案的爆发和迅速处置得到化解，反而成为下一场动乱的前奏。

义和团运动的主战场

义和团运动又称庚子事变、庚子之乱，是 19 世纪末中国发生的

---

① "35. 威妥玛先生致克拉伦登伯爵文（摘录）"（北京，1870 年 7 月 16 日）。中国第一历史档案馆、福建师范大学历史系编，《清末教案·第六册，英国议会文件选译》，中华书局，2006 年，第 415—420 页。

that the people of Tianjin were misled by anti-Christian posters from other places. Subsequently, the bodies of the victims were buried in Tianjin, and the funeral ceremony was attended by acting consuls of France and Britain, commanders of the French and British navies, Chonghou, as well as the newly appointed Taotai, prefect, and county magistrate. Chonghou, who was spared from punishment, carried the letter of apology to France, but due to France's ongoing war with Germany (the Franco-Prussian War), he could not find a responsible official to present the letter. Eventually, President Adolphe Thiers received him.

From the perspective of today's cultural exchange, the Tianjin Incident was undoubtedly a conflict that arose during the integration of Chinese and Western cultures in late Qing Dynasty. Christianity, as a foreign culture, was incompatible with the indigenous thoughts, beliefs, and customs of China. Missionaries labeled deeply ingrained Buddhism and Taoism among the masses as cults, causing resentment among the people. Churches were spread throughout urban and rural areas, interfering with local customs of worshiping gods and ancestors, often resulting in friction with the local populace. The resistance of the people also received support from some gentry, with many conflicts initially instigated by local officials and gentry. Representing the Confucianist class, the gentry mostly held a stance of rejection towards heterogeneous cultures, staunchly upholding traditional culture and opposing Christian beliefs. They used Confucian temples and academies as rallying points, supporting the anti-Christian actions of the people, and even instigating disputes between believers and non-believers, leading to conflicts between the two. Moreover, with a few followers of the church exploiting the power of the church to act wantonly in the countryside, it further fueled the hatred of the masses towards missionaries. This hatred would not be resolved simply by the outbreak and swift handling of a single incident, but rather serve as a prelude to the next upheaval.

The Main Battleground of the Boxer Rebellion

The Boxer Rebellion, also known as the National Disturbances of the Year Gengzi, was a peasant movement in late 19th-century China with the slogan "Support the Qing, Exterminate the Foreign." It was a significant chapter in the history of the late Qing Dynasty. In the painful process of both accepting and rejecting Western culture and constructing modern self-identity in 20th-century China, the Boxer Rebellion played a unique and symbolic role. Tianjin was the main battleground of the Boxer Rebellion.

一场以"扶清灭洋"为口号的农民运动，是清朝末年历史画卷中的重要篇章。在 20 世纪中国人既接受又排斥西方文化、构建现代自我认同的痛苦历程中，义和团运动扮演了独一无二的具有象征意义的角色。而天津正是义和团运动的主战场。

义和团的排外与传教士的殖民

义和团运动是之前天津教案以及其他教案的延续，是之前埋下的各种隐患的集中爆发。"它表现了被侵略者对于侵略者郁积已久的愤怒；同时又包含着一种文化对另一种文化的抵抗，包含着旧式小农和手工业者因自然经济分解而蒙受的痛苦；并与百日维新失败后的政局变动牵连相结。"①

义和团又称义和拳，源自山东、直隶一带民间练拳习武的团体组织，有的具有民间宗教色彩，还有的则是打着"反清复明"旗号的秘密结社组织。义和团的团民，多是因 19 世纪 90 年代初以来持续不断的自然灾害而变得赤贫的农村青壮年。义和团运动的中心是华北平原，那里土地平坦肥沃、人口稠密，是中国重要的农业区之一。但是，清朝末年朝政腐败，官府无心也无力管理农田水利，广大的平原没有任何人工灌溉系统，农民完全靠天吃饭。而大陆性气候使得那里天气变幻莫测，不仅有严寒冬季所造成的大段农闲期，而且经常遭受水旱灾害，土地盐碱化严重。在这片平原上，除了北京、天津以及大运河沿岸的若干城镇之外，少有城镇，商业化程度很低，农民普遍贫穷，经济上几乎完全是低水平的自给自足。鸦片战争之后，西方的工业制成品随着坚船利炮而深入内陆，一步步摧毁了几千年以来的自然经济。"洋布、洋纱、洋花边、洋袜、洋巾入中国而女红失业"，"洋铁、洋针、洋钉入中国而业冶者多无事投闲"。②轮船火车的引进不仅帮助工业品迅速抢占了内陆市场，亦且夺走了船夫、纤夫、脚夫、水手、驿站店员的饭碗。正处于萌芽期的民族工业尚无力吸纳更多来

---

① 陈旭麓，《近代中国社会的新陈代谢》，上海人民出版社，1992 年，第 183 页。

② 夏东元编，《郑观应集》，上海人民出版社，1982 年，第 715 页。

The Exclusivism of the Boxers and the Colonialism of the Missionaries

The Boxer Rebellion was a culmination of various latent issues that had been brewing since the Tianjin Incident and other similar incidents. "It represented the long-suppressed anger of the invaded against the invaders; at the same time, it embodied a cultural resistance to another culture, encompassing the suffering of old-style peasants and artisans due to the breakdown of the natural economy; and it was intertwined with the political changes following the failure of the Hundred Days' Reform."[1]

The Boxer Movement, also known as the Righteous and Harmonious Fists, originated from grassroots martial arts groups in the Shandong and Zhili provinces. Some had folk religious elements, while others were secret societies operating under the banner of "Overthrow the Qing, Restore the Ming." The adherents of the Boxer Movement were mostly young rural adults who had become impoverished due to continuous natural disasters since the early 1890s. The movement's epicenter was the North China Plain, a region characterized by flat, fertile land and dense population, making it one of China's important agricultural areas. However, during the late Qing Dynasty, government corruption and neglect led to ineffective management of farmland irrigation. The vast plains lacked any artificial irrigation systems, and farmers relied entirely on unpredictable weather conditions for agriculture. The region experienced prolonged periods of agricultural downtime during severe winters and frequent water shortages and droughts, leading to serious salinization of the land. Apart from several towns such as Beijing, Tianjin, and some along the Grand Canal, there were few urban centers, and commercialization was minimal. The majority of the population lived in poverty, relying almost entirely on subsistence farming. After the Opium Wars, Western industrial goods penetrated the inland regions, gradually destroying the natural economy that had existed for thousands of years. "Foreign cloth, yarn, lace, socks, and towels entered China, leading to unemployment in the textile industry." "Foreign iron, needles, and nails entered China, causing many blacksmiths to lose their livelihoods."[2] The introduction of steamships and railways not only allowed industrial products to quickly dominate the inland market but also took away the livelihoods

---

① Chen Xulu. *The Metabolism of Modern Chinese Society*. Shanghai People's Publishing House, 1992, p.183.

② Xia Dongyuan (ed.). *The Collected Works of Zheng Guanying*. Shanghai People's Publishing House, 1982, p.715.

在国外出版的一幅国内少见的义和团年轻首领照片。头巾上的"佛"字表明，在那个时代，无论在东方还是西方，宗教的力量都是强大的。鉴于义和团反对洋人洋物，此照片应为义和团少年被俘后由外国人所拍

A rare photograph of a young Boxer leader, published abroad and seldom seen in China. The character "Fo" (Buddha) on his headscarf indicates that, during that era, the influence of religion was strong both in the East and the West. Given the Boxers' opposition to foreigners and foreign goods, this photograph was likely taken by foreigners after the young Boxer was captured

自农村的剩余劳动力。经济转轨的时代尘埃落在破产而生计断绝的农民身上，骤然变成他们无法承受的大山。他们无法理解工业文明代替农耕文明的必然性，只将生路的断绝归咎于身边可见的洋人洋货。于是，他们仇视一切外来之物，进而加入身边原有的义和团组织。本来只是"反清复明"、练拳强身、保卫乡里的义和团，至此演变为"最恶洋货，如洋灯、洋瓷盆，见即怒不可遏，必毁而后快"，甚至遇到路人身上有洋物，"皆毁物杀人"。^① 由此可见，这种仇恨所导致的排外，是小农生产者对机器文明的抵制，是底层民众在新旧时代转折时期的迷惘和盲目的反抗。

义和团排斥的不仅是象征西方工业文明的洋货洋物，还有作为外来文化的基督教。近代，天主教和新教传教士来到中国，目的就是用基督教文化征服和取代中国文化。但是在有着悠久文化积淀的中国社会，这几乎是一项不可能完成的任务。教会和传教士遭到中国人的不断抵制，甚至受到人身威胁。因此，传教士不得不更多依靠国家的力量以获得支持和保护，他们不可避免地与各自的国家利益联系在一起，成为一种政治化的力量，并受到殖民主义和强权政治理念的浸染，充当了征服殖民地的先锋。此外，在18世纪末19世纪初的欧洲，民族主义和自由主义的思想大行其道，对本民族文化的自豪感和优越感导致种族主义的倾向和"欧洲中心论"的确立。特别是19世纪中叶达尔文发表了著名的"物竞天择，适者生存"的进化论思想后，"生物进化论"很快被借用来解释人类社会的基本构成及行为准则：社会发展的规律同生物进化的规律一样，也是优胜

of boatmen, porters, carriers, sailors, and innkeepers. The nascent national industry was unable to absorb surplus labor from the countryside. The transition of the economy fell heavily on bankrupt farmers, leading to their livelihoods being cut off abruptly, which they found unbearable. They could not understand the inevitability of industrial civilization replacing agrarian civilization; instead, they blamed visible foreigners and foreign goods for cutting off their means of survival. Consequently, they harbored animosity towards all foreign items and joined existing Boxer organizations in their vicinity. What originally started as groups opposing the Qing Dynasty and practicing martial arts for self-defense and local protection evolved into a violent hatred for foreign goods, such as foreign lamps and porcelain basins, which upon sight would provoke uncontrollable anger and lead to destruction. They even resorted to destroying property and killing individuals found with foreign items.^① This hatred-driven xenophobia represented the resistance of small-scale agricultural producers against industrial civilization and the bewildered and blind resistance of the lower classes during the transition from the old to the new era.

The Boxers not only rejected foreign goods and products symbolizing Western industrial civilization but also Christianity as a foreign culture. In modern times, Catholic and Protestant missionaries came to China with the aim of using Christian culture to conquer and replace Chinese culture. However, in a society with a long cultural heritage like China, this was almost an impossible task. The Church and missionaries faced continuous resistance from the Chinese people, and even threats to their lives. Consequently, missionaries had to rely more on the power of their respective countries to obtain support and protection. They inevitably became associated with national interests, becoming a politicized force and succumbing to the influence of colonialism and hegemonic political ideas, acting as vanguards of colonial conquest. Additionally, in late 18th and early 19th century Europe, nationalist and liberal ideas flourished, leading to a sense of pride and superiority in one's own culture and the establishment of racist tendencies and the "Eurocentric" worldview. Especially after Darwin published his famous theory of evolution—"survival of the fittest"—in the mid-19th century, social Darwinism was quickly borrowed to explain the basic composition and behavioral norms of human society: the law of social development, like biological evolution, is also one of survival of the fittest. During the same period, the Industrial Revolution greatly developed the productivity and

---

① 中国史学会主编，中国近代史资料丛刊《义和团》，上海人民出版社，1957年，第一卷第347页，第二卷第146页。

---

① Association of Chinese Historians (ed.). Chinese Modern Historical Data Series *Boxer Rebellion*. Shanghai People's Publishing House, 1957, Vol.1, p.347; Vol.2, p.146.

义和团小孩。鉴于义和团反对洋人洋物，此照片应为义和团小孩被俘后由外国人所拍

A Boxer child. Given the Boxers' opposition to foreigners and foreign goods, this photograph was likely taken by foreigners after the child was captured

劣汰，适者生存。同一时期，工业革命使西欧的生产力和科学得到了极大发展，这为欧洲优越的理念提供了有力的支持。欧洲的进步是如此明显，以致不论"东方诸民族"的文明在古代如何辉煌，他们在近代都必须被认定为是"野蛮人，或儿童"①。有了国家力量的支持，教会和传教士的态度变得越来越强横，使传统文化背景下的中国民众对基督教的厌恶日益增长。由上可知，义和团反洋教的斗争毫无疑问具有反侵略的性质，并通过捍卫传统文化和排外主义而表现出来。

义和团运动是在民族矛盾日益激化下的另一种选择，是对洋务运动、戊戌变法的"一种历史回流"②。两次鸦片战争失败以后，民族矛盾凸显，洋务派官员提出"师夷长技以制夷"的应对策略。在这一策略中，反抗西方列强侵略和学习西方先进科学技术，两者是统一的。甲午战争失败后，逐渐向资产阶级转化的士大夫及知识分子群体发起的维新变法，也在不同程度上反映了这种统一。但在主动学习西方工业文明的过程中，不仅顽固派认为搞洋务和变法是"以夷变夏"，小农阶级也因利益受损而痛恨洋人、洋教，并旁及洋务派、改良派，一概视之为异类。洋务运动和戊戌维新的失败，使上至最高统治阶层的顽固派、下至义和团民众都认为，只有恢复到过去的自然经济、小农社会和陈腐的旧制度，

science of Western Europe, providing strong support for the idea of European superiority. The progress of Europe was so obvious that regardless of how brilliant the civilizations of the "Eastern nations" were in ancient times, they had to be considered as "barbarians or children"[1] in modern times. With the support of state power, the attitudes of the Church and missionaries became increasingly domineering, leading to growing resentment among the Chinese people against Christianity within their traditional cultural context. It is evident that the Boxer Rebellion's anti-Christian struggle undoubtedly had an anti-aggression nature and was manifested through the defense of traditional culture and xenophobia.

The Boxer Rebellion was another choice made under the escalating ethnic conflicts, representing a "historical regression" in response to the Westernization Movement and the Hundred Days' Reform.[2] After the failures of the two Opium Wars, ethnic conflicts became more pronounced, and officials of the Westernization Movement proposed the strategy of "learning western science and technology to counter imperialist encroachment." In this strategy, resistance against Western aggression and the learning of advanced Western science and technology were seen as unified. The Hundred Days' Reform initiated by the gentry and intellectuals gradually transitioning to the bourgeoisie after the defeat of the First Sino-Japanese War also reflected this unity to varying degrees. However, during the process of actively learning from Western industrial civilization, not only did the conservatives believe that engaging in the Westernization Movement and reforms was "sinicization through barbarianization," but the peasant class also harbored hatred towards foreigners and Christianity due to their losses of interests, targeting both the Westernization Movement and reformists as well, viewing them all as outsiders. The failures of the Westernization Movement and the Hundred Days' Reform led both the conservative elements at the highest ruling levels and the Boxers to believe that the fundamental solution lay only in restoring the past natural economy, peasant society, and obsolete old systems, and expelling all foreigners and Christianity from China. At that time, both reformists and revolutionaries negated the Boxers, pointing out that "if we follow their intentions, they probably think that the so-called foreigners are nothing more than six or seven diplomats, dozens of merchants, and hundreds of missionaries... If we can unite and drive out the Europeans and

① （加）卜正民、格力高利·布鲁主编，古伟瀛等译，《中国与历史资本主义：汉学知识的系谱学》，新星出版社，2005年，第90页。

② 陈旭麓，《近代中国社会的新陈代谢》，上海人民出版社，1992年，第195页。

① Timothy Brook, Gregory Blue (eds.). *China and Historical Capitalism: Genealogies of Sinological Knowledge*, translated by Gu Weiying, et al. New Star Press, 2005, p.90.

② Chen Xulu. *The Metabolism of Modern Chinese Society*. Shanghai People's Publishing House, 1992, p.195.

并将一切洋人洋教赶出中国，才是根本解决之道。对此，当时的改良派和革命派都对义和团持否定态度，指出："揣若辈之意，殆谓所谓洋人者不过六七公使，数十商人，数百教士云耳。……苟其一鼓作气，聚而歼旃，使欧美诸人之足迹，永不复见于中国，而后可以复大一统之旧观，而后可以遂闭关独立之夙愿"，[①] 这显然是不现实的。

本来，处庙堂之高的以慈禧太后为首的守旧派与处江湖之远的义和团民众，是两个互相隔绝的阶级。但因戊戌变法而几乎丧失最高权力的慈禧意图废黜支持改革派的光绪皇帝，遭到八国公使的反对，由此痛恶洋人。这样一来，共同的敌人使清朝皇族与义和团走到一起。而义和团为了获得官方认可，将运动宗旨和口号更改为"扶清灭洋"。于是，得到清朝贵族支持的义和团，很快将其斗争活动一路向北延烧而去，矛头直指外国势力的中心——北京使馆区、天津的领事馆和租界。

义和团是一群"乌合之众"吗？

《马关条约》签订、1897 年德国传教士在山东被杀、法国要求割让广州湾等事件后，义和团的风暴慢慢开始聚集。在天津，1897 年望海楼教堂重建完工后，本已销声匿迹 28 年之久的拐骗儿童谣言又流传起来。1899 年春天开始，运河沿岸的天津西郊、南郊和北郊都有义和团团民在秘密练习神拳。1900 年 1 月 11 日，慈禧太后颁布上谕，承认义和团团民是"安分良民"，"习技艺以自卫身家"的举动是"守望相助"之义，义和团不是"邪教"，无须查拿。直隶总督裕禄完全遵照谕旨行事，之后义和团在直隶蔓延，1900 年 2 月发展到天津县城，当时已有不少团民在天津公开活动。

1900 年 5 月，华北平原大旱。无法耕作的农民眼见饥荒将至，将满腔怒火投向洋人和洋教。他们在揭帖中写道："天无雨、地焦旱，全是教堂止住天。"绝望的饥饿游民加入义和团，从四面八方涌入天津。义和团在天津城西吕祖堂内设总坛口，又在老爷庙、老母庙、

Americans permanently from China, then we can return to the old concept of reunification, and then we can fulfill the long-cherished dream of closing our country off and remaining independent."[①] This was clearly unrealistic.

Originally, the conservative faction led by Empress Dowager Cixi, who held the highest position in the imperial court, and the Boxers, who were far removed from official circles, were two mutually isolated classes. However, Empress Dowager Cixi, who almost lost the highest authority due to the Hundred Days' Reform, intended to depose Emperor Guangxu, who supported the reformists, but faced opposition from the Eight-Nation Alliance ministers, thus developing a strong hatred towards foreigners. As a result, the common enemy brought together the Qing imperial family and the Boxers. In order to gain official recognition, the Boxers changed their movement's purpose and slogan to "Support the Qing, exterminate the foreigners." Consequently, with the support of the Qing nobility, the Boxers quickly extended their campaign northward, directing their attacks towards the heart of foreign influence—the legation quarter in Beijing, the consulates in Tianjin, and the concessions.

Were the Boxers a "Rabble"?

After the signing of the *Treaty of Shimonoseki*, the killing of German missionaries in Shandong in 1897, and France's demand for the cession of Guangzhou Bay, the storm of the Boxers slowly began to gather. In Tianjin, after the completion of the reconstruction of the Wanghailou Church (also known as Notre Dame des Victoires) in 1897, rumors of child abduction, which had been silent for 28 years, resurfaced. In the spring of 1899, Boxer members secretly practiced martial arts in the western, southern, and northern suburbs along the canal in Tianjin. On January 11, 1900, Empress Dowager Cixi issued an edict acknowledging Boxer members as "law-abiding citizens" whose practice of martial arts for self-defense was an act of "neighborhood watchfulness." The Boxers were not considered a "cult" and did not need to be apprehended. Viceroy of Zhili Province, Yulu, fully complied with the edict, and thereafter, the Boxers spread in Zhili Province, reaching Tianjin County in February 1900, where many Boxer members were already openly active.

In May 1900, there was a severe drought in the North China Plain. Farmers, unable to cultivate their land, saw famine looming and directed

---

① 《论中国欲自立宜先求开民智之策》。中国史学会主编，中国近代史资料丛刊《义和团》（四），上海人民出版社，1957 年，第 211 页。

① *On the Strategy of Enlightening National Wisdom for China's Independence*. Association of Chinese Historians (ed.). Chinese Modern Historical Data Series *Boxer Rebellion* (4). Shanghai People's Publishing House, 1957, p.211.

玉皇庙等处设立分坛。据不完全统计，当时天津各处共设坛口三百余个，人数很快从不到万人发展到四万人左右，大街小巷都可以见到义和团团民的踪影。他们按八卦分支，设有乾、坤、震、巽、坎、离、艮、兑。以"乾"字团和"坎"字团为主，其中"乾"字团有两万余人，以曹福田、刘呈祥为首领；"坎"字团有一万四千人左右，以张德成为首领；"离"字团有一千余人；"震"字团人数几百，其他各分支加在一起有一千多人；"红灯照"坛口数个，人数有一二百人。曹福田、张德成和"红灯照"领袖"黄莲圣母"林黑儿等人成为天津义和团的中心人物。①

当时，不仅劳动群众踊跃加入义和团，就是统治阶级中的人物以及驻津的清军，如练军、水师营和武备学堂的学生，也有不少人加入义和团或参加其活动。6月14日，曹福田率领义和团数千人，从西门进入天津，直隶总督裕禄率领百官亲自出迎。据天津租界的外国侨民描绘："至于义和团运动的情况，天津城已经成为他们的中心，……我们或者其他人所看到的却是什么呢？——（1）海关道台向傲慢的无赖叩头；（2）扎着黄色、红色和蓝色腰带的人进入店铺，随意吃住；（3）士兵们怕得发抖，跪地叩头嘭嘭作响；（4）普遍的惶恐不安。我的一位中国朋友昨天看见一件奇怪的事情。在总督衙门附近，有两个扎着蓝腰带的十二三岁的小孩，大声喊叫：'你们谁想避免灾难，就上大街听大师兄讲话去吧！'接着就有两个扎红腰带戴红帽子的人宣布集会的地点和时间，最后还举行了乱七八糟的神秘仪式。我听说这样的事已经持续四五天了。"②外国侨民的叙述固然有其偏见，但也从侧面印证了当时天津义和团发展的状况，特别是官员和军队士兵对义和团的态度。

天津义和团的领袖较之其他地区义和团领袖有独特之处。他们走南闯北，阅历丰富，善于宣传和鼓动，其组织能力和领导水平比世代固守于村庄的农民要强许多。他们不仅在行动之前运用揭帖进行广泛的反洋人反洋教宣传，引导社会舆论；而且在行动当日，对

① 来新夏主编，《天津近代史》，南开大学出版社，1987年，第150—151页。

② （英）雷穆森著，许逸凡等译，《天津租界史（插图本）》，天津人民出版社，2009年，第114页。

their anger towards foreigners and foreign religions. In posters, they wrote, "No rain from the heavens, scorched earth, all because churches block the sky." Desperate hungry wanderers joined the Boxers, pouring into Tianjin from all directions. The Boxers established a central altar in the Lüzu Temple in the west outside of Tianjin city, and set up branch altars in places like Laoye Temple, Laomu Temple, and Jade Emperor Temple. According to incomplete statistics, there were over three hundred altars set up across Tianjin at that time, with the number of people quickly growing from less than ten thousand to around forty thousand. The presence of Boxer members could be seen everywhere in the streets and alleys. They were organized according to the eight trigrams, with branches such as Qian, Kun, Zhen, Xun, Kan, Li, Gen, and Dui. The Qian faction and Kan faction were the main ones, with over twenty thousand members in the Qian faction led by Cao Futian and Liu Chengxiang, and around fourteen thousand members in the Kan faction led by Zhang Decheng. The Li faction had over a thousand members, while the Zhen faction had several hundred, and the other branches had over a thousand members altogether. There were also several "Red Lantern" altar sites with about one to two hundred members. Cao Futian, Zhang Decheng, and leaders of the "Red Lantern" faction like "Holy Mother of the Yellow Lotus" Lin Hei'er became central figures of the Tianjin Boxers.①

At that time, not only did the laboring masses eagerly join the Boxers, but also figures from the ruling class and Qing troops stationed in Tianjin, such as the trainees of military camps, naval barracks, and the military academy, joined the Boxers or participated in their activities. On June 14th, Cao Futian led thousands of Boxers into Tianjin from the west gate, where Viceroy Yulu personally went out to greet them along with hundreds of officials. According to descriptions by foreign residents of the Tianjin concessions: "As for the situation with the Boxer rebellion, Tianjin has become their center... What did we or others see?—(1) Customs officials kowtowing to arrogant ruffians; (2) People wearing yellow, red, and blue sashes entering shops, eating and

明信片上的手中握枪的义和团团练。鉴于义和团反对洋人洋物，此照片应为义和团团民被俘后由外国人所拍

A Boxer militia member holding a gun on a postcard. Given the Boxers' opposition to foreigners and foreign goods, this photograph was likely taken by foreigners after the militia member was captured

① Lai Xinxia. *Modern History of Tianjin*. Nankai University Press, 1987, pp.150-151.

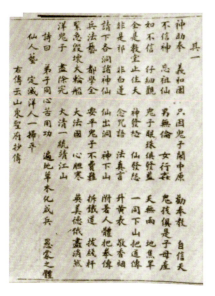

义和团揭帖
Boxer Proclamation

神助拳、义和团，只因鬼子闹中原。
劝奉教、自信天，不信神、忘祖仙。
男无伦、女行奸，鬼孩俱是子母产。
如不信、仔细观，鬼子眼珠俱发蓝。
天无雨、地焦旱，全是教堂止住天。
神发怒、仙发怒，一同下山把道传。
非是邪、非白莲，念咒语、法真言。
升黄表、敬香烟，请下各洞诸神仙。
仙出洞、神下山，附着人体把拳传。
兵法艺、都学全，要平鬼子不费难。
拆铁道、拔线杆，紧急毁坏火轮船。
大法国、心胆寒，英美德俄尽消然。
洋鬼子、尽除完，大清一统靖江山。
诗曰：
弟子同心苦用功，遍地草木化成兵；
愚蒙之体仙人艺，定灭洋人一扫平。

义和团团民进行了目标和组织明确、充满鼓动性的战前动员。义和团首领之一说："几十年来他们侵吞了我们的田地和窃取了金银财宝，把魔爪伸进胶州、旅顺口和威海卫。……现在轮到收拾这些住在天津的二毛子的时候了。我们今天内就要把到这儿来的外国军队消灭掉，不让它跟被包围在廊坊的洋鬼子会合。……要是你们坚如仙山磐石，勇如龙虎，那末你们就能克敌制胜，刀枪不入。要是你们象信天地那样相信你们的心，要是你们的心洁如山泉，要是你们信仰赤诚，那你们就是神圣的！不能伤害的，永生的。"他对慈禧太后和清政府摇摆不定的态度也有清醒的认知，并不抱幻想："皇上的官兵会跟我们一块儿打仗。皇上和西太后，还有我们的大首领端王爷在庇护我们。但要是清朝廷不再帮我们，不站在我们一边，那你们得明白，我们就推翻朝廷，拯救中华黎民，免遭洋鬼子蹂躏。"[①]话语中充满了强烈的爱国主义精神和斗争到底的坚定决心。

---

① （俄）德米特里·扬契维茨基著，许崇信等译，《八国联军目击记》，福建人民出版社，1983年，第83—84页。

lodging at will; (3) Soldiers trembling in fear, kneeling and bowing with loud thumps; (4) Widespread anxiety and unease. One of my Chinese friends saw something strange yesterday. Near the Governor's yamen, two twelve or thirteen-year-old children wearing blue sashes were shouting loudly: 'Whoever wants to avoid disaster, come to the streets to listen to Big Brother's speech!' Then two people wearing red sashes and red hats announced the location and time of the assembly, and finally, some chaotic and mysterious rituals were performed. I heard that such things had been going on for four or five days."[①] While the accounts of foreign residents may be biased, they also indirectly confirm the situation of the development of the Boxers in Tianjin at that time, especially the attitudes of officials and soldiers towards the Boxers.

The leaders of the Boxers in Tianjin have unique characteristics compared to leaders in other regions. They had traveled extensively, gained rich experiences, were skilled in propaganda and incitement, and their organizational ability and leadership level were much stronger than the farmers who have been entrenched in villages for generations. They not only used posters for extensive anti-foreign and anti-Christian propaganda before taking action, guiding public opinion, but also on the day of action, they provided clear targets and organization for the Boxer members, with pre-battle mobilization full of excitement. One of the Boxer leaders said: "For decades, they have encroached upon our land and plundered our gold and silver treasures, extending their claws into Jiaozhou, Lüshun Port, and Weihaiwei... Now it's time to deal with these 'Er Maozi' living in Tianjin. Today, we must eliminate the foreign troops that have come here, preventing them from joining the foreign devils surrounded in Langfang... If you are as firm as the mountains and rocks, brave as dragons and tigers, then you can defeat the enemy, impervious to swords and spears. If you believe in yourselves like you believe in the heavens and earth, if your hearts are as pure as mountain springs, if your faith is sincere, then you are sacred, invulnerable, and eternal!" He also had a clear understanding of the ambivalent attitude of Empress Dowager Cixi and the Qing government, harboring no illusions: "The Emperor's soldiers will fight with us. The Emperor, the Empress Dowager, and our great leader Prince Duan are protecting us. But if the Qing court no longer supports us, if it does not stand with us, then you must understand, we will overthrow the court, save the Chinese people from being ravaged by the

---

① O. D. Rasmussen. *Tientsin: An Illustrated Outline History*, translated by Xu Yifan, et al. Tianjin People's Publishing House, 2008, p.114.

一般认为，义和团的整个运动并无严密的组织或统一的领袖，而是一场自发的群众行动，行为矛盾且混乱。然而，当慈禧太后决定暂时利用义和团打击外国人后，清朝贵族及其幕僚就明目张胆地支持义和团的活动。在北京，认为义和团所谓"神功"皆为虚假的官员被撤换，在慈禧太后许可之下，大批拳民开始进入北京；义和团的"龙团"驻在端王载漪府邸，"虎团"驻在庄王府，"仙团"驻在大公主府邸；[①]顺天府尹还奏请清政府发给义和团口粮。慈禧太后调董福祥的武卫后军进城，董军中不少士兵参加了义和团，董福祥还与义和团首领李来中结拜为兄弟。因此，贵族官员及其幕僚以及军队将领必然为义和团的活动出谋划策，甚至可能掌握了部分领导权。从京津一带义和团与清军配合所进行的一系列军事行动可以看出，义和团是有一定的组织性纪律性的。但是由于后来战争失利，八国联军占领京津，坚持要求惩办祸首，清政府便将所有行动尽量归咎于义和团，加上在当时和其后一段时间内知识分子甚至革命党人对义和团的愚昧落后和盲目排外大加挞伐，"乌合之众"的帽子才被扣在义和团身上。

在战争中，交通通信往往是决定胜利的关键因素。在义和团与清军结成同盟之后，北京的义和团首先在 6 月 9 日推倒电线杆，切断了东交民巷外国使馆区的对外通信，同时拆毁京津之间的铁路。清军聂士成部和义和团在廊坊勇敢阻击了之前由天津派出的英国海军中将西摩尔（Edward Hobart Seymour）率领的八个国家的联军，这便是史上著名的"廊坊大捷"。随后义和团和清军合力将这支由 2157 名各国海军及海军陆战队人员组成的援军围困在杨村附近。最后用了整整一个星期的时间，西摩尔联军才撤回租界。6 月 17 日，联军攻占大沽炮台，得到消息的驻津清军开始炮轰租界，拆毁通往塘沽的铁路，并切断了电报线路。同时，为阻止八国联军进军北京，义和团于 6 月 18 日发起攻打老龙头车站（今天津站前身）的战斗，给驻守车站的沙俄侵略军以很大杀伤，并一度占领了车站。由此可见，义和团与清军在战争初期的配合较为成功，虽然拆毁铁路和电报线

---

① 《庚子诗鉴》，中国社会科学院近代史研究所《近代史资料》编辑组编，《义和团史料》（上），中国社会科学出版社，1982 年，第 125 页。

foreign devils."[①] His words are filled with a strong spirit of patriotism and a determined resolve to fight to the end.

It is generally believed that the entire Boxer rebellion lacked strict organization or unified leadership, and was instead a spontaneous mass action characterized by contradictory and chaotic behavior. However, when Empress Dowager Cixi decided to temporarily utilize the Boxers to strike against foreigners, Qing aristocrats and their aides openly supported the Boxers' activities. In Beijing, officials who considered the Boxers' so-called "divine feats" to be false were replaced, and with the permission of Empress Dowager Cixi, large numbers of Boxer adherents began to enter Beijing. The "Dragon Unit" of the Boxers was stationed at the residence of Prince Zaiyi, the "Tiger Unit" at the residence of Prince Zhuang, and the "Immortal Unit" at the residence of the Grand Princess.[②] The magistrate of Shuntian Prefecture even requested the Qing government to provide rations for the Boxers. Empress Dowager Cixi deployed Dong Fuxiang's Westernized Rear Division into the city, and many soldiers from Dong's army joined the Boxers. Dong Fuxiang even swore brotherhood with the Boxer leader Li Laizhong. Therefore, aristocratic officials and their aides, as well as military leaders, were undoubtedly plotting and possibly even exercising some leadership over the Boxers' activities. A series of military actions coordinated between the Boxers and Qing troops in the Beijing-Tianjin area indicates that the Boxers had a certain level of organizational discipline. However, due to subsequent military defeats, the occupation of Beijing and Tianjin by the Eight-Nation Alliance, and their insistence on punishing the perpetrators, the Qing government sought to blame all actions on the Boxers. Moreover, at the time and for some time afterward, intellectuals and even revolutionaries criticized the Boxers as ignorant, backward, and blindly xenophobic, leading to the label of "rabble" being applied to the Boxers.

In war, transportation and communication are often decisive factors in determining victory. After the Boxers formed an alliance with the Qing army, the Boxers in Beijing first toppled telegraph poles on June 9, cutting off external communication in the foreign legation quarter of Dongjiaominxiang, and simultaneously dismantled the railway between Beijing and Tianjin. The Qing army under General Nie Shicheng bravely resisted the eight-nation

---

① Dmitry Yanchevetsky. *Eyewitness Records of the Eight-Nation Alliance*, translated by Xu Chongxin, et al. Fujian People's Publishing House, 1983, pp.83-84.

② *Poetry about Disturbances of the Year Gengzi*. Editorial Section of *Historical Data*, the Institute of Modern History of the Chinese Academy of Social Sciences (ed.). *Historical Data of the Boxer Rebellion (Vol.1)*. China Social Sciences Press, 1982, p.125.

义和团团民。此照片应为团民被俘后被迫拍摄
Boxer militia members. This photograph was likely taken under coercion after the militia members were captured

运动后被清政府用站笼处死的义和团团民
Boxer militia members who were executed by the Qing government using standing cages after the movement

杆有迷信排外的成分，但是也不能排除其出于作战方面考虑的因素。

面对拥有近代火炮快枪的强大敌人，大部分普通团民所谓的"武器"，除了口中的咒语、臆想中的附体神灵、手中的火把之外，几乎一无所有。6月15日夜间，天津义和团和清军开始攻击教堂和租界。义和团焚毁了基督教堂、圣母得胜堂以及城里和城外的其他许多建筑。据租界里的外国侨民日记记录："6月16日，星期六，上午9点。昨夜，我们第一次经历了严重的惊恐。在半夜1点时，四处可见大火烧起，同时由9处增加到13处。距离我们最近的一处大火是马家口（Machiakou）的福音堂（London Mission Chapel），离租界只有一里地左右。……放哨的人看见，在皎洁的月色下，成群的大人和孩子从不同方向向我们走来；他们手中拿着火把、刨花和油，朝着租界涌来，似乎想烧掉一切可烧的东西。当距我们只有500码的时候，他们肆意地发出可怕的喊叫声。各国水手和士兵们立刻用来复枪射击，而且有两处是用机枪扫射。"真正对外国军队和租界造成危害的则是聂士成的军队。"6月18日，星期一，上午10点钟……各国的军队都被派出到租界四周的每个地点与敌人交火。……与俄军对阵的有两千名中国军队。"与清军并肩作战的义和团率先出战，"今天有一个穿着考究的义和团首领，独自一个人庄严地朝着俄国步兵

coalition led by British Rear Admiral Edward Hobart Seymour, who had been dispatched from Tianjin, in the Battle which became known as the famous Great Victory at Langfang in history. Subsequently, the Boxers and the Qing army besieged this support force, consisting of 2,157 personnel from various naval forces and marine contingents, near Yangcun Village. It took a whole week before the Seymour Expeditionary Force retreated to the concession area. On June 17, the coalition forces captured the Taku Forts. Upon receiving this news, the Qing troops stationed in Tianjin began bombarding the concession area, dismantling the railway leading to Tanggu, and cutting off telegraph lines. Meanwhile, to prevent the Eight-Nation Alliance from advancing towards Beijing, the Boxers launched an attack on the Old Dragon Head Railway Station (predecessor of Tianjin Station) on June 18, inflicting significant casualties on the Russian aggressors stationed at the station and briefly occupying it. This indicates that the coordination between the Boxers and the Qing army was relatively successful in the early stages of the war. Although the dismantling of railways and telegraph poles had elements of superstition and xenophobia, it cannot be ruled out that they were also considered from a strategic perspective.

Facing the formidable enemy armed with modern artillery and rifles, the majority of ordinary Boxer adherents had little in the way of conventional "weapons" besides their chants, imagined possessed spirits, and torches in hand. On the night of June 15, the Boxers in Tianjin, along with the Qing army, began attacking churches and the concession area. The Boxers set fire to Christian

义和团运动期间京汉铁路的比利时职工及其家属在天津合影。1900年5月29日,在保定的京汉铁路比利时、意大利工程师和他们的眷属接到警告,当天即匆忙乘船出发赶往天津。这是一支41人的队伍,包括33名男子、7名女子和1个小孩。保定府的官员一开始派了一队士兵护送他们,但是后来借故离开了。第二天早晨,他们遭到一群义和团的袭击。这一小队人且战且走,舍弃了船只,冒着风沙和烈日,带着极少的干粮,徒步走完了其余的路程,终于在6月4日下午4时到达天津。这一队人中,有9人"失踪",23人受伤,只有9人没有受到伤害。这件事极大地震撼了天津租界的外国侨民。照片下文字说明,他们是被友好的中国人在晚上偷偷救出来的

A group photo of Belgian employees of the Beijing-Hankou Railway and their families in Tianjin during the Boxer Uprising. On May 29, 1900, Belgian and Italian engineers and their families in Baoding received a warning and hastily set off for Tianjin by boat the same day. The group consisted of 41 people: 33 men, 7 women, and 1 child. Initially, Baoding officials assigned a unit of soldiers to escort them, but the soldiers later left under various pretexts. The next morning, the group was attacked by a band of Boxers. Forced to fight while retreating, they abandoned their boats and continued their journey on foot, braving sandstorms, scorching heat, and with only minimal food supplies. After days of hardship, they finally reached Tianjin at 4:00 PM on June 4. Of the 41 travelers, 9 went "missing," 23 were injured, and only 9 remained unharmed. This incident deeply shocked the foreign community in Tianjin's concessions. The caption under the photograph states that the survivors were secretly rescued at night by friendly Chinese

义和团运动中被清军炮火摧毁的法租界
The French Concession destroyed by Qing army artillery during the Boxer Rebellion

义和团运动中被清军炮火摧毁的租界
The concession destroyed by Qing army artillery during the Boxer Rebellion

阵地前面的浮桥走来。这无疑是他们的狂热的盲信使他有了这样英雄式的无畏。他挥舞着饰带，做着他的仪式。当然，在几秒钟内他就变成了一具死尸。"① 令人悲叹的是，在这场反洋教反侵略斗争中，"深沉的爱国主义情感是同植根于自然经济的保守意识连在一起的；抵御外侮的强烈愿望是同陈旧的天朝观念和华夷之见连在一起的。这种矛盾，显示了一场正义的反帝群众运动中落后的封建主义内容。"代表旧生产力的农民，"只能找到中世纪的社会理想，也只能找到中世纪的精神武器和物质武器"②。

义和团运动与北洋大学、庚子赔款

在洋务运动中，教育是一项重要内容。李鸿章希望培养出能够实现他富国强兵梦想的"学贯中西"的新型人才，以及可以在近代工业和科技领域中替代洋人洋匠的实用型人才。但限于"中学为体，西学为用"和"师夷长技以制夷"的教育思想，近代洋务学堂设立20余年后，皆收效不大，所培养的能够在洋务事业中真正发挥作用的学生寥寥无几。在甲午战争败于日本后，康有为等人"公车上书"，举国上下要求自强的呼声日高。在李鸿章幕府中多年从事洋务活动的盛宣怀以此为契机，上书清政府要求设立现代大学性质的北洋大学堂（或称北洋西学学堂）。盛宣怀在奏折中特别指出："自强之道以作育人才为本，求才之道以设立学堂为先"；"日本援照西法，广开学堂书院，不特陆军海军将弁取材于学堂，即外部出使诸员及制造开矿等工，亦皆取材于学堂"，委婉地指出甲午之战败在缺乏现代人才；且"学堂迟设一年，则人材迟出一年"，当务之急是建立现代大学，培养精通西学的综合型人才。③ 清政府终于认识到："自

① （英）雷穆森著，许逸凡等译，《天津租界史（插图本）》，天津人民出版社，2009年，第115、118-119页。

② 陈旭麓，《近代中国社会的新陈代谢》，上海人民出版社，1992年，第194页。

③ 中国第一历史档案馆、天津大学，《中国近代第一所大学——北洋大学（天津大学）历史档案珍藏图录》，天津大学出版社，2005年，第6页。

churches, including the Church of Our Lady of Victories, as well as many other buildings both inside and outside the city. According to diary entries from foreign residents in the concession area: "Saturday, June 16th, 9 a.m. We had our first serious alarm last night. At 1 a.m. fires were seen on all sides, varying from nine to thirteen at one time. The nearest to us was that of the great London Mission Chapel at Machiakou, about one li distant from the Settlements... Bodies of men and boys were seen by the pickets to be approaching us on many sides in the bright moonlight; they carried torches, shavings and oil, and as they came on towards the Settlements tried to fire everything they could indulging in hideous yelling when about 500 yards off. The sailors and soldiers of all nationalities were instantly in action with rifles and, in two places, machine guns." The real harm to foreign troops and the concession area was caused by Nie Shicheng's army. "Monday, 18th June, 10 a.m. ...All forces went out and engaged the enemy at all points of the compass... Two thousand Chinese are opposed to them." The Boxers, fighting alongside the Qing army, took the initiative, "Today a well-dressed Boxer leader came impressively down alone towards the bridge of boats in front of the Russian infantry. There could be no doubt that fanaticism lent him heroic courage. He waved his sash and went through his ceremony, but of course he was a corpse in a few seconds."① It is lamentable that in this struggle against foreign religions and aggression, "profound patriotic sentiments were intertwined with conservative notions rooted in the natural economy; the strong desire to resist aggression was intertwined with outdated celestial dynasty concepts and the distinction between China and the barbarians. This contradiction reveals the backward feudal content in a just anti-imperialist mass movement." Representing the old means of production, the farmers "could only find medieval social ideals and could only find medieval spiritual and material weapons"②.

The Boxer Rebellion, Peiyang University, and the Boxer Indemnity

In the Wesernization Movement, education was an important aspect. Li Hongzhang hoped to cultivate a new type of talent capable of realizing his dream of enriching the country and strengthening the military, one that was proficient in both Chinese and Western knowledge, as well as practical talents who could replace foreign experts in modern industry and technology.

① O. D. Rasmussen. *Tientsin: An Illustrated Outline History*, translated by Xu Yifan, et al. Tianjin People's Publishing House, 2008, p.115,pp.118-119.

② Chen Xulu. *The Metabolism of Modern Chinese Society*. Shanghai People's Publishing House, 1992, p.194.

盛宣怀（1844—1916），江苏常州府武进人，清末政治家，洋务运动的代表人物。北洋大学堂（今天津大学）和南洋公学（今西安交通大学、上海交通大学、西南交通大学、台湾交通大学）创始人，同时也是一位实业家和慈善家

Sheng Xuanhuai (1844-1916), a native of Wujin, Changzhou Prefecture, Jiangsu, was a late Qing dynasty statesman and a leading figure in the Self-Strengthening Movement. He was the founder of Peiyang University (now Tianjin University) and Nanyang Public School (which later evolved into Xi'an Jiaotong University, Shanghai Jiao Tong University, Southwest Jiaotong University, and National Chiao Tung University in Taiwan). Sheng was also a prominent industrialist and philanthropist

来求治之道必当因时制宜"（光绪皇帝谕曰）[1]，把立学堂列为应及时办理的实政之一。

此后，盛宣怀与李鸿章的家庭教师、熟悉西方现代高等教育体系的美国人丁家立（Charles D. Tenney）通力合作，成功创办了中国第一所大学——北洋大学堂。北洋大学堂在中国第一次完全引进了近代西方的大学制度，初创法律、土木、矿冶、机械四科，皆为国家现代化所亟须科目。毕业的学生被资送出国留学，都能学有所成，为近代中国各方面事业的发展和进步作出了极大的贡献。

义和团运动中，洋务运动时期创办的几所学堂尽皆受创，相继停办。1885 年创办的中国第一所陆军军官学校——北洋武备学堂，在八国联军入侵天津时奋起参战，学堂内留校的 90 余名学员顽强抵抗，最后全部壮烈牺牲。他们的英勇行为，即便是当时在天津的外国侨民也大为肯定："他们与许多正规军一起，进行了值得赞扬的抵抗。"[2] 不过，北洋大学堂的命运则有所不同。义和团由于落后封闭的观念，认为凡是跟西洋有关的事物皆是邪恶的而加以毁灭，于

However, due to the educational philosophy of "Chinese learning for the essence, Western learning for practical application" and the idea of "learning from the west to counter the foreigners," the modern Western-style schools established for over 20 years yielded little effect. Few students trained in these institutions were able to truly contribute to the Wesernization Movement. After the defeat in the First Sino-Japanese War, calls for self-strengthening became louder across the nation, with Kang Youwei and others petitioning the government for reforms. Seizing this opportunity, Sheng Xuanhuai, who had long been involved in the Wesernization Movement under Li Hongzhang's administration, petitioned the Qing government to establish a modern university-like institution called the Peiyang University (also known as the Peiyang Western Study School). In his memorial, Sheng Xuanhuai emphasized, "The path to self-strengthening lies in nurturing talents, and the method to seek talents starts with establishing schools"; "Japan, emulating the West, widely establishes schools and academies. Not only do they draw military and naval officers from these institutions, but also staff for external missions and various industrial sectors such as mining and manufacturing." He delicately pointed out that our defeat in the First Sino-Japanese War was due to a lack of modern talents and that "a year's delay in establishing schools means a year's delay in producing talents." The urgent task was to establish modern universities and cultivate comprehensive talents proficient in Western learning.[1] Finally, the Qing government realized that "the way to seek governance must adapt to the times" (Emperor Guangxu's decree)[2], and establishing schools was listed as one of the timely policies to be implemented.

Subsequently, Sheng Xuanhuai collaborated closely with Charles D. Tenney, an American who served as the family tutor for Li Hongzhang and was well-versed in the modern Western higher education system. Together, they successfully established China's first university, Peiyang University. Peiyang University introduced the complete modern Western university system to China for the first time, initially offering courses in law, civil engineering, mining and metallurgy, and mechanical engineering, all of which were urgently needed subjects for the modernization of the country. Graduates were sponsored to study abroad and achieved remarkable success, making significant contributions to the development and progress of various

① 中国第一历史档案馆、天津大学，《中国近代第一所大学——北洋大学（天津大学）历史档案珍藏图录》，天津大学出版社，2005 年，第 6 页。

② （英）雷穆森著，许逸凡等译，《天津租界史（插图本）》，天津人民出版社，2009 年，第 117 页。

① The First Historical Archives of China, Tianjin University. *Collection of Historical Archives of Peiyang University (Tianjin University) - the First University of Modern China*. Tianjin University Press, 2005, p.6.

② The First Historical Archives of China, Tianjin University. *Collection of Historical Archives of Peiyang University (Tianjin University) - the First University of Modern China*. Tianjin University Press, 2005, p.6.

盛宣怀（端坐者右起第二）与丁家立（端坐者左起第二）等人合影
Sheng Xuanhuai (seated, second from the right) and Charles Daniel Tenney
(seated, second from the left) in a group photo with others

义和团运动之前北洋大学学生身穿制服在军训。图片来源：美国华盛顿大学图书馆
Peiyang University students in uniform during military training before the Boxer Uprising.
Source: University of Washington Library, U.S.

是对北洋大学进行了围攻。为了师生人身安全，学校被迫停办。八国联军占领天津后，校园被德军征作军营，学校师生四处星散，教学设施损毁殆尽。联军占领后期，北洋大学创办人、校长丁家立协同直隶总督兼北洋大臣袁世凯向德方索要校址不得。丁家立自告奋勇，亲赴柏林，援引德国法律，讨回赔偿费白银五万两。袁世凯又拨出西沽武器库旧址和部分款项，由丁家立组织复校。1903 年 4 月 27 日，北洋大学堂在西沽新址重建后正式开学。

袁世凯急于用人，未等义和团运动后首批北洋学生毕业，即于 1906 年和 1907 年连续两批资送近 50 名学生赴美留学。丁家立以"留美学堂监督"身份带领学生赴美，其间安排学生起居、联系入学。许多学生进入哈佛、耶鲁、康奈尔等名校攻读硕士和博士学位，其中就有中国近代医学及公共卫生先驱刘瑞恒、交通名宿刘景山、数学家和天文学家秦汾、经济学家马寅初、实业家和北洋大学校长冯熙运诸人。至 1908 年丁家立完全脱离北洋大学堂时，中国与美国政府间就退还部分义和团运动后的"庚子赔款"用于留美事宜的外交谈判方才正式启动。美国将当时尚未付足的 1078 万从 1909 年 1 月

aspects of modern China.

During the Boxer Rebellion, several schools established during the Wesernization Movement were heavily damaged and subsequently shut down. The Beiyang Military Academy, founded in 1885 as China's first military academy, rose up to fight when the Eight-Nation Alliance invaded Tianjin. More than 90 students who remained at the academy fought bravely and eventually sacrificed their lives. Their courageous actions were praised even by foreign residents in Tianjin at the time: "They, along with many regular soldiers, conducted commendable resistance."[1] However, the fate of Peiyang University was different. Due to the backward and closed-minded ideology of the Boxers, who believed that anything related to the West was evil and should be destroyed, Peiyang University was besieged. To ensure the safety of the faculty and students, the school was forced to close. After the Eight-Nation Alliance occupied Tianjin, the campus was turned into a military camp by the German forces, and the faculty and students scattered while the teaching facilities were severely damaged. In the later stages of the occupation by the Allied forces, Charles D. Tenney, the founder and president of Peiyang University, along with the Viceroy of Zhili Province and Minister of Beiyang,

---

[1] O. D. Rasmussen. *Tientsin: An Illustrated Outline History*, translated by Xu Yifan, et al. Tianjin People's Publishing House, 2008, p.117.

起退还，帮助中国建立海外留学教育系统。清华大学最初称为"清华学堂"，即为留美预备学校，后来成为中国最优秀的高等学府之一。此后，其他收款各国也都陆续模仿这一模式进行了不同程度的退款，用于特定的在华文化事业。这些教育活动是义和团运动盲目排外之后的又一个回流，对中国社会的未来产生了深远影响。

对义和团运动的多方评价

义和团运动的高潮虽说为期不过三个月，并且最终还在清政府的叛卖下，在中外反动势力的合力绞杀下失败，但是它的丰功伟绩却是昭昭在人耳目的。概括起来说，义和团运动阻止了帝国主义列强瓜分中国，保存了中国几千年来的悠久文化，加快了清王朝的覆灭，促进了中国广大人民群众的觉醒，并成为五十年后中国人民伟大胜利的奠基石之一。

这一运动在当时的直接后果是，粉碎了帝国主义列强瓜分中国的狂妄计划。当时的八国联军统帅、德国元帅瓦德西（Alfred von Waldersee）在其《瓦德西拳乱笔记》中总结说："吾人对于中国群众，不能视为已成衰弱无德行之人；彼等在实际上，尚含有无限蓬勃之生气，无论欧美日本各国，皆无此脑力与兵力，可以统治此天下生灵四分之一！"① 尽管有少数同时代富有正义感的西方人对义和团运动表示肯定和支持，如美国著名作家马克·吐温于 1900 年 11 月 23 日，在纽约公共教育协会上发表《我是一名拳民》（又译《我也是义和团》）的演讲："为什么不让中国人摆脱那些外国人？既然我们并不准许中国人到我们这儿来，我愿郑重声明，让中国人自己去决定，哪些人可以到他们那里去，拳民（义和团）是爱国者，他们爱他们自己的国家胜过爱别的民族的国家，我们祝愿他们成功。拳民主张把我们赶出他们的国家，我也是拳民，因为我也主张把他们赶出我们的国家。"但是在 20 世纪前半期的西方，人们普遍认为义和团是"黄祸的化身"，认为义和团的言行是危险、排外、非理性和野蛮的。

---

① 中国史学会主编，中国近代史资料丛刊《义和团》（三），上海人民出版社，2000 年，第 244 页。

Yuan Shikai, demanded the return of the campus from the Germans. Tenney bravely went to Berlin himself, cited German law, and successfully obtained compensation of fifty thousand taels of silver. Yuan Shikai also allocated the former site of the Xigu Arsenal and some funds for the reconstruction of the university. On April 27, 1903, Peiyang University officially reopened at its new location in Xigu.

Yuan Shikai urgently needed talents. Without waiting for the first batch of students from the Peiyang University to graduate after the Boxer Rebellion, he sent nearly 50 students to study in the United States in 1906 and 1907. Charles D. Tenney, in his capacity as "Supervisor of American Schools," led the students to the United States, arranging their daily lives and assisting with enrollment. Many students went on to pursue master's and doctoral degrees at prestigious institutions such as Harvard, Yale, and Cornell. Among them were pioneer in modern Chinese medicine and public health Liu Ruiheng, transportation expert Liu Jingshan, mathematician and astronomer Qin Fen, economist Ma Yinchu, and industrialist and president of Peiyang University Feng Xiyun. By 1908, when Charles D. Tenney completely disassociated himself from Peiyang University, formal diplomatic negotiations between China and the United States regarding the return of part of the Boxer Indemnity for educational purposes finally commenced. The United States began returning the outstanding balance of $10.78 million from January 1909, assisting China in establishing an overseas education system for studying abroad. Tsinghua University, initially known as "Tsing Hua College," served as a preparatory school for studying abroad in the United States before evolving into one of China's premier institutions of higher learning. Subsequently, other recipient countries also followed suit, returning varying degrees of funds for specific cultural endeavors in China. These educational initiatives represented a resurgence after the blind xenophobia of the Boxer Rebellion and had a profound impact on the future of Chinese society.

Various Evaluations of the Boxer Rebellion

Although the climax of the Boxer Rebellion lasted only three months and ultimately ended in failure under the betrayal of the Qing government and the joint suppression by reactionary forces at home and abroad, its remarkable achievements are evident to all. In summary, the Boxer Rebellion prevented the imperialist powers from partitioning China, preserved China's ancient culture spanning thousands of years, hastened the downfall of the Qing Dynasty, spurred the awakening of the vast Chinese population, and became one of the cornerstones of the great victory of the Chinese people fifty years later.

中国宣传画中的义和团
The Boxers in Chinese propaganda posters

义和团的招贴画
Poster of the Boxers

在 20 世纪 20 年代之前，中国的旧知识分子对义和团也抱有这种负面的看法，并增加了"迷信"和"落后"两条。例如，近代杰出思想家、政治家、文学家梁启超抨击道："夫今日拳匪之祸，论者皆知为一群愚昧之人召之也。然试问全国之民庶，其不与拳匪一般见识者几何人？全国之官吏，其不与通拳诸臣一般见识者几何人？国脑不具，则今日一拳匪去，明日一拳匪来耳。"① 邹容在《革命军》中说："有野蛮之革命，有文明之革命。野蛮之革命有破坏，无建设，横暴恣睢，适足以造成恐怖之时代，如庚子之义和团，意大利加波拿里，为国民添祸乱。"但是，到了 20 世纪 20 年代中国的民族主义和排外主义发展的高潮阶段，虽然许多西方人试图以"义和团主义"的复活为说辞来诋毁中国的民族主义，但中国的革命者已开始正面评价义和团，认为义和团运动的实质是"爱国主义"和"反对帝国主义"。例如，陈独秀在转向共产主义后完全改变了对义和团的评价：义和团事件的起因十分明白：一是经济上的原因——农民对于帝国主义侵略的反抗；一是政治上的原因——清廷反动政局趋于极端之结果。"若因为参加义和团运动者为全民中之少数，则参加辛亥革命与五四运动者，也是全民中之少数，我们决不能只据实际参

① 梁启超，《中国积弱溯源论·积弱之源于风俗者》，《饮冰室合集·文集之五》，中华书局，1936 年，第 22 页。

The immediate consequence of this movement was the shattering of the arrogant plans of the imperialist powers to partition China. The commander-in-chief of the Eight-Nation Alliance at the time, German Field Marshal Alfred von Waldersee, summarized in his *A Field Marshal's Memoirs*: "We cannot regard the Chinese masses as weak and immoral; in reality, they possess boundless vitality. None of the European, American, or Japanese nations have the intellectual and military power to dominate a quarter of the world's population!"[1] A few Westerners with a sense of justice at the time expressed affirmation and support for the Boxer Rebellion, such as the renowned American writer Mark Twain, who delivered a speech titled *I am a Boxer, too* on November 23, 1900, at a meeting of the Public Education Association in New York City: "Why should not China be free from the foreigners, who are only making trouble on her soil? We do not allow Chinamen to come here, and I say in all seriousness that it would be a graceful thing to let China decide who shall go there. The Boxer is a patriot. He loves his country better than he does the countries of other people. I wish him success. The Boxer believes in driving us out of his country. I am a Boxer too, for I believe in driving him out of our country." However, in the Western world of the first half of the 20th century, the Boxers were generally regarded as the "incarnation of the Yellow Peril." Their actions and words were seen as dangerous, xenophobic, irrational, and barbaric.

Before the 1920s, Chinese intellectuals held negative views towards the Boxers, adding "superstition" and "backwardness" to their criticisms. For example, the eminent modern thinker, politician, and writer Liang Qichao criticized, "Today's Boxer calamity, everyone knows it was summoned by a group of ignorant people. But let me ask, how many common people in the entire nation do not share the same views as the Boxers? How many officials in the entire nation do not share the same views as those who sympathize with the Boxers? Without a national intellect, when today's Boxers are gone, tomorrow's Boxers will come."[2] Zou Rong in *The Revolutionary Army* said, "There are savage revolutions and civilized revolutions... Savage revolutions are destructive without construction, rampant and violent, enough to create an era of terror, like the Boxers of the Gengzi year and Italy's Giuseppe Garibaldi, adding calamity and chaos to the nation." However, in the 1920s, during the peak development of Chinese nationalism and xenophobia,

① Association of Chinese Historians (ed.). Chinese Modern Historical Data Series *Boxer Rebellion (Vol.3)*. Shanghai People's Publishing House, 2000, p.244.

② Liang Qichao. *On the Trace of China's Accumulated Weakness: Due to the Customs. Ice-drinking Room Combined Collected Works: Volume 5*. Zhonghua Book Company, 1936, p.22.

加者之数量，便否认其质量上代表全民族的意识与利益。文明的绅士学者们，说义和团事件是少数人之罪恶，说列强不应该惩罚到义和团以外的人，不啻是向列强跪着说：我们是文明人，我们不曾反抗；汝们惩罚少数的义和团，不应该皂白不分连累到我们大多数安分屈服的良民。情形如果是这样，还幸亏有野蛮的义和团少数人，保全了中国民族史上一部分荣誉！"[1]

老西开事件

欧洲 14 世纪开始的文艺复兴运动，不仅带来了思想启蒙，更释放了人们的欲望，这种欲望很快变成对黄金的追求和对殖民地的征服。在天津，外国侵略者对土地的欲望并不因各国租界划定而停止，他们利用一切机会拓展租界，占有更多的土地。而在这种掠夺中，教会几乎总是冲在最前面。

西开教堂的兴修与城市精英领导下的抗争

老西开位于当时法租界旁，原是城市以外的一片沼泽地，但随着天津市区发展，成了法国觊觎之地。1912 年，梵蒂冈教廷颁发诏书，宣布从直隶北境代牧区分设直隶海滨代牧区，主教府设在天津三岔河口的望海楼教堂。首任主教杜保禄（法国遣使会会士）认为望海楼教堂地处旧市区，不便于今后扩展，于是在紧邻法租界西南面的老西开地区购买了一片沼泽洼地，兴建新的主教座堂——西开教堂。

津代牧区的法国司铎，先与中国政府协议，将教堂建于路旁，道路归中国政府所有；但同时又与法方协议，请其出钱筑路。路旁零星土地则由教会卖给中国商人。西开教堂于 1913 年 8 月开始动土兴建，1916 年竣工建成。最初称圣味增爵堂，后改为圣约瑟堂（St. Joseph Cathedral），一般天津人称为"法国教堂""西开教堂"或"老西开教堂"。西开教堂落成后，周围形成一大片教会建筑群，这里

---

① 陈独秀，《我们对于义和团两个错误的观念》，《向导》1924 年 9 月 3 日。

── 254 ──

---

although many Westerners attempted to denigrate Chinese nationalism by reviving the "Boxerism," Chinese revolutionaries had started to positively evaluate the Boxers, considering the essence of the Boxer Rebellion as "patriotism" and "opposition to imperialism." For instance, after shifting towards communism, Chen Duxiu completely changed his evaluation of the Boxers, stating, The causes of the Boxer Rebellion are very clear: one is economic—peasants' resistance to imperialist aggression; the other is political—the reactionary situation of the Qing court leading to extreme outcomes. "If participation in the Boxer Rebellion was by a minority among the population, then participants in the 1911 Revolution and the May Fourth Movement were also minorities among the population. We cannot deny their representing the consciousness and interests of the entire nation solely based on the number of actual participants. Civilized gentlemen scholars who claim that the Boxer Rebellion was the wrongdoing of a minority and that the foreign powers should not punish anyone beyond the Boxers, are essentially kneeling before the foreign powers, saying: we are civilized people, we never rebelled; you punish the minority Boxers, without distinguishing, implicating most of us law-abiding citizens. If that were the case, fortunately, there were a few savage Boxers who preserved some honor in Chinese national history!"[1]

The Laoxikai Incident

The Renaissance movement that began in Europe in the 14th century not only brought about intellectual enlightenment but also unleashed people's desires, which quickly turned into pursuits of gold and conquest of colonies. In Tianjin, the desire of foreign aggressors for land did not cease with the demarcation of various countries' concessions; they seized every opportunity to expand their concessions and occupy more land. In this plunder, the church was almost always at the forefront.

The Renovation of Xikai Church and the Resistance Led by Urban Elites

Laoxikai was located adjacent to the French Concession at that time, originally a swampy area outside the city, but as Tianjin developed, it became coveted by France. In 1912, the Vatican issued a decree announcing the establishment of the Vicar Apostolic of Maritime Zhili, with the bishop located

---

① Chen Duxiu. Our Two Mistaken Conceptions Concerning the Boxers. *The Guide Weekly*, September 3, 1924.

1918 年的天津西开教堂。西开教堂初建时，这里还是一片苇塘，地势较其附近的墙子河低四五尺。因地势低洼，每逢大雨，堂前堂后便水漫金山

Xikai Church in Tianjin, 1918. When the church was first built, the area was still a reed marsh, with the terrain about four to five feet lower than the nearby Qiangzi River. Due to the low-lying land, heavy rains often caused flooding around the church

不仅成为天津天主教会的中心，也成为天主教徒聚集居住区。当年，很多来自河北乡村的教徒，通过传教士的介绍到天津谋生，其中不少人在教堂附近定居。教会为了增加自己的社会影响力，往往在其教区内开办学校和医院，例如基督教伦敦会在津创办的新学书院，美以美会创办的中西女中和汇文中学。法国天主教会也不例外，他们以西开教堂为核心，在其附近形成了一个包括教堂、修道院、学校、医院的天主教社区。教会医院即位于今营口道上的天津市中心妇产科医院，学校则有法汉学校（1952 年后改为天津市第二十一中学，现为天津市中心小学校区）以及陆续开办的西开小学、若瑟小学、圣功小学等。

教堂开始动工后，天津法租界工部局声称保护教堂，派巡捕进驻该地区。对于这种公然侵犯我国主权的行径，天津人民强烈反对，并要求北洋政府制止这一行为。天津警察厅派遣 9 名警察驻守从法

at the Wanghailou Church at Tianjin's Sancha estuary. The first bishop, Paul-Marie Dumond (a member of the Congregation of the Mission), believed that Wanghailou Church, situated in the old city area, was not conducive to future expansion. Therefore, he purchased a swampy lowland area adjacent to the southwest of the French Concession in Laoxikai and built a new cathedral—the Xikai Church.

The French priests of the Zhili Vicariate first reached an agreement with the Chinese government to build the church along the roadside, with the road belonging to the Chinese government. At the same time, they also reached an agreement with the French side who shall fund the construction of the road. The sporadic land along the road was sold by the church to Chinese merchants. Xikai Church began construction in August 1913 and was completed in 1916. Initially called the Church of St. Vincent de Paul, it was later renamed St. Joseph's Cathedral. It is commonly referred to by Tianjin locals as the "French Church," "Xikai Church," or "Laoxikai Church." After the completion of Xikai Church, a large complex of church buildings formed around it, not only becoming the center of Tianjin Catholicism but also a gathering area for Catholics. Many believers from rural Hebei came to Tianjin to make a living through the introduction of missionaries, and many settled near the church. In order to increase their social influence, churches often opened schools and hospitals within their dioceses. For example, the London Missionary Society established the Anglo-Chinese College in Tianjin, and the Methodist Episcopal Church founded the Keen Girls' School and Huiwen Middle School. The French Catholic Church was no exception. They formed a Catholic community around Xikai Church, including churches, monasteries, schools, and hospitals. The church hospital is now located on Yingkou Road and is known as the Tianjin Central Hospital of Gynecology Obstetrics. The schools included the Ecole Municipale Francaise (which became Tianjin No.21 High School after 1952, now the Tianjin Zhongxin Primary School of Heping District), as well as the subsequent establishment of Xikai Primary School, St. Joseph Primary School, and Sheng Kung Primary School, among others.

After the construction of the church began, the Tianjin French Municipal Council claimed to protect the church and sent patrols to the area. The people of Tianjin strongly opposed this blatant infringement of our country's sovereignty and demanded that the Beiyang government stop this behavior. The Tianjin Police Department dispatched nine police officers to guard the Zhangzhuang Bridge (wooden bridge), which was a necessary passage from the French Concession to Laoxikai. This bridge was located on the Qiangzi River on the Sino-French border. Thus, a situation of mutual confrontation between the police of France and China was formed in the Laoxikai area.

1920 年左右西开教堂周围还是一片相对荒芜的开洼
Around 1920, the area surrounding Xikai Church was still a
relatively desolate and open lowland

从营口道方向看到的西开教堂，照片右下角为教会医院（今天津市中心妇产科医院）
Xikai Church as seen from Yingkou Road. The lower right corner of the photograph shows the
missionary hospital, which is now Tianjin Central Obstetrics and Gynecology Hospital

张庄大桥
Zhangzhuang Bridge

租界通往老西开所必经的张庄大桥（木桥），该桥位于华法交界墙
子河上。这样，在老西开地区形成中法两国警察相互对峙的局面。

　　这种局面维持一年后，1914 年 7 月，法国驻天津领事宝如华致
函直隶交涉署，主张由于中国方面未答复法国领事的照会，后来对
法租界在老西开派设巡捕、修筑道路也未提出异议，即表示中国方
面已经默认了老西开地区为法国推广租界，因此要求中国方面撤走
警察。对此直隶交涉署当即驳复，1902 年法国的所谓"照会"仅为
法国单方面要求，中国方面并没有同意，自不能发生效力。不过，
直隶交涉署并未采取任何实际行动。

　　翌年，即 1915 年 5 月 9 日，袁世凯为推动帝制，接受日本提出

After maintaining this situation for a year, in July 1914, Paul Beau, the French Consul in Tianjin, wrote to the Zhili Negotiation Office, claiming that due to China's failure to respond to the French Consul's inquiries and the subsequent lack of objections to the French Concession's deployment of patrols and construction of roads in Laoxikai, it indicated that China had tacitly accepted the extension of the French Concession into the Laoxikai area. Therefore, they demanded that China withdraw its police. The Zhili Negotiation Office promptly responded, refuting that the so-called "inquiries" from France in 1902 were merely unilateral demands from France, which China did not agree to and thus had no legal effect. However, the Zhili Negotiation Office did not take any practical action in response.

The following year, on May 9, 1915, Yuan Shikai, in his efforts to promote monarchy, accepted Japan's proposed "Twenty-One Demands," granting

的"二十一条"，给予日本种种特权。其他欧美列强乃随之心动而后行动。1915年9月，天津法租界工部局在老西开地区散发传单，要求当地居民向租界当局纳税。天津人民闻之大哗，坚决不答应。同月，天津一批爱国绅商组织成立了"维持国权国土会"对租界当局提出抗议，会长为卞月亭（天津商会会长），副会长为赵天麟（北洋大学校长、新教徒）、孙子文，委员为刘子鹤、刘俊卿（《益世报》经理、天主教徒）、宋则久（新教徒）、杜小琴，与法国侵略者展开针锋相对的斗争。

1916年1月，法国政府通过其驻北京公使多次照会中国政府外交部，蛮横要求北洋政府饬令天津地方当局撤回老西开的中国警察，以将老西开据为己有。6月，老西开主教座堂及其附属建筑全部竣工，教会机构正式迁入。法租界工部局在教堂前方今独山路、营口道和西宁道之间近50亩的三角地带安插法国国旗，设置界牌，表示此地已划入法租界，并派安南（今越南）兵把守。天津人民异常愤怒，将界牌木标统统拔掉。"维持国权国土会"和当地居民向当局提出要求，立即制止法国人的越轨行为。但北洋政府一边安抚劝谕市民"静候中央解决，勿得暴动，以兹口实"，一边已经动摇，准备答允法方要求。6月20日，外交部电告直隶省省长，要求地方官从速疏通

Japan various privileges. Other Western powers followed suit after being similarly influenced. In September 1915, the Tianjin French Municipal Council distributed leaflets in the Laoxikai area, demanding that local residents pay taxes to the concession authorities. Upon hearing this, the people of Tianjin reacted strongly and refused to comply. In the same month, a group of patriotic gentry and merchants in Tianjin formed the "National Territorial Rights Preservation Association" to protest against the concession authorities. The president of the association was Bian Yueting (President of the Tientsin Chamber of Commerce), the vice presidents were Zhao Tianlin (President of Peiyang University, a Protestant), and Sun Ziwen. Committee members included Liu Zihe, Liu Junqing (Manager of *Social Welfare*, a Catholic), Song Zejiu (a Protestant), and Du Xiaoqin. They engaged in a fierce struggle against the French aggressors.

In January 1916, the French government repeatedly demanded through its Minister in Beijing that the Chinese Ministry of Foreign Affairs order the local authorities in Tianjin to withdraw the Chinese police from Laoxikai in a brazen attempt to claim Laoxikai for themselves. In June, the Xikai Cathedral and its affiliated buildings were all completed, and the church institutions officially moved in. The Tianjin French Municipal Council planted the French flag and set up boundary markers in the triangular area of nearly 50 mu between Dushan Road, Yingkou Road, and Xining Road in front of the church, indicating that this area had been annexed into the French Concession, and stationed Annamese (now Vietnamese) troops to

卞月亭（1866—1926），爱国实业家。清末任职户部、工部、法部。1904年任天津商务总会协理。辛亥革命后出任天津商团团长、天津红十字会执行委员。1913年任直隶商务联合会会长，同年以中国代表团团长名义参加巴拿马博览会。在1916年的"老西开事件"中，以卞月亭为核心的天津商会发挥了重要的组织、领导作用

Bian Yueting (1866-1926) was a patriotic industrialist. During the late Qing dynasty, he held positions in the Ministry of Revenue, the Ministry of Works, and the Ministry of Justice. In 1904, he became the associate director of the Tianjin General Chamber of Commerce. After the 1911 Revolution, he served as the commander of the Tianjin Merchants Group and an executive member of the Tianjin Red Cross Society. In 1913, he was appointed president of the Zhili Commercial Federation and led the Chinese delegation to the Panama-Pacific Exposition. During the 1916 "Old Xikai Incident," the Tianjin Chamber of Commerce, under Bian Yueting's leadership, played a crucial role in organizing and directing efforts to address the crisis

赵天麟（1886—1938），爱国教育家。毕业于北洋大学法律系，后成为北洋大学首批派往美国的留学生，1909年毕业于美国哈佛大学法律科，获法学博士学位。1914年被任命为北洋大学校长。1920年辞去北洋大学校长职务，1934年出任天津耀华中学校长。因支持抗日活动，1938年被日本宪兵队特务暗杀，后被追认为革命烈士

Zhao Tianlin (1886-1938) was a patriotic educator. He graduated from the law department of Peiyang University and was among the first group of students sent to the United States. In 1909, he graduated from Harvard University with a doctorate in law. In 1914, he was appointed president of Peiyang University. In 1920, he resigned from his position as president of Peiyang University and, in 1934, became the principal of Tianjin Yao Hua Middle School. Zhao was an active supporter of anti-Japanese activities and was assassinated by the Japanese military police in 1938. He was posthumously honored as a revolutionary martyr

教堂前独山路
Dushan Road in front of the Church

guard it. The people of Tianjin were extremely angry and pulled out all the boundary markers. The "National Territorial Rights Preservation Association" and local residents demanded that the authorities immediately stop the French's transgressive actions. However, the Beiyang government tried to placate and urge the citizens to "wait quietly for government resolution, avoid riots to offer an excuse for them." Meanwhile, it was already wavering and preparing to acquiesce to the French demands. On June 20, the Ministry of Foreign Affairs instructed the Viceroy of Zhili Province to swiftly control public opinion and accept the unreasonable demands of France. On October 17, the French Municipal Council issued a final ultimatum to Zhili Province, demanding that China cede Laoxikai within 48 hours. On the night of October 20, the French Consul in Tianjin, along with French Municipal Council patrols and Annamese troops, blatantly disarmed the Chinese police stationed at Zhangzhuang Bridge, detained them at the French Municipal Council, and set up guards in the Laoxikai area, declaring the occupation of this region, which became known as the "Laoxikai Incident" in history.[1]

The aggression of the French and the retreat of the Beiyang government sparked fierce anger among the citizens of Tianjin, leading to large-scale protest activities. The morning after the incident, the "National Territorial Rights Preservation Association" held a general meeting at the Tientsin Chamber of Commerce. At the meeting, President Bian Yueting first spoke, revealing the process of the French occupation of Laoxikai. Then, Liu Junqing, the manager of *Social Welfare*, delivered a speech, angrily condemning the aggression of French imperialism. He said, "The French consul detained Chinese police officers, insulting our country. Although our country has not perished, the treatment of our country by foreigners is as if it were a fallen nation. This is intolerable. Who can tolerate it?" He expressed the determination to "fight to preserve national rights rather than live in disgrace forever."[2] After the meeting, thousands of people went to the Zhili Provincial Office, the Negotiation Office, and the Provincial Council to protest and petition. On October 23, the Tientsin Chamber of Commerce held a meeting and unanimously passed resolutions: boycott paper currency issued by French banks; boycott French goods; and request the government to telegram the French government to demand the replacement of the French envoy to China.[3] On October 25, more than 8,000 people from all walks of life gathered at the Nanshi Grand Stage, announcing the establishment of the "Tianjin Assembly"

舆论，接受法国无理要求。10 月 17 日，法租界工部局向直隶省发出最后通牒，限中国在 48 小时内让出老西开。10 月 20 日晚，法国驻津领事带领法租界巡捕和安南兵，悍然将驻守张庄大桥的中国警察缴械，拘禁至法国工部局，并在老西开地区设岗警戒，宣告对这一地区的占领，史称"老西开事件"。[1]

法方的侵略与北洋政府的退让，引发了天津市民的熊熊怒火，天津市民随即举行大规模抗议活动。事件发生的第二天清晨，"维持国权国土会"在天津商会总会召开全体大会。会上，会长卞月亭

① 来新夏主编，《天津近代史》，南开大学出版社，1987 年，第 251、252 页。

① Lai Xinxia. *Modern History of Tianjin*. Nankai University Press, 1987, p.251,252.

② *Social Welfare*, October 21, 1916.

③ *Social Welfare*, October 24, 1916.

西开教堂是华北地区最大的罗曼式教堂建筑，建筑面积 1891.95 平方米，可同时容纳 1500 人。西开教堂建筑平面呈拉丁"十"字形构图，正面顶部的两座高大的塔楼，与楼体中央的后塔楼形成呼应。三个高达 45 米的巨型圆顶，错落排列成"品"字形，圆顶内部为木结构支撑，每座圆顶上有一个青铜十字架。据老教徒介绍，早年塔楼圆顶表面覆盖的是铜片，在阳光下熠熠闪光，风采独特。西开教堂的建筑外墙面主体是用红黄色花砖相间清水砌筑的，檐口下采用扶壁连列柱券做装饰带。建筑外立面以圆形窗和列柱券形窗组成的半圆形叠砌拱窗为要素，教堂内有许多壁画和大管风琴，前面院中有圣水坛，有左右两道大门，信徒分男女从不同的门入内

Xikai Church is the largest Romanesque church in northern China, covering an area of 1,891.95 square meters and capable of accommodating 1,500 people at once. The church's floor plan is designed in the shape of a Latin "cross," with two towering spires at the front that echo the central rear tower. The three massive domes, each reaching 45 meters in height, are arranged in a staggered "品" shape. The domes are supported by a wooden structure inside, with a bronze cross on top of each dome. According to longtime parishioners, the dome surfaces were originally covered with copper sheets, which gleamed brilliantly in the sunlight, creating a unique and striking appearance. The church's exterior walls are primarily constructed of alternating red and yellow decorative bricks with exposed concrete. The eaves are adorned with a decorative band of buttress columns and arches. The facade features semicircular, stacked arched windows, formed by circular windows and columned arches. Inside the church, there are numerous murals and a large pipe organ. The front courtyard has a font for holy water, and there are two large doors on the left and right sides for male and female worshippers to enter separately

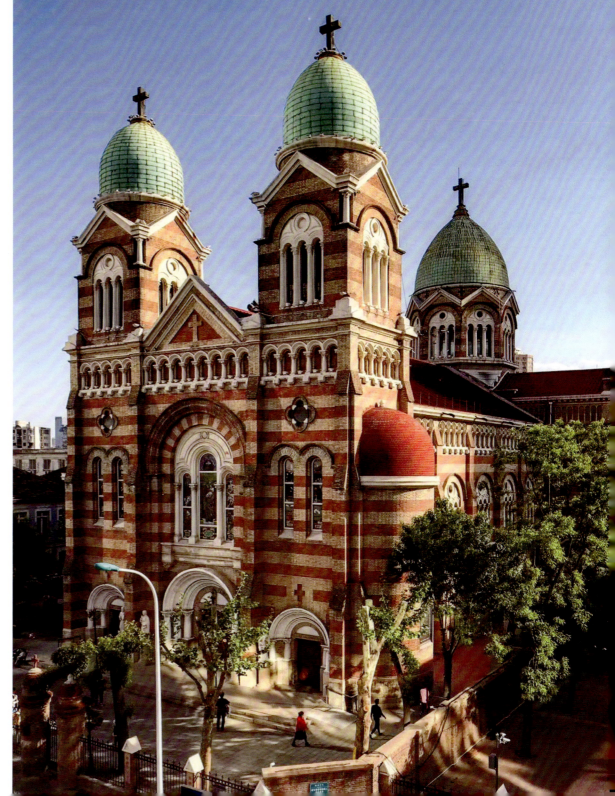

西开教堂。张建勇摄
Xikai Church. Taken by Zhang Jianyong

首先发言，揭露法国人强占老西开的经过。然后，《益世报》经理刘俊卿发表演说，愤怒谴责法国帝国主义的侵略行动，他说："法领事拘留华警，侮辱我国，莫此为甚。我国虽未亡，而外人对待我国，如亡国一般，是可忍也，孰不可忍也"，表达了"与其苟且图存，贻羞于永久，何若舍命力争以维国权"的决心。① 会后，数千人前往直隶省公署、交涉署和省议会示威、请愿。10 月 23 日，天津商会召开会议，全体决议：抵制法国银行所发行的纸币；抵制法国货；并请政府致电法国政府，要求撤换法国驻华公使。②10 月 25 日，八千余名各界人士聚集在南市大舞台，宣布成立"天津公民大会"，并一致决议：通电全国，宣布与法国断绝贸易；不使用法国银行纸币；解散法国在中国招募华工的机构，不准招募华工；中国货不售与法国；中国人敢替法国为侦探者一经查出，予以相当处分；电告驻法公使，要求法国政府撤换公使与驻津领事等。③ 由此天津掀起了一场历时四个月的声势浩大的反帝爱国运动。

工人罢工、学生罢课、商人支持与传教士声援

近代城市中的反帝爱国群众运动，往往由学生、工人、市民和商人集结起来，形成合力，"老西开事件"中也是如此。在这场反帝爱国运动中，学生充当先导力量，四处讲演，宣传鼓动；知识分子精英出谋划策，引导舆论，对外交涉；商人是强大的后援，募集经费，提供物质支持和保障；工人则是最直接和最有力的斗争力量，不仅有产业工人，还有夫役、人力车工人、女佣工、职员等各阶层各行业劳动者都直接参与罢工，组成联合一致行动。长达四个月的罢工导致法租界内的电灯厂停电，商店停业，道路、垃圾无人清扫，租界的商业活动和日常生活几乎完全陷于瘫痪。最后，法国代理公使不得不允诺归还老西开土地。

学生一直是近代爱国运动的先导者。当时正在南开中学就读的

---

① 《益世报》1916 年 10 月 21 日。

② 《益世报》1916 年 10 月 24 日。

③ 《益世报》1916 年 10 月 26 日。

and unanimously resolved: to issue a nationwide telegram announcing the cessation of trade with France; to refrain from using French banknotes; to dissolve French organizations recruiting Chinese laborers in China and prohibit the recruitment of Chinese laborers; to refuse to sell Chinese goods to France; to severely punish any Chinese individuals found working as spies for France; and to telegram the French envoy, demanding the replacement of the envoy and the consul in Tianjin, among other measures.[1] Thus, Tianjin launched a massive anti-imperialist and patriotic movement that lasted for four months.

Workers on Strike, Students Boycotting Classes, Merchants Providing Support, and Missionaries Expressing Solidarity

In modern urban anti-imperialist and patriotic movements, students, workers, citizens, and merchants often gather together, forming a collective force. The "Laoxikai Incident" was no exception. In this anti-imperialist and patriotic movement, students acted as the vanguard, giving speeches and mobilizing; intellectual elites provided guidance and directed public opinion, as well as engaged in diplomatic negotiations; merchants provided strong support, raising funds and providing material support and security; workers were the most direct and powerful force of resistance. Not only industrial workers but also laborers, rickshaw pullers, maids, clerks, and workers from various sectors participated directly in strikes, forming united actions. The four-month-long strike led to power outages in the power plant, closures of shops, roads and trash left unattended, and commercial activities and daily life in the French concession almost completely paralyzed. Eventually, the French acting consul had to promise to return the land of Laoxikai.

Students have always been the vanguard of modern patriotic movements. At the time, Zhou Enlai, who was studying at Nankai Middle School, delivered a speech titled *The Current Crisis in China* at a school-wide assembly, pointing out that "China is currently in an extremely dangerous position," "the Beiyang government is corrupt and incompetent," the president "lacks decisive leadership," the premier "lacks political common sense," there is "a president who is just a figurehead, lacking experience in governance," there are "members of parliament who have experienced worldly changes but lack sincere patriotism," and bureaucrats "only know how to maintain their power and positions," resulting in such a humiliating situation for the country. Zhou Enlai called on his fellow students to shoulder the responsibility of defending national dignity and to join the struggle against

---

① *Social Welfare*, October 26, 1916.

周恩来，在全校召开的大会上发表题为《中国现时之危机》演说，指出"中国现时已处于极危险地位"，"北洋政府腐败无能"，总统"无绝断之伟力"，总理"无政治之常识"，"有徒负虚名之总长，而无办事之经验"，"有饱经世变之议员，而无谋国之忠忱"，大小官僚"仅知固其势保其位"，造成国家如此难堪的局面。周恩来号召同学们肩负起维护民族尊严的重任，投入反对帝国主义制造的"老西开攘土之事"的斗争中去。① 与此同时，老西开法汉学校② 的学生于 10 月 26 日罢课，甚至宣布退学，率先点燃了市民反帝斗争的火焰。随后其他老西开地区的中小学也都纷纷声援，并一起罢课。③

近代中国的工人阶级具有广泛的行业构成，他们在遭受资产阶级剥削压迫的同时，还具有朴素的爱国热情，因而展现出强大的力量。11 月 12 日，法比义品公司和义善实业铁厂的工人开始罢工，一场轰轰烈烈的反法罢工运动由此展开。随后，法租界内的各个工厂、洋行、电灯房、饭店、俱乐部的中方员工群起罢工。罢工的浪潮还波及法租界的行政管理机构，包括法租界工部局和兵营，一向唯法国人之命是从的中国籍巡捕侦探、职员、消防员及兵营工役，都纷纷离职。法国人家里的厨师、保姆、马夫、苦力等也都相继告退。据公民大会负责人之一吴子铭回忆："某法人欲留中国女工，允许每月工资增加到四十元，遭到该女工的严词拒绝。"后来，粪夫、清道夫也罢了工，不肯上班清扫。甚至由于电灯房工人罢工，"法国人只好自己动手，因不懂技术，结果触电而死"④。因为缺少警力，法租界当局不得不让"法国商人也穿上军装在租界里维持治安"⑤。昔日繁华热闹的法国街市，彻底变成萧条冷清、垃圾遍地、入夜则一片漆黑的污秽之处。

---

① 这篇檄文刊登在周恩来任主编的学生会刊物《校风》杂志 11 月期上，见《校风》第 2、5 页。

② 天津法汉学校隶属于天主教会，是专门为中国学生开办的中学。

③ 北京《益世报》1916 年 11 月 26 日。

④ 吴子铭，《法帝侵占老西开事件回忆》（未刊稿）。转引自杨大辛《津门古今杂谭》，天津人民出版社，2015 年，第 94、95 页。

⑤ 吴子舟，《回忆"老西开事件"》（未刊稿）。转引自杨大辛《津门古今杂谭》，天津人民出版社，2015 年，第 95 页。

---

the "Laoxikai Incident" orchestrated by imperialism.[1] Meanwhile, on October 26th, students at the Ecole Municipale Francaise (French Chinese School)[2] went on strike, even announcing their withdrawal from school, igniting the flames of anti-imperialist struggle among the citizens. Subsequently, students from other primary and secondary schools in the Laoxikai area also expressed their support and joined the strike.[3]

In modern China, the working class had a wide range of industries, and while they suffered from bourgeois exploitation and oppression, they also possessed a simple patriotism, demonstrating powerful strength. On November 12th, workers from the Crédit Foncier d'Extrême-Orient and the Yishan Industrial Ironworks went on strike, initiating a vigorous anti-French strike movement. Subsequently, Chinese employees from various factories, foreign firms, electric power plants, restaurants, and clubs within the French Concession also joined the strike. The wave of strikes even affected the administrative institutions of the French Concession, including the Municipal Council, and barracks. Chinese police detectives, clerks, firefighters, and barracks workers, who had always followed French orders, all resigned. Even cooks, nannies, stable hands, and laborers working in French households tendered their resignations one after another. According to Wu Ziming, one of the leaders of the Tianjin Assembly, "Some French wanted to retain Chinese female workers, offering to increase their monthly wages to forty yuan, but they were sternly refused by the workers." Later, even scavengers and street sweepers went on strike, refusing to work. Due to the strike by electric power plant workers, "the French had to do it themselves, but not understanding the technology, they ended up being electrocuted to death."[4] Due to the lack of police forces, the French Concession authorities had to let "French merchants wear military uniforms to maintain order within the concession."[5] The once bustling streets of the French Concession turned into desolate, garbage-strewn, filthy places, pitch black at night.

---

① This proclamation was published in the November issue of the Student Union magazine *Xiaofeng* (School Spirit), edited by Zhou Enlai, on pages 2 and 5.

② Tianjin Ecole Municipale Francaise was affiliated with the Catholic Church and was a high school specifically for Chinese students.

③ *Social Welfare*, Beijing, November 26, 1916.

④ Wu Ziming. *Reminiscences of the French Occupation of Laoxikai* (unpublished manuscript). Cited in Yang Daxin. *Miscellaneous Tales of Tianjin Through the Ages*. Tianjin People's Publishing House, 2015, p.94, 95.

⑤ Wu Zizhou. *Reminiscences of the "Laoxikai Incident"* (unpublished manuscript). Cited in Yang Daxin. *Miscellaneous Tales of Tianjin Through the Ages*. Tianjin People's Publishing House, 2015, p.95.

公民大会与罢工团代表合影
A group photo of the representatives of Tianjin
Assembly and the Strike Committee

罢工开始的一星期之内，参与罢工的总人数就达到1400余人。[①]
为了声援罢工工人，罢工团于11月18日成立，下设文牍、会计、招待、
调查、庶务、稽查、演说等八个部门，对所有罢工的工人登记造册，
妥善解决他们的生活困难，并为他们介绍工作。公民大会还为罢工
团赶制了工团代表徽章，发给罢工工人证书，载明工人们"牺牲职业，
热心爱国，凡有证书者，官府应认真保护"，无论天津还是外地的厂矿，
"见此证书，应优先录用，以示优异"。公民大会还为罢工工人解
决生活困难而"照章发薪"。[②]随后，热心国事的仁人志士组成的"爱
国团""保卫社"等纷纷成立，协助公民大会进行宣传、组织工作。
11月23日又成立了演说团，聘请演说员20人，分成十组，在天津
城关内外戏院、茶园轮流演讲，观者如堵。同时，居住在法租界内
的中国居民、商人也掀起迁居华界的运动。他们在报纸上刊登广告，
呼吁居住在法租界的其他国人迁出，"以免受庇于欺我辱我者之宇
下，被同胞之唾骂也"，指出"津地广大，均属乐土，尤望坚持到底，

① 《益世报》1916年11月24日。

② 《益世报》1916年11月24日。

Within the first week of the strike's commencement, the total number of participants reached over 1,400.[①] To support the striking workers, a strike committee was formed on November 18th, consisting of eight departments: correspondence, accounting, reception, investigation, general affairs, inspection, and speeches. They registered and documented all striking workers, effectively addressed their living difficulties, and helped them find employment. The Assembly also hurriedly produced badges for the strike committee representatives, issued certificates to the striking workers, stating that those "who sacrifice their works and are zealous patriots, the authorities should seriously protect." Regardless of whether they were from Tianjin or elsewhere, factories and mines were encouraged to "prioritize hiring those with this certificate, to demonstrate their excellence." The Assembly also ensured that striking workers had their salaries paid according to regulations.[②] Subsequently, patriotic individuals formed organizations such as the "Patriotic League" and the "Defense Society" to assist the Assembly in publicizing and organizing work. On November 23rd, a speaking group was formed, employing 20 orators divided into ten groups, who took turns giving speeches at theaters and teahouses inside and outside the city walls of Tianjin, drawing large crowds of spectators. Meanwhile, Chinese residents and merchants living in the French Concession also initiated a movement to relocate to the Tianjin old city. They published advertisements in newspapers, urging other nationals residing in the French Concession to move out "to avoid being sheltered by those who insult and ridicule us, and being cursed by our compatriots," emphasizing that "Tianjin is vast and belongs to everyone's enjoyment. We especially hope to persevere to the end and not let those who insult us turn us into objects of ridicule."[③]

The workers' strike received vigorous support from the entire population of the city, especially in terms of material support, which allowed the strike movement to consolidate its achievements and achieve its goals. On the second day of the strike (November 13th), the striking workers held a general meeting at the Tientsin Chamber of Commerce. The President of the Provincial Assembly, Bian Jieqing, delivered a speech, repeatedly encouraging everyone to persevere to the end. The President of the Tientsin Chamber of Commerce, Bian Yueting, expressed the hope that the strike movement would have a clear beginning and end. Regarding the living expenses of the striking workers, he firmly stated that, in support of the strike, even if it meant "losing everything,

① *Social Welfare*, November 24, 1916.

② *Social Welfare*, November 24, 1916.

③ *Social Welfare*, November 18, 1916.

勿令欺我者转而笑我也"。[1]

工人罢工得到了全市人民的有力支持，特别是物质上的保障，由此使罢工运动能够巩固成果、达到斗争目标。罢工的第二天（11月13日）上午，罢工工人在天津商会会场开全体大会。省议会会长边洁卿上台演说，一再勉励大家坚持到底。天津商会会长卞月亭表示，希望罢工运动有始有终，对于罢工工人的生活费用，他斩钉截铁地表示，为支援罢工，即使"倾家荡产，亦绝不辞其责任"，"闻者莫不动容，全体鼓掌不绝"。11月16日下午，公民大会在南市大舞台特地为罢工工人维持生计商筹经费召开大会，决定邀请京津地区著名演员举行联合义演，收入全部作为罢工经费。商会准备房间为工人提供休息场所，并馈赠食物和提供取暖设备。三条石街隆兴煤厂捐献硬煤两千斤，分文不取。甚至还有车夫也捐出自己微薄的收入。不到一个星期，天津各界共捐款超过四万元。[2] 房产公司为使迁出法租界的迁居者有安身之地，宣布提供房屋，并租金"一律减价三成"。[3]

本来天津人民寄希望于北洋政府的外交交涉，然而中国政府最初准备与法国妥协，接受法国占据老西开的现实。来到天津的北洋政府代理外交次长夏诒霆等人态度敷衍塞责，厚颜无耻。被激怒的民众召开18000余人大会，通电要求北洋政府惩办夏诒霆等人。这使广大民众意识到不能寄希望于腐败无能的政府，只有依靠自身力量才能维护自己的国土。随着天津的反法运动日趋激烈，外交部长陈锦涛提出辞职，代理外交次长夏诒霆不久也被撤换。

天津人民的斗争长达四个月，不仅造成了法租界的瘫痪，还使法国在华的商业利益受到巨大损失。中国人抵制法货，拒绝使用法国货币，许多天津商店的门口都贴有"凡法国货币概不收用"的告示。法国人为了解决供电问题，高薪招聘工人却无一人应聘，不得已向英国电灯公司求告借人。天津英国电灯公司的工人严厉警告英国人："如果帮助法人，将用对待法人办法对待之。"结果英国人不敢答应法国人的要求。就连法租界内的他国商行也唯恐受到殃及，亨达

① 《益世报》1916年11月18日。

② 《益世报》1916年11月25日。

③ 来新夏主编，《天津近代史》，南开大学出版社，1987年，第258页。

he would not shirk his responsibility," which "moved everyone who heard it, and the whole audience applauded continuously." On the afternoon of November 16th, the Assembly held a meeting at the Nanshi Grand Stage specifically to raise funds for the livelihood of the striking workers, deciding to invite famous actors from the Beijing-Tianjin area to hold a joint performance, with all proceeds going towards strike funds. The Chamber of Commerce prepared rooms to provide resting places for the workers and offered food and heating equipment. Longxing Coal Yard on Santiaoshi Street donated two thousand jin (0.5 kilo) of hard coal without asking for a penny. Even cart drivers donated their meager earnings. In less than a week, donations from all sectors of Tianjin amounted to over forty thousand yuan.[1] Real estate companies announced that to provide resettlement for those leaving the French Concession, they would offer housing with rents reduced by thirty percent.[2]

Originally, the people of Tianjin placed their hopes on the Beiyang Government's diplomatic negotiations. However, the Chinese government initially prepared to compromise with France and accept the reality of France occupying Laoxikai. The Deputy Minister of Foreign Affairs of the Beiyang Government, Xia Yiting, and others who came to Tianjin had an indifferent and shameless attitude. Enraged citizens convened a mass meeting of over 18,000 people and issued a public demand for the Beiyang Government to punish Xia Yiting and others. This made the general public realize that they could not rely on a corrupt and incompetent government, and only by relying on their own strength could they defend their homeland. As the anti-French movement in Tianjin intensified, Foreign Minister Chen Jintao tendered his resignation, and Acting Deputy Minister of Foreign Affairs Xia Yiting was soon replaced.

The struggle of the people of Tianjin lasted for four months, not only causing paralysis in the French Concession but also inflicting enormous losses on French commercial interests in China. Chinese people boycotted French goods and refused to use French currency. Many shops in Tianjin had notices posted at their entrances stating, "No French currency accepted." In order to solve the power supply problem, the French offered high salaries to recruit workers, but no one applied. They had to reluctantly ask the British Tianjin Gas and Electric Light Company for help. Workers of the British Tianjin Gas and Electric Light Company in Tianjin sternly warned the British, "If you help the French, we will treat you the same way we treat the French." As a result, the British dared not comply with the French's request. Even other foreign businesses within the French Concession feared being affected. The

① *Social Welfare*, November 25, 1916.

② Lai Xinxia. *Modern History of Tianjin*. Nankai University Press, 1987, p.258.

利洋行郑重请美国领事向公民大会声明，其为瑞士洋行，不是法国商人，以平息行内已开始酝酿的罢工行动。[1] 与此同时，法国正全力投入第一次世界大战，无力干预东方事务。1916年底，法国政府电令驻华公使尽快结束老西开事件。于是法国公使向中国政府提出暂时维持原状的要求，原公使被召回国，代理公使允诺将归还老西开土地。11月19日，被拘捕的中国警察尽数送回，"老西开事件"至此落幕。但老西开地区事实上仍长期维持中法共管局面。

在反对法帝国主义侵占老西开的斗争中，天津的资产阶级和知识精英充当了运动的领导者。"它的种种活动远远超出了'天津教案'和义和团运动的斗争水平。"这场城市中的革命，广泛地团结了全市各个阶级、阶层的民众，形成了强大的合力，恰当地运用了不同的斗争的策略，集中力量打击法帝国主义，最终利用欧战的有利时机取得了斗争胜利。这次运动是中国共产党成立以前工人阶级与民族资产阶级自发合作的一次政治斗争，说明在半殖民地半封建社会国家，建立最广泛统一战线的重要性，在中国工人运动史上也有着重要意义。

值得一提的是，在老西开事件中，天主教会内部出现明显对立的两个阵营。天津教区的比利时籍副主教雷鸣远（Vincent Lebbe）批评由外国各个修会代表本国利益控制中国天主教的做法，反对法国人扩展天津法租界的行动，提出"中国归中国人"的口号。雷鸣远于1915年10月1日在南市荣业大街创办《益世报》，利用这个舆论阵地大力呼吁、报道和支持天津人民的反抗。他在《益世报》上登出致法国领事公开信，吁请其放弃妄想。1916年5月，租界中连接道路的桥筑好，法方派出士兵巡逻。在雷鸣远提醒下，中方也派出警察设岗，形成双方对峙。法国领事向天主教教会抗议雷鸣远的作为，主教于是命令雷鸣远不许再就老西开问题发言。为此他还被法国籍主教杜保禄（Paul–Marie Dumond）降职调往外地，1920年更遭遣送回欧洲。[2]

① 来新夏主编，《天津近代史》，南开大学出版社，1987年，第258页。

② 杨大辛，《津门古今杂谭》，天津人民出版社，2015年，第98、99页。

Hope Bros. &. Co. solemnly requested the American Consul to declare to the Assembly that they were a Swiss firm, not French, in order to quell the brewing strike action within the company.[1] At the same time, France was fully engaged in World War I and had no power to intervene in Eastern affairs. At the end of 1916, the French government ordered the French Minister to China to quickly resolve the Laoxikai Incident. Consequently, the French Minister requested the Chinese government to maintain the status quo temporarily. The former Minister was recalled to France, and the acting Minister promised to return the land of Laoxikai. On November 19th, all the arrested Chinese police were returned, marking the end of the "Laoxikai Incident." However, the Laoxikai area continued to be effectively under joint control by China and France for an extended period.

In the struggle against French imperialist occupation of Laoxikai, Tianjin's bourgeoisie and intellectual elites played the role of leaders in the movement. "Its various activities far exceeded the level of struggle seen in the 'Tianjin Missionary Case' and the Boxer Rebellion." This urban revolution extensively united people from all classes and strata of Tianjin, forming a powerful collective force. It effectively utilized different strategies of struggle, focusing its efforts on combating French imperialism. Ultimately, it seized the opportunity presented by the favorable conditions of the European War to achieve victory in the struggle. This movement was a political struggle in which the working class and the national bourgeoisie cooperated spontaneously before the establishment of the Communist Party of China. It demonstrates the importance of establishing the broadest united front in semi-colonial and semi-feudal societies and holds significance in the history of the Chinese labor movement.

It's worth mentioning that during the Laoxikai Incident, there were two distinct factions within the Catholic Church. Belgian Vice-Bishop Vincent Lebbe of the Tianjin Diocese criticized the practice of foreign religious orders representing their own countries' interests in controlling Chinese Catholicism. He opposed French expansion of the Tianjin Concession and advocated for the slogan "China for the Chinese." On October 1, 1915, Lebbe established the *Social Welfare* on Rongye Street in Nanshi, using this platform to vigorously advocate for, report on, and support the resistance of the Tianjin people. He published an open letter to the French Consul in *Social Welfare*, urging him to abandon his delusions. In May 1916, when the bridges connecting the roads in the concession were completed, French soldiers were sent to patrol. At Lebbe's reminder, the Chinese side also deployed police to set up posts, leading to a

① Lai Xinxia. *Modern History of Tianjin*. Nankai University Press, 1987, p.258.

雷鸣远（1877—1940），天主教遣使会神父。1877年出生于比利时。1901年被比利时教会派往中国传教。1906年来津任天主教天津教区总铎。1915年在天津创办《益世报》。1916年爆发"老西开事件"，他站在中国人民一方反对扩展法租界，受到法国当局迫害达10年之久。在此期间被遣返欧洲，后又被派到河北传教。他热爱中国，于1927年改入中国籍，自称"天津人"

Vincent Lebbe (1877-1940) was a Lazarists priest. Born in Belgium in 1877, he was assigned to China in 1901 by the Belgian Church. In 1906, he arrived in Tianjin to serve as the Vicar of the Catholic Diocese of Tianjin. In 1915, he founded the *Social Welfare* in Tianjin. During the 1916 "Laoxikai Incident," he supported the Chinese people's opposition to the expansion of the French Concession and was persecuted by the French authorities for nearly 10 years. During this period, he was deported to Europe, but was later sent to preach in Hebei. He developed a deep love for China and, in 1927, became a Chinese citizen, declaring himself a "Tianjinese"

穿中国服装的雷鸣远
Vincent Lebbe in Chinese clothing

《益世报》是近代天津最有名的报纸之一，是罗马天主教教会在华出版的中文日报。1915年10月1日创刊于天津，罗马天主教天津教区副主教雷鸣远和中国教徒刘守荣创办并主持。20世纪三四十年代，《益世报》持自由主义倾向，在反对国民党的腐败统治和抵抗帝国主义国家的侵略方面，《益世报》的立场是鲜明的，成为国内反抗日本侵略最激烈的大报。1949年停刊

Social Welfare, was one of the most famous newspapers in modern Tianjin, and it was the Chinese daily newspaper published by the Roman Catholic Church in China. It was founded on October 1, 1915, in Tianjin by Vicent Lebbe, the Vice Bishop of the Roman Catholic Diocese of Tianjin, and Liu Shourong, a Chinese Catholic layman. In the 1930s and 1940s, *Social Welfare* held liberal views and took a strong stance against the corruption of the Kuomintang government and the imperialist powers' aggression. It became one of the most prominent newspapers in China in its resistance to Japanese invasion. The newspaper ceased publication in 1949

五四运动中的天津

第一次世界大战结束后，中国派出外交代表团参加巴黎和会，本以为可以借战胜国身份，收回战败国德国在山东的权益。不料"公理"不能战胜"强权"，参会列强将山东权益转让给日本。于是，中国民众长久以来积蓄的爱国热情被点燃。1919 年 5 月 4 日，北京的学生游行示威，抗议和会上有关山东问题的决议，敦促当时的北洋政府不可签约，并要求惩处相关官员。由此引发了一系列的全国性游行示威、罢课、罢市、罢工及抵制日货活动，进而导致影响深远的整个社会变革。

新式知识分子、新思想与新文化运动

任何一项政治运动的发生发展都有其思想根源。自鸦片战争后，一部分知识分子睁眼看世界，从那时起，很多西方近代思想开始传入中国。在天津，随着洋务运动的开展，大量留学生归国后效力于洋务事业，同时开办报纸刊物，并在其上译介了大量在近代非常有影响的思想，使逐渐开放的中国社会经历了一系列思想潮流的洗礼。

严复
Yan Fu

与此同时，1907 年以后新式西方教育制度开始大规模施行。此后十年间，大约有 1000 万人接受了各种方式的新式教育。① 在现代西方文明的影响下，他们与传统思想意识渐渐背道而驰，走上新式知识分子阶层走向寻找有效路径"救中国"的道路。

1880 年严复来到天津，任北洋水师学堂所属驾驶学堂的"洋文正教习"，后成为水师学堂会办、总办（相当于副校长、校长）。甲午战争之后，激愤不已的严复在天津《直报》发表《论世变之亟》《原强》《辟韩》《救

① （美）周策纵著，陈永明等译，《"五四"运动史》，世界图书出版公司，2016 年，第 9 页。

---

standoff between the two sides. The French Consul protested Lebbe's actions to the Catholic Church, prompting the Bishop to order Lebbe not to speak out on the Laoxikai issue anymore. As a result, he was demoted and transferred to a distant location by French Bishop Paul-Marie Dumond, and in 1920, he was deported back to Europe.[1]

Tianjin in the May Fourth Movement

After the end of World War I, China sent a diplomatic delegation to participate in the Paris Peace Conference, hoping to reclaim the rights in Shandong Province held by the defeated country Germany under the identity of a victorious nation. However, "justice" was unable to overcome "power," and the participating powers transferred the rights in Shandong to Japan. As a result, the long-held patriotic fervor of the Chinese people was ignited. On May 4, 1919, students in Beijing staged protests and demonstrations, protesting the resolutions regarding the Shandong issue at the conference, urging the then Beiyang government not to sign any agreements, and demanding punishment for relevant officials. This triggered a series of nationwide protests, strikes, boycotts of Japanese goods, and other activities, leading to profound social changes and ideological revolutions.

New Intellectuals, New Ideas, and the New Culture Movement

The occurrence and development of any political movement have their ideological roots. Since the Opium War, some intellectuals have begun to open their eyes to the world, and from then on, many Western modern thoughts have begun to enter China. In Tianjin, with the development of the Westernization Movement, a large number of students returning from abroad have devoted themselves to the cause of self-strengthening, while also launching newspapers and periodicals, through which a large number of influential modern Western thoughts have been introduced, leading to a series of ideological trends in gradually opening Chinese society. At the same time, after 1907, the new Western-style education system began to be implemented on a large scale. Over the next decade, approximately 10 million people received various forms of modern education.[2] Under the influence of modern Western civilization, they

① Yang Daxin. *Miscellaneous Tales of Tianjin Through the Ages*. Tianjin People's Publishing House, 2015, p.98. 99.

② Zhou Cezong. *The May Fourth Movement: Intellectual Revolution in Modern China*, translated by Chen Yongming, et al. World Publishing Company, 2016, p.9.

亡决论》等文，主张变法维新、武装抗击外来侵略。1897 年参与创办《国闻报》和《国闻汇编》，宣传变法维新。同时，他翻译《天演论》，并在《国闻报》报上连续发表，大力介绍和宣传进化论学说，主张社会变革和唤起民族觉醒。从此，"物竞天择，适者生存"的观念日益深入人心，成为那个时代人民救亡图存的思想武器和上层阶级占据统治性的意识形态。这种意识形态落实在政体上，往往被解读为民主共和优于君主立宪，君主立宪优于君主专制，成为以后维新和革命运动的思想理论基础。

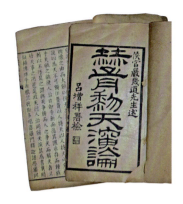

严复翻译的《天演论》
Evolution and Ethics translated by Yan Fu

辛亥革命后，中国社会原本面临的各种内忧外患并未减少。在国内，经历了两次复辟帝制的失败，中国随即陷入军阀混战、地方割据的状态；国际上，列强之间对中国的瓜分和侵略虽然告一段落，但是彼此的争权夺利并未减少，直至矛盾激化引发了第一次世界大战。趁西方列强无暇东顾之机，日本想要全面控制中国。而当时的大总统袁世凯为了复辟帝制需要得到日本支持，接受了日本妄图独霸中国的"二十一条"。这个消息一经泄露，立即引起全国舆论大哗，几乎所有中国报章杂志都表现出强烈的反日情绪，引发了强烈的民族主义情绪，"勿忘国耻"的标语在全国随处可见，甚至事件经过也被写进教科书。[1] 这次事件可以说是中国民众、特别是新式知识分子在近代史上第一次大规模公开表达自己的意见，这也成为五四运动的先声。1915 年 12 月 12 日袁世凯复辟帝制，只当了 83 天皇帝，就被迫结束闹剧。此后，1917 年安徽军阀张勋拥立清朝末代皇帝溥仪复辟，仅仅坚持了 12 天而迅速失败。

然而，第一次世界大战的爆发，使曾对中国社会产生过巨大影响、

gradually diverged from traditional ideology, joining the ranks of the new intellectual class and seeking effective paths to "save China."

In 1880, Yan Fu arrived in Tianjin and served as the "Western Language Chief Instructor" at the Navigation School affiliated with the Beiyang Naval Academy, later becoming the manager and director (equivalent to vice principal and principal) of the Naval Academy. After the First Sino-Japanese War, the enraged Yan Fu published articles such as *On the Speed of World Change*, *On the Origin of Strength*, *Refutation of Han Yu*, and *On Our Salvation* in the Tianjin *Chih Pao*, advocating reform and renewal, and armed resistance against foreign aggression. In 1897, he participated in the founding of *Kwo Wen Pao* and *Compilation of Kwo Wen Pao*, advocating reform and renewal. At the same time, he translated *Evolution and Ethics* and published it serially in *Kwo Wen Pao*, vigorously introducing and promoting evolutionary theory, advocating social change, and arousing national awakening. From then on, the concept of "the survival of the fittest" increasingly penetrated people's hearts, becoming the ideological weapon of the people of that era striving for survival, and the dominant ideology of the upper class. This ideology was implemented in the political system, often interpreted as democracy and republicanism being superior to constitutional monarchy, and constitutional monarchy being superior to absolute monarchy, becoming the theoretical basis for subsequent reform and revolutionary movements.

After the Revolution of 1911, the various internal and external challenges facing Chinese society did not diminish. Domestically, following two failed attempts to restore the monarchy, China plunged into a state of warlordism and regional division. Internationally, although the partition and aggression of China among the great powers came to a temporary halt, their competition for power and profit did not decrease, eventually leading to the escalation of tensions and the outbreak of the First World War. Taking advantage of the distraction of the Western powers, Japan sought to gain full control over China. At that time, President Yuan Shikai, in need of Japanese support to restore the monarchy, accepted Japan's attempt to dominate China with the "Twenty-One Demands." Upon the leakage of this news, it immediately caused nationwide uproar, with almost all Chinese newspapers and magazines expressing strong anti-Japanese sentiment, igniting intense nationalist fervor. Slogans like "Never Forget National Humiliation" could be seen everywhere in the country, and the incident itself was even written into textbooks.[1] This event can be considered the first large-scale public expression of opinion by

① （美）周策纵著，陈永明等译，《"五四"运动史》，世界图书出版公司，2016 年，第 22 页。

① Zhou Cezong. *The May Fourth Movement: Intellectual Revolution in Modern China*, translated by Chen Yongming, et al. World Publishing Company, 2016, p.22.

并推动了社会变革和进步的进化论，遭到不少思想家的反思和批判。他们认为，进化论鼓吹"弱肉强食""优胜略汰"，为帝国主义推行强权政治、侵略弱小民族提供了理论依据，是导致欧战爆发的重要原因；而国内的军阀混战，大军阀吞并小军阀、强人欺压弱者，也正是建立在这种观念之上。后来定居天津的梁启超在 1920 年《欧游心影录》中指出："谓剿绝弱者为强者之天职，且为世运进化所必要。这种怪论，就是借达尔文的生物学做个基础。"①

欧战爆发和反日浪潮，还直接导致了大批海外留学生回到祖国，投身新文化运动。近代中国自"留美幼童"开始派遣留学生。19 世纪末、20 世纪初，更多留学生赴日本、美国或者欧洲大陆，特别是法国留学。新文化运动的很多倡导者，都是自欧美日归来的留学生，如留学日本的陈独秀、鲁迅、钱玄同、周作人，留学美国的胡适、蒋梦麟，留学法国的蔡元培等。这些国家的思想文化、社会政治被深受其影响的留学生带回祖国，在新文化运动及其后的五四运动中留下了深刻的印迹。

1915 年 9 月，陈独秀在上海创办《青年杂志》（后改名《新青年》），意味着新文化运动由此发端。新文化运动提出了拥护"德先生"和"赛先生"的口号，即提倡民主与科学。中国人对民主与科学的了解，源自鸦片战争中外国人的坚船利炮，经历了洋务运动的"师夷长技以制夷"和戊戌维新的"兴民权""设议院"的尝试后，因辛亥革命，而使民主思想得到进一步传播，科学的重要性也为越来越多的人所认识。陈独秀在《青年杂志》创刊号上发表《敬告青年》一文，疾呼："只有这两位先生（指民主与科学），可以救治中国政治上道德上学术上思想上的一切的黑暗。"他认为，民主是一种个人独立自主的观念，具有不迷信不盲从的独立思考的自我意识和敢担干系的负责态度。李大钊则指出，"现代生活的种种方面都带有 Democracy 的颜色，……Democracy 就是现代唯一权威"②。新文化运动对科学的理解和认识是广义上的，不仅是科学技术或科学思

---

① 梁启超，《欧游心影录》，《饮冰室合集》第 7 册，专集之二十三，第 9 页。

② 李大钊，《劳动教育问题》，《李大钊文集》（上），人民出版社，1984 年，第 632 页。

the Chinese people, especially the new intellectuals, in modern history, laying the groundwork for the May Fourth Movement. On December 12, 1915, Yuan Shikai restored the monarchy, becoming emperor for only 83 days before being forced to end the farce. Subsequently, in 1917, Anhui Clique warlord Zhang Xun supported the restoration of the last Emperor of the Qing Dynasty, Puyi, which lasted only 12 days before quickly failing.

However, the outbreak of the First World War led to considerable reflection and criticism of Darwinian evolution, which had previously exerted a significant influence on Chinese society and had promoted social change and progress. Many intellectuals argued that Darwinian evolution, with its promotion of "survival of the fittest" and "natural selection," provided a theoretical basis for imperialism's practice of power politics and aggression against weaker nations, making it an important cause of the outbreak of the European war. Moreover, the internal warlord conflicts in China, characterized by large warlords swallowing up smaller ones and the strong oppressing the weak, were also seen as being based on this ideology. Liang Qichao, who later settled in Tianjin, pointed out in his 1920 work *Reflections on My Travels in Europe*: "The belief that it is the duty of the strong to exterminate the weak is essential for the progress of the world. This absurd theory is based on Darwin's biology."[1]

The outbreak of the European War and the anti-Japanese wave also directly led to a large number of overseas students returning to their homeland and joining the New Culture Movement. Modern China began sending students abroad with the "Boxer Indemnity Scholarship Program" to the United States. In the late 19th and early 20th centuries, more students went to Japan, the United States, or Europe, especially France, for further studies. Many advocates of the New Culture Movement were returning students from Europe, America, and Japan, such as Chen Duxiu, Lu Xun, Qian Xuantong, and Zhou Zuoren, who studied in Japan; Hu Shi and Jiang Menglin, who studied in the United States; and Cai Yuanpei, who studied in France. Influenced by the ideologies, cultures, and social politics of these countries, these returning students left a profound imprint on China during the New Culture Movement and the subsequent May Fourth Movement.

In September 1915, Chen Duxiu founded the *Youth Magazine* (later renamed *New Youth*) in Shanghai, marking the beginning of the New Culture Movement. The New Culture Movement advocated the slogans of embracing "Mr. Democracy" and "Mr. Science," promoting democracy and

---

① Liang Qichao. *Reflections on My Travels in Europe*. Ice-drinking Room Combined Collected *Works: Volume 7*. Special Collection 23, p.9.

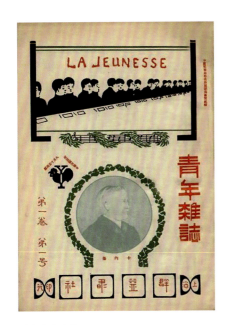

《青年杂志》
Youth Magazine

想，而且是一种世界观和方法论，一种与迷信、盲从、愚昧相对立的崇尚实证的理性精神。正因为新文化运动将民主与科学作为其核心观念和基本价值，反对封建专制主义、迷信愚昧思想以及旧伦理道德，甚至将其与对传统文化的反思和批判联系在一起，所以极大地解放了人们尤其是年轻人的思想，使其激发起强烈的社会责任感，进而投身社会变革的浪潮。

1917年十月革命爆发，这个消息被迅速传递给中国的知识分子。革命爆发后第三天，上海《民国日报》就以《突如其来的俄国大政变》对其加以介绍。之后，《时报》《申报》《晨钟报》《太平洋》《劳动》《东方杂志》等纷纷对十月革命过程、劳工政权、反地主反资本主义基本方针及和平友好外交政策等进行报道。受到革命胜利启发的李大钊，在《新青年》和《每周评论》等阵地上奋笔疾书，大量宣传介绍十月革命和马克思列宁主义的文章、演说，并且发起组织马克思学说研究会。十月革命以及战后其他国家爆发的社会主义革命，给中国相当一部分新式知识分子带来了"自由的曙光"①。

第一次世界大战与新阶级、新经验

五四运动中，有很多具有一定知识甚至有海外经历的工人发挥了重要作用。他们中有一些是通商口岸中各中外工厂中的雇工，也有一些是曾在欧洲参加过第一次世界大战的华工，还有的则是曾留学海外半工半读的"学生工人"。他们与青年学生、广大市民、工商人士等阶层一起共同参与，通过罢工、示威等方式有力地声援了

---

① 李大钊，《布尔什维克主义的胜利》，《新青年》1918年11月15日，第五卷第五号。

science. Chinese understanding of democracy and science stemmed from the experience of foreign powers' superior military technology during the Opium War, followed by attempts such as the Westernization Movement and the Hundred Days' Reform to adopt Western methods, and further spread after the 1911 Revolution. The importance of science became increasingly recognized. In the inaugural issue of *Youth Magazine*, Chen Duxiu published an article titled *Advice for Youth*, urging, "Only these two gentlemen (referring to democracy and science) can cure all the darkness in China politically, morally, academically, and intellectually." He believed that democracy was a concept of individual independence, characterized by independent thinking free from superstition and blind obedience, and a responsible attitude towards oneself. Li Dazhao pointed out, "Various aspects of modern life are tinged with the color of Democracy... Democracy is the sole authority of modernity."① The New Culture Movement's understanding of science was broad, encompassing not only scientific technology or scientific thought but also a worldview and methodology, advocating empirical rationality opposed to superstition, blind obedience, and ignorance. Because the New Culture Movement took democracy and science as its core concepts and fundamental values, opposing feudal autocracy, superstition, and old ethical morals, and even linking them to reflection and criticism of traditional culture, it greatly liberated people's, especially young people's, thinking, instilling them with a strong sense of social responsibility and leading them to engage in the tide of social change.

The October Revolution broke out in 1917, and this news was swiftly transmitted to Chinese intellectuals. Three days after the revolution broke out, the Shanghai *Republican Daily News* introduced it with the headline *Sudden Russian Political Upheaval*. Subsequently, newspapers such as *The Eastern Times*, *The Shun Pao*, *The Morning Post*, *The Pacific Ocean*, *Labor*, and *The Eastern Miscellany* reported on various aspects of the October Revolution, including the process, the labor government, the basic policies against landlords and capitalism, and the policy of peaceful and friendly diplomacy. Inspired by the success of the revolution, Li Dazhao vigorously wrote articles in publications such as *New Youth* and *The Weekly Review*, extensively promoting and introducing articles and speeches on the October Revolution and Marxism-Leninism, and even initiated the organization of the Marxist Research Society. The October Revolution, along with socialist revolutions in other countries after the revolution, brought a "dawn of freedom" to a

---

① Li Dazhao. *Labor Education Issues. Li Dazhao Collected Works* (vol.1). People's Publishing House, 1984, p.632.

一战中的中国劳工。图片来源：比利时法兰德斯一战战地博物馆
Chinese laborers during the First World War. Source: In Flanders Fields Museum, Belgium

这场爱国运动，同时也标志着中国工人阶级开始登上政治舞台，并逐渐成为斗争主力。

　　早在洋务运动中，各个洋务企业开始将一些工人送往欧洲学习工业技能。例如，1892 年张之洞在创办汉阳铁厂时，曾经派遣 40 名中国工匠赴比利时列日省的郭格里尔（Cockerill，也译作克革列）钢铁厂学炼钢铁，回国后成为技术骨干。民国建立之后，1912 年李石曾、蔡元培等人组织建立了"留法学生会"，开展勤工俭学运动。旅欧学潮兴起后，天津、北京、上海和保定等地纷纷建立"俭学会"，组织者在当地开办法语预备班，为留学做准备。从 1912 年到 1913 年的一年间，共有大约 120 名学生赴法。① 第一次世界大战期间，勤工俭学的学生人数开始增加，于是蔡元培和一些朋友在法国成立了华法教育会以帮助在法学生。1919 年年底，在法勤工俭学者已达 400 人，翌年又增加了 1200 人。这些学生中只有小半进了学校，大半则是在工厂或其他地方打工。②

①　舒新城，《近代中国留学史》，1933 年，第 86—88 页。张允侯等编，《留法勤工俭学运动》（一），上海人民出版社，1980 年，第 12—14 页。

②　陈学恂、田正平编，《留学教育》，上海教育出版社，2007 年，第 518—529 页。

considerable number of new intellectuals in China.[1]

The First World War and the New Class, New Experience

In the May Fourth Movement, many workers with certain knowledge or overseas experiences played significant roles. Among them were some employed in various Chinese and foreign factories in the treaty ports, some were Chinese laborers who had participated in the First World War in Europe, and others were "student workers" who had studied overseas while working. They, together with young students, the general public, businessmen, and others, participated actively in this patriotic movement through strikes, demonstrations, and other means, marking the beginning of the Chinese working class stepping onto the political stage and gradually becoming the main force in the struggle.

As early as the Westernization Movement, various enterprises began sending some workers to Europe to learn industrial skills. For example, in 1892, when Zhang Zhidong established the Hankou Iron and Steel Works, he sent 40 Chinese craftsmen to study steelmaking at the Cockerill Iron and Steel Works in Liège Province, Belgium. After returning to China, they became the backbone of the technical workforce. After the establishment of the Republic of China, in 1912, Li Shizeng, Cai Yuanpei, and others organized the "Association of Students Studying in France" to promote the Diligent Work-Frugal Study Movement. With the rise of the trend of studying abroad in Europe, associations promoting frugal study were established in Tianjin, Beijing, Shanghai, Baoding, and other places. Organizers set up preparatory French classes locally to prepare students for studying abroad. From 1912 to 1913, approximately 120 students went to France within a year.[2] During the First World War, the number of students participating in frugal study began to increase. Consequently, Cai Yuanpei and some friends established the Sino-French Education Association in France to assist students there. By the end of 1919, the number of students working diligently and studying frugally in France had reached 400, and the following year, an additional 1,200 students joined. Only a small portion of these students attended school, while the majority worked in factories or other places.[3]

①　Li Dazhao. The Victory of Bolshevism. *New Youth*, Vol.5, No.5, November 15, 1918.

②　Shu Xincheng. *A History of Studying Abroad in Modern China*. 1933, pp.86-88. Zhang Yunhou (eds.). *Diligent Work-Frugal Study Movement in France* (1). Shanghai People's Publishing House, 1980, pp.12-14.

③　Chen Xuexun, Tian Zhengping (eds.). *Study Abroad.* Shanghai Educational Publishing House, 2007, pp.518-529.

第一次世界大战期间，在欧洲的中国工人，除了以上那些"学生工人"，还有被中国政府派到欧洲参战的劳工。1914年大战爆发后，有国内政治家鼓动袁世凯参战，声称一旦成为战胜国，不但可以提高中国的国际地位，还可借机收回一部分中国以前被列强攫取的特权和领土。起初，在日本的反对下，协约国不希望中国加入战斗并获得平等地位。但随着战争机器对士兵和劳动力的不断绞杀，法国、英国和俄国政府都不得不与中国政府签订输入劳工的长期合同。法国政府和英国政府在1916年和1920年之间雇用了14万或者15万中国劳工，俄国则在1915年和1917年之间雇用了5万中国劳工。[①]

劳工们抵达欧洲后，有的在冶金、化工和兵工厂工作，有的则前往战场服务。尽管合同上规定，中国劳工原则上不应该参与"军事活动"，但北洋政府对德宣战后，中国劳工几乎全部被送往前线。在那里，他们主要负责挖战壕、运送伤员、补给等体力劳动，虽然没有直接参与作战，但他们的工作依然繁重且极具危险性。中国劳工需要帮助当地人继续清理战场的废墟，搬运安葬尸体，修建桥梁、公路、铁路。战后工作的危险程度一点儿不亚于战时，搬运埋在土地里未爆炸的弹药时稍有疏忽便可能伤亡，战场上腐烂的尸体滋生细菌也可能导致他们染上疾病。[②]

如此众多的出身于农村的中国人一下子成为工人，并被派往西方国家工作，在中国历史上是破天荒的。在留法俭学会的帮助下，中国政府与协约国商定，在招募的华工中须有学生和教师作为通译员一起来到欧洲，从事体力劳动之余，还要教导华工识字。这使中国知识分子有机会与工人一起生活劳动，并肩负起领导组织的责任。因此，这些华工是受到教育的能识字有文化的工人。"根据合约，他们还有权组织工会，并且和其他公民同样享有法国法律所保障的

During the First World War, in addition to the "student workers" mentioned above, Chinese workers in Europe also included laborers sent by the Chinese government to participate in the war. After the outbreak of the war in 1914, some domestic politicians advocated for Yuan Shikai's participation in the war, claiming that once China became victorious, it could not only enhance China's international status but also seize back some of the privileges and territories previously taken by foreign powers. Initially, due to opposition from Japan, the Allied Forces did not want China to join the combat and obtain equal status. However, as the war machine continued to demand soldiers and labor, the governments of France, Britain, and Russia were compelled to sign long-term contracts with the Chinese government for importing labor. Between 1916 and 1920, the French and British governments hired approximately 140,000 to 150,000 Chinese laborers, while Russia employed 50,000 Chinese laborers between 1915 and 1917.[①]

After arriving in Europe, some laborers worked in metallurgy, chemical, and munitions factories, while others went to serve on the battlefield. Although the contracts stipulated that Chinese laborers should not be involved in "military activities" in principle, after the Beiyang government declared war on Germany, almost all Chinese laborers were sent to the front lines. There, they were mainly responsible for digging trenches, transporting wounded soldiers, and supplying goods, among other physical tasks. Although they did not directly engage in combat, their work was still strenuous and extremely dangerous. Chinese laborers needed to help locals continue clearing battlefield debris, moving and burying bodies, and constructing bridges, roads, and railways. The danger of post-war work was no less than that during the war; even a slight negligence while handling unexploded ammunition buried in the ground could lead to casualties, and the bacteria breeding in the decaying bodies on the battlefield could also expose them to diseases.[②]

So many rural Chinese suddenly becoming workers and being sent to Western countries for work was unprecedented in Chinese history. With the assistance of the French Diligent Work-Frugal Study Organization, the Chinese government reached an agreement with the Allied Forces that among the recruited Chinese laborers, there must be students and teachers serving

① （法）多米尼克·马亚尔、曲辰，《第一次世界大战期间在法国的中国劳工》，《国际观察》2009年第2期，第74页。（比）邓杜文，皮特·奇连斯，《第一次世界大战：五大洲前线》（拉辛版本，2008年），第136—144页。

② （法）多米尼克·马亚尔、曲辰，《第一次世界大战期间在法国的中国劳工》，《国际观察》2009年第2期，第74—75页。比利时驻华大使馆、《使馆商社贸易快讯》杂志社编，《走进比利时》，世界在线外交传媒集团，2004，第141页。

① Dominigue Maillard. China's Laborers in France in World War I. *International Review*, 2009(02), p.74. Dominiek Dendooven & Piet Chielens. *La Premiere Guerre Mondiale: Cinq Continents au Front* (Editions Racine, 2008), pp.136-144.

② Dominigue Maillard. China's Laborers in France in World War I. *International Review*, 2009(02), pp.74-75. Embassy of Belgium in China, *Trade News of Embassy Commercial Organization* (eds.). *A Passage to Belgium*. World Online Media and Entertainment Group, 2004, p.141.

自由。"① 在知识分子的协助下，一战期间在法国的华工组织了很多自助、互助机构，如职业介绍所、工会、工人社团、中国劳工社、储蓄会、读书会等，帮助华工向所在地政府争取福利。至 1918 年战争结束，华工依照合约规定回到中国时，相当多的人已成为有知识有组织的工人阶级，而且知识分子开始关注劳工阶级，并有意识地组织和帮助工人阶级学文化、谋福利。1918 年，曾在法国参与过华工教育工作的晏阳初，利用在法教育工人的经验，领导和推动了五四运动后期曾风行一时的平民教育运动。

战后回到中国的华工和"勤工俭学生"们给国内带来了新思想、新经验。他们不但体验到西方工业革命后较高的生活水平，还亲历了当时欧洲的社会革命和劳工运动，民族主义意识变得十分强烈。中国共产党的创始人和早期领导者中，有相当一部分是在法国勤工俭学中得以接触到资本主义的阴暗面，从而印证了马克思主义的科学性，日后成为中国革命坚定的核心。这些人中包括陈延年、陈乔年、王若飞、刘伯坚、陈毅、李维汉、李富春、蔡和森、向警予、李立三、聂荣臻等。1917 年十月革命爆发后，在俄国的华工亲身经历和感受了这场革命。革命中，大批旅俄华工参加了红军。苏联红军第三军二十九师后备团、乌拉尔中国团、莫斯科中国团等全体成员都是华工。在莫斯科、彼得堡，华工组织的赤卫队，直接参加了夺取冬宫的战斗和莫斯科的十月武装起义。② 1919 年 3 月 2 日第三国际第一次代表大会在莫斯科召开，旅俄华工联合会会长刘绍周代表中国，与来自欧洲、亚洲和美洲的 21 个国家的 52 名代表参加了此次会议。③ 从欧洲战场上回国的华工和学生，聚集在天津、上海、青岛等沿海城市的工厂中。他们带回了罢工和革命斗争的经验，成为日后五四运动后期发挥重要作用的工人运动的领导者和参与者，有力地推动了运动的发展。

---

① （美）周策纵著，陈永明等译，《"五四"运动史》，世界图书出版公司，2016 年，第 39 页。

② 姚涵、潘乐，《十月革命"一声炮响"怎样传入中国》，《解放日报》，2021 年 6 月 29 日。

③ 李玉贞，《国民党与共产国际（1919—1927）》，人民出版社，2012 年，第 34 页。

as interpreters to Europe. In addition to engaging in physical labor, they were also required to teach literacy to the Chinese workers. This provided Chinese intellectuals with the opportunity to live and work together with workers, taking on the responsibility of organizing and leading. Consequently, these Chinese laborers were educated and literate workers. "According to the contract, they also had the right to organize trade unions and enjoy the same freedoms guaranteed by French law as other citizens."[1] With the assistance of intellectuals, during World War I, Chinese laborers in France organized many self-help and mutual aid institutions, such as employment agencies, unions, worker associations, Chinese labor societies, savings clubs, and reading clubs, to help Chinese workers seek benefits from local governments. By the end of the war in 1918, when the Chinese laborers returned to China according to the contract, many of them had become educated and organized members of the working class. Intellectuals began to pay attention to the working class and consciously organized and assisted them in cultural learning and welfare. In 1918, Yan Yangchu, who had been involved in educating Chinese workers in France, used his experience in educating workers in France to lead and promote the grassroots education movement that was prevalent during the later stages of the May Fourth Movement.

The Chinese laborers and the "Diligent Work-Frugal Study" students who returned to China after the war brought new ideas and experiences to the country. They not only experienced the higher living standards after the Western Industrial Revolution but also witnessed the social revolutions and labor movements in Europe at that time, which intensified their nationalist consciousness. Among the founders and early leaders of the Chinese Communist Party, a considerable number had the opportunity to encounter the dark side of capitalism through their experiences in frugal study programs in France, which confirmed the scientific nature of Marxism and later became the steadfast core of the Chinese revolution. These individuals include Chen Yannian, Chen Qiaonian, Wang Ruofei, Liu Bojian, Chen Yi, Li Weihan, Li Fuchun, Cai Hesen, Xiang Jingyu, Li Lisan, Nie Rongzhen, and others. After the outbreak of the October Revolution in 1917, the Chinese workers in Russia personally experienced and felt the revolution. During the revolution, a large number of Chinese workers in Russia joined the Red Army. All members of the Reserve Regiment of the Third Army, Twenty-Ninth Division, the Chinese Units in the Urals, and in Moscow were Chinese workers. In Moscow and St. Petersburg, the Red Guard organized by Chinese workers directly participated

---

[1] Zhou Cezong. *The May Fourth Movement: Intellectual Revolution in Modern China*, translated by Chen Yongming, et al. World Publishing Company, 2016, p.39.

知识分子与工人阶级、工商业者的结合

1918 年 11 月 11 日，第一次世界大战结束。消息传来，中国作为战胜国之一，政府宣布放假三天庆祝。战后和会于次年 1 月在巴黎召开。中国人民普遍对此报以极大期许。国人的喜悦溢于言表，北京市民举行大游行，北京政府早在参战之后即设立筹备参与战后媾和的小组，收集驻外公使的报告和意见，研究未来在和会上提出的所要收回的利权。①

1919 年 1 月 11 日由外交总长陆征祥率领的中国代表团抵达巴黎。1 月 18 日和会开幕，26 个战胜国派代表出席，商议战后世界秩序的重建问题。在会议上，尽管中国全权代表、时任驻美公使的顾维钧在会议上发表了慷慨激昂的关于"山东问题"主张，然而，列强却在会议中秘密决定把德国在山东的利益全部转让给日本。中国代表团还在和会上提出要求废除根据"二十一条"签订的 1915 年中日条约，以及收回外国在华特权，但均遭和会拒绝。"弱国无外交"在巴黎和会上再一次得到印证。

1919 年 4 月下旬，和会要把德国在山东的权益让给日本的消息传回国内时，中国人民的愤怒终于如火山一样喷发了。5 月 4 日，包括北京大学在内的北京 13 所大专学校的学生代表召开了学生代表会，决定会后举行示威游行，抗议巴黎和会关于山东的决议案。下午 1 时 30 分，3000 多名学生聚集在天安门前广场，游行示威、分发传单，要求"外争主权，内除国贼"，矛头指向北京政府里的三名亲日分子曹汝霖、章宗祥和陆宗舆。随后，由于军警阻拦，学生情绪转而激动，直奔曹汝霖家，殴伤正在他家的章宗祥，并放火烧了曹家。最后，警察逮捕了几十名学生。

和会期间，天津的学生和民众一直极为关注和会议程。国内外的中国人联合起来，组织了很多民间团体，研究讨论外交问题，并致电巴黎的中国代表团进行监督。5 月 5 日，天津学生得到来自北京的消息，迅速反应。当天，北洋大学以全体学生的名义，致电北京

---

① 中国社会科学院近代史研究所译，《顾维钧回忆录》第 1 分册，中华书局，1983 年，第 162—164 页。

in the battles to seize the Winter Palace and the October Armed Uprising in Moscow.[1] On March 2, 1919, the First Congress of the Third Communist International was held in Moscow. Liu Shaozhou, the president of the Union of Chinese Workers in Russia, represented China and attended the conference along with 52 representatives from 21 countries in Europe, Asia, and the Americas.[2] Chinese workers and students returning from the European battlefield gathered in factories in coastal cities such as Tianjin, Shanghai, and Qingdao. They brought back their experiences of strikes and revolutionary struggles, becoming leaders and participants in the later stages of the May Fourth Movement, and effectively driving the development of the movement.

The Integration of Intellectuals with the Working Class, Industrialists and Businessmen

On November 11, 1918, the First World War came to an end. Upon hearing the news, the Chinese government, as one of the victorious nations, declared a three-day holiday for celebration. The post-war peace conference was held in Paris in January of the following year. The Chinese people generally anticipated this with great hope. The joy of the people was evident, with large parades held by the citizens of Beijing. The Beijing government had set up a team to prepare for participation in post-war negotiations soon after joining the war, collecting reports and opinions from its foreign envoys and studying the interests to be reclaimed at the conference.[3]

On January 11, 1919, the Chinese delegation, led by Foreign Minister Lu Zhengxiang, arrived in Paris. The conference opened on January 18, with representatives from 26 victorious nations attending to discuss the reconstruction of the post-war world order. Despite the impassioned advocacy of the "Shandong Issue" by Gu Weijun, the Chinese plenipotentiary and then Minister to the United States, the great powers secretly decided during the conference to transfer all of Germany's interests in Shandong to Japan. The Chinese delegation also demanded the annulment of the 1915 Sino-Japanese Treaty based on the "Twenty-One Demands" and the recovery of foreign privileges in China, but both requests were rejected by the conference. The

---

① Yao Han, Pan Le. How the Salvoes of October Revolution to be Introduced to China. *Jiefang Daily*, June 29, 2021.

② Li Yuzhen. *The Kuomintang and the Communist International (1919-1927)*. People's Publishing House, 2012, p.34

③ *Memoirs of Gu Weijun (vol.1)*, translated by Institute of Modern History, Chinese Academy of Social Sciences. Zhonghua Book Company, 1983, pp.162-164.

"五四"运动期间北洋大学
学生游行示威
Peiyang University students
marching in protest during
the May Fourth Movement

1919年5月北洋大学的学
生在举行抗议活动
Peiyang University students
staging a protest in May 1919

图片来源：天津大学档案馆
Source: Tianjin University Archives

大学，电文的内容是："北京大学转各学校钧鉴：惩贼有勇，极表赞同，以后共同进行。"同时致电北京政府："北京大总统、国务院钧鉴：北京学生举动情殷爱国，所拘十九人恳请释放。"5月6日，北洋大学又以全体学生名义致电巴黎和会中国专使团，电文的内容是："为谋世界悠久之和平，贯彻公理战胜之精神，青岛、胶济铁路应直接返还我国，'二十一条'条约亦当然废除，务望诸公力持到底，不获所愿，不签和约，全国人民实同此意。"[1]5月7日，北洋大学全体学生和天津各界代表近千人，聚集在北洋大学礼堂，声

---

① 《益世报》1919年5月6日、5月7日。

principle of "Might makes Right" was once again affirmed at the Paris Peace Conference, demonstrating the plight of weaker nations in diplomacy.

In late April, when news spread back home that the Paris Peace Conference intended to transfer Germany's rights in Shandong to Japan, the anger of the Chinese people finally erupted like a volcaNo.On May 4th, student representatives from 13 institutions of higher learning in Beijing, including Peking University, convened a student assembly. They decided to hold a demonstration and protest march after the meeting to oppose the resolutions of the Paris Peace Conference regarding Shandong. At 1:30 p.m., more than 3,000 students gathered in Tiananmen Square, marching and distributing leaflets, demanding "defend sovereignty externally, expel traitors internally," targeting three pro-Japanese figures within the Beijing government: Cao Rulin, Zhang Zongxiang, and Lu Zongyu. Subsequently, as the students were blocked by police and military forces, their emotions escalated, and they headed straight to Cao Rulin's residence. They assaulted Zhang Zongxiang, who was present at Cao's house, and set fire to Cao's home. Eventually, the police arrested dozens of students.

During the Paris Peace Conference, students and the public in Tianjin were closely monitoring the conference proceedings. Chinese people at home and abroad united to organize many civil groups to study and discuss diplomatic issues and sent telegrams to the Chinese delegation in Paris to supervise. On May 5th, Tianjin students swiftly responded to news from Beijing. That day, Peiyang University, on behalf of all its students, telegraphed Peking University with the message: "Peking University, to all schools, for consideration: Punishing traitors requires courage, and we fully endorse it. Let us act together in the future." Simultaneously, they telegraphed the Beijing government: "To the President of Beijing Government, State Council: The actions of Beijing students show their deep patriotism. We earnestly request the release of the nineteen detainees." On May 6th, Peiyang University, again on behalf of all its students, telegraphed the Chinese Special Envoy in Paris with the message: "In order to achieve lasting world peace and uphold the spirit of justice in victory, Qingdao and the Jiaozhou-Jinan Railway should be directly returned to our country, and the Twenty-One Demands should be naturally abolished. Please persevere and do not sign any treaty if our wishes are not met. The people nationwide share this sentiment."[1] On May 7th, all students of Peiyang University and representatives from various sectors in Tianjin, nearly a thousand people, gathered in the university auditorium to express support for the patriotic movement of Beijing students and announced the establishment

---

① *Social Welfare*. May 6-7, 1919.

援北京学生的爱国运动，同时宣告成立天津学生临时联合会。他们的这一举动，对响应北京学生的爱国运动和发动天津各界人士参加爱国运动起到了积极作用。

在天津学生临时联合会的组织下，5月12日，1000余名学生为纪念五四事件中殉难的北大学生郭钦光举行了追悼会，会后在城内外进行了街头演讲。14日，正式成立了"天津中等以上学校学生联合会"，学生来自南开学校①、直隶高等工业专门学校、北洋法政专门学校、水产学校、新学书院、北洋大学和唐山工业专门学校（即唐山交通大学，现西南交通大学）。学生会的领袖有来自直隶高等工业专门学校的谌志笃、南开学校的马骏和周恩来、北洋大学的张太雷和孙越崎、直隶省第一中学的于方舟等。大会决定即日起组织各校学生讲演队，上街讲演，宣传运动主张。5月23日，直隶省第一女子师范学校的刘清扬、王天麟、郭隆真、邓颖超等人又组织成立了"天津女界爱国同志会"，壮大了学生群体的力量。同一日，天津学生联合会开始举行全体大罢课。最先参加的有14所学校，包括北洋大学、直隶法政学校、直隶第一师范学校、高等工业学校、南开中学、省立中学、孔德中学、成美中学、大营门中学、直隶水产学校、育才中学、私立法政学校、新学书院、甲种商业学校等，共计10000余名学生宣布罢课，声援北京学生的罢课斗争（后有英华中学加入）。②

学生群体是一个特殊的社会群体，他们没有资本、没有权力也没有社会地位，但却是一群有热血有头脑、能迅速集中组织动员并发挥宣传鼓动作用的群体。罢课后，天津大中学校学生在两会的领导下，分别组织了大批的讲演团、新剧团、义勇队，上街讲演、散发传单，提出要求恢复青岛主权、拒绝承认基于"二十一条"和其他密约所签订的中日协定，并鼓励民众抵制日货、购买国货，齐心协力救中国。仅北洋大学就组织了44个讲演团分赴杨柳青、北仓、南仓、塘沽等地的工厂和农村，开展演讲活动，宣传爱国。《益世报》

① 南开大学创立于1919年2月，9月25日举行开学典礼。所以五四时期应为南开中学学生参与学生运动。
② 《申报》1919年5月26日。

of the Tianjin Student Provisional Union. Their actions played a positive role in responding to the patriotic movement of Beijing students and mobilizing people from all walks of life in Tianjin to participate in the patriotic movement.

Under the organization of the Tianjin Student Provisional Union, on May 12th, more than 1,000 students held a memorial service to commemorate Guo Qinguang, a Peking University student who died during the May Fourth Movement. After the meeting, they conducted street speeches both within and outside the city. On the 14th, the "Tianjin Federation of Students from Intermediate and Higher Schools" was formally established. Students came from Nankai School①, Zhili Higher Industrial Specialized School, Beiyang School of Law and Politics, Zhili Aquaculture Institute, Anglo-Chinese College, Peiyang University, and Tangshan School of Technology (Tangshan Institute of Jiaotong University, currently Southwest Jiaotong University). Leaders of the student union included Chen Zhidu from Zhili Higher Industrial Specialized School, Ma Jun and Zhou Enlai from Nankai School, Zhang Tailei and Sun Yueqi from Peiyang University, and Yu Fangzhou from Zhili Provincial First High School. The meeting decided to immediately organize student lecture teams from various schools to give street speeches and promote the movement's principles. On May 23rd, Liu Qingyang, Wang Tianlin, Guo Longzhen, Deng Yingchao, and others from Zhili Provincial First Women's Normal School established the "Tianjin Patriotic Women's Association," further strengthening the student community's power. On the same day, the Tianjin Student Federation began a full-scale strike. The first to participate were 14 schools, including Peiyang University, Zhili Law and Politics School, Zhili First Normal School, Zhili Higher Industrial Specialized School, Nankai Middle School, Provincial High School, Kongde Middle School, Tientsin Intermediate School for Chinese Boys, Dayingmen Middle School, Zhili Aquaculture Institute, Yucai Middle School, Private Law and Politics School, Anglo-Chinese College, and First-Class Commercial School, totaling more than 10,000 students who declared their strike in support of the Beijing students' strike movement (later joined by Yinghua Middle School).②

The student body is a special social group. They have no capital, no power, and no social status, but they are a group with passion and intelligence, able to quickly organize and mobilize, and play a role in publicity and mobilization. After the strike, under the leadership of student representatives,

① Nankai University was founded in February 1919 and held its opening ceremony on September 25 of the same year. Therefore, during the May Fourth Movement, it was the students of Nankai Middle School who participated in the student protests

② *The Shun Pao*. May 26, 1919.

曾报道了张太雷参加的北洋大学讲演第二团一行四人，一日之内不畏风雨，先赴塘沽两等小学校讲演，后又到东大沽、西大沽和塘沽火车站等地，先后讲演六次，每次听众少则几十人、多达六百余人。有的人听后十分感动地说道："先生们讲的话真对，如果能一个月来一次，使大家永远不忘才好。"学生们感到，"我国人民非无爱国心，第无人开导之耳"，由此更加坚定了与工农相结合的决心。①

天津的学生运动震动了军阀政府。时任直隶省长曹锐为直系军阀首领曹锟之弟，天津是直系军阀的大本营。虽然与皖系军阀段祺瑞控制的北京政府貌合神离，但天津直接控制北京的经济命脉，所以北京政府严令天津警方限制学生运动。6月5日，天津15所罢课学校的学生们聚集在南开中学操场，举行"六五"大集会。会后学生们准备赴省公署请愿。为了阻止学生，曹锐派出武装警察封锁了南开中学和北洋大学，不准学生们游行。学生面对荷枪实弹的军警，动之以情晓之以理："诸君非中国人邪？""我等既非土匪，又非大盗，何所持之枪咸上刺刀？"负责的警官听到这些，只得命警士等将刺刀取下。最终，经学生再三恳请，曹锐只得允许学生在警察的监视下游行至省公署，并接见了5名学生代表。当然，曹锐并没有接受学生的要求。②学生们遂决定第二天继续举行游行示威。6月7日上午，北洋大学的全体学生聚集在校门内准备外出，被武装军警阻拦。于是双方发生了冲突，学生们边向警察宣传共同救国，边向校门外冲去，警察极力阻止，学生们人多势众，爱国心切，眼看着就要冲出校门。这时曹锐又增派了步兵、马队近三百人，再度将北洋大学校舍包围住，学生们无法走出校门游行宣传。天津《益世报》记者一直随行报道学生的活动，见此情景道："不意人文荟萃之所，一变为狉獉之地。"③

学生的力量终究有限，但他们的热血行动却感染、动员了大众，通过各阶层之间的合作，学生运动初步达到了效果。6月9日，天津市各界群众两万多人，在河北公园召开公民大会，呼吁各界民众联合起来，用学生罢课、工人罢工、商界罢市等种种强力手段，敦请

① 《益世报》1919年6月2日。

② 《益世报》1919年6月6日。

③ 《益世报》1919年6月8日。

students from major schools in Tianjin organized numerous lecture groups, new drama troupes, and volunteer teams. They took to the streets to give speeches, distribute leaflets, and demanded the restoration of Qingdao's sovereignty, refused to recognize the Sino-Japanese agreements based on the "Twenty-One Demands" and other secret treaties, and encouraged the public to boycott Japanese goods and buy domestic products, urging everyone to work together to save China. Just Peiyang University alone organized 44 lecture groups to factories and rural areas in places like Yangliuqing, Beicang, Nancang, and Tanggu, carrying out speaking activities to promote patriotism. The *Social Welfare* once reported on a group led by Zhang Tailei from Peiyang University. On one day, despite the wind and rain, they first went to two primary schools in Tanggu to give lectures, then to East Dagu, West Dagu, and Tanggu railway stations, giving six speeches in total, with audiences ranging from dozens to over six hundred people. Some listeners were deeply moved and said, "The gentlemen speak the truth. If they could come once a month, it would be wonderful for everyone to never forget." The students felt that "the Chinese people are not without patriotism, but lack guidance," which further strengthened their determination to unite with workers and peasants.①

The student movement in Tianjin shook the warlord government. Cao Rui, the Viceroy of Zhili Province at the time, was the younger brother of the leader of the Zhili warlords, Cao Kun, and Tianjin was the stronghold of the Zhili warlords. Although the Beijing government controlled by the Anhui Clique warlords led by Duan Qirui appeared to be at odds with them, Tianjin directly controlled the economic lifeline of Beijing. Therefore, the Beijing government strictly ordered the Tianjin police to restrict the student movement. On June 5th, students from 15 schools on strike in Tianjin gathered at the playground of Nankai Middle School for the "June 5th" mass rally. After the meeting, the students prepared to march to the provincial office to petition. In order to stop the students, Cao Rui sent armed police to blockade Nankai Middle School and Peiyang University, prohibiting the students from marching. Faced with the armed police, the students appealed emotionally and reasoned logically: "Are you not Chinese?" "We are neither bandits nor thieves, why do you brandish bayonets at us?" Hearing this, the responsible officer had to order the soldiers to remove their bayonets. In the end, after repeated pleas from the students, Cao Rui had to allow the students to march to the provincial office under police surveillance and met with 5 student representatives. Of course, Cao Rui did not accept the students' demands.② The students then decided

① *Social Welfare*. June 2, 1919.

② *Social Welfare*, June 6, 1919.

北洋政府释放被捕学生，罢免三个卖国贼职务，拒绝在《巴黎和约》上签字。天津商会在学生们爱国激情的影响推动下，决定从 6 月 10 日起发动罢市，天津的工人们随之宣布于同日举行罢工。天津的经济直接影响着北京政权的稳定，罢市罢工给北京政府施加了巨大的压力。"各绸缎洋布庄等，其罢市景象尤觉可敬，诚不愧为头等商号。""宫北之各家银号，均为本埠巨商，其一日出入即可获巨额之利息，今亦毅然决然全体罢市，虽为重大牺牲，亦所不惜，其爱国救亡之观念似又加人一等矣。"① 眼见天津城里的所有公用事业都要停止，金融业也发生动荡，北京政府不得不于 9 日、10 日连夜召开会议，12 日正式下令罢免曹汝霖、章宗祥、陆宗舆三人。②

学生们的行为还感动了在华外国人，使他们认识到中国民众尤其是年轻人强烈的爱国心和社会责任感。例如，美国实用主义哲学家杜威（John Dewey）当时恰在北京访问，他在 6 月 20 日寄给女儿的信中评价道："想想我们国内 14 岁以上的孩子，有谁思考国家的命运？而中国学生负起一个清除式的政治改革运动的领导责任，并且使得商人和各界人士感到惭愧而加入他们的运动。这实在是一个了不起的国家。"③

抵制日货运动与拒绝和约签字

抵制日货是由学生与商会及工人联合开展的运动，是工人阶级和民族资产阶级参加时间最长、次数最多的反帝爱国运动。天津距离日本很近，日本在天津的势力很大、商民很多、双方经贸往来密切，还驻扎有大批军队。在当时国人的认知中，认为日本第一要靠中国的大米，第二要靠中国的市场，如果中国人不买他们的东西，日本就会变穷甚至衰落。因此，学生与商会达成共识，"抵制日货，

① 《益世报》1919 年 6 月 11 日。
② （美）周策纵著，陈永明等译，《"五四"运动史》，世界图书出版公司，2016 年，第 105 页。
③ 转引自（美）周策纵著，陈永明等译，《"五四"运动史》，世界图书出版公司，2016 年，第 105 页。

to continue the protest march the next day. On the morning of June 7th, all students of Peiyang University gathered inside the school gate, preparing to go out, but were blocked by armed police. A conflict broke out between the two sides. While the students were promoting patriotism to the police and rushing towards the school gate, the police tried to stop them. With the students being numerous and eager to express their patriotism, they were on the verge of breaking out of the school gate. At this moment, Cao Rui dispatched nearly 300 infantry and cavalry to surround the Peiyang University campus again, making it impossible for the students to leave the school gate for the march. A reporter from the Tianjin *Social Welfare*, who had been accompanying the students, witnessed the scene and commented, "Unexpectedly, a place of intellectual gathering has turned into a place of oppression."[1]

The students' power was ultimately limited, but their passionate actions touched and mobilized the masses. Through cooperation between various social classes, the student movement initially achieved results. On June 9th, more than 20,000 people from all walks of life in Tianjin gathered at Hebei Park for an Assembly, calling on people from all walks of life to unite. They urged the release of arrested students, the dismissal of three traitors, and the refusal to sign the *Treaty of Versailles*. Influenced by the patriotic fervor of the students, the Tientsin Chamber of Commerce decided to launch a city-wide strike starting from June 10th. The workers in Tianjin announced that they would strike on the same day. Tianjin's economy directly affected the stability of the Beijing regime, and the strike and boycott exerted tremendous pressure on the Beijing government. "The scene of the boycott, especially by various silk and foreign cloth shops, is particularly admirable. It is truly worthy of being the top businesses." "The money shops north of the Tianhou Temple are all operated major merchants in the city. They earn huge interest from their daily transactions. Today, they have resolutely joined the city-wide boycott. Although it is a major sacrifice, it is worth it. Their patriotic and salvationist ideas seem to be even more admirable."[2] Seeing that all public utilities in Tianjin were about to stop, and the financial industry was in turmoil, the Beijing government had to convene meetings overnight on the 9th and 10th and officially ordered the dismissal of Cao Rulin, Zhang Zongxiang, and Lu Zongyu on the 12th.[3]

The students' actions also touched the foreigners in China, making them realize the strong patriotism and sense of social responsibility among the

① *Social Welfare*, June 8, 1919.
② *Social Welfare*, June 11, 1919.
③ Zhou Cezong. *The May Fourth Movement: Intellectual Revolution in Modern China*, translated by Chen Yongming, et al. World Publishing Company, 2016, p.105.

诚为自救第一要著"①。抵制日货是当时国人用来对日本表示抗议的唯一办法，是所谓"弱者的武器"②。

6月中旬，北京政府无视全国人民的反对，悍然决定在《巴黎和约》上签字。天津人民随即展开了更大规模的斗争。6月18日天津各界救国联合会成立，这是一个包括170余个教育、经济、社会和宗教团体在内的力量更加强大的社会团体组织。6月20日起，天津学联、天津织布工人联合会、天津电车工人联合会、天津总商会相继组织了罢课、罢工和罢市活动。6月24日，北京政府通电各省，要求地方政府镇压群众运动。③天津各界联合会和天津学生联合会立即决定发动更大规模的抗议活动，通过抵制日货方式对日本进行经济制裁。他们共同组织了抵制日货委员会，到市内各处检查日货，各行业的商人积极予以配合。例如，绸缎、棉纱、洋布同业公布拟定抵制日货简章12条，表示"自议定之日起，同业各号对于日行货物现买批定，概行停止"④；五金铁行同业表示"同是国民，应发天良，各尽个人之天职，虽忍痛须臾，牺牲营业上之利益，在所不惜，俾免贻害于子孙，永为他人之奴隶"⑤；茶商、海货商、糖杂物商、洋纸商、灰煤商、木商、水火保险业、颜料等商行，也都拟定简章、坚决抵制日货。对于个别继续订购日货图谋厚利的商号，总商会提出并经各界联合会讨论通过，处罚其3万元。⑥抵制日货最坚定的一直都是学生。很多学生从一开始就把自己和家里人所有的日货统统烧毁。甚至小学生也将自己的日本生产的文具盒、书包、纸笔、橡皮、墨水等都捣毁并付之一炬。学生们还组织起来，到各条街上的店铺和仓库里，通过验看商标、包装、品种等等项目，进行认真检查标注，

---

① 天津市档案馆等编，《天津商会档案汇编（1912—1928）》第4册，天津人民出版社，1992年，第4748页。

② 张鸣，《北洋裂变：军阀与五四》，广西师范大学出版社，2010年，第148—149页。

③ 《北京政府国务院通电各省训令签字的电文》（1919年6月24）。熊志勇、苏浩、陈涛编，《中国近现代外交史资料选辑》，世界知识出版社，2012年，第232—233页。

④ 天津市档案馆等编，《天津商会档案汇编（1912—1928）》第4册，天津人民出版社，1992年，第4747页。

⑤ 《益世报》1919年7月24日。

⑥ 宋美云，《近代天津商会》，天津社会科学院出版社，2002年，第346—347页。

Chinese people, especially the youth. For example, the American pragmatist philosopher John Dewey happened to be visiting Beijing at the time. In a letter to his daughter dated June 20th, he remarked, "Just think of our children over 14 years old back home, who among them ponders the fate of the nation? Yet, Chinese students have taken on the leadership responsibility of a radical political reform movement and have made businessmen and people from all walks of life feel ashamed to join their cause. This is truly an extraordinary country."[1]

The Movement to Boycott Japanese Goods and Refusal to Sign the Treaty

Boycotting Japanese goods was a movement jointly launched by students, chambers of commerce, and workers. It was the longest and most frequent anti-imperialist patriotic movement in which the working class and the national bourgeoisie participated. Tianjin is very close to Japan, and the Japanese had a strong influence there with many merchants and civilians. The two sides had close economic and trade exchanges, with a large number of Japanese troops stationed there as well. In the eyes of the Chinese at that time, Japan relied heavily on Chinese rice and markets. It was believed that if the Chinese did not buy Japanese goods, Japan would become poor or even decline. Therefore, students and chambers of commerce reached a consensus that "boycotting Japanese goods is the first step for self-rescue".[2] Boycotting Japanese goods was seen as the only way for the Chinese to protest against Japan and was considered the "weapon of the weak".[3]

In mid-June, disregarding the opposition of the people nationwide, the Beijing government decided to sign the *Treaty of Versailles*. The people of Tianjin then launched a larger-scale struggle. On June 18, the Tianjin United Patriotic Association was established, comprising more than 170 educational, economic, social, and religious organizations. Starting from June 20, the Tianjin Student Union, Tianjin Weaving Workers Union, Tianjin Tram Workers Union, and Tientsin Chamber of Commerce successively organized strikes, protests, and boycotts. On June 24, the Beijing government issued telegrams

---

① Quoted in Zhou Cezong. *The May Fourth Movement: Intellectual Revolution in Modern China*, translated by Chen Yongming, et al. World Publishing Company, 2016, p.105.

② Tianjin Archives (ed.). *Compilation of Archives of Tientsin Chamber of Commerce (1912-1928) (Vol.4)*. Tianjin People's Publishing House, 1992, p.4748.

③ Zhang Ming. *Beiyang Split: Warlords and the May Fourth Movement*. Guangxi Normal University Press, 2010, pp.148-149.

National Célébration. 1919. - TIENTSIN

1919 年 10 月 10 日，天津市各界人民数万人在南开大学操场举行盛大的 "双十节"
庆祝大会，痛斥北洋政府镇压爱国运动的罪行。会后群众举行游行示威，反动军警
进行镇压，学生英勇反抗，在搏斗中，多人受伤。学生们决定到警察厅找厅长杨以
德抗议，杨以德拒不接见，于是学生们包围了警察厅，直到第二天凌晨才返回学校

On October 10, 1919, tens of thousands of people from all walks of life in Tianjin
gathered at the Nankai University sports field for a grand "Double Tenth Festival"
celebration. During the event, they vehemently denounced the Beiyang government's
suppression of the patriotic movement. After the assembly, the crowd took to the
streets in a protest march. In response, reactionary military police attempted to
suppress the demonstrators, but the students bravely resisted. Many were injured in
the clashes. Determined to voice their opposition, the students decided to confront
Police Commissioner Yang Yide at the police department. However, Yang refused to
meet them. In protest, the students surrounded the police department, maintaining
their demonstration until the early hours of the following day before returning to their
schools

to various provinces, requesting local governments to suppress the mass
movement.[1] The Tianjin United Patriotic Association and Tianjin Student
Union immediately decided to launch larger-scale protest activities, imposing
economic sanctions on Japan by boycotting Japanese goods. They jointly
organized a committee to boycott Japanese goods and inspected Japanese
goods throughout the city. Merchants from various industries actively
cooperated. For example, the silk, cotton yarn, and foreign cloth industry
publicly announced a draft of the 12 articles for boycotting Japanese goods,
stating that "from the date of self-determination, all stores in the industry
shall cease buying and ordering Japanese goods"[2]; the hardware and iron
industry stated "as fellow nationals, we should have a conscience, fulfill our
individual duties, endure the pain for a while, sacrifice the business interests,
and not spare any effort to avoid harm to future generations, and be slaves to
others forever"[3]; tea merchants, seafood merchants, sugar and sundry goods
merchants, foreign paper merchants, coal ash merchants, wood merchants,
fire insurance, paint, and other business sectors also drafted regulations and
resolutely boycotted Japanese goods. For individual merchants who continued
to order Japanese goods for profit, the Chamber of Commerce proposed and,
after discussion by the United Patriotic Association, imposed a fine of 30,000
yuan.[4] Students were the most steadfast in boycotting Japanese goods. Many
students burned all the Japanese goods belonging to themselves and their
families from the beginning. Even elementary school students destroyed their
Japanese-made stationery boxes, school bags, paper, pens, erasers, and ink,
and set them ablaze. Students also organized themselves to inspect shops and
warehouses on various streets, carefully examining trademarks, packaging,
varieties, and other items to prevent merchants from reselling new goods.[5]

Due to the strict supervision by students, merchants dealing in various
Japanese goods suffered heavy losses. In the later stages of the boycott of
Japanese goods, the Chamber of Commerce gradually shifted its attitude from

① *Telegram sent by the State Council of the Beijing Government for all Provinces on Instructions to Sign* (June 24, 1919). Xiong Zhiyong, Su Hao, and Chen Tao (eds.). *Selected Materials on Chinese Modern and Contemporary Diplomatic History*. World Affairs Press, 2012, pp.232-233.

② Tianjin Archives (ed.). *Compilation of Archives of Tientsin Chamber of Commerce (1912-1928) (Vol.4)*. Tianjin People's Publishing House, 1992, p.4747.

③ *Social Welfare*. July 24, 1919.

④ Song Meiyun. *Modern Tianjin Chamber of Commerce*. Tianjin Academy of Social Sciences Press, 2002, pp.346-347.

⑤ Tianjin Museum, Faculty of History, Nankai University. *May Fourth Movement in Tianjin*. Tianjin People's Publishing House, 1979, pp.69-71.

防止商人再售新货。[1]

由于学生的严格监督，经营各种日货的商人损失严重。在抵制日货活动后期，商会因担心商人利益受损而对抵制的态度逐渐由主动变为被动。与商会相反，天津的民族工业者则对抵制日货、提倡国货大力支持。第一次世界大战中，日本产业在没有竞争的条件下突飞猛进，中国市场成为日货倾销地，严重阻碍了中国民族工业的发展。当时的国货很难同物美价廉的日本货尤其是日用品竞争，因此抵制日货、提倡国货的运动，给国货生产带来了一个机遇。在天津，北洋第一商业纺织有限公司在此期间成立，另有 20 余家商号联合开办纺纱厂。[2]这场运动使天津乃至全国的民族工业得到发展，而对日本对华贸易则造成沉重打击。据日本方面统计，自运动发生以来，1919 年 5 月出口中国的商品较之平时减少 30%，运动持续的一年里，日本对华贸易输出总量减少 40%。[3]

在民众团结一心争取民族权益的斗争下，五四运动取得了胜利。由于国内民众的坚决抵制，北京政府亦不敢公然违背民意。6 月 24 日以后，外交部竟然电告中国代表团，签字一事由其"自行决定"。[4] 在国内舆论的巨大压力下，6 月 28 日巴黎和会《凡尔赛和约》签字当日，中国代表团最终发表声明和宣言，拒绝在和约上签字。[5]这一决定大大出乎美、英、法、日等国的意料，将协约国内部的裂痕暴露于世，陷于他们所谓的"窘境"。中国此举，也使日本处于尴尬境地，没有中国的签字同意，它在对德和约中所获权利就不能合法继承。中国人民的坚定立场赢得了广大支持公平正义的世界人民的支持，也在协约国内部产生深远影响，动摇了第一次世界大战后列

① 天津历史博物馆、南开大学历史系《五四运动在天津》编辑组编，《五四运动在天津——历史资料选辑》，天津人民出版社，1979 年，第 69—71 页。

② 天津历史博物馆、南开大学历史系《五四运动在天津》编辑组编，《五四运动在天津——历史资料选辑》，天津人民出版社，1979 年，第 273、274 页。

③ 张鸣，《北洋裂变：军阀与五四》，广西师范大学出版社，2010 年，第 159、160 页。

④ 中国社会科学院近代史研究所译，《顾维钧回忆录》第 1 分册，中华书局，1983 年，第 206 页。

⑤ 《中国代表团拒签〈凡尔赛和约〉的声明和宣言》（1919 年 6 月 28）。熊志勇、苏浩、陈涛编，《中国近现代外交史资料选辑》，世界知识出版社，2012 年，第 233—234 页。

proactive to passive due to concerns about the interests of merchants being harmed. In contrast to the Chamber of Commerce, Tianjin's national industrialists strongly supported the boycott of Japanese goods and advocated for domestic products. During the First World War, Japanese industries made rapid progress under conditions of no competition, and the Chinese market became a dumping ground for Japanese goods, seriously hindering the development of China's national industry. At that time, domestic products were difficult to compete with cheap and good-quality Japanese goods, especially daily necessities. Therefore, the movement to boycott Japanese goods and promote domestic products provided an opportunity for the production of domestic goods. In Tianjin, the Beiyang First Commercial Textile Company was established during this period, and more than 20 businesses jointly operated spinning mills.[1] This movement facilitated the development of national industries in Tianjin and even across the country, while dealing a heavy blow to Japan's trade with China. According to Japanese statistics, since the start of the movement, the export of goods to China decreased by 30% compared to usual in May 1919, and during the year-long movement, Japan's total exports to China decreased by 40%.[2]

Under the united struggle of the people to fight for national rights, the May Fourth Movement achieved victory. Due to the resolute resistance from the domestic population, the Beijing government dared not openly defy public opinion. After June 24th, the Ministry of Foreign Affairs unexpectedly informed the Chinese delegation via telegram that the decision to sign the treaty was left to their "own discretion."[3] Under immense domestic pressure, on June 28th, the day of signing the *Treaty of Versailles* at the Paris Peace Conference, the Chinese delegation finally issued a statement and declaration, refusing to sign the treaty.[4] This decision greatly surprised countries such as the United States, Britain, France, and Japan, exposing rifts within the Allied Forces and putting them in what they called a "dilemma." China's action also embarrassed Japan because without China's consent, its rights obtained in the *Treaty of Versailles* could not be legally inherited. China's firm stance won broad support from fair-minded people worldwide and had a profound

① Tianjin Museum, Faculty of History, Nankai University. *May Fourth Movement in Tianjin*. Tianjin People's Publishing House, 1979, p.273, 274.

② Zhang Ming. *Beiyang Split: Warlords and May Fourth Movement*. Guangxi Normal University Press, 2010, pp.159,160.

③ *Memoirs of Gu Weijun (vol.1)*, translated by Institute of Modern History, Chinese Academy of Social Sciences. Zhonghua Book Company, 1983, p.206.

④ *Declaration of the Chinese Delegation's Refusal to Sign the Treaty of Versailles* (June 28, 1919). Xiong Zhiyong, Su Hao, and Chen Tao (eds.). *Selected Materials on Chinese Modern and Contemporary Diplomatic History*. World Affairs Press, 2012, pp.233-234.

强建立起的国际"新秩序"基础，为第二次世界大战的爆发埋下了伏笔，成为当时极为引人注目的"国际性事件"。[①]

在五四运动中，一大批后来成为中国革命骨干的新青年，以"天下兴亡，匹夫有责"的使命感积极投身运动。周恩来、张太雷、邓颖超等，都曾在天津求学时积极参加五四运动。运动爆发后，21 岁的周恩来创办"觉悟社"，并负责主编《天津学生联合会报》，揭露时政黑暗，唤醒民众觉悟，传播马克思主义思想，总共出版 100 多期。作为学生领袖之一，他还带头与警察厅长交涉。同为 21 岁的张太雷，积极参加街头演讲，在学生联合会里被选为该会讲演委员会筹备委员。年仅 15 岁的邓颖超参与组织"女界爱国同志会"，在成立会上发表了激动人心的演说并被推举为评议委员、讲演队长。他们经过斗争洗礼，得到了锻炼，进一步接受了马克思主义。在运动中他们还认识到，没有组织的运动是不可能成功的，"一个群众运动没有有主义的政党领袖，他既不能走入正轨，亦更不能继续发展"，而"中国资产阶级因为太幼稚与软弱，没有维持这运动的力量"，因此"有革命觉悟及了解世界革命意义的青年要纠正五四运动的错误，逐渐集合在革命党的旗子之下，在劳动阶级中间尽宣传与组织之力，以求中国民族革命的胜利，且更进而求世界革命的成功"[②]。此后，他们投身到建立中国共产党、与工农相结合、领导中国新民主主义革命取得胜利的伟大斗争实践中去。从这个意义来说，五四运动实开中国革命之新纪元。

impact within the Allied Forces, shaking the foundation of the international "new order" established by the great powers after World War I and laying the groundwork for the outbreak of the Second World War, making it an extremely notable "international event" at the time.[①]

In the May Fourth Movement, a large number of young intellectuals who later became the backbone of the Chinese revolution actively joined the movement with a sense of mission embodied by the phrase "The fate of the nation concerns every individual." Zhou Enlai, Zhang Tailei, Deng Yingchao, and others actively participated in the May Fourth Movement while studying in Tianjin. After the outbreak of the movement, 21-year-old Zhou Enlai founded the "Awakening Society" and served as the chief editor of the *Tientsin Student*, exposing political darkness, awakening public consciousness, spreading Marxist thought, and publishing more than 100 issues in total. As one of the student leaders, he also took the lead in negotiating with the police chief. Similarly, at the age of 21, Zhang Tailei actively participated in street speeches and was elected as a member of the preparatory committee of the Student Union Speech Committee. At the age of only 15, Deng Yingchao participated in the organization of the "Women's Patriotic Association" and delivered an inspiring speech at the founding meeting, being elected as an appraisal committee member and head of the speech team. Through the baptism of struggle, they were tempered and further embraced Marxism. During the movement, they also realized that a movement without organization could not succeed. "A mass movement without leaders of a party with an ideology cannot go on the right track, let alone continue to develop." The "Chinese bourgeoisie, being too immature and weak, cannot sustain the strength of this movement." Therefore, "youth with revolutionary consciousness and an understanding of the world revolution must correct the mistakes made by the May Fourth Movement, gradually gather under the banner of the revolutionary party, and exert efforts in mobilization and organization among the working class to achieve the victory of the Chinese national revolution, and further seek the success of the world revolution."[②] Subsequently, they immersed themselves in the great struggle to establish the Communist Party of China, unite with the workers and peasants, and lead the victorious practice of the Chinese new democratic revolution. In this sense, the May Fourth Movement marks the dawn of a new era in the Chinese revolution.

① 中国社会科学院近代史研究所译，《顾维钧回忆录》第 1 分册，中华书局，1983 年，第 212 页。

② 张太雷，《五四运动的意义与价值》，《张太雷文集》，人民出版社，2013 年，第 198 页。

① *Memoirs of Gu Weijun (vol.1)*, translated by Institute of Modern History, Chinese Academy of Social Sciences. Zhonghua Book Company, 1983, p.212.

② Zhang Tailei. *The Significance and Value of the May Fourth Movement*. In *Collected Works of Zhang Tailei*. People's Publishing House, 2013, p.198.

日租界旭街街景
A street view of Asahi Road in the
former Japanese Concession

第七章 国际战争与城市的沦陷

Chapter Seven: International Wars and the Fall of the City

中日甲午战争中的天津

战争是作战双方力量消长的指示器，它有助于确定国家的特征。[①] 日本通过甲午战争一役，打败清朝，一跃成为东亚强国；而中国则完全显示了其武力乃至国力的衰弱，国际地位一落千丈，进一步引起了西方列强瓜分中国的狂潮。

大沽船坞、北洋海军与中国的海防建设

在东亚地区，至少自明朝以来就已奠定了以中国为中心和顶点的国际秩序，并通过朝贡体系发挥着相应的作用。这种国际秩序在明朝灭亡后被清朝所继承，但日本是个例外。因为僻居海外，日本列岛大部分地区自统一之后，一直没有与明清两朝建立正式外交关系，并且奉行"锁国"政策，直至1853年"黑船来航"[②]，被迫向西方列强打开国门。从那以后，他们不仅开始睁眼看世界，而且更进一步通过"明治维新"，确立了"脱亚入欧""开拓万里波涛，布国威于四方"的"国策"。其计划第一步就是征服朝鲜，然后占领中国东北，进而独占中国扩充实力，获取争霸世界的各种资源。为此，日本发动甲午战争是蓄谋已久的必然步骤。

---

① （法）费尔南·布罗代尔著，顾良等译，《十五至十八世纪的物质文明、经济与资本主义》第三卷，生活·读书·新知三联书店，2002年，第45页。

② 1853年，美国海军准将马休·佩里（Matthew Calbraith Perry）率舰队驶入江户湾浦贺海面，佩里带着美国总统的国书向江户幕府致意，最后双方于次年签订了不平等条约《神奈川条约》（日本通称为《日美和亲条约》）。此事件一般被视作日本幕末时代的开端。

Tianjin in the Sino-Japanese War of 1894

War is an indicator of the waxing and waning of the strengths of the warring parties, and it helps determine the characteristics of a nation.[①] Through the Sino-Japanese War of 1894, Japan defeated the Qing Dynasty, rising as a strong nation in East Asia; whereas China fully displayed its weakness in terms of military and national strength, plummeting its international status, further fueling the frenzy among Western powers to carve up China.

Taku Shipyard, Beiyang Fleet, and China's Naval Defense Construction

In the East Asian region, at least since the Ming Dynasty, an international order centered around China and based on the tribute system has been established and played a corresponding role. This international order was inherited by the Qing Dynasty after the fall of the Ming Dynasty. However, Japan is an exception. Due to its geographical isolation and being situated overseas, most of the Japanese archipelago did not establish formal diplomatic relations with the Ming and Qing Dynasties after unification. Moreover, Japan pursued a policy of isolation known as "sakoku" until the arrival of the "Black Ships"[②] in 1853, which forced Japan to open its doors to Western powers. Since then, Japan not only began to perceive the world but also further solidified its "Leave Asia and Enter Europe" and "Spread the National Prestige Far and

---

① Fernand Braudel. *Civilisation Materielle, Economie et Capitalisme: XVe-XVIIIe Siècle* (vol.3), translated by Gu Liang, et al. SDX Joint Publishing Company, 2002, p.45.

② In 1853, U.S. Navy Commodore Matthew Calbraith Perry led a fleet into Edo Bay, off the coast of Uraga. Carrying a letter from the President of the United States, Perry extended greetings to the Edo Shogunate. The following year, both parties signed the unequal Treaty of Kanagawa (commonly known in Japan as the *Japan-U.S. Treaty of Peace and Amity*). This event is generally regarded as the beginning of the Bakumatsu period in Japan.

海防建设一般包括陆上防御设施和海军建设两大部分。晚清的海防，大体上是根据 1860 年南北洋通商大臣的设置而划分。南洋包括广东、福建、浙江、江南（江苏）四省，北洋包括山东、直隶（河北）、奉天（辽宁）三省。起初，南北洋的防务大多由各地的督抚负责，南北洋大臣只负责通商与洋务等。[2] 1874 年日本借"牡丹社事件"[1] 侵略台湾。虽然清政府并没有真正将崛起不久的日本放在眼里，不过洋务派还是借此掀起了海防建设的大讨论。此后，清政府将南北洋的海防明令交给两江总督兼南洋大臣沈葆桢与直隶总督兼北洋大臣李鸿章二人督办。[2] 而北洋可称为京师门户，以大沽、天津为枢纽。作为拱卫京畿的战略要地，大沽口的战略位置极为重要。为了建设海防，李鸿章于 1874 年开始以天津大沽口为基地，创建北洋海军，同时修筑大沽船坞。

1874 年之后，通过中国海关设在伦敦的办事处，李鸿章先后向英国阿姆斯特朗公司（Armstrong Co.）订购蚊子船（即炮艇）和快碰船（即撞击巡洋舰）达十余艘，耗资近 200 万两。[3] 1880 年之后，李鸿章又通过驻德公使李凤苞和使馆二等参赞徐建寅二人在德国什切青[4] 的伏尔铿船厂（Vulcan Co.）订购了三艘铁甲舰。这几艘铁甲舰成为北洋水师的主力战舰，即"定远号""镇远号"和"济远号"。从 1876 年至 1880 年，从英国、德国订购的炮艇相继驶回大沽口，北洋水师初具规模，拥有各类舰船 25 艘。为了使日益庞大的北洋海军的舰船能够就近维修，1880 年，李鸿章奏请光绪皇帝批准，于大沽海口选购民地 110 亩，建起一座船坞，命名为"北洋水师大沽船坞"，也称海神庙船坞。这是中国北方最早的船舶修建厂和重要的军火基地。

大沽船坞甲坞位于大沽口海神庙的东北，长 320 尺、宽 92 尺、

---

① 1874 年，日本舰队以琉球船民事件为由，入侵台湾。沈葆桢带舰入台交涉退兵，形成中日双方的第一次正面冲突。

② 张侠等编，《清末海军史料》，海洋出版社，1982 年，第 12—13 页。

③ 1874 年 9 月 4 日赫德致金登干第 95 号函件注②。陈霞飞主编，《中国海关密档——赫德、金登干函电汇编（1874—1907）》第一卷，中华书局，1990 年，第 141 页。

④ 现为波兰城市，德语称为"斯德丁"。

Wide" national policies through the Meiji Restoration. The first step of this plan was to conquer Korea, then occupy Northeast China, and subsequently monopolize China to expand its power and acquire various resources to vie for world dominance. Therefore, Japan's initiation of the First Sino-Japanese War was a long-planned and inevitable step in this direction.

Maritime defense construction generally includes two main parts: land-based defense facilities and naval construction. During the late Qing Dynasty, maritime defense was broadly divided based on the establishment of the Nanyang and Beiyang Ministers of Trade in 1860. Nanyang included four provinces: Guangdong, Fujian, Zhejiang, and Jiangnan (Jiangsu), while Beiyang included three provinces: Shandong, Zhili (Hebei), and Fengtian (Liaoning). Initially, the defenses of Nanyang and Beiyang were mainly the responsibilities of local governors, with the Nanyang and Beiyang Ministers only overseeing matters related to trade and Westernization. In 1874, Japan invaded Taiwan in the "Mudan Incident"[1]. Although the Qing government did not take the newly rising Japan seriously, the Westernization faction seized the opportunity to spark a major discussion on maritime defense construction. Subsequently, the Qing government officially entrusted the maritime defenses of Nanyang and Beiyang to the two governors-general: The Shun Paozhen, who concurrently served as the Nanyang Minister, and Li Hongzhang, who concurrently served as the Beiyang Minister.[2] Beiyang can be referred to as the gateway to the capital, with Taku and Tianjin as its hubs. As a strategically important area for defending the capital region, the strategic position of Taku was extremely crucial. To develop maritime defense, Li Hongzhang began establishing the Beiyang Navy and constructing the Taku Shipyard in Tianjin's Taku in 1874.

After 1874, through the Chinese customs office in London, Li Hongzhang successively ordered more than ten mosquito boats (gunboats) and ram cruisers from the British Armstrong Co., totaling nearly 2 million taels of silver.[3] After 1880, Li Hongzhang, through the Minister to Germany Li Fengbao and the Second Counsellor at the Embassy Xu Jianyin, ordered

---

① In 1874, the Japanese fleet, using the Mudan Incident as a pretext, invaded Taiwan. Shen Baozhen led a fleet to Taiwan to negotiate the withdrawal of Japanese forces, resulting in the first direct confrontation between China and Japan.

② Zhang Xia, Yang Zhiben, Luo Shuwei, et al. *Historical Materials of the Navy in the Late Qing Dynasty*. China Ocean Press, 1982, pp.12-13.

③ The No.95 letter of Robert Hart to James Duncan Campbell on September 4, 1874 (Note 2). Chen Xiafei (ed.). *Chinese Customs Confidential Files—Compilation of Letters and Telegrams by Robert Hart and James Duncan Campbell (1874-1907)*. Vol.1. Zhonghua Book Company, 1990, p.141.

大沽船坞
Taku shipyard

深 20 尺。自 1880 年 5 月起兴建，用了大约 6 个月的时间大致建造起轮机厂房、马力房、抽水房、码头、起重架、绘图楼、办公房、库房、木厂、模具厂、铸铁厂、熟铁厂、熟铜厂、锅炉厂等，其中机床 20 余台、马力机、锅炉等皆由外国购买。全厂工人 600 余名、工匠 300 余名，皆由福建、广东、宁波等早期沿海开放港口征调而来。以后，又逐年修建了乙、丙、丁等坞，以备舰艇修理避冻之用。直至 1886 年，全部工程告竣。[1]

竣工后的大沽船坞已成为具有相当规模的近代船舶修造工厂，"能在同一时间装配和修理六艘船舶"。不仅可以修船而且可以自己造船，1882 年至 1900 年，大沽船坞共造杆雷艇、挖泥船等 18 艘，造河驳船 145 艘，修理大小船舶 70 余艘。从 1884 年起，大沽船坞还承修海防工程。如修理大沽海口各营雷电炮械及电灯，承造炮台炮洞、铁门等。1886 年，中国海军第一艘潜水艇在这里研制成功。1890 年以后，船坞除了继续修、造舰船外，还开始生产军火。1891 年仿造德国 1 磅后膛炮 90 余尊，1892 年在船坞院内设修炮厂兼造水雷，大沽口水域布置的水雷大部分由该厂制造。从此，大沽船坞建成一个集合了修船、造船、生产枪炮军火的综合军事基地。[2]

---

① 张侠等编，《清末海军史料》，海洋出版社，1982 年，第 156—160 页。

② 张侠等编，《清末海军史料》，海洋出版社，1982 年，第 156—160 页。

three armored ships from the Vulcan Co. in Szczecin[1], Germany. These three armored ships became the main battleships of the Beiyang Fleet, namely the "Dingyuan", "Zhenyuan", and "Jiyuan". From 1876 to 1880, gunboats ordered from England and Germany successively returned to Taku, and the Beiyang Fleet began to take shape with a total of 25 ships of various types. In order for the increasingly large Beiyang Navy ships to be repaired nearby, Li Hongzhang requested Emperor Guangxu's approval in 1880 to purchase 110 mu of land at the mouth of the Taku, where a shipyard was constructed, named the "Beiyang Fleet Taku Shipyard", also known as the "Temple of Sea Goddess Shipyard". This was the earliest shipbuilding yard in northern China and an important military base.

The dock Jia of the Taku Shipyard is located northeast of the Temple of Sea Goddess at Taku, measuring 320 feet long, 92 feet wide, and 20 feet deep. Construction began in May 1880 and it took about 6 months to roughly complete the construction of the engine factory, power house, pumping house, wharf, crane, drafting office, office building, warehouse, carpentry shop, die plant, foundry, wrought iron shop, coppersmith shop, boiler shop, and other facilities. More than 20 lathes, steam engines, boilers, and other equipment were all purchased from abroad. The entire workforce comprised over 600 workers and more than 300 artisans, recruited from early open ports along the coast such as Fujian, Guangdong, and Ningbo. Subsequently, docks Yi, Bing, Ding, and Ji were gradually built for ship repair and wintering. By 1886, all construction was completed.[2]

After completion, the Taku Shipyard had become a relatively large modern shipbuilding factory, "capable of assembling and repairing six ships at the same time." Not only could it repair ships, but it could also build them. From 1882 to 1900, the Taku Shipyard constructed a total of 18 spar torpedo boats, dredgers, 145 river barges, and repaired more than 70 ships of various sizes. From 1884 onwards, the Taku Shipyard also undertook naval defense projects, such as repairing the machine cannons and lights of various camps at Taku, and constructing gun emplacements and iron gates. In 1886, China's first submarine was successfully developed here. After 1890, in addition to ship repairs and construction, the shipyard began producing military supplies. In 1891, over 90 replicas of German 1-pound breech-loading guns were produced, and in 1892, a gun repair factory was established within the shipyard premises, which also manufactured torpedoes. Most of the mines

---

① Now a Polish city, known in German as "Stettin."

② Zhang Xia, et al (eds.). *Historical Materials of the Navy in the Late Qing Dynasty*. China Ocean Press, 1982, pp.156-160.

在近代海防设施建设中，构筑海岸炮台至关重要。自1870年李鸿章出任直隶总督兼北洋大臣后，就立即对大沽原有炮台进行了整修和扩建，新建了三座炮台。日本侵台之后，又于1879年3月入侵琉球，将其变为冲绳县。面对日本不断升级的侵略行动，李鸿章下令修建旅顺和威海卫基地，历时8年终于建构成大沽、旅顺、威海的三角防御体系。

海军建设，除了需要有舰艇，更要训练出一支海军队伍。北洋水师购买船舰的同时，在英国招募了一批外籍教官和炮手，然后由他们驾驶所购船舰来到中国，在水师提督丁汝昌麾下负责驾驶船舰并训练中国水师。1880年李鸿章将烟台的艇船及已由德国教官训练多年的水勇调来天津，划归到北洋海军序列之中。第二年，李鸿章派丁汝昌率领拨自山东的两百多名中国水师官兵，先期乘坐兵船或雇用商船前往英国，到船厂和炮厂观摩学习，"以扩眼界而增学识"，随后由这些中国水师官兵自行驾驶所购船舰回中国。于是，高高悬挂清朝龙旗的中国舰队首次航行在大西洋，一路经由大西洋、地中海、埃及、苏伊士运河、新加坡等地，再经香港、上海，最后抵达大沽。此次航行令创立不久的清朝海军扬威海外，"阅历数万里风涛形势，教练熟悉，保护平稳，卓著勋劳，实为中国前此未有之事，足以张国体而壮军声。"欧洲诸国也由此"知道中国亦有水师群起，而尊敬之"。①

不过，令人痛心的是，虽然投资巨大，但是清朝军队中固有的弊端在这支现代化海军中仍然存在。清军内部派系林立，尔虞我诈互相猜忌互相排斥，同乡之谊远重于建制上应有的团结一致。北洋舰队中，任人唯亲，拉帮结派。每艘战舰上的管带（即舰长）都对自己的战舰拥有一定的管理权和招募军官的权力，他们总是从自己的乡亲中挑选军官，而不是看重他们所掌握的海军知识和实际作战指挥能力。而且，北洋海军高官带头腐败，将领之间争权夺利，也严重削弱了战斗力。所以这支海军虽有先进的武器舰船，却没有组织训练有素的作战指挥队伍，再加上缺少经费拨款无法购买新舰与炮弹，导致这支重金打造的现代化军队在甲午战争中全军覆没。

---

① 顾廷龙、戴逸主编，《李鸿章全集》（奏议九），安徽教育出版社，2008年，第507、508页。

laid in the waters of Taku were manufactured by this factory. Since then, the Taku Shipyard has become a comprehensive military base for ship repair, shipbuilding, and the production of firearms and military equipment.[1]

In the construction of modern coastal defense facilities, the construction of coastal batteries is crucial. Since Li Hongzhang became the Viceroy of Zhili Province and the Minister of Beiyang in 1870, he immediately repaired and expanded the existing batteries at Taku and built three new ones. After Japan invaded Taiwan in 1879, it invaded Ryukyu in March of that year, turning it into Okinawa Prefecture. Faced with Japan's escalating aggression, Li Hongzhang ordered the construction of the bases at Lüshun and Weihaiwei. After eight years, the triangular defense system of Taku, Lüshun, and Weihai was finally constructed.

In naval construction, besides having ships, it is also necessary to train a navy. The Beiyang Fleet not only purchased ships but also recruited a group of foreign instructors and gunners from Britain. They then sailed the purchased ships to China and, under the command of Admiral Ding Ruchang, were responsible for piloting the ships and training the Chinese navy. In 1880, Li Hongzhang transferred the boats from Yantai and the Chinese marines trained by German instructors for many years to Tianjin, incorporating them into the Beiyang Navy. The following year, Li Hongzhang dispatched Ding Ruchang to lead over two hundred Chinese naval officers and soldiers from Shandong, who initially traveled to Britain by troop ships or hired merchant ships to visit shipyards and gun factories for observation and learning, "to broaden their horizons and increase their knowledge." Subsequently, these Chinese naval officers and soldiers piloted the purchased ships back to China themselves. Thus, for the first time, the Chinese fleet, flying the Qing Dynasty dragon flag high, sailed across the Atlantic Ocean, passing through the Atlantic, the Mediterranean Sea, Egypt, the Suez Canal, Singapore, and other places, before finally reaching Tianjin via Hong Kong and Shanghai. This voyage showcased the newly established Qing Dynasty navy's prowess overseas, "traversing tens of thousands of miles, mastering the winds and waves, becoming familiar with the situation, ensuring smooth navigation, and achieving remarkable achievements, which had never happened before in China, enough to show the nation's strength and enhance the military's prestige." European countries also "came to know that China also had a rising navy and respected it."[2]

---

① Zhang Xia, et al (eds.). *Historical Materials of the Navy in the Late Qing Dynasty*. China Ocean Press, 1982, pp.156-160.

② Gu Tinglong, Dai Yi (eds.). *The Collected Works of Li Hongzhang (Memorials 9)*. Anhui Education Press, 2008, pp.507, 508.

世界史上第一次铁甲战舰海战

甲午战争中，日本是举国之力，而中国方面则只有李鸿章的北洋系参与。因此天津成为中日甲午战争的中方大本营，不仅战前的外交调停、战争中的军事调动命令乃至战后的求和，几乎一切行动的指令都从位于天津的直隶总督府发出。

中日甲午之战起因于朝鲜问题。日本对朝鲜觊觎已久，从1875年到1885年的10年间，不断在朝鲜制造事端，逼迫朝鲜签订多个不平等条约，以使朝鲜沦为日本殖民地。朝鲜不得已向中国求援，李鸿章即派在小站驻扎屯田的淮军赴朝，驻军汉城。此后，中日两国代表李鸿章、伊藤博文于1885年在天津签订《中日天津条约》，约定如果将来朝鲜有事，中日两国如要派兵，应先知会对方。1894年，朝鲜爆发东学党起义，朝鲜政府再次向北京乞援，李鸿章即派提督叶志超率数营北洋兵驰赴朝鲜。日本以保护商民为由乘机也派兵到朝鲜，蓄意挑起战争。李鸿章发觉事态不妙，急调总兵卫汝贵、提督马玉崑率军火速由大东沟登陆，进驻平壤；另调北洋陆军十余营分批渡海驰援朝鲜。

李鸿章虽然调兵遣将奔赴朝鲜，却并没有下定作战的决心，也无战胜的信心。多年来，李鸿章致力于北洋海防的建设，但随着北洋舰队的日益壮大，虽然引起皇帝的重视以及随之产生许多权利双收的职位，但也引发了其他当权者的嫉妒。大敌当前，清朝的大臣之间矛盾不断"升级"。政敌翁同龢对李鸿章多加掣肘，百般阻挠拨付海军军费。而海军是高消耗兵种，在一定意义上说，海战打的就是钱，必须有强大的财政支持。加上海防建设过程中，迭逢光绪皇帝大婚和慈禧太后的六十大寿庆典，所费何止几千万两。所以，筹集资金是最令李鸿章头疼的事。北洋水师初建时，舰队实力优于日本海军。然而明治维新后的日本倾其国力发展海军。到甲午战前，不仅日舰数量超过北洋舰队，且多是铁甲快船，速度达到每小时23海里，而北洋舰队最高速度只有18海里。北洋舰队不仅数量、速度不如日舰，各种口径的火炮有的竟没有炮弹，难以应对即将到来的恶战。李鸿章无力挽回北洋海军军力不断下降的局面，因此从朝鲜

However, it is heartbreaking to note that despite the massive investment, the inherent flaws within the Qing Dynasty army persisted within this modernized navy. The Qing military was plagued by internal factions, deceit, mutual suspicion, and mutual exclusion, with loyalty to hometowns often outweighing the unity that should have existed within the establishment. In the Beiyang Fleet, nepotism and cliques were rampant. Each ship's officer (the captain) had a certain degree of authority over their vessel and the power to recruit officers. They often selected officers from their own hometowns rather than based on their naval knowledge and actual combat command abilities. Moreover, corruption among senior officers of the Beiyang Navy, along with their power struggles for personal gain, severely undermined its combat effectiveness. Consequently, despite possessing advanced weaponry and ships, this navy lacked a well-organized and trained combat command team. Additionally, the lack of funding to purchase new ships and ammunition further contributed to the downfall of this heavily funded modernized military force in the First Sino-Japanese War.

The First Armored Warship Naval Battle in World History

In the First Sino-Japanese War, Japan mobilized its entire nation, while China only had the participation of Li Hongzhang's Beiyang faction. Therefore, Tianjin became the headquarters of the Chinese side in the First Sino-Japanese War. Almost all instructions, including pre-war diplomatic mediation, military mobilization orders during the war, and post-war peace negotiations, were issued from the office of the Viceroy of Zhili Province located in Tianjin.

The Sino-Japanese War of 1894 began with the Korean issue. Japan had long coveted Korea and, from 1875 to 1885, for a period of ten years, continuously stirred up trouble in Korea, forcing it to sign multiple unequal treaties, with the aim of making Korea a Japanese colony. Korea had no choice but to seek help from China. Li Hongzhang dispatched the Huai Army stationed in Xiaozhan to Korea, stationed in Seoul. Subsequently, representatives from China and Japan, Li Hongzhang and Ito Hirobumi, signed the *Treaty of Tianjin* in 1885, which stipulated that if there were any issues in Korea in the future and either China or Japan intended to send troops, they must notify the other party first. In 1894, the Donghak Peasant Revolution broke out in Korea, and the Korean government once again sought assistance from Beijing. Li Hongzhang immediately dispatched Admiral Ye Zhichao with several battalions of Beiyang Army to Korea. Japan, under the pretext of protecting its merchants and citizens, also sent troops to Korea, deliberately provoking war. Li

发生事端之后，他的基本态度就是消极避战，一味仰赖列强调停，通过在天津的各国领事馆，请求英国、俄国、德国、法国和美国出面进行调停。而列强又怎会为了所谓公理和正义介入中日之间的纷争呢？！不过，预期有可能发生大规模海战，而这将是铁甲舰面世以来的第一次作战，列强都纷纷派出军舰到战场附近水域观战。

1894 年 7 月 23 日上午 9 点 50 分，赴朝清军搭乘向怡和洋行租来的英籍"高升号"运输船，从大沽口出发去朝鲜。船上悬挂英国旗，载有 1200 余名清军、12 门火炮以及枪支弹药等，并由北洋舰队的"济远""广乙"二舰护航。① 这个情报立即被长期潜伏、无孔不入的日本间谍探听清楚，并由日本驻津领事馆发出电报。7 月 23 日当天，日本联合舰队就接到大本营的密令，如在牙山附近遇有清国军舰，可进行攻击。25 日晨 8 点左右，日本海军派出三艘巡洋舰，预先埋伏在北洋舰队必经之路的朝鲜牙山湾入口处丰岛海域。双方遭遇之后，日方率先开火。激战约一小时，"广乙"舰负伤败走，后搁浅焚毁。"济远"舰以小击大、以一敌三，遭重创，败退的过程中，将追击的日舰"吉野"击伤。日舰"浪速"号遇到"高升号"，将其逼停，船上清军官兵宁死不降。"浪速"舰长东乡平八郎悍然下令将"高升"击沉，清军除 200 余人获救生还外，余皆殉难。

这一日，日军不仅在海上袭击了"高升号"，还出动 4000 多人的陆军准备在牙山偷袭清军陆军。29 日，日本陆军与聂士成率领的千余清军发生激战。聂士成部拼死作战，终因兵力相差悬殊，后援不力告败。1894 年 8 月 1 日，中日两国政府宣战，甲午战争开始。

中日宣战后，两国军队在平壤对峙。由于陆军实力上敌强我弱，9 月 13 日，李鸿章派招商局"新裕""图南""镇东""利运""海定"五艘轮船，载运总兵刘盛休率领的铭军八营兵力自大沽口出发赴大东沟登陆，以援助驻朝清军。鉴于"高升号"惨案，李鸿章命北洋舰队的"定远""震远""致远""靖远""经远""来远""济

---

① 汉纳根的誓词，"美国外交关系"，1894 年，附录一，第 45 页；船长高惠悌和大副田泼林 8 月 17 日的抗议照会，《北华捷报》，1894 年 8 月 24 日。转引自（美）马士著，张汇文等译，《中华帝国对外关系史》（第三卷），上海书店出版社，2006 年，第 27 页，注释 1。

Hongzhang realized the danger and urgently ordered General Wei Rugui and Admiral Ma Yukun to quickly land at Dadonggou and occupy Pyongyang; meanwhile, he dispatched over ten battalions of the Beiyang Army to Korea in batches to reinforce them.

Although Li Hongzhang dispatched troops to Korea, he did not have the determination to engage in battle, nor did he have confidence in victory. Over the years, Li Hongzhang had been dedicated to the construction of the Beiyang Navy. However, as the Beiyang Fleet grew stronger, it not only attracted the attention of the emperor and led to the creation of many lucrative positions but also aroused jealousy among other powerful figures. In the face of a formidable enemy, conflicts among the Qing Dynasty's ministers escalated continuously. Li's political rival, Weng Tonghe, placed numerous obstacles in the disbursement of naval funds, hindering the navy's development. Naval warfare is a high-cost endeavor, and in a sense, battles at sea are fought with money, requiring strong financial support. Additionally, during the process of naval construction, the lavish expenditures for Emperor Guangxu's wedding and Empress Dowager Cixi's sixtieth birthday celebration amounted to tens of millions of taels of silver. Therefore, raising funds was the most troublesome issue for Li Hongzhang. When the Beiyang Navy was initially established, its strength exceeded that of the Japanese navy. However, after the Meiji Restoration, Japan poured its national strength into naval development. By the eve of the Sino-Japanese War, not only did the number of Japanese ships exceed that of the Beiyang Fleet, but many were ironclad cruisers capable of reaching speeds of up to 23 knots, while the highest speed of the Beiyang Fleet was only 18 knots. The Beiyang Fleet not only lagged behind the Japanese fleet in terms of quantity and speed but also lacked ammunition for some of its cannons, making it difficult to face the impending battle. Unable to reverse the decline of the Beiyang Navy's strength, Li Hongzhang's basic attitude since the outbreak of the Korean incident was to passively avoid war, relying solely on the intervention of the great powers. Through the various consulates in Tianjin, he requested mediation from Britain, Russia, Germany, France, and the United States. However, why would the great powers intervene in the dispute between China and Japan for the sake of justice and righteousness? Nevertheless, with the prospect of a large-scale naval battle looming, the first since the introduction of ironclad ships, the great powers sent their warships to the waters near the battlefield to observe.

On the morning of July 23, 1894, at 9:50 a.m., Qing troops headed to Korea boarded the British-chartered "Kowshing" transport ship leased from the Jardine, Matheson & Co., departing from Taku. The ship flew the British flag and carried over 1,200 Qing soldiers, 12 cannons, firearms, and ammunition,

旗舰定远号
Flagship Dingyuan

镇远号
Battleship Zhenyuan

远""广甲""超勇""扬威"十艘战舰随行护航，这几乎是北洋舰队的全部主力舰艇。9月17日，十艘战舰抵达目的地，停泊于距陆地12海里之外，陆军及武器装备连夜登岸。早在三天前的9月14日，日军特务机关即已探得消息，决定派出12艘日舰在鸭绿江的出海口——大东沟海域袭击北洋舰队。9月18日上午9时，提督丁汝昌下令，午饭后完成运兵任务的舰队返航驶回旅顺港。10点左右，北洋舰队发现远方天际的一缕黑烟。

12点50分左右，激战开始。丁汝昌排出以"定远"担任旗舰的10艘北洋舰队主力舰组成的人字形战斗队形。双方舰队相距约5000多米时，旗舰"定远"率先发炮，然后各舰相继发炮。稍后日舰还击。战斗从中午开始，震耳欲聋的炮声、横飞的弹片、滚滚浓烟烈火交织出一幅激战的场面。海战持续到下午，北洋舰队已有"超勇"和"扬威"两艘舰艇沉没，而日舰"扶桑"号的大炮集中火力攻击"定

escorted by the Beiyang Fleet's "Jiyuan" and "Guangyi" ships.[1] This information was immediately intercepted by long-term infiltrated Japanese spies and relayed by the Japanese consulate in Tianjin. On the same day, the Japanese Combined Fleet received a secret order from headquarters that if they encountered Qing warships near Asan, they could attack. Around 8 a.m. on the 25th, the Japanese navy dispatched three cruisers to ambush in the Pungdo at the entrance of the Bay of Asan in Korea, a route that the Beiyang Fleet must pass through. After the encounter, the Japanese fired first. After about an hour of fierce fighting, the "Guangyi" ship was wounded and fled, later grounding and burning. The "Jiyuan" ship, facing three enemies alone, suffered heavy damage. During its retreat, it wounded the pursuing Japanese ship "Yoshino." The Japanese ship "Naniwa" encountered the "Kowshing" and forced it to stop. The Qing soldiers on board chose death over surrender. The captain of the "Naniwa," Togo Heihachiro, boldly ordered the sinking of the "Kowshing." Except for over 200 rescued Qing soldiers, the rest perished.

On that day, not only did the Japanese navy attack the "Kowshing," but they also deployed over 4,000 troops to prepare for a surprise attack on the Qing army at the Bay of Asan. On the 29th, fierce fighting erupted between the Japanese army and the Qing army led by Nie Shicheng. Despite Nie Shicheng's unit fighting bravely, they were ultimately defeated due to the vast difference in strength and lack of reinforcements. On August 1, 1894, the governments of China and Japan declared war, marking the beginning of the First Sino-Japanese War.

After the declaration of war between China and Japan, the two armies confronted each other in Pyongyang. Due to the disparity in military strength, with the enemy stronger than us, on September 13th, Li Hongzhang dispatched five steamships from the China Merchants Steamship Company—the "Xinyu," "Tunan," "Zhendong," "Liyun," and "Haiding"—carrying the forces of General Liu Shengxiu's Ming Army's Eight Battalions from Taku to land at Dadonggou in support of the Qing army stationed in Korea. In light of the tragedy of the "Kowshing," Li Hongzhang ordered the ten main battleships of the Beiyang Fleet—the "Dingyuan," "Zhenyuan," "Zhiyuan," "Jingyuan," "Jingyuan," "Laiyuan," "Jiyuan," "Guangjia," "Chaoyong," and "Yangwei"—to accompany and escort them. This almost constituted the entire main force of the Beiyang Fleet. On September 17th, the ten battleships arrived at their

---

[1] Sworn statement of Constantin von Hanneken, *U.S. For. Rel.*, 1894, App. i, p.45; Note of Protest of Captain Thomas Ryder Galsworthy and Lieutenant Lewis Henry Tamplin, Aug. 17th, in *North China Herald*, August 24, 1894. Quoted in Hosea Ballou Morse. *The International Relations of the Chinese Empire* (vol.3), translated by Zhang Huiwen, et al. Shanghai Bookstore Publishing House, 2006, p.27, Note 1.

远"舰的前部，多亏"致远"舰奋不顾身、牺牲自己，保护了"定远"舰没有遭受致命打击。此时，战斗出现了转折——日方旗舰"松岛号"被击中爆炸，"比睿""赤城"等多艘日舰也被击伤；而日舰队长时间围攻北洋舰队的两艘主力舰"定远"和"镇远"，却久攻不下。终于，由于担心夜幕降临后遭到北洋舰队鱼雷艇的攻击，日本舰队主动撤出了战斗，双方基本战平。北洋舰队共损失超勇、扬威、致远、经远、广甲五舰，死伤兵员千余人。日本联合舰队官兵死伤六百余人，舰队五艘军舰受重伤，但未沉一艘。

这次海战持续了5个多小时，北洋舰队官兵奋勇作战。战斗中，北洋水兵精神饱满、斗志昂扬，意欲为"高升号"死难的士兵们报仇雪恨。他们毫不畏惧，"一兵负重伤，同侣嘱其入内休养，及予重至此炮座，见彼虽已残废，仍裹创工作如常"。作为主帅的丁汝昌，重伤后拒绝入舱内休息，虽不能站立，却仍然坐在甲板上微笑着鼓励士兵。① 李鸿章在《大东沟战状折》中总结黄海海战时说："各将士效死用命，愈战愈奋，始终不懈，实属勇敢可嘉。"② 但是此战之后，李鸿章却再也不敢让海军出战，丁汝昌率领舰队退入威海卫军港，黄海制海权落入日本海军手中。1895 年 1 月，日军登陆荣成湾，像登陆辽东半岛花园口一样如入无人之境，轻而易举地占领了威海卫炮台，然后用炮台堡垒上的重炮轰击被包围在威海港内的北洋舰队。这支中国近代装备最好的海军覆灭了。

马关议和及日租界的开辟

甲午之战爆发前，清政府内部意见不统一，和战不定。一方面，中国对崛起的日本缺乏一定程度的重视，另一方面寄希望于俄国干涉和英国牵制，因此根本没有做好军事上的必要准备。随着朝鲜战场上的失败，战火一路烧过鸭绿江到了中国东北。旅顺失守后，日

---

① （英）泰莱著，张荫麟译，《泰莱甲午中日海战见闻记》。中国史学会主编，《中日战争》第六册，新知识出版社，1956 年，第 50 页。

② 顾廷龙、戴逸主编，《李鸿章全集》（奏议十五），安徽教育出版社，2008 年，第 449 页。

destination, anchoring 12 nautical miles from the shore, while the army and weapons and equipment landed overnight. Three days earlier, on September 14th, the Japanese espionage agency had already obtained information and decided to send 12 Japanese warships to ambush the Beiyang Fleet in the Dadonggou area at the mouth of the Yalu River. At 9 a.m. on September 18th, Admiral Ding Ruchang ordered the fleet to return to Lüshun Port after completing the transportation mission after lunch. At around 10 a.m., the Beiyang Fleet spotted a wisp of black smoke on the distant horizon.

Around 12:50 p.m., the fierce battle began. Ding Ruchang deployed the main force of the Beiyang Fleet, consisting of ten ships with the "Dingyuan" serving as the flagship, in a formation resembling the Chinese character " 人 " (ren). When the two fleets were approximately 5,000 meters apart, the flagship "Dingyuan" opened fire first, followed by successive salvos from each ship. Shortly after, the Japanese ships retaliated. The battle commenced at noon, with deafening cannon fire, flying shrapnel, and thick smoke and flames weaving a scene of intense combat. The naval battle continued into the afternoon, with the Beiyang Fleet losing two ships, the "Chaoyong" and "Yangwei," while the Japanese battleship "Fuso" concentrated its firepower on the bow of the "Dingyuan." Thanks to the self-sacrifice of the "Zhiyuan," which bravely shielded the "Dingyuan," the latter was spared from a fatal blow. At this juncture, the tide of battle turned as the Japanese flagship "Matsushima" was hit and exploded, and several other Japanese ships such as the "Hiei" and "Akagi" were also damaged. Meanwhile, the two main Beiyang Fleet ships, the "Dingyuan" and "Zhenyuan," withstood prolonged attacks from the Japanese fleet without being overwhelmed. Eventually, fearing an attack from the Beiyang Fleet torpedo boats after nightfall, the Japanese fleet voluntarily withdrew from the battle, resulting in a stalemate between the two sides. The Beiyang Fleet lost five ships—the "Chaoyong," "Yangwei," "Zhiyuan," "Jingyuan," and "Guangjia"—with over a thousand casualties. The Japanese Combined Fleet suffered over six hundred casualties, with five warships heavily damaged but none sunk.

The naval battle lasted for over 5 hours, during which the officers and soldiers of the Beiyang Fleet fought bravely. In the midst of the battle, the sailors of the Beiyang Fleet were full of spirit and morale, determined to avenge the soldiers who perished on the "Kowshing." They showed no fear, and an English officer Tyler recorded, "one was wounded somewhat badly as I looked on and was told to go below and stay there. On the next visit to this gun the wounded man—bandaged and partly disabled—was busy with his work. " As the commander, Ding Ruchang, refused to rest in the cabin even after being seriously wounded. Though unable to stand, he sat on the deck smiling,

天津原日租界
Former Japanese Concession in Tianjin

军更是向北京进犯而来。清政府急于请列强调停议和。1894 年 11 月 3 日，总理衙门正式召见英、法、德、俄、美等国驻京使节，吁请他们努力争取和平。

清政府软弱的态度令列强不齿。战争中，各国政府都在观望中国是否能够战斗到底，因为只有血战到底，才能博得一向以实力为唯一衡量标准的列强的尊重。中国妥协避战并公开向各国呼吁请求干涉的举动，令外国政府以及在华外国人极为鄙视。德国政府明确告诉向其请求调停的中国驻柏林公使说，"如中国坚决作战到底，则长期战争的危害可能诱使有约各国更有力地为中国而行动，但中国自己却住手不打，它能指望英国或德国代它作战吗？"[1] 然而，清政府却从未认真地想要战斗到底。于是，"全世界又一次目睹了一个庞大的、支离破碎的、有着丰富的资源但是没有很好地开发的帝国，败给一个小得多的、但是更加军事化的、组织得更好、领导得更好

---

① 中国近代经济史资料丛刊编辑委员会主编，《中国海关与中日战争》，中华书局，1983 年，第 75 页。

encouraging the soldiers.[1] In his summary of the *Battle of the Yalu River*, Li Hongzhang remarked, "Our soldiers fought bravely, becoming more spirited as the battle progressed, showing unyielding courage throughout, which is truly commendable."[2] However, after this battle, Li Hongzhang dared not let the navy engage in combat again. Ding Ruchang led the fleet to retreat to the Weihaiwei naval base, and control of the Yellow Sea fell into the hands of the Japanese navy. In January 1895, Japanese troops landed at Rongcheng Bay, entering the Weihaiwei fortress as easily as entering an unmanned territory, effortlessly occupying the Weihaiwei fortifications. Then, they used the heavy guns on the fortress to bombard the Beiyang Fleet trapped in Weihaiwei Port. Thus, this once modern and well-equipped Chinese navy met its demise.

The *Treaty of Shimonoseki* and the Establishment of Japanese Concession

Before the outbreak of the First Sino-Japanese War, there was internal disagreement within the Qing government, and the decision to go to war was uncertain. On the one hand, China lacked a certain degree of attention to the rising power of Japan, while on the other hand, it relied on Russian intervention and British restraint, thus failing to make necessary military preparations. With the failure on the battlefield in Korea, the flames of war spread from the Yalu River to northeastern China. After the fall of Lüshun Port, the Japanese forces advanced towards Beijing. The Qing government urgently sought peace negotiations with the Great Powers. On November 3, 1894, the Ministry of Foreign Affairs summoned the envoys of Britain, France, Germany, Russia, the United States, and other countries in Beijing, urging them to strive for peace.

The weak attitude of the Qing government was held in contempt by the Great Powers. During the war, governments of various countries were watching to see if China could fight to the end because only by fighting fiercely to the end could China earn the respect of the Great Powers, who always measured strength as the sole criterion. China's compromising and openly appealing to foreign intervention during the war were viewed with extreme contempt by foreign governments and foreigners in China. The German government explicitly told the Chinese envoy in Berlin who requested mediation,

---

① William Ferdinand Tyler. *Pulling Strings in China*, translated by Zhang Yinlin. Association of Chinese Historians (ed.). *Sino-Japanese Wars*. Vol.6. New Knowledge Publishing House, 1956, p.50.

② Gu Tinglong, Dai Yi (eds.). *The Collected Works of Li Hongzhang (Memorials 15)*. Anhui Education Press, 2008, p.449.

原日租界武德殿今景。航鹰摄于 2002 年
The present view of the Wude Hall in the former Japanese
Concession. Taken by Hang Ying in 2002

"If China resolutely fights to the end, the dangers of a prolonged war may prompt the contracting powers to act more forcefully for China, but if China refrains from fighting, can it expect England or Germany to fight on its behalf?"[1] However, the Qing government never seriously intended to fight to the end. Thus, "the world witnessed once again a vast, fragmented empire with abundant resources but poorly developed, being defeated by a much smaller but more militarized, better organized, better led, and more cohesive power."[2]

Japan hinted to China through the United States that China should first propose peace talks and send envoys to Japan to discuss terms. However, at this time, no Qing government officials were willing to go to Japan because negotiating peace was an extremely difficult task, and the Ministry of Foreign Affairs, in particular, feared being coerced by Japan during the negotiations.[3] Li Hongzhang, along with officials of the Ministry of Foreign Affairs, decided to send a foreign adviser serving the Qing government to Japan to seek peace and understand the conditions for negotiations from the Japanese side. Li Hongzhang recommended his own foreign adviser, a German named Gustav Detring, for this task. Detring's personal secretary, a British man named Charles Henry Brewitt-Taylor, accompanied him, along with Alexander Michie, the correspondent of *The Times in China*, and the editor of the *The Eastern Times* in Tianjin. By sending Detring, a German, along with other foreign assistants to Japan, it implied to the Japanese that Germany and other great powers were prepared to intervene in the Sino-Japanese War. The intervention of the great powers was what Japan was keen to avoid in this war, but what the Qing government hoped for. However, the Qing government did not give Detring diplomatic authorization to conduct formal negotiations when sending him to Japan for peace talks. Li Hongzhang and the Ministry of Foreign Affairs believed that "the other side is currently arrogant, and if we hastily send a high-ranking official for negotiation, they may despise us."[4] Therefore, sending a foreigner employed by China rather than an official representative of the Qing government to Japan to seek peace could save some

并且更加团结的强国"。[1]

日本通过美国向中国示意，中国应首先提出讲和并派员赴日商议条件。然而清政府官员此时没有人愿意赴日，因为议和是一件极其艰难的事，总理衙门尤其害怕在日本议和容易受其胁迫。[2]李鸿章与总理衙门的大臣们商议，决定派一位为清政府服务的外国洋员赴日求和并了解日方和谈的条件。李鸿章举荐了自己的洋务顾问、津海关税务司德国人德璀琳担当此任，并由德璀琳的私人秘书英国人泰勒（Charles Henry Brewitt-Taylor）与伦敦《泰晤士报》驻华通讯员及天津《时报》的编辑密嘉（Alexander Michie）随行。德璀琳作为一名德国人，与同样属于外籍的助手赴日，即暗示日本人德国及其他强国都准备对中日战争进行干涉。而列强的干涉，是此次战争中日方所极力避免而清政府所寄予希望的。不过，清政府派德璀琳赴日议和，却没有给予他进行正式谈判的外交授权。李鸿章与总理衙门认为，"目下彼方志得气盈，若遽由我特派大员往商，转虑

① （英）魏尔特著，陈敉才等译，《赫德与中国海关》，厦门大学出版社，1993 年，第 283 页。

② 赫德致金登干第 2279、2363 号函件。陈霞飞主编，《中国海关密档——赫德、金登干函电汇编（1874—1907）》第六卷，中华书局，1995 年，第 87、244 页。

① Editorial Committee of the Modern Chinese Economic Historical Data Series (ed.). *Chinese Customs and the Sino-Japanese War*. Zhonghua Book Company, 1983, p.75.

② Stanley F. Wright. *Hart and the Chinese Customs*, translated by Chen Yangcai, et al. Xiamen University Press, 1993, p.283.

③ The No.2279 and 2363 letter of Robert Hart to James Duncan Campbell. Chen Xiafei (ed.). *Chinese Customs Confidential Files - Compilation of Letters and Telegrams by Robert Hart and James Duncan Campbell (1874-1907)*. Vol.6. Zhonghua Book Company, 1995, p.87, 244.

④ Gu Tinglong, Dai Yi (eds.). *The Collected Works of Li Hongzhang* (Letters 8). Anhui Education Press, 2008, pp.55-56.

为彼轻视"①，而派一个受雇于中国的外国人却不是正式的清政府官员赴日乞和，可以保存一些清政府的面子。

于是，1894 年 11 月 22 日，德璀琳以李鸿章特使的名义，一行三人乘德国商船从大沽出发前往日本。他们于四日后抵达神户，并立即拜访了当地知事，要求面见伊藤博文呈递李鸿章信函。由于担心清政府任命外国人为全权代表有可能给列强间接干涉的机会，日本首相和外相考虑再三，以德璀琳没有正式的委任为由拒绝接见他。②之后，指名要恭亲王奕䜣或李鸿章到日本议和。1895 年 3 月 14 日，李鸿章迫不得已启程赴日，3 月 20 日在马关开始谈判，4 月 17 日最终签订了丧权辱国的《马关条约》。

对于东方人来说，面子很重要。德璀琳之所以被清政府选择充当赴日求和的代表，是由于清政府方面不想失去面子；而日本通过美国向中国提出必须由中国首先提出讲和，所争的也是面子。日本坚持让李鸿章赴日进行和谈，就达到了羞辱中国的目的。③作为曾经被中国人轻蔑地呼为"倭人""倭寇"的日本，一旦把曾经当作偶像来仰视和学习的中国打败，这种胜利当然令其志得意满、兴奋难掩。日本人不但要在战场上打败中国，还要中国人到日本来乞求和平，借此在全世界面前羞辱中国、令其彻底折服。从中国战败和签订《马关条约》后国内的群情激愤来看，中国人所恼怒和痛心的也正是被日本这样一个自己素来瞧不起的小国所打败，而以前的两次鸦片战争和中法战争的失败都不能使国人如此痛心疾首。所以，关键还是一个面子问题。当然，对日本人来说，不仅争得了面子，还获得台湾及其附属岛屿一大片土地、2 亿两白银军费补偿以及得以在增开的通商口岸开设工厂等许多实惠。

1896 年，清政府与日本签订《中日通商行船条约》。1898 年，

① 顾廷龙、戴逸主编，《李鸿章全集》（信函八），安徽教育出版社，2008 年，第 55—56 页。

② "美国外交文件"，1894 年，附录一，第 83 页。转引自（英）菲利浦·约瑟夫著，胡滨译，《列强对华外交（1894—1900）——对华政治经济关系的研究》，商务印书馆，1959 年，第 55 页。

③ （英）菲利浦·约瑟夫著，胡滨译，《列强对华外交（1894—1900）——对华政治经济关系的研究》，商务印书馆，1959 年，第 57—58 页。

face for the Qing government.

So, on November 22, 1894, Detring, in the capacity of Li Hongzhang's envoy, set off for Japan aboard a German merchant ship from Taku, accompanied by two others. Four days later, they arrived in Kobe and immediately visited the local governor, requesting an audience with Ito Hirobumi to deliver Li Hongzhang's letter. Concerned that the appointment of foreigners as plenipotentiary representatives by the Qing government might indirectly invite interference from the great powers, the Japanese Prime Minister and Foreign Minister deliberated and ultimately refused to meet him, citing Detring's lack of formal appointment.[1] Subsequently, Prince Yixin or Li Hongzhang was named to negotiate with Japan. On March 14, 1895, Li Hongzhang reluctantly set off for Japan, and negotiations began in Shimonoseki on March 20. On April 17, the humiliating *Treaty of Shimonoseki* was finally signed.

For Easterners, saving face is crucial. Detring was chosen by the Qing government to represent them in negotiations with Japan because they didn't want to lose face. Japan, through the United States, insisted that China must initiate peace talks, also a matter of saving face. Japan's insistence on Li Hongzhang going to Japan for negotiations served the purpose of humiliating China.[2] Japan, once derogatorily referred to by the Chinese as "dwarf pirates," found immense satisfaction and excitement in defeating China, a country they had previously admired and learned from. The victory not only meant defeating China on the battlefield but also making the Chinese come to Japan to beg for peace, thus humiliating China before the world and making it completely submissive. Judging from the intense anger and sorrow within China following its defeat and the signing of the *Treaty of Shimonoseki*, what truly infuriated and grieved the Chinese was being defeated by such a small country as Japan, which they had always looked down upon. The defeats in the Opium Wars and the Sino-French War did not evoke such deep anguish and indignation among the people. Therefore, the key issue remains saving face. Of course, for the Japanese, it was not just about saving face; they also gained a large piece of land including Taiwan and its adjacent islands, compensation of 200 million taels of silver for military expenses, and many other benefits such as opening factories in newly established treaty ports.

In 1896, the Qing government signed the *Sino-Japanese Treaty of Com-*

① "American Diplomatic Documents", 1894, Appendix I, p. 83. Philip Joseph. *Foreign Diplomacy in China (1894-1900)—A Study in Political and Economic Relations with China,* translated by *Hu Bin*. The Commercial Press, 1959, p.55.

② Philip Joseph. *Foreign Diplomacy in China (1894-1900)—A Study in Political and Economic Relations with China,* translated by Hu Bin. The Commercial Press, 1959, pp.57-58.

原日租界大和公园内的天津神社。这些建筑今已不存，旧址位于今和平区鞍山道八一礼堂及其周边的位置
The Tianjin Shrine, formerly located within the Yamato Park of the Japanese Concession, no longer exists. Its former site is now situated in and around the Bayi Auditorium on Anshan Road in Heping District

在此条约基础上又签订了《天津日本租界协议书及附属议定书》，就此奠定天津日租界雏形。日租界有着严谨的规划，至今道路肌理基本保存。租界内建有神社与大和公园，是作为日本居留民精神依托的特殊存在。据《天津日本居留民团资料·民团事务报告》记载，大和公园由首任天津总领事伊集院彦吉命名，其内设有公会堂、租界局、图书馆，还有以首任领事命名的音乐堂等设施。每逢日本节日，也在此张灯结彩、大肆庆祝，平常则对外开放，多有居留民在此休闲娱乐。近代日本在华开辟的五个租界中，天津日租界是"发展最快、经营最好"的租界。由于天津作为华北地区重要交通枢纽的地位，日本人利用在租界开办的商店、旅馆、饭店从事秘密特务活动，为后来的日俄战争、九一八事变直至七七事变，搜集了大量的情报，使日租界成为日本侵略华北的前沿阵地。所以，天津日租界既是日本侵华的产物，又是近代日本侵华的物证和象征。①

八国联军与都统衙门

义和团运动期间的天津之战，从 1900 年 6 月 14 日开始到 7 月 14 日结束，历时一个月。中经大沽炮台之战、老龙头火车站争夺战、紫竹林租界攻坚战和八里台保卫战，天津最后于 7 月 14 日经过惨烈战斗被八国联军攻陷。联军占领天津后，组织了一个占领军临时政府，中文名为都统衙门，自此天津经历了两年时间的殖民统治。

merce and Navigation with Japan. In 1898, based on this treaty, the *Tianjin Japanese Concession Agreement and Supplementary Protocal* were signed, laying the groundwork for the formation of the Tianjin Japanese Concession. The concession was meticulously planned, and to this day, the layout of the roads remains largely preserved. Within the concession, there were shrines and the Yamato Park, serving as a special place of spiritual support for Japanese residents. According to records from the *Tianjin Japanese Residents Association Materials—Association Affairs Report*, Yamato Park was named by the first Tianjin consul-general, Ijūin Hikokichi. It contained a public hall, Japanese Residents' Corporation, library, and facilities like a music hall named after the first consul-general. During Japanese festivals, the park would be adorned with decorations and celebrations were held, while on regular days, it was open to the public, often frequented by residents for leisure and entertainment. Among the five concessions opened by modern Japan in China, the Tianjin Japanese Concession was considered the "fastest developing and best managed" concession. Due to Tianjin's strategic position as a vital transportation hub in North China, the Japanese utilized the shops, hotels, and restaurants they established in the concession to conduct clandestine espionage activities. This provided them with a wealth of intelligence leading up to events like the Russo-Japanese War, the Mukden Incident, and eventually the Marco Polo Bridge Incident, making the Japanese concession a frontline stronghold for their aggression in North China. Therefore, the Tianjin Japanese Concession was not only a product of Japanese aggression in China but also evidence and a symbol of Japan's modern aggression in China.①

The Eight-Nation Alliance and the Tianjin Provisional Government

The Battle of Tianjin during the Boxer Rebellion began on June 14, 1900, and ended on July 14, lasting for a month. It included the battles of Taku Fort, the struggle for control of the Old Dragon Head Railway Station, the assault on the Zizhulin Concession, and the defense of Balitai. After fierce fighting, Tianjin was ultimately captured by the Eight-Nation Alliance on July 14. Following the occupation of Tianjin, the Alliance established a provisional government known in Chinese as the "Dutong Yamen." Thus, Tianjin experienced two years of colonial rule thereafter.

① 万鲁建，《近代天津日本租界研究》，天津社会科学院出版社，2022 年，第 527—534 页。

① Wan Lujian. *Research on the Japanese Concession in Modern Tianjin*, Tianjin Academy of Social Sciences Press, 2022, pp.527-534.

日本人画的联军攻打天津机器局
A depiction by a Japanese artist of the Allied Forces attacking Tianjin Arsenal

一个城市与八个国家

　　1900 年 4 月，英、美、德、法、意五国使团联合发出照会，限令清政府在"两月以内，悉将义和团'匪'一律剿除，否则将派水陆各军驰入山东、直隶两省，代为剿平"[1]。彼时，天津一带义和团运动越来越高涨，外县及天津城郊有不少外国传教士纷纷逃往天津紫竹林租界以求庇护。5 月 19 日，驻北京的法国主教樊国梁写信给法国公使，说义和团"主要的目的是要消灭外国人"，当下的处境已和 1870 年天津惨案前夕相似，要求派遣海军卫队来华。[2]6 月 4 日，英、法、美、日、俄、德、意、奥公使向本国政府电告，要求八国政府派遣军队"采取联合行动救援我们"[3]，这就是八国联军侵华的由来。

① 来新夏主编，《天津近代史》，南开大学出版社，1987 年，第 154 页。

② （俄）德米特里·扬契维茨基著，许崇信等译，《八国联军目击记》，福建人民出版社，1983 年，第 51—52 页。

③ （美）马士著，张汇文等译，《中华帝国对外关系史》第三卷，上海书店出版社，2006 年，第 218 页。

One City and Eight Countries

In April 1900, the diplomatic envoys of Britain, the United States, Germany, France, and Italy jointly issued a note, demanding that the Qing government "eliminate all Boxers within two months, otherwise troops will be dispatched to Shandong and Zhili provinces to suppress them."[1] At that time, the Boxer movement around Tianjin was escalating, with many foreign missionaries in Tianjin and its outskirts fleeing to the Zizhulin Concession for refuge. On May 19, the French bishop stationed in Beijing, Pierre-Marie-Alphonse Favier-Duperron, wrote to the French envoy, stating that the Boxers' "main purpose is to eliminate foreigners," and the situation was similar to the eve of the Tianjin Missionary Case in 1870, requesting the dispatch of a naval contingent to China.[2] On June 4, the envoys of Britain, France, the United States, Japan, Russia, Germany, Italy, and Austria telegraphed their respective governments, requesting the dispatch of troops to "take concerted measures for our relief,"[3] thus laying the foundation for the invasion of China by the Eight-Nation Alliance.

Starting from May 28, the railway transportation and telegraph communication between Beijing and Tianjin were continuously disrupted by the Boxers. On June 10, Vice Admiral Edward Hobart Seymour, commander of the British China Relief Expedition, received the final plea for help from Beijing and led an expeditionary force of over 2,000 men organized from personnel aboard various naval vessels of the participating countries to Beijing by train.[4] Boxers along the Beijing-Tianjin railway line swiftly reacted to stop Seymour's expeditionary force by destroying railways and bridges, forcing the enemy to repair the railway while advancing, causing a significant delay in their movement. On June 11, the allied forces' train barely reached near Langfang, where they were attacked by Boxers wielding swords, spears, and wooden sticks during railway repair, forcing them to retreat to Langfang station. Despite the rudimentary weapons of the Boxers, they bravely charged forward in the face of gunfire from the invading forces armed with rifles. "But what they lacked in drill they made up for in courage and dash, their bravery

① Lai Xinxia. *Modern History of Tianjin*. Nankai University Press, 1987, p.154.

② Dmitry Yanchevetsky. *Eyewitness Records of the Eight-Nation Alliance*, translated by Xu Chongxin, et al. Fujian People's Publishing House, 1983, pp.51-52.

③ Hosea Ballou Morse. *The International Relations of the Chinese Empire (vol.3)*, translated by Zhang Huiwen, et al. Shanghai Bookstore Publishing House, 2006, p.218.

④ Hosea Ballou Morse. *The International Relations of the Chinese Empire (vol.3)*, translated by Zhang Huiwen, et al. Shanghai Bookstore Publishing House, 2006, p.224.

5月28日开始，京津之间的火车运输和电报通信不断遭到义和团破坏。6月10日，英国海军中国舰队司令西摩尔中将接到发自北京的最后一封求救电报后，率领从各国海军舰上人员组织起的一支2000多人的八国联军远征队，搭乘火车前往北京。[①]京津铁路沿线各村庄的义和团团民迅速做出反应，为阻止西摩尔远征队，他们拆毁铁路、桥梁，使敌人不得不边修铁路边前进，行动极为缓慢。11日，联军火车勉强开到廊坊附近，修路时遭到手持大刀、长矛和木棍的义和团攻击，不得不退回廊坊车站。尽管义和团的武器简陋，但面对装配了来复枪的侵略军的射击，他们还是勇猛冲锋，"他们在训练上所缺少的东西，却由他们的勇猛来补足了。他们在优势的敌人面前表现出的勇敢，不断地使我们信服：中国人并不像我迄今为止所认为的那样，他们很少怯懦，而更多的却是爱国心和信念"。[②]在董福祥的甘军、直隶提督聂士成所部清军与义和团的连日阻击下，西摩尔远征队被围困在廊坊不能前进一步。由此也创造了近代世界战争史上乘火车进军速度的"奇迹"，三天仅仅前进了50多千米。在中国军民的联合打击之下，西摩尔远征队弹尽粮绝、进退两难，完全与天津失去了联系。当时的外国人揶揄说，西摩尔远征队与北京的使团、京津两地的侨民、传教士一样，成为需要八国联军后续部队解救和保护的人。[③]后来他们于6月26日被救援部队救回天津。

6月16日，为了使更多的军队得以顺利登陆，各国舰队司令决定夺取大沽炮台，并向守卫炮台的天津镇总兵罗荣光发出最后通牒。遭到拒绝后，战斗于6月17日凌晨打响。激战6个多小时，清军官兵打死打伤敌军130多人，击伤敌舰6艘，最终因敌我力量悬殊、腹背受敌，大沽炮台陷于敌手，守将罗荣光自刎殉国。[④]列强军队占领大沽炮台后，分兵攻占塘沽、北塘、新河等村镇，屠杀数万平民，

in the face of heavy odds continually convincing us that there is much less cowardice and much more patriotism or faith among the Chinese than has hitherto been believed."[①] Under relentless attacks from Dong Fuxiang's Gan Army, Nie Shicheng's Qing Army, and the Boxers, Seymour's expeditionary force was besieged in Langfang, unable to advance further. This also created a "miracle" in the speed of marching by train in modern world war history; in three days, they only advanced more than 50 kilometers. Under the joint attacks of the Chinese military and civilians, Seymour's expeditionary force ran out of ammunition and food, trapped, and completely lost contact with Tianjin. At that time, foreigners ridiculed that Seymour's expeditionary force, like the diplomatic envoys in Beijing, overseas residents and missionaries in Beijing and Tianjin, became people in need of rescue and protection by the follow-up forces of the Eight-Nation Alliance.[②] They were eventually rescued and returned to Tianjin on June 26.

On June 16th, in order to facilitate the smooth landing of more troops, the commanders of the various naval fleets decided to seize the Taku Forts and issued a final ultimatum to General Luo Rongguang, the commander guarding the forts in Tianjin. After being refused, the battle broke out in the early hours of June 17th. After more than six hours of intense fighting, the Qing soldiers killed and wounded more than 130 enemy soldiers, damaged 6 enemy ships. Eventually, due to the disparity in strength and being surrounded, the Taku Forts fell into the hands of the enemy, and its defender Luo Rongguang committed suicide.[③] After occupying the Taku Forts, the allied forces divided their troops to capture villages such as Tanggu, Beitang, and Xinhe, massacring tens of thousands of civilians. Many villages were burned and slaughtered, turning into ruins along the route from Tanggu to Tianjin city. The entire west bank of the Peiho became a wasteland (including the present-day Haihe Education Park).[④] The fall of the Taku Forts was equivalent to the Eight-Nation Alliance's undeclared war. On June 21st, the Qing government was forced to issue a "declaration of war," urging the Qing army to resist foreign aggression alongside the Boxers, and notifying the various foreign legations in China of the declaration of war.

① （美）马士著，张汇文等译，《中华帝国对外关系史》第三卷，上海书店出版社，2006年，第224页。

② （英）壁阁衔，《在华一年记》。天津社会科学院历史研究所编，《八国联军在天津》，齐鲁书社，1980年，第232页。

③ （美）马士著，张汇文等译，《中华帝国对外关系史》第三卷，上海书店出版社，2006年，第227页。

④ 来新夏主编，《天津近代史》，南开大学出版社，1987年，第163页。

① Clive Bigham. *A Year in China*. Institute of History, Tianjin Academy of Social Sciences (ed.). *The Eight-Nation Alliance in Tianjin*. Qilu Press, 1980, p.232.

② Hosea Ballou Morse. *The International Relations of the Chinese Empire (vol.3)*, translated by Zhang Huiwen, et al. Shanghai Bookstore Publishing House, 2006, p.227.

③ Lai Xinxia. *Modern History of Tianjin*. Nankai University Press, 1987, p.163.

④ Dmitry Yanchevetsky. *Eyewitness Records of the Eight-Nation Alliance*, translated by Xu Chongxin, et al. Fujian People's Publishing House, 1983, p.160.

八国联军在塘沽登陆
The Eight-Nation Alliance landed in Tanggu

八国联军中的德军在海河边码头上集结。摄于 1900 年
The German army of the Eight-Nation Alliance gathering at
the dockside along the Hai River, taken in 1900

八国联军中的美国陆军。约摄于 1900—1902 年
The U. S. Army of the Eight-Nation Alliance. Taken around 1900-1902

八国联军中的日本兵。摄于 1900 年
The Japanese soldiers of the Eight-Nation Alliance. Taken in 1900

图片来源：德国 "东亚之友" 协会
Source: StuDeo

很多村庄被烧光杀光，从塘沽到天津城沿路村庄变成废墟，整个白河左（西）岸变成一片荒野（包括今海河教育园区）。① 大沽炮台的失陷等于八国联军的不宣而战，清政府被迫于6月21日发布"宣战"上谕，要求清军与义和团一起抵抗外侮，并将宣战书通知各国驻华使馆。

在此之前，天津市内的战斗已经打响。5月底，沙俄侵略军攻占了老龙头火车站（今天津站）。老龙头火车站是京津重要的交通枢纽，也是列强沿津塘铁路运兵到津、京的必经之路。而且它隔海河与紫竹林租界相对，是租界北面的门户，因此义和团、清军与占据此处的沙俄军队展开了多次激战。6月5日，聂士成率领2000名配有火炮的清军发动进攻，试图夺回被俄军占领的老龙头火车站。在清军激烈的炮火之下，火车站被流弹击中烧毁，后来沙俄援军从塘沽赶来，清军夺回车站的努力失败，但他们打死打伤八国官兵百余人。② 6月18日，义和团领袖曹福田率义和团数千人，协同部分清军，合力攻打火车站，双方激战十多个小时，义和团尽管武器落后，但人人奋勇冲杀，使联军军队伤亡惨重，仅俄军就死伤500多名。③ 6月29日，义和团与清军再次向火车站发起进攻，双方在车站展开了拉锯战，但未能夺回火车站。7月1日至3日，义和团与清军奋战两昼夜之后，短暂占领车站，但不久被八国联军反扑夺回。7月11日清晨，一部分义和团团民冲进车站，抢占了一部分火车车厢，与联军展开肉搏。同时，清军向车站开炮轰击，战斗持续数小时，击毙敌军40人、击伤100余人、④

---

① （俄）德米特里·扬契维茨基著，许崇信等译，《八国联军目击记》，福建人民出版社，1983年，第160页。

② （俄）德米特里·扬契维茨基著，许崇信等译，《八国联军目击记》，福建人民出版社，1983年，第113—118页。

③ 也有俄军随军记者统计伤亡俄军100多人。前一数字来自（日）佐原笃介，《拳匪纪事》卷四：《八国联军志》，转引自来新夏主编，《天津近代史》，南开大学出版社，1987年，第166页。后一数字来自（俄）德米特里·扬契维茨基著，许崇信等译，《八国联军目击记》，福建人民出版社，1983年，第194页。

④ 也有说伤亡人数在80到100人。前一数字来自（日）佐原笃介，《拳匪纪事》卷四：《八国联军志》，转引自来新夏主编，《天津近代史》，南开大学出版社，1987年，第167页。后一数字来自（英）雷穆森著，许逸凡等译，《天津租界史（插图本）》，天津人民出版社，2009年，第169页。

Prior to this, battles had already begun within the city of Tianjin. At the end of May, the Russian invading forces captured the Old Dragon Head Railway Station (now Tianjin Station). Old Dragon Head Railway Station was an important transportation hub between Beijing and Tianjin and a necessary route for the great powers to transport troops along the Tianjin-Tanggu Railway to Tianjin and Beijing. Moreover, it was situated across the Hai River from the Zizhulin Concession, serving as the gateway to the north of the concessions. Therefore, the Boxers, Qing Army, and the Russian forces stationed here engaged in multiple fierce battles. On June 5th, General Nie Shicheng led 2,000 Qing soldiers equipped with artillery to launch an attack in an attempt to retake the Old Dragon Head Railway Station occupied by the Russian troops. Under the intense artillery fire from the Qing Army, the station was hit and burned by shrapnel. Later, Russian reinforcements arrived from Tanggu, and the Qing Army's efforts to retake the station failed, but they managed to kill and wound more than 100 soldiers from the Eight-Nation Alliance.[1] On June 18th, Boxer leader Cao Futian led thousands of Boxers, along with some Qing troops, to launch a coordinated attack on the railway station. After more than ten hours of fierce fighting, despite the Boxers' inferior weapons, they fought bravely, inflicting heavy casualties on the allied forces, with over 500 Russian soldiers[2] killed or wounded. On June 29th, the Boxers and Qing Army launched another attack on the railway station, engaging in a tug-of-war battle, but failed to retake it. From July 1st to 3rd, after two days and nights of fierce fighting, the Boxers and Qing Army briefly occupied the station, but were soon counterattacked and driven out by the Eight-Nation Alliance. On the early morning of July 11th, some Boxers rushed into the station, occupying some of the train cars, and engaged in hand-to-hand combat with the allied forces. Meanwhile, the Qing Army bombarded the station with artillery fire, resulting in the death of 40 enemy soldiers and more than 100 wounded after several hours of fighting.[3] The battle at Old

---

[1] Dmitry Yanchevetsky. *Eyewitness Records of the Eight-Nation Alliance*, translated by Xu Chongxin, et al. Fujian People's Publishing House, 1983, pp.113-118.

[2] A Russian military journalist reported Russian army suffered more than 100 casualties. The former figure comes from Sawara Tokusuke, *Boxers Miscellanies*. Quoted in Lai Xinxia, *Modern History of Tianjin*. Nankai University Press, 1987, p.166. The latter figure comes from Dmitry Yanchevetsky, *Eyewitness Records of the Eight-Nation Alliance*, translated by Xu Chongxin, et al. Fujian People's Publishing House, 1983, p.194.

[3] It was also said that the number of casualties was between 80 and 100 people. The former figure comes from Sawara Tokusuke, *Miscellaneous Notes about the Boxers*. Quoted in Lai Xinxia, *Modern History of Tianjin*. Nankai University Press, 1987, p.167. The latter figure comes from O. D. Rasmussen, *Tientsin: An Illustrated Outline History*, translated by Xu Yifan, et al. Tianjin People's Publishing House, 2008, p.169.

聂士成〔1836—1900〕，淮军著名将领。中法之战中增援台湾，防守台北，力保不失。中日甲午之战中率领部队参加鸭绿江防御战，打退日军进攻。后又取得摩天岭大捷，为甲午战场上少有的胜利。八国联军侵华战争中，率部打败西摩尔远征队，史称"廊坊大捷"。1900年7月8日在进攻租界的战斗中，与联军鏖战一昼夜，殉难于八里台

Nie Shicheng (1836-1900) was a prominent general of the Huai Army. During the Sino-French War, he reinforced Taiwan, defended Taipei, and ensured it remained secure. In the First Sino-Japanese War, he led his troops in the defense of the Yalu River, successfully repelling Japanese forces. Later, he achieved a significant victory at Motianling, one of the few Chinese successes in the war. During the Boxer Rebellion and the Eight-Nation Alliance's invasion of China, he led his troops to defeat the Seymour Expedition, an event known as the "Victory at Langfang." On July 8, 1900, while attacking the foreign concessions, he fought fiercely against the Allied forces for an entire day before sacrificing his life at Balitai

2000年，天津市政府在聂士成为国捐躯100周年之际主持修建铜像和纪念碑，铜像高4.18米

In 2000, on the 100th anniversary of Nie Shicheng's sacrifice for the nation, the Tianjin Municipal Government oversaw the construction of a bronze statue and a memorial monument. The bronze statue stands 4.18 meters tall

聂公祠
Shrine of Nie Shicheng

义和团攻打天津车站时被毁的火车车厢。摄于 1900 年。
图片来源：美国国会图书馆
Train cars destroyed during the Boxer Rebellion's attack on Tianjin Railway Station. Taken in 1900. Source: Library of Congress, U.S.

一直到 7 月 14 日天津城陷落，老龙头火车站的战斗始终没有停止。当然，义和团的伤亡也很大，但没有具体统计数字。

海河东岸老龙头火车站附近还有两处重要的军事设施，一处是天津武备学堂，另一处是北洋机器局东局。武备学堂是一所培训军官的学校，学堂内有不少枪炮和弹药，又正位于紫竹林外国租界的河对岸，直接威胁租界。6 月 17 日大沽炮台被占领后，八国联军中的英国兵和德国兵便组成联队渡河去攻打武备学堂。学堂的学生在两天前已被疏散，但有 90 余名学生留下来，与正规军一起进行了殊死抵抗，最后全部殉国。

6 月 27 日，联军计划进攻机器东局。东局是当时华北最大的军火制造厂，规模庞大，占地约 1.5—1.85 平方千米，雇用工人将近 2000 名，制造地雷、炮弹、毛瑟枪子弹和各种火药，有 1000 名清军驻防。为了保卫机器局，聂士成的清军与东郊的义和团也集结了数千人进行防守。八国联军方面主要以 2000 人的沙俄军队为首，300 名德国海军陆战队士兵和 600 名英国海军陆战队士兵为接应。[1] 双方激战和对峙了三天，联军未能拿下东局，但随着敌人援兵不断增加，加上俄军大炮轰击导致东局内火药爆炸，清军和义和团被迫撤离。据王恩普回忆："当外国人挨近东局子时，其他人都撤退了。一个小官没走，大家劝他撤退，他说：'我末了走，我和外国人一块儿走（意思是说和外国人一块儿同归于尽）。'等大家撤退完后，他独自把火线拉好，并且跑到房顶上呆着。等到外国人都来齐了，他把火线一拉，

Dragon Head Railway Station continued until the fall of Tianjin on July 14th. Of course, the casualties among the Boxers were also considerable, but specific figures are not available.

On the east bank of the Hai River near Old Dragon Head Railway Station, there were two other important military facilities: one was the Beiyang Military Academy, and the other was the Tianjin Arsenal East Bureau. The Military Academy was a school for training officers, and it housed many firearms and ammunition. Located directly across the river from the Zizhulin Foreign Concession, it posed a direct threat to the concessions. On June 17th, after the capture of the Taku Forts, British and German soldiers from the Eight-Nation Alliance formed a joint force to cross the river and attack the Military Academy. The students had been evacuated two days earlier, but more than 90 students remained behind and fought alongside regular soldiers in a desperate resistance, all of them sacrificing their lives. On June 27th, the Allied Forces planned to attack the Tianjin Arsenal East Bureau. The East Bureau was the largest munitions factory in North China at that time, with a large scale and an area of approximately 1.5 to 1.85 square kilometers. It employed nearly 2,000 workers and manufactured landmines, shells, Mauser rifle bullets, and various types of gunpowder. It was defended by 1,000 Qing soldiers. To defend the Arsenal, Nie Shicheng's Qing Army and the Boxers from the eastern suburbs also assembled thousands of people for defense. The main force of the Eight-Nation Alliance consisted mainly of 2,000 Russian troops, with 300 German marines and 600 British marines as support.[1] After three days of fierce fighting and standoff, the Alliance failed to capture the East Bureau, but with the continuous arrival of enemy reinforcements and the bombardment by Russian artillery leading to explosions of gunpowder inside the Arsenal, the Qing Army and the Boxers were forced to withdraw. According to Wang Enpu's recollection: "When foreigners approached the Arsenal, everyone else retreated, but one junior officer stayed behind. Others advised him to retreat, but he said, 'I'll leave last. I'll leave with the foreigners.' After everyone else had retreated, he alone set the fuse and waited on the roof. When all the foreigners had gathered, he pulled the fuse, and suddenly there was a deafening explosion, and he perished along with many foreigners."[2]

Another battlefield in Tianjin that witnessed fierce fighting for over a month was the foreign concessions. On June 2nd, the Boxers launched their

① （英）雷穆森著，许逸凡等译，《天津租界史（插图本）》，天津人民出版社，2009 年，第 146—147 页。

① O. D. Rasmussen. *Tientsin: An Illustrated Outline History*, translated by Xu Yifan, et al. Tianjin People's Publishing House, 2008, pp.146-147.

② Faculty of History, Nankai University (ed.). *Investigation of the Tianjin Boxers*. Tianjin Ancient Books Publishing House, 1990, p.152.

按身高排列的八国联军士兵,其国籍从左至右依次为英国、美国、澳大利亚、印度、德国、法国、奥匈帝国、意大利和日本

Eight-Nation Alliance soldiers arranged by height. Their nationalities, from left to right, are British, American, Australian, Indian, German, French, Austro-Hungarian, Italian, and Japanese

霎时间'轰'声震天,炸死了不少外国人。"①

　　天津市内另一处激战长达一个多月的战场就是外国租界。6月2日,义和团开始首次进攻租界。6月初,列强调遣本国海军运送军队源源不断地从大沽口登陆,随后乘火车从塘沽到达天津租界。租界内集中了八国军队2000余人。各国租界实行联防,由现有联军昼夜巡逻,晚上九点后实行宵禁;各洋行联合组织义勇队(志愿兵),在各主要路口设置工事,配合联军;各国传教士组织界内的中国教民抢修工事,为联军服役;拆除连接租界和车站等处的桥梁,并在租界四周设立岗哨,以防义和团民接近租界。大沽炮台陷落后,清军和义和团开始进攻租界。他们从租界南面和西面进攻,同时还从海河对岸炮轰租界。6月18日,天津老城的守卫清军在南门城墙上架起多门大炮向位于老城外南边的租界轰击,造成很多联军士兵伤亡,很多建筑物被炸毁,尤其是更靠近老城的法租界,几乎成为一片废墟。租界里的妇女儿童纷纷躲进英租界工部局办公大楼戈登堂和利顺德饭店的地下室,后来被送到大沽乘船前往上海。英租界内布置了联军的战地医院,挤满了伤员,截至6月26日即超过300人。②7月1日开始,张德成率领的义和团与聂士成的清军联合攻打租界,他们在城内街巷与联军进行巷战和肉搏,虽付出巨大代价,但也令敌人损失惨重。随着敌人后援的到来,双方的战斗以炮击为主。"在

first attack on the concessions. In early June, foreign powers dispatched their naval forces to continuously land from Taku, who then arrived at Tianjin concessions by train from Tanggu. Over 2,000 troops from the Eight-Nation Alliance were concentrated within the concessions. The concessions implemented joint defense, with patrols by the existing allied forces day and night, curfew after 9 p.m., joint organization of voluntary corps by various foreign firms at major intersections to assist the allied forces, organization of Chinese Christians by missionaries within the concessions for fortification work to serve the allied forces, demolition of bridges connecting the concessions and the railway station, and the establishment of outposts around the concessions to prevent Boxers militia from approaching. After the fall of the Taku Forts, Qing Army and Boxers began to attack the concessions. They attacked from the south and west of the concessions, while also bombarding them from across the Hai River. On June 18th, Qing Army guarding the southern gate of the old city of Tianjin mounted multiple cannons on the city wall and bombarded the concessions located to the south of the old city, causing many casualties among the allied soldiers and destroying many buildings, especially the French concession closer to the old city, which was almost reduced to rubble. Women and children from the concessions sought refuge in the basements of the Gordon Hall British Municipal Council and the Astor House Hotel, and were later sent to Shanghai by boat from Taku. A field hospital for the Allied forces was set up in the British concession, which was crowded with casualties, exceeding 300 people as of June 26th.① On July 1st, Zhang Decheng led the Boxers to join forces with Nie Shicheng's Qing Army to attack the concessions. They engaged in street fighting and close

① 南开大学历史系编,《天津义和团调查》,天津古籍出版社,1990年,第152页。

② (英)雷穆森著,许逸凡等译,《天津租界史(插图本)》,天津人民出版社,2009年,第145页。

① O. D. Rasmussen. *Tientsin: An Illustrated Outline History*, translated by Xu Yifan, et al. Tianjin People's Publishing House, 2008, p.145.

清军与八国联军激战后的废墟。摄于 1900 年
The ruins after fierce battles between the Qing Army and
the Eight-Nation Alliance. Taken in 1900

联军占领天津。摄于 1900 年
The Eight-Nation Alliance occupied Tianjin. Taken in 1900

天津被围 27 天中落在租界的炮弹要比在布尔战争①中莱迪史密斯城被围四个月落下的炮弹还要多。"② 由此可见战况之激烈。

天津陷落与第一次世界大战的预演

7 月 13 日清晨 5 点，八国联军集中了各种火炮几十门，全力进攻天津城，天津战役开始了。一个多小时的炮击后，城外的一座军火库发生爆炸，天空上升起了一朵巨大的蘑菇云。巨大的爆炸使天津城内和租界里的很多房屋都被震毁。上午 7 点，枪声代替了炮声，由美、英、法、日、奥五国军队 5130 名步兵组成的南路军，从南面和西南面向老城发起进攻。守城清军也向租界进行了炮击，并居高临下从城墙的枪眼向攻城的联军射击。联军陷入正面纵射的火力之中，死伤惨重。他们被困在南门外的臭水坑里一整天。直到第二天

---

combat with the Allied Forces in the streets and alleys of the city. Although they suffered heavy losses, they also inflicted severe casualties on the enemy. As reinforcements of enemy arrived, the battle shifted to mainly artillery bombardment. "During the twenty-seven days of the siege of Tianjin, more shells fell than during the four-month siege of Ladysmith in the Boer War①."② This indicates the intensity of the battle.

The Fall of Tianjin and the Prelude to the First World War

On the morning of July 13th at 5 o'clock, the Eight-Nation Alliance concentrated dozens of various cannons and launched a full-scale attack on Tianjin City, marking the beginning of the Battle of Tianjin. After more than an hour of bombardment, an explosion occurred in a military arsenal outside the city, creating a huge mushroom cloud in the sky. The massive explosion destroyed many buildings in Tianjin City and the concessions. At 7 o'clock in the morning, the sound of gunfire replaced the sound of cannons. The Southern Route Army, consisting of 5,130 infantries from the United States,

---

① 指第二次布尔战争。1899 年 10 月 11 日—1902 年 5 月 31 日发生于南非的一场英国与德兰士瓦共和国和奥兰治自由邦之间的战争。第二次布尔战争也是象征大英帝国由盛而衰的开始。

② （英）雷穆森著，许逸凡等译，《天津租界史（插图本）》，天津人民出版社，2009 年，第 192 页。

---

① Referring to the Second Boer War (October 11, 1899 - May 31, 1902), a conflict in South Africa between Britain and the Transvaal Republic and Orange Free State. The war is also seen as the beginning of the decline of the British Empire.

② O. D. Rasmussen. *Tientsin: An Illustrated Outline History*, translated by Xu Yifan, et al. Tianjin People's Publishing House, 2008, p.192.

拂晓，日本人炸开了南城门，天津城才最终被联军攻陷。与此同时，4000 名俄军和 700 多名法军、德军组成的东路军，则向老城的东面或东南面前进，很快夺取了三岔河口附近水师营的黑炮台和芦台运河沿岸的大炮阵地。①

八国联军占领天津后，仅在城墙上，他们就发现了 150 具清军尸体。从北门到南门的大街两旁的房屋已全被烧毁，城里居民几乎逃走了一半。联军在位于市中心的鼓楼上架起大炮，向城里未来得及逃走的居民人群里发炮，城里"死尸山积"，海河中漂浮的尸体阻塞了河道。联军方面的伤亡也很惨重，不到 24 小时，死伤 882 人。② 其中，伤亡最大的是日军和美军，日军死伤人数有 300 多人，一个大队长、两个中队长均被击毙。战斗中，美军指挥官当场被打死，他们还损失了 33% 的军官和 21% 的士兵。曾参加此战、后成为驻津美军第十五步兵团团长的奈勒（William K. Naylor）上校，1925 年将天津战役与第一次世界大战所经历的战斗相比时说，"我曾经在法国参加过若干次最残酷的战役，也曾经陷入危险的境地，然而在天津这短短一天的战役，却是我曾经遇到过的最激烈的一场战斗"③。

八个国家的驻津军队名为保护本国侨民，实则各怀鬼胎。虽然，在面对共同的敌人——清军和义和团时，他们能够暂时联合起来、协同作战。但是，很快就暴露了彼此的矛盾。他们承认，"天津解围之后才是最危险的时期"。国家间的竞争与猜忌经常导致敌对行动的发生，而以流血事件结束。"最严重的一次争斗的结果是，20 名法国阿尔萨斯士兵被打死和打伤，2 名英国皇家威尔士燧发枪团士兵被打伤。1 名英军印度士兵（帕坦人）由于受到德国士兵的嘲弄和

---

① 《天津海关 1892—1901 年十年调查报告书》。北京市政协文史资料研究委员会、天津市政协文史资料研究委员会编，《京津蒙难记——八国联军侵华纪实》，中国文史出版社，1990 年，第 152—153 页。（英）雷穆森著，许逸凡等译，《天津租界史（插图本）》，天津人民出版社，2009 年，第 171—175 页。（俄）德米特里·扬契维茨基著，许崇信等译，《八国联军目击记》，福建人民出版社，1983 年，第 237—240 页。

② （俄）德米特里·扬契维茨基著，许崇信等译，《八国联军目击记》，福建人民出版社，1983 年，第 239 页。

③ （英）雷穆森著，许逸凡等译，《天津租界史（插图本）》，天津人民出版社，2009 年，第 178、181—182 页。

天津城墙上牺牲的清军。摄于 1900 年
The Qing soldiers who sacrificed on the Tianjin city wall. Taken in 1900

被摧毁的天津城。摄于 1900 年
The destroyed city of Tianjin. Taken in 1900

图片来源：美国波士顿公共图书馆
Source: Boston Public Library in the United States

Britain, France, Japan, and Austria, launched an attack from the south and southwest towards the old city. The defending Qing Army also bombarded the concessions and fired at the attacking allied forces from the gun holes on the city walls. The allied forces were caught in the crossfire, suffering heavy casualties. They were trapped in the foul-smelling ditch outside the south gate for the whole day. It wasn't until dawn the next day that the Japanese blew open the south gate, and Tianjin City was finally captured by the allied forces. At the same time, the Eastern Route Army, consisting of 4,000 Russian troops and over 700 French and German troops, advanced towards the east or southeast of the old city. They quickly captured the Black Fort near Sancha estuary and the artillery positions along the Lutai Canal.①

After the Eight-Nation Alliance occupied Tianjin, they found 150 Qing soldiers' bodies just on the city walls. Houses along the main streets from the north gate to the south gate were completely burnt, and almost half of

---

① *The Ten-year Report of Tianjin Customs from 1892 to 1901.* Cultural and Historical Data Research Committee of Beijing Municipal Committee of the CPPCC and Cultural and Historical Data Research Committee of Tianjin Municipal Committee of the CPPCC. *The Suffering of Beijing and Tianjin: An Actual Record of the Eight-Nation Alliance's Invasion of China.* China Literature and History Press, 1990, pp.152-153. O. D. Rasmussen. *Tientsin: An Illustrated Outline History*, translated by Xu Yifan, et al. Tianjin People's Publishing House, 2008, pp.171-175. Dmitry Yanchevetsky. *Eyewitness Records of the Eight-Nation Alliance*, translated by Xu Chongxin, et al. Fujian People's Publishing House, 1983, pp.237-240.

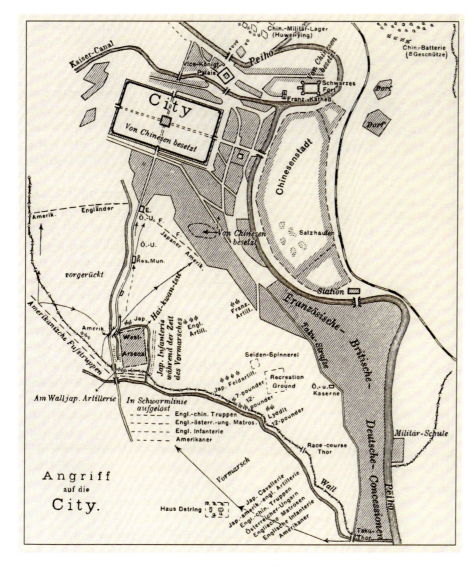

八国联军进攻天津城路线图。出自《地图中的近代天津城市》
（天津大学出版社，2018）
The route map of the Eight-Nation Alliance attacking Tianjin. Source: *Modern Tianjin City in the Map* (Tianjin University Press, 2018)

the city's residents had fled. The allied forces mounted cannons on the Drum Tower in the city center and fired at the residents who hadn't managed to escape, causing a "mountain of corpses" in the city, with bodies floating in the Hai River blocking the waterway. The casualties on the side of the alliance were also severe, with 882 killed or wounded in less than 24 hours.[1] Among them, the Japanese and American forces suffered the most casualties, with over 300 Japanese soldiers killed or wounded, including a major and two lieutenants killed. During the battle, an American commanding officer was killed on the spot, and they lost 33% of their officers and 21% of their soldiers. Colonel William K. Naylor, who participated in the battle and later became the commander of the 15th Infantry Regiment stationed in Tianjin, compared the Battle of Tianjin to the battles he experienced in World War I in France, saying, "I have participated in several of the most brutal battles in France and have been in dangerous situations, but the Battle in Tianjin on that short day was the most intense battle I have ever encountered"[2] in 1925.

The armies stationed in Tianjin from the eight countries were ostensibly there to protect their own nationals, but each had its own agenda. Although they were able to temporarily unite and cooperate in the face of a common enemy—the Qing Army and the Boxers—their underlying contradictions were quickly exposed. They acknowledged that "the period after the relief of Tianjin was the most dangerous." Competition and suspicion among the nations often led to hostile actions, culminating in bloody incidents. "The most serious clash resulted in 20 French soldiers from Alsace being killed or wounded, and two soldiers from the British Royal Welsh Fusiliers being injured. One British Indian soldier (a Pathan) lost control due to taunts and insults from German soldiers, and he wildly charged into the German camp, shooting at anyone he saw. Three German soldiers were killed on the spot, and two others were injured and later died, while the Pathan was also killed"[3]. At the time, Western expatriates believed that the Japanese army was the most courageous and disciplined in combat. During the Battle of Tianjin, Japanese soldiers led the way, while the discipline and combat effectiveness of the armies of other countries paled in comparison. "The Japanese soldiers earned praise, ... while

---

[1] Dmitry Yanchevetsky. *Eyewitness Records of the Eight-Nation Alliance*, translated by Xu Chongxin, et al. Fujian People's Publishing House, 1983, p.239.

[2] O. D. Rasmussen. *Tientsin: An Illustrated Outline History*, translated by Xu Yifan, et al. Tianjin People's Publishing House, 2008, p.178, pp.181-182.

[3] O. D. Rasmussen. *Tientsin: An Illustrated Outline History*, translated by Xu Yifan, et al. Tianjin People's Publishing House, 2008, p.101.

八国联军中的炮队。摄于 1900—1902 年。
图片来源：德国"东亚之友"协会
The artillery of the Eight-Nation Alliance.
Taken around 1900-1902. Source: StuDeo

PLAN OF TIENTSIN, SHOWING POSITIONS OF ALLIED ARMIES.

八国联军驻扎图。出自《地图中的近代天津城市》
（天津大学出版社，2018）
Plan of Tientsin, Showing Position of Allied Armies.
Source: *Modern Tianjin City in the Map* (Tianjin
University Press, 2018)

侮辱而失控，疯狂地冲进德国兵营见人就开枪。3 名德国兵当场被打死，另外两名也受伤而死，这个帕坦人也被打死"①。当时西方侨民认为，日本军队是作战最勇猛和军纪最好的。天津战役中，日本军人身先士卒，其他国家军队的军纪和战斗力则相形见绌。"日本兵赢得了赞誉，……其他各国的军队都成了支援队伍。"②

老城陷落后，城内外的银行、钱庄和各个商铺都被洗劫一空。起初去抢的是撤退前的义和团、士兵和暴民，继则是联军，在天津的外国侨民也参与了抢劫。负责征收盐税的盐道金库被日本人宣布没收，他们抢走了价值几百万鹰洋的纹银，美军、英军也分别从废墟里挖出价值几百万元的纹银。普通士兵的劫掠更比比皆是，"满载着抢来的毛皮、丝绸、瓷器等物的军人和文职人员随处可见③"。当时在华外国人都认为，他们所造成的天津居民生命损失无法估计，至于财产损失，仅一个城郊所毁坏的财产保守估计就价值好几千万两白银。可以说，"这些军队在 19 世纪末几乎是世界上最能干的抢劫者"④。

由于天津的特殊地位，这"短短一天的战役"成为义和团运动中的转折点。天津城被攻陷，"不仅打通了通往北京的道路，而且也使烟台和上海从日益加剧的危险中解脱了出来"。"在天津及其周围的战斗，以及这些战斗的重大战略意义，都由于北京发生的引人瞩目的事件而失去了它们真正的重要地位。"⑤事实上，八国联军攻陷天津，标志着义和团运动的失败。

① （英）雷穆森著，许逸凡等译，《天津租界史（插图本）》，天津人民出版社，2009 年，第 101 页。

② （英）雷穆森著，许逸凡等译，《天津租界史（插图本）》，天津人民出版社，2009 年，第 167 页。

③ 《俄国在远东》第 9 章；《中国与联军》上册第 35 至 38、40、41 章。北京市政协文史资料研究委员会、天津市政协文史资料研究委员会编，《京津蒙难记——八国联军侵华纪实》，中国文史出版社，1990 年，第 175—193 页。

④ （美）马士著，张汇文等译，《中华帝国对外关系史》第三卷，上海书店出版社，2006 年，第 264 页。

⑤ 《1892—1901 年津海关十年报告》（一）；1900 年 7 月 5 日沃伦爵士致索尔斯伯里勋爵函。（英）雷穆森著，许逸凡等译，《天津租界史（插图本）》，天津人民出版社，2009 年，第 189 页。

the armies of other countries became support units"[1].

After the fall of the old city, banks, money shops, and various shops both inside and outside the city were plundered. Initially, it was the retreating Boxers, soldiers, and mobs who went to loot, followed by the allied forces, with foreign expatriates in Tianjin also participating in the looting. The salt treasury responsible for collecting salt taxes was declared confiscated by the Japanese, who seized ingots worth of millions of taels of silver. The American and British forces also dug out ingots worth millions of taels of silver from the ruins. Plundering by ordinary soldiers was widespread, with "soldiers and civilian seen everywhere loaded with looted furs, silks, porcelain, and other goods."[2] At the time, foreigners in China believed that the loss of life among Tianjin residents caused by them was incalculable, and as for property damage, the conservative estimate was that just the property destroyed in the suburbs was worth tens of millions of taels of silver. It could be said that "the imperial troops, who, at the close of the nineteenth century, were the most accomplished plunderers in the world.[3]"

Due to Tianjin's special status, this "short battle" became a turning point in the Boxer Rebellion. With Tianjin captured, "not only was the road to Beijing opened up, but also Yantai and Shanghai were relieved from the increasing danger." "The battles in and around Tianjin, and the significant strategic implications of these battles, lost their true significance due to the remarkable events in Beijing."[4] In fact, the capture of Tianjin by the Eight-Nation Alliance marked the failure of the Boxer Rebellion.

The Tianjin campaign also provided a practical rehearsal for the subsequent First World War. The first Industrial Revolution made possible the development of military industry, with a wide range of weapons being used extensively in the Tianjin campaign, from ironclad warships transporting combat personnel to repeating rifles, various caliber cannons, machine guns,

① O. D. Rasmussen. *Tientsin: An Illustrated Outline History*, translated by Xu Yifan, et al. Tianjin People's Publishing House, 2008, p.167.

② *Far East in Russia*, Chapter 9; *China and the Eight-Nation Alliance* (vol.1), Chapter 35-38, 40, 41. Cultural and Historical Data Research Committee of Beijing Municipal Committee of the CPPCC and Cultural and Historical Data Research Committee of Tianjin Municipal Committee of the CPPCC. *The Suffering of Beijing and Tianjin: An Actual Record of the Eight-Nation Alliance's Invasion of China*. China Literature and History Press, 1990, pp.175-193.

③ Hosea Ballou Morse. *The International Relations of the Chinese Empire* (vol.3), translated by Zhang Huiwen, et al. Shanghai Bookstore Publishing House, 2006, p.264.

④ *The Ten-year Report of Tianjin Customs from 1892 to 1901*; Sir Warren's Letter to Marquess of Salisbury on July 5, 1900. (Britain) O. D. Rasmussen. *Tientsin: An Illustrated Outline History*, translated by Xu Yifan, et al. Tianjin People's Publishing House, 2008, p.189.

天津战役还为后来的第一次世界大战提供了一次实战演练。第一次工业革命为军事工业的发展提供了可能，从运送作战人员的铁甲战舰，到连发步枪、各种口径大炮、速射炮和各种火药，无不在天津战役中得到大量使用。尽管义和团的装备只有大刀、木棍等简陋的冷兵器，但李鸿章多年训练并投入大量资金的淮军，却是用来复枪、克虏伯大炮、马克西姆速射炮等武装起来的一支精锐部队。尤其是聂士成麾下部队在对八国联军的作战中战绩辉煌。"天津的战斗再次印证了南非战役的经验教训，现代化的武器显然可以使士气高下不相等的士兵在作战能力上趋于相等，一个中国人在 2 英里外打炮或在 1 英里外打枪，可以差不多和欧洲人一样，如果武器稍好一点，他们就完全等于一个上等的士兵。"① 因此，尽管程度不高，但西方列强在世界范围进行殖民战争得出的旧有规律随之加以改变。另外，大规模炮兵与步兵的配合作战在此次战役中得以再次验证。此前的布尔战争中，英军就曾大规模使用速射炮、野战炮，但并没有取得明显战果。天津战役中最先使用炮击的是清军，给租界和八国联军造成巨大伤亡。后来的第一次世界大战中，现代火炮成为战场上的绝对主力，造成交战双方的极大损失。还有，几个国家之间的协同作战也在这次战争中得以再次实践。八国联军侵华之后，大规模的国际联盟之间的战争拉开序幕，一战中是协约国与同盟国，二战中则是反法西斯同盟与轴心国。

除了武器和战术改良，天津战役还为一战提供了作战指挥人员的准备。第一次世界大战中有许多指挥官甚至发挥重要影响的人物都曾参加过天津战役。除了上文提到的天津美军第十五步兵团团长的奈勒上校，著名的还有美国的巴特勒将军（Smedley Butler）②、德国的法根海上将（Erich von Falkenhayn）③ 和法国的德斯佩雷元帅

---

① （英）雷穆森著，许逸凡等译，《天津租界史（插图本）》，天津人民出版社，2009 年，第 172 页。

② 巴特勒将军是美国海军陆战队史上最有名望的将军，在天津战役中负伤，后被任命为上尉，第一次世界大战中参加西线作战。

③ 法根海曾任德国东亚远征队参谋，瓦德西元帅离开后成为驻津德军最高指挥官，后来在一战中任德军总参谋长。

and various types of gunpowder. Despite the Boxers' equipment being limited to crude cold weapons such as swords and wooden sticks, the Huai Army trained for many years and invested heavily by Li Hongzhang was an elite force armed with Mauser rifles, Krupp guns, Maxim machine guns, and more. Especially the achievements of the forces under Nie Shicheng's command in their battles against the Eight-Nation Alliance were outstanding. "Tientsin emphasizes the lessons of South Africa that modern arms of precision tend to equate soldiers unequal in morale; a Chinaman with a gun at two miles, or a rifle at one, is almost as good a man as a European, and if his weapons are slightly better, he is quite as good man."① Therefore, although to a lesser extent, the old rules drawn from colonial wars waged by Western powers around the world were subsequently changed. In addition, the coordinated operations of large-scale artillery and infantry were validated once again in this battle. In the previous Boer War, the British army had used rapid-firing guns and field guns on a large scale but did not achieve significant results. The Qing Army was the first to use artillery in the Tianjin Battle, causing massive casualties to the concessions and the Eight-Nation Alliance. In the subsequent First World War, modern artillery became the absolute main force on the battlefield, causing great losses to the warring parties. Also, coordinated operations between several countries were once again practiced in this war. After the invasion of China by the Eight-Nation Alliance, the stage was set for large-scale wars between international alliances, with the First World War being fought between the Triple Entente and the Central Powers, and the Second World War between the Allies and the Axis powers.

In addition to improvements in weapons and tactics, the Tianjin Battle also prepared commanders for the First World War. Many commanders who played important roles in the First World War had participated in the Tianjin Battle. In addition to Colonel Naylor, commander of the US 15th Infantry Regiment in Tianjin mentioned earlier, notable figures included General Smedley Butler② of the United States, Admiral Erich von Falkenhayn③ of Germany,

---

① O. D. Rasmussen. *Tientsin: An Illustrated Outline History*, translated by Xu Yifan, et al. Tianjin People's Publishing House, 2008, p.172.

② General Smedley Butler was the most distinguished general in the history of the United States Marine Corps. He was wounded during the Battle of Tianjin and was later promoted to the rank of captain. He also served on the Western Front during the First World War.

③ Erich von Falkenhayn served as a staff officer with the German East Asia Expeditionary Force. After the departure of Marshal Waldersee, he became the highest-ranking German officer in Tianjin. Later, during the First World War, he was appointed as the Chief of Staff of the German Army.

（Louis Franchet d'Espèrey）^①等。在天津租界中被义和团和清军围困、朝不保夕的 27 天经历，成为许多在津外国人的深刻记忆。义和团运动期间署天津领事的德国外交官齐默曼（Arthur Zimmermann）见证了义和团运动在天津的发展过程。1902 年他回到德国，1911 年成为外交部副部长。第一次世界大战时期，他任德意志帝国外交大臣，是第一次世界大战的策动者之一，以"齐默曼电报"^②闻名。缘于在天津经历的影响，一战中，齐默曼热衷于在世界各地煽动叛乱，曾参与策划支持爱尔兰叛乱、印度叛乱以及沙俄的动乱。

都统衙门的殖民统治

1900 年，八国联军攻陷天津，随后于 7 月 30 日成立了一个军事政府——"天津临时政府"，中文名"天津都统衙门"，对当时的天津城、静海和宁河等地区实行军事统辖。都统衙门的市政委员会，

都统衙门印鉴
The seal of the Tianjin
Provisional Government

天津都统衙门
Tianjin Provisional Government

---

① 德斯佩雷早年曾参加对义和团作战，后累升至军团指挥官，在一战中成功指挥了马其顿战役，导致同盟国南部战线的崩溃，促成了一战停战。

② 1917 年 2 月 24 日，美国驻英大使佩奇收到齐默曼于 1 月 16 日发出的著名的"齐默曼电报"，称如果墨西哥对美国宣战，德国将协助把美国西南部归还给墨西哥。于是美国以此为借口，在该年 4 月 6 日向德国宣战。此举使协约国实力大增，一战得以提早结束。同年 8 月 6 日，齐默曼辞去外交大臣一职。1940 年因肺病逝于柏林。

and Marshal Louis Franchet d'Espèrey^① of France. The 27-day ordeal of being besieged and uncertain of the future in the Tianjin Concessions left a deep impression on many foreigners in Tianjin. Arthur Zimmermann, a German diplomat who served as consul in Tianjin during the Boxer Rebellion, witnessed the development of the Boxer Rebellion in Tianjin. He returned to Germany in 1902 and became Deputy Minister of Foreign Affairs in 1911. During the First World War, he served as Foreign Minister of the German Empire and was one of the instigators of the war, famous for the "Zimmermann Telegram."^② Influenced by his experiences in Tianjin, Zimmermann was enthusiastic about fomenting rebellions around the world during the First World War, and was involved in planning and supporting rebellions in Ireland, India, and the unrest in Tsarist Russia.

Colonial Rule by the Provisional Government

In 1900, the Eight-Nation Alliance captured Tianjin and subsequently established a military government called the "Tianjin Provisional Government" on July 30th. Known in Chinese as the "Tianjin Dutong Yamen," it exercised military jurisdiction over Tianjin City, Jinghai, Ninghe, and other areas. The Municipal Committee of the Provisional Government, the highest decision-making body, consisted of representatives from Russia, Britain, Japan, Germany, France, and the United States, totaling six members. It had subordinate offices including the Police Bureau, Health Bureau, Treasury Department, Public Food Supply Office, Judiciary Department, Public Works Bureau, as well as the General Secretariat and Chinese Secretariat.^③ The officials heading these offices, except for the Police Bureau Chief who was a British officer, were

---

① Louis Franchet d'Espèrey participated in the campaign against the Boxers in his early years. He later rose to the rank of corps commander. During the First World War, he successfully commanded the Macedonian Front, leading to the collapse of the Central Powers' southern front and contributing to the eventual armistice that ended the war.

② On February 24, 1917, Walter H. Page, the U.S. Ambassador to the United Kingdom, received the famous Zimmermann Telegram, which had been sent by Arthur Zimmermann on January 16, 1917. The telegram stated that if Mexico declared war on the United States, Germany would assist Mexico in reclaiming the southwestern territories of the U.S. This message served as a pretext for the United States to declare war on Germany on April 6, 1917. This move significantly boosted the strength of the Allied Powers, helping to bring about an early end to the First World War. On August 6, 1917, Zimmermann resigned from his post as German Foreign Minister. He passed away in Berlin in 1940 due to lung disease.

③ Minutes of the 67th meeting: *Administrative Regulations of Tianjin*; Minutes of the 71st meeting: *Administrative Regulations (Revised Draft)*. Liu Haiyan, et al. *Record of the Eight-Nation Alliance's Occupation—Minutes of the Tianjin Provisional Government Meeting*. Tianjin Academy of Social Sciences Press, 2004, pp.1-3, 88-91.

都统衙门巡捕局的巡捕们

The constables of the Provisional Government Police Bureau

都统衙门最高委员会成员由八国联军驻津最高指挥官组成

The Supreme Council of the Provisional Government was composed of the highest-ranking commanders of the Eight-Nation Alliance stationed in Tianjin

即最高决策机构，由俄国、英国、日本、德国、法国和美国代表共6人组成，下设巡捕局、卫生局、库务司和公共粮食供应署、司法部、公共工程局以及总秘书处和中文秘书处。① 各机构为首的官员，除了巡捕局局长是一名英国军官外，其他都是具有专门资格和能力、有的还是久居天津、对中国情况比较熟悉的外国人，甚至是能讲一口汉语的"中国通"。例如，被任命为临时政府秘书长的田夏礼（Charles Jr. Denby）是美国驻华大使田贝（Charles Denby）之子，当时正在天津经商；担任汉文秘书长的丁家立是久居天津的美国人，创办北洋大学堂并任总教习，也曾担任过美国驻天津领事馆副领事。丹麦工程师林德（A. de Linde）受聘担任公共工程局的局长，他长期生活在天津英租界从事公用事业，曾参与海河治理工程。

临时政府实行委员会"集权制"，委员会集立法、司法和行政权力于一身。根据联军司令官会议通过的"天津行政条例"，委员会有权制定和公布具有法律效用的各种条例、有施行治安管理的权力和司法权力、有权向中国人征税、有权支配中国政府的财产以及没收和出售中国人的私人财产。临时政府设有法庭并任命了法官，

① 第67次会议纪要：《天津城行政条例》；第71次会议纪要：《行政条例（修订稿）》。刘海岩等编，《八国联军占领实录：天津临时政府会议纪要》，天津社会科学院出版社，2004年，第1—3、88—91页。

individuals with specialized qualifications and abilities, some of whom had long resided in Tianjin and were familiar with the situation in China. Some were even "China experts" who could speak Chinese fluently. For example, Charles Jr. Denby, appointed as Secretary-General of the Provisional Government, was the son of Charles Denby, the American ambassador to China, and was engaged in business in Tianjin at the time. Charles Daniel Tenney, serving as the Chinese Secretary-General, was an American who had long resided in Tianjin, founded the Peiyang University, served as its dean, and also worked as the Deputy Consul at the American Consulate in Tianjin. Danish engineer A. de Linde was hired as the Director of the Public Works Bureau. He had lived in the British concession in Tianjin for a long time, engaged in public utilities, and had participated in the management of the Hai River project.

The Provisional Government implemented a "centralized system" by the Executive Committee, which consolidated legislative, judicial, and administrative powers. According to the "Tianjin Administrative Regulations" passed by the Allied Forces Commanders' Conference, the committee had the authority to enact and promulgate various regulations with legal effect, exercise public security management, and judicial powers, impose taxes on Chinese people, dispose of Chinese government property, and confiscate and sell private property of Chinese individuals. The Provisional Government established courts and appointed judges, with all criminal and civil cases being tried by the courts. However, all judgments had to be approved by the committee before being executed, and the committee had the authority to modify and make different decisions regarding the court's judgments. Ac-

Un exemplaire sera remis à chacun des Plénipotentiaires étrangers et un exemplaire sera remis aux Plénipotentiaires chinois.

Pekin, le 7 Septembre, 1901

光緒二十七年七月二十五日

一千九百零一年九月初七日

在北京定立

《辛丑条约》
The *Boxer Protocol*

拆除大沽炮台。约摄于 1900—1902 年
Demolition of Taku Forts. Taken around 1900-1902

从大沽炮台上拆卸下来的克虏伯大炮。约摄于 1900—1902 年
The Krupp cannons dismantled from the Taku Forts. Taken around 1900-1902

cording to the provisions of the "Administrative Regulations," the Provisional Government had the power to sentence Chinese people to exile or death, and impose fines or confiscate property. However, for foreigners, according to extraterritoriality, they only had the right to arrest them and then hand them over to the military or consular authorities of their respective countries for trial.[1] The patrols were not only responsible for judicial and public security matters but also for managing public affairs such as transportation and health, which was significantly different from the management of traditional "yamen", strengthening the government's control over society.[2] At that time, the first fixed-location patrols were established to maintain public order on the streets, marking the beginning of police maintaining traffic and public security through "standing guard."

After the establishment of the Provisional Government committee, suppressing the Boxers became the primary task, and most captured Boxers were summarily executed after simple interrogation.[3] To prevent Chinese resistance, the Tianjin Provisional Government also destroyed military facilities in the local area. The earliest dismantled were the Tianjin Arsenal East and West

所有刑事和民事案件均由法庭审判。但是，各项判决都要经委员会批准后才能执行，委员会对法庭的判决有权修改和做出不同的决定。按照"行政条例"的规定，临时政府有权判处华人流放直至死刑、有权处以罚款或没收财产。但对于外国人，则按照治外法权，只有权将其逮捕，然后送交其所属国的军事或领事当局审判。[1] 巡捕不仅负责司法、治安，还负责交通、卫生等公共事务的管理，这与传统衙门的管理有明显的不同，政府对社会的控制职能强化了。[2] 当时，首次出现专门在街头固定位置站岗维持治安的巡捕，是警察以"站岗"

---

① 第 67 次会议纪要：《天津城行政条例》；第 71 次会议纪要：《行政条例（修订稿）》。刘海岩等编，《八国联军占领实录：天津临时政府会议纪要》，天津社会科学院出版社，2004 年，第 1—3、88—91 页。

② 第 2 次会议纪要。刘海岩等编，《八国联军占领实录：天津临时政府会议纪要》，天津社会科学院出版社，2004 年，第 4—5 页。

---

① Minutes of the 67th meeting: *Administrative Regulations of Tianjin*; Minutes of the 71st meeting: *Administrative Regulations (Revised Draft)*. Liu Haiyan, et al (eds.). *Record of the Eight-Nation Alliance's Occupation: Minutes of the Tianjin Provisional Government Meeting*. Tianjin Academy of Social Sciences Press, 2004, pp.1-3, 88-91.

② Minutes of the 2nd meeting. Liu Haiyan, et al (eds.). *Record of the Eight-Nation Alliance's Occupation: Minutes of the Tianjin Provisional Government Meeting*. Tianjin Academy of Social Sciences Press, 2004, pp.4-5.

③ No.42 of *Appendix 1: Compilation of Announcements from Tianjin Provisional Government*. Liu Haiyan, et al (eds.). *Record of the Eight-Nation Alliance's Occupation: Minutes of the Tianjin Provisional Government Meeting*. Tianjin Academy of Social Sciences Press, 2004, p.808.

方式维持交通、治安的肇始。

临时政府委员会成立后，镇压义和团成为首要任务，抓到的团民大都经简单审讯即处决。[1] 为了防范中国人的反抗，天津临时政府还摧毁了本地区的军事设施。最早拆毁的是天津东、西机器局和西沽武库。在 19 世纪，天津曾是中国北方规模最大的军火生产基地，建于 1867 年的西机器局主要生产枪炮，建于 1869 年的东机器局主要生产弹药，1873 年建成的西沽武库则是大型军火库。从此天津的军火工业不复存在。都统衙门还下令拆除了天津城墙，天津成了不设防的城市。[2] 在海河沿岸，从大沽口到天津城分布着的多处炮台也成为八国联军摧毁的主要对象。[3]

20 世纪初的天津，既遭遇了灾祸，也迎来了历史的转折。在城墙旧址上，都统衙门下令铺筑了东、西、南、北四条马路，还修筑了排水系统。[4] 伴随道路改造的是电车的出现。1906 年，天津开通了一条公共有轨电车路线。这一时期老城区也有了城市照明，出现了路灯。[5] 为老城区供应自来水和电话系统也在这一时期开始提出。[6] 为了防疫，老城区建起了多处公共厕所，并设有清洁夫按时清扫。都统衙门专门发布告谕，要求人们必须到厕所"出恭"，在厕所以外便溺要受重罚。同时，还将所有粪厂迁到郊外。这些强制性的措施对城市环境的改善产生了很大的影响。此外，临时政府时期，还建立消防队、制定交通法规、建立公共墓地等。

① 《附录一：天津都统衙门告谕汇编》第 42 号。刘海岩等编，《八国联军占领实录：天津临时政府会议纪要》，天津社会科学院出版社，2004 年，第 808 页。

② 刘海岩等编，《八国联军占领实录：天津临时政府会议纪要》，天津社会科学院出版社，2004 年，第 85、139、231、273、301 页。

③ 第 227 次会议纪要。刘海岩等编，《八国联军占领实录：天津临时政府会议纪要》，天津社会科学院出版社，2004 年，第 494—497 页。

④ 刘海岩等编，《八国联军占领实录：天津临时政府会议纪要》，天津社会科学院出版社，2004 年，第 24、30、71、92、94、129、136、232、253、298、302、392 页。（英）雷穆森著，许逸凡等译，《天津租界史（插图本）》，天津人民出版社，2009 年，第 198 页。

⑤ 刘海岩等编，《八国联军占领实录：天津临时政府会议纪要》，天津社会科学院出版社，2004 年，第 8、101、127、300、315、404、505、602、721、742、754 页。

⑥ 刘海岩等编，《八国联军占领实录：天津临时政府会议纪要》，天津社会科学院出版社，2004 年，第 185、188、191、207、216、317、329、351、423 页。

Bureaus and the Xigu Arsenal. In the 19th century, Tianjin was once the largest military production base in northern China. The West Bureau, established in 1867, mainly produced firearms, while the East Bureau, built in 1869, mainly produced ammunition. The Xigu Arsenal, completed in 1873, was a large-scale military arsenal. Since then, Tianjin's military industry ceased to exist. The Provisional Government also ordered the dismantling of the Tianjin city wall, turning Tianjin into an undefended city.[1] Along the Hai River, several forts distributed from Taku to Tianjin became the main targets destroyed by the Eight-Nation Alliance.[2]

In early 20th century, Tianjin experienced both disasters and historical turning points. On the site of the old city wall, the Provisional Government ordered the construction of four roads: East, West, South, and North, and also built a drainage system.[3] Accompanying the road renovations was the appearance of electric trams. In 1906, Tianjin opened a public tram line. During this period, the old city area also saw urban lighting with the introduction of street lamps.[4] The provision of tap water and telephone systems for the old city area also began during this period.[5] To prevent epidemics, multiple public toilets were built in the old city area, and sanitation workers were employed to clean them regularly. The Provisional Government specifically issued decrees requiring people to use the toilets properly, imposing heavy penalties for urination outside of designated areas. At the same time, all manure plants were relocated to the outskirts. These compulsory measures had a significant impact on improving the urban environment. Additionally, during the period of the Provisional Government, firefighting teams were established, traffic regulations were enacted, and public cemeteries were established.

In May 1902, Yuan Shikai, then Viceroy of Zhili Province, negotiated with

① Liu Haiyan, et al (eds.). *Record of the Eight-Nation Alliance's Occupation: Minutes of the Tianjin Provisional Government Meeting*. Tianjin Academy of Social Sciences Press, 2004, p.85,139,231,273,301.

② Minutes of the 227th meeting. Liu Haiyan, et al (eds.). *Record of the Eight-Nation Alliance's Occupation: Minutes of the Tianjin Provisional Government Meeting*. Tianjin Academy of Social Sciences Press, 2004, pp.494-497.

③ Liu Haiyan, et al (eds.). *Record of the Eight-Nation Alliance's Occupation: Minutes of the Tianjin Provisional Government Meeting*. Tianjin Academy of Social Sciences Press, 2004, p. 24,30,71,92,94,129,136,232,253,298,302,392. O. D. Rasmussen. *Tientsin: An Illustrated Outline History*, translated by Xu Yifan, et al. Tianjin People's Publishing House, 2008, p.198.

④ Liu Haiyan, et al (eds.). *Record of the Eight-Nation Alliance's Occupation: Minutes of the Tianjin Provisional Government Meeting*. Tianjin Academy of Social Sciences Press, 2004, p.8, 101,127,300,315,404,505,602,721,742,754.

⑤ Liu Haiyan, et al (eds.). *Record of the Eight-Nation Alliance's Occupation: Minutes of the Tianjin Provisional Government Meeting*. Tianjin Academy of Social Sciences Press, 2004, p.1 85,188,191,207,216,317,329,351,423.

袁世凯创办的中国最早的警察机构接管天津。摄于 1902 年
The earliest police organization in China, founded by Yuan Shikai, took over the administration of Tianjin. Taken in 1902

袁世凯与都统衙门的官员谈判交接天津管辖权后合影。摄于 1902 年
Yuan Shikai took a group photo with officials of the Provisional Government after negotiating the transfer of Tianjin's jurisdiction. Taken in 1902

　　1902 年 5 月，时任直隶总督的袁世凯和各国驻天津都统会商收回天津，得到了各国驻天津都统会议的批准。但都统衙门以清军只能驻扎在距天津 20 里外为由——根据《辛丑条约》的规定，作为战败国的中国，不能在天津城及京津铁路沿线驻兵——拒绝将天津的行政管理权和警察管理权交还给当时的清政府。于是，袁世凯从保定新军中挑了 3000 人，换上警察制服，改编为巡警派驻天津，接手了天津的防务，变相收回了京津沿线主权，并组成天津南北段巡警局，这支部队就是中国最早的警察队伍。1902 年 8 月 15 日，袁世凯代表清政府接管天津政权，撤除都统衙门这一殖民机构。天津被联军占领达两年之久后，终于回到中国人手中。为此，天津各住户、店铺高挂龙旗，悬灯结彩三日，庆贺天津城管理权的收回。北洋新政的推行，社会出现的种种变革，使得天津的经济、社会以及城市建设等方面，都出现了新的局面。

the heads of various countries stationed in Tianjin to reclaim the city, which was approved by the conference of heads of various countries stationed in Tianjin. However, the colonial office refused to return the administrative and police powers of Tianjin to the Qing government at the time, citing the provision of the *Boxer Protocol* that the Qing troops could only be stationed 20 li away from Tianjin—as a defeated country, China could not station troops in Tianjin City or along the Beijing-Tianjin railway. Consequently, Yuan Shikai selected 3,000 soldiers from the New Army in Baoding, dressed them in police uniforms, and reorganized them into a police force stationed in Tianjin, taking over the city's defense. This effectively regained sovereignty over the Beijing-Tianjin railway line. He established the Tianjin North and South Police Bureaus, forming China's earliest police force. On August 15, 1902, Yuan Shikai represented the Qing government in taking over the Tianjin administration, abolishing the colonial institution of the Provisional Government. After being occupied by the Allied Forces for two years, Tianjin finally returned to Chinese hands. In celebration, households and shops in Tianjin displayed

二战爆发前列强在华的军事存在

近代史上战争结束后的通常惯例就是割地赔款，天津租界的设立及其扩张也与战争直接相关。各国租界设立之初，本无驻扎军队的权力。义和团运动之后，通过《辛丑条约》的签订使各国在华大规模驻军合法化，因此天津有八国租界，八个国家在天津的各租界内设立兵营，常驻军队。[①] 列强拥有在华驻军权，对中国人民形成武装威慑，是中国半殖民地社会形态的深刻体现。

军队、兵营与租界的扩张

义和团运动后，列强之间设立和扩张租界的"攫取竞赛"便开始了。[②] 八国联军侵华期间，俄国军队占领了天津火车站及海河左岸（东岸）的大片土地。战后俄国人宣称"这是根据军队占领和俄国人所付出的血的代价而取得的财产"，是"征服者的权利"。由于这一区域阻隔了自紫竹林法租界和英租界至火车站的通道，引起两国不满。经德国从中调停，俄国同意改划原定租界范围，将火车站地区交还中国，俄租界遂分为东、西两区。1901 年 5 月 30 日，清政府与沙俄在天津签订协定，正式划定俄租界，面积仅次于英租界。[③] 继俄国之后，八国联军中的意、奥匈两国，甚至连未出兵参战的比利时也纷纷乘机在天津强占租界。法国则趁机将大片土地划为"扩充界"；英国也再次扩张租界，并擅自将原美租界并入英租界。德国自 1895 年借口甲午战争中迫使日本将辽东半岛归还中国有功，向清政府索取天津租界，之后趁镇压义和团向租界北面和西南方向扩

---

① 美国派兵参加了八国联军，在天津有美国兵营，但美租界在 1902 年并入英租界。比利时虽未派兵参加联军，但趁机划定了比租界。

② （英）雷穆森著，许逸凡等译，《天津租界史（插图本）》，天津人民出版社，2009 年，第 202 页。

③ 天津市地方史志编修委员会编著，《天津通志·附志·租界》，天津社会科学院出版社，1996 年，第 54—57 页。（英）雷穆森著，许逸凡等译，《天津租界史（插图本）》，天津人民出版社，2009 年，第 203 页。刘海岩等编，《八国联军占领实录：天津临时政府会议纪要》，天津社会科学院出版社，2004 年，第 75 页。

各国驻津部队军官合影。摄于 1905 年
Group photo of military officers from various countries stationed in Tianjin. Taken in 1905

dragon flags and illuminated lanterns for three days, commemorating the return of Tianjin's administrative authority. The implementation of the Beiyang New Policies and various social changes ushered in a new era in Tianjin's economy, society, and urban development.

The Military Presence of the Great Powers in China Before the Outbreak of the Second World War

The usual practice after wars in modern history is territorial cession and indemnities. The establishment and expansion of the Tianjin Concessions are directly related to wars. Initially, there was no authority for military presence in the concessions of various countries. After the Boxer Rebellion, the signing of the *Boxer Protocol* legalized the large-scale military presence of various countries in China. Therefore, there were eight foreign concessions in Tianjin, with each country establishing barracks and maintaining a permanent military presence within their respective concessions.[①] The presence of foreign troops in China, with the right to station soldiers, formed an armed deterrent

---

① The United States sent troops to join the Eight-Nation Alliance and established American Barracks in Tianjin, but the American Concession was merged into the British Concession in 1902. Although Belgium did not send troops to join the Alliance, it took the opportunity to obtain the Belgian Concession.

张。日本将天津城厢东南繁华区列为扩张租界。

各国在津扩张租界的理由和依据，均以本国军队在镇压义和团运动中的"贡献"大小来证明。驻军的多少即是各国实力的象征，是列强不断攫取在华利益的保证。1901 年 4 月，在八国联军最高统帅瓦德西元帅的主持下，联军召开会议，决定了平常时期各国驻屯军的人数，多余兵力陆续在临时政府撤销前后开始从京津一带撤离。瓦德西去职后，各国军队由驻军的高级将领进行协商，在编制、给养、卫生、守备等方面协同行动。八国军队中，除了奥匈帝国因天津租界侨民极少而把兵力主要部署在北京保护使馆以外，其他 7 个国家驻军的司令部都设在天津，以便于协调联动。①除了在天津设立兵营之外，八国联军还在天津附近的军粮城、塘沽直到山海关一线设置兵营，驻扎军队，并且按期换防。

由于沙俄的在华势力范围在东北、德国的势力范围在山东，距离京津很近，而现代战争主要依靠铁路和军舰运输军队，从旅顺或青岛、烟台进行海上陆上运输都非常便捷，可以随时调兵增援，加之海外驻军需要大量资金支持，因此，除了美国、英国、法国、意大利、日本等在天津设立长期的兵营以外，德国、沙俄和奥匈基本上都从天津撤回了驻军，只保留有限兵力作为在津领事馆的卫兵。一战爆发后，以上三国即撤走了全部在华驻军。

各国兵营大都建在原来天津的各个学堂校址上，主要是原有校舍便于利用为集体宿舍，而操场便于演兵训练，食堂、浴室等设施也比较齐全。例如，德军占领了北洋大学堂位于梁家园的最初校址，使得北洋大学不得不另择被德军摧毁的西沽武库重建校园；沙俄军队则占领了原北洋武备学堂的校址以作兵营；法国军队因原有兵营容纳不下增加的军队，强占了原北洋水师学堂校舍设为"东局子兵营"。后来，这些兵营又大都恢复为校舍。比如，为了满足德国侨民子女入学的需要，天津德国领事馆于 1907 年将兵营改为学校，创办天津德华普通中学堂（今海河中学）；英国兵营在 1947 年后被划给天津市第一中学和实验小学作为校园；法国"东局子兵营"现为中国人民解放军陆

---

① 天津市地方史志编修委员会总编辑室编，《二十世纪初的天津概况》，内部发行，1986 年，第 155—160 页。

---

against the Chinese people, reflecting profoundly the semi-colonial nature of Chinese society.

Armies, Barracks, and the Expansion of Concessions

After the Boxer Rebellion, a "race for seizure" of concessions and their expansion among the Great Powers began.[1] During the invasion of China by the Eight-Nation Alliance, Russian troops occupied a large area of land including the Tianjin railway station and the left bank (east bank) of the Hai River. After the war, the Russians claimed this territory as "property acquired at the cost of military occupation and the blood of Russians," asserting it as the "right of conquerors." This area, blocking the passage from the French and British Concessions to the railway station, caused dissatisfaction between the two countries. With mediation from Germany, Russia agreed to redraw the original concession boundaries, returning the railway station area to China. The Russian Concession was then divided into east and west zones. On May 30, 1901, an agreement was signed in Tianjin between the Qing government and Russia, formally delineating the Russian Concession, second in size only to the British Concession.[2] Following Russia, Italy and Austria-Hungary, even Belgium, which did not send troops to participate in the war, seized concessions in Tianjin. France took advantage of the situation to designate a large area as the "extra extension," while Britain expanded its concession once again, incorporating the original American Concession into the British one. Germany, since 1895, under the pretext of merit for forcing Japan to return the Liaodong Peninsula to China during the First Sino-Japanese War, demanded the Tianjin concession from the Qing government. Subsequently, it expanded northward and southwestward during the suppression of the Boxer Rebellion. Japan designated the prosperous southeastern urban area of Tianjin as an expanded concession zone.

The reasons and justifications for the expansion of concessions by various countries in Tianjin all relied on the "contributions" of their own troops in suppressing the Boxer Rebellion. The number of troops stationed was a symbol of the strength of each country and ensured the continuous acquisition of

---

① O. D. Rasmussen. *Tientsin: An Illustrated Outline History*, translated by Xu Yifan, et al. Tianjin People's Publishing House, 2008, p.202.

② Tianjin Chorography and History Compilation Committee. *Tianjin Chorography Supplementary: Concessions*. Tianjin Academy of Social Sciences Press, 1996, pp.54-57. O. D. Rasmussen. *Tientsin: An Illustrated Outline History*, translated by Xu Yifan, et al. Tianjin People's Publishing House, 2008, p.203. Liu Haiyan, et al (eds.). *Record of the Eight-Nation Alliance's Occupation: Minutes of the Tianjin Provisional Government Meeting*. Tianjin Academy of Social Sciences Press, 2004, p.75.

英国兵营。俗称英国营盘，始建于 1900 年，坐落在当时的天津英租界推广界内。最初建立时该兵营占地面积为 124 市亩，为一层建筑，面积为 23500 平方米。英国兵营的驻军为营的建制，司令官为上校军衔。兵营分为两个部分，一为英国兵营，另一为印度兵营。英国兵营旧址现为天津市第一中学和实验小学

The British Barracks, commonly known as the British Camp, was established in 1900 within the expanded area of the British concession in Tianjin. Initially, the barracks covered an area of 124 Chinese mu (approximately 8.27 hectares) and featured a single-story structure with a total building area of 23,500 square meters. The barracks housed troops organized at the battalion level, with a colonel serving as the commanding officer. It was divided into two sections: one for British troops and the other for Indian troops. The site of the former British Barracks is now home to Tianjin No.1 High School and Tianjin Experimental Primary School

1934 年英国兵营里的鼓乐队。营房后面的三个圆顶为西开教堂

In 1934, the military band inside the British Barracks performed within the camp. Behind the barracks, the three distinctive domes of Xikai Church (St. Joseph's Cathedral) could be seen

法国兵营。法国兵营前身为李鸿章于1879年设立的北洋水师营务处，所在街道即为水师营路（今赤峰道）。因李鸿章创办北洋水师的经费主要来自海关税收，经管北洋海防经费的是外国人控制下的津海关税务司，所以日常管理水师的营务处就设在离津海关几步之遥的地方。1900年八国联军侵华期间，这里被法国军队占领用作兵营，因这一带在划为租界前有个叫"紫竹林"的村庄，所以该兵营又被称为"紫竹林兵营"。1915年，天津法租界工部局重建这处兵营，新建营房包括士兵宿舍和驻军司令部等，占地11亩，建筑面积6203平方米。现已被列为重点保护等级历史风貌建筑和天津市文物保护单位。"紫竹林兵营"今已成为民居

The French Barracks were originally the Beiyang Fleet Operations Office, established by Li Hongzhang in 1879. It was located on Shuishiying Road (now Chifeng Road). Since the funding for the Beiyang Fleet mainly came from customs tax revenue, which was managed by foreign-controlled Tianjin Customs, the operations office was strategically placed near the customs office for financial oversight. During the 1900 Boxer Rebellion, the site was seized by French troops and converted into a military barracks. Since the area was previously home to a village called "Zizhulin" (Purple Bamboo Forest) before being incorporated into the French concession, the barracks became known as the "Zizhulin Barracks." In 1915, the French Municipal Council in Tianjin rebuilt the barracks, adding new military facilities, including soldiers' dormitories and the headquarters for the stationed troops. The compound covered 11 mu (approximately 7,330 square meters) with a total building area of 6,203 square meters. Today, the former Zizhulin Barracks has been designated as a historically significant architectural site and a protected cultural heritage site in Tianjin. It has since been repurposed into residential housing

由越南兵站岗的法国"紫竹林兵营"。1901年经八国联军指挥官会议协商规定，法国当时在天津驻扎约1400人。1902年，八国联军结束对天津的占领时又议定额外驻扎1007人，因此，法国当局在天津实际驻扎达2000余人，司令官为将军衔。由于当时的紫竹林兵营容纳不了太多的士兵，因此法国军队强占了已毁于炮火的天津机器局旁边的北洋水师学堂作为"东局子兵营"（现为陆军军事交通学院校址），并将附近荒地辟为靶场

French "Zizhulin Barracks" guarded by Vietnamese Soldiers. In 1901, following discussions among the Eight-Nation Alliance commanders, it was agreed that France would station approximately 1,400 troops in Tianjin. By 1902, when the Eight-Nation Alliance ended its occupation of Tianjin, an additional 1,007 French troops were approved for continued presence. This brought the total number of French troops in Tianjin to over 2,000, under the command of a general. Due to the limited capacity of the Zizhulin Barracks, the French military forcibly occupied the remains of the Beiyang Naval Academy, which had been destroyed by artillery fire near the Tianjin Arsenal, and established the "Dongjuzi Barracks" there. Additionally, the French troops converted nearby wasteland into a shooting range. Today, the former Dongjuzi Barracks is the site of the PLA Army Military Transportation University

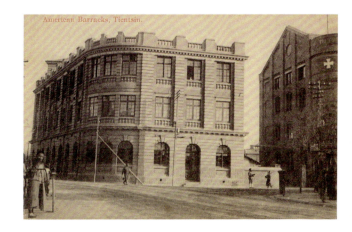

博罗斯道（今烟台道）上的美国兵营，后方为美国军医院。义和团运动之后，天津美国兵营最初设在英租界海大道（今烟台道与大沽北路交口），直到一战爆发，迁往原德租界

The American Barracks in Tianjin were located on Bruce Road (now Yantai Road), with the American military hospital situated behind them. After the Boxer Rebellion, the initial American Barracks were established on Taku Road in the British Concession (near the intersection of Yantai Road and Taku North Road). However, with the outbreak of the First World War, the barracks were relocated to the former German Concession

美国兵营。第一次世界大战结束后，美国驻军迁到原属于德国租界的马场道与广东路交口的兵营（现为天津医科大学东院），天津人称为"美国营盘"。兵营占地205公顷，兵营院内设有大操场和一些西式楼房，均为3层砖木混合结构楼房，带地下室，现存3座建筑。摄于1927年

American Barracks in Tianjin. After the First World War, the U.S. military garrison in Tianjin was relocated to a barracks at the intersection of Race Course Road and Guangdong Road in the former German Concession. Locals referred to this site as the "American Camp". The barracks covered an area of 205 hectares and included a large parade ground along with several Western-style buildings. These three-story brick-wood structures were built with basements and served as military facilities. Today, the site of the former American barracks is home to Tianjin Medical University's East Campus, with three of the original buildings still standing. Photograph taken in 1927

本书作者刘悦与《扛龙旗的美国大兵：美国第十五步兵团在中国1912~1938》原作者阿尔弗雷德·考尼比斯教授于2010年参观原美国兵营

Liu Yue, the author of this book, and Professor Alfred Cornebise, the original author of *The United States 15th Infantry Regiment in China 1912~1938*, visited the former American Barracks in 2010

军乐队。摄于1927年
Military Band. Taken in 1927

德国兵营。1900 年德军将北洋大学堂校舍占为兵营，教学楼成为德军司令部。1907 年天津德国领事馆将兵营改为学校，创办天津德华普通中学堂（今海河中学）

German Barracks. In 1900, the German army occupied the Peiyang University campus as its barracks, and the teaching building became the German headquarters. In 1907, the German Consulate in Tianjin converted the barracks into the Tianjin German-Chinese Middle School (now Haihe High School)

20 世纪初德国海军在兵营的教堂外

German Navy by the Barracks church in the early 20th century

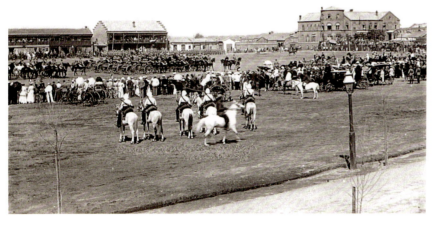

为欢迎普鲁士王子阿达尔贝特（Adalbert）访问天津，在德国兵营里举行的阅兵式。摄于 1904 年 5 月 18 日

The military parade held in the German Barracks to welcome Prussian Prince Adalbert's visit to Tianjin. Taken on May 18, 1904

德军在北洋大学堂所在梁家园扩建的营房（明信片上面贴着大龙邮票）

Barracks extension by the German army in Liangjiayuan, where the Peiyang University was located (with a Large Dragon Postage stamp on the postcard）

图片来源：德国"东亚之友"协会

Source: StuDeo

意大利兵营。始建于 1902 年，位于意租界营盘小马路（今河北区光明道 20 号）。兵营有宽阔的操场和呈直角的两幢高大的三层坡顶楼房，各层楼前都有三米宽（约一丈）的走廊，建筑至今保存完好。兵营驻扎一个营，有官兵约 300 人，司令官为中校军衔。1940 年意大利撤回天津驻军，意国兵营曾交与日本兵驻扎

Italian Barracks. Founded in 1902, it is located on Via Matteo Ricci in the Italian Concession (now No.20 Guangming Road, Hebei District). The barracks have a wide sports field and two tall 3-story buildings with sloping roofs at right angles. Each floor has a corridor over three meters wide, and the buildings are still well preserved to this day. A battalion was stationed in the barrack, with about 300 officers and soldiers, and the Commander held the rank of colonel. In 1940, Italy withdrew its troops from Tianjin and the Italian Barracks were handed over to Japanese troops for garrisoning

意大利兵营今景
Italian Barracks today

意大利兵营
Italian Barracks

日本兵营。天津人称为"海光寺兵营"。八国联军占领天津后，日本将天津城南海光寺夷为平地，于1901年修建了中国驻屯军司令部和兵营，并将其营造成侵略中国的桥头堡和大本营，开始了长达45年的军事驻扎。占地面积97700平方米，建筑面积5434平方米，后因日本不断向天津增兵而随之改建和增扩。最初驻军2600人，至1937年已达8000余人，司令官为中将军衔。兵营内设施齐全，有司令部、宿舍、宪兵队、军医院、火药库和附属建筑多座。部分遗址现为中国医学科学院血液病医院和二七二医院

Japanese Barracks, also known as the "Haiguang Temple Barracks" in Tianjin. After the Eight-Nation Alliance occupied Tianjin, Japan leveled the Haiguang Temple in south Tianjin and built the headquarters of Japanese Forces in China and barracks in 1901. The barracks became a bridgehead for invading China, stationing troops for 45 years. It covers an area of 97,700 square meters with the construction area of 5,434 square meters. It was later renovated and expanded with the continuous increase of its troops in Tianjin. At first, it stationed in Tianjin with 2,600 soldiers, but by 1937 the number had reached over 8,000, with the Commander holding the rank of Lieutenant General. The well-equipped barracks had the headquarters, dormitories, military police, military hospital, gunpowder depot, and many other buildings. Part of it are currently the Hematology Hospital of the Chinese Academy of Medical Sciences and No.272 Hospital of Tianjin

天津海光寺日本中国驻屯军司令部外景。1935年后改名为华北驻屯军司令部，七七事变后司令部迁往北平，改名为华北方面军。抗战胜利后被远东国际法庭定为甲级战犯的日本陆军大将南次郎、梅津美治郎以及冈村宁次等都曾先后在此担任司令官。另外，日军还在塘沽南站对面设有日本塘沽驻屯军兵营，占地约一万平方米，本地人称"日本大院"

Exterior view of the Japanese garrison headquarters at Tianjin Haiguang Temple. After 1935, it was renamed as the North China garrison headquarters. After the Marco Polo Bridge Incident, the headquarters moved to Beiping and was renamed as the Northern China Army. After the victory of the War of Resistance Against Japan, Japanese army generals Jiro Minami, Yoshijiro Umezu, and Yasuji Okamura, who successively served as commanders in Tianjin, were convicted as Class-A war criminals by the Far East International Court. In addition, the Japanese army also set up a Tanggu garrison across Tanggu South Railway Station, covering an area of about 10,000 square meters, which was called the "Japanese Courtyard" by natives

俄国兵营设在海河东岸的原北洋武备学堂旧址，与紫竹林租界隔河相望（俄国兵营的原建筑今已不复存在）

Russian Barracks were located on the former site of the Beiyang Military Academy on the east bank of the Hai River, facing the Zizhulin concession across the river (the original building of the Russian Barracks no longer exists)

奥匈帝国派兵短暂驻扎，人数不多，所以没有兵营
The Austro-Hungarian Empire sent troops to stay for a short period of time, but the number of troops was small, so there was no barracks

火车站台上的英国印度锡克士兵
British Indian Sikh soldiers on a railway platform

图片来源：德国"东亚之友"协会
Source: StuDeo

interests in China by the Great Powers. In April 1901, under the leadership of Marshal Alfred von Waldersee, the supreme commander of the Eight-Nation Alliance, a conference was convened where it was decided the number of troops each country could station during peacetime. Excess troops began to gradually withdraw from the Beijing-Tianjin area with the dissolution of the Provisional Government. After von Waldersee resigned, the senior military commanders of the various countries negotiated with each other on matters such as organization, supplies, hygiene, and defense. Among the Eight-Nation Alliance forces, except for the Austro-Hungarian Empire, which deployed most of its forces in Beijing to protect its embassy due to the small number of expatriates in the Tianjin concession, the headquarters of the other seven countries' troops were located in Tianjin for coordination purposes.[1] In addition to setting up camps in Tianjin, the Eight-Nation Alliance also established camps in nearby areas such as Junliangcheng, Tanggu, and even as far as Shanhaiguan, stationed troops, and rotated them periodically.

Due to Russia's influence in the northeast of China and Germany's influence in Shandong, which is close to Beijing and Tianjin, and modern warfare relying mainly on railway and naval transport of troops, it is very convenient to transport troops by sea and land from Lüshun or Qingdao, Yantai to Beijing-Tianjin, allowing for rapid reinforcement. In addition, maintaining overseas garrisons requires significant financial support. Therefore, apart from the United States, the United Kingdom, France, Italy, Japan, and others establishing long-term barracks in Tianjin, Germany, Russia, and Austria-Hungary basically withdrew their stationed troops from Tianjin, retaining only limited forces as guards for their consulates in Tianjin. After the outbreak of World War I, these three countries withdrew all their stationed troops in China.

Most of the barracks of various countries were built on the original sites of schools in Tianjin. This was mainly because the existing school buildings were convenient to use as collective dormitories, while the playgrounds were suitable for military training. Additionally, facilities such as canteens and bathrooms were relatively complete. For example, the German army occupied the original site of the Peiyang University in Liangjiayuan, forcing the university to rebuild its campus at the site of the destroyed Xigu Arsenal; the Russian army occupied the original site of the Beiyang Military Academy as its barracks; the French army, unable to accommodate the increased troops in the original barracks, forcibly occupied the premises of the Beiyang Naval Academy and established the "Dongjuzi Barracks." Later, most of these barracks were restored

---

① Editorial Office of the Tianjin Chorography and History Compilation Committee (ed.). *Overview of Tianjin in the Early 20th Century*. Published internally in 1986, pp.155-160.

乔治·卡特莱特·马歇尔（George Catlett Marshall, Jr., 1880—1959），美国军事家、战略家、政治家、外交家、陆军五星上将。毕业于弗吉尼亚军事学院，参加过第一次世界大战。1924 年夏到 1927 年春末在美军驻天津第十五步兵团任副团长，同时学习汉语。1939 年任美国陆军参谋长，其间，美国的陆、空军经他筹划，人数大规模扩充，由他一手提拔的将军就有 160 多人。在第二次世界大战中帮助罗斯福总统出谋划策，坚持先进攻纳粹德国再攻打日本的战略方针。1945 年退役，后被任命为美国驻华特使，还以"调处"之名参与国共和谈。1947 年，马歇尔出任美国国务卿。为稳定世界局势，提出援助欧洲经济复兴的"马歇尔计划"，效果显著，因此获得 1953 年诺贝尔和平奖

约瑟夫·华伦·史迪威（Joseph Warren Stilwell，1883—1946），美国陆军四星上将。1904 年毕业于美国西点军校。曾参加过第一次世界大战，战后被选派到北京学习汉语，三年后回国。1926 年史迪威到天津，接任驻津美军第十五步兵团的营长。时值中国第一次国内革命战争北伐军挺进山东，为了解北伐军的真实情况，史迪威化装只身赴徐州，后向美国驻华使馆提交了一份出色的报告。不久，他便以中校军衔担任了驻津美军第十五兵团的参谋长。三年后，史迪威奉调回国，在本宁堡步兵学校任教官。1935 年调任美国驻华使馆陆军武官，被公认为美军内研究中国问题的权威。二战期间，他出任美国第三军司令。1942 年由美国政府派遣来华，任中印缅战区美军司令、美国驻华军事代表、对华军事物资统制人、中国战区统帅顾问及参谋长。其间，因他对中国共产党领导的民族解放事业持同情态度，以至在作战部署、作战物资分配等方面，常与蒋介石发生矛盾，于 1944 年被调回美国，后任太平洋战场司令。1946 年因病去世

Joseph Warren Stilwell (1883-1946) was a four-star general in the United States Army. He graduated from U.S. Military Academy at West Point in 1904, participated in the World War I, and then was selected to study Chinese in Beijing after the war. He returned home three years later. In 1926, Stilwell went to Tianjin and took over as the Battalion Commander of the 15th Infantry Regiment stationed in Tianjin. At the time of the First Chinese Revolutionary Civil War, the Northern Expedition Army advanced into Shandong Province. In order to understand the true situation of the Northern Expedition Army, Stilwell went to Xuzhou alone in disguise and later submitted an excellent report to the U.S. Legation in China. Soon, he was promoted to the Chief of Staff of the 15th Infantry Regiment with the rank of Lieutenant Colonel. Three years later, Stilwell was recalled to U.S. and served as an instructor at the Army Infantry School (Fort Benning). In 1935, he was transferred to the U.S. Legation in China as Military Attaché and was recognized as an authority on China issues. During the Second World War, he served as the Commander of the United States Third Army. In 1942, he was sent by the U.S. government to China and served as the Commander of the U.S. Army in China-Burma-India Theater, the U.S. military representative in China, the controller of Military supplies to China, the Advisor to the Commander of the Chinese Theater, and the Chief of Staff. During this period, because he sympathized with the national liberation cause led by the Communist Party of China, he often had conflicts with Chiang Kai-shek in terms of combat deployment and distribution of combat supplies. He was transferred back to the United States in 1944 and later served as the Commander in the Pacific War Zone. He died of an illness in 1946

1924 年马歇尔在美国驻津第十五步兵团担任代理团长
In 1924, George Marshall served as Acting Commander of the 15th Infantry Regiment in Tianjin

George Catlett Marshall, Jr. (1880-1959) was an American military strategist, statesman, diplomat, and a five-star general of the Army. Graduated from Virginia Military Institute, he had participated in World War I. From the summer of 1924 to the end of spring 1927, he served as Acting Commander in the United States 15th Infantry Regiment stationed in Tianjin, while learning Chinese. In 1939, he served as the Chief of Staff of the United States Army. During this period, he managed to expand the military and air forces, and promoted more than 160 generals. In the Second World War, he helped President Roosevelt to make plans and insisted on the strategic policy of attacking Nazi Germany first and then Japan. He retired in 1945. Later he was appointed as the U.S. Special Envoy to China, and mediated in the peace talk between the Nationalists and Communists. In 1947, Marshall was appointed as the United States Secretary of State. To stabilize the world situation, he proposed the Marshall Plan to assist Europe's economic recovery, which had a significant effect, and was thus awarded the Nobel Peace Prize in 1953

第十五步兵团军官合影，前排右五为史迪威
Group photo of 15th Infantry Regiment officers, with Joseph Stilwell in the front row, fifth from the right

斯梅德利·达灵顿·巴特勒（Smedley Darlington Butler，1881—1940），美国海军陆战队少将（当时陆战队的最高军衔）。美国海军陆战队史上最有名望的人，荣获 16 枚勋章。服役 34 年，随海军陆战队参加了对菲律宾、中国、洪都拉斯、古巴、尼加拉瓜、多米尼加、海地、巴拿马、墨西哥和危地马拉的无数次小规模殖民主义战争以及在法国的第一次世界大战。1927 年北伐期间，美国向中国派驻旅级的海军陆战队中国远征军，兵力超过 4000 人，由巴特勒任司令官，并统一指挥驻天津第十五步兵团和驻北京的海军陆战队特遣队。1931 年退役后，成为反战、反大资本的社会活动家。1935 年出版了影响深远的著作《战争是一场骗局：拥有最多荣誉的美国士兵的反战经典》（*War is a Racket: The Antiwar Classic by America's Most Decorated Soldier*），其中称自己是"一直为资本家敲诈勒索、巧取豪夺"的"十足的骗子"，是"资本主义的匪徒"

Smedley Darlington Butler (1881-1940) was a Major General of the U.S. Marines Corps (the highest rank in the Marines at the time). He was the most prestigious person in the history of the U.S. Marine Corps, and was awarded 16 medals. He served for 34 years, and participated in numerous small-scale colonial wars against the Philippines, China, Honduras, Cuba, Nicaragua, Dominican Republic, Haiti, Panama, Mexico, and Guatemala, as well as the World War I in France. During the Northern Expedition in 1927, the United States sent a brigade-level Marine Corps to China Expeditionary, with a strength of more than 4,000 soldiers. Butler was the commander, and unified the command the 15th Infantry Regiment in Tianjin and the Marines Corps Contingent in Beijing. After retiring in 1931, he became a social activist against war and big capitalist. In 1935, he published the *War is a Racket: The Antiwar Classic by America's Most Decorated Soldier*, in which he described himself as a racketeer for capitalism who had been extorting and seizing money for capitalists, and could be called as the "Gangsters of Capitalism"

阿尔伯特·科蒂·魏德迈（Albert Coady Wedemeyer，1897—1989），美国陆军上将。1918 年毕业于美国陆军军官学校（西点军校）。1929 年，以中尉军衔到驻津美军第十五步兵团服务。1931 年调至菲律宾。二战中，魏德迈为著名的英国海军元帅蒙巴顿将军所赏识，被提升为盟军东南亚总部副总参谋长。1944 年底接任史迪威为盟军中国战区参谋长及驻中国美军指挥官，至 1946 年 3 月卸任。1947 年再度来华，作为美国特使主持所谓"军事调查团"，回国后写了一份著名的《魏德迈报告》，抨击国民党政治军事腐败无能。1948 年爆发"柏林危机"，魏德迈支持进行"柏林空运"，以稳定欧洲

Albert Coady Wedemeyer (1897-1989), General of U.S. Army, graduated from the U.S. Military Academy at West Point in 1918. In 1929, he served as a lieutenant in the 15th Infantry Regiment stationed in Tianjin. In 1931, he was transferred to Philippines. During the Second World War, Wedemeyer was appreciated by the famous British Admiral Mountbatten and was promoted to the Deputy Chief of Staff of the Supreme Allied Commander of the South East Asia Command. At the end of 1944, he replaced Stilwell as the Chief of Staff of the Chinese Theater and the Commander of the U.S. military stationed in China until the March 1946. In 1947, he returned to China as a special envoy to lead the so-called "Fact-Finding Mission to China" and wrote a famous *Wedemeyer Report*, criticizing the political and military corruption and incompetence of the Kuomintang. In 1948, in face with the "Berlin Crisis", Wedemeyer supported the "Berlin Airlift" to stabilize Europe

马修·邦克·李奇微（Matthew Bunker Ridgway，1895—1993），美国陆军上将。1917 年毕业于美国陆军军官学校。1918—1926 年在其母校和本宁堡步兵学校任教官。后在驻天津的第十五步兵团任职。之后，被派往尼加拉瓜、巴拿马、玻利维亚、菲律宾、巴西和美国各地服役，1937 年毕业于陆军军事学院。第二次世界大战爆发后不久，马歇尔将李奇微调到战争计划处。1942 年晋升为准将，受命指挥美军最早的空降师，协助筹划了 1943 年在西西里岛的空降作战。诺曼底登陆时，他随部队一起伞降在法国，率部进入德国。后在朝鲜战争中与中国人民志愿军作战

Matthew Bunker Ridgway (1895-1993) was a U.S. Army general. He graduated from the United States Military Academy in 1917. From 1918 to 1926, he served as an instructor at his school and the Fort Benning Army Infantry School. Afterwards, he served in the 15th Infantry Regiment stationed in Tianjin. Later, he was sent to serve in Nicaragua, Panama, Bolivia, the Philippines, Brazil, and various places of the United States. Shortly after the outbreak of the Second World War, Marshall assigned Ridgway to the War Plans Division. In 1942, he was promoted to brigadier general and was appointed to command the earliest airborne division of the U.S. military, assisting in planning the airborne operations in Sicily in 1943. During Normandy landing, he parachuted with his troops in France and led them into Germany. Later in the Korean War, he fought against the Chinese People's Volunteer Corps

军军事交通学院校址；美国兵营现为天津医科大学广东路校区。

不同种族的英国兵营和将星闪耀的美国兵营

英国兵营和美国兵营是在天津存在时间最长的外国兵营。作为当时最大的殖民国家，英国部队兵源来自世界上各个地方的不同种族。因此，英国派往天津的驻军也来自本土不同的郡和海外的殖民地。比如，参加八国联军的英军中不仅有来自本土的海军，还有来自澳大利亚的水兵、来自印度的锡克兵、来自新加坡和香港的军团，甚至有来自威海卫的"华勇营"。为了保卫殖民利益，英国的各支军队需要在海外各殖民地的军事基地换防。例如，1930 年英国皇家军团第一营从马耳他被派往天津。他们搭乘拥挤简陋的运输舰，经过大约一个月艰苦的海上航程后抵达秦皇岛港，其中一个连和机枪排被派往北京保护公使馆，其余前往天津。京津之间的士兵每半年换防一次。四年后，这个营又被调往印度奎达（今属巴基斯坦）驻防。^①在天津的英国兵营由两个兵营组成，一个是给白色人种的英国营房，一个是给印度兵住宿的印度营房，形成事实上的种族隔离。

天津英国兵营在他们的记述中是非常令人满意的："兵营的住宿条件非常好。营房和办公室是平房，配有厨房、餐厅和浴室，都有集中供暖。有一个比较大的体育馆和操练场。军官宿舍在不远处的英租界里，由三栋两层小楼组成。"京津两地的物价便宜、设施齐全，天津甚至"有大量的酒吧和白俄姑娘与各国军人厮混"，所以他们认为，"这两个城市对于我们的部队来说是世界上最好的驻地"。而由于拥有治外法权，天津的中国警察无权管辖他们，于是这些"丘八"们在这个地方"度过了一段有趣的时光"。不过，尽管生活条件很好，但天津兵营的训练条件并不好。城市被切分成众多块租界，在街区里设靶场是非常危险的。所以英军每年都前往山海关附近的海边夏季营地进行射击训练，其他驻军也在山海关设有

---

① "女王重访中国：1930 年"。https://www.queensroyalsurreys.org.uk/1661to1966/hongkong_china/hkc08_1.shtml.

---

to school buildings. For instance, to meet the educational needs of German immigrants' children, the German Consulate General in Tianjin converted its barracks into a school in 1907, establishing the Tianjin German-Chinese Middle School (now Haihe High School); the British barracks were allocated to Tianjin No.1 High School and Experimental Primary School as campuses after 1947; the French "Dongjuzi Barracks" now serves as the campus of the PLA Army Military Transportation University; and the American barracks now house the Guangdong Road Campus of Tianjin Medical University.

The British Barracks of Different Ethnicities and the Star-studded American Barracks

The British barracks and the American barracks were the longest-standing foreign barracks in Tianjin. As the largest colonial power at the time, the British forces were composed of troops from various ethnicities around the world. Therefore, the British troops stationed in Tianjin came from different counties in the United Kingdom and overseas colonies. For example, among the British troops in the Eight-Nation Alliance, there were not only navies from the homeland but also navies from Australia, Sikh soldiers from India, troops from Singapore and Hong Kong, and even the "Chinese Regiment" from Weihaiwei. To defend colonial interests, British military units needed to rotate through military bases in various colonies overseas. For instance, in 1930, the First Battalion of the Royal Regiment was dispatched from Malta to Tianjin. They traveled on crowded and rudimentary transport ships, enduring about a month of arduous sea voyage before arriving at Qinhuangdao Port. One company and a machine gun platoon were sent to Beijing to protect the legation, while the rest went to Tianjin. Soldiers between Beijing and Tianjin rotated every six months. Four years later, this battalion was transferred to Quetta, India (now part of Pakistan), for duty.^① In Tianjin, the British barracks comprised two separate areas: one for the barracks of white soldiers and another for the barracks of Indian soldiers, effectively creating a form of racial segregation.

The British barracks in Tianjin were described as very satisfactory: "The accommodation conditions in the barracks were excellent. The barracks and offices were bungalows equipped with kitchens, dining rooms, and bathrooms, all centrally heated. There was a relatively large gymnasium and drill ground. The officers' quarters were located in the nearby British concession,

---

① "The Queen's rejoin the China Station: 1930". https://www.queensroyalsurreys.org.uk/1661to1966/hongkong_china/hkc08_1.shtml.

夏季营地。[1]

在天津驻防最久的美国军队，是第十五步兵团。第十五团从1912年至1938年驻扎在天津，隶属于美国国务院，总部设在天津。部队部署在京沈铁路沿线，使命是保护美国在华利益。1938年，日本侵略华北，迫使美国把第十五团撤回美国，接管天津兵营的是负责保卫北京使馆的美海军陆战队，后于珍珠港事件当天全部被俘。

第十五团在军阀混战期间的中国得到历练。两次世界大战之间是一段短暂的和平时期，对于缺乏实战机会的美军官兵来说，"在中国服役至少有一个好处，我们总有机会看到一些真正的军事行动。这一点意义重大，我们经历的各种训练像是为了一个特定的目标，它并非遥不可及"[2]。第十五团这段经历为美国了解中国和远东起到重要作用，也为评估中美关系和制定相关外交、军事政策提供了帮助。天津美国营盘前后存在了30多年，涌现出几十位日后获得将军头衔的杰出军官。回国后，他们在美国陆军和陆军学校中发挥了重要作用，因此该团是培养美国陆军中大量关键领导者实际经验的场所。因为欣赏中国文化并具有很高的汉语水平以及共同的履历，他们被称之为"该死的中国帮"，其中包括马歇尔、史迪威、巴特勒、李奇微、魏德迈、麦克安德鲁、沃克（朝鲜战争指挥官）、卡斯特纳等人。

列强在华角力场

天津租界是近代中国政治舞台的"后台"，乃至国际政治和世界战争的组成部分。国际关系的复杂不可避免地体现在天津的各国军队和不同国籍的侨民之间。面对中国人民、军阀及其军队时，不仅列强政府、军队彼此协同以维护在华"共同利益"，在华外国侨民也能团结互助。义和团运动之后，在联军司令部的协调下，八国军队逐渐形成了彼此之间的协同行动机制，租界的安全稳定得到保

consisting of three two-story buildings." Prices were cheap and facilities were complete in both Beijing and Tianjin. Tianjin even had "a large number of bars and White Russian girls mingling with soldiers from various countries," so they believed that "these two cities were the best stations in the world for our troops." And because they had extraterritoriality, Chinese police in Tianjin had no authority over them, so these "Tommies" spent "an interesting time" there. However, despite the good living conditions, the training conditions in the Tianjin barracks were not good. The city was divided into many leased areas, and setting up shooting ranges in the neighborhoods was very dangerous. Therefore, the British troops went to seaside summer camps near Shanhaiguan every year for shooting training, and other garrisons also had summer camps in Shanhaiguan.[1]

The longest-serving American military unit stationed in Tianjin was the 15th Infantry Regiment. The 15th Regiment was stationed in Tianjin from 1912 to 1938, under the jurisdiction of the U.S. State Department, with its headquarters located in Tianjin. The unit was deployed along the Beijing-Shenyang Railway to protect American interests in China. In 1938, with the Japanese invasion of northern China, the United States was forced to withdraw the 15th Regiment back to the United States. The United States Marine Corps, responsible for defending the Beijing Legation, took over the Tianjin barracks and was captured in its entirety on the same day as the Pearl Harbor incident.

The 15th Regiment gained experience during the warlord era in China. The period between the two World Wars was a brief period of peace, and for American military personnel lacking real combat opportunities, "serving in China had at least one benefit—we always had the opportunity to witness some real military action. This was significant, as the various training experiences we went through seemed to be aimed at a specific goal, which was not beyond reach."[2] The experience of the 15th Regiment played an important role in America's understanding of China and the Far East, and also assisted in assessing Sino-American relations and formulating relevant diplomatic and military policies. The presence of the American barracks in Tianjin for over 30 years produced dozens of outstanding officers who later achieved the rank of general. Upon returning home, they played important roles in the U.S. Army and Army schools, making the regiment a place where a large number of key leaders in the U.S. Army gained practical experience. Because of their appreciation for

---

[1] "女王重访中国：1930 年"。https://www.queensroyalsurreys.org.uk/1661to1966/hongkong_china/hkc08_1.shtml.

[2] （美）阿尔弗雷德·考尼比斯著，刘悦译，《扛龙旗的美国大兵：美国第十五步兵团在中国 1912~1938》，作家出版社，2011 年，第 262 页。

[1] "The Queen's rejoin the China Station: 1930". https://www.queensroyalsurreys.org.uk/1661to1966/hongkong_china/hkc08_1.shtml.

[2] Alfred Cornebise. *The United States 15th Infantry Regiment in China 1912~1938*, translated by Liu Yue. The Writers Publishing House, 2011, p.262.

障。这种平静期只是偶尔被混战的北洋军阀所打断，直至第一次世界大战结束。战胜国侨民对战败国的耀武扬威持续时间也并不长，租界很快又恢复了其乐融融的"国际大家庭"状态。真正的改变是在第二次世界大战爆发才到来。

1911 年辛亥革命爆发，袁世凯凭借"小站练兵"掌握的北洋陆军，在列强的支持下，逼清帝退位，攫取了中华民国大总统职位，篡夺了辛亥革命的成果。为了不离开北洋势力盘踞的北方，袁世凯唆使亲信部队发动了"壬子兵变"（又称"天津兵变"）。兵变前，社会上谣言纷纭。"许多官商富户携带金银细软避往各国租界。奥国租界毗邻城厢，华界居民前往运存箱笼者络绎不绝。"[1]1912 年 3 月 2 日时值壬子年正月十四日晚八时许，袁世凯的党羽、天津镇守使张怀芝所统领的天津巡防营倾巢出动，直接扑向天津商业最繁荣、铺户最集中的北大关、河北大街和老城内外，鸣枪呼啸，沿途抢掠。事后，据天津商会统计，被抢劫的天津商户多达 2385 户、居民 639 户、当铺 15 家，总计损失达到了 1280 余万两白银。[2]而一早得到消息的租界，由于有驻兵保护，没有任何损失。随即，日、俄、德列强从东北、青岛等地调军队两千余人来津，加上天津租界原有的驻兵，一起对南京临时政府施加压力。在此"内忧外患"之下，南京方面不得不做出让步，3 月 10 日袁世凯在北京就任临时大总统，中华民国首都亦定为北京。

袁世凯死后，北洋军阀四分五裂，各派军阀之间钩心斗角，割据一方，不断爆发争权夺利的战争。仅大的战争就有直皖战争、第一次直奉战争、第二次直奉战争。尤其是 1924 年 9—11 月的第二次直奉战争影响较大。它的主战场虽不在天津附近，但是各方军阀都使用火车调动兵力，因此天津仍不免遭池鱼之殃。直系军阀的两支队伍分别由津浦铁路和京汉铁路北上，与冯玉祥的部队争夺京津一带的控制权。随后，奉系军阀截断了山海关—天津的交通线，直军

① 华克格、杨绍周，《天津壬子兵变纪事》，中国人民政治协商会议全国委员会文史资料研究委员会编，《辛亥革命回忆录·第八集》，中国文史出版社，2012 年，第 443 页。

② 涂小元等，《辛亥革命后天津兵变发生的缘起及影响》，《天津史志》1998 年第 4 期。

Chinese culture, high proficiency in the Chinese language, and shared experiences, they were called the "Damned China Crowd," including figures such as George Catlett Marshall, Joseph Warren Stilwell, Smedley Darlington Butler, Matthew Bunker Ridgway, Albert Coady Wedemeyer, Joseph A. McAndrew, Walton Harris Walker (commander in the Korean War), and Joseph C. Castner.

The Battleground Between Great Powers in China

The Tianjin Concessions were the "backstage" of modern Chinese political stage, and even part of international politics and world wars. The complexity of international relations was inevitably reflected in the interactions between the various foreign military forces and nationals of different countries in Tianjin. Faced with the Chinese people, warlords, and their armies, not only did the governments and military forces of the great powers coordinate with each other to maintain their "common interests" in China, but also foreign nationals in China could help each other and unite in friendship. After the Boxer Rebellion, under the coordination of the Allied Command, the military forces of the eight countries gradually formed a mechanism for coordinated action among themselves, ensuring the security and stability of the concessions. This period of calm was only occasionally interrupted by the skirmishes of the warlord factions until the end of the First World War. The period of boasting and dominance of the victorious country nationals over the defeated nations was also short-lived, and the concessions quickly returned to harmonious "international family" status. The real change came with the outbreak of the Second World War.

After the 1911 Revolution broke out, Yuan Shikai, with the support of the Beiyang Army trained through the "Xiaozhan Troop Training" and the backing of the Great Powers, forced the Qing Emperor to abdicate and seized the position of President of the Republic of China, usurping the achievements of the 1911 Revolution. In order to maintain his influence in the northern region where the Beiyang faction was entrenched, Yuan Shikai instigated his loyal troops to launch the "Renzi Coup" (also known as the "Tianjin Coup"). Prior to the coup, there were various rumors circulating in society. "Many officials, merchants, and wealthy families carried gold and silver with them to flee to various foreign concessions. The Austrian concession was adjacent to the city, and residents of the Chinese quarter flocked there to store their belongings."[1] On the evening

① Hua Kege, Yang Shaozhou. *Records of the Tianjin Munity in the Year of Renzi*. Cultural and Historical Data Research Committee of National Committee of the CPPCC (ed.). *Memoirs of the 1911 Revolution* (Vol.8). China Literature and History Publishing House, 2012, p.443.

天津东站被军阀军队征用的火车
The train requisitioned by the warlord army at Tianjin East Railway Station

天津街道上的中国军阀部队。摄于 1925 年
The Chinese warlord troops on the street of Tianjin. Taken in 1925

of March 2, 1912, at around 8 p.m. on the fourteenth day of the first month of the Renzi year, the Tianjin Patrol Battalion, commanded by Zhang Huaizhi, a supporter of Yuan Shikai and the garrison commander of Tianjin, launched a massive assault directly on the most prosperous commercial areas of Tianjin, including Beidaguan, Hebei Street, and the old city. Gunshots and shouts echoed as they plundered along the way. Afterwards, according to statistics from the Tientsin Chamber of Commerce, a total of 2,385 Tianjin merchants, 639 households, and 15 pawnshops were robbed, resulting in a total loss of over 12.8 million taels of silver.[1] However, the concessions, which received early warning, suffered no losses due to the protection of stationed troops. Subsequently, the Great Powers of Japan, Russia, and Germany dispatched over two thousand troops from Northeast China, Qingdao, and other places to Tianjin, along with the existing garrison in the Tianjin Concessions, to exert pressure on the Nanjing Provisional Government. Under this "internal and external troubles," the Nanjing side had to make concessions, and on March 10th, Yuan Shikai assumed the position of Provisional President in Beijing, with Beijing also designated as the capital of the Republic of China.

After Yuan Shikai's death, the Beiyang Warlords fragmented, and the various factions engaged in intrigue and power struggles, continuously erupting into wars for supremacy and profit. There were major conflicts such as the Zhili-Anhui War, the First Zhili-Fengtian War, and the Second Zhili-Fengtian War. Particularly significant was the Second Zhili-Fengtian War that took place between September and November 1924. Although its main battlefield was not near Tianjin, the warlords from all sides used trains to mobilize their forces, inevitably affecting Tianjin. Two factions of the Zhili Clique Warlords moved northward along the Tianjin-Pukou Railway and the Beijing-Hankou Railway respectively, vying with Feng Yuxiang's forces for control over the Beijing-Tianjin area. Subsequently, Fengtian Clique Warlords cut off the transportation line between Shanhaiguan and Tianjin, causing the Zhili Clique to retreat in disarray. Foreign troops began running international trains regularly between Tianjin and Shanhaiguan, transporting troops to the Tianjin Concessions for defense until the end of the year when Zhang Zuolin, Feng Yuxiang, and others convened a meeting in Tianjin and elected Duan Qirui, the leader of the Anhui Clique, as the "Interim President of the Republic of China," thus ending the war. During this war, the high-level commanders of the foreign troops in China "shrewdly" utilized the situation to conduct reconnaissance, patrols, and rotation training for their

①　Tu Xiaoyuan, et al. The Origins and Effects of the Tianjin Mutiny after the 1911 Revolution. *Tianjin Historical Records*, 1998 (4).

纷纷溃退。各国军队开始在天津和山海关之间定期运行国际列车，运兵到天津租界内进行防范，直至年底张作霖、冯玉祥等在天津召开会议，推举皖系首领段祺瑞为"中华民国临时执政"，战争结束。此次战争中，各国驻华军队的高层指挥"精明"地利用当时的局势对军队进行了侦察、巡逻和换防训练。美国第十五步兵团指挥官曾说："该团在这一时期获得了实战锻炼。"① 由于布防得力，各国租界免受侵犯。但战争造成天津华界社会动荡，"城头变幻大王旗"使经济遭到严重破坏，很多老字号商家都改到租界开设店面，使租界更加繁荣。

　　尽管面对中国的军阀混战，八国军队尚能协同一致、保护租界和侨民，但是第一次世界大战的爆发，还是改变了租界的形态，打破了各国在华的力量平衡。第一次世界大战爆发后，美国驻军借列强在欧洲混战，主动向在津拥有租界的八个国家发出通报，要求各国允许美军"在必要的时候采取行动镇压各国租界里的任何起义或暴乱"。虽然只有奥地利人、德国人和比利时人表示同意，但美国在津军事力量还是悄然扩大了。② 中国政府于 1917 年 8 月 14 日向德国和奥匈帝国宣战，收回了两国租界，接管了德华银行，解除了两国在华士兵的武装。作为敌国侨民，德奥两国的侨民先是受到监视，继而被政府收容，移送到专门看管敌国侨民的暂居地。战争结束后，德奥两国的侨民被遣送回国，他们在中国的所有不动产、债券、股票等，都作为敌国财产被没收。当德、奥战败投降消息传来，英法侨民走上街头，欢庆胜利。他们涌入德租界，用砖头石块砸碎德国人房子的窗户，将义和团运动后在德租界主要路口立起的一尊战争纪念碑——身穿铠甲、手持利剑的"罗兰德骑士"立像推倒，砸成碎块。曾经在义和团运动中组成义勇队并肩对抗中国军民的各国侨民，依照他们的国籍形成不同的阵营，壁垒森严，不复其乐融融的侨民大家庭。不过，仇恨持续的时间并不长。战争结束后，事业、财产都

---

troops. The commander of the American 15th Infantry Regiment said, "the regiment received actual field training during this period."[1] Due to effective defense measures, the concessions of various countries remained inviolate. However, the war caused social unrest in the Chinese quarter of Tianjin. The fluctuating situation led to serious economic damage, prompting many well-established businesses to relocate to the concessions, further enhancing their prosperity.

Despite the warlord conflicts in China, the Eight-nation Allied Forces were able to coordinate and protect the concessions and nationals. However, the outbreak of World War I changed the landscape of the concessions and disrupted the balance of powers among the countries in China. After the outbreak of World War I, the American troops took advantage of the chaos in Europe and actively notified the eight countries with concessions in Tianjin, requesting permission for the U.S. military to "might take such steps in their respective concessions as were necessary adequately to suppress any uprising or riot." Although only the Austrians, Germans, and Belgians agreed, the military presence of the United States in Tianjin quietly expanded.[2] On August 14, 1917, the Chinese government declared war on Germany and Austria-Hungary, reclaiming their concessions, taking over the Deutsch-Asiatische Bank, and disarming the soldiers of the two countries in China. As enemy nationals, the German and Austrian nationals were initially under surveillance, then detained by the government and transferred to temporary residences designated for enemy nationals. After the war, German and Austrian nationals were repatriated, and all their immovable property, bonds, stocks, etc., in China were confiscated as enemy property. When news of Germany and Austria's surrender came, British and French nationals took to the streets to celebrate victory. They flooded into the German concession, smashing windows of German houses with bricks and stones, and toppling a war memorial erected at a major intersection in the German concession after the Boxer Rebellion—the statue of Roland clad in armor and holding a sword, smashing it into pieces. The nationals of various countries who had formed volunteer Corps and fought alongside against Chinese soldiers and civilians during the Boxer Rebellion formed different camps based on their nationalities, creating barriers and divisions in the once harmonious community of expatriates. However, the duration of the animosity was not long-lasting. After the war, the nationals of

---

① （美）阿尔弗雷德·考尼比斯著，刘悦译，《扛龙旗的美国大兵：美国第十五步兵团在中国 1912~1938》，作家出版社，2011 年，第 47 页。

② （美）阿尔弗雷德·考尼比斯著，刘悦译，《扛龙旗的美国大兵：美国第十五步兵团在中国 1912~1938》，作家出版社，2011 年，第 38 页。

① Alfred Cornebise. *The United States 15th Infantry Regiment in China 1912~1938*, translated by Liu Yue. The Writers Publishing House, 2011, p.47.

② Alfred Cornebise. *The United States 15th Infantry Regiment in China 1912~1938*, translated by Liu Yue. The Writers Publishing House, 2011, p.38.

义和团运动后在德租界主要路口立起的战争纪念碑——罗
兰德骑士像
The War Memorial - Statue of Knight Roland - erected at
major intersections in the German Concession after the Boxer
Rebellion

图片来源：德国"东亚之友"协会
Source: StuDeo

1918 年一战结束后被英法两国侨民捣毁的罗兰德纪念碑
The Roland Statue, demolished by British and French expatriates after
the end of the First World War in 1918

一战结束后被英法侨民砸毁破坏的德侨开的饭店
The German expatriate-owned restaurant vandalized and destroyed by
British and French expatriates after the end of the First World War

在中国的战败国侨民很快返回天津，重新开启他们的生活，租界又逐渐恢复繁荣，仿佛战争并未发生过。

中国政府曾在 1920—1921 年的华盛顿会议上要求撤离在华外国军队，这个要求当然被列强拒绝。他们甚至坚持认为，他们的军队没有对中国施加任何威胁，相反，"北京使馆区、天津租界和京沈铁路的相对安全要归功于外国兵营的存在"。几年后，北伐战争期间发生的"南京事件"，又给予列强证明外国军队存在"必要性"的机会。1927 年 3 月北伐军驱逐北洋军阀后控制了南京，随后一些流氓劫掠租界和外国使馆，造成外国使馆和侨民的财产损失及人员伤亡。英美两国遂指挥游弋在长江上的一艘英舰和两艘美舰，于当日下午炮轰南京城，致使百余人伤亡、大量房屋和村庄被毁坏。随着"二次北伐"的局势，列强纷纷出兵平津，借口保护使领馆与外侨及教民，干预中国革命，当时从其他地区及海外调集的外国军队总人数达几万人。其中，美国在天津进驻旅级的海军陆战队中国远征军，加上常年驻扎天津的美国陆军第十五步兵团、驻北京专职守卫美国公使馆与教堂教区的海军陆战队特遣队，兵力总共近 6000 人，并装备了大量的装甲车、野榴炮、越野卡车，甚至还配备了 20 架作战飞机，均由巴特勒准将统一指挥。尽管实力强大，但巴特勒将军却是军人中少有的温和派，他对英国人和日本人侵略中国的图谋保持警惕，多次拒绝参加日本人为最高指挥官的驻津盟军的计划和行动。他对长期遭受苦难的中国人表示同情，认为："我们的暴行给中国和中国人留下的痕迹和创伤越少，我们留给中国人去抚平的伤痛也就越少。"蒋介石于 1928 年进军北京后，建立南京国民政府，天津所在的直隶省改名为河北省。1929 年 1 月，除了驻扎上海的第四团以外，巴特勒率其余海军陆战队撤离中国，以示友好。①

动荡危险的军阀混战时期之后，从 1927 年至 1937 年，各国驻军在天津度过了一段舒适而平静的海外驻军生活。这十年中，各国驻军在天津的主要活动基本上就是提供大型仪仗队，在高级军官和外国政要访问时接受检阅。例如，英军军乐队每个周日都要在教堂

① （美）阿尔弗雷德·考尼比斯著，刘悦译，《扛龙旗的美国大兵：美国第十五步兵团在中国 1912~1938》，作家出版社，2011 年，第 56—60 页。

the defeated countries who had their careers and property in China quickly returned to Tianjin, restarting their lives, and the concessions gradually regained prosperity, as if the war had never happened.

The Chinese government had previously requested the withdrawal of foreign troops from China at the Washington Conference in 1920-1921, but this request was naturally rejected by the great powers. They even insisted that their military presence posed no threat to China; on the contrary, they claimed that the relative security of the Beijing Legation Quarter, the Tianjin Concessions, and the Beijing-Shenyang Railway was attributed to the presence of foreign garrisons. Several years later, during the Northern Expedition in 1927, the "Nanking Incident" provided the great powers with an opportunity to justify the "necessity" of foreign military presence. In March 1927, after the Northern Expedition army expelled the Beiyang warlords and took control of Nanjing, some rogues looted concessions and foreign embassies, resulting in property damage and casualties among embassy staff and nationals. In response, Britain and the United States directed one British warship and two American warships patrolling the Yangtze River to bombard Nanjing that same afternoon, causing over a hundred casualties and extensive damage to houses and villages. As the situation unfolded during the "Second Northern Expedition," the great powers sent troops to Tianjin under the pretext of protecting embassies, nationals, and missionaries, interfering in the Chinese revolution. The total number of foreign troops mobilized from other regions and overseas reached tens of thousands. Among them, the United States stationed the Marine Corps China Expeditionary Force in Tianjin, comprising a brigade, along with the long-standing presence of the 15th Infantry Regiment and a Marine detachment dedicated to guarding the U.S. Legation and church district in Beijing. The total force amounted to nearly 6,000 personnel, equipped with a large number of armored vehicles, field howitzers, off-road trucks, and even 20 combat aircraft, all under the unified command of Brigadier General Smedley Butler. Despite their formidable strength, General Butler was one of the few moderate military leaders. He remained vigilant against British and Japanese aggression in China and repeatedly refused to participate in plans and actions proposed by the Japanese to establish a joint allied force with the Japanese as the supreme commander in Tianjin. He sympathized with the long-suffering Chinese people, believing, "the fewer marks or scars of violence we make on China or the Chinese people, the fewer wounds we leave to heal." After Chiang Kai-shek marched into Beijing in 1928 and established the Nanjing National Government, Zhili Province, where Tianjin was located, was renamed Hebei Province. In January 1929, apart from the Fourth Regiment stationed in Shanghai, General Butler led the rest of the

里进行演出，然后驻军在教堂前举行阅兵，各国侨民纷纷涌向街边围观。每年国王的生日、一战停战日以及其他大型国际聚会上，他们也都会举行游行和阅兵式。[①]

抗日战争中的天津

抗日战争的伟大胜利，是中国人民自 1840 年第一次鸦片战争以来，第一次反对外敌侵略所取得的全面胜利，是中华民族重新走向振兴的重大转折。抗日战争中，中国以巨大的民族牺牲，抗击和牵制了占日本军力近三分之二的侵略者，为世界反法西斯战争的胜利、争取世界和平作出了不可磨灭的贡献。

"天津事变""华北独立"与"卢沟桥事变"

日本自 1875 年开始在天津设立领事馆，1898 年设立租界。日租界内不仅设有领事馆、警察署、居留民团等一般行政机构，还隐藏了许多以各种面目为掩护的特务机关和情报机关。八国联军侵华战争中，日军充当了攻打天津的急先锋。联军占领天津后，日本在天津海光寺设中国驻屯军司令部。其后，逐年在天津及周边地区增兵和扩充军事基地，于 1928 年起在城南修建军用机场、军用仓库并扩建兵营，为发动全面侵华战争做持续的准备。1902 年天津的领事馆升格为总领事馆，管辖青岛、济南、太原、张家口等地领事馆（战后出任日本首相的吉田茂曾于 1922—1924 年在天津担任过总领事）。天津由此成为日本控制华北地区的中枢和发动全面侵华战争的桥头堡。

1931 年日本在沈阳刚刚发动九一八事变后不到两个月，在关东军的支持下，日军特务头子土肥原贤二就在天津策划并发动了天津便衣队暴乱，史称"天津事变"。目的是转移国际上对九一八事变的关注视线，掩盖其侵略真相，同时趁乱将蛰居在津的清逊帝溥仪挟持到东北充当伪满洲国的傀儡皇帝。

---

① "女王重访中国：1930 年"。https://www.queensroyalsurreys.org.uk/1661to1966/hongkong_china/hkc08_1.shtml.

Marine Corps to withdraw from China as a gesture of goodwill.[①]

After the turbulent and perilous warlord era, from 1927 to 1937, the foreign troops stationed in Tianjin experienced a comfortable and peaceful overseas military life. During these ten years, the main activity of the foreign troops in Tianjin was essentially to provide large ceremonial guards and undergo inspections during visits by senior military officers and foreign dignitaries. For example, the British military band performed every Sunday in the church, followed by a parade in front of the church by the stationed troops, attracting crowds of foreign nationals to gather and watch along the streets. They also held parades and military reviews on the King's birthday, World War I Armistice Day, and other major international gatherings each year.[②]

Tianjin During the War of Resistance Against Japan

The great victory of the War of Resistance Against Japan was the first comprehensive victory achieved by the Chinese people against foreign aggression since the First Opium War in 1840, marking a significant turning point for the rejuvenation of the Chinese nation. During the War of Resistance Against Japan, China made enormous national sacrifices to resist and contain the invaders, who accounted for nearly two-thirds of Japan's military strength, making an indelible contribution to the victory of the World Anti-Fascist War and the pursuit of world peace.

"The Tianjin Incident," "North China Independence," and "The Marco Polo Bridge Incident"

Japan established a consulate in Tianjin in 1875 and a concession in 1898. Within the Japanese concession, besides typical administrative institutions such as consulate, police station, and Japanese Residents' Corporation, there were also numerous covert agencies and intelligence bureaus hidden under various disguises. During the invasion of China by the Eight-Nation Alliance, Japanese troops acted as the vanguard in attacking Tianjin. After the alliance occupied Tianjin, Japan established the headquarters of its garrison forces in China at the Haiguang Temple in Tianjin. Subsequently, they gradually increased troops and expanded military bases in Tianjin and surrounding areas. Starting from 1928,

---

① Alfred Cornebise. *The United States 15th Infantry Regiment in China 1912~1938*, translated by Liu Yue. The Writers Publishing House, 2011, pp.56-60.

② "The Queen's rejoin the China Station: 1930". https://www.queensroyalsurreys.org.uk/1661to1966/hongkong_china/hkc08_1.shtml.

"天津事变"时中国保安队在所筑街垒后警戒
During the "Tianjin Incident," the Chinese security forces standing guard behind the barricades they had built

11月8日夜间，以汉奸、土匪和地痞流氓两千余人组成的"便衣队"在日军枪炮的支援下，分三路冲出日租界，向省政府、公安局及其他重要机关发起攻击。在东北军第二集团军军长、河北省政府主席王树常和天津市市长兼公安局局长张学铭的指挥下，天津保安队给予了坚决反击。这场由日本人出钱、出武器并以日军为后盾制造的暴乱，在遭到中国保安队的坚决镇压后，日本领事馆和驻屯军司令部反诬中国方面制造事端、破坏治安，并以动用武力相威胁，提出中国军队退出天津、天津民众不得有反日行为等无理要求。南京国民政府为防止事态扩大，采取忍让妥协态度，最终主要由东北军组成的保安队退出天津，将王树常调职，张学铭辞职下野。动乱爆发当日夜晚，溥仪按照土肥原的精心安排潜出家门，经舟车辗转秘密到达旅顺。在近一个月的暴乱中，天津华界居民每日处于惊恐不安之中，财产也遭受严重损失。

"天津事变"，日本人不胜而胜。此后，为实现进占华北、吞并全中国的目的，日本人不断在华北制造事端，并引起战火。1933年日军占领热河后，开始在长城沿线发起全面攻击。中国守军被迫反击，在义院口、冷口、喜峰口、古北口等地顽强抗击、浴血奋战。长城抗战得到了全国爱国同胞的强烈声援和支持，但国民政府坚持"攘外必先安内"政策，对日本侵略者采取妥协退让方针，1933年5月与日本在天津塘沽签订了丧权辱国的《塘沽协定》，承认日本占领东三省和热河合法化，同时将冀东划为"非武装区"，使华北门

they built military airfields, warehouses, and expanded barracks in the southern part of the city, making continuous preparations for launching a comprehensive war of aggression against China. In 1902, the consulate in Tianjin was upgraded to a consulate-general, overseeing consulates in places such as Qingdao, Jinan, Taiyuan, and Zhangjiakou (Yoshida Shigeru, who later became Prime Minister of Japan, served as Consul-General in Tianjin from 1922 to 1924). Tianjin thus became the center of Japanese control in North China and a springboard for launching a full-scale war of aggression against China.

In 1931, less than two months after Japan initiated the September 18 Incident (also known as the Mukden Incident) in Shenyang, with the support of the Kwantung Army, Japanese spy chief Doihara Kenji orchestrated and launched the Tianjin Incident in Tianjin. The purpose was to divert international attention from the Mukden Incident, conceal its aggressive nature, and at the same time, take advantage of the chaos to abduct the Qing dynasty's exiled emperor, Puyi, who was residing in Tianjin, and use him as a puppet emperor for the pseudo-Manchukuo state.

On the night of November 8th, more than 2,000 collaborators, bandits, and thugs formed a "plainclothes squad" with the support of Japanese guns and cannons, breaking out of the Japanese concession in three directions to launch attacks on the provincial government, the public security bureau, and other important institutions. Under the command of Wang Shuchang, the commander of the Northeastern Army's Second Army Group and the chairman of the Hebei Provincial Government, and Zhang Xueming, the mayor of Tianjin and the director of the public security bureau, the Tianjin Security Corps resolutely counterattacked. This riot, financed and armed by the Japanese and backed by the Japanese army, was vigorously suppressed by the Chinese security forces. However, the Japanese consulate and the garrison command falsely accused the Chinese side of creating disturbances and disrupting public order, threatening to use force and demanding unreasonable concessions such as the withdrawal of Chinese troops from Tianjin and prohibiting anti-Japanese activities by Tianjin residents. In order to prevent the situation from escalating, the Nanjing National Government adopted a conciliatory attitude. Eventually, the security forces, mainly composed of the Northeastern Army, withdrew from Tianjin, and Wang Shuchang was reassigned, while Zhang Xueming resigned and went into exile. On the night of the outbreak of the riot, Puyi, following Doihara's careful arrangements, secretly left his home and secretly arrived in Lüshun after traveling by boat and car. During the unrest, the residents of Tianjin's Chinese quarter lived in fear and anxiety every day, and their properties suffered severe losses.

During Tianjin Incident, Japanese achieved his purposes despite being

日租界旭街明信片
A postcard of Asahi Road in the Japanese
Concession

日租界寿街
Kotobuki Road in the former Japanese Concession

天津日本公会堂明信片
A postcard of Japanese public hall in Tianjin

日本驻津总领事馆
The Japanese Consulate-General in Tianjin

户洞开，平津地区危在旦夕。1935 年 5 月日军再次制造事端，以天津亲日分子被杀以及中国政府支持抗日义勇军为由，向中国政府提出禁止河北省境内一切抗日团体和反日活动，并接管华北统治权等各种无理要求，同时向天津、山海关等地大量调集军队。国民政府军事委员会北平分会代理委员长何应钦于 6 月与日军华北驻屯军司令梅津美治郎秘密签署了《何梅协定》，驻天津周边地区的中国军队撤出河北省，省政府也从天津迁至保定，从而将河北和平津地区拱手送给了日本。

1935 年 8 月 1 日，中国共产党发表了《为抗日救国告全体同胞书》，提出全国人民团结一致、共同抗日的主张。同年 10 月日本策划香河汉奸暴动，大搞"华北自治运动"；11 月在通县又炮制了以汉奸殷汝耕为首的"华北防共自治政府"，煽动"华北独立"。在策划武装侵略的同时，自 1932 年起，日本在天津、青岛以及山海关至天津沿线疯狂走私棉布、棉纱、人造丝、砂糖、纸烟等商品，给天津和青岛的支柱产业——纺织业造成严重打击，扰乱了市场，并使华北白银大量外流。至七七事变前，日本走私活动给华北经济造成严重损失。以南满洲铁道株式会社（简称"满铁"）为代表的日本官商和民间资本加大在天津的投资规模，有计划有目的地控制各项重要产业，包括发电业、盐业、矿山、棉花和交通等重要国防资源和基础部门。同一时期，日本驻屯军还抵制破坏南京政府于 1935 年开始

defeated. Subsequently, in pursuit of their goal to occupy North China and annex the entire country, the Japanese continued to stir up troubles in North China, sparking off conflicts. In 1933, after the Japanese occupation of Rehe, they launched a full-scale attack along the Great Wall. Chinese defenders were forced to retaliate, fiercely resisting and fighting bloody battles at Yiyuankou, Lengkou, Xifengkou, and Gubeikou, among other places. The defense of the Great Wall received strong support from patriots nationwide. However, the Nationalist government adhered to the policy of "First Internal Pacification, Then External Resistance" and adopted a policy of compromise and concession towards the Japanese aggressors. In May 1933, the humiliating *Tanggu Agreement* was signed in Tianjin between China and Japan, recognizing Japan's occupation of the Northeastern Provinces and Rehe as legitimate. Simultaneously, the government designated eastern Hebei as a "demilitarized zone," leaving North China vulnerable and the Tianjin area on the brink of danger. In May 1935, the Japanese provoked another incident, citing the killing of pro-Japanese individuals in Tianjin and the Chinese government's support for anti-Japanese guerrillas. They demanded the cessation of all anti-Japanese activities and organizations in Hebei Province and the transfer of control over North China, among other unreasonable demands. Meanwhile, they massed troops in Tianjin, Shanhaiguan, and other areas. In June, the Acting Chairman of Military Commission Beijing Branch of the Nationalist government, He Yingqin, secretly signed the *He–Umezu Agreement* with the commander of the Japanese forces in North China, Umezu Yoshijiro. This agreement led to the withdrawal of Chinese troops from the areas surrounding Tianjin and the relocation of the provincial government from Tianjin to Baoding, effectively

进行的币制改革，他们制定了《华北自主币制施行计划纲领方案》，提出以天津为新的金融中心，意图使华北与华中、华南金融相分离，驱除南京政府的法币，破坏中国金融稳定。①

日本人处心积虑经营多年，以天津为大本营，从策动华北独立到发动全面侵华战争。经济、军事的多重努力之下，他们认为时机已经成熟，全面侵华的序幕徐徐拉开。1936 年 10 月，日本华北驻屯军举行了以北平为进攻目标的大规模军事演习。1937 年 3 月，日军数十艘军舰在青岛举行了大规模的登陆演习。之后，华北驻屯军又在天津、北平郊区及通县分别举行了数次军事演习。7 月 7 日，日军发动了震惊世界的卢沟桥事变。7 月 8 日当天，中国共产党第一时间通电全国："平津危急！华北危急！只有全民族实行抗战，才是我们的出路！"中国全面抗战爆发。

七七事变后中国军队主动出击的第一战

抗日战争中，天津再次沦陷。此前，天津军民进行了英勇的抵抗。1937 年 7 月 29 日爆发的天津抗战，是卢沟桥事变后中国军队大规模对日主动出击的第一战。

七七事变后，天津形势十分危急。作为日本华北驻屯军司令部所在地，驻津的侵略军不断演习，加紧进行攻击天津的准备。日军首先控制了天津的海陆交通。将塘沽沿海码头完全占用，并在塘沽设立了运输部，在北岸修筑军用码头，驻在塘沽的日军有 1000 多人。天津铁路东站和总站（即北站）也被日军派兵占领，并且修建轻便铁路运兵，路线系由东站直达东局子兵营，全线长 20 余里。同时，日军大量增兵天津，7 月 12 日 15 列装甲运兵车载 4600 名日军开抵天津；同日 3500 名日军从塘沽登陆；之后几乎每天都有日军进入天津；特别是还有大批飞机飞抵天津，截至 27 日，天津市共停日机 60 余架；28 日下午 4 时，日军"临时航空兵团"团长德川好敏中将又督机百余架抵达东局子机场。日军还不分昼夜地进行着侵占天津的

---

① 张利民、刘凤华，《抗战时期日本对天津的经济统制与掠夺》，社会科学文献出版社，2016 年，第 44—64 页。

handing over Hebei and the Tianjin area to Japan.

On August 1, 1935, the Communist Party of China issued the *Message to all Compatriots on Resistance against Japanese and National Salvation*, proposing the unity of the people nationwide and the joint resistance against Japan. In October of the same year, Japan planned the traitor riot in Xianghe and launched the "North China Autonomy Movement." In November, it concocted the "North China Anti-Communist Autonomous Government" headed by the traitor Yin Rugeng in Tong County to incite "North China Independence." While planning armed aggression, since 1932, Japan has been smuggling large quantities of cotton, cotton yarn, rayon, sugar, and cigarettes from Tianjin, Qingdao, and Shanhaiguan to Tianjin along the railway line, severely damaging the pillar industries of Tianjin and Qingdao, particularly the textile industry, disrupting the market, and causing a massive outflow of silver from North China. Before the Marco Polo Bridge Incident, Japan's smuggling activities had caused severe economic losses to North China. Represented by the South Manchuria Railway Company (known as "Mantetsu"), Japanese official, commercial, and private capital increased their investment in Tianjin, systematically controlling various important industries, including electricity, salt, mines, cotton, and transportation, which were vital defense resources and infrastructure sectors. During the same period, the Japanese garrison also resisted and sabotaged the currency reform initiated by the Nanjing government in 1935. They formulated the *Outline for the Implementation of the Autonomous Currency System in North China*, proposing Tianjin as the new financial center, with the intention of separating North China from the financial systems of Central and South China, driving out the legal currency of the Nanjing government, and destabilizing China's financial stability.①

The Japanese meticulously operated for many years, using Tianjin as their headquarters, from instigating North China's independence to launching a full-scale invasion of China. Under their economic and military efforts, they believed the timing was ripe, and the prelude to a full-scale invasion of China began gradually. In October 1936, the Japanese garrison in North China conducted large-scale military exercises with Beijing as the target of attack. In March 1937, dozens of Japanese warships held large-scale landing exercises in Qingdao. Subsequently, the garrison in North China conducted several military exercises in Tianjin, the outskirts of Beijing, and Tong county. On July 7, the Japanese launched the shocking Marco Polo Bridge Incident. On July 8, the Communist Party of China immediately telegraphed the entire country: "Beijing and Tianjin

---

① Zhang Limin, Liu Fenghua. *Japan's Economic Domination and Plunder of Tianjin during the War of Resistance Against Japan*. Social Science Academic Press, 2016, pp.44-64.

日军向天津增加军备
The Japanese army reinforced its military presence in Tianjin

战术演习，从 25 日起已发展到演习巷战；26 日日军向华北中国军队发出最后通牒，要求中国军队立即南撤，在遭到中国军队拒绝后，日军 10 万人分数路对北平、天津实行包围和攻击；27 日日军占领了天津各车站，切断了平津两地中国军队间的联系。[1]

面对此种危局，驻华北第 29 军军长宋哲元于 27 日向全国发出通电："决心尽力自卫，守土有责。" 29 军驻津守军第 38 师副师长李文田兼天津市警察局长（师长张自忠兼任天津市市长，此时在北平与日本人谈判）代理天津军政事务，接到通电后，于 28 日凌晨召集在津的主要军政负责人开会，决定立即反击日军。会议的参加者包括：第 38 师副师长兼市警察局局长李文田、第 112 旅旅长黄维纲、独立第 26 旅旅长李致远、第 38 师手枪团团长祁光远、天津保安司令刘家鸾、天津保安总队队长宁殿武以及市政府秘书长马彦翀等七人，史称 "七人会议"。当时，因天津日军以一部增援北平，天津市内及郊区的兵力有 5000 人左右，在数量上稍多于日军，而在武器装备和训练上却又落后日军许多。然而，广大官兵对于当局的消极抵抗政策早已不满，抗日情绪高涨，纷纷请缨杀敌。会后李文田发出通电："誓与天津市共存亡！"打响了天津主动抗战第一枪。

29 日凌晨 2 时，中国军队对海光寺日本兵营、火车站、东局子机场以及市区日租界等重要目标进行了突袭。开始战事进展顺利，

---

① 刘景岳，《天津沦陷前的最后一战》。中国人民政治协商会议天津市委员会文史资料研究委员会编，《沦陷时期的天津》，内部发行，1992 年，第 1—8 页。

are in danger! North China is in danger! Only by implementing a national resistance can we find a way out!" China's full-scale resistance broke out.

The First Battle in Which the Chinese Army Took the Initiative to Attack After the Marco Polo Bridge Incident on July 7th

During the War of Resistance Against Japan, Tianjin fell once again. Prior to this, the military and civilians of Tianjin had bravely resisted. The Tianjin resistance that broke out on July 29, 1937, was the first major counterattack by Chinese forces against Japan following the Marco Polo Bridge Incident.

After the Marco Polo Bridge Incident, the situation in Tianjin became extremely critical. As the location of the headquarters of the Japanese North China Garrison Army, the invading forces stationed in Tianjin continued their exercises and intensified preparations for attacking Tianjin. The Japanese army first seized control of the sea and land transportation in Tianjin. They fully occupied the coastal docks in Tanggu and set up a transportation department there. They also constructed military docks on the north bank of Tanggu. There were about 1,000 Japanese soldiers stationed in Tanggu. The East Railway Station and the Main Station (also known as the North Station) in Tianjin were also occupied by the Japanese army, and they built a light railway for transporting troops from the East Station directly to the Dongjuzi Barracks, with a total length of about 20 li. Meanwhile, the Japanese army massively reinforced Tianjin. On July 12th, 15 armored trains carrying 4,600 Japanese soldiers arrived in Tianjin. On the same day, 3,500 Japanese soldiers landed in Tanggu, and almost every day thereafter, Japanese troops entered Tianjin. In particular, a large number of aircraft also arrived in Tianjin. By the 27th, there were over 60 Japanese aircraft parked in Tianjin. At 4 p.m. on the 28th, Lieutenant General Tokugawa Yoshitoshi, the commander of the "Provisional Air Corps," arrived at Dongjuzi Airport with over a hundred planes under his command. The Japanese army conducted tactical exercises to occupy Tianjin day and night, escalating to street combat exercises starting from the 25th; on the 26th, the Japanese issued a final ultimatum to the Chinese forces in North China, demanding an immediate withdrawal to the south. After being refused by the Chinese forces, the Japanese army, consisting of 100,000 troops, began to encircle and attack Beijing and Tianjin along several routes. On the 27th, the Japanese occupied various stations in Tianjin, cutting off the communication between the Chinese forces in Beijing and Tianjin.[1]

---

① Liu Jingyue. *The Last Battle Before the Fall of Tianjin*. The Cultural and Historical Data Research Committee of the Tianjin Municipal Committee of the Chinese People's Political Consultative Conference (ed.). *Tianjin during Its Occupation*. Published internally in 1992, pp.1-8.

张自忠（1891年8月11日—1940年5月16日），山东临清人，第五战区右翼集团军兼第三十三集团军总司令，抗日战争时期张自忠是国军中第一位以身殉国的高级将领，后被追授陆军二级上将。1936年张自忠任天津市市长，对天津市的吏治、工商财政、文化教育、社会福利和社会治安等各项事业进行了大刀阔斧的整顿。从1925年到1935年，天津市经历了长达10年的萧条，经过张自忠的整顿，天津经济首次出现了增长。1937年至1940年先后参与临沂保卫战、徐州会战、武汉会战、随枣会战与枣宜会战等。1940年在襄阳与日军战斗中，不幸牺牲

Zhang Zizhong (August 11, 1891 - May 16, 1940), a native of Linqing, Shandong, was the commander of the Right-wing Army Group of the Fifth Theater and the 33rd Army. During the War of Resistance Against Japan, he became the first high-ranking general in the Nationalist Army to sacrifice his life for the country, and was posthumously awarded the rank of Second-Class Army General. In 1936, Zhang Zizhong was appointed Mayor of Tianjin, where he carried out significant reforms in the civil service, industry, commerce and finance, culture and education, social welfare, and public security. From 1925 to 1935, Tianjin had endured a decade of economic decline, but under his leadership, the city's economy experienced its first growth. From 1937 to 1940, Zhang participated in several key battles, including the Campaigns of Linyi, Xuzhou, Wuhan, Suizhou, and Zaoyang. Unfortunately, he was killed in action while fighting the Japanese army in Xiangyang in 1940

位于海河边的张自忠雕像
The statue of Zhang Zizhong on the bank of the Hai River

李文田（1894—1951），河南浚县人，国民党二级上将、原第三十三集团军副司令。1937年4月至5月张自忠赴日访问期间，李文田任天津市代理市长，领导天津抗战。1940年他与张自忠共同指挥了随枣战役、襄樊战役。1940年至1946年任第三十三集团军副总司令。1947年任第三绥靖区副司令长官。由于不愿打内战，1948年脱离军队任总统府参军（虚职），1951年逝世

Li Wentian (1894-1951), from Jun County, Henan Province, was a 2nd Class General of the Kuomintang and a former Deputy Commander of the 33rd Army Group. During Zhang Zizhong's visit to Japan from April to May 1937, Li served as the acting Mayor of Tianjin and led the city's resistance against Japanese aggression. In 1940, he, along with Zhang Zizhong, jointly commanded the Suizhou-Zaoyang Campaign and the Xiangyang-Fancheng Campaign. From 1940 to 1946, Li was the Deputy Commander in Chief of the 33rd Army Group. In 1947, he was appointed Deputy Commander of the Third Pacification Area. Due to his unwillingness to engage in the civil war, he left the military in 1948 and took on a nominal position as a staff member of the Presidential office. He passed away in 1951

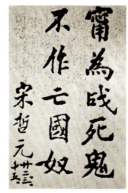

宋哲元（1885—1940），山东乐陵县人。中国军事家，抗战名将。他治军严谨，作战勇敢，为西北军五虎之一。1935年被授为陆军二级上将，任平津卫戍司令、冀察绥靖主任和冀察政务委员会委员长兼河北省政府主席。1938年春，宋哲元将军改任一战区副司令，不久染上肝病，于1940年3月辞职改任军事委员会委员，4月5日病逝

Song Zheyuan (1885-1940), a native of Laoling County, Shandong Province, was a Chinese military strategist and a famous general in the War of Resistance against Japanese Aggression. He was known for his strict military discipline and bravery in battle, and was one of the "Five Tigers" of the Northwest Army. In 1935, he was promoted to the rank of 2nd Class Army General, serving as the Commander of the Beiping-Tianjin Garrison, the Director of the Hebei-Chahar Pacification Area, the Chairman of the Hebei-Chahar Political Affairs Committee, and the Chairman of the Hebei Provincial Government. In the spring of 1938, General Song Zheyuan was appointed Deputy Commander of the First Theater. He soon contracted a liver disease and, in March 1940, he resigned from his post and became a member of the Military Commission. He passed away on April 5, 1940

被日军飞机炸毁的南开大学校舍
The Nankai University buildings destroyed by
Japanese aircraft bombing

被日军掠走熔化做炮弹的南开校钟
Nankai School Bell, which was looted and melted by
the Japanese army to make artillery shells

Facing this crisis, General Song Zheyuan, the commander of the 29th Army stationed in North China, issued a nationwide telegram on the 27th, stating, "We are determined to do our best to defend ourselves and fulfill our responsibility to defend our territory." Li Wentian, the deputy commander of the 38th Division stationed in Tianjin and the acting director of the Tianjin Municipal Police Bureau (the division commander Zhang Zizhong concurrently served as the mayor of Tianjin and was negotiating with the Japanese in Beiping at this time), took charge of military and political affairs in Tianjin after receiving the telegram. In the early morning of the 28th, he convened a meeting of the main military and political leaders in Tianjin to decide to immediately counterattack the Japanese. The participants of the meeting included Li Wentian, Deputy Division Commander of the 38th Division and Director of the Municipal Police Bureau; Huang Weigang, Commander of the 112th Brigade; Li Zhiyuan, Commander of the Independent 26th Brigade; Qi Guangyuan, Commander of the 38th Pistol Regiment; Liu Jialuan, Tianjin Security Commander; Ning Dianwu, Chief of Staff of the Tianjin Security General Command; and Ma Yanchong, Secretary-General of the Municipal Government, a total of seven individuals, known as the "Seven-Person Meeting." At that time, due to the Japanese reinforcements sent to Beiping, there were about 5,000 Chinese troops in Tianjin and its suburbs, slightly more in number than the Japanese forces. However, they were far behind the Japanese in terms of weapon equipment and training. Nevertheless, the majority of officers and soldiers were dissatisfied with the passive resistance policy of the authorities and were eager to fight the Japanese. After the meeting, Li Wentian issued a telegram declaring, "We swear to live or die together with Tianjin!" This marked the beginning of Tianjin's active resistance against the Japanese.

At 2 a.m. on the 29th, the Chinese army launched a surprise attack on key targets such as the Japanese barracks in Haiguang Temple, the railway station, Dongjuzi Airport, and the Japanese concession in the city. The battle began smoothly, and Chinese army recaptured two railway stations. By dawn, Chinese army had penetrated Dongjuzi Airport and destroyed more than a dozen Japanese planes; the enemy in the Japanese concession was surrounded on three sides, and Japanese expatriates organized volunteer teams to join the battle; the Japanese troops in Haiguang Temple barracks were holed up in fortifications awaiting rescue; the Tianjin Main Station was occupied by the Chinese army, and the Japanese troops at the East Station were forced to retreat to a warehouse. This was the final battle before the fall of Beiping and Tianjin, and it was also the only battle initiated by Chinese army since the Marco Polo Bridge Incident. Historians of the resistance movement called it the "Tianjin Great Offensive." At the same time as the attack was launched, Chinese army

中国军队夺回了两个车站。到拂晓，中国军队攻进东局子机场，并烧毁了十几架日机；日租界的敌人被三面包围，日本侨民组织了义勇队上战场；海光寺日本兵营的日军龟缩在工事内等待援救；天津总站被中国军队占领，东站日军被逼退到一个仓库中。这是北平和天津陷落前的最后一战，也是卢沟桥事变以来中国军队主动进攻的唯一战斗，抗战史家称之为"天津大出击"。发动攻击的同时，中国军队向全国发布抗日通电，电文称"日人日日运兵，处处挑衅"，"我方为国家民族图生存，当即分别应战，誓与津市共存亡，喋血抗日，义无反顾"。天津《益世报》7月29日发表了通电全文。

29日上午，日军紧急从外围调集军队分四路进入天津，同时调集飞机对中国军队和阵地进行扫射轰炸，中国军队伤亡很大。29日傍晚，日本大批援军从北平等地陆续开来。在没有兵力增援的情况下，中国军队不得不于当日下午撤出市区，转赴静海一带作战。30日中国军队撤出后，日军以疯狂报复的方式，派飞机对天津东站、北站、省政府和市政府、警察局、南开大学、北宁铁路局及电台、造币厂、法院等重要目标进行狂轰滥炸。日军进入市区后，在街头对手无寸铁的居民随意开枪开炮，很多地方被炸为废墟，天津群众罹难者两千多人，街道遍布死尸，到处是无家可归的难民。日军的暴行给天津和天津人民造成的损失与痛苦罄竹难书。7月31日，天津沦陷。

当时的报纸曾报道："我当局所属之保安队警及各部队，久历戎行，迭遭巨变，对于日军之一再压迫，容忍已久，一旦参予守土卫国之战役，无不奋勇当先，踊跃效死。"如进攻公大七厂（天津印染厂旧址）的五名战士，在撤退令下达后仍不下战场，登上厂内水楼与敌一拼到底，最后均壮烈殉国。

这次抗战还得到了天津人民群众的全力支持。市民在战斗中为部队送上茶饭、西瓜，公私汽车都组织起来为前线运送弹药，有的商店还把门板卸下来运到前沿充作工事。特别是中国共产党领导的学生组织，他们以南开大学为基地，进行宣传鼓动、救护伤员、运送弹药等工作，有力地支持了战斗，南开大学因此被日军视为"保安队及中国军队攻击日军的中心地"而遭到轰炸。直到8月1日，日军才宣布基本完成市区扫荡，但中国保安队最后坚持到8月5日才

issued a nationwide anti-Japanese telegram, stating, "The Japanese transport troops every day and provoke everywhere," "We are fighting for the survival of our nation and our country, and we vow to live or die together with Tianjin, shedding blood to resist Japan without hesitation." The full text of the telegram was published in the Tianjin newspaper *Social Welfare* on July 29th.

In the morning of the 29th, the Japanese urgently mobilized troops from the periphery and entered Tianjin from four directions, while deploying airplanes to strafe and bomb the Chinese army and positions, resulting in heavy casualties among the Chinese army. In the evening of the 29th, large numbers of Japanese reinforcements arrived from Beiping and other places. Without additional reinforcements, the Chinese army had to withdraw from the city in the afternoon and move to fight in the Jinghai area. After the Chinese army withdrew on the 30th, the Japanese launched a frenzied retaliation, sending planes to indiscriminately bomb important targets in Tianjin such as the East Station, North Station, provincial government, municipal government, police station, Nankai University, Beijing-Liaoning Railway Bureau, radio station, mint, court, and others. After entering the city, the Japanese indiscriminately shot and shelled unarmed residents on the streets, and many areas were turned into ruins, with more than two thousand Tianjin residents killed and streets littered with corpses, leaving countless homeless refugees. The atrocities committed by the Japanese caused immeasurable losses and suffering to Tianjin and its people. On July 31st, Tianjin fell.

The newspapers of the time reported: "Our security teams and various units under the authority have experienced many changes and endured prolonged oppression from the Japanese army. Once they participated in the battle to defend the homeland, they all bravely took the lead and eagerly sacrificed themselves." For example, five soldiers who attacked Gongda Seventh Factory (former site of Tianjin Printing and Dyeing Factory), despite receiving the order to retreat, remained on the battlefield, climbed onto the water tower inside the factory, and fought the enemy to the end, eventually sacrificing themselves heroically.

This resistance also received full support from the people of Tianjin. Citizens provided tea, meals, and watermelons to the troops during the battle. Public and private vehicles were organized to transport ammunition to the front lines, and some shops even dismantled their doors and sent them to the front lines to be used as fortifications. Particularly, student organizations led by the Communist Party of China, based at Nankai University, engaged in mobilization, first aid for the wounded, and transporting ammunition, providing strong support for the battle. Nankai University was consequently bombed by the Japanese army, which regarded it as "the center of the security

向日军缴械。根据日军统计，战斗中日军被击毙127人，348人负伤。尽管天津抗战仅仅坚持了三天便宣告失败，却让南京政府丢掉了与日和谈的妄想，蒋介石也公开表示："现在既然和平绝望，只有抗战到底，举国一致，不惜牺牲，来和倭寇死拼，以驱逐倭寇，复兴民族"。

"孤岛"上的抗日活动

天津沦陷后，具有反帝爱国斗争传统的天津人民以各种方式与日本法西斯统治者进行了长达8年的艰苦卓绝的斗争，为正面战场的抗战作出了重要贡献。七七事变后，日本大举入侵华北，之后于12月占领上海。但此时第二次世界大战尚没有开始，日方当时还没有准备好与英、美、法等国对抗，列强在天津的租界和治外法权得以保留，英、法租界成为"孤岛"。中国人民利用这种特殊环境和条件，开展了一系列抗日活动。

1937年8月至1940年9月天津电话局职工的"抗交"活动，就是"孤岛"上中国人的不屈抗争。天津电话局三分局设在英租界内，四分局设在意租界，电报局设在法租界，其他分局遍及市区。日本占领天津后，接管了除三分局和四分局以外的其他分局。这两个电话局的广大职工拒绝将电话局交给日本人，当时的电话局局长国民党员张子奇也表示"抗交"到底。日本宪兵队不能公然进入租界内接管和逮捕中国人，于是在租界外的地方大肆逮捕三、四分局职工。居住在租界外的职工纷纷携眷进入租界居住，找不到住处的就住到局里。技术工人不足，总工程师朱彭寿就培训员工亲属子女，成立短期培训班，学成后补充缺额。日本人指使汉奸潜入租界破坏电缆线箱，电话局工人及时抢修。英租界当局唯恐日本人控制租界里的电话，所以也暗中支持电话局员工的"抗交"活动。后在日本人的武力威胁下，英租界当局同意由英、法、意三国从形式上接管电话局。1939年日本宪兵绑架了朱彭寿，要他交出机线图，并对他实施了各种酷刑，但他宁死不屈，最后惨死在日军宪兵队中。在日方的不断施压之下，英、法、意租界当局最终于1940年9月将电话局管理权

forces and Chinese troops attacking the Japanese army." It wasn't until August 1st that the Japanese army announced the completion of the sweep of the city, but the Chinese security forces persisted until August 5th before surrendering their weapons to the Japanese. According to Japanese statistics, 127 Japanese soldiers were killed, and 348 were wounded in the battle. Although the Tianjin resistance lasted only three days before it was declared a failure, it shattered the Nanjing government's illusions of peace talks with Japan. Chiang Kai-shek publicly stated, "Since peace is hopeless now, we must fight to the end, unite the whole country, spare no sacrifice, confront the Japanese invaders head-on, expel them, and revive the nation."

The Anti-Japanese Activities on the "Isolated Islands"

After the fall of Tianjin, the people of Tianjin, who had a tradition of anti-imperialist and patriotic struggle, engaged in a difficult and remarkable struggle against the Japanese fascist rulers for eight years through various means, making important contributions to the resistance on the main battlefield. Following the Marco Polo Bridge Incident, Japan launched a large-scale invasion of North China, and later in December, occupied Shanghai. However, at this time, the Second World War had not yet begun, and Japan was not yet prepared to confront countries like Britain, the United States, and France. As a result, the concessions and extraterritorial rights of the Western powers in Tianjin were preserved, and the British and French concessions became "isolated islands." Chinese people utilized this unique environment and conditions to carry out a series of anti-Japanese activities.

The "anti-transfer" activities of Tianjin Telephone Bureau workers from August 1937 to September 1940 were the indomitable struggle of the Chinese people on the "isolated islands." The Tianjin Telephone Bureau had its Third Division in the British Concession, its Fourth Division in the Italian Concession, and its Telegraph Bureau in the French Concession, with other divisions spread throughout the city. After the Japanese occupation of Tianjin, they took control of all divisions except the Third and Fourth Divisions. The vast majority of workers in these two branch offices refused to hand over the branch office to the Japanese. The bureau's director at the time, Zhang Ziqi, a member of the Kuomintang, also expressed full support for the "anti-transfer" movement. The Japanese military police could not openly enter the concessions to take over or arrest Chinese people, so they began to arrest workers from the Third and Fourth Divisions outside the concessions. Workers living outside the concessions brought their families into the concessions, and those who couldn't find housing stayed in the bureau. Due to a shortage of technical workers, the Chief

大光明电影院
The Gaiety Theater

交予对方。"抗交"运动最终以英租界当局的妥协而告终。①

1939年英租界还发生了一起震惊全国、影响波及世界的重大案件，亲日的新任津海关监督兼伪中国联合准备银行天津分行经理程锡庚，被爱国抗日志士刺杀。此后引发了一系列中英日之间长达一年多时间的外交交涉。国民党政府为了打击破坏伪临时政府，命令军统天津站利用其外围团体"抗日锄奸暗杀团"（也叫"抗日杀奸团"，简称"抗团"），于1939年4月9日晚7点30分在英租界大光明影院将正在观影的程锡庚枪杀。消息传出后，伪天津市市长温世珍致函英总领事抗议。英租界迫于压力同意接受日本"协力"，共同搜捕暗杀案犯，随后逮捕了4名中国男性嫌疑犯，扣押在租界警局。在日本宪兵队的强烈要求下，英驻天津领事同意将4名嫌疑犯暂时"借"给日本宪兵队审问。日本宪兵队严刑逼供，终于得到4人的口供，并到案发现场进行了所在位置、逃走线路等勘查、取证。之后将4人返还给英租界警方收押。可是4人回到工部局警务处后，全员翻供，拒不承认自己是暗杀关联者。同时，重庆政府方面也展开营救，要求英方不要将这4人交给日方。英国方面

Engineer, Zhu Pengshou, trained the relatives and children of employees, forming short-term training classes to fill the vacancies. The Japanese instigated collaborators to sabotage the cable boxes in the concessions, but the telephone bureau workers promptly repaired the damage. The British Concession authorities, fearing Japanese control over telephones within the concession, secretly supported the "anti-transfer" activities of the telephone bureau staff. Later, under Japanese military pressure, the British Concession authorities agreed to formally hand over the management of the telephone bureau to the British, French, and Italian authorities. In 1939, the Japanese military police kidnapped Zhu Pengshou, demanding him to surrender the machine line map and subjected him to various tortures, but he chose to die rather than surrender and eventually died miserably in the hands of the Japanese military police. Under continuous pressure from the Japanese, the British, French, and Italian Concession authorities eventually handed over the management of the telephone bureau to the Japanese in September 1940. The "anti-transfer" movement ended with the compromise of the British Concession authorities.①

In 1939, a major incident occurred in the British Concession that shocked the nation and had worldwide repercussions: Cheng Xigeng, a pro-Japanese newly appointed supervisor of the Tianjin Customs and manager of the Tianjin branch of the Federal Reserve Bank of China, was assassinated by patriotic anti-Japanese activists. This incident triggered a series of diplomatic negotiations between China, Britain, and Japan lasting over a year. The Nationalist government, in order to combat and undermine the Puppet Provisional Government, instructed the Military Statistics Bureau Tianjin Branch to utilize its peripheral group "Anti-Japanese Traitor-Extermination Assassination Group" (also known as "Anti-Japanese Assassination Group," abbreviated as "Anti-Group") to assassinate Cheng Xigeng on the evening of April 9, 1939, at 7:30 p.m. while he was watching a movie at the Grand Cinema in the British Concession. Upon the news spreading, the puppet-mayor of Tianjin, Wen Shizhen, protested to the British Consul General. Under pressure, the British Concession agreed to cooperate with Japan to jointly search for the assassins. Subsequently, four male Chinese suspects were arrested and detained at the concession police station. At the strong request of the Japanese military police, the British Consul in Tianjin agreed to temporarily "borrow" the four suspects for interrogation by the Japanese military police. After subjecting them to severe interrogation, the Japanese military police finally obtained confessions

① 吴云心，《沦陷时期天津电话局"抗交"事件》。中国人民政治协商会议天津市委员会文史资料研究委员会编，《沦陷时期的天津》，内部发行，1992年，第27—30页。

① Wu Yunxin. *The Anti-Transfer Activities of Tianjin Telephone Bureau during its Occupation*. The Cultural and Historical Data Research Committee of the Tianjin Municipal Committee of the Chinese People's Political Consultative Conference (ed.). *Tianjin During Its Occupation*. Published internally in 1992, p.27-30.

1939年6月14日日本华北地区驻屯军包围并封锁了英法租界
On June 14, 1939, the Japanese garrison troops in North China surrounded and blockaded the British and French concessions

为了切断租界之间的联系，日军在租界周围架起了电气化铁丝网
In order to sever the contact between the concessions, the Japanese army erected electrified barbed wire around them

日本兵对出入英、法租界的行人进行盘问和检查
Japanese soldiers questioned and inspected pedestrians entering and exiting the British and French concessions

from the four individuals and conducted investigations and evidence collection at the scene of the incident regarding their locations and escape routes. The four suspects were then returned to the custody of the British concession police. However, upon returning to the police department of the Municipal Council, all four individuals recanted their confessions and refused to admit any involvement in the assassination. Simultaneously, the Chongqing government initiated rescue efforts and requested that the British refrain from handing over the four individuals to the Japanese. Due to restrictions and damage to activities and interests in the Japanese-occupied areas, the British side adopted a non-cooperative attitude towards the issue of extradition to the Japanese puppet regime, emphasizing insufficient evidence and refusing to extradite the four individuals.

On the Japanese occupation side, seeing that negotiations were ineffective, they decided to take a tough stance by imposing a blockade on the British Concession and demanding that the British hand over the individuals within a specified period. On June 14, the Japanese military implemented a comprehensive blockade on seven roads surrounding the British and French concessions, conducting questioning and inspections of pedestrians entering and exiting from the concessions. They also implemented a permit system

祝宗梁（1920—2020），"抗日锄奸团"主要成员及后期负责人之一。当时被逮捕的4人其实并不是程锡庚事件的直接刺杀者。日本史料中记载：1939年8月下旬重庆等地有新闻报道说：刺杀程锡庚的是南开中学学生祝宗梁、袁汉俊。此二人后到香港警方自首，声明他们在电影院刺杀了程锡庚。可是香港警方以此二人为暗杀者证据不足，拒绝了二人的自首。台湾历史馆里也有档案《祝宗梁锄奸告》，记载了是爱国志士、南开学生祝宗梁刺杀了程锡庚。祝宗梁1920年出生在北京，中学就读于天津南开中学，南开被炸后改读天津工商学院附中。七七事变后加入"抗日锄奸团"（集会地设在英租界松寿里）。他第一次持枪杀奸，是在刺杀天津伪商会会长王竹林的行动中。此后天津的多起刺杀日伪汉奸的行动，都有祝宗梁参与，不少行动令日伪汉奸闻风丧胆

Zhu Zongliang (1920-2020) was one of the key members and later leaders of the "Anti-Japanese Traitor-Extermination Group." The four individuals arrested at that time were not the direct assassins of the Cheng Xigeng incident. According to Japanese historical records, in late August 1939, news reports in places like Chongqing stated that the assassins of Cheng Xigeng were Zhu Zongliang and Yuan Hanjun, students of Nankai Middle School. The two later turned themselves in to the Hong Kong police, claiming they had assassinated Cheng Xigeng in a movie theater. However, the Hong Kong police rejected their confession due to insufficient evidence. The National History Museum of Taiwan also holds an archive titled *Zhu Zongliang's Traitor-Extermination Report*, which records that Zhu Zongliang, a patriotic Nankai student, was the one who assassinated Cheng Xigeng. Zhu Zongliang was born in Beijing in 1920 and attended Nankai Middle School in Tianjin. After Nankai was bombed, he transferred to the Affiliated Middle School of Tientsin Kung Shang College. After the Marco Polo Bridge Incident, he joined the "Anti-Japanese Traitor-Extermination Group" (whose meetings were held in Songshouli, the British Concession). His first act of using a gun to kill a traitor was during the assassination of Wang Zhulin, the president of the Tianjin Puppet Chamber of Commerce. Following this, he participated in several other assassinations of puppet traitors in Tianjin, many of which made the puppet collaborators tremble in fear

由于在日军占领区域内第三国的活动和权益受到限制和损坏，所以在引渡问题上对日伪摆出了不合作态度，强调犯罪证据不足，拒绝引渡4人。

日占领军方面见交涉无效，决定采取对英租界进行封锁的强硬手段，令英方限期交人。6月14日，日军对英、法租界外围的7条道路实施全面封锁，对出入租界的行人进行盘问和检查。又在两个租界沿岸的从万国桥（今解放桥）起到白河下游的水域，实行水上船舶许可证通行；在临近英法租界的其他区域增设监视口。翌日，英租界驻兵在马场道检查口架起机枪并呐喊，双方出现剑拔弩张、一触即发之势。日军随即调来坦克助威，对峙4个小时后，英兵无奈地撤去。其后在检查口检查行人时，日军变得气焰嚣张，经常在大庭广众之下对进出租界的英国人加以羞辱，不论男女实行近于裸体的脱衣检查。日军甚至不允许将食物和燃料运进租界里。

当时，第二次世界大战爆发在即，德意日结成三国轴心，而英法两国则站在对立的一方。英国无法兼顾东西两个半球的窘境，只得同意在东京进行外交谈判。1939年7月15日9时，世界瞩目的日英会谈在东京日本外务官邸举行，日本有田外务大臣和英国驻日大使克莱琪（Robert Leslie Craigie）开始就原则问题进行谈判。经过3

for waterborne vessels in the waterways from the International Bridge (now Jiefang Bridge) to the downstream area of the Peiho along the banks of the two concessions, and increased surveillance in other areas near the British and French Concessions. The next day, British concession troops erected machine guns and shouted slogans at the inspection point on Race Course Road, leading to a tense standoff and potential confrontation between the two sides. The Japanese promptly brought in tanks to bolster their position, and after a four-hour standoff, the British troops reluctantly withdrew. Subsequently, during the inspection of pedestrians at the checkpoint, the Japanese became increasingly arrogant, often humiliating British individuals entering and exiting from the concessions in full view of the public, subjecting them to strip searches regardless of gender. The Japanese even prohibited the transportation of food and fuel into the concessions.

At that time, with the outbreak of the Second World War imminent, the Axis Powers of Germany, Italy, and Japan had formed, while Britain and France stood on the opposing side. Britain found itself in a dilemma, unable to manage its interests in both the Eastern and Western Hemispheres, and reluctantly agreed to diplomatic negotiations in Tokyo. On July 15, 1939, at 9 o'clock in the morning, the highly anticipated Japan-UK talks were held at the Japanese Foreign Office in Tokyo, with Japanese Minister of Foreign Affairs Hachiro Arita and British Ambassador to Japan Robert Leslie Craigie initiating negotiations on principle issues. After three rounds of talks, Britain finally made concessions to Japan. An agreement was reached, and the *Crai-*

纳粹德国的旗帜飘扬在英租界标志性建筑戈登堂的屋顶上。日本与德国和意大利结成"轴心国"后，日本人邀请德国和意大利的军队到天津接收英、法租界。1941 年 12 月 8 日太平洋战争爆发，日本为报复美国限制日裔美籍人在美国本土活动，于 1942 年 3 月在山东潍县设立了一座外侨集中营，将两千多名包括京津和华北地区的欧美侨民关押其中，西方人称为"潍县集中营"。直到 1945 年，集中营被解放。德国侨民的命运也好不到哪里去，他们并未因远离欧洲战场而幸免于战争之外。纳粹政府在天津、上海设立了纳粹分部以控制侨民的思想，军队甚至出动舰艇来到中国运送被征召入伍的适龄青壮年回欧洲参战。一些德国侨民家中悬挂着希特勒的照片，但是也有西门子公司南京分公司经理德国人拉贝（John Rabe），在南京大屠杀中冒着生命危险援救中国难民，将记录日军暴行的信件寄给妻子，著名的《拉贝日记》直到 1997 年才首次出版。照片由德国"东亚之友"协会提供

The flag of Nazi Germany flying on top of the iconic Gordon Hall in the British Concession. After Japan formed the Axis powers with Germany and Italy, the Japanese invited German and Italian forces to take over the British and French concessions in Tianjin. On December 8, 1941, the Pacific War broke out. In retaliation for the United States restricting the activities of Japanese expatriates on American soil, Japan established an internment camp in Weixian, Shandong Province, in March 1942. More than 2,000 European and American expatriates, including those from Beijing, Tianjin, and North China, were detained in the camp, which Westerners referred to as the "Weixian Internment Camp." The camp remained in operation until 1945 when it was liberated. The fate of German expatriates was little better, as they were not spared from the war simply by being far from the European battlefield. The Nazi government set up Nazi branches in Tianjin and Shanghai to control the thoughts of the expatriates. The military even dispatched ships to China to transport young conscripts back to Europe to fight. Some German expatriates displayed photos of Hitler in their homes, but there were exceptions, such as John Rabe, a German manager of Siemens' Nanjing branch. Rabe risked his life to rescue Chinese refugees during the Nanjing Massacre and sent letters to his wife documenting the atrocities committed by the Japanese army. *The Good Man of Nanking: The Diaries of John Rabe* was first published in 1997. Source: StuDeo

次会谈，英国终于对日本让步。双方达成协议，签订了《有田—克莱琪协定》，就日军在其占领区的治安管辖权予以确认（其间，英国还曾求助于美国，但遭到拒绝。这给日本人留下了一个美国人软弱的印象，即美国人害怕对日开战，愿意付出任何代价来避免战争，就此为后来的珍珠港事件埋下了祸根）。《有田—克莱琪协定》发表后，日本举国欢腾，认为这是继日俄战争后日本对西方列强的又一次胜利。中国国内也反应强烈，各界申明这就是英国的"东方慕尼黑方案"。中国共产党于7月29日在延安《新中华报》发表社论，一针见血地指出：英国与日寇订立这一协定，则无异是赞助日本在中国的掳掠、屠杀、奸淫、侮辱和占领，无异赞助日本消灭我国的抗战力量。

1940年4月，希特勒的坦克横扫西欧，英国也面临德国入侵。英国决定在中国战场向日本妥协，从华北和上海撤军。而法国已被德国打败，法租界成了准沦陷区。为了体现友好和国际性，日本人邀请德国和意大利的军队到天津接收英、法租界，一战战败的德国陆海军趾高气扬地重返天津。"孤岛"不复存在，日本占领军对天津的统治日益严酷。太平洋战争爆发前后，日本人在天津和整个华北地区先后进行了五次"治安强化运动"，城市里的抗日活动变得非常困难。

为坚持长期抗战，中国共产党在天津北部山区——盘山，建立了抗日根据地，在八路军十三团团长包森领导下，积极开展武装斗争。在天津南部平原水乡活跃的津南支队，也是中共领导下赫赫有名的八路军武工队，他们利用青纱帐和水网纵横的有利地形，神出鬼没地开展武装斗争。国民党天津地方组织则在城市里的爱国学生、工商业者和知识分子中寻求热血志士，为打击汉奸败类和支援抗战作出贡献。抗战期间天津出现的烧毁敌军仓库、抢劫敌军物资、暗杀汉奸日特、袭扰重要目标等行动，既有共产党地下组织领导的，也有国民党地下组织领导的。在当时历史条件下，正面战场对于歼灭敌军有生力量起决定性作用，但敌后战场对敌军持久有效的牵制和打击，对缓解正面战场压力也起到了重要作用。因此，正面战场与敌后战场都为抗战胜利作出了重要贡献。

gie-Arita Agreement was signed, confirming Japan's jurisdiction over public security in its occupied territories. (During this time, Britain had also sought assistance from the United States, but was refused. This left the Japanese with an impression of American weakness, believing that Americans were afraid of war with Japan and were willing to pay any price to avoid it, laying the seeds for the later Pearl Harbor incident.) After the *Craigie-Arita Agreement* was announced, Japan rejoiced nationwide, viewing it as another victory over Western powers after the Russo-Japanese War. There was also a strong reaction within China, with various sectors declaring it as Britain's "Eastern Munich Agreement." The Chinese Communist Party published an editorial in the Yan'an *Xin Zhonghua Bao* on July 29, bluntly pointing out, The agreement between Britain and Japan is nothing short of endorsing Japan's plunder, massacre, rape, insult, and occupation in China, endorsing Japan's efforts to eliminate our country's resistance forces.

In April 1940, Hitler's tanks swept through Western Europe, and Britain also faced the threat of German invasion. Britain decided to compromise with Japan on the Chinese battlefield and withdrew its troops from North China and Shanghai. Meanwhile, France had been defeated by Germany, and the French Concession became a quasi-occupied area. To demonstrate friendship and international cooperation, the Japanese invited German and Italian forces to Tianjin to take over the British and French Concessions. The triumphant German army and navy from World War I proudly returned to Tianjin. The "isolated islands" no longer existed, and the rule of the Japanese occupation forces in Tianjin became increasingly harsh. Before and after the outbreak of the Pacific War, the Japanese conducted five "security enhancement campaigns" in Tianjin and the entire North China region, making anti-Japanese activities in the city very difficult.

To sustain the long-term resistance against Japan, the Communist Party of China established an anti-Japanese base in the mountainous area of Mountain Panshan, northern Tianjin. Under the leadership of Bao Sen, the commander of the 13th Regiment of the Eighth Route Army, they actively engaged in armed struggle. In the southern plains and water towns of Tianjin, the Jinnan Brigade, also known as the renowned Eighth Route Army detachment under the leadership of the Communist Party, made use of advantageous terrain with the curtain of tall crops and its intricate network of waterways and canals, conducting guerrilla warfare with agility and stealth. The local organizations of the Kuomintang in Tianjin sought patriotic students, businessmen, and intellectuals in the city to contribute to the fight against traitors and to support the resistance against Japan. During the resistance, actions such as burning enemy warehouses, looting enemy supplies, assassinating collabora-

日本对天津的八年殖民统治

日本对中国的侵略是蓄谋已久的。占领天津后，日本人立即对天津这个北方最重要的工商业中心进行了全方位的控制，实行名义上的"自治"事实上的殖民统治。他们将天津定位为华北的经济中心，对其进行经济剥削，以达到"以战养战"的目的。

七七事变后，日本军占领北京和天津，将日本统治华北地区的政治军事和经济机构迁至北京，如华北方面军司令部和特务部等；日伪政权——"中华民国临时政府"和"华北政务委员会"也都设立在北京。天津于 1937 年 8 月 1 日，宣布成立汉奸傀儡组织"天津治安维持会"；于 12 月成立"天津特别市公署"。1940 年 3 月汪精卫在南京成立"国民政府"后，设立华北政务委员会，天津从此隶属其下。1943 年天津特别市公署改名为"天津特别市政府"。不管名称、人员如何变动，实际上，它都不过是日本特务机关的执行机构，完全听命于日本人，对天津人民实行法西斯统治。

为了镇压抗日活动，日本军国主义者 1941 年 3 月至 1942 年 12 月进行了五次"治安强化运动"，加速沦陷区的殖民化。与此同时，为维持其对中国及东南亚国家发动的侵略战争，日军在中国推行"以经济战为主体"的策略，一方面疯狂地从中国掠夺各种战略物资和资源，另一方面在其统治地区成立"圣战献金动员总会"，强迫机关团体、企业、商号、全体市民，甚至小学生和幼稚园学童，"献铜、献铁、献金、献锡"，以此弥补其军需资源匮乏。自 1941 年 12 月至 1944 年 2 月，日伪当局从天津商会、工厂联合会掠得"献机金"125 万元，从钱业、五金业公会掠得 130 万元，从银行业同业公会掠得 100 万元；搜刮铜 60 多万千克，铁 41 万多千克，锡纸 1.5 万张。[①] 日伪统治当局还成立了各种"统制会"，将所有重要工业原料和重要企业以军管方式强行霸占。例如，化学工业是近代天津的支柱产业，在华北地区乃至全国居于领先地位。沦陷后，久大精盐公司和永利制碱公司都被实行军事管理，后交由日资企业负责产销运

[①] 黎始初，《日军控制下的天津伪政权》。中国人民政治协商会议天津市委员会文史资料研究委员会编，《沦陷时期的天津》，内部发行，1992 年，第 55—66 页。

tors and Japanese spies, and attacking key targets occurred in Tianjin. These actions were led by both underground Communist Party organizations and underground Kuomintang organizations. In the historical context of the time, while the frontal battlefield played a decisive role in annihilating enemy forces, the guerrilla warfare behind enemy lines provided sustained and effective pressure and strikes against the enemy, thereby alleviating the pressure on the frontal battlefield. Therefore, both the frontal battlefield and the guerrilla warfare behind enemy lines made significant contributions to the victory in the resistance against Japan.

Japan's Eight-year Colonial Rule over Tianjin

Japan's aggression against China was premeditated. After occupying Tianjin, the Japanese immediately exerted comprehensive control over this crucial industrial and commercial center in the north, implementing a nominal "autonomy" that was, in fact, colonial rule. They positioned Tianjin as the economic hub of North China, subjecting it to economic exploitation to achieve the goal of "waging war by sustaining war."

After the Marco Polo Bridge Incident, the Japanese military occupied Beijing and Tianjin, relocating the political, military, and economic institutions governing North China to Beijing, such as the North China Area Army Command and the Special Service Department. Additionally, the puppet regimes—the "Provisional Government of the Republic of China" and the "North China Political Council"—were also established in Beijing. On August 1st, 1937, Tianjin announced the establishment of the collaborationist puppet organization "Tianjin Public Security Maintenance Committee," and in December, the "Tianjin Special Municipality Office" was established. After Wang Jingwei established the "National Government" in Nanjing in March 1940, the North China Political Council was set up, with Tianjin subsequently falling under its jurisdiction. In 1943, the Tianjin Special Municipality Office was renamed the "Tianjin Special Municipal Government." Regardless of the changes in names and personnel, in reality, it was merely an executive organ of the Japanese secret service, completely obedient to the Japanese, implementing fascist rule over the people of Tianjin.

To suppress anti-Japanese activities, Japanese militarists conducted five "security enhancement campaigns" from March 1941 to December 1942, accelerating the colonization of occupied areas. At the same time, to sustain their aggressive war against China and Southeast Asian countries, the Japanese military implemented a strategy of "economic warfare" in China. On one hand, they plundered various strategic materials and resources from China, and on

1943 年日伪组织献纳活动
The donation campaign organized by the
Japanese puppet regime in 1943

营。好在永利制碱公司在沦陷前即已将机器设备和技术人员等南迁，但其他大多数企业和重要资源，如煤、铁、盐、棉，即"二黑二白"等军需物资，还是被日军牢牢控制。①

为大肆掠夺中国的资源，日本在中国滥发纸币和战争债券，导致通货膨胀，据统计，1943 年中国物价是抗战前的 35 倍。不仅物价高涨，而且很多生活必需品难以买到。例如，粮食不仅是人民生活资料，还是重要的军用物资。日伪政权对市民实行"配给制"，没有日军的特别许可证就无法购买，一旦发现"走私"行为，性命难保。1942 年 12 月 25 日伪市公署宣布在市民"居住证"上附加"配卖证"，实行按户发票购买粮食。日伪政权把配给对象分为上、中、下三等。上等人是日军、日侨，中等人是伪政府的官吏，下等人则指天津平民百姓，根据不同等级定量定质分配售卖粮食。起初，天津普通市民的粮食配卖标准是：无论老少，每月一律配给面粉 0.5 千克、高粱 1.22 千克、玉米 1.22 千克、谷子 1.25 千克、绿豆 1.78 千克、黑豆 1.44

---

① 张利民、刘凤华，《抗战时期日本对天津的经济统制与掠夺》，社会科学文献出版社，2016 年，第 88 页。

the other hand, they established the "Holy War Fund Mobilization Association" in their controlled territories, coercing government agencies, organizations, businesses, all citizens, and even elementary school students and kindergartners to "donate copper, iron, money, and tin" to compensate for their shortage of military resources. From December 1941 to February 1944, the puppet authorities looted 1.25 million yuan in "donation funds" from the Tientsin Chamber of Commerce and Industrial Union, 1.3 million yuan from the monetary and hardware industry guilds, and 1 million yuan from the banking industry guilds; they also confiscated over 600,000 kilograms of copper, over 410,000 kilograms of iron, and 15,000 sheets of tin foil.[1] The puppet authorities also established various "control associations" to forcibly seize all important industrial raw materials and enterprises through military management. For example, the chemical industry was a pillar industry in modern Tianjin and held a leading position in North China and even the whole country. After the occupation, the Chiuta Refined Salt Company and Yungli Alkali Manufacturing Corporation were placed under military administration and later handed over to Japanese-owned enterprises for production, sales, and operation. Fortunately, the Yungli Alkali Manufacturing Corporation had already relocated its machinery, equipment, and technical personnel southward before the occupation, but most other enterprises and important resources, such as coal, iron, salt, and cotton, known as the "two blacks and two whites" military supplies, were still firmly controlled by the Japanese military.[2]

To plunder Chinese resources extensively, Japan flooded China with paper currency and war bonds, leading to inflation. According to statistics, by 1943, prices in China had increased 35 times compared to that before the war. Not only did prices soar, but many essential goods became difficult to obtain. For instance, grains were not only essential for people's livelihoods but also important military supplies. The puppet regime implemented a rationing system for citizens, requiring special permits from the Japanese military for purchases. Engaging in "smuggling" activities meant risking one's life. On December 25, 1942, the puppet municipal authority announced the addition of "rationing certificates" to citizens' "residential permits," implementing a household-based system for purchasing grains. The puppet regime classified ration recipients into three categories: upper, middle, and lower. The upper

---

[1] Li Shichu. *Tianjin Puppet Regime under the Japanese Control*. The Cultural and Historical Data Research Committee of the Tianjin Municipal Committee of the Chinese People's Political Consultative Conference (ed.). *Tianjin during Its Occupation*. Published internally in 1992, p.55-66.

[2] Zhang Limin, Liu Fenghua. *Japan's Economic Domination and Plunder of Tianjin during the War of Resistance Against Japan*. Social Science Academic Press, 2016, p.88.

千克。①农村则实行"计口授粮"，即将粮食全部收走，然后按壮年、幼年、老年或丧失劳动力三等配卖粮食。壮年每人每年售原粮 1 石 5 斗；幼年每人每年售原粮 1 石 3 斗；老年或丧失劳动力的每人每年售原粮 8 斗或 1 石。按照以上标准，基本上难以糊口。事实上，就连如此可怜的配给粮食，普通市民也根本买不到，只好到市场上购买高价粮食。在汉奸和奸商的控制下，粮店囤积居奇，每日只出售很少的粮食，多数市民都是在饥饿中度日。②

控制粮食的同时，日本人却大肆贩卖鸦片，攫取巨额利润，瓦解中国人的反抗意志。九一八事变前，日租界街道上，"白面庄和吗啡馆林立两旁，总数有 170 家之多"。七七事变后，"日本在中国占领区公布了鸦片法……根据这一法律，设置了政府统治的专卖机关，经过许可的专卖店可销售由官方配给的鸦片和麻醉品（吗啡、海洛因）。为了从麻醉品中增加收入，这些专卖机关成了奖励使用麻醉品的征税机关。在被日本占领的所有地区，从占领之时直到日本投降，鸦片的使用都在增加"③。

经济掠夺的同时，日军还以天津为据点，在附近的郊县农村抓捕劳工。据抗战胜利后国民党天津警察局的统计，从 1940 年至 1945 年 8 月，伪政府在天津骗招和强征的劳工有 73347 人之多。④而天津作为劳工掠夺和转运中心，从这里押运前往日本、东北和其他占领区的各地劳工，人数就更多了，仅 1942 年的前七个月，就多达 70 余万人。⑤劳工处于日军的严密看管之下，劳动和生活环境恶劣，很多人有去无回。

此外，日伪当局还通过强化"保甲制""自肃自励""勤劳俸仕"

① 天津市地方史志编修委员会编著，《中国天津通鉴》上卷，中国青年出版社，2005 年，第 276 页。

② 罗澍伟主编，《近代天津城市史》，中国社会科学出版社，1993 年，第 700 页。

③ 1948 年《远东国际军事法庭判决书》B 部第 5 章"日本对中国的侵略"。转引自郭登浩、周俊旗主编，《日本占领天津时期罪行实录》，社会科学文献出版社，2016 年，第 173 页。

④ 《天津市警察局呈报沦陷期间本市被征劳工人数及经济损失概算表》（1946 年 9 月 2 日），天津市档案馆藏，档案号：J2—2—1474，第 21—22 页。

⑤ 李秉新、徐俊元、石玉新主编，《侵华日军暴行总录》，河北人民出版社，1995 年，第 161 页。

class included the Japanese military and Japanese expatriates, the middle class comprised officials of the puppet government, and the lower class referred to ordinary Tianjin civilians. Different quantities and qualities of grains were distributed and sold based on these classifications. Initially, the ration standards for grains for ordinary Tianjin citizens were as follows: regardless of age, each person received 0.5 kilograms of flour, 1.22 kilograms of sorghum, 1.22 kilograms of corn, 1.25 kilograms of millet, 1.78 kilograms of mung beans, and 1.44 kilograms of black beans per month.[1] In rural areas, a "calculated allocation based on household size" system was implemented, where all grains were confiscated and then distributed based on age groups (adults, children, elderly, or those incapable of labor). Adults received 15 dou of grain per person per year, children received 13 dou per person per year, and the elderly or those incapable of labor received 8 dou or 1 dan per person per year. Even with such meager rationing standards, ordinary citizens could hardly make ends meet. In reality, most ordinary citizens couldn't even obtain the allotted grains and were forced to purchase expensive grains from the market. Under the control of traitors and profiteers, grain stores hoarded their stocks, selling only a small portion daily, leaving most citizens to endure hunger.[2]

While controlling grains, the Japanese aggressively sold opium, reaping huge profits and undermining the resistance of the Chinese people. Before the September 18 Incident, "Heroin shops and opium dens lined the streets of the Japanese concession, totaling as many as 170." After the Marco Polo Bridge Incident, "Japan promulgated the Opium Law in the occupied areas of China... According to this law, a government monopoly agency was established, and licensed monopoly stores were permitted to sell opium and narcotics (morphine, heroin) provided by the authorities. To increase revenue from narcotics, these monopoly agencies became tax authorities rewarding the use of narcotics. In all areas occupied by Japan, from the time of occupation until Japan's surrender, opium use increased"[3].

While engaging in economic plunder, the Japanese military used Tianjin as a base to capture laborers from nearby rural counties. According to statistics from the Tianjin Police Bureau after the victory of the Anti-Japanese War, from 1940 to August 1945, the puppet government deceived and forci-

① Editorial Office of the Tianjin Chorography and History Compilation Committee (ed.). *The General History of China: Tianjin*. Vol.1. China Youth Publishing Group, 2005, p.276.

② Luo Shuwei. *Modern History of Tianjin*. China Social Sciences Press, 1993, p.700.

③ The Chapter 5 of Part B of the 1948 *Judgment of the International Military Tribunal for the Far East*: Japan's Aggression against China. Quoted in Guo Denghao, Zhou Junqi (eds.). *Record of Crimes during Japan's Occupation of Tianjin*. Social Sciences Academic Press (China), 2016, p.173.

等各种名目以及强力推行殖民奴化教育，严格控制市民的思想和行为。尤其在思想教育方面，日本人深谙"欲灭其族，必先灭其文化"。他们强令各级各类学校的教育全部纳入"大东亚圣战"的轨道之中，规定"全市各级学校一律增设日语课程"，并成立了"日语专科学校"，胁迫教师学生和公务员学习日语。此外，还规定各学校每天都要举行"朝会"，校长必须宣讲"圣战思想"10分钟。通过规定"青年必读书目""各科研究书目"等，对青少年进行洗脑教育，灌输"亲日""反共"思想。[①] 对于不服从者，轻者关押刑罚，重者秘密枪决。天津沦陷后，爱国教育家、曾任北洋大学校长并担任过反对法国强占老西开的"维持国权国土会"副会长、时任耀华学校校长赵天麟，因收留被日军炸毁校园的南开大学师生、拒绝换用日方用来进行奴化教育的教材并支持学校师生的爱国举动，遭到日本人仇恨，于1938年6月27日清晨被暗杀于上班途中。

日本统治天津的八年时间里，日本情报机关极力利用青帮这种黑社会性质的民间秘密团体，为日方打探情报、伪造"民意"、贩卖华工、制毒贩毒。早在1915年，大特务土肥原贤二被派到中国，潜伏渗透、搜集情报，并于1921年加入青帮。卢沟桥事变前夕，日本黑社会组织黑龙会成员奉土肥原命令来津，将青帮各个帮口头目组织起来，在日租界内成立以青帮组织为基础的"普安协会"，在日方煽动"华北自治"时制造舆论，参与"便衣队"暴乱，为日本侵吞华北的阴谋效力。1939年汪精卫建立伪政权、倡导"和平"时，一众天津青帮头目也都加以响应。[②] 天津被占领后，日本侵略者重用青帮头目袁文会搜集情报，袁本人向日本宪兵队、茂川特务机关、驻津总领事馆、日本守备队和日本海军武官府等不同部门的情报机构提供情报。他也在日本人的庇护下经营赌场妓院，拐卖人口，贩

bly recruited 73,347 laborers in Tianjin.[①] As a hub for labor exploitation and transportation, Tianjin dispatched over 700,000 laborers to Japan, Northeast China, and other occupied areas during the first seven months of 1942.[②] These laborers were tightly supervised by the Japanese military, subjected to harsh working and living conditions, and many never returned.

Additionally, the puppet authorities strengthened various measures such as the "Baojia system," "self-restraint and self-improvement," and "work hard to make salary," as well as forcefully promoting colonial indoctrination education, tightly controlling the thoughts and behaviors of the citizens. Especially in terms of ideological education, the Japanese understood well that "to destroy a nation, one must first destroy its culture." They forcibly incorporated all levels and types of education into the orbit of the "Greater East Asia Holy War," requiring "the addition of Japanese language courses in all schools in the city" and establishing "Japanese language specialized schools," coercing teachers, students, and civil servants to learn Japanese. Additionally, they mandated that every school hold a "morning assembly" daily, during which the principal must preach "holy war ideology" for 10 minutes. Through prescribing "required reading for youth" and "research reading lists for various subjects," they brainwashed young people, instilling pro-Japanese and anti-communist ideologies.[③] For those who disobeyed, lighter punishments included imprisonment, while more severe cases resulted in secret executions. After the fall of Tianjin, Zhao Tianlin, a patriotic educator who had served as president of Peiyang University and vice president of the "National Territorial Rights Preservation Association" opposing French occupation of the Laoxikai, and was the current principal of Yaohua School, was hated by the Japanese for sheltering teachers and students from Nankai University whose campus had been bombed by the Japanese, refusing to use textbooks provided by the Japanese for indoctrination education, and supporting patriotic actions of the school's faculty and students. He was assassinated on the morning of June 27, 1938, on his way to work.

During the eight years of Japanese rule in Tianjin, Japanese intelligence

---

① 黎始初，《日军控制下的天津伪政权》。中国人民政治协商会议天津市委员会文史资料研究委员会编，《沦陷时期的天津》，内部发行，1992年，第55—66页。

② 胡君素、李树棻，《日军对天津青帮的控制和利用》。中国人民政治协商会议天津市委员会文史资料研究委员会编，《沦陷时期的天津》，内部发行，1992年，第176—179页。

---

① *General Estimate on the Number of Conscripted Laborers and Economic Losses of Tianjin during Its Occupation Submitted by the Tianjin Police Bureau* (September 2, 1946). In the collection of Tianjin Municipal Archives. File number J2-2-1474, pp.21-22.

② Li Bingxin, Xu Junyuan, and Shi Yuxin (eds). *General Collection of the Atrocities of the Japanese Invaders in China*. Hebei People's Publishing House, 1995, p.161

③ Li Shichu. *Tianjin Puppet Regime under the Japanese Control*. The Cultural and Historical Data Research Committee of the Tianjin Municipal Committee of the Chinese People's Political Consultative Conference (ed.). *Tianjin during Its Occupation*. Published internally in 1992, p.55-66.

卖毒品，无恶不作，大发横财。[1]美国财政代表尼科尔森（Nicholson）在1938年12月16日给美国麻醉药品局的报告中说："日本人方面，始终要求保证与黑社会势力的长期合作。他们相信，这是保证控制上海外国人地区的最好方法，因为一旦他们得以调动这些黑社会力量，他们就能制造动乱，骚扰警方，逮捕抗日分子和中国政府的代表，攻击中国政府的银行、法庭与反日的报纸，以及破坏中国货币的稳定。……而日本人保障黑社会分子与其合作的唯一武器，便是鸦片和赌博业。"[2]事实上，不仅在上海如此，日本特务机关对与其情况相似的天津同样采取了这种策略和手段，并且有过之无不及。

战争带来的问题只有用战争来解决

中国人民的抗日战争是世界反法西斯战争的一部分，随着日军在太平洋战场上的节节溃败和德国宣布无条件投降，中国的抗战也迎来了最后的胜利。1945年7月7日，国民政府军事委员会宣布中国战区进入反攻阶段。8月9日中国共产党由毛泽东发表《对日寇最后一战》，号召"八路军、新四军及其他人民军队，应在一切可能条件下，对于一切不愿意投降的侵略者及其走狗实行广泛的进攻"。接着，朱德又于10日接连发出了七道反攻作战命令。与此同时，国际上，中、美、英三国于7月26日发表《波茨坦公告》，敦促日本无条件投降。8月6日，为了避免大量伤亡的登陆战以及抢先苏联一步拿下日本本土，美军在广岛投下第一枚原子弹，3天后又在长崎投下第二枚原子弹。8月9日苏联百万大军越过中苏、中蒙边境，向远东的日本关东军发起进攻。

1945年8月14日，日本政府照会美、英、苏、中四国政府，表示接受《波茨坦公告》，向盟军投降。15日，日本裕仁天皇发布诏书，向全世界宣布无条件投降。9月2日，日本代表在美国密苏里战舰上

agencies vigorously utilized the Qing Gang, a clandestine civilian organization with a mafia-like nature, to gather intelligence for the Japanese, fabricate "public opinion," traffic in Chinese laborers, and engage in drug production and trafficking. As early as 1915, the chief spy, Doihara Kenji, was dispatched to China to infiltrate and gather intelligence, joining the Qing Gang in 1921. On the eve of the Marco Polo Bridge Incident, members of the Japanese criminal organization, the Black Dragon Society, acting on Doihara's orders, came to Tianjin to organize leaders of various Qing Gang factions and establish the "Pu'an Association" based on the Qing Gang in the Japanese concession, stirring up public opinion when Japan incited "autonomy in North China," participating in riots by "plainclothes squads," and aiding Japan's conspiracy to annex North China. In 1939, when Wang Jingwei established the puppet regime and advocated for "peace," many Tianjin Qing Gang leaders responded positively.[1] After Tianjin was occupied, the Japanese aggressors employed Qing Gang leader Yuan Wenhui to gather intelligence. Yuan himself provided intelligence to various Japanese intelligence agencies, including the military police, the Shigekawa Secret Service Agency, the Japanese consulate general in Tianjin, the Japanese garrison, and the Japanese naval attaché office. Under Japanese protection, he operated casinos and brothels, engaged in human trafficking, and drugs trafficking, committing various atrocities to amass wealth.[2] In a report to the United States Narcotics Bureau on December 16, 1938, M. R. Nicholson, U.S. Treasury Agent, stated: "On the part of the Japanese, they have been wanting to secure the cooperation of the underworld influences for a long time. They believe this is the best way to secure control of the foreign areas (of Shanghai), for once they can secure these underworld forces, they will be able to create disturbances, to harass the police, to arrest anti-Japanese elements and Chinese government agents, attack Chinese government banks, law courts, and anti-Japanese newspapers, and damage the stability of the Chinese currency... The only weapons left for the Japanese to secure the cooperation of these gangsters are opium and gambling business."[3] In fact, not only in Shanghai,

---

① 刘静山，《依附日本势力的汉奸恶霸袁文会》。中国人民政治协商会议天津市委员会文史资料研究委员会编，《沦陷时期的天津》，内部发行，1992年，第180—184页。

② 转引自（美）魏斐德著，芮传明译，《上海歹土——战时恐怖活动与城市犯罪，1937—1941》，上海古籍出版社，2003年，第5页。

---

① Hu Junsu, Li Shufen. *The Japanese Army's Control and Utilization of the Tianjin Qing Gang*. The Cultural and Historical Data Research Committee of the Tianjin Municipal Committee of the Chinese People's Political Consultative Conference (ed.). *Tianjin during Its Occupation*. Published internally in 1992, pp.176-179.

② Liu Jingshan. *Yuan Wenhui, A Traitor and Bully Who Surrendered to Japanese Forces*. The Cultural and Historical Data Research Committee of the Tianjin Municipal Committee of the Chinese People's Political Consultative Conference (ed.). *Tianjin during Its Occupation*. Published internally in 1992, pp.180-184.

③ Quoted in Frederic Wakeman. *The Shanghai Badlands—Wartime Terrorism and Urban Crime, 1937-1941*, translated by Rui Chuanming. Shanghai Ancient Books Publishing House, 2003, p.5.

正式签署了停战投降书。至此，第二次世界大战以日本战败投降而宣告结束，中国人民英勇顽强、不屈不挠长达14年的抗日战争也宣告取得胜利。

天津作为中国北方最大的城市，作为日本盘踞经营长达45年的军事基地，由谁来接受日军投降是一件重大且慎重的事。中国共产党领导的抗日武装力量长期在北方进行敌后抗战，大反攻后八路军将原本分散的抗日根据地一一连通，并控制了大量铁路干线，为接收北京和天津等大城市创造了条件。8月23日，八路军收复张家口。为了不让大城市落入中国共产党军队的手中，国民党方面请求美国帮助，动用美国空军和海军的力量，迅速占领各大城市，接受日本投降。蒋介石与美国政府商议，决定授权由美军驻冲绳的海军陆战队第三师前往天津接受日军投降。于是，9月，美国海军陆战队一万多人，在天津的塘沽港登陆，前往天津、秦皇岛等地驻扎，随后在天津接受了日军的投降。

1945年10月6日上午9时，天津日军受降仪式在美国海军陆战队第三军团司令部（原法租界工部局、天津数字艺术博物馆）门前广场举行。国民政府受降代表施奎龄、天津市市长张廷谔、副市长杜建时参加了受降仪式。仪式开始后，日本天津驻屯军司令官内田银之助及另外6名日本军官依次将各自佩刀放到签字桌上，然后美军骆基少将（Major General Keller Rockey）和日军内田银之助分别在投降备忘录上签了字。之后，内田等人被美军送往关押地点。天津被日军占领八年的历史终于结束。

租界的割据是列强侵略战争的产物，天津租界的收回也与战争紧密相关。第一次世界大战中，中国加入协约国一方，向奥匈帝国和德国宣战。战后，中国作为战胜国收回了这两个国家在天津的租界。俄国十月革命取得胜利后，苏维埃政权声明放弃沙俄在华取得的一切特权。（由于美、英、法等国施加压力，直至1924年8月天津地方当局才正式接管俄租界。）1931年，比利时政府将在津租界交还给当时的国民政府。第二次世界大战中，日本偷袭珍珠港后第二天，中国政府向德国、意大利、日本三国宣战，宣布收回日租界和意租界。1942年1月1日，由中国领衔，美国、英国、苏联等24个国家在美

but Japanese intelligence agencies adopted similar strategies and methods in Tianjin, and even exceeded them.

The Problems Brought by War Can Only Be Solved by War

The Chinese people's War of Resistance Against Japan was part of the global anti-fascist war. As the Japanese suffered successive defeats on the Pacific front and Germany declared unconditional surrender, China's resistance war also ushered in its final victory. On July 7, 1945, the Military Affairs Commission of the National Government announced that the Chinese theater of war had entered the counteroffensive phase. On August 9, the Communist Party of China, represented by Mao Zedong, issued *The Last Round with the Japanese Invaders*, calling on the Eighth Route Army, the New Fourth Army, and other people's army units to "launch extensive attacks against all aggressors and their lackeys who are unwilling to surrender under all possible conditions." Subsequently, Zhu De issued seven consecutive counteroffensive orders on the 10th. Meanwhile, internationally, on July 26, China, the United States, and Britain issued the *Potsdam Declaration*, urging Japan to surrender unconditionally. On August 6, in order to avoid massive casualties in a land invasion and to preempt the Soviet Union in taking control of Japan's mainland, the U.S. military dropped the first atomic bomb on Hiroshima, followed by the second atomic bomb on Nagasaki three days later. On August 9, the Soviet Union's million-strong army crossed the Sino-Soviet and Sino-Mongolian borders, launching an attack on the Japanese Kwantung Army in the Far East.

On August 14, 1945, the Japanese government notified the governments of the United States, Britain, the Soviet Union, and China that it accepted the *Potsdam Declaration* and surrendered to the Allies. On the 15th, Emperor Hirohito of Japan issued a proclamation to the world announcing an unconditional surrender. On September 2, Japanese representatives officially signed the surrender documents aboard the USS Missouri in the United States. With this, the Second World War was declared over with Japan's defeat and surrender, marking the end of the valiant and relentless 14-year-long resistance of the Chinese people in the War of Resistance Against Japan.

As the largest city in northern China and a military base occupied and operated by Japan for 45 years, deciding who would accept the surrender of the Japanese military in Tianjin was a significant and cautious matter. The armed forces led by the Communist Party of China had been engaged in anti-Japanese resistance in the northern regions for a long time, and after the major counter-offensive, the Eighth Route Army connected the previously scattered anti-Japanese base areas one by one and controlled a large number of railway

天津日军受降仪式现场。摄于 1945 年 10 月 6 日
The Japanese surrender ceremony in Tianjin. Taken on October 6, 1945

天津人民早早来到现场围观庆祝胜利。摄于 1945 年 10 月 6 日
The people of Tianjin arrived early to watch and celebrate the victory.
Taken on October 6, 1945

mainlines, creating conditions for the takeover of major cities like Beijing and Tianjin. On August 23, the Eighth Route Army recaptured Zhangjiakou. In order to prevent major cities from falling into the hands of the Communist Party of China's forces, the Nationalist government requested assistance from the United States and mobilized the U.S. Air Force and Navy to quickly occupy major cities and accept the surrender of Japan. Chiang Kai-shek negotiated with the U.S. government and decided to authorize the Third Marine Division of the U.S. Marines stationed in Okinawa to go to Tianjin to accept the surrender of the Japanese military. Therefore, in September, over ten thousand U.S. Marines landed at the Tanggu Port in Tianjin and proceeded to stations in Tianjin, Qinhuangdao, and other places. Subsequently, they accepted the surrender of the Japanese military in Tianjin.

On the morning of October 6, 1945, at 9 o'clock, the surrender ceremony of the Tianjin Japanese troops was held at the square in front of the headquarters of the Third Marine Division of the United States Marine Corps (formerly the French Municipal Council, now Tianjin Digital Art Museum). Representatives of the Nationalist government, Shi Kuiling, Tianjin Mayor Zhang Ting'e, and Deputy Mayor Du Jianshi, attended the surrender ceremony. During the ceremony, Japanese Commander of the Tianjin Garrison, Ginnosuke Uchida, and six other Japanese officers each placed their swords on the signing table in turn. Then, Major General Keller Rockey of the U.S. military and Japanese Commander Uchida signed the surrender memorandum respectively. Afterwards, Uchida and others were taken by the U.S. military to the detention location. The eight-year history of Tianjin's occupation by the Japanese finally came to an end.

The concession system was a product of the aggression of the great powers, and the reclamation of the Tianjin concessions was closely related to the war. During World War I, China joined the Allied Forces and declared war on Austria-Hungary and Germany. After the war, China, as one of the victorious countries, reclaimed the concessions held by these two countries in Tianjin. After the success of the Russian October Revolution, the Soviet government declared the abandonment of all privileges obtained by Tsarist Russia in China. (Due to pressure from countries like the United States, Britain, and France, it was not until August 1924 that the Tianjin local authorities formally took over the Russian concession.) In 1931, the Belgian government returned the concession in Tianjin to the then Nationalist government. During the Second World War, the day after Japan's attack on Pearl Harbor, the Chinese government declared war on Germany, Italy, and Japan, announcing the reclamation of the Japanese and Italian concessions. On January 1, 1942, led by China, 24 countries including the United States, Britain, and the Soviet Union signed the

国华盛顿签订了《联合国家宣言》，标志着世界反法西斯同盟的最后形成。反法西斯同盟对抗德国、日本和意大利的轴心国，不仅是为了自卫，也是为了各国的人权、尊严，以及政治、经济和社会制度中的平等。因此，战争中当中国政府提出立即废弃不平等条约特权时，美国政府同意放弃在华特权，英国同意将英租界交还给中国，法国维希政府则将法租界交还给天津伪政府。1945 年 8 月日本投降后，天津地方政府得以实际收回日、意、英、法四国租界。至此，天津的所有租界全部正式收回。中国人民在抗日战争中浴血奋战，付出了巨大的代价，但也赢得了全世界爱好和平人们的尊重。

中国近代史上，从鸦片战争开始直到抗日战争之前的历次战争，几乎都以签订"割地赔款"为主要内容的不平等条约结束。八国租界是近代天津的独特现象，是近代中国屈辱的直接体现。"一个国家如被迫将其领土一些部分租给他国，或给予他国任何形式的治外法权，那么该国的'领土完整'即令未被破坏也受到了限制。"① 租界设置不久，中国人就为收回租界进行了不屈不挠的斗争。随着中国民族主义的觉醒，中国历届政府（包括北洋政府和国民政府）都在为收回租界而与租借国展开谈判，经历了废除不平等条约及提升国际地位的艰难历程。北洋政府提出"修约外交"，国民政府倡导"革命外交"，直至中国人民取得民族解放战争的胜利之后，才彻底废除了所有不平等条约。因此，总结中国废除不平等条约之经验，那就是：由战争带来的问题只有用战争去解决。

United Nations Declaration in Washington, D.C., marking the final formation of the World Anti-Fascist Alliance. The anti-fascist alliance against the Axis powers of Germany, Japan, and Italy was not only for self-defense but also for the rights, dignity, and equality in the political, economic, and social systems of all countries. Therefore, during the war, when the Chinese government proposed the immediate abolition of unequal treaty privileges, the US government agreed to relinquish its privileges in China, Britain agreed to return the British concession to China, and the Vichy government in France agreed to return the French concession to the puppet government in Tianjin. After Japan surrendered in August 1945, the Tianjin local government was able to effectively reclaim the concessions of Japan, Italy, Britain, and France. With this, all concessions in Tianjin were officially reclaimed. The Chinese people fought bravely in the War of Resistance Against Japan, paying a huge price, but also earning the respect of peace-loving people around the world.

In modern Chinese history, from the Opium War to the period just before the War of Resistance Against Japan, almost all wars ended with unequal treaties focusing on "territorial cession and indemnity" as their main contents. The presence of the Eight-Nation Concessions was a unique phenomenon in modern Tianjin and a direct manifestation of China's humiliation. "If a country is forced to lease parts of its territory to other countries or grant extraterritorial rights to other countries, then the 'territorial integrity' of that country, even if not destroyed, is still restricted."① Shortly after the concessions were established, Chinese people began an unwavering struggle to reclaim them. With the awakening of Chinese nationalism, successive Chinese governments (including the Beiyang government and the Nationalist government) negotiated with the concession powers to reclaim the concessions, undergoing the arduous process of abolishing unequal treaties and elevating international status. The Beiyang government proposed "diplomatic negotiation," and the Nationalist government advocated "revolutionary diplomacy," until the Chinese people achieved victory in the War of Liberation, finally all unequal treaties were abolished. Therefore, summarizing the experience of China's abolition of unequal treaties, it can be concluded that: the problems caused by war can only be resolved through war.

---

① （美）威罗贝著，王绍坊译，《外人在华特权和利益》，生活·读书·新知三联书店，1957 年，第 33 页。

① Westel W. Willoughby. *Foreign Rights and Interests in China*, translated by Wang Shaofang. SDX Joint Publishing Company, 1957, p.33.

天津五大道。刘悦摄于 2005 年
Panoramic view of the Five Great Avenues
area. Taken by Liu Yue in 2005

第 八 章　中西合璧的近代天津城市文化

Chapter Eight: The Modern Tianjin Urban Culture with a Fusion of Chinese and Western Elements

近代天津人的日常生活

当一个地方用一道长长的四方城墙将自己包围起来与其他地方隔离，它就逐渐成为一个封闭的系统，进而由于内部频繁的互动交往而衍生出自己独特的地域文化。近代天津城市的发展兴盛于开埠后中西文化的碰撞与交流，它的居民来自国内各个省份和世界各个地方，它的围墙在20世纪初被大炮轰开并被彻底拆毁，因此中西合璧、兼容并蓄就成为近代以来天津城市文化最明显的特征。

在天津城市发展的漫长历史中，相比于政治局势的风云变幻、革命的激情澎湃和战争的巨大破坏力，城市居民的日常活动似涓涓细流般悄无声息，但唯有它才是塑造一个城市文化基因并代代相传的根本元素。

"当当吃海货，不算不会过"

历史学家布罗代尔（Fernand Braudel）说："食物是每个人社会地位的标志，也是他周围的文明或文化的标志。"[①] 天津居民饮食习惯和特征具有明显的地域性。从食材来说，一方水土养一方人，天津地处九河下梢、渤海之滨，物产丰富，特产质优量大的河海两鲜和飞禽野味等。食材新鲜是制作美食的首要条件。坐在桌旁就餐的居民，看着在自己家门口河中成百上千渔船上的渔民，从河里捞起满网活蹦乱跳的鱼虾，被家里大师傅简单烹制后端上餐桌，这种美

① （法）费尔南·布罗代尔著，顾良等译，《十五至十八世纪的物质文明、经济与资本主义》第一卷，生活·读书·新知三联书店，2002年，第118页。

The Daily Life of Modern Tianjin Residents

When a place isolates itself from others by surrounding itself with a long, square-shaped wall, it gradually becomes a closed system, and because of frequent internal interaction and communication, it develops its own unique regional culture. The development and prosperity of modern Tianjin city were catalyzed by the collision and exchange of Chinese and Western cultures after the opening of the port. Its residents come from various provinces within China and from all around the world. The city wall was breached by artillery in the early 20th century and completely demolished, hence the blending of Chinese and Western cultures has become the most prominent feature of Tianjin's urban culture since modern times.

In the long history of Tianjin's urban development, compared to the turbulent political situation, the passionate revolution, and the immense destructive power of war, the daily activities of urban residents flow quietly like a trickle. However, it is precisely these activities that shape the fundamental elements of a city's cultural genes and are passed down from generation to generation.

"When You Pawn Your Stuff in Order to Eat Seafood, No One Will Think You Unable to Make Ends Meet"

Historian Fernand Braudel once said, "Food is a symbol of everyone's social status and also a symbol of the civilization or culture around him."[①] The dietary habits and characteristics of Tianjin residents have obvious regional features. In terms of ingredients, the land nourishes its people, and Tianjin, located at the confluence of nine rivers and the Bohai Bay, boasts abundant natural resources, including freshwater and marine products, as

① Fernand Braudel. *Civilisation Materielle, Economie et Capitalisme: XVe-XVIIIe Siècle* (vol.1), translated by Gu Liang, et al. SDX Joint Publishing Company, 2002, p.118.

味是天津人以及所有河湖边上居民的最爱。① 天津还有句俗话说"当当吃海货，不算不会过"，形象地说明了天津人重视"吃"，特别是爱吃海产品的程度——为了吃新鲜海货，不惜把家当送入当铺换钱；当然，从另一方面也证明了当时海货丰富、价格平实，大部分人都吃得起海货。20世纪20年代，熟对虾一块大洋60对，半斤左右的大海蟹四五只一个铜板，麻蛤、皮皮虾等在过去是上不了席面的。除了河海两鲜，天津人还喜欢各种飞禽，如野鸭、大雁、铁雀等野味② 和鸡、鸭、鹅、鸽等家禽。银鱼、紫蟹和铁雀，号称天津的冬令"三珍"。天津人的饮食习惯还讲究"应时到节"，即到什么时令、气候、节气和节日就吃什么食物。在天津，按时令来说，春天吃海里的黄花鱼、鲙鱼，夏天吃鳎目鱼，秋天吃河里的鲤鱼，冬天吃银鱼。农历七月吃河蟹，要吃母蟹，满黄特肥；八月吃公蟹，蟹膏肥腻。不同的季节吃不同的东西，这也符合没有现代仓储条件的农耕渔猎时代的食物生产和供应特点。

"民以食为天"，中国传统餐饮文化历史悠久，菜肴在烹饪做法上有许多流派。在清代逐渐形成鲁、川、粤、苏四大菜系，后来更细分为八大菜系、十二大菜系等。但是，其中从来都没有"天津菜"的一席之地。这是为什么呢？天津和上海从人口上来讲，都属于五方杂处的移民城市，市民中各个阶层各个地域的都有，既有北京来的遗老遗少，又有山南海北的军阀富商，还有留学归来的新派知识分子。虽然底层民众只能勉强果腹，但上层社会则继承了"食不厌精，脍不厌细"的中国传统，形成了以"宫、商、馆、门、家"著称的天津菜系门类，即由宫廷菜、商埠菜、公馆菜、宅门菜和家庭菜构成，每个公馆宅门的厨师都有自己的拿手菜。而面向公众的饭店，则有口味之分，大致分为天津馆、羊肉馆、北京馆、扬州馆、宁波馆、川菜馆、山东馆、山西馆、广东馆及西餐馆等数种。③ 可以说，人们

① 张畅、刘悦，《李鸿章的洋顾问：德璀琳与汉纳根》，台北传记文学出版社，2012年，第375页。（法）费尔南·布罗代尔著，顾良等译，《十五至十八世纪的物质文明、经济与资本主义》第二卷，生活·读书·新知三联书店，2002年，第18页。

② 笔者年少时常听家中长辈谈及野味的鲜美，尤爱食铁雀。后来野味都被列为国家野生保护动物，不再捕猎，这是文明的进步。

③ 张仲编著，《天津早年的衣食住行》，天津古籍出版社，2004年，第74页。

well as wild game. Fresh ingredients are the primary requirement for making delicious food. Residents dined at the table, watching fishermen from their own doorsteps haul in fish and shrimp by the hundreds or thousands of boats from the river, cooked simply by the master chefs at home and served on the table, and this delicacy is loved by Tianjin locals and all residents living by rivers and lakes.[1] There is a saying in Tianjin, "When you pawn your stuff in order to eat seafood, no one will think you unable to make ends meet." This vividly illustrates the extent to which Tianjin people value "eating," especially their love for seafood. To eat fresh seafood, some are willing to pawn their belongings for money. Of course, from another perspective, it also proves that seafood was abundant and affordable at that time, and most people could afford it. In the 1920s, 60 pairs of prawns cost 1 silver dollar, and four or five large crabs weighing around half a pound cost only a copper coin. Clams, mantis shrimps, and other seafood were hardly considered luxuries in the past. In addition to freshwater and marine delicacies, Tianjin residents also enjoy various wild birds such as wild ducks, wild geese, and sparrows[2], as well as domestic poultry like chickens, ducks, geese, and pigeons. Whitebait, purple crabs, and sparrows are known as the "Three Treasures" of Tianjin in winter. Tianjin people's dietary habits also emphasize eating according to the season and occasion, meaning they eat foods that match the season, climate, solar terms, and festivals. In Tianjin, for example, in spring, people eat yellow croaker and Chinese herring from the sea; in summer, they eat sole fish; in autumn, they eat carp from the river; and in winter, they eat whitebait. In the seventh lunar month, people eat river crabs, preferring female crabs that are full of roe; in the eighth month, they eat male crabs, which are rich and oily. Eating different foods in different seasons also aligns with the food production and supply characteristics of the agricultural and hunting eras when modern warehousing conditions were not available.

"The people regard food as paramount." China's traditional culinary culture has a long history, with various schools of cooking techniques for dishes. During the Qing Dynasty, four major culinary styles emerged gradually: Shandong, Sichuan, Guangdong, and Jiangsu. Later, they were further divided into eight major styles, twelve major styles, and so on.

[1] Zhang Chang, Liu Yue. *Li Hongzhang's Foreign Consultants: Gustav Detring and Constantin von Hanneken*. Taipei: Biographies Publishing House, 2012, p.375. Fernand Braudel. *Civilisation Materielle, Economie et Capitalisme: XVe-XVIIIe Siècle* (vol.2), translated by Gu Liang, et al. SDX Joint Publishing Company, 2002, p.18.

[2] When the author was a teenager, she often heard her elders speak of the deliciousness of wild game, particularly the sparrows. Later, wild game was classified as a nationally protected species and was no longer hunted. This marked progress in civilization.

无需出远门就可以在津城吃到最地道的各色菜系，这就是天津饮食的特点，八大菜系里没有"津菜"也就不足为奇了。

近代天津人也喜食西餐。天津是近代文明传入中国北方的窗口，受欧风美雨的侵袭最久，是西餐、洋酒、西点最早进入中国北方的基地。当时中国人称西餐叫"番菜""大餐"或"大菜"。开埠之初，天津的西餐店基本上是由外国人在租界里开设的旅馆经营，如利顺德、起士林、帝国饭店等，供应初来天津的外国人或者年轻单身汉们食宿，此外还出现一些西点店、日料店。随着城市人口的激增，为了快速便捷地提供日常食物供应，租界区内还出现了现代化的菜市场。20世纪初，天津就已有了英租界、法租界及华界的三处菜市场，它们不仅建筑规模宏大、设备完善，而且有非常详细的卫生管理章程。租界当局甚至还在原德租界、靠近租界地中心的一处地方设置了新式屠宰场，耗资五万元。所有牲畜围栏、屠宰房、冷藏间，都是在外国专家的监督下建成，冷藏设备也是专门从国外订购的。运进这里的牲畜和运出的肉都要进行医学检验。[①]菜市场和屠宰场供应的肉类品质丰富，包括：鸡、鸭、鹅、野鸡、小野鸟、洋鸡、鸽子等禽类，兔、牛、猪、羊、野羊等肉类，鸡蛋、鸭蛋、鸽蛋等蛋类；从平均日消费量来看，禽类1950只，肉类531头（只），蛋类20500只。[②]当时的各种水果也价廉物美，葡萄、香蕉、橘子、梨、苹果应有尽有，而且南边产的香蕉每斤只要4分钱，每捆只卖10分钱。[③]

来自本地的供应之外，开埠之后，天津还从欧洲大量进口食品饮料。在海关免税物品清单中，食品位列榜首，其种类纷繁复杂，包括：鱼、肉、禽、各种野味罐头、鱼子酱、香肠、面饼、葡萄干、蛋糕、夹心糖、咖啡、可可、黄油、牛奶酥等，各种新鲜的蔬菜、水果、蜜饯、咸菜等，光是面粉就有粗磨粉（包括粟米粉及燕麦粉）和砂谷粉（葛粉、玉米粉等），还有酸辣酱、各种香料、调味汁、

① （英）雷穆森著，许逸凡等译，《天津租界史（插图本）》，天津人民出版社，2009年，第336页。

② 天津市地方史志编修委员会总编辑室编，《二十世纪初的天津概况》，内部发行，1986年，第354页。

③ （比）约翰·麦特勒等著，刘悦等译，《比利时—中国：昔日之路（1870—1930）》，社会科学文献出版社，2021年，第200页。

However, there has never been a place for "Tianjin cuisine" among them. Why is that? Tianjin and Shanghai, in terms of population, are both immigrant cities where people come from various regions and social classes. There are survivals of bygone ages from Beijing, warlords and wealthy merchants from all over the country, and new intellectuals returning from studying abroad. Although the lower class can barely make ends meet, the upper class inherited the traditional Chinese ethos of "the finer the grain, or the more finely chopped, the better the dishes are," forming the renowned Tianjin cuisine categories known as "Palace, Merchant, Mansion, Gate, and Home," with each mansion and household having its own specialty dishes. As for restaurants catering to the public, there are distinctions in taste, roughly categorized into Tianjin-style restaurants, lamb restaurants, Beijing-style restaurants, Yangzhou-style restaurants, Ningbo-style restaurants, Sichuan-style restaurants, Shandong-style restaurants, Shanxi-style restaurants, Guangdong-style restaurants, and Western-style restaurants, among others.[①] It can be said that one does not need to travel far to taste the most authentic dishes of various styles in Tianjin, which is the characteristic of Tianjin's cuisine. So, it's not surprising that there's no "Tianjin cuisine" among the eight major culinary styles.

In modern times, Tianjin residents also enjoyed Western cuisine. Tianjin served as the gateway for modern civilization to enter northern China, enduring the longest influence of European culture and the earliest introduction of Western cuisine, wine, and pastries to northern China. At that time, Chinese people referred to Western cuisine as "Fan Cai", "Da Can", or "Da Cai." At the beginning of the port opening, most of the Western restaurants in Tianjin were operated by foreigners in the concessions, such as Astor House Hotel, Kiessling & Bader, and Imperial Hotel, providing accommodation and food for foreigners or young bachelors. Additionally, there were also some pastry shops and Japanese restaurants. With the rapid increase in urban population, to provide daily food supplies quickly and conveniently, modernized markets emerged within the concessions. In the early 20th century, Tianjin already had three markets: the British Concession Market, the French Concession Market, and the Chinese Market. These markets were not only large in scale and well-equipped but also had very detailed sanitation regulations. The concession authorities even established a new-style slaughterhouse in the original German concession, near the center of the concession area, at a cost of fifty thousand yuan. All livestock pens,

① *The Clothing, Food, Shelter, and Transportation in the Early Days of Tianjin*, compiled by Zhang Zhong. Tianjin Ancient Books Publishing House, 2004, p.74.

威尔逊路上的起士林饭店。摄于 20 世纪三四十年代
Kiessling & Bader on Woodrow Wilson Street. Taken in the 1930s and 1940s

迁址后的今日起士林。安红摄于 2024 年
Today's Kiessling, after its relocation. Taken by An Hong in 2024

展示在起士林橱窗内的俄国宫殿式
蛋糕。摄于 20 世纪二三十年代
Russian palace-style cake displayed in
the Kiessling showcase. Taken in the
1920s and 1930s

位于威尔逊路上的起士林饭店虽然只有一层，但内部规模较大。不仅居住在天津、北京、上海的欧美人常到起士林用餐、聚会，天津本地各界人士也喜欢起士林的各种糕点美食。著名作家张爱玲对起士林的面包有过这样一段描述："在上海我们家隔壁就是战时天津新搬来的起士林咖啡馆，每天黎明制面包，拉起嗅觉的警报，一股喷香的浩然之气破空而来。"

The one-story Kiessling & Bader on Woodrow Wilson Street had a spacious interior. Not only did Europeans and Americans living in Tianjin, Beijing, and Shanghai frequently dine and gather at Kiessling, but local residents from all walks of life in Tianjin also enjoyed its various pastries and delicacies. The famous writer Eileen Chang once described Kiessling's bread as follows: "Next to our house in Shanghai was the Kiessling Cafe, which had just moved in from Tianjin during the war. Every day at dawn, they made bread, which triggered the olfactory alarm and a fragrant aroma broke through the air."

法国大菜市
French market

日本菜市
Japanese market

西北角菜市
The market at the northwest corner of the old Chinese City

slaughterhouses, and cold storage rooms were built under the supervision of foreign experts, and the refrigeration equipment was specially ordered from abroad. Medical examination will be made of all cattle coming in and all meats sent out.[1] The quality of meat supplied by the markets and slaughterhouses was abundant, including poultry such as chickens, ducks, geese, wild chickens, small wild birds, foreign chickens, and pigeons; meats such as rabbit, beef, pork, lamb, and wild goat; and eggs such as chicken eggs, duck eggs, and pigeon eggs. In terms of average daily consumption, there were 1,950 of poultry, 531 of livestock, and 20,500 eggs.[2] Various fruits were also affordable and of good quality at that time, with grapes, bananas, oranges, pears, and apples readily available. Bananas from the south, for example, were only 4 cents per pound or 10 cents per bundle.[3]

In addition to local supplies, after the port opened, Tianjin also imported a large quantity of food and beverages from Europe. In the customs duty-free list, food items ranked first, with a wide variety including fish, meat, poultry, various canned game, caviar, sausages, pastries, raisins, cakes, candies, coffee, cocoa, butter, milk biscuits, etc. Various fresh vegetables, fruits, preserves, pickles, etc., were available, along with different types of flour such as coarse flour (including millet flour and oat flour) and fine flour (arrowroot flour, corn flour, etc.), as well as hot sauce, various spices, sauces, seasonings, essences, etc. Beverages ranked second, including foreign bitter beer, sweet wine, cordials, raspberry wine, soda water, mineral water, and lemon soda.[4] These imported goods were not only consumed by foreign expatriates but also sought after by middle and high-income Chinese families. When friends came from afar, it was customary to treat them to a Western meal at a restaurant. Gifts exchanged between relatives and friends were also highly esteemed if they were Western delicacies. Tianjin's upper-class society often indulged in Dutch water, ale (popular in England, a fermented malt beverage), soda, coffee, and other Western beverages. Red wine or champagne were commonly used for gatherings or celebrations among friends.[5] For example, in the diary

[1] O. D. Rasmussen, *Tientsin: An Illustrated Outline History*, translated by Xu Yifan, et al. Tianjin People's Publishing House, 2008, p.336.

[2] Editorial Office of the Tianjin Chorography and History Compilation Committee (ed.). *Overview of Tianjin in the Early 20th Century*. Published internally in 1986, p.354.

[3] Johan J. Mattelaer, et al. *A Belgian Passage to China (1870-1930)*, translated by Liu Yue, et al. Social Sciences Academic Press (China), 2021, p.200.

[4] Zhang Chang, Liu Yue. *Li Hongzhang's Foreign Consultants: Gustav Detring and Constantin von Hanneken*. Taipei: Biographies Publishing House, 2012, p.321.

[5] Guo Lizhen. Exploring the Changes and Effects of Diet Expenditure among Modern Tianjin Residents - Based on Ying Lianzhi's Diary. *History Teaching*, 2011(3), pp.20-26.

英国大菜市
British market

意国菜市
Italian market

奥国菜市
Austrian market

调料、香精等；饮品列在次位，包括：外国苦啤酒、甜露酒、甘露酒、树莓酒、苏打矿泉水、矿泉水及柠檬汽水等。① 这些洋货不仅供应外国侨民消费，也受到中高收入阶层的中国家庭追捧。有朋自远方来，一般要请到西餐馆吃大餐，亲朋好友之间馈送礼品也以送洋食为尊贵。天津的上流社会还常品尝荷兰水、麦酒（流行于英国，经发酵的麦芽饮料）、汽水、咖啡等洋饮料，朋友们聚会、朋友家有红白喜事均使用红酒或香槟酒。② 例如，《大公报》创办人英敛之在日记中就常常记录与朋友们出入西餐馆和日本料理店吃饭，或者携妻带子到饭店喝汽水、饮咖啡。1902 年 9 月 9 日的日记中记录，他到朋友家贺喜，"饮香蘋酒数十瓶"（即香槟酒）。西餐与中餐的价格相当，丰俭由人，个人一餐五六角，请客的话，一席少则二三元，多则 20 元（银元）以上，是普通劳动者一个月甚至几个月的收入。

19 世纪末 20 世纪初天津中上流社会饮食消费的一个基本特征是，宴饮往往与逛商店、看戏、看电影等娱乐消费相结合。因为这些在当时属于新鲜事物，所以在那一时期的名人日记中，对于这种

① 张畅、刘悦，《李鸿章的洋顾问：德璀琳与汉纳根》，台北传记文学出版社，2012 年，第 321 页。

② 郭立珍，《近代天津居民饮食消费变动及影响探究——以英敛之日记为中心》，《历史教学》，2011 年第 3 期，第 20—26 页。

of Ying Lianzhi, the founder of *Ta Kung Pao*, he frequently recorded dining out with friends at Western restaurants and Japanese cuisine restaurants, or taking his wife and children to drink soda and coffee at restaurants. On September 9, 1902, he recorded in his diary that he visited a friend's house for a celebration and "drank dozens of bottles of Champagne." The prices of Western and Chinese meals were comparable, varying according to one's means. A meal for one person could cost five or six jiao (jiao, 1/10 of a yuan). If hosting guests, a dinner could range from as low as 2 or 3 yuan to over 20 yuan (silver dollar), equivalent to the income of an ordinary laborer for a month or even several months.

In the late 19th and early 20th centuries, a fundamental characteristic of the dining consumption of Tianjin's middle and upper-class society was that banquets were often combined with entertainment such as shopping, theater, and watching movies. Because these were considered novel activities at the time, they were extensively documented in the diaries of celebrities during that period. In 1897, Na Tong, Minister of the Military Affairs Office, wrote in his diary about traveling to Tianjin with friends by train. Upon arriving, they took a brief rest and then "took a rickshaw to Deyi Lou Restaurant to drink Western liquor and dine on Western dishes," feeling it was "quite exotic." After enjoying drinks and conversation, they "strolled through the foreign shops in the French Concession." The next day, they went shopping first, "purchasing odds and ends at the Japan Cotton Company and French trading company," then had breakfast, "took a rickshaw to Liu Laoji's lamb restaurant outside the north gate of Tianjin for breakfast, purely Western Regions flavor dishes,

饮食、购物加娱乐活动的记载比比皆是。1897 年，军机处大臣那桐在日记中说，与友人乘火车来津游玩，一下火车稍作休息，即"乘东洋车（即人力车）至第一楼（德意楼）饮洋酒、餐洋馔"，感觉"别具风味"；"欢饮畅谈"之后，"在法租界踏月游洋货店"。第二天是先购物，"至日本棉花公司及法国洋行购买零物"，然后吃早餐，"乘东洋车至天津北门外刘老纪羊肉馆早饭，纯是西域菜样，别有风味"。晚上到裕泰饭馆赴约吃饭，仍是西餐，散席后"同至鸣和戏园观灯戏"。① 几年后，电影在天津流行起来，餐后的娱乐活动就变成了看电影。1906 年的闰五月初六，英敛之"偕内人邀朋友及其夫人品昇楼饭，饭后同看美国活动影戏，内容精妙入神，其运转活动情形，与真人无异"，这是他们第一次观影。以后这样的娱乐活动成为他日记中的生活常态，直到后来忙于吃喝玩乐，感觉无聊乏味了。②

随着天津工商业的发展，餐饮业呈现出前所未有的繁荣景象。饭店、酒楼、乳品店、冷饮店、咖啡厅、面包房林立，全国各大菜系、小吃遍地开花。不仅传统中餐馆日益繁荣，而且象征现代生活的西餐业也发展迅速。1922 年《天津指南》中记录比较著名的酒店 13 家，其他酒馆菜饭店 47 家；据不完全统计，到 20 世纪 30 年代，天津约有西餐馆 38 家，洋酒馆、咖啡馆、洋点心铺 13 家。民国时期天津的旅馆基本上都提供中西两餐，还出现一批兼卖中西两餐的小食堂。③ 西式餐饮打破了中国餐饮业一统天下的旧格局，不仅丰富了中国居民饮食内容，使传统的餐饮观念得以改良，最重要的就是女性可以参加宴会。西方宴会礼仪是夫妇共同出席重要活动，且男女可以同席，而中国古代妇女一般不参加正式宴饮活动，即使参加也是男女宾客分席而坐。清末上海、天津等主要城市受西方文化影响较大，一批与外国人打交道较多的中产阶级知识分子、买办和留学归国者率先

quite distinctive." In the evening, they went to Yutai Restaurant for dinner, still having Western cuisine. After the meal, they "went to Minghe Theater to watch a lantern show."[1] A few years later, movies became popular in Tianjin, and post-dinner entertainment activities shifted to watching movies. On the sixth day of the intercalary fifth month of the lunar calendar in 1906, Ying Lianzhi "invited friends and their wives to dine at Shenglou Restaurant, followed by watching an American motion picture. The content was exquisitely captivating, and the movement of the characters was no different from real life," marking their first time watching a film. Such entertainment activities became a regular part of their lives as recorded in his diary, until later when they became too preoccupied with indulgence and felt bored and dull.[2]

With the development of industry and commerce in Tianjin, the catering industry has witnessed unprecedented prosperity. Restaurants, taverns, dairy shops, cold drink shops, coffee houses, and bakeries abound, with various cuisines and snacks from all over the country flourishing. Not only have traditional Chinese restaurants thrived, but also the symbol of modern life, the Western catering industry, has developed rapidly. In 1922, *Tianjin Guide* recorded 13 relatively famous hotels and 47 other taverns and eateries. According to incomplete statistics, by the 1930s, there were approximately 38 Western restaurants, 13 liquor bars, coffee houses, and pastry shops in Tianjin. During the Republic of China era, most hotels in Tianjin provided both Chinese and Western meals, and there emerged a batch of small canteens that sold both Chinese and Western meals.[3] Western-style dining broke the old pattern of dominance in the Chinese catering industry. It not only enriched the dietary choices of Chinese residents and improved traditional dining concepts but also, most importantly, allowed women to participate in banquets. In Western banquet etiquette, couples attend important events together, and men and women can sit together. In contrast, in ancient China, women generally did not participate in formal banquets, and if they did, they sat separately from men. By the late Qing Dynasty, major cities such as Shanghai and Tianjin were greatly influenced by Western culture, and a group of middle-class intellectuals, compradors, and returned overseas students

① 见那桐在光绪二十三年（1897 年）八月十七日和十八日日记。北京市档案馆编，《那桐日记》上册，新华出版社，2006 年，第 251、252 页。

② 方豪编录，《英敛之先生日记遗稿》，文海出版社，1974 年，第 771—788 页。

③ 郭立珍，《近代天津居民饮食消费变动及影响探究——以英敛之日记为中心》，《历史教学》，2011 年第 3 期，第 20—26 页。

① See Na Tong's diary on August 17th and 18th in the 23rd year of the Emperor Guangxu reign (1897). Beijing Municipal Archives. *The Diary of Na Tong*. Vol.1. Xinhua Publishing House, 2006, p.251, 252.

② Fang Hao (ed.). *Unpublished Diary of Ying Lianzhi*. Wenhai Publishing House, 1974, pp.771-788.

③ Guo Lizhen. Exploring the Changes and Effects of Diet Expenditure among Modern Tianjin Residents - Based on Ying Lianzhi's Diary. *History Teaching*, 2011(3), pp.20-26.

打破这一藩篱。比如，英敛之就常常偕夫人赴朋友的宴会。

由于餐饮业的繁荣，自明末清初以来，天津人即已养成喜好美食、崇尚奢华的民风食俗。例如，集中华美食之精华于一席的"满汉全席"，在天津早有流传。虽然在正史里不见记录，但在一些中外人士的笔记文集和文艺作品中则有记载。20 世纪 20 年代在北京和天津献艺的著名相声演员万人迷编了一段相声名为"报菜名"，罗列大量菜名作为"贯口"词，颇受听众欢迎，虽有艺术想象却也来源于生活。20 世纪初，一位在比商天津电车电灯公司创办时任职的比利时工程师在他的日记中，详细记载了受邀赴宴的情形。从他记述的食物内容来看，应该是一整套经过天津厨师改良的津味大餐，其中包罗各种山珍海味，疏不逊于"满汉全席"。这位外国人观察到，"等待上菜期间，餐桌上摆着干果与西瓜子。晚餐通常先供应各式各样的果脯、苹果、梨等等。换言之，就是我们欧洲人的甜点。随后有炖鱼、鲜虾、腌虾、鱼翅、河豚鱼白①、鹿脊髓、海龟、燕窝、藕和莲子等。所有菜品均为水煮，带着汤汁被端上来。接着为无骨鸭，或炖或炸，然后就是所谓的汤，但实际上又是煮过各种食物的汤汁。因此，这里吃东西的顺序与我们的习惯正好相反"。宴席的丰盛无与伦比，"用餐过程中，所有菜品或盘子都不会撤走。全部都将摆放在桌子上，必要时，会把一个盘子堆在另一个上面。你根本无法想象高级饭店里晚餐的菜品数量和种类的丰富程度"。酒水是米酒或高粱酒，"酒是温热的，盛在小锡壶里，你可以倒进极其小的酒杯里再喝下去。这种酒的味道像杜松子酒"。餐具是中式的，"吃饭时使用筷子，均由骨头、竹子或黄檀木制成。每人还有一把瓷勺，用来舀酱汁或汤，此外，还有一把两齿叉子。这种叉子是铜制的，用来吃水果等"。当然初来乍到的外国人并不习惯用筷子，不过这正好给了他一个拒绝不喜欢食物的委婉理由，"出于餐桌礼节，中国人喜欢将自己认为好吃的菜夹给客人。但经常客人不得不将其扔于桌下。若被人看到，你可以装作笨手笨脚，不善于使用筷子！其他东西都是预料之内的

---

① 河豚的鱼白，即雄性河豚鱼的精巢，又名西施乳。世间天津产河豚最有名，其味道最鲜美之处便是鱼白，其质地甘腻细嫩，味为海产品之冠，以至民间有"不食鱼白，不知鱼味。食过鱼白，百鱼无味"的谚语。

---

who interacted more with foreigners took the lead in breaking this barrier. For example, Ying Lianzhi often attended banquets with his wife.

Due to the prosperity of the catering industry, since the late Ming and early Qing dynasties, Tianjin people have developed a fondness for gourmet food and a penchant for luxury in their culinary culture. For example, the "Manchu Han Imperial Feast," which gathers the essence of Chinese cuisine, has long been circulated in Tianjin. Although not recorded in official history, it is mentioned in the notes, collections, and literary works of some Chinese and foreigners. In the 1920s, Wan Ren Mi, a famous crosstalk comedian who performed in Beijing and Tianjin, compiled a skit called "Bao Cai Ming" (Naming Dishes), listing a large number of dish names as a "running gag," which was quite popular among audiences. Though it involved artistic imagination, it was rooted in real life. In the early 20th century, a Belgian engineer working for CTET recorded in his diary the details of an invitation to a banquet. From his description of the food, it seemed to be a set of Tianjin-style grand banquet dishes modified by Tianjin chefs, including various delicacies from both land and sea, rivaling the "Manchu Han Imperial Feast." The foreigner observed that "While waiting to be served, there are dry nuts on the table, as well as watermelon seeds, called 'sigwa' in Chinese. The meal invariably begins with all kinds of candied fruits, apples, pears, etc. In other words, what usually constitutes dessert for us Europeans. This is followed by stewed fish, fresh shrimps, pickled shrimps, shark fins, whale sperm①, doe nerves, sea turtles, birds' nests, roots and the fruits of the water lily, etc. All this is served in the water in which these foods have been cooked. After that, come boneless ducks, stewed or fried, and then the so-called soups, which again is only the water that has been used to cook all the various foods. The order of eating is therefore the reverse of what we are used to". The banquet was lavish beyond compare. "During the meal, none of the dishes or plates are taken away. Everything stays on the table, piled one on top of the other, if necessary. You simply cannot imagine the number and the types of food that are served for a good supper in a good hotel." The drinks served were rice wine or sorghum wine, "It is served hot in little tin cans and you drink it in extremely small cups. It tastes like gin." The tableware was Chinese-style, "You eat with chopsticks made of bone, bamboo or rosewood. You also have a porcelain spoon to scoop up the sauce and the soup, as well as

---

① It refers to the milt of male pufferfish, also known as 'Xishi's milk.' Tianjin's pufferfish is world-renowned, and its milt is considered the most delicious part, with a sweet, rich, and delicate texture that is regarded as the finest among seafood. There is even a folk saying that goes, "If you haven't tasted the milt, you don't truly know the taste of fish. Once you've eaten it, all other fish will seem tasteless."

常规食物，基本上每次都一样，有些非常可口"。① 宴席丰盛既表明了天津人的热情好客，也是中国人普遍的虚荣好面子在餐饮聚会上的体现。另一点值得注意的是，请客的人只是任职电车公司仓库管理员的普通中国职员，说明菜价并没有高到不可接受。

"人配衣裳马配鞍"

在各种现代花样炫富的方式出现以前，古代和近代社会的人们展示自身财富地位和风度仪表的最佳方式，莫过于穿衣打扮。根据一个人的衣着来判断一个人的社会地位等级，是最简单方便的方法。最典型的例子是清朝官员的官服，从帽子上的顶戴花翎到衣服的颜色、前胸上的补子，都明确标示着官员的品级爵位，令人一望而知。普通人的服饰则从面料和式样上昭示着穿着者的身份。封建时代，社会地位低下的人，即使富有资产，也不被允许穿戴绫罗绸缎或者某种颜色的衣料。在近代工业革命以前，由于生产力落后，中国历朝历代服装的式样很少有流行一时的风尚，也不会由于个别人的喜好而改变。什么身份、什么职位、什么季节应该穿什么衣服，都有定规。妇女最多在发型和首饰上翻新花样。只有当政治改革或动乱打破了整个社会秩序时，穿着才会发生改变，比如赵武灵王的"胡服骑射"，还有不同朝代崇尚不同的颜色，以及清朝入关后强迫汉族男人剃发等。

天津虽然与北京近在咫尺，但近代之前天津地区的服饰却与北京服饰有着明显的差别。北京作为帝都、满族特权阶层的统治中心，服装服饰明显具有满族服饰的特点，女子普遍穿着各式旗袍，男子则"筒身箭袖"满袍马褂，即便汉族男女的穿着多数也是如此。而天津此时却呈现出女子"上袄下裙"的汉族传统服饰特征，男子的袍服也更多地体现满汉结合的特点。② 晚清时的天津官员群体，为了

---

① （比）约翰·麦特勒等著，刘悦等译，《比利时—中国：昔日之路（1870—1930）》，社会科学文献出版社，2021年，第206—207页。

② 杨丽娜、孙世圃，《浅论天津近代服饰变革及其在我国服装发展演变中的重要影响》，《中国轻工教育》，2009年第1期，第5—6页。

a fork with two prongs. This fork is made from copper and is used to eat the fruits, etc." Of course, newly arrived foreigners were not accustomed to using chopsticks, which gave them a polite excuse to reject food they didn't like. "One of the things the Chinese find very polite is to serve you their own favorite food, which often forces you to drop it under the table. If they see it, you can always pretend that this was due to your clumsiness in handling the sticks! Everything else is the regular standard food you might expect, which is always the same and some of which is quite tasty."[1] The lavish banquet not only showed the warmth and hospitality of Tianjin people but also reflected the common vanity and face-saving behavior of Chinese people in dining gatherings. Another noteworthy point is that the host was just an ordinary Chinese employee working as a warehouse manager for the tram company, indicating that the prices of the dishes were not so high as to be unacceptable.

"The Clothes Fit the Person, and the Saddle Fits the Horse"

Before various modern ways of flaunting wealth emerged, the best way for people in ancient and modern societies to display their wealth, status, and demeanor was through their clothing. Judging a person's social status based on their attire was the simplest and most convenient method. The most typical example is the official robes of Qing Dynasty officials, from the feathered hat ornament to the color of the garments and the patches on the front chest, all clearly indicating the official's rank and title, easily recognizable at a glance. The clothing of ordinary people revealed the wearer's identity through the fabric and style. During the feudal era, even if someone had wealth, they were not allowed to wear luxurious fabrics or certain colors if their social status was low. Before the modern industrial revolution, due to backward productivity, there were few fleeting fashion trends in the clothing styles of China's past dynasties, and they would not change due to individual preferences. There were strict rules regarding what clothes should be worn for different identities, positions, and seasons. Women mainly innovated in hairstyles and jewelry. Only when political reforms or upheavals disrupted the entire social order did clothing change, such as King Wuling of Zhao's adoption of "barbarian clothing and horse riding," the preference for different colors in different dynasties, and the forced shaving of Han Chinese men's heads after the Qing Dynasty came to power.

Although Tianjin is close to Beijing, the clothing styles in the Tianjin

---

① Johan J. Mattelaer, et al. *A Belgian Passage to China (1870-1930)*, translated by Liu Yue, et al. Social Sciences Academic Press (China), 2021, pp.206-207.

晚清汉女装（1875）
Han Chinese Women clothing in the
Late Qing Dynasty (1875)

清末汉女装（1909）
Han Chinese Women clothing in the
late Qing Dynasty (1909)

遵从服饰制度、迎合中央集权的审美喜好，一般穿着满汉结合的服饰和改良的旗装。初到中国且具有好奇心的外国人，他们眼中中国男性的"长袍马褂"是："裤子宽松肥大，没有裤门。裤腿上宽下窄，里面穿着内裤。裤腿口缠着宽绑带。裤腰翻折，用棉布或丝做的腰带系住"；衬衫"是一种类似于马甲的短衣，为白色棉质。侧面系扣，衣长至中腹部。立领设计，始终敞着口，与其余服饰的款式搭配有致"；衬衫的外面"套着棉质、丝质或其他布料的长袍，颜色一般较为鲜艳，有紫罗兰、天蓝等"；有时，长袍外面再套一件马褂（马褂有袖，无袖的称作马甲），"类似教士穿的长袍，衣长至腰部，颜色多为黄、红或其他醒目的颜色，并镶着黑色或蓝色的衣边"；帽子也有季节的区分，冬天戴暖帽（多用毛皮和呢缎），夏天戴凉帽（藤编，外裹白色绫罗），帽顶有不同颜色的"扣子"（即顶珠，以不同颜色宝石区分品级）；靴子均由丝绸制成，或长或短，他们的长袜多为白色亚麻布或棉布材质；冬季时，所有衣物之外都会披上一层又一层的棉毛或皮毛，裤子外也套上保护小腿和臀部的护腿片，"中国男性会套着一件又一件的大衣，有时多达 7 件"。女士的服装在外国人眼里与男性基本相同，只是外衫更长、盖住臀部，"下摆缝

region before modern times were significantly different from those in Beijing. As the imperial capital and the ruling center of the privileged Manchu class, Beijing's clothing clearly bore the characteristics of Manchu attire, with women commonly wearing various types of Cheongsam and men wearing "tube-bodied, arrow-sleeved" Manchu robes or mandarin jackets. Even the attire of Han Chinese men and women mostly followed this pattern. However, Tianjin at this time exhibited the traditional Han Chinese clothing characteristic of women wearing "upper jackets and lower skirts," while men's robes more often reflected a combination of Manchu and Han styles.[①] During the late Qing Dynasty, Tianjin's official class, to comply with clothing regulations and cater to the aesthetic preferences of centralized authority, generally wore a combination of Manchu-Han attire and modified Manchu clothes. To curious foreigners newly arrived in China, the attire of Chinese men appeared as follows: "The trousers were loose and baggy, with no opening. The legs were wide at the top and narrow at the bottom, with underwear worn underneath. The bottom of trousers were tied with wide bands. The waist of the trousers was folded over and tied with a cotton or silk belt." The shirt was described as "a short garment similar to a waistcoat, made of white cotton. It was buttoned on the side and reached the mid-abdomen. It had a standing collar that remained open, complementing the style of the other garments." Outside the shirt, they "wore long robes made of cotton, silk, or other fabrics, usually brightly colored, such as violet or sky blue." Sometimes, they would wear a mandarin jacket (with sleeves; sleeveless ones were called waistcoats) over the robe, "similar to the robes worn by priests, reaching to the waist, often in yellow, red, or other bright colors, with black or blue trim." Hats also varied by season, with fur-lined caps worn in winter and woven hats covered with white silk worn in summer, with different colored "buttons" on top (denoting rank with different colored gemstones). Boots were all made of silk, either tall or short, and their stockings were mostly made of white linen or cotton fabric. During winter, layers of cotton or fur were added outside all clothing, and leg guards were worn over the trousers to protect the calves and buttocks. "Chinese men would layer one coat over another, sometimes up to seven layers." Women's clothing, according to foreigners, was basically the same as men's, except that the outer garments were longer, covering the buttocks, with "colored embroidered pleats" sewn at the hem. The colors were also brighter, with Tianjin women particularly fond of red,

---

① Yang Lina, Sun Shipu. A Brief Discussion on the Transformation of Modern Clothing in Tianjin and Its Important Influence on the Evolution of Clothing in China. *China Education of Light Industry*, 2009(1), pp. 5-6.

有彩色绣花褶边"。颜色也都较为鲜艳，他观察到，天津妇女尤其喜欢红色。这一点确实是天津女服的一个特点。[1] 通常令来华外国人大为震惊的是中国风俗对女性脚部的残害，即缠足。[2] 后来，慈禧太后在推行"新政"时，废除了这一陋俗。不过，她也对从法国回来的女侍德龄说过，欧洲女性穿的紧身衣，腰部勒得让人喘不过来气，不如中国服装舒服。[3] 从对女性的束缚来说，两者本质上是一样的。

天津成为通商口岸后，大量外国侨民涌入，带来了西方服饰文化。天津人的穿衣打扮逐渐表现出明显的"现代性"，实现了款式、工艺、装饰的快速简化，并充分考虑到将服装的功能与美观相结合。例如，当北京女子普遍穿着宽身、"十八镶滚"的旗袍时，天津女子的袄、裙已经开始明显向窄身、展现曲线美的方向发展；到了辛亥革命之后，天津地方女子学校兴起，新文化、新思潮唤起和鼓舞着天津女子走出闺房、独立工作、自由恋爱、投身革命，此间代表新时代风貌的女学生着装在各个阶层普遍呈现，不仅衣身合体，彰显女性的身材，且上衣（袄）达到了有史以来的最短——仅及臀部，下裙摆提高到露出脚踝的高度，百褶裙、马面裙也已被简洁、素色的"A"字长裙所代替，呈现出明确的功能性和现代美感。[4]

而下层民众的服装更多从服装的功能性和实用性出发，这方面的代表是天津漕运服饰——"短打儿"。"短打儿"是天津特有的一种劳动者穿着服饰，夏季的"短打儿"上衣类似于坎肩，下配裤子，上衣前后两片在腋下用布条相系，河北、山东等地也有类似装扮；冬季"短打儿"是指头戴毡帽，耳戴灰鼠护耳，上身穿"二大棉袄"（比棉袍短、比棉袄长），下身穿空裆棉裤。"短打儿"着装是从搬运为生的漕运脚夫穿着演化而来，是下层劳动人民的耐用服饰。[5]

开埠后，外国侨民涌入天津。租界内的西式服装店生意兴隆，

① 张仲编著，《天津早年的衣食住行》，天津古籍出版社，2004年，第22页。

② （比）约翰·麦特勒等著，刘悦等译，《比利时—中国：昔日之路（1870—1930）》，社会科学文献出版社，2021年，第209—211页。

③ （美）德龄著，顾秋心译，《清宫二年记》，中国人民大学出版社，2012年，第47页。

④ 杨丽娜、孙世圃，《浅论天津近代服饰变革及其在我国服装发展演变中的重要影响》，《中国轻工教育》，2009年第1期，第5—6页。

⑤ 张仲编著，《天津早年的衣食住行》，天津古籍出版社，2004年，第23页。

which was indeed a characteristic of Tianjin women's attire.[1] What often shocked foreigners coming to China was the custom of foot binding inflicted on women.[2] Later, Empress Dowager Cixi abolished this barbaric practice when she implemented the "New Policies." However, she also remarked to Lady-in-waiting Deling, who had returned from France, that the tight-fitting dresses worn by European women, which cinched the waist so tightly that one could hardly breathe, were not as comfortable as Chinese clothing.[3] In terms of the constraints imposed on women, both practices were essentially the same.

After Tianjin became a treaty port, many foreign expatriates poured in, bringing Western clothing culture with them. The attire of Tianjin residents gradually exhibited a distinct "modernity," achieving rapid simplification in style, craftsmanship, and decoration, while fully considering the combination of clothing functionality and aesthetics. For example, while women in Beijing commonly wore wide-bodied, "eighteen trimming and piping" Cheongsam, Tianjin women's jackets and skirts had already begun to noticeably evolve towards narrow-bodied styles, highlighting curves; after the 1911 Revolution, local women's schools in Tianjin flourished, and the new culture and ideologies inspired Tianjin women to step out of the traditional confines, work independently, engage in free love, and join the revolution. The attire of female students representing the new era was prevalent across all social classes, with snug-fitting tops accentuating the female figure, and jackets reaching historically unprecedented short lengths—barely covering the buttocks—while skirts were raised to ankle-length, pleated skirts and horse-face skirts were replaced by simple, monochrome A-line skirts, demonstrating clear functionality and modern aesthetic.[4]

For the lower-class population, clothing is more often approached from the perspective of functionality and practicality, exemplified by the Tianjin canal transport attire known as "Duan Da'er." "Duan Da'er" is a unique type of attire worn by laborers in Tianjin. In the summer, the top of "Duan Da'er" is similar to a sleeveless jacket, paired with trousers. The front and back pieces

① *The Clothing, Food, Shelter, and Transportation in the Early Days of Tianjin*, compiled by Zhang Zhong. Tianjin Ancient Books Publishing House, 2004, p.22.

② Johan J. Mattelaer, et al. *A Belgian Passage to China (1870-1930)*, translated by Liu Yue, et al. Social Sciences Academic Press (China), 2021, pp.209-211.

③ Deling. *Two Years in the Forbidden Palace*, translated by Gu Qiuxin. China Renmin University Press, 2012, p.47.

④ Yang Lina, Sun Shipu. A Brief Discussion on the Transformation of Modern Clothing in Tianjin and Its Important Influence on the Evolution of Clothing in China. *China Education of Light Industry*, 2009(1), pp.5-6.

旗袍。照片由刘悦提供
Cheongsam. Courtesy of Liu Yue

穿"短打儿"的人力车夫
Rickshaw pullers wearing "Duan Da'er" outfits

穿长袍马褂与穿西装的学校教师。摄于约 20 世纪 10—30 年代
Teachers wearing long gowns and mandarin jackets, as well as suits. Taken in the 1910s-1930s

男学生的冬季穿着，裤腿口缠着宽绑带。摄于 1908 年
Schoolboys' winter uniforms with wide straps wrapped around their trouser legs. Taken in 1908

民国时期女学生装
Schoolgirl uniform during the Republic of China era

图片来源：联合卫理公会档案和历史总委员会
Source: The General Commission on Archives and History of The United Methodist Church

来自巴黎的时装装饰着橱窗。欧洲人尤其对时装有一种历史悠久的特殊偏爱。17世纪的一位欧洲使节说："一个人如果没有二十五到三十套各式各样的衣服就算不上有钱，有钱人必须每天换装。"①这里的绅士们制定了一整套穿着规矩。他们的衣着不仅严格地因时令而异，而且因一天内的不同时间和服装的不同用途而异。他们依据所做的事情和所到的场合，在一天内仔细换装数次，极为重视穿着打扮的各种细枝末节。一位义和团时期到访天津的细心的观察者这样描述道："如果领带的色调和样式同皮带、袜子的不相协调，那将被认为是严重地有损风雅和身份。在天津，从来没有一个珍惜自己的尊严和声誉的大人阁下或先生不是穿着运动服来到打网球的recreation-ground（休息场）。他从来不会犯那种和男宾吃饭时穿燕尾服，而和女宾吃饭时却穿着晚礼服这种颠三倒四、不可饶恕的乱穿衣服的错误。"②

为了满足侨民们在衣着上的讲究，租界里有各种服装商店，专门为侨民们制作和进口时装，其款式来自时尚之都巴黎的当季流行样式。在1928年出版的天津租界英文洋行目录中，经营服装和女帽的商店有7家、鞋店4家、百货商店22家、专营珠宝手表的商店有8家，基本能够满足侨民们日常的服装要求。在中国人看来，这些商店的数目简直是大大超过需求了。③西装讲究量体裁衣，侨民在天津也能找到非常好的中国裁缝、鞋匠为他们制作西装、鞋帽，而且价格大大低于欧洲人经营的时装店，其实后者除了裁缝来自欧洲，制衣工作仍是由中国人来完成。精打细算的外国工薪阶层发现，"花55法郎就能买到一套海蓝色三件式西装"，而且剪裁精致，中国裁缝的手艺"堪比比利时的裁缝"。夏季穿的浅色西服更便宜一些，"白色服装需要8到9.5元，卡其色只需7.5元"。中国鞋匠制作的皮靴"做法与欧洲一样专业"，甚至"比我从比利时买来的那些工艺更好，

---

① （法）费尔南·布罗代尔著，顾良等译，《十五至十八世纪的物质文明、经济与资本主义》第一卷，生活·读书·新知三联书店，2002年，第373页。

② （俄）德米特里·扬契维茨基著，许崇信等译，《八国联军目击记》，福建人民出版社，1983年，第38页。

③ 张畅、刘悦，《李鸿章的洋顾问：德璀琳与汉纳根》，台北传记文学出版社，2012年，第318—319页。

---

of the top are tied together under the armpits with cloth strips, a style also found in regions such as Hebei and Shandong. In winter, "Duan Da'er" refers to wearing a felt hat, with ear flaps made of gray fur, an upper body clad in "medium long padded jackets" (shorter than a padded robe but longer than a padded jacket), and the lower body dressed in crotchless padded trousers. The attire of "Duan Da'er" originated from the clothing worn by canal porters who made a living from carrying goods, evolving into durable attire for the lower-class laboring people.①

After the opening of the port, foreign expatriates flooded into Tianjin. Western-style clothing stores thrived within the concessions, with showcases adorned with fashion from Paris. Europeans, in particular, had a long-standing special preference for fashion. A European envoy from the 17th century once said, "A person cannot be considered wealthy without having twenty-five to thirty sets of various clothes; wealthy individuals must change outfits every day."② Gentlemen here established a set of dressing rules. Their attire not only varied strictly according to the seasons but also differed depending on the time of day and the purpose of the clothing. They changed clothes several times a day with great emphasis on the minutiae of dressing according to their activities and the occasions they attended. A careful observer visiting Tianjin during the Boxer Rebellion period described it like this: "If the tone and style of the tie do not match the belt and socks, it will be considered a serious breach of elegance and status. In Tianjin, there has never been a gentleman or sir who values his dignity and reputation who would not wear sportswear to a tennis recreation-ground. He would never commit the unforgivable mistake of wearing a tuxedo while dining with male guests and an evening suit while dining with female guests."③

To meet the expatriates' refined tastes in clothing, there were various clothing stores within the concessions, specializing in producing and importing fashionable attire for expatriates, with styles sourced from the fashion capital, Paris. In the 1928 Hong-List about the foreign firms in Tianjin concessions, there were 7 shops selling clothing and women's hats, 4 shoe shops, 22 department stores, and 8 shops specializing in jewelry and watches, essentially meeting the daily clothing needs of the expatriates. From

---

① *The Clothing, Food, Shelter, and Transportation in the Early Days of Tianjin*, compiled by Zhang Zhong. Tianjin Ancient Books Publishing House, 2004, p.23.

② Fernand Braudel. *Civilisation Materielle, Economie et Capitalisme: XVe-XVIIIe Siècle* (vol.1), translated by Gu Liang, et al. SDX Joint Publishing Company, 2002, p.373.

③ Dmitry Yanchevetsky. *Eyewitness Records of the Eight-Nation Alliance*, translated by Xu Chongxin, et al. Fujian People's Publishing House, 1983, p.38.

东亚毛纺厂车间旧照
Old photo of the workshop at the Oriental
Wool Manufacturers Company

估衣街
Gu Yi Street

原谦祥益绸缎庄。安红摄于 2006 年
Former Qian Xiangyi Silk Village. Taken by An
Hong in 2006

舒适性更强"。①

　　近代社会风起云涌，服饰文化呈现出异彩纷呈的局面。不仅是外国侨民，还有 20 世纪初大批从海外归来的留学生、受过教会教育的洋派人物、在洋行供职的职员、追求时髦的年轻人，都热衷于穿西式服装，西装男女在天津街头随处可见。不同的文化相互碰撞、相互交融，使天津成为近代中国服饰文化的前沿，呈现出亦"土"亦"洋"、亦"古"亦"今"、亦"满"亦"汉"的服饰风貌。

　　天津在近代引领服饰变革，更成为一个纺织业非常发达的城市，拥有华新纺织、恒源纺织、北洋纱厂、裕大纱厂、东亚毛呢、仁立纺织等众多纺织企业。其中，东亚毛呢厂生产的"抵羊牌"毛线更是享誉国内外。到 1931 年 9 月，因纺织业发达而兴起的服装相关商业店铺已经达到鼎盛时期。当时天津估衣街店铺最多的就是服装店与绸缎庄。据统计，绸布棉纱呢绒布庄、裘皮商店及服装商店就有：谦祥益、敦庆隆、元隆、华祥、瑞蚨祥、绵章、宝丰、崇庆、万聚恒、庆德成、恒泰庆等近百家。②天津已经成为一个包括棉、毛、丝、印染、

the Chinese perspective, the number of these shops far exceeded demand.[1] Tailoring was highly valued for suits, and expatriates in Tianjin could find excellent Chinese tailors and shoemakers to tailor suits, shoes, and hats for them, at prices much lower than those of European-operated fashion stores. In reality, besides the tailors being from Europe, the garment-making process of the latter was still carried out by Chinese workers. The frugal foreign working-class discovered that they could "buy a navy-blue three-piece suit for just 55 francs," and the tailoring was exquisite, with the craftsmanship of Chinese tailors being "comparable to Belgian tailors." Light-colored suits for summer were even cheaper, with "white clothing costing 8 to 9.5 yuan, and khaki only 7.5 yuan." Leather boots made by Chinese shoemakers were crafted "with the same professionalism as in Europe," and were even "better than those I bought from Belgium, with stronger comfort."[2]

In the tumultuous winds of modern society, the clothing culture presents a diverse and colorful scene. Not only foreign expatriates but also a large number of returnee students from overseas, Westernized individuals educated by the church, employees working for foreign firms, and fashion-conscious young people in the early 20th century were enthusiastic about wearing Western-style clothing. Men and women in suits could be seen everywhere on the streets of Tianjin. The collision and integration of different cultures

①　（比）约翰·麦特勒等著，刘悦等译，《比利时—中国：昔日之路（1870—1930）》，社会科学文献出版社，2021 年，第 201 页。

②　谢鹤声、刘嘉琛，《六十年前的天津估衣街》。中国人民政治协商会议天津市委员会、南开区委员会文史资料委员会合编，《天津老城忆旧》，天津人民出版社，1997 年，第 74—83 页。

①　Zhang Chang, Liu Yue. *Li Hongzhang's Foreign Consultants: Gustav Detring and Constantin von Hanneken*. Taipei: Biographies Publishing House, 2012, pp.318-319.

②　Johan J. Mattelaer, et al. *A Belgian Passage to China (1870-1930)*, translated by Liu Yue, et al. Social Sciences Academic Press (China), 2021, p.201.

针织和服装等各个行业的近代纺织工业基地。

戏园、电影院、舞厅和俱乐部

看戏是近代天津人日常生活中的主要娱乐活动。因地近首都，所以发源于北京的京剧也深得天津人喜爱。天津人也非常懂戏，在京剧界流传着这样一句话："北京学戏，天津走红，上海赚包银"，即是说一名京剧演员必须在天津赢得好评，才能成为全国公认的"红角"。因为天津有大量有钱有闲的京剧爱好者，票房可观，所以几乎所有的京剧表演艺术家，如四大名旦、四大须生等，都经常在天津演出，马连良、张君秋更是定居这里。在津居住的王公大臣、军阀富商的家里常有戏台或临时搭设戏台，比如庆王府的一楼大厅就是办寿宴时搭临时戏台的地方。家中举办喜庆宴会时，请戏班艺人来演出助兴，称之为"唱堂会"。还有一些公馆宅院或者会馆则建有专门的戏楼，比如杨柳青石家大院的戏楼和广东会馆的戏楼，而更多的天津普通民众看戏则是去公共娱乐场所——戏园。

天津的戏园设施先进，照明良好。所有的戏园都是正方形，前方正中是戏台，周围有两层看台，楼上一般都设有包厢。19 世纪末天津开始引入煤气灯照明，这是北方最早的，所以"园中煤气灯极多，明如白昼，一大观也"。[①] 演出一般从晚上五点开始，到凌晨一两点才结束，一幕紧接另一幕，中间没有间隔。20 世纪初，坐在可容纳 6 人到 8 人的楼上包厢内，每人需要支付 5 元或 3.5 元，其他座位的价格为 3.5 元。"演出期间，戏园服务员会售卖坚果、干瓜子、茶水等等。同时还会分发毛巾，这些毛巾浸在温水中，被紧紧地拧在一起，供观众来擦脸和手。毛巾用过之后，服务员会收回，将毛巾再次放入热水中，拧干，然后重新分发给其他观众。这一幕整晚不断重复。这些毛巾擦成一大堆，服务员们互相扔来扔去，从戏院一边抛到另一边。"观众还可以随意闲聊、走动，既为休闲娱乐，也可进行社交。所以，中式戏园的秩序是非常混乱的，演员的首要能力就是嗓音足

---

① 光绪二十三年（1897 年）八月十八日日记。北京市档案馆编，《那桐日记》上册，新华出版社，2006 年，第 252 页。

---

made Tianjin the forefront of modern Chinese clothing culture, presenting a clothing style that is both "local" and "Western," both "ancient" and "modern," and reflecting elements of both the Manchu and Han cultures.

In modern times, Tianjin has led the way in clothing reform and has become a city with a highly developed textile industry, boasting numerous textile enterprises such as Hua Xin, Heng Yuan, Beiyang, Yu Da, Oriental Wool, and Ren Li. Among them, the "Diyang" wool yarn produced by the Oriental Wool Manufacturers Company is renowned both domestically and internationally. By September 1931, the clothing-related commercial establishments that had arisen due to the developed textile industry had reached their heyday. At that time, the largest number of shops on Tianjin's Gu Yi Street were clothing stores and silk shops. According to statistics, there were nearly a hundred shops including those specializing in silk fabric, cotton yarn, woolen fabric, fur, and clothing, such as Qinxiangyi, Dunqinglong, Yuanlong, Huaxiang, Ruifuxiang, Mianzhang, Baofeng, Chongqing, Wanjuheng, Qingdecheng, Hengtaiqing, and many others.[①] Tianjin has become a modern textile industrial base encompassing industries such as cotton, wool, silk, printing and dyeing, knitting, and clothing.

Opera Theaters, Movie Theaters, Dance Halls, and Clubs

Watching opera was the main entertainment activity in the daily lives of modern Tianjin residents. Due to its proximity to the capital, Peking opera, originating from Beijing, was also deeply loved by the people of Tianjin. Tianjin residents were very knowledgeable about opera, and there was a saying in the Peking opera circle: "Study opera in Beijing, become famous in Tianjin, and make money in Shanghai." This means that a Peking opera performer must win acclaim in Tianjin to become a nationally recognized "popular performer." Because there were many wealthy and leisurely Peking opera enthusiasts in Tianjin, ticket sales were considerable, so almost all Peking opera performers, such as the Four Great Dan (Female Role) Performers, Four Great Bearded Male Performers, etc., often performed in Tianjin. Performers like Ma Lianliang and Zhang Junqiu even settled here. In the homes of aristocrats, warlords, and wealthy merchants living in Tianjin, there were often opera stages or temporary stages set up. For example, the first-floor hall of Prince Qing's Mansion was the place where temporary

---

① Xie Hesheng, Liu Jiachen. *Tianjin Gu Yi Street in Sixty years ago*. Tianjin Municipal Committee of CPPCC and Cultural and Historical Research Committee of Nankai District. *Memories of the Old City of Tianjin*. Tianjin People's Publishing House, 1997, pp.74-83.

比利时侨民内恩斯拍摄的中国京剧照片。约摄于 1905—1906 年。图片来源：比利时根特大学档案馆
Chinese Peking Opera photo taken by Belgian expatriate Francois Nuyens, circa 1905-1906. Source: Archives of Ghent University, Belgium

广东会馆。刘悦摄于 2024 年
Guangdong Guild Hall. Taken by Liu Yue in 2024

够大。"如果哪位艺人能够一口气喊得时间特别长且声音洪亮的话，观众会认为这是一位很好的表演者，他会得到大家的喝彩。"① 相声大师侯宝林的经典《关公战秦琼》对那时北京戏园的场景有极其相似的描述。可见，戏园是当时中国中下层民众的主要娱乐社交场所，观众之间、观众与服务人员之间以及观众与演员之间的互动都是同时进行的，因此难免秩序混乱。

天津的戏园主要分布在城厢和南市一带，20 世纪二三十年代，随着城市中心的转移，而集中到商业繁荣、交通便利的法租界。这一时期，由于经济的发展，加上很多清朝贵族、遗老遗少、军阀督军、买办富商都定居天津。他们投入大量的时间精力和金钱来支持和赞

stages were set up for birthday banquets. When hosting celebratory banquets at home, opera troupes were invited to perform to enliven the atmosphere, referred to as "Tang Hui." Some mansions or guild halls had dedicated opera houses, such as the opera houses in the Yangliuqing's Shi Family Courtyard and the Guangdong Guild Hall. However, for the majority of ordinary Tianjin residents, watching opera meant going to public entertainment venues—opera theaters.

The opera theaters in Tianjin were well-equipped and well-lit. All the opera theaters were square-shaped, with a stage in the center, surrounded by two tiers of seating, and generally, there were private boxes on the upper level. In the late 19th century, Tianjin began to introduce gas lighting, which was the earliest in the northern region, hence "there were many gas lamps in the theater, bright as daylight, making for a grand spectacle."[1] Performances usually started around 5:00 in the evening and lasted until one or two in the morning, with one act following another without interruption. In the early 20th century, sitting in a private box upstairs, which could accommodate 6 to 8 people, required each person to pay 5 yuan or 3.5 yuan, while seats in other areas were priced at 3.5 yuan. "During the performance, theater attendants sold nuts, dried melon seeds, tea, and so on. They also distributed towels, which were soaked in warm water, tightly wrung out, and provided for the audience to wipe their faces and hands. After the towels were used, the attendants would collect them, soak them in hot water again, wring them out, and then redistribute them to other audience members. This scene repeated throughout the night. The towels were stacked in a large pile, and the attendants threw them back and forth to each other, from one side of the theater to the other." Audiences could freely chat and move around, engaging in both leisure and socializing. Therefore, the order in the Chinese-style opera theater was very chaotic, and the primary skill of the actors was to have a loud voice. "An artist who can shout and yell sufficiently long and hard in a single breath is considered to be a very good performer and is rewarded by the public's calls of approval."[2] The classic sketch *Guan Gong Fights Qin Qiong* by the master of cross-talk, Hou Baolin, describes a scene in Beijing opera theaters at that time that is extremely similar. It can be seen that the opera theater was the main entertainment and social venue for the middle and lower

---

① （比）约翰·麦特勒等著，刘悦等译，《比利时—中国：昔日之路（1870—1930）》，社会科学文献出版社，2021 年，第 207—209 页。

---

① See Na Tong's diary on August 18th in the 23rd year of the Emperor Guangxu reign (1897). Beijing Municipal Archives. *The Diary of Na Tong*. Vol.1. Xinhua Publishing House, 2006, p.252.

② Johan J. Mattelaer, et al. *A Belgian Passage to China (1870-1930)*, translated by Liu Yue, et al. Social Sciences Academic Press (China), 2021, pp.207-209.

助京剧艺术，有的甚至自己装扮登场，称之为"票友"，比如袁世凯的二公子袁克文常以"寒云主人"的名号登台演出。南开大学的倡议人、张伯苓校长的胞弟张彭春，是哥伦比亚大学硕士，精通西洋戏剧，曾两次协助梅兰芳赴海外演出，对京剧艺术的海外传播起到积极作用。当时的新闻界也对京剧给予关注和支持，报纸上常常刊登评论文章。由于上述内容，这一时期京剧演员的表演水平大幅提高，剧本和音乐的创作有名家指点，服装、化妆、道具更加精美，一件绣满了金线和宝石的戏服需要几千元，京剧表演艺术几乎登峰造极。1936 年"中国大戏院"在法租界落成，拥有 2000 个座位，设备完善，开幕广告中号称"冠绝华北，唯我独尊"。四大名旦、四大须生等名角都曾在此登台演出。在"中国大戏院"一炮而红，成为每一位京剧表演者的心愿。以此为标志，在抗战爆发前，京剧在天津的发展达到鼎盛。①

比京剧更受年轻人欢迎的娱乐消遣是看电影。电影于 1895 年由美国传入欧洲，1896 年即传入天津，在天丰舞台、天仙茶园等处，使用手摇电影机放映无声"外洋电戏"。1905 年 6 月 16 日，天津《大公报》首次使用"电影"一词。《大公报》是北方地区最重要的报纸之一，由于它的影响力，"电影"一词很快在京津地区乃至全国流行开来。1906 年 12 月，权仙影院开始放映电影，当年名为"天津权仙茶园"，位于原法租界紫竹林附近的葛公使路（今滨江道）与巴黎路（今吉林路）交口处，名曰"茶园"，实际是以放电影为主的电影院。银幕用白布做成，有几排长板凳，可容纳近 300 名观众。楼上是雅座，票价也是按照观影的位置、角度不同，从 3 角到 1 元不等。当时院方邀美国电影商人来津放映最新电影，影片每三天更换一次，每晚 9 点到 11 点放映，多为世界各地名胜和滑稽短剧片，也有打斗片、侦探片、歌舞片等，使得人们大开眼界，不仅中国观众，侨民也非常踊跃地去观看。两年后的 1908 年 2 月，"权仙"在南市分设一座新电影院，俗称"上权仙"。1929 年，彩色有声电影传入中国，"权仙"生意更旺。"权仙"经理特向电车公司订下专车，

classes in China at that time, and interaction among the audience, between the audience and the attendants, and between the audience and the actors all took place simultaneously, inevitably leading to disorder.

The opera theaters in Tianjin were mainly distributed in the urban area and the Nanshi area. In the 1920s and 1930s, with the shift of the city center and the concentration in the French Concession with commercial prosperity and convenient transportation, opera theaters also moved there. During this period, economy developed and many Qing Dynasty nobles, survivals of bygone ages, warlord governors, and comprador merchants settled in Tianjin, investing a lot of time, energy, and money to support and sponsor Peking opera art. Some even took to the stage themselves, known as "Piao You." For example, Yuan Kewen, the second son of Yuan Shikai, often performed under the name "Hanyun Zhuren." Zhang Pengchun, the younger brother of Chang Poling, the founder and president of Nankai University, held a Master's degree from Columbia University and was proficient in Western drama. He assisted Mei Lanfang twice in overseas performances, playing a positive role in the overseas dissemination of Peking opera art. The news industry at the time also paid attention to and supported Peking opera, often publishing commentary articles in newspapers. Due to these reasons, the performance level of Peking opera actors improved significantly during this period, with guidance from famous playwrights and musicians. Costumes, makeup, and stage props became more exquisite. A costume embroidered with gold thread and gems cost several thousand yuan. Peking opera performance art almost reached its pinnacle. In 1936, the "China Theater" was completed in the French Concession, with 2,000 seats and advanced facilities. The opening advertisement claimed to be "unrivaled in North China, unique and supreme." Famous actors such as the Four Great Dan Performers and the Four Great Bearded Male Performers have performed here. Becoming popular overnight at the "China Theater" became the dream of every Peking opera performer. As a symbol of this, before the outbreak of the War of Resistance Against Japan, Peking opera reached its peak development in Tianjin.①

A more popular form of entertainment among young people than Peking opera was watching movies. Movies were introduced to Tianjin from the United States in 1896, appearing at venues like Tianfeng Stage and Tianxian Teahouse, where hand-cranked projectors screened silent "foreign films." On June 16, 1905, the term "dian ying", meaning "film," was first used in the Tianjin *Ta Kung Pao* newspaper. The *Ta Kung Pao* was one of the most

① 尚克强、刘海岩主编，《天津租界社会研究》，天津人民出版社，1996 年，第 258—260 页。

① Shang Keqiang, Liu Haiyan (eds.). *Research on Tianjin Concession Society*. Tianjin People's Publishing House, 1996, pp. 258-260.

平安电影院。摄于 20 世纪 30 年代
Empire Theatre. Taken in the 1930s

每晚 11 点散场后，蓝牌电车特设"权仙"一站。[1] 这一时期在南市还有"新明"和"皇宫"两家电影院，设施更先进，银幕由美国进口，场内有电扇，场外备有咖啡西点。

20 世纪 30 年代初，电影院开始集中到法租界劝业场一带的商业中心。"明星""光明社"（今光明影院）"新新""春和""天宫""天丰"等影院，相距不过一两百米，形成了档次不同的影院群，且经常上映国产片。因为相互竞争，票价都比较低廉，多在 2 角到 4 角，一般大众都能接受。另一个影院汇集的商业娱乐中心在英租界的"小白楼"一带。这里有"平安"（今音乐厅）"大光明""大华"三家影院。这个影院群的档次更高、设备和环境更好，票价从 5 角到 2 元左右，观众多为外国侨民和欧化的中国人，主要上映进口的美国影片。这一时期，"平安影院"和"新新影院"与世界大电影公司发行网建立了直接联系，欧美最流行的新片往往半年左右即可引进天津放映。天津大众对当时的好莱坞影星如卓别林、嘉宝、秀兰·邓波、琼克·劳馥等都非常熟悉喜爱，到电影院观影成为天津大众尤

influential newspapers in the northern region, and due to its influence, the term "dian ying" quickly became popular in the Beijing-Tianjin region and even nationwide. In December 1906, the Quanxian Cinema began showing films. Originally named "Tianjin Quanxian Teahouse" that year, it was located near the original French Concession's Zizhulin area at the intersection of Rue de Baron Gros (now Binjiang Road) and Rue de Paris (now Jilin Road). Though named "Teahouse," it was actually a cinema mainly focused on showing movies. The screen was made of white cloth, with several rows of long benches accommodating nearly 300 spectators. Upstairs were private boxes, and ticket prices varied from 3 jiao to 1 yuan depending on the viewing position and angle. At that time, the theater invited American film merchants to Tianjin to show the latest movies. Films changed every three days, with screenings from 9 to 11 p.m., featuring world-famous scenic spots, comedic shorts, as well as action, detective, and musical films, broadening people's horizons. Both Chinese audiences and expatriates eagerly attended. In February 1908, Quanxian opened a new cinema in the Nanshi area, commonly known as "Shang Quanxian." In 1929, color sound films were introduced to China, further boosting business at "Quanxian." The theater manager arranged special tram services with the tram company. After the 11 p.m. show, blue-line trams would stop at a dedicated "Quanxian" station.[1] During this period, there were also two cinemas in the Nanshi area, "Xinming" and "Huanggong," with more advanced facilities. Their screens were imported from the United States, and the theaters were equipped with electric fans, while coffee and pastries were available outside the venues.

In the early 1930s, cinemas began to concentrate in the commercial center of the French Concession's Quanye Bazaar. Cinemas such as "Mingxing," "Guangming She" (now Guangming Cinema), "Xinxin," "Chunhe," "Tiangong," and "Tianfeng" were all located within a short distance of one or two hundred meters from each other, forming a group of cinemas with different grades, often screening domestic films. Due to competition, ticket prices were relatively low, ranging from 2 to 4 jiao, which was generally affordable for the public. Another commercial entertainment center where cinemas gathered was in the British Concession's area near the "Xiao Bailou" (Little White Building). Here, there were three cinemas: "Empire Theater" (now the Music Hall), "Gaiety Cinema," and "Majestic Theater." The cinemas in this group had higher grades, better equipment, and environment, with ticket prices ranging from 5 jiao to 2 yuan. The audience mainly consisted of foreign expatriates

① 　王述祖、航鹰编著，《近代中国看天津：百项中国第一》，天津人民出版社，2007 年，第 203 页。

① 　*Modern China through the Eyes of Tianjin: 100 Firsts*, compiled by Wang Shuzu, Hang Ying. Tianjin People's Publishing House, 2007, p.203.

乡谊俱乐部弹簧地板舞厅
Ballroom with sprung floor in Tientsin Country Club

其是年轻人娱乐生活的主要内容。①

深受时髦青年喜欢的另一项近代娱乐活动是跳舞。这一娱乐活动很早即由西方侨民引入到天津租界。租界内的各个俱乐部里都设有舞厅，虽然只有俱乐部成员能参加，但这是天津交谊舞和舞厅的滥觞。娱乐是分阶层的，也是由上至下逐渐普及的。交谊舞由旅欧回来的清政府外交官家属带到宫廷，受到追求享乐的皇室贵族的欣赏，逐渐又被军阀权贵带到天津，成为上流社会的时髦娱乐项目。后来这种娱乐活动蔓延到中产阶层。为了招揽生意，很多中外人士常常光顾的西式饭店也都开设舞厅，如利顺德、起士林、西湖饭店、大华饭店等。1923 年开在法租界内的国民饭店，面向社会开放它的"皇宫舞厅"，这是天津第一家营业性舞厅。此后，利顺德饭店的"天升舞厅"、英国乡谊俱乐部的"南楼舞厅"、德租界"大华影院"二楼的"圣安娜舞厅"这几家高档舞厅相继开业，法租界的"福禄林"、中原公司（今百货大楼）的"巴黎跳舞场"、惠中饭店的舞场、百乐门舞场等面向大众的舞厅也日渐增多，到 20 世纪 20 年代天津

① 尚克强、刘海岩主编，《天津租界社会研究》，天津人民出版社，1996 年，第 255—258 页。

and westernized Chinese people, and the cinemas primarily screened imported American films. During this period, both "Empire Theater" and "Xinxin Cinema" established direct connections with the distribution network of major film companies worldwide, enabling the introduction of the latest and most popular Hollywood films to Tianjin for screening within about six months. The people of Tianjin were very familiar with and fond of Hollywood stars of the time, such as Charlie Chaplin, Greta Garbo, Shirley Temple, and Joan Crawford, making going to the movies a major part of entertainment for Tianjin residents, especially the young.①

Another modern entertainment activity highly favored by fashionable youth is dancing. This form of entertainment was introduced to the Tianjin Concessions by Western expatriates at an early stage. Dance halls were established in various clubs within the concessions. Although only club members could participate, this marked the beginning of social dancing and dance halls in Tianjin. Entertainment was hierarchical and gradually became popular from the top down. Social dancing was brought to the court by diplomats returning from Europe, appreciated by pleasure-seeking nobility, and eventually introduced to Tianjin by warlords and dignitaries, becoming a trendy leisure activity for the upper class. Later, this form of entertainment spread to the middle class. To attract business, many Western-style restaurants frequented by both Chinese and foreigners also opened dance halls, such as the Astor House Hotel, Kiessling, West Lake Hotel, and Cafe Riche. In 1923, the National Grand Hotel opened its "Imperial Palace Dance Hall" in the French Concession, making it the first commercially operated dance hall in Tianjin open to the public. Afterwards, the upscale dance halls like the "Tiansheng Dance Hall" at Astor House Hotel, the "South Wing Dance Hall" at the British County Club, and the "St. Anna Dance Hall" on the second floor of the Majestic Theater in the German Concession opened successively, and there was an increasing number of public dance halls in the French Concession, such as the "Fululin," the "Paris Dance Hall" at the Chungyuen Co. (now the Tianjin Department Store), the dance hall at the Hui Chung Hotel, and the Paramount Dance Hall. By the 1920s, the number of dance hall in Tianjin was over 20. In addition to the early returnees and diplomats and their families dancing, some Russians who fled to Tianjin after the October Revolution began opening dance schools to teach the Chinese people dances like the waltz and tango. Social dancing gradually became one of the essential skills for gentlemen and ladies in high society.

① Shang Keqiang, Liu Haiyan (eds.). *Research on Tianjin Concession Society*. Tianjin People's Publishing House, 1996, pp. 255-258.

的舞厅达到 20 多家。除了早期留学归来的新派人物和驻外使节及其家属会跳舞之外，一些十月革命后流亡到天津的俄国人开始开办舞蹈学校，教国人跳华尔兹、探戈等交谊舞。交谊舞逐渐成为上流社会绅士淑女的必备技能之一。

20 世纪 20 年代天津舞厅中的名人以溥仪和张学良为最。1924 年被冯玉祥部队士兵赶出紫禁城迁居天津的末代皇帝溥仪，如离开牢笼的金丝雀，一头扎进天津的灯红酒绿。在皇宫中，溥仪早已在英国教师教导下学会跳舞、打网球，来津后他带着"皇后"婉容，几乎日日去利顺德饭店吃饭跳舞。奉系军阀张作霖的儿子"少帅"张学良因时常流连于天津的舞厅，在 1931 年九一八事变之后背负骂名，被马君武写诗讽刺道："赵四风流朱五狂，翩翩胡蝶最当行。温柔乡是英雄冢，哪管东师入沈阳。告急军书夜半来，开场弦管又相催。沈阳已陷休回顾，更抱佳人舞几回。"

1931 年"巴黎跳舞场"开业，从上海、北平引入"职业舞女"。另外还有很多流亡来津的白俄女性，其中不乏贵族后裔，被生计所迫沦为舞女，主要招待驻津外国军队士兵。所以天津的舞厅，尤其是中下层舞厅，鱼龙混杂，曾引发社会名流们的激烈反对，指其"有伤风化"。1927 年的《大公报》上连续刊登"跳舞问题"专号，对舞厅状况进行分析，指出交际舞对社交也有好处，不可一概否定。著名教育家严修也在报上说，他认为跳舞是一种娱乐，不能不加分析地一概反对。[①]

天津中上层外国侨民的主要社交娱乐场所是各个俱乐部。19世纪忙于在全世界进行殖民扩张的英国人，为了在异域他乡排解寂寞、互通声气、加强联系，在远东各主要港口城市都开办了俱乐部。天津最早的俱乐部就叫"天津俱乐部"，也叫"万国俱乐部"。它在租界建立的早期已经扎根，是由最早在天津设立租界的英国人设立的。作为当时最有实力的殖民国家，英国人订立了早期俱乐部的规定：当地土著——中国人、朝鲜人和日本人，以及 half-castes（混血儿）不得进入俱乐部。"只有白色人种才能成为它的

① 《大公报》1927 年 7 月 1 日、8 月 9 日。

In the Tianjin dance halls of the 1920s, the most famous figures were Puyi and Zhang Xueliang. Puyi, the last emperor, who was expelled from the Forbidden City by Feng Yuxiang's troops in 1924, moved to Tianjin, where he indulged in the city's nightlife like a caged canary released into a world of revelry. Having been taught to dance and play tennis by British teachers in the Forbidden City, Puyi continued his passion for these activities in Tianjin, often dining and dancing at the Astor House Hotel with his "empress" Wanrong. Zhang Xueliang, the son of Fengtian Clique warlord Zhang Zuolin, known as the "Young Marshal," gained notoriety for his frequenting of Tianjin's dance halls. After the September 18th Incident in 1931, he became the subject of criticism. Ma Junwu wrote a poem mocking him: "Zhao and Zhu, debonair and wild, flutter like butterflies in the wind. The land of tenderness becomes a hero's grave, regardless of the Japanese troops entering Shenyang. Urgent military dispatches arrive in the dead of night, urging the start of the show with stringed instruments. Shenyang has fallen, no need to look back, just dance a few more rounds with your beloved."

In 1931, the "Paris Dance Hall" opened, importing "professional dancers" from Shanghai and Beiping (now Beijing). Additionally, there were many White Russian women who had fled to Tianjin, among them were descendants of nobility who, due to economic necessity, became dancers, mainly entertaining foreign soldiers stationed in Tianjin. Consequently, Tianjin's dance halls, especially those catering to the middle and lower classes, were a mixed bag, which sparked intense opposition from social elites, who criticized them as "damaging to morality." In 1927, the *Ta Kung Pao* newspaper ran a series of special issues on the "dancing problem," analyzing the situation in dance halls and pointing out that social dancing also had its benefits for social interaction, which couldn't be entirely dismissed. Renowned educator Yan Xiu also commented in the newspaper, stating that he believed dancing was a form of entertainment and should not be blindly opposed without proper analysis.[①]

The main social and entertainment venues for the upper-middle-class foreign expatriates in Tianjin were various clubs. In the 19th century, the British, busy with colonial expansion worldwide, established clubs in major port cities in the Far East to alleviate loneliness, facilitate communication, and strengthen connections in foreign lands. The earliest club in Tianjin was called the "Tientsin Club," also known as the "Club of All Nations." It was established early in the history of the concessions and was founded by the earliest British settlers in Tianjin. As the most powerful colonial nation at the

① *Ta Kung Pao*, July 1st and August 9th, 1927

高贵的会员。俱乐部事务由各国代表选举产生的委员会管理。"①俱乐部里的各种设施齐全，设有餐厅、台球场、九柱戏场（类似保龄球）、图书室和拥有很多报刊的阅览室。俱乐部的仆役是中国人，所有会员都是经过挑选的，同时，他们也都有权推荐宾客，但必须严格注意他的社会等级。只有各国军官可以被认为是俱乐部的常客。义和团运动之后，德国俱乐部、法国俱乐部、日本俱乐部、意大利俱乐部和美国俱乐部纷纷成立。每个国家俱乐部都有它的网球会和运动俱乐部。②但是最有影响力的仍然是英国人建立的各种俱乐部，所以天津的各国侨民所遵循的是英式社交娱乐法则。英国人的赛马俱乐部直接被命名为"天津赛马会"，英国人的各种运动俱乐部被称作"天津草地网球会""天津冰球会""天津马球会""天津高尔夫球会""天津板球会"等，还有女性侨民组织的"天津妇女俱乐部"，每周聚会。体育项目的俱乐部主要组织各种比赛，而妇女俱乐部除了学习中文和法语会话、戏剧、体操、研习《圣经》之外，还开展各种慈善活动。③

由于贸易的繁荣，以英国人为代表的外国商人在天津经商很快就积累了大笔财富，而且他们大都依靠买办筹措各种事宜，自然拥有大把空闲时间。初到天津的外来者观察到，天津侨民一天的生活离不开各种俱乐部。他们的生活很规律：一上午繁忙紧张的工作后，中午"坐人力车或骑脚踏车去天津俱乐部，在那里互相见面，读电讯和报纸，交换消息"。下午"四点钟办公室结束工作。欧洲人骑自行车或骑马到郊外的休息场打网球，在那里和妇女们见面"。晚上八时进晚餐后，年轻人和单身汉去俱乐部或旅馆玩台球、打牌或者痛饮威士忌，常常到深更半夜。④20世纪初电力照明设施普及后，

①（俄）德米特里·扬契维茨基著，许崇信等译，《八国联军目击记》，福建人民出版社，1983年，第36页。

②（英）雷穆森著，许逸凡等译，《天津租界史（插图本）》，天津人民出版社，2009年，第265页。

③（英）雷穆森著，许逸凡等译，《天津租界史（插图本）》，天津人民出版社，2009年，第223—224、264—281页。

④（俄）德米特里·扬契维茨基著，许崇信等译，《八国联军目击记》，福建人民出版社，1983年，第36—38页。

time, the British established rules for the early clubs: Local natives — Chinese, Koreans, and Japanese, as well as half-castes, were not allowed to enter the club. "Only white people could become its distinguished members. The affairs of the club were managed by a committee elected by representatives from various countries."① The clubs were fully equipped with various facilities, including restaurants, billiards rooms, nine-pin alleys (similar to bowling alleys), libraries with many newspapers and periodicals. The club servants were Chinese, and all members were carefully selected. At the same time, they also had the right to recommend guests, but they had to strictly observe their social status. Only military officers from various countries could be considered regulars at the club. After the Boxer Rebellion, German, French, Japanese, Italian, and American clubs were established. Each nationality has its tennis and sporting clubs.② However, the most influential clubs were still those established by the British, so the various foreign expatriates in Tianjin followed British-style social and entertainment rules. The British horse racing club was directly named the "Tientsin Race Club," and various sports clubs for the British were called the "Tientsin Lawn Tennis Club," "Tientsin Ice Hockey Club," "Tientsin Polo Club," "Tientsin Golf Club," "Tientsin Cricket Club," and so on. There was also the "Tientsin Woman's Club" for female expatriates, which met weekly. Sports clubs primarily organized various competitions, while women's clubs, in addition to learning Chinese and French conversation, drama, gymnastics, and studying the Bible, also conducted various charitable activities.③

Due to the prosperity of trade, foreign businessmen represented by the British quickly accumulated vast wealth in Tianjin, and most of them relied on compradors to handle various matters, naturally having plenty of leisure time. Observers who arrived in Tianjin noticed that the daily lives of expatriates in Tianjin revolved around various clubs. Their lives were very regular: after a busy and tense morning of work, they would "take a rickshaw or ride a bicycle to the Tientsin Club at noon, where they would meet each other, read telegrams and newspapers, and exchange news." In the afternoon, "work in the office ends at four o'clock. Europeans ride bicycles or horses to the countryside recreation-groud for playing tennis, where they meet women."

① Dmitry Yanchevetsky. *Eyewitness Records of the Eight-Nation Alliance*, translated by Xu Chongxin, et al. Fujian People's Publishing House, 1983, p.36.

② O. D. Rasmussen, *Tientsin: An Illustrated Outline History*, translated by Xu Yifan, et al. Tianjin People's Publishing House, 2008, p.265.

③ O. D. Rasmussen, *Tientsin: An Illustrated Outline History*, translated by Xu Yifan, et al. Tianjin People's Publishing House, 2008, pp.223-224, 264-281.

天津的市民，无论中外，都更有条件开展丰富多彩的休闲娱乐活动，从此开始了真正的"夜生活"。

赛马、体育活动和奥运会

近代天津在各方面开风气之先，许多当时在世界范围流行的体育运动纷纷在天津对外开放后传入，参加者从租界的侨民扩展到本地居民，体育运动也成为天津市民日常休闲活动的一项重要内容。

天津的外国侨民最热衷的运动是赛马和草地网球。一种运动之所以会受到侨民的推崇，主要在于其能炫耀财富和社会地位。"一项高级别的运动项目，从定义上说，就是一种要求大批昂贵用具或者昂贵设施或二者兼备的运动。"[1]赛马和草地网球与一般运动相比，都需要更大的专业性场地、昂贵的设施、专业的训练以及相配套的服装等等。所以，天津上流社会的侨民非常热爱这两种"烧钱"的运动。

草地网球很早就已经是侨民中最流行的户外运动。在 20 世纪 20 年代，天津有 8 个草地网球俱乐部，打球的成员有约 1500 人。[2]"草地网球吸引着所有的人：儿童、青年人、成年人，乃至老头子和老太婆。他们一清早就手执球拍来回奔跑，一直打到天黑。……会打网球被认为是好风度的标志。……一个人必须打网球，就象一个人必须遵守礼节和装束入时一样。"[3]天津的草地网球俱乐部还经常与北京的俱乐部在春秋两季各举行一次比赛，6 月份在北京，9 月份在天津。在温布尔登网球赛上获得过世界冠军的运动员也曾于 1922 年访问天津，并在海关俱乐部球场进行了表演赛。[4]

---

[1] （美）保罗·福塞尔著，梁丽真等译，《格调：社会等级与生活品味》，中国社会科学出版社，1998 年，第 156 页。

[2] （英）雷穆森著，许逸凡等译，《天津租界史（插图本）》，天津人民出版社，2009 年，第 269 页。

[3] （俄）德米特里·扬契维茨基著，许崇信等译，《八国联军目击记》，福建人民出版社，1983 年，第 37 页。

[4] （英）雷穆森著，许逸凡等译，《天津租界史（插图本）》，天津人民出版社，2009 年，第 272—273 页。

After dinner at eight o'clock, young people and bachelors go to clubs or hotels to play billiards, cards, or indulge in whiskey drinking, often until late at night.[1] With the widespread adoption of electric lighting facilities in the early 20th century, Tianjin's citizens, both Chinese and foreigners, were more able to engage in a variety of leisure and entertainment activities, thus beginning a true "nightlife."

Horse Racing, Sports Activities, and the Olympic Games

In modern times, Tianjin took the lead in various aspects, and many sports popular worldwide at the time were introduced to Tianjin after its opening to the outside world. Participants expanded from the expatriates in the concessions to local residents, making sports activities an important part of daily leisure for Tianjin citizens.

The favorite sports of foreign expatriates in Tianjin were horse racing and lawn tennis. The reason why a sport was highly regarded by expatriates mainly lies in its ability to flaunt wealth and social status. "A high-status sport, by definition, is one that requires a great deal of expensive equipment or an expensive setting or both."[2] Compared to general sports, both horse racing and lawn tennis require larger professional venues, expensive facilities, professional training, and matching attire, among other things. Therefore, the expatriates of Tianjin's upper-class society were very fond of these two "money-burning" sports.

Lawn tennis had long been the most popular outdoor sport among expatriates. In the 1920s, Tianjin had eight lawn tennis clubs, with about 1,500 members playing tennis.[3] "Lawn tennis attracts everyone: children, young people, adults, and even old men and old women. They start running back and forth with their rackets early in the morning and keep playing until dark. ... Playing tennis is considered a sign of elegance. ... A person must play tennis, just as a person must observe etiquette and dress appropriately."[4] Tianjin's lawn tennis clubs also often held matches with clubs in Beijing in the spring and autumn seasons, in June in Beijing and September in Tianjin. Athletes

---

[1] Dmitry Yanchevetsky. *Eyewitness Records of the Eight-Nation Alliance*, translated by Xu Chongxin, et al. Fujian People's Publishing House, 1983, pp.36-38.

[2] Paul Fussell. *Class: A Guide through The American Status System*, translated by Liang Lizhen, et al. China Social Sciences Press, 1988, p.156.

[3] O. D. Rasmussen, *Tientsin: An Illustrated Outline History*, translated by Xu Yifan, et al. Tianjin People's Publishing House, 2008, p.269.

[4] Dmitry Yanchevetsky. *Eyewitness Records of the Eight-Nation Alliance*, translated by Xu Chongxin, et al. Fujian People's Publishing House, 1983, p.37.

赛马就更不用说了。这项运动在天津、上海、北京和香港等通商口岸的侨民中非常流行，是天津侨民开展最早的休闲运动。天津赛马会（Tientsin Race Club）在 1863 年 5 月举行了第一次赛马，一位路过天津的旅行者发现，"天津处于极度的兴奋状态中"①。在天津骑马并非完全为了运动，还因为开埠早期道路状况极差，侨民出行时主要依靠骑马，而买马、养马的费用极低廉，所以几乎每个侨民家里都会养上一两匹马。1886 年，天津赛马会接管了英租界以南的"养心园"，并在那里修建了新的固定赛马场。新赛马场"赛道周长一点五英里，赛道极宽，可轻易容纳十四匹马并肩赛跑，十八匹的话也并不嫌拥挤。赛道里是一圈同样长度的训练用跑道。再里面是一条防洪用的排水沟以保持赛道干燥。排水沟里是一条煤渣路。赛马场的最外面环绕着一条小河"②。马场设有看台，老的看台在 1900 年被烧毁，第二年就立刻重建了一座新看台，一直使用到 1925 年才被三座混凝土看台所取代。③ 这座跑马场在许多方面，是中国所有赛马场中最好的，也是远东第一流的。

骑马是一种体育运动，赛马则是一种休闲娱乐，同时也是一项赌博活动。当道路情况改善后，人们出行有了更多的交通工具，马匹就更多地被用来进行比赛了。富有者养马参赛，中产者骑马运动，没有马的人可以赌马。赌徒们在速度的刺激下，游走在倾家荡产的边缘，感受肾上腺素飙升带来的快感。天津最早的赛马场设在海光寺一带，赛马会每年在那里举行一次只有欧洲人参加的马赛。④ 英商天津赛马俱乐部一年举行春季和秋季两次赛会。1893 年举行的一次会议上，天津赛马会决定在每个赛会期间为中国骑手举行两次比赛。后来由天津道台向这两场中国骑手的比赛捐赠了一个奖杯，所以比赛被称作"道台杯"（Taotai's Cup），该项赛事一直是中国最好的

① （英）雷穆森著，许逸凡等译，《天津租界史（插图本）》，天津人民出版社，2009 年，第 40 页。

② （英）奥斯汀·科茨，《中国赛马》，牛津大学出版社，1983 年，第 93 页。

③ （英）雷穆森著，许逸凡等译，《天津租界史（插图本）》，天津人民出版社，2009 年，第 267 页。

④ 1880 年 11 月 24 日汉纳根致父母的信函。摘译自康斯坦丁·冯·汉纳根。《1879—1886 发自中国的书信》。

who won world championships at Wimbledon had also visited Tianjin in 1922 and played exhibition matches at the Customs Club tennis court.①

Horse racing goes without saying. This sport was extremely popular among the expatriates in commercial ports such as Tianjin, Shanghai, Beijing, and Hong Kong, and it was the earliest leisure activity engaged in by the Tianjin expatriates. The Tientsin Race Club held its first horse race in May 1863, where a passing traveler noted that "I found Tientsing in a great state of excitement."② Riding horses in Tianjin was not only for sport but also because the roads were in poor condition in the early days of opening up to foreign trade. Expatriates primarily relied on horseback for transportation, and the cost of buying and keeping horses was extremely low, so almost every expatriate household would keep one or two horses. In 1886, the Tientsin Race Club took over the "Yang Xin Garden" south of the British Concession and built a new permanent racecourse there. The new racecourse had "The course was a 1.5-mile circuit, wide enough to start 14 horses abreast with ease, 18 without undue difficulty. Within it there was a training track of similar length. Within this there ran a canal, one of the many that were essential in keeping the earth dry in this exceptionally flat region. Inside the canal was a cinder track. Creeks surrounded the entire racecourse area."③ The racetrack had grandstands; the old grandstand was burned down in 1900 and immediately replaced the following year with a new one, which was used until 1925 when it was replaced by three concrete grandstands.④ This racetrack, in many respects, was the best among all racetracks in China and was first-rate in the Far East.

Riding horses is a sport, while horse racing is a form of leisure entertainment and also a form of gambling. With improvements in road conditions, people had more transportation options for travel, so horses were increasingly used for racing. The wealthy would raise horses for competition, the middle class would engage in equestrian sports, and those without horses could place bets on races. Under the thrill of speed, gamblers teetered on the edge of financial ruin, experiencing the adrenaline rush of excitement. The earliest racecourse in Tianjin was located around the Haiguang Temple area,

① O. D. Rasmussen, *Tientsin: An Illustrated Outline History*, translated by Xu Yifan, et al. Tianjin People's Publishing House, 2008, pp.272-273.

② O. D. Rasmussen, *Tientsin: An Illustrated Outline History*, translated by Xu Yifan, et al. Tianjin People's Publishing House, 2008, p.40.

③ Austin Coates, *China Races*, Cambridge: Oxford University Press, 1983, p.93.

④ O. D. Rasmussen, *Tientsin: An Illustrated Outline History*, translated by Xu Yifan, et al. Tianjin People's Publishing House, 2008, p.267.

赛马场
The Race Course

获胜赛马及其主人。照片摄于 20 世纪初，由德依信先生提供
The winning racehorse and its owner. Taken in the early 20th century.
Courtesy of Mr. Bruce Eason

赛马场看台上的中外观众。照片摄于 20 世纪二三十年代
Chinese and foreign spectators in the stands of the racecourse.
Taken in the 1920s-1930s

乡谊俱乐部。照片摄于 20 世纪二三十年代
Tientsin Country Club. Taken in the 1920s-1930s

乡谊俱乐部室外休息区
The outdoor lounge area of Tientsin Country Club

乡谊俱乐部室内游泳馆
Indoor swimming pool of Tientsin Country Club

乡谊俱乐部餐厅
Restaurant in Tientsin Country Club

乡谊俱乐部休息室
The lounge at Tientsin Country Club

图片来源：德国"东亚之友"协会
Source: StuDeo

赛事之一。[1] 抗日战争结束前，天津先后有过 7 个赛马会，其中天津赛马会的经济效益是最好的。马会还将原来马场旁的乡谊俱乐部（Tientsin Country Club）并入到马场，使人们在赛马之余有了一个休息娱乐的去处。改建后的乡谊俱乐部拥有室内舞厅、室内游泳池、保龄球场、壁球场，另外还设有餐厅、茶厅、剧场、台球房、露天舞池等多功能设施，成为京津中外人士聚会休闲的高级娱乐场所。

外国侨民中还曾流行过板球、曲棍球、橄榄球、足球、棒球、游泳、冰球、冰帆、滑冰、马球和高尔夫球，并都有相应的俱乐部。这些俱乐部还经常与北京、上海、汉口的侨民俱乐部进行比赛交流，或者与当地驻军军人进行比赛。[2] 这些体育运动项目虽然没有或少有中国人参加，但通过教会学校、留学归国者的引荐，越来越多的中国年轻人了解、喜爱并投入其中。尤其是网球和游泳在天津的中国人中也很流行。网球也是天津的达官贵人和中产阶层热衷的运动，中华人民共和国第一支网球队于 1950 年在天津组建并进行日常训练。在解放前，天津体育界"张家的网球"和"穆家的游泳"已颇负盛名，两家私交甚好，既

张大陆，1965 年摄于北京
Zhang Dalu, taken in Beijing in 1965

是邻居，子一辈也是同学，后都为新中国体育事业的蓬勃发展作出了卓越贡献。张大陆的父亲张植久曾于 1935 年、1936 年力克中外群雄两度获得天津市网球双打冠军。在父亲的影响下，张大陆 10 几岁开始接触网球，曾师从末代皇帝溥仪的教练兼专职陪打吴少香，他很快就展现出过人的天赋。1953 年全国四项球类（篮、排、网、羽）比赛在天津的干部俱乐部举行，这也是中华人民共和国成立后的第一次全国网球比赛，年仅 19 岁的张大陆代表华北队参赛，是当时年纪最小的队员。由此，张大陆一路代表华北地区、北京市、河北省多次参加全国比赛，直至 20 世纪 60 年代初担任国家网球队总教练。1963 年的新兴力量运动会是亚洲、非洲、拉

---

① （英）奥斯汀·科茨，《中国赛马》，牛津大学出版社，1983 年，第 95 页。
② （英）雷穆森著，许逸凡等译，《天津租界史（插图本）》，天津人民出版社，2009 年，第 273—280 页。

where the race club held an annual horse race exclusively for Europeans.[1] The British Tientsin Race Club held races twice a year in spring and autumn. At a meeting held in 1893, the Tientsin Race Club decided to hold two races for Chinese riders during each race meeting. Later, the Tianjin Taotai donated a trophy for these two races, hence they were called the "Taotai's Cup", and this event has always been one of the best races in China.[2] Before the end of the War of Resistance Against Japan, Tianjin had a total of seven race clubs, among which the Tientsin Race Club had the best economic performance. The club also incorporated the Tientsin Country Club, which was originally located next to the racecourse, providing people with a place for relaxation and entertainment besides horse racing.

The renovated Tientsin Country Club had indoor ballroom, indoor swimming pool, bowling alley, and squash court as well as restaurant, tea room, theaters, billiard room, outdoor dance floor, and other multifunctional facilities, making it a high-class entertainment venue for gatherings and leisure for people from Beijing, Tianjin, and abroad.

Among foreign expatriates, cricket, field hockey, rugby, football, baseball, swimming, ice hockey, ice yachting, ice skating, polo, and golf were once popular, each with its corresponding clubs. These clubs often competed and exchanged matches with expatriate clubs in Beijing, Shanghai, and Hankou, or with local military personnel.[3] Although these sports had few or no Chinese participants, through the introduction of church schools and returning overseas students, more and more young Chinese came to understand, love, and engage

张植久在 1935 年和 1936 年获得天津市网球双打冠军的奖杯
Trophies won by Zhang Zhijiu in Tianjin Tennis Doubles Championship in 1935 and 1936

---

① Letter from Constantin von Hanneken to his parents on November 24, 1880. Constantin von Hanneken: *Briefe aus China: 1879–1886; als deutscher Offizier im Reich der Mitte*.
② Austin Coates, *China Races*, Cambridge: Oxford University Press, 1983, p.95.
③ O. D. Rasmussen, *Tientsin: An Illustrated Outline History*, translated by Xu Yifan, et al. Tianjin People's Publishing House, 2008, pp.273-280.

1951 年天津苏联俱乐部网球友谊赛。前排左二为张植久，后排左一为吴少香，后排左二为张大陆，前排居中者为印度裔网球名将小龙乾

Tianjin Soviet Club Tennis Friendly Match in 1951. The second person from the left in the front row is Zhang Zhijiu, and the first and second from the left in the back row are Wu Shaoxiang and Zhang Dalu, respectively. The person in the center of the front row is the Indian tennis star, A. L. Rumjahn

丁美洲各新兴国家为冲破西方大国体育垄断而举办的世界性体育赛事，也是中华人民共和国成立后第一次正式全面参加的国际体育比赛，张大陆作为总教练带领中国网球队 7 名队员获得两银四铜的佳绩。改革开放初期，1979 年张大陆首次率领中国网球队赴美国网球公开赛观摩，后又分别率领国家男子、女子网球队出征世界大学生运动会、戴维斯杯等重大国际赛事，培养了刘树华、马克勤、谢昭、胡娜等一代网球名将。天津人穆成宽是我国第一位参加国际游泳比赛、与外国人同场竞技并获得过冠军的人，他的儿子穆祥雄也从小练习游泳，曾经打破过世界蛙泳纪录，被称为中国"蛙王"。

近代天津的洋务学堂非常注重学生的身体素质，一般都将体育课

穆祥雄
Mu Xiangxiong

in them. Particularly, tennis and swimming were also popular among the Chinese in Tianjin. Tennis was also a sport favored by Tianjin's elites and middle class. The first tennis team of the People's Republic of China was established and trained daily in Tianjin in 1950. During pre-1949 period, the "Zhang Family's Tennis" and "Mu Family's Swimming" were already well-known in Tianjin's sports circles, and the two families had good personal relationships. They were neighbors and their children were classmates. Later they all made great contributions to the vigorous development of sports in People's Republic of China. Zhang Dalu's father, Zhang Zhijiu, won the Tianjin Tennis Doubles Championship twice in 1935 and 1936, defeating both Chinese and foreign competitors. Under the influence of his father, Zhang Dalu began to play tennis in his teens. He learned tennis under Wu Shaoxiang, the coach and practice partner of the last Emperor Puyi, and quickly showed his extraordinary talent. In 1953, the National Four Balls Games (basketball, volleyball, tennis, and badminton) was held at the Tianjin Cadre Club, which was also the first national tennis game after the founding of New China. At the age of only 19, Zhang Dalu represented the North China team, and was the youngest player at that time. From then on, Zhang Dalu participated in many national competitions representing North China, Beijing, and Hebei Province, until he became the head coach of the China National Tennis Team in the early 1960s. Games of the New Emerging Forces in 1963 was a global sports event held by emerging countries in Asia, Africa, and Latin America to break the sports monopoly of Western powers. It was also the first international sports competition that China officially participated after her founding. Zhang Dalu, as the head coach, led seven players of the China National Tennis Team to win two silver and four bronze medals. In the early days of Reform and Opening-up, Zhang Dalu led the China National Tennis Observation Group to the U.S. Open for the first time in 1979. He later led the National Men's and Women's Tennis Teams respectively to participate in various major international events such as the World University Games and the Davis Cup, and trained a generation of tennis stars such as Liu Shuhua, Ma Keqin, Xie Zhao, and Hu Na. Mu Chengkuan, a Tianjin native, was China's first participant in international swimming competitions, competing against foreigners and winning championships. His son, Mu Xiangxiong, also practiced swimming from a young age, once breaking the world breaststroke record, earning him the title of "Frog King" of China.

In modern Tianjin, Western-style schools paid significant attention to students' physical fitness, often making physical education a compulsory subject. Sports classes in schools particularly emphasized team sports that helped foster team spirit. Football and basketball were introduced to Tianjin

作为必修课程之一。学校的体育课尤其重视有助于培养团队精神的球类运动。足球和篮球运动分别于 1864 年和 1895 年传入天津。北洋水师学堂、电报学堂、武备学堂、北洋大学堂、高等工业学堂、新学书院、汇文中学、南开学校等众多学校也相继设立足球课和篮球课，并成立球队。京津之间的学校经常举办埠际比赛。1915 年南开学校足球队经常赴京参赛。20 世纪 30 年代，足球和篮球运动成为天津的群众性体育活动，全市各处空地建有篮球场，当时的媒体称天津为"篮球城"。1910 年至 1948 年，全国共举办过七届运动会，天津男篮蝉联一至六届冠军，并多次在国际比赛中获胜，其中主力队员出自南开学校篮球队，即著名的"南开五虎"。南开大学篮球队教练董守义曾赴美国专门学习篮球理论，训练之余于 1928 年出版了篮球专著《篮球术》一书，推动了我国篮球运动的正规化、科学化。天津的足球运动水平也很高，1935 年，以天津河东大直沽球员为主的中华足球队战胜西洋各国联队，夺得国际"爱罗鼎杯"足球大赛的冠军。1937 年该队赴日本参赛，以四战四捷的战绩挫败日本各队，在抗日战争前夕引起全国各界轰动。①

三大球类运动中，天津的排球运动起步虽晚于足球、篮球，但自 20 世纪初传入至今依然有近百年历史。早期，排球作为一种游戏形式在学校内流行，南开中学、汇文中学、新学书院、铃铛阁中学、南开大学与北洋大学等均是开展排球运动较早的学校。1927 年，张伯苓等人发起成立天津体育协进会，举办多场全市排球公开赛，一举推动了排球运动的普及。1931 年，南开大学学生组建南敏排球队，屡战屡胜横扫全国，天津排球运动进入兴盛时期，一时间涌现出各种民间体育社团，促进了天津乃至全国排球事业的发展。中华人民共和国成立后，随着中华全国体育总会号召开展"6 人制"排球运动，1956 年，天津市选拔建立了第一支男、女排球队，开始参加全国排球联赛并崭露头角。1950 年，首批国字号代表队"中国大学生排球代表队"组建，北洋大学学生李安格入选，翌年毕业后他正式进入国家队担任男排二传手，后成为新中国首任女排教练。1979 年，李安格研发了有"中国排球杀

① 王述祖、航鹰编著，《近代中国看天津：百项中国第一》，天津人民出版社，2007 年，第 217、219、221 页。

董守义（居中左三着西装者）与南开大学篮球队
Dong Shouyi (in suit, third from the left in the middle row) and the Nankai University basketball team

in 1864 and 1895, respectively. Many schools such as the Beiyang Naval Academy, Telegraph School, Military Academy, Peiyang University, Higher Industrial School, Anglo-Chinese College, Huiwen Middle School, and Nankai Schools successively offered football and basketball classes and formed teams. Inter-school competitions between Beijing and Tianjin were frequent. In 1915, the Nankai School football team frequently traveled to Beijing for matches. In the 1930s, football and basketball became popular mass sports activities in Tianjin. Basketball courts were built in various places throughout the city, earning Tianjin the nickname "Basketball City" by the media of the time. From 1910 to 1948, seven national sports meets were held, where the Tianjin men's basketball team won the championship for six consecutive times, and they also won many international matches. The main players were from the Nankai School basketball team, famously known as the "Five Tigers of Nankai." Dong Shouyi, the coach of Nankai University basketball team, went to the United States to study basketball theory. In addition to training, he published the basketball book *Basketball Skills* in 1928, promoting the regularization and scientization of basketball in China. Tianjin's football level was also high. In 1935, the Chinese football team, mainly composed of players from Dazhigu in Hedong District, Tianjin, defeated teams from various Western countries and won the championship of the international "Eilers Trophy" football tournament. In 1937, the team went to Japan to compete, defeating all Japanese teams in four matches, causing a sensation throughout the country

手铜"之称的"单脚背飞"技术，20 世纪 80 年代，作为技术顾问、科研攻关组长助力女排蝉联"五连冠"，培养了冯坤、赵蕊蕊等一代名将。天津排球的荣光一直闪耀至今，天津女排 20 余年间勇夺 16 次全国联赛冠军，更于 2024 年刷新了亚洲俱乐部在世俱赛的最佳成绩，已在世界舞台上成为中国排球运动的一面旗帜。

田径运动是最古老的体育运动项目，在天津也非常具有群众基础。不仅学校一般将其列入体育课程以提高学生身体素质，而且各国侨民和驻军也都在每年（一战期间中断）举行公开运动会，各国选手都可以参加。1902 年在天津出生的苏格兰人埃里克·利迪尔（Eric Liddell，中文名李爱锐），曾在 1924 年 7 月巴黎奥运会 400 米赛跑中夺得金牌，并打破奥运会纪录和世界纪录。后利迪尔回到天津任教于新学书院。在他的建议下，民园体育场被改建成为当时世界一流的赛场，每年在这里都会举行众多的体育比赛。太平洋战争爆发后，他与其他英美籍侨民被关押到山东潍县集中营，战争结束前夕因病去世。1982 年，以埃里克·利迪尔体育生涯为真实背景的英国影片《烈火战车》，获得美国奥斯卡奖的最佳影片、最佳配乐等四项大奖，至今仍为世界各地久演不衰的经典影片。

体育运动既是强身健体、摆脱无聊的休闲娱乐活动，也是和平时期国家之间进行竞争的一种方式。因此，国内有识之士认为中国应当参加世界奥林匹克运动会，南开大学校长张伯苓便是其中之一。1907 年 10 月 24 日，他在天津第五届学校运动会颁奖仪式上发表演说，指出："此次运动会的成功，使我对吾国选手在不久的将来参加奥林匹克运动充满了希望。""我国应立即成立一奥林匹克运动会代表队。"1928 年，张伯苓任名誉会长的"中华全国体育协进会"，派代表出席观摩了第 9 届国际奥林匹克运动会。1945 年抗战胜利，他组织召开体育协进会会议，申办第 15 届奥运会，这是中国历史上第一次申奥活动。近代著名外交家王正廷，在北洋大学求学期间，开始了解奥林匹克运动。1912 年，他和张伯苓等人，与菲律宾、日本的体育界人士协议，发起举办"远东运动会"。1920 年"远东运动会"被国际奥林匹克委员会正式承认为区域性国际体育赛事，舆论称之为"远东奥林匹克运动会"。1922 年，王正廷被选为国际奥

on the eve of the War of Resistance Against Japan.[1]

Among the three major ball games, volleyball started later than football and basketball in Tianjin, but it has a history of nearly a hundred years since it was introduced in the early 20th century. In the early days, volleyball was popular as a form of game in schools, including Nankai Middle School, Huiwen Middle School, Anglo-Chinese College, Lingdanggao Middle School, Nankai University, and Peiyang University, which were among the earliest schools to play volleyball. In 1927, Chang Poling and others initiated the establishment of the Tianjin Amateur Athletic Federation, which held many citywide volleyball open tournaments, promoting the popularization of volleyball sports. In 1931, students from Nankai University formed the Nanmin Volleyball Team, which swept across the country with repeated victories. Tianjin volleyball entered a period of prosperity, and various non-government sports clubs emerged at one time, contributing to the development of volleyball in Tianjin and even the whole country. After the founding of the People's Republic of China, with the call of the All-China Sports Federation to launch the "6-person" volleyball movement, in 1956, Tianjin selected and set up the first Men's and Women's Volleyball Teams, and began to participate in the National Volleyball League and make a name for themselves. In 1950, the first national team "China College Volleyball Team" was formed, and Li Ange, a student from Peiyang University, was selected. After graduation the following year, he officially joined the national team as a setter for the Men's Volleyball Team and later became the first coach of the Women's Volleyball Team in People's Republic of China. In 1979, Li Ange invented the "backward flight spiking with one foot taking-off", known as the "trump card of China volleyball". In the 1980s, as a technical consultant and research team leader, he helped the Women's Volleyball Team win five consecutive championships and trained a generation of famous players such as Feng Kun and Zhao Ruirui. The glory of Tianjin volleyball has continued to shine to this day. Tianjin Women's Volleyball Team has won 16 national league championships in more than 20 years. It has become a banner of China volleyball on the world stage.

Track and field is the oldest sports event, also

利迪尔在天津
Eric Liddell in Tianjin

① *Modern China through the Eyes of Tianjin: 100 Firsts*, compiled by Wang Shuzu, Hang Ying. Tianjin People's Publishing House, 2007, pp.217,219,221.

中华全国体育协进会董事王正廷授旗给中国参加奥运会第一人刘长春。摄于 1932 年

Wang Zhengting, the director of the China National Amateur Athletic Federation, presented a flag to Liu Changchun, the first Chinese athlete to participate in the Olympic Games. Taken in 1932

委会委员，他也是中国历史上第一位国际奥委会委员。1936 年第 11 届奥运会和 1948 年第 14 届奥运会，中国均派出代表团参加，王正廷两次担任总领队。中国第二位国际奥委会委员是南开大学篮球队教练董守义。此外，天津的中华基督教青年会（YMCA）也积极推动奥林匹克运动在中国青年中的发展，并将其与爱国主义精神联系起来。1908 年青年会刊物《天津青年》（*Tientsin Young Men*）上的一篇文章提出了著名的"奥林匹克三问"："1. 中国何时能派一名能赢得金牌的运动员参加奥林匹克竞赛？ 2. 中国何时能派一支能获得金牌的代表团参加奥林匹克竞赛？ 3. 中国何时能邀请全世界到北京来参加一场国际奥林匹克竞赛，改变奥运会一直在雅典举办的局面？"整整 100 年之后，2008 年中国终于成功举办了北京奥运会。

近代天津人的精神世界

文化，是构成一个城市时空概念的范畴之一，它不仅包括生活方式，还包括人们的精神面貌、宗教信仰以及文学、艺术等。它源远流长，与城市共生，是城市记忆的延续。

very popular among the masses in Tianjin. Not only were schools generally including it in physical education to improve students' physical fitness, but also foreign nationals and stationed troops held public sports meetings annually (interrupted during World War I), where athletes from various countries could participate. Eric Liddell, a Scottish born in Tianjin in 1902 (Chinese name Li Airui), won the gold medal and broke the Olympic and world records in the 400-meter race at the Paris Olympics in July 1924. Later, Liddell returned to Tianjin to teach at Anglo-Chinese College. At his suggestion, the Minyuan Recreation Ground was renovated into a world-class venue, hosting numerous sports competitions every year. After the outbreak of the Pacific War, Liddell, along with other British and American expatriates, was interned in a concentration camp in Wei County, Shandong Province. He passed away due to illness shortly before the end of the war. In 1982, the British film "Chariots of Fire," based on Eric Liddell's sports career, won four Academy Awards including Best Picture and Best Original Score, and remains a classic film widely acclaimed worldwide.

Sports are not only activities for physical fitness and leisure, but also a way for countries to compete during peacetime. Therefore, enlightened individuals in China believed that China should participate in the Olympic Games. Chang Poling, the president of Nankai University, was one of them. On October 24, 1907, during the fifth school sports meeting in Tianjin, he stated in his speech, "The success of this sports meeting fills me with hope for our country's athletes to participate in the Olympic Games in the near future." "Our country should immediately establish an Olympic team." In 1928, Chang Poling served as the honorary president of the "China National Amateur Athletic Federation" and sent representatives to observe the 9th International Olympic Games. After the victory in the War of Resistance Against Japan in 1945, he organized a meeting of the Amateur Athletic Federation to bid for the 15th Olympic Games, marking the first Olympic bid in Chinese history. Wang Zhengting, a famous diplomat in modern times, began to learn about the Olympic Games during his studies at Peiyang University. In 1912, he and Chang Poling, among others, reached an agreement with sports figures from the Philippines and Japan to initiate the "Far East Games." In 1920, the "Far East Games" was formally recognized by the International Olympic Committee as a regional international sports event, known in public opinion as the "Far East Olympic Games." In 1922, Wang Zhengting was elected as a member of the International Olympic Committee (IOC), becoming the first Chinese member of the IOC in history. China participated in the 11th and 14th Olympic Games in 1936 and 1948, respectively, with Wang Zhengting serving as the head of the delegation twice. The second Chinese member of

多元化、分阶层的宗教信仰

　　宗教在工业革命以前的人类社会生产生活中占有重要地位。它起源于社会生产力水平低下的时期，是原始人类对各种自然现象的神秘想象和解释。中国人的宗教主要有道教、佛教、伊斯兰教、天主教、基督教新教和民间信仰。其中，道教、佛教、伊斯兰教以及各种民间信仰在天津都有悠久的发展历史，构成了天津人丰富的精神世界。近代以来，随着西方殖民主义的入侵和资本主义生产方式的发展，天主教、基督教新教、东正教、犹太教、锡克教等也都传入天津，为天津的宗教发展留下了丰富的印迹，充分体现了这座近代大都市的国际化程度。

　　前文中讲到，天津素有"先有天后宫，后有天津卫"的说法，天后宫里供奉的是妈祖。妈祖本是民间信仰的神，后来被道教吸收成为"天后娘娘"和"护国天妃"。距离现在的天后宫不远处还有一处历史悠久的道院叫"玉皇阁"，它曾是天津城内最大的道教庙宇。清人有诗云："直在云霄上，蓬瀛望可通；万帆风汇舞，一镜水涵空。"从明至清，佛教寺院遍布天津地区，其中影响较大的有孤云寺、海光寺、大悲禅院、紫竹林庙宇等。伊斯兰教在天津的发展也有几百年的历史。天津最早的清真寺建于永乐二年（1404），与天津城的历史一样悠久。1655年荷兰使团来到天津时就发现，"这个地方到处是庙宇，人烟稠密"[1]。以上能够说明在西方殖民主义的入侵和资本主义生产方式到来以前，天津地区民众的主要信仰是佛教、道教、伊斯兰教以及民间信仰。至近代，玉皇阁的绝大部分建筑被废，现仅存主体建筑。而佛教寺院除了大悲禅院香火依旧之外，孤云寺（天津人后来称为白庙）[2]、海光寺和紫竹林的庙宇被外国侵略者拆毁，只剩下地名留存。明清两代中国的道教发展陷入停滞僵化，天津的

---

① （荷）约翰·纽霍夫，《荷兰联邦东印度公司使节哥页和开泽阁下在北京紫禁城晋谒大鞑靼可汗（顺治）》，1669年。转引自（英）雷穆森著，许逸凡等译，《天津租界史（插图本）》，天津人民出版社，2009年，第11页。

② 1900年义和团运动期间，被沙俄军队烧毁。辛亥革命后，庙宇曾做过小学。1948年平津战役前夕，国民党为了修筑城防壕，再度将白庙村放火焚毁。天津解放后，白庙村重建。1958年白庙被拆除。2001年，白庙得到复建。

the IOC was Dong Shouyi, the coach of the Nankai University basketball team. Additionally, the Young Men's Christian Association (YMCA) in Tianjin actively promoted the development of the Olympic movement among Chinese youth and associated it with patriotic spirit. An article in the 1908 YMCA publication *Tientsin Young Men* raised the famous "Three Olympic Questions": "1. When will China send an athlete who can win a gold medal to the Olympic Games? 2. When will China send a delegation that can win gold medals to the Olympic Games? 3. When will China invite the world to Beijing to participate in an international Olympic Games and change the situation where the Olympics have always been held in Athens?" Exactly 100 years later, China successfully hosted the Beijing Olympics in 2008.

The Spiritual World of Modern Tianjin Residents

Culture is one of the categories that constitute the temporal and spatial concept of a city. It encompasses not only lifestyle but also people's spiritual outlook, religious beliefs, as well as literature, art, and so forth. It has a long history, coexists with the city, and is the continuation of urban memory.

Diverse and Stratified Religious Beliefs

Religion played a significant role in human society's production and livelihood before the Industrial Revolution. It originated during periods of low levels of social productivity and constituted primitive human beings' mysterious imagination and explanations of various natural phenomena. The main religions in China include Taoism, Buddhism, Islam, Catholicism, Protestantism, and folk beliefs. Among them, Taoism, Buddhism, Islam, and various folk beliefs have a long history of development in Tianjin, forming a rich spiritual world for Tianjin residents. In modern times, with the intrusion of Western colonialism and the development of capitalist modes of production, Catholicism, Protestantism, Eastern Orthodoxy, Judaism, Sikhism, and other religions have also been introduced to Tianjin. They have left rich traces in Tianjin's religious development, fully reflecting the level of internationalization of this modern metropolis.

As mentioned earlier, Tianjin is known for the saying "First come the Tianhou Temple, then come the Tianjin Wei," where the Tianhou Temple worships Mazu. Mazu was originally a deity of folk belief and later absorbed into Taoism as "Heavenly Empress" and "Protective Deity of the Nation." Not far from the present Tianhou Temple, there is another historic Taoist temple called "Jade Emperor Pavilion," which was once the largest Taoist

弘一法师李叔同
Master Hongyi (Li Shutong)

《送别》
The poetry of *Send-off*

长亭外，
古道边，
芳草碧连天。
晚风拂柳笛声残，
夕阳山外山。
天之涯，
地之角，
知交半零落。
一瓢浊酒尽余欢，
今宵别梦寒。

道教在近代逐渐与民间信仰融合、难分彼此，而天津佛教在近代的式微则与国运的衰败密切相关。

　　近代中国佛教史上著名高僧、文化奇才——弘一法师，是天津文化史和佛教史上的杰出人物。"半世风流半世僧"的他，一生充满了传奇色彩，以卓越的才华照耀了一个时代。弘一法师，俗名李叔同，1880 年生于天津官宦富商之家。前半生的他是中国新文化运动的前驱，是卓越的音乐家、美术教育家、书法家、戏剧活动家，是中国话剧事业的开拓者之一。他是第一个向中国传播西方音乐的先驱者，作词的歌曲《送别》，历经几十年传唱经久不衰，成为经典名曲，几乎没有一个人在学校毕业时没唱过这首歌。同时，他也是中国第一个开创裸体写生的教师，潘天寿、丰子恺都是他的入室弟子。他的书法朴拙圆满、浑然天成。弘一法师可谓是集各个领域才华于一身的不可多得的全才。在人生达到顶峰时，他却选择遁入空门，于 1918 年在杭州虎跑寺正式出家，在灵隐寺受戒。出家后，他恪守佛教的清规戒律，一心钻研律宗，并到各地去弘法，大力振兴律宗，普度众生出苦海，被尊为律宗第十一代世祖。1942 年，弘一法师功德圆满，在圆寂前写下"悲欣交集"四个字，完美诠释了他追求丰富精神生活、达至灵魂升华的一生。

temple in Tianjin. During the Ming and Qing dynasties, Buddhist temples were widespread in the Tianjin area, with significant ones including Guyun Temple (later referred to as the White Temple), Haiguang Temple, Dabei Temple (The Temple of Great Compassion), and Zizhulin Temple. Islam has also had a history of development in Tianjin for several hundred years. The earliest mosque in Tianjin was built in the second year of Yongle (1404), which is as old as the history of Tianjin city. When the Dutch delegation arrived in Tianjin in 1655, they found, "Temples and people are everywhere in this place."[1] The above examples illustrate that before the intrusion of Western colonialism and the arrival of capitalist modes of production, the main beliefs of the people in the Tianjin area were Buddhism, Taoism, Islam, and folk beliefs. In modern times, most of the buildings of Jade Emperor Pavilion were abandoned, leaving only the main structure. Buddhist temples, except for the Dabei Temple, were destroyed by foreign aggressors, leaving only the place names, such as White Temple[2], Zizhulin Temple, and Haiguang Temple. During the Ming and Qing dynasties, Taoism in China stagnated, and Tianjin's Taoism gradually merged with folk beliefs in modern times, becoming indistinguishable from each other. The decline of Tianjin Buddhism in modern times is closely related to the decline of the country's fortunes.

In modern Chinese Buddhist history, the famous monk and cultural genius, Master Hongyi, is an outstanding figure in Tianjin's cultural history and Buddhist history. With a life filled with legends, he illuminated an era with exceptional talent. Master Hongyi, whose secular name was Li Shutong, was born in 1880 into a wealthy official family in Tianjin. In the first half of his life, he was a pioneer of the New Culture Movement in China, an outstanding musician, art educator, calligrapher, and theater activist, and one of the pioneers of China's drama. He was the first to introduce Western music to China, and the song "Farewell," which he wrote, became a classic that lasted for decades, almost everyone sang this song when graduating from school. At the same time, he was also the first teacher in China to introduce nude figure drawing, with Pan Tianshou and Feng Zikai among his disciples. His calligraphy was simple, perfect, and natural. Master Hongyi was indeed a

---

①　Johan Nieuhof. *An Embassy from the East-India Company of the United Provinces*, 1669. O. D. Rasmussen, *Tientsin: An Illustrated Outline History*, translated by Xu Yifan, et al. Tianjin People's Publishing House, 2008, p.11.

②　During the Boxer Rebellion in 1900, it was burned down by the Russian army. After the 1911 Revolution, the temple was repurposed as a primary school. On the eve of the Beiping-Tianjin Campaign in 1948, the Kuomintang set fire to White Temple Village once more in order to build defense trenches. After the liberation of Tianjin, White Temple Village was rebuilt. The White Temple was demolished in 1958 and was reconstructed in 2001.

天主教传入中国是在明朝，但它在天津的发展则是在开埠以后。第一位来华传教士利玛窦在天津滞留了半年，但没有在此传教。由他开创的中国传教方法，后来被称作"利玛窦规矩"①，决定了天主教的传教对象一开始是皇室贵族和士大夫等上层人士，以获得保护并提高影响力。因此天津作为一个小城镇，并不是早期天主教的理想传教地。直到近代被开放为通商口岸之后，在军队枪炮的保护和威胁下，天主教才在天津打下了第一根桩。法国支持的天主教会拆除了望海楼和紫竹林的佛教寺庙，建起教堂、修道院、孤儿院、医院、学校等一系列宗教场所和公共设施，并通过各种手段来吸引底层民众加入，由此引发天主教教徒与普通民众之间的各种冲突，从而酿成"教案"，其中最著名的莫过于1870年的"望海楼教案"，或称"天津教案"。

与天主教挟外国军队保护而自重的做法不同，基督教新教在天津的传播更加温和。新教的传播主要来自英美系统的几大教派，其中美国传教士在近代天津的影响力更大。19世纪80年代开始，美国兴起了学生海外传教运动，其领导者和推动者主要是大学生，而非旧有的保守的上层宗教人士。这项传教运动，在方向上直指中国，"中国就是目标，就是指路星辰，就是吸引我们所有人的巨大的磁铁"；在方法上"强调关注社会问题，参与社会改革"，"不急于拯救个人灵魂，而企图用西方文化改造中国文化"。②新教在天津的传教方式主要是兴教育、办医院和赈济灾民等，传教对象主要是中国的知识分子阶层。近代天津最有影响力的外国人中，就有曾经由学生海外传教运动派遣来华，后一心兴办教育，创办了中国近代第一所大学的美国人丁家立（Charles Daniel Tenney）。

1882年25岁的丁家立由美国出发前往山西传教。到达中国后不久，虽充满宗教热情但不乏独立思考和探索精神的丁家立就意识到：

---

① "利玛窦规矩"，决定了天主教传教士的传教方法：1. 学汉语、改装易服、习新礼，以利沟通，方便中国人接纳；2. 结交皇室贵族、士大夫等上层人士，以获得保护和提高影响力；3. 改编《圣经》故事，迎合中国人的道德观和宿命论；4. 注重传授西方科学知识，借此得到中国人对西方科学的关注以接受基督教信仰；5. 发展天主教徒要重质不重量。

② 王立新，《美国传教士与晚清中国现代化》，天津人民出版社，1997年，第14—15页。

rare talent in various fields. When he reached the peak of his life, he chose to enter the monastic life. In 1918, he officially became a monk at Hupao Temple in Hangzhou and received precepts at Lingyin Temple. After ordination, he strictly adhered to the Buddhist precepts, devoted himself to the study of the Vinaya, and traveled to various places to spread Buddhism, vigorously revitalizing the Vinaya and helping sentient beings out of suffering, being honored as the 11th patriarch of the Vinaya lineage. In 1942, Master Hongyi passed away, writing the four characters "Bei Xin Jiao Ji" (a mixture of sorrow and joy) before his final moments, perfectly interpreting his pursuit of a rich spiritual life and the elevation of his soul throughout his life.

The introduction of Catholicism to China occurred during the Ming Dynasty, but its development in Tianjin took place after the city's opening to foreign trade. The first missionary to come to China, Matteo Ricci, stayed in Tianjin for six months but did not preach there. The missionary methods he initiated in China later became known as the "Ricci method,"[1] which initially targeted the royal nobility, scholars, and upper-class individuals to gain protection and increase influence. Therefore, Tianjin, being a small town, was not an ideal missionary ground for early Catholicism. It was not until modern times, after being opened as a treaty port, that Catholicism established its foothold in Tianjin under the protection and threat of military force. The Catholic Church supported by France demolished Buddhist temples such as Wanghailou and Zizhulin, replacing them with a series of religious facilities and public institutions including churches, convents, orphanages, hospitals, and schools. They used various means to attract lower-class people to join, leading to conflicts between Catholic followers and the common people, resulting in various incidents known as "missionary cases." The most famous of these incidents was the "Wanghailou Incident" in 1870, also known as the "Tianjin Missionary Case."

Unlike the Catholic practice of relying on foreign military protection and asserting dominance, the spread of Protestantism in Tianjin was more moderate. The propagation of Protestantism mainly came from several major denominations within the British and American systems, with American missionaries having a greater influence in modern Tianjin. In the

---

① The "Matteo Ricci Rules" determined the missionary approach of Catholic missionaries: 1. Learn Chinese, adopt Chinese clothing, and practice new customs to facilitate communication and make it easier for the Chinese to accept Christianity; 2. Befriend the royal family, nobility, and intellectuals to gain protection and enhance influence; 3. Adapt *The Holy Bible* to align with Chinese moral views and fatalism; 4. Focus on imparting Western scientific knowledge to garner Chinese interest in Western science, thus fostering acceptance of Christianity; 5. Emphasize quality over quantity in the development of Catholic followers.

在具有悠久文化传统的中国传教几乎是一项不可能完成的任务，中国人所迫切需要的是将西方科学的精密性和确定性融入他们巨大的思想宝库中去。[1] 丁家立认为天津会是自己发挥才能最理想的舞台。这里是手握军政大权的直隶总督兼北洋通商大臣李鸿章的衙署所在地，被视为中国的第二政府和影子内阁。1886年夏天，丁家立在天津建立中西书院（Anglo-Chinese School），专门教授中国学生西学，此后他又成为李鸿章子孙的家庭教师。1895年，借由李鸿章，丁家立协助盛宣怀创办了中国第一所大学——北洋大学。在创办过程中，他以美国哈佛、耶鲁大学为蓝本，规定学制四年，分为土木工程、冶金矿务、机械、法律四门专业。此后北洋大学向美国输送了第一批公派大学留学生，这些学生中有很多人后来成为民国时期的重要人物，其中一些人也成为新教徒。1915年反对法国天主教会的"老西开事件"中，斗争组织者"维持国权国土会"的副会长赵天麟即为丁家立的学生。他是留美海归，时任北洋大学校长，也是一名新教徒。此次斗争不失为天津基督教新教和天主教之间的一次较量。

在中国传统社会的民众日常生产生活中，宗教信仰当然是非常重要的，但是它的重要程度不如基督教在欧洲或伊斯兰教在阿拉伯社会那样占有独立的重要地位。中国的"天子"代替"天"在人间进行统治，主持国家级的各种祭祀和祈福活动，但是日常的各种规范却并不要求人民对天子的绝对信仰。"忠孝节义"是中国古代所提倡的道德准则。《尚书·仲虺之诰》中说："佐贤辅德，显忠遂良。"意即：帮助贤能之人，辅佐仁德之人，表彰忠诚之人，起用善良之人。可见，"忠"在封建社会里特指为君主尽心尽责，"忠诚"只是对于皇帝本身的。自汉武帝推行"罢黜百家，独尊儒术"的政策以来，儒家思想与中央集权的封建专制制度相辅相成。其结果是，在中国没有任何一种宗教偶像可以超越帝王的权威。同时，儒家思想成为居于统治地位的上层社会的信仰，其维护社会秩序的功能和使命与基督教和伊斯兰教不相上下，对"君君臣臣父父子子"这种规则和秩序的维护达到了宗教狂热的程度。

1880s, the United States saw the rise of the Student Volunteer Movement for Foreign Missions, led and driven primarily by college students rather than conservative religious figures from the upper class. This missionary movement was explicitly aimed at China, with the country being seen as the goal, the guiding star, and the immense magnet attracting all of them. The approach emphasized addressing social issues and participating in social reform, rather than hastily trying to save individual souls, with the intent to transform Chinese culture with Western culture.[1] The Protestant missionary methods in Tianjin mainly focused on promoting education, establishing hospitals, and providing relief to disaster victims, targeting primarily the intellectual class of China. Among the most influential foreigners in modern Tianjin was Charles Daniel Tenney, an American who was sent to China by the Student Volunteer Movement for Foreign Missions and later devoted himself to establishing education, eventually founding China's first modern university.

In 1882, at the age of 25, Charles Daniel Tenney set out from the United States to Shanxi for missionary work. Shortly after arriving in China, although filled with religious fervor, Tenney, who possessed an independent spirit of thought and exploration, realized that missionary work in China, with its long cultural traditions, was almost an impossible task. What the Chinese urgently needed was to integrate the precision and certainty of Western science into their vast treasure trove of ideas.[2] Tenney believed Tianjin would be the ideal stage for him to showcase his talents. It was the location of the yamen of Li Hongzhang, the Viceroy of Zhili and the Beiyang Minister of Commerce, which was regarded as the second government and shadow cabinet of China. In the summer of 1886, Tenney established the Anglo-Chinese School in Tianjin, specializing in teaching Chinese students Western knowledge. Later, he became a private tutor for Li Hongzhang's descendants. In 1895, with Li Hongzhang's assistance, Tenney helped Sheng Xuanhuai establish the first university in China, Peiyang University. In the establishment process, he modeled it after Harvard and Yale University in the United States, setting the curriculum for four years, divided into four majors: civil engineering, metallurgy and mining, machinery, and law. Subsequently, Peiyang University sent the first group of government-sponsored overseas students to the United States. Many of these students later became important figures

---

[1] 美国达特茅斯学院未刊档案：丁家立的论文集，约1900—1920。

[1] Wang Lixin. *American Missionaries and China Modernization in Late Qing*. Tianjin People's Publishing House, 1997, pp.14-15.

[2] Unpublished Archives of Dartmouth College in the U.S.: Charles Daniel Tenney Papers, ca. 1900-1920.

玉皇阁原由山门、钟楼、鼓楼、大殿、配殿、清皇阁、六角亭等建筑组成，现仅存主体建筑。玉皇阁是天津市区现存年代最早的木结构高层建筑。安红摄于 2006 年

The Jade Emperor Pavilion originally consisted of a mountain gate, a bell tower, a drum tower, a main hall, side halls, the Qinghuang pavilion, and hexagonal pavilion, but now only the main building remains. Jade Emperor Pavilion is the oldest surviving high-rise wooden building in Tianjin. Taken by An Hong in 2006

很多近代来华外国人也观察到了这一点，他们意识到儒家思想就是中国人的信仰。例如，丁家立认为，尽管佛教和道教的寺庙遍及中国各地，"但这些并不是中国上层社会所信奉的宗教，他们仅仅满足了无知者对盲目迷信的本能渴望"。他甚至认为，儒家思想可以被视为上层社会所信奉的占统治地位的宗教，孔子"是中国伟大的道德及宗教领袖"，只不过孔子"从不灌输任何超越生命的东西，从不发表有关来世和神灵的言论"。子曰："未知生，焉知死。""务民之义，敬鬼神而远之，可谓知矣。"与其他宗教创始人的不同在于，"他不创造奇迹，只限于讨论有生命的人之间的关系"，"子不语怪力乱神"。[①] 丁家立的观点与著名社会学家马克斯·韦伯不谋而合。在比较宗教社会学的经典著作《世界宗教的经济伦理·儒教与道教》一书中，韦伯指出，儒家思想所具有的理性主义，使中国社会破除了"迷信"、摆脱了巫术，它所发展起来的伦理道德在规范人们的

---

① 美国达特茅斯学院未刊档案：丁家立的论文集，第 12 号，约 1900—1920，《丁家立关于中国教育的演说》，第 1—4 页。

during the Republic of China period, with some also becoming Protestant Christians. In the "Laoxikai Incident" of 1915, an anti-French Catholic movement, Zhao Tianlin, the vice chairman of the organization "National Territorial Rights Preservation Association," was a student of Tenney. He was a returned student from the United States, serving as the president of Peiyang University and was also a Protestant Christian. This struggle was a confrontation between Protestantism and Catholicism in Tianjin.

In traditional Chinese society, religion is certainly very important in the daily production and life of the people, but its importance is not as independent as Christianity in Europe or Islam in Arab society. In China, the "Son of Heaven" replaces "Heaven" in ruling on earth, presiding over various national sacrifices and blessing activities, but the various norms of daily life do not require the people to have absolute faith in the Son of Heaven. "Loyalty, Filial Piety, Benevolence, and Righteousness" are the moral principles advocated in ancient China. As stated in the *Shang Shu: Zhonghuizhigao*: "Assist the wise and virtuous, promote loyalty and good." This indicates that "loyalty" in feudal society specifically refers to serving the monarch wholeheartedly, and "loyalty" is only for the emperor himself. Since Emperor Wu of Han Dynasty implemented the policy of "eliminating the Hundred Schools and promoting Confucianism", Confucianism has complemented the centralized feudal autocratic system. As a result, in China, no religious idol can surpass the authority of the emperor. At the same time, Confucianism has become the belief of the upper ruling class in society, and its function and mission of maintaining social order are no less than those of Christianity and Islam, reaching the level of religious fanaticism in upholding the rule and order of "Let the emperor be a emperor, the minister a minister, the father a father, and the son a son."

Many foreigners who came to China in modern times also observed this point, realizing that Confucianism is the belief of the Chinese people. For example, Charles Daniel Tenney believed that although Buddhist and Taoist temples were widespread throughout China, "these are not the religions revered by the upper class of China; they only satisfy the instinctive desires of the ignorant for blind superstition." He even believed that Confucianism could be regarded as the dominant religion revered by the upper class of society, and Confucius was "China's great moral and religious leader," except that Confucius "never instill anything beyond life, never make any statements about the afterlife and deities." Confucius said: "How can you know death without knowing life?" "The righteousness of serving the people, respecting ghosts and gods and staying away from them, can be considered as knowing the truth." Unlike other religious founders, "he did not perform miracles,

吕祖堂。为供奉仙人吕洞宾的道观，1433 年（明宣德八年）始称为吕祖堂，后多次重修。1900 年义和团运动兴起，将总坛口设在此处

Lüzu Temple. This Taoist temple is dedicated to the immortal LüDongbin. It was named Lüzu Temple in 1433 (the eighth year of the Xuande Emperor of the Ming Dynasty) and has undergone several renovations. In 1900, during the Boxer Rebellion, the main altar was established here

清真大寺始建于清顺治年间，康熙、嘉庆、咸丰、同治、光绪、宣统年间曾进行多次扩建。三百多年以来，寺内保存了阿文匾额 32 块、阿文楹联 4 幅；汉字匾额 64 块、楹联 8 幅；清代汉白玉石匾 1 块、砖匾 2 块；辛亥革命时期木匾 1 块。堪称清代书法展览。保存如此众多的匾额楹联墨宝、石刻、砖刻，在全国清真寺中是罕见的

The Grand Mosque was first built during the Shunzhi reign of the Qing Dynasty and underwent multiple expansions during the reigns of Kangxi, Jiaqing, Xianfeng, Tongzhi, Guangxu, and Xuantong. Over the course of more than 300 years, the mosque has preserved 32 Arabic plaques and 4 Arabic couplets; 64 Chinese plaques and 8 couplets; 1 white marble plaque and 2 brick plaques from the Qing Dynasty; and 1 wooden plaque from the 1911 Revolution. It can be considered a calligraphy exhibition of the Qing Dynasty. The preservation of such a large number of plaques, couplets, stone carvings, and brick inscriptions is rare among mosques across the country

大悲禅院。始建于明代，清朝时期两次扩建，是天津唯一的十方丛林寺院。1983 年，被列为全国重点佛教寺院之一。大悲殿的两侧设有玄奘法师纪念堂和弘一法师纪念堂。大悲院原先供奉着玄奘法师的灵骨。1956 年，遵照周恩来总理的安排，玄奘灵骨移供印度那烂陀寺，成为中印传统友谊的象征

Dabei Buddhist Temple (The Temple of Great Compassion) was founded in the Ming Dynasty and expanded twice during the Qing Dynasty. It is the only Shifang Conglin temple in Tianjin. In 1983, it was designated as one of the key Buddhist temples in China. Memorial halls for Master Xuanzang and Master Hongyi are located on either side of the temple. Originally, the temple housed the skull relic of Master Xuanzang, which was moved to Nalanda, India, in 1956, in accordance with the instructions of Premier Zhou Enlai. The relocation of the relic became a symbol of the traditional friendship between China and India

以上照片由安红摄于 2006 年

Photos taken by An Hong in 2006

独乐寺山门。刘悦摄于 2024 年
The mountain gate of Dule Temple. Taken by Liu Yue in 2024

独乐寺为天津现存最早的佛教寺庙，坐落于蓟州区，是中国仅存的三大辽代寺院之一。寺庙历史最早可追至唐贞观十年（公元 636 年），而寺内现存最古老的两座建筑物山门和观音阁为辽圣宗统和二年（公元 984 年）重建。这是佛教在天津发展的最早见证。独乐寺山门为中国现存最早的庑殿顶山门，也是最早的屋顶鸱吻、"分心斗底槽"殿堂实例、木构建筑直斗实例；最早的 45 度斜拱、45 度线出角华拱、山门转角斗拱。观音阁为中国现存最古老的木结构楼阁，由里外两圈柱子组成，分别限定出内、外槽空间；最早的空井结构实例，阁内长方形的空井结构，容有高大的观音像；最早的斗八藻井实例，特别是斗八藻井与平闇、梁架、斗拱的巧妙配合，形成阁内空间艺术的高潮，突出了观音主像；寺内供奉的十一面观音主像，总高 16.08 米，是我国现存最大的彩色泥塑站像。全阁有三层柱框、三层斗拱和上层梁架，历经了千年风雨和 28 次地震的考验

Dule Temple is the earliest existing Buddhist temple in Tianjin, located in Jizhou District. It is one of the three existing temples of the Liao Dynasty in China. Its history can be traced back to the tenth year of the Emperor Taizong of Tang (636 AD), and the two oldest existing buildings in the temple, mountain gate and Guanyin Pavilion, were rebuilt in the second year of the Emperor Shengzong of Liao Dynasty (984 AD). It's the witness of the earliest development of Buddhism in Tianjin. The mountain gate of Dule Temple is the earliest existing mountain gate with a hip roof in China, and it is also the earliest example of a roof gargoyle, a hall with a structure of equally dividing from the middle by columns, and a straight bracket in a wooden structure; the earliest 45-degree inclined arch, 45-degree corner arch, and mountain gate corner bracket. Guanyin Pavilion is the oldest existing wooden structure tower in China, consisting of two circles of columns inside and outside, respectively defining the inner and outer spaces. It's the earliest rectangular empty-well structure with a tall statue of Guanyin. It's also the first temple with Douba caisson ceiling, especially its ingenious combination with caisson ceiling decoraiton, beam frames and brackets, highlighting the main statue of Guanyin. The eleven-face Guanyin statue enshrined in the temple, with a total height of 16.08 meters, is the largest existing colored-clay standing statue in China. The pavilion has three layers of column frames, brackets and upper beam frames, which have withstood the test of thousands of years of wind and rain and 28 earthquakes

独乐寺内观音阁。刘悦摄于 2024 年
Guanyin Pavilion in Dule Temple. Taken by Liu Yue in 2024

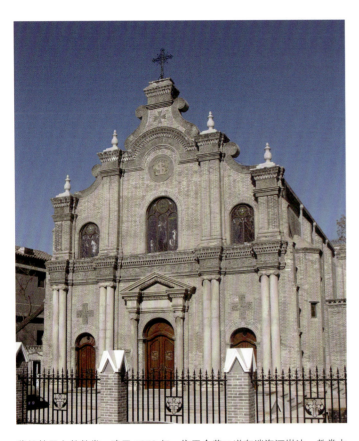

紫竹林天主教教堂。建于 1872 年，位于今营口道东端海河岸边。教堂占地 6.8 亩，建筑面积 779 平方米。教堂内有西洋古典管风琴赫然耸立，紫铜音管靠墙壁排列，直向屋顶。演奏时，声音宏大丰满，浑厚和谐，音域宽广，伴和唱诗班的歌声时，神圣而庄严。安红摄于 2015 年

Zizhulin Catholic Church. Built in 1872, it is located at the eastern end of Yingkou Road, on the bank of the Hai River. The church covers an area of 6.8 mu, with a building area of 779 square meters. Inside, there is a classical organ standing tall, with copper pipes arranged against the wall, extending towards the ceiling. When played, its sound is grand and full, rich and harmonious, with a wide range. When accompanied by the choir's singing, it creates a sacred and solemn atmosphere. Taken by An Hong in 2015

安里甘教堂。由基督教圣公会创办，建筑风格为典型的英国乡村教堂风格。教堂用地由 1893 年英租界工部局捐赠，1903 年正式落成，位于现在的泰安道和浙江路的交界。安红摄于 2007 年

Anglican Church. Founded by the Anglican Church, the architectural style is typical of British country churches. The land for the church was donated by the British Municipal Council in 1893, and the church was officially completed in 1903. It is located at the intersection of Tai'an Road and Zhejiang Road. Taken by An Hong in 2007

犹太会堂。1940 年 9 月，犹太人公会在天津落成一座大教堂，是中国留存至今的建筑规模最大的犹太会堂。历史上犹太人涌入天津曾有三次浪潮：1860 年天津开埠以后，犹太商人来津经商；1901 年俄租界在天津划定了大片土地，俄籍犹太人陆续来津落脚谋生；1931 年，九一八事变日本侵占东北，大批"白俄"中的犹太人由东北迁居到天津。据 20 世纪 30 年代末美国《犹太年鉴》记载，1935 年天津的犹太人多达 3500 人。犹太会堂坐落于旧英租界 32 号路，今南京路与郑州道交口

Jewish Synagogue. In September 1940, the Tientsin Jewish Union completed the construction of a large synagogue in Tianjin, which remains the largest Jewish synagogue in China today. There were three significant waves of Jewish immigration to Tianjin: After the opening of Tianjin in 1860, Jewish merchants came to the city to engage in business; in 1901, when Russia established a concession in Tianjin, Russian Jews gradually settled in the city to seek livelihoods; and in 1931, following the September 18 Incident, when Japan occupied Northeast China, a large number of Jewish White Russians migrated to Tianjin. According to the American *Jewish Yearbook* in the late 1930s, there were as many as 3,500 Jews in Tianjin by 1935. The Jewish synagogue is located on No. 32 Road in the former British Concession, at the present-day intersection of Nanjing Road and Zhengzhou Road

俄国东正教教会在天津举办宗教活动
Religious activities held by the Russian Orthodox Church in Tianjin

建于 1925 年的天津东正教纪念堂
The Tianjin Orthodox Memorial Hall, built in 1925

天津基督教青年会。1895 年，北美基督教青年会派人来天津组建青年会，为中国第一个基督教青年会。1911 年，张伯苓当选为董事长，梅贻琦（后任清华大学校长）任干事。1913 年，天津成立基督教女青年会。青年会是世界性的社会团体，主要致力于社会服务工作，组织青年开展文化、教育、体育、慈善等活动

Tianjin Young Men's Christian Association (YMCA). In 1895, the North American YMCA sent representatives to Tianjin to establish the first YMCA in China. In 1911, Chang Poling was elected as the chairman, and Mei Yiqi (who later became the president of Tsinghua University) served as the secretary. In 1913, the Young Women's Christian Association was founded in Tianjin. The YMCA is a global social organization primarily focused on social service, organizing youth activities in culture, education, sports, charity, and more

日常行为中起到与宗教相似的作用，在这一点上，它与基督教新教具有多方面内在联系。① 比如，儒学核心原则就是孝敬父母，而"孝顺父母"也是"十诫"之一。儒家思想的统治地位，在普通人日常生活中的影响力更大，所以中国人对于佛教或者道教等宗教信仰并不那么虔诚，而是抱持一种功利主义的态度，总是"临时抱佛脚"。尤其是在近代，当西方殖民者的"坚船利炮"摆在面前时，天津人更是把"有用""灵验"放到第一位，从而把各种宗教信仰，甚至神话传说混为一体。无论是义和团拳民们附体的各路神仙，还是娘娘宫里供奉的八方神祇，都是这种"功利主义"最直观的体现。

报人与报纸

随着租界人口的不断增长，人们相互联系、沟通信息的需求也日益增多，于是外国侨民在英租界创办了天津第一份报纸。随着经济社会的繁荣，近代天津出现了各种语言的新闻媒体，其中中文报纸的发展，更是使天津成为北方的新闻传播中心。在印刷媒介繁荣的同时，新的传播技术如广播无线电和新闻电影等也在租界内得到应用和推广。

天津第一份报纸是英文报纸《中国时报》（*China Times*），创办者之一是津海关税务司（海关关长）德璀琳。他还参与创办了第一份中文报纸《时报》，同时他也是出版发行这两份报纸的天津印刷公司（Tientsin Printing Company）的创办人和股东之一。《中国时报》每周出版一份，三栏十二页，1886年11月6日开始出版，1891年3月28日停刊。一些当时比较了解中国情况的在华外国人曾为它充当撰稿人，如丁韪良（W. A. P. Martin）、明恩溥（A. H. Smith）、李提摩太（T. Richard）、丁家立、濮兰德（J. O. P. Bland）等人。因此，它的社论被认为是比较公允而有分寸的，"可以列入远东迄今最好的报纸之列"。"报纸大量关注与公共利益有关的事物而不是如有些人所期望的只关注某些人或团体"，因

---

① （德）马克斯·韦伯著，王容芬译，《世界宗教的经济伦理·儒教与道教》，广西师范大学出版社，2008年，第263页。

only discussing relationships between living beings," "the Master did not speak of extraordinary abilities or supernatural powers."① Tenney's views coincided with those of the renowned sociologist Max Weber. In Weber's classic work of comparative religious sociology, *Economic Ethics of World Religion—Confucianism and Taoism*, he pointed out that the rationality of Confucianism enabled Chinese society to dispel "superstition" and rid itself of witchcraft. The ethical morality it developed played a role similar to religion in regulating people's daily behavior. In this respect, it has multiple inherent connections with Protestant Christianity.② For example, the core principle of Confucianism is filial piety, and "honoring one's parents" is also one of the Ten Commandments. The dominance of Confucianism has a greater influence on the daily lives of ordinary people, so Chinese people are not so devout in their religious beliefs such as Buddhism or Taoism, but hold a utilitarian attitude, always resorting to last-minute actions. Especially in modern times, when Western colonialists' "powerful navy with excellent weaponry" were looming, the people of Tianjin prioritized "usefulness" and "efficacy," thus blending various religious beliefs, and even mythical legends, together. Whether it was the various gods possessed by the Boxers during the Boxer Rebellion or the deities worshipped in the Sea Goddess Temple, they were the most direct manifestations of this "utilitarianism."

Journalists and Newspapers

As the population of the concessions continued to grow, the demand for mutual contact and communication of information also increased. Therefore, foreign residents in the British concession founded the first newspaper in Tianjin. With the prosperity of the economy and society, various language news media emerged in modern Tianjin, among which the development of Chinese newspapers made Tianjin a news dissemination center in the north. Alongside the flourishing of print media, new communication technologies such as radio broadcasting and newsreels were also applied and promoted within the concessions.

The first newspaper in Tianjin was the English newspaper *China Times*, one of the founders being Gustav Detring, the Commissioner of the Tianjin Customs. He also participated in the establishment of the first Chinese

---

① Unpublished Archives of Dartmouth College in the U.S.: Charles Daniel Tenney Papers, ca. 1900-1920, carbon of proposed entry for Dictionary of American Biography, carbon, pp.1-4.

② Max Weber. *Economic Ethics of World Religion · Confucianism and Taoism*, translated by Wang Rongfen. Guangxi Normal University Press, 2008, p.263.

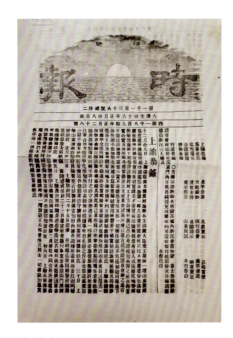

《时报》
The Eastern Times

此这份报纸主要是一份地方性报纸，办报宗旨是为租界建设和公共事业服务。例如在报纸的建议下，很多租界的重要机构和公共事业建成了，包括天津商会（Tientsin Chamber of Commerce）、天津文学辩论会、某些河道与港口改进工程，以及各种土地、道路和公用事业计划等。天津第一份中文报纸《时报》的创办曾得到直隶总督李鸿章的大力支持，有两年时间是由传教士李提摩太担任主编。报纸登载中国的新闻、上谕以及其他中文刊物不会有的综合信息，约在 1900 年停刊。①

《中国时报》停刊后，它的继承者《京津泰晤士报》（Peking & Tientsin Times）于 1894 年创刊，吸收了《中国时报》的一些成功经验，且它的关注面更广，因此很快成为中国北方最具影响力的英文报纸。许多有留学背景的中国人都是它的订阅者和读者，在长江以北，它几乎是无处不见。而且，它发行到国外的数量是近代所有在华出版的英文报纸中最大的，由此可见其影响力。②该报名义上是份商业报纸，但它接受英租界工部局的资助，实际上是份半官方报纸。《时报》的继承者是《直报》，由德璀琳资助于 1895 年正月创刊，为中文日报，共八版。甲午战争期间，《直报》以积极的态度报道战争。刊物还连续登载了以严复为代表的维新派知识分子为挽救民族危机所撰写的一系列时事政治评论文章，如《论世变之亟》《原强》《辟韩》《原强续篇》《救亡决论》等，力主变法图强，以西方科学取代八股文章，力倡新学和废除专制政治，

---

① （英）雷穆森著，许逸凡等译，《天津租界史（插图本）》，天津人民出版社，2009 年，第 76 页。

② "中国北方外国人的'圣经'：《京津泰晤士报》"。http://www.022tj.net/tianjinwei/article.php?itemid-12-type-news.html.

newspaper *The Eastern Times* and was one of the founders and shareholders of the Tientsin Printing Company, which published both newspapers. *China Times* was published weekly, consisting of three columns and twelve pages. It began publication on November 6, 1886, and ceased on March 28, 1891. Some foreigners in China who were familiar with the situation in China served as contributors, such as W. A. P. Martin, A. H. Smith, T. Richard, Charles Daniel Tenney, and J. O. P. Bland. Therefore, its editorials were considered fair and balanced, and it was regarded as "one of the best newspapers in the Far East." The newspaper focused heavily on matters related to public interest rather than catering to specific individuals or groups, making it primarily a local newspaper aimed at serving the interests of the concessions and public affairs. For example, many important institutions and public projects in the concessions were established based on the newspaper's suggestions, including the Tientsin Chamber of Commerce, Tianjin Literary and Debating Society, improvements projects of waterways and ports, as well as various land, road, and public utility plans. The establishment of the first Chinese newspaper *The Eastern Times* in Tianjin received strong support from Li Hongzhang, the Viceroy of Zhili Province. It was edited by missionary Timothy Richard for two years. The newspaper published news, imperial edicts, and other comprehensive information from China not found in other Chinese publications, and it ceased publication around 1900.①

After the cessation of the *China Times*, its successor, the *Peking & Tientsin Times*, was founded in 1894. It absorbed some successful experiences from the *China Times*, and its coverage was broader, quickly becoming the most influential English newspaper in northern China. Many Chinese with overseas education backgrounds were subscribers and readers, and it was nearly ubiquitous north of the Yangtze River. Moreover, it had the largest circulation overseas among all modern English newspapers published in China, indicating its influence.② While nominally a commercial newspaper, it received funding from the British Municipal Council, making it essentially a semi-official newspaper. The successor to the *The Eastern Times* was the *Chih Pao*, sponsored by Gustav Detring and launched in the first lunar month of 1895 as a Chinese daily newspaper with eight editions. During the First Sino-Japanese War, the *Chih Pao* reported on the war with a positive attitude. The publication also serialized a series of political commentaries by reformist

---

① O. D. Rasmussen, *Tientsin: An Illustrated Outline History*, translated by Xu Yifan, et al. Tianjin People's Publishing House, 2008, p.76.

② The "Bible" for Foreigners in Northern China: *Peking & Tientsin Times*. http://www.022tj.net/tianjinwei/article.php?itemid-12-type-news.html.

是反省甲午战争、探讨强国之路的重要论坛。因为报道袁世凯部哗变的消息，1904 年 3 月《直报》被袁世凯命令停止发行，当年六月、九月两度易名为《商务日报》《中外实报》继续出版。[①] 外国人在华创办中文报纸，当然是为了控制舆论，为其在华利益服务，因此办报需要了解和尊重中国人和中国文化，这样才能不致引起反感而达不到预期效果。1927 年出版的《中国新闻发达史》曾评价说，"外国在中国宣传，不独为其自国报纸（外文报纸），即在中国报纸亦可宣传。德国的《中外实报》（天津）得有极大的效果"；并认为其成功之处在于，"他能猜出中国人心理，将内容形式，处处都迎合着中国人的心理而编辑。所以就是中国人自己亦往往不知读的是外国报"。[②] 这可以说是对外国侨民发起创办中文报纸一事的极高评价了。

近代天津有外国人创办的多种语言的报纸，如法文的《中国回声》、俄文的《霞报》、德文的《德华日报》和多种日文报刊。其中，《京津泰晤士报》之外另一份具有全国影响力的英文报纸是《华北明星报》。它于 1918 年 8 月在津出版，太平洋战争爆发后停刊。其董事长和总编辑是北洋大学法学教授、美国人福克斯（Charles J. Fox）。福克斯拥有德国海德堡大学哲学博士学位，曾在纽约和华盛顿的报社工作达 10 年之久，具有丰富的办报经验，结束在北洋大学的教职后，他创办了《华北明星报》。《华北明星报》定价低廉，一般日报订阅费是二三十元，而它只需十元，且全年无休，一天也不停刊，很快就成为"华北发行量最大的外国日报"[③]。它的信息量大、视野广阔，新闻来源主要是路透社发布的消息，使天津本地的中外读者能及时准确地了解全世界正在发生的重大新闻。例如，天津人最早得知俄国十月革命的信息即是通过《华北明星报》。它的介绍公正客观，对中国先进知识分子了解接受马克思主义思想指导下的无产

① 天津市地方史志编修委员会总编辑室编，《二十世纪初的天津概况》，内部发行，1986 年，第 333 页。

② 蒋国珍，《中国新闻发达史》，世界书局，1927 年，第 66 页。

③ （英）雷穆森著，许逸凡等译，《天津租界史（插图本）》，天津人民出版社，2009 年，第 227 页。

intellectuals like Yan Fu aimed at saving the nation from crisis, such as *On the Speed of World Change*, *On the Origin of Strength*, *Refutation of Han Yu*, *On the Speed of World Change Sequel*, and *On Our Salvation*, advocating for reform and strengthening the country, replacing classical literature with Western science, promoting new learning, and abolishing autocratic politics. It served as an important forum for reflection on the First Sino-Japanese War and the exploration of the path to a strong nation. Due to its coverage of the mutiny in Yuan Shikai's army, *Chih Pao* was ordered to cease publication by Yuan Shikai in March 1904. It was renamed twice that year, as *Shang Wu Ri Bao* (Commerce Daily) in June and *Zhong Wai Shi Bao* (Domestic and Foreign Real Report) in September, continuing publication.[①] Foreigners establishing Chinese newspapers in China, of course, did so to control public opinion and serve their interests in China. Therefore, publishing required an understanding of and respect for the Chinese people and culture to avoid causing resentment and failing to achieve the desired effect. *The Development History of Chinese News* published in 1927, praised, "Foreign propaganda in China is not only in its own newspapers (foreign-language newspapers) but also in Chinese newspapers. Germany's *Domestic and Foreign Real Report* (Tianjin) had a great effect," and believed its success lay in, "It could guess the Chinese people's psychology and tailor the content and form to cater to the Chinese people's psychology everywhere. So even the Chinese themselves often didn't know they were reading a foreign newspaper."[②] This can be considered a high praise for the initiative of foreign expatriates to establish Chinese newspapers.

In modern Tianjin, there were newspapers in various languages established by foreigners, such as the French-language *Echo de Chine*, the Russian-language *The Dawn*, the German-language *Deutsch-Chinesische Nachrichten*, and several Japanese-language newspapers and periodicals. Among them, another English newspaper with nationwide influence besides the *Peking & Tientsin Times* was the *North China Star*. It was published in Tianjin in August 1918 and ceased publication after the outbreak of the Pacific War. Its chairman and editor-in-chief was Charles J. Fox, a law professor at Peiyang University and an American. Fox held a Ph.D. in Philosophy from Heidelberg University in Germany and had worked for newspapers in New York and Washington for up to 10 years, possessing extensive experience in newspaper management. After leaving his position at Peiyang University, he founded the *North China Star*. The *North China Star* was priced affordably,

① Editorial Office of the Tianjin Chorography and History Compilation Committee (ed.). *Overview of Tianjin in the Early 20th Century*. Published internally in 1986, p.333.

② Jiang Guozhen. *The Development History of Chinese News*. World Press, 1927, p.66.

《华北明星报》
North China Star

《益世报》报馆
The office of *Social Welfare*

with a general daily newspaper subscription fee being two or three dozen yuan, while it only required ten yuan and operated all year round without a day off, quickly becoming the "largest foreign daily newspaper in North China" in terms of circulation.[1] It provided extensive information and a broad perspective, with news primarily sourced from Reuters, allowing local and foreign readers in Tianjin to timely and accurately understand major global news events. For example, Tianjin residents first learned about the October Revolution in Russia through the *North China Star*. Its objective and fair reporting played an important role in introducing and disseminating Marxist revolutionary ideology among progressive intellectuals in China. During the May Fourth Movement, the newspaper provided real-time coverage of student protests in the Beijing-Tianjin region, especially concerning Peiyang University, often being reprinted by important Chinese-language newspapers in Tianjin such as the *Social Welfare*. Moreover, Peiyang University students used the telephone at the *North China Star* office to communicate with the Beijing Student Union. Fox was a liberal intellectual who sympathized with the unequal treatment suffered by the Chinese people. He represented Americans in China at the Washington Conference and delivered a speech, later serializing the conference proceedings in the *North China Star* under the title *Struggle for China's Tariff Autonomy*. In 1925, he also wrote a series on *Arms Embargoes against China*, serialized in the newspaper, and the following year authored a book exposing imperialist unequal treaties titled the *Boxer Protocol*. In 1927, he was commissioned by student Zhang Tailei to serve as a lawyer defending the wife of the arrested Soviet advisor Borodin.[2]

Zhang Tailei was one of the early important leaders of the Chinese Communist Party, a founding member of the Communist Youth League of China, and a prominent leader in the youth movement. He was also a student of Fox at Peiyang University. Zhang Tailei excelled academically, particularly in English, which was greatly admired by Fox. After graduation, Zhang Tailei took a job at the *North China Star* to facilitate revolutionary work. His main responsibility was translating Chinese information and presenting it to senior foreign editors after revision and editing. Through this work, Zhang Tailei improved his English proficiency, laying the language foundation for his future work in the Communist International (Comintern). Additionally, he enhanced his skills in news writing, which proved beneficial for his future involvement

阶级革命起到了重要作用。五四运动时期，该报实时报道京津地区学生的斗争消息，尤其是北洋大学的有关情况，时常被天津重要的中文报纸《益世报》所转载，并且北洋大学学生还借用《华北明星报》报馆的电话与北京学联进行联络。福克斯是一位自由派知识分子，同情中国人民所遭受的不平等待遇，曾代表在华美国人参加"华盛顿会议"并作发言，并将会议内容整理后在《华北明星报》上连载，题为《为争取中国关税自主权而斗争》。1925年他还撰写了《针对中国的武器禁运》，连载于报纸上，次年撰写了揭露帝国主义不平等条约的专著《辛丑条约》。1927年他接受学生张太雷的委托，

① O. D. Rasmussen, *Tientsin: An Illustrated Outline History*, translated by Xu Yifan, et al. Tianjin People's Publishing House, 2008, p.227.

② Ding Yanmo. *Biography of Zhang Tailei*. Shanghai Lexicographical Publishing House, 2011, pp.29-32.

作为律师为被捕的苏联顾问鲍罗廷的夫人辩护。①

张太雷是中国共产党早期的重要领导人之一，是中国共产主义青年团的创始人之一和青年运动的卓越领导人，也曾经是福克斯在北洋大学教过的学生。张太雷的学业成绩优异，特别是英语非常好，深受福克斯欣赏。毕业后，张太雷为了方便革命工作，到《华北明星报》任职，主要工作是翻译中文信息，整理修改后交给外籍资深编辑。通过这项工作的训练，张太雷提高了英语读写水平，为日后在共产国际（第三国际）工作打下了语言基础；同时，还提升了新闻写作能力，对于日后参与编辑中共重要刊物《向导》、主编《人民周刊》以及撰写国内外新闻评论和起草党内报告等大有裨益。② 可以说，《华北明星报》不仅为外国侨民及时了解世界消息提供了方便，更为中国先进青年打开了通向世界无产阶级革命的一扇窗。

张太雷
Zhang Tailei

外侨在天津创办报纸，不仅推动了租界文化事业的发展，还促进了天津本地文化事业的发展。严复在《直报》上发表一系列倡导维新的文章后，声名大振，享誉全国，对报纸所产生的社会影响深感振奋，同时报纸"通外情"、通民智、引导舆论的功能也日益为新派知识分子所重视，于是严复等人于 1897 年 10 月 26 日在英租界创办了天津第一份中国人自办报纸《国闻报》。其增刊《国闻汇编》曾刊载严复所译《天演论》，阐发保种保群、自强进化之公理，与上海梁启超主编的《时务报》南北呼应，在维新运动中发挥了很大的舆论宣传作用。随着《时报》《直报》《国闻报》等中文报纸的出版发行，让中国社会上层人士，无论官员还是商人，都已习惯了"人在家中坐，便知天下事"的便利，对信息获取的需求不断增长。报纸这种由外国侨民引进创办的大众信息传播工具，在义和团运动后

in editing important Communist publications such as *Guide*, serving as editor-in-chief of *People's Weekly*, and writing domestic and international news commentaries as well as drafting internal party reports.① It can be said that the *North China Star* not only provided convenience for foreign residents to timely access world news but also opened a window to the world proletarian revolution for progressive Chinese youth.

Foreign residents founding newspapers in Tianjin not only propelled the development of cultural initiatives in the concessions but also stimulated the growth of local cultural endeavors in Tianjin. After Yan Fu published a series of articles advocating for reform in the *Chih Pao*, his reputation soared, gaining nationwide acclaim. He was deeply encouraged by the social impact of the newspaper. The function of newspapers to inform about foreign affairs, enlighten the people, and guide public opinion increasingly gained the attention of progressive intellectuals. Therefore, on October 26, 1897, Yan Fu and others founded Tianjin's first Chinese-run newspaper, *Kwo Wen Pao*, in the British Concession. Its supplement, *Compilation of Kwo Wen Pao*, published Yan Fu's translation of *Evolution and Ethics*, expounding on principles of protection and evolution, echoing the northern and southern trends in the Reform Movement along with *Chinese Progress* edited by Liang Qichao in Shanghai, thus playing a significant role in the dissemination of public opinion during the reform movement. With the publication and distribution of Chinese newspapers such as *The Eastern Times*, *Chih Pao*, and *Kwo Wen Pao*, the upper-class individuals in Chinese society, including officials and merchants, became accustomed to the convenience of "knowing the world's affairs while sitting at home," leading to a continuous increase in demand for information. This mass medium of information dissemination introduced by foreign residents flourished after the Boxer Rebellion. In 1902, after Yuan Shikai took over Tianjin, the first government-issued newspaper in China, the *Beiyang Official Gazette*, appeared in Tianjin. It was an authoritative official newspaper during late Qing Dynasty. On June 17, 1902, *Ta Kung Pao* was founded by Ying Lianzhi in Tianjin, with a daily circulation of 5,000 copies, becoming a prominent newspaper in the country. In December 1912, Liang Qichao established the academic publication *The Justice* magazine in Tianjin, achieving an unprecedented distribution of 10,000 copies in its inaugural issue. After the seventh issue, it surged to 15,000 copies, becoming the largest-circulating publication in China at the time and effectively

---

① 丁言模，《张太雷传》，上海辞书出版社，2011 年，第 29—32 页。

② 丁言模，《张太雷传》，上海辞书出版社，2011 年，第 32 页。

① Ding Yanmo. *Biography of Zhang Tailei*. Shanghai Lexicographical Publishing House, 2011, p.32.

蓬勃发展起来。1902年袁世凯接管天津后，中国有史以来第一份由政府发行的报纸——《北洋官报》在天津出现，这是清朝末年一份颇具权威性的官方报纸。1902年6月17日，英敛之在天津创办《大公报》，日发行量达5000份，一举成为国内令人瞩目的报纸。1912年12月，梁启超在天津创办了学术性刊物《庸言》杂志，创刊号即取得发行万份的空前成绩，第七期后激增至1.5万份，是当时中国发行量最大的刊物，有力地推动了新文化运动的开展。①

20世纪二三十年代是天津报业的鼎盛时期。当时有《大公报》《益世报》《庸报》《商报》四份大报和几十份小报。1931年天津报纸发行量达29万份，除发往外地10万余份外，市内流通18万余份，按当时有阅读能力人口计算，大约每天平均2.5人便拥有一份报纸。与此同时天津涌现出一大批杰出的报人，如《大公报》的张季鸾、胡政之、王芸生、张琴南、曹谷冰、徐铸成、汪桂年、萧乾、孟秋江等，《益世报》的刘豁轩、唐梦幻、谢幼圃、马彦祥、生宝堂等，《新天津报》的刘髯公，《新民意报》的马千里、孟震侯，《商报》的邰光典、秦丰川，《东方时报》的萨空了，以及在各报刊上连载小说的刘云若、宫白羽，画漫画的赵望云、高龙生、冯朋弟，写天津民俗掌故的戴愚庵（娱园老人），还有《博陵报》的刘震中、《北洋画报》的冯武越等。②他们是"无冕之王"，怀抱强烈的社会责任感，用所掌握的舆论工具批判执政当局政策、揭露社会丑恶面，宣传新思想新文化。他们是中国新闻事业的先驱者，是令近代津门文坛熠熠生辉的一群报人。

九一八事变后，民族危机日益严重，新闻记者的民族使命感驱使他们走出书斋、编辑部，投身到现实的抗战中。他们有的投身战场成为战地记者，采写新闻通讯，如《大公报》张高峰报道黄泛区的灾民；有的深入西北内陆，调查抗战后方，如曾在《益世报》和《大公报》撰写新闻通讯的范长江，报道西北人民的困苦生活和红军长征的真实情况，在西安事变后亲赴现场调查事实还原真相，使全国

---

① 王述祖、航鹰编著，《近代中国看天津：百项中国第一》，天津人民出版社，2007年，第201、199、195页。

② 徐景星，"序"。天津市政协文史资料委员会编，《近代天津十二大报人》，天津人民出版社，2001年，第5—7页。

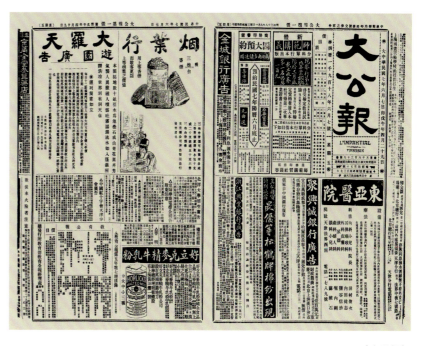

《大公报》
Ta Kung Pao

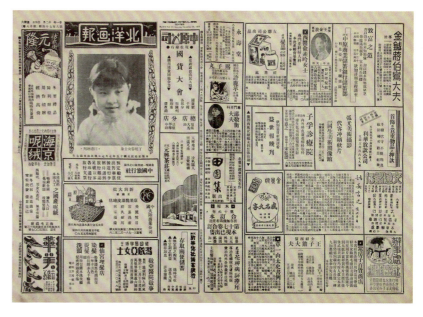

《北洋画报》
Beiyang Pictorial News

人民从报道通讯中，第一次了解中国共产党的抗日民族统一战线政策，看到了中华民族的希望。日后，他们当中的很多人成为中华人民共和国新闻事业的开拓者，如范长江后来担任了新华社总编辑、人民日报社社长。

女子教育与职业女性

近代天津开放以后，风气日新，社会日渐开化，妇女解放的思想也开始出现。清末民初一些非常具有知名度的职业女性很多出自天津。她们大都出自高官显宦之家，本就拥有较多较好的社会资源，加上出身家庭思想开明，使得她们接受了新式教育，从而走出家庭，拥有个人事业和社会影响力，成为妇女表率，为近代社会发展作出了杰出贡献。

范长江
Fan Changjiang

吕碧城
Lü Bicheng

吕碧城（1883—1943）是中国近代史上一位卓越的职业女性，在她身上集合了诸多闪闪发光的头衔，如词人、作家、教育家、政治活动家等。她亦在诸多领域引领潮流，是中国近代女权运动的首倡者之一，女子教育的先驱，中国新闻史上最早的几位女报人之一，也是在欧美倡导动物保护主义的先驱。吕碧城出身于安徽一个官宦家庭，自小受家庭熏陶，因诗词书画才名远播。父亲去世后家道中落，来到塘沽投奔舅父，接受了新式学校教育。1904年，吕碧城离家出走来到天津，受到《大公报》创办人英敛

promoting the development of the New Culture Movement.[1]

The 1920s and 1930s were the heyday of the newspaper industry in Tianjin. At that time, there were four major newspapers, including *Ta Kung Pao*, *Social Welfare*, *Yung Pao*, and *Shang Bao*, as well as dozens of smaller newspapers. In 1931, the circulation of Tianjin newspapers reached 290,000 copies, with over 100,000 copies distributed outside the city and over 180,000 copies circulating within the city. Calculated based on the population capable of reading at the time, approximately every 2.5 people in the city had access to a newspaper on average each day. At the same time, Tianjin saw the emergence of a large number of outstanding journalists, such as Zhang Jiluan, Hu Zhengzhi, Wang Yunsheng, Zhang Qinnan, Cao Gubing, Xu Zhucheng, Wang Guinian, Xiao Qian, Meng Qiujiang, and others from *Ta Kung Pao*; Liu Huoxuan, Tang Menghuan, Xie Youpu, Ma Yanxiang, and Sheng Baotang from *Social Welfare*; Liu Rangong from *Xin Tianjin Bao*; Ma Qianli and Meng Zhenhou from *Xin Min Yi Pao*; Tai Guangdian and Qin Fengchuan from *Shang Bao*; Sa Kongliao from *Oriental Affairs*; as well as novelists like Liu Yunruo and Gong Baiyu, cartoonists like Zhao Wangyun, Gao Longsheng, and Feng Pengdi, and folklorists like Dai Yu'an (Yu Yuan Lao Ren) who wrote about Tianjin customs and anecdotes, and others such as Liu Zhenzhong from *Bo Ling Bao* and Feng Wuyue from *Beiyang Pictorial News*.[2] They were the "uncrowned kings," embracing a strong sense of social responsibility, using the power of public opinion to criticize government policies, exposing social evils, and promoting new ideas and cultures. They were pioneers of Chinese journalism, a group of journalists who illuminated the modern literary scene of Tianjin.

After the September 18th Incident, the national crisis became increasingly severe, and the sense of national mission among journalists compelled them to leave their studies and editorial offices, and immerse themselves in the reality of the resistance against Japan. Some of them joined the battlefield as war correspondents, reporting news and dispatches, such as Zhang Gaofeng from *Ta Kung Pao* reporting on the refugees in the Yellow River flood area. Some ventured deep into the northwest hinterland to investigate the rear area of the resistance against Japan. For example, Fan Changjiang, who wrote news dispatches for both *Social Welfare* and *Ta Kung Pao*, reported on the hardships of the people in the northwest and the true situation of the Red

---

[1] *Modern China through the Eyes of Tianjin: 100 Firsts*, compiled by Wang Shuzu, Hang Ying. Tianjin People's Publishing House, 2007, pp.201,199,195.

[2] Xu Jingxing. "Preface". Cultural and Historical Data Research Committee of Tianjin Municipal Committee of CPPCC. *The Twelve Major Journalists of Modern Tianjin*. Tianjin People's Publishing House, 2001, pp.5-7.

之的赏识，被聘为报社编辑。吕碧城入职后，先后在《大公报》上刊载诗词，获得盛名，同时她还发表了《论提倡女学之宗旨》《敬告中国女同胞》《兴女权贵有坚忍之志》《教育为立国之本》在内的一系列倡导女子教育、呼吁女权的文章，轰动京津，得到许多官绅名流的赏识和支持。1904年5月，秋瑾从北京来到天津，慕名拜访吕碧城，成为文友。秋瑾起义失败遇难后，吕碧城冒着生命危险派人到绍兴为挚友收尸，并为其作传。1906年著名教育家傅增湘奉袁世凯之命创办中国第一所女子公立学校——北洋女子师范学堂，特聘请吕碧城为校长。她还一度受袁世凯赏识而任总统府秘书。因袁世凯复辟，她辞职赴上海，成功投身商界而成为富甲一方的女商人。再之后，她赴美国哥伦比亚大学留学旁听，还曾游历欧美，在奥地利维也纳参加世界动物保护大会，宣扬动物保护主义。1930年皈依佛教，成为居士。吕碧城一生丰富多彩，于文学、教育、政治、商业等方面皆成就斐然，被誉为女词人中"三百年来第一人"①。她以自身经历很好地诠释了什么是"知识改变命运"，率先垂范了女子应当通过教育获得自身独立。

中国历史上第一位女博士、女律师，也是清末第一女刺客的郑毓秀（1891—1959），同样出身官宦，天性具有反叛精神，十几岁时到天津读女校，在美国传教士开办的崇实女塾教会学校念书，开始接触西方教育。1907年她到日本留学，期间经廖仲恺介绍加入同盟会。1911年回国后，参加京津同盟会分会，曾计划暗杀袁世凯，1912年参与刺杀清末立宪派大臣良弼并取得成功。同年赴法勤工俭学，1917年获巴黎大学法学硕士学位。1919年曾组织留学生抗议，阻止出席巴黎和会的中国代表团在和约上签字。1924年获巴黎大学法学博士学位，成为中国历史上第一位女博士。回国后在上海开办律师事务所，成为中国历史上第一

郑毓秀
Zheng Yuxiu

①　王忠和，《吕碧城传》，百花文艺出版社，2010年，第129页。

Army's Long March. After the "Xi'an Incident," he personally went to the scene to investigate and reveal the truth, allowing the people of the whole country to understand for the first time the Communist Party of China's policy of the Anti-Japanese National United Front through his reports and dispatches, and see the hope of the Chinese nation. Later on, many of them became pioneers in the news industry of People's Republic of China, such as Fan Changjiang, who later served as the chief editor of Xinhua News Agency and the editor-in-chief of *People's Daily*.

Women's Education and Professional Women

After Tianjin opened up in modern times, the atmosphere became increasingly progressive, and society gradually modernized, with the idea of women's liberation beginning to emerge. Many highly prominent professional women from Tianjin emerged during the late Qing Dynasty and early Republic of China period. Most of them came from prestigious families with abundant social resources. Coupled with the progressive thinking in their families, they received modern education, enabling them to step out of their families and pursue personal careers and social influence. They became role models for women, making outstanding contributions to the development of modern society.

Lü Bicheng (1883–1943) was an outstanding professional woman in modern Chinese history, holding numerous shining titles such as poet, writer, educator, political activist, and more. She led the trend in various fields and was one of the pioneers of the modern Chinese women's movement, a pioneer in women's education, one of the earliest female journalists in Chinese journalism history, and also a pioneer in advocating animal protectionism in Europe and America. Born into a scholarly family in Anhui, Lü Bicheng gained fame for her poetry, calligraphy, and painting skills from an early age. After her father's death and the family's decline, she went to Tianjin to live with her uncle in Tanggu, where she received a modern education. In 1904, Lü Bicheng left home and arrived in Tianjin, where she was appreciated by Ying Lianzhi, the founder of the *Ta Kung Pao* newspaper, and was hired as an editor. During her tenure at *Ta Kung Pao*, Lü Bicheng published poems and gained great renown. At the same time, she also wrote a series of articles advocating women's education and women's rights, including *On Advocating the Purpose of Female Education*, *An Advice to Chinese Female Compatriots*, *The Nobility of Feminism Requires Perseverance*, and *Education Is the Foundation of a Nation*, which caused a sensation in Beijing and Tianjin, earning her recognition and support from many officials and celebrities.

丁懋英
Ding Maoying

丁懋英著作
The work of Ding Maoying

位女律师、第一位女法院审判厅厅长，还曾兼任上海法政大学校长。她还于 1929 年参与起草南京国民政府《民法典》，特别提出增加多条女性权利保护条文。①

　　近代留学生中，有很多女留学生学习医学，在近代中国公共卫生领域扮演了重要角色。妇产科专家丁懋英（1892—1969）于民国初年随家人来津定居，后入严氏女学读书。她虽身为女性却胸怀大志，深得教育家严修器重。在其资助下，丁懋英于 1913 年考取公费留美生，进入美国密歇根大学医学院专修妇科和产科专业。她在国外学习时刻苦努力，成绩优异，为一生的事业打下了坚实基础。学成归国后，于 1923 年进入天津公立女医院（原名北洋女医院，俗称"水阁医院"）任院长。这所医院始建于 1903 年，是中国第一家公立妇产专科医院，曾有 10 万人在此出生。在公立女医院出现之前，当地都是由接生婆走街入户帮助产妇分娩。由于各种因素，那时候的产妇和婴儿的死亡率很高。在丁懋英担任院长期间，天津的女医事业得到了很大的发展。1936 年，她在英租界伦敦路（今成都道 106 号）创建了水阁医院分院，俗称"丁懋英女医院"，内设挂号室、诊室、化验室和住院室。此后，她上午在水阁医院应诊，下午在分院应诊，以产科为主，兼治妇科。1945 年日本投降后，丁懋英在联合国救济

---

①　郑毓秀，《不寻常的玫瑰枝：郑毓秀自述》，中国法制出版社，2018 年。

In May 1904, Qiu Jin came to Tianjin from Beijing and visited Lü Bicheng, becoming her friend. After Qiu Jin's failed uprising and subsequent death, Lü Bicheng sent people to Shaoxing at great personal risk to collect her body and wrote her biography. In 1906, the famous educator Fu Zengxiang, at the behest of Yuan Shikai, founded the first public girls' school in China, the Beiyang Women's Normal School, and hired Lü Bicheng as its principal. Lü Bicheng was also once appreciated by Yuan Shikai and served as a secretary at the presidential palace. After Yuan Shikai's restoration, she resigned and went to Shanghai, successfully entering the business world and becoming a wealthy female entrepreneur. Later, she went to the United States to study at Columbia University and also traveled to Europe and America, attending the World Animal Protection Conference in Vienna, Austria, to promote animal protectionism. In 1930, she converted to Buddhism and became a lay Buddhist. Lü Bicheng's life was rich and colorful, and she achieved remarkable success in literature, education, politics, business, and other fields. She was hailed as the "first one in nearly three hundred years"[1] among the female poets. She perfectly exemplified the concept of "knowledge changes destiny" through her own experience, setting an example for women to gain independence through education.

Zheng Yuxiu (1891–1959), the first female Ph.D. holder and lawyer in Chinese history, and also the first female assassin of the late Qing Dynasty, was born into a prominent family with a rebellious spirit. In her early teens, she attended a girls' school in Tianjin and studied at the Keen School (Chung Hsi), founded by American missionaries, where she was introduced to Western education. In 1907, she went to Japan to study and, during this time, joined the Tongmenghui upon the recommendation of Liao Zhongkai. After returning to China in 1911, she participated in the Beijing-Tianjin Alliance branch and was involved in a plot to assassinate Yuan Shikai. In 1912, she successfully assassinated Liang Bi, a constitutionalist minister of the late Qing Dynasty. Later that year, she went to France to study under a work-study programme, and in 1917, she obtained a Master of Law from the University of Paris. In 1919, she organized protests by overseas students to prevent the Chinese delegation from signing the treaty at the Paris Peace Conference. In 1924, she obtained a Ph.D. in Law from the University of Paris, becoming the first female Ph.D. holder in Chinese history. Upon returning to China, she opened a law firm in Shanghai, becoming the first female lawyer and the first female president of a court chamber in Chinese history. She also served as the

---

①　Wang Zhonghe. *Biography of Lü Bicheng*. Baihua Literature and Art Publishing House, 2010, p.129.

凌叔华
Ling Shuhua

总署、国民政府行政院救济总署华北国际救济会担任公职。她还担任天津女青年会董事，凭借她的资历、能力和声望从事社会公益事业和慈善事业。1950 年，丁懋英把救济总署所余物资及医院的全部资产，交给了天津市人民政府。

五四运动以来的中国文坛上很有名气的女作家凌叔华（1900—1990），是清末天津知府凌福彭的女儿。受父亲影响，她自幼喜欢画画，曾师从著名女画家缪素筠，还曾师从学贯中西的辜鸿铭学英文，跟周作人学写白话文。1922 年考入燕京大学外文系，并开始在《晨报副镌》《现代评论》《新月》等刊物发表小说、散文。1925 年以短篇小说《酒后》一举成名，鲁迅称其小说描写的是"高门巨族的精魂"。后与冰心、林徽因一同被誉为 20 世纪 30 年代"北方文坛的三位才女"。她的家是北京最早的文人沙龙。后随丈夫陈西滢赴武汉大学任教，与女作家苏雪林、袁昌英合称"珞珈三女杰"。1935 年任《武汉日报》副刊《现代文艺》的主编。1953 年她在英国出版英文自传体小说《古韵》（*Ancient Melodies*，又译作《古歌集》）。书中描绘了清末时社会风俗、人情世故，并无之前作品中反抗父权制度的精神，但因其新奇而引起重视，成为畅销书，被称为"第一位征服欧洲的中国女作家"。《泰晤士报》文学副刊的评论说："叔华平静、轻松地将我们带进那座隐蔽着古老文明的院落。她向英国读者展示了一个中国人情感的新鲜世界。高昂的调子消失以后，古韵犹存，不绝于耳。"[1]

近代天津之所以涌现出以上出色的职业女性，源自清末以来天

---

① 傅光明，《凌叔华：古韵精魂》，大象出版社，2004 年，第 67 页。

president of the Shanghai School of Law and Politics. In 1929, she participated in the drafting of the *Civil Code* of the Nanjing National Government, proposing several provisions to protect women's rights.[1]

In modern times, many female students studying abroad chose to study medicine and played significant roles in the field of public health in modern China. Obstetrics and gynecology expert Ding Maoying (1892–1969) settled in Tianjin with her family in the early years of the Republic of China and later attended the Yan Family Girls' School. Despite being a woman, she harbored ambitious aspirations and gained the respect of educator Yan Xiu. With his support, Ding Maoying was awarded a government scholarship in 1913 to study in the United States, where she specialized in obstetrics and gynecology at the University of Michigan Medical School. She studied diligently abroad, achieving excellent results and laying a solid foundation for her career. Upon returning home after completing her studies, she became the director of the Tianjin Public Women's Hospital (formerly known as the Beiyang Women's Hospital, colloquially known as the "Shuigao Hospital") in 1923. Established in 1903, this hospital was the first public specialized obstetrics and gynecology hospital in China, where 100,000 people were born. Before the establishment of the public women's hospital, midwives assisted in childbirth in the local area. Due to various factors, the maternal and infant mortality rates were very high at that time. During Ding Maoying's tenure as director, the women's medical profession in Tianjin experienced significant development. In 1936, she established a branch of the Shuigao Hospital on London Road in the British Concession (now No.106 Chengdu Road 106), commonly known as the "Ding Maoying Women's Hospital," which had registration rooms, consultation rooms, laboratories, and wards. Subsequently, she consulted at the Shuigao Hospital in the morning and at the branch in the afternoon, mainly specializing in obstetrics and gynecology. After the surrender of Japan in 1945, Ding Maoying held public positions at the United Nations Relief and Rehabilitation Administration, the Relief Administration of the Cabinet of the National Government, and the North China International Relief Association. She also served as a director of the Tianjin Young Women's Association, engaging in social welfare and charitable activities based on her qualifications, abilities, and reputation. In 1950, Ding Maoying handed over all the remaining supplies of the relief agencies and all the assets of the hospital to the Tianjin Municipal People's Government.

Ling Shuhua (1900–1990), a well-known female writer in the Chinese

---

① Zheng Yuxiu. *An Unusual Rose: Zheng Yuxiu's Self Narration.* China Legal Publishing House, 2018.

邓颖超
Deng Yingchao

津女子教育所取得的巨大成就。1898 年至 1917 年，中国近代教育先驱严修、张伯苓在天津以严氏家馆为基地，改革旧式教育，推进新学。1905 年严修将严氏女塾改为严氏女学，设保姆科和幼稚园，后又开设南开女中，形成了"南开系列"学校。1906 年 6 月 13 日中国第一所女子师范学校在天津创办，首任校长即为吕碧城。辛亥革命后学堂扩大规模，更名为北洋女子师范学校、直隶第一女子师范学校、河北省立第一女子师范学院（原校址在河北区天纬路，现为天津美术学院）。从 1906 年至 1928 年，该校培养出 698 位师范本科毕业生，许多学生后来都成为中国杰出的女权革命家、教育家、艺术家，如刘清扬、许广平、郭隆真、周道如等。其中，无产阶级革命家邓颖超同志是其中的佼佼者。除了这两所学校，天津还有成立于 1908 年附设于北洋女医院、专门培养护士的北洋女医学堂（后更名为北洋女子医学校）和多所教会女子学校，这都为培养具有男女平等意识、思想解放的新女性创造了条件。

天津宽松开放的城市社会风气，为女性的教育和职业发展提供了一个良好环境，同时贫富悬殊的社会环境、日益严重的民族危机也使一批先进女青年知识分子觉醒，走上职业革命家道路。邓颖超（1904—1992）的革命生涯开启于天津。1915 年，年仅 12 岁的邓颖超进入直隶第一女子师范学校。这一年，张伯苓代理天津直隶第一女子师范学校校长，马千里也随同前往，任学校学监并执行校务。由于马千里的倡导，进步思想得以在女师传播，学校里也充满着一

literary world since the May Fourth Movement, was the daughter of Ling Fupeng, the magistrate of Tianjin during the late Qing Dynasty. Influenced by her father, she had a fondness for painting from a young age and studied under the famous female painter Miao Suyun. She also studied English under the guidance of the bilingual scholar Gu Hongming and learned to write vernacular Chinese from writer Zhou Zuoren. In 1922, she enrolled in the Foreign Language Department of Yenching University and began publishing novels and essays in publications such as *Morning News Supplement*, *Modern Review*, and *New Moon*. In 1925, she rose to fame with the short story *After Drinking*, which Lu Xun praised for depicting the "essence of the noble families". Later, she was acclaimed alongside Bing Xin and Lin Huiyin as the "three talented women of the northern literary world" of the 1930s. Her home was one of the earliest literary salons in Beijing. Later, she accompanied her husband Chen Xiying to teach at Wuhan University, where she, along with female writers Su Xuelin and Yuan Changying, were collectively known as the "three outstanding women of Wuhan". In 1935, she became the editor-in-chief of the supplement *Modern Literature* of the *Wuhan Daily*. In 1953, she published the English autobiographical novel *Ancient Melodies* in the United Kingdom. The book depicted the social customs and human sentiments of the late Qing Dynasty, lacking the spirit of resisting patriarchal authority found in her previous works. However, due to its novelty, it attracted attention and became a bestseller, earning her the title of the "first Chinese female writer to conquer Europe". The *Literary Supplement of The Times* commented, "Shuhua calmly and lightly leads us into the secluded courtyard of ancient civilization. She shows British readers a fresh world of Chinese emotions. After the lofty tones disappear, the ancient melodies linger, echoing in our ears."[1]

The outstanding professional women that emerged in modern Tianjin can be attributed to the significant achievements made in women's education in Tianjin since the late Qing Dynasty. From 1898 to 1917, pioneers of modern education in China, Yan Xiu and Chang Poling, used Yan's family school in Tianjin as a base to reform traditional education and promote new learning. In 1905, Yan Xiu transformed the Yan family's girls' school into the Yan family's girls' academy, introducing courses in childcare and kindergarten education. Later, he established Nankai Girls' High School, forming the "Nankai series" of schools. On June 13, 1906, the first women's normal school in China was founded in Tianjin, with Lü Bicheng serving as its first principal. After the 1911 Revolution, the school expanded and was renamed as Beiyang Women's Normal School, Zhili First Women's Normal School, and Hebei Provincial

---

① Fu Guangming. *Ling Shuhua: The Essence of Ancient Melodies*. Elephant Press, 2014, p.64.

种自由、向上的风气，邓颖超在这里开始吸收新知识，寻求救国救民的真理，逐渐成长为一位学生运动的领袖。1919年，五四运动爆发，直隶第一女子师范学校也成为天津乃至全国妇女运动的核心。5月25日，刘清扬、郭隆真和邓颖超等人成立了天津第一个妇女爱国团体"天津女界爱国同志会"，宗旨是"提倡国货并唤起女界之爱国心"。女界爱国同志会尤其关注女性自身的问题，譬如男女自由平等、妇女解放、反对包办婚姻等。她们采取组织演讲、举办女子学校、出版刊物等多种形式向广大民众特别是妇女进行深入浅出、通俗易懂的教育和爱国宣传。之后，爱国同志会和天津学生联合会合并，组成了觉悟社。觉悟社成立伊始便明确宣布，倡导男女平等。之后，经过与反动政府长达半年的斗争，觉悟社里的知识青年认识到，仅靠个人和小团体的力量难以完成改造旧中国、挽救中国危亡的任务，只有对各种团体进行改造，才能真正团结起来。1922年，邓颖超毕业两年后再次回到天津，在达仁女校任教，同时从事天津的妇女运动。1924年，邓颖超在天津参加中国社会主义青年团，并担任特支宣传委员。1925年3月，邓颖超正式加入中国共产党，成为一名坚定的革命家。①

除了参加社会工作，女子解放的另一个重要标志是恋爱、婚姻、家庭观念的更新。自由恋爱、宽容离婚、妇女再婚成为社会时尚。1913年《大公报》载："近代法庭诉讼，男女之请离婚者，实繁有徒。"②1931年秋天津发生了一桩轰动一时的离婚案，"前无古人，后无来者"。末代皇帝溥仪携皇后和妃子离开北京故宫来到天津寓居后，"淑妃"文绣受到新思潮的影响，毅然离家出走，聘请律师起诉与溥仪离婚，最后离婚成功并获得"赡养费"。20世纪二三十年代，天津女性的"时髦"程度居于全国前列，很多受过新式教育的女性，不仅在衣着打扮上越加时髦和西化，她们的思想也更加开放、更加富有个性、更加追求人格独立和自由。这个群体的变化发展，折射出近代天津社会转型时期社会文化的多元、开放和包容。

---

① 金凤，《邓颖超传》，人民出版社，1993年。

② 《大公报》1913年9月15日。

First Women's Normal College (originally located on Tianwei Road in Hebei District, now Tianjin Academy of Fine Arts). From 1906 to 1928, the school graduated 698 normal school undergraduates, many of whom later became outstanding female revolutionary activists, educators, and artists in China, such as Liu Qingyang, Xu Guangping, Guo Longzhen, and Zhou Daoru. Among them, comrade Deng Yingchao, a proletarian revolutionary, stood out. In addition to these two schools, Tianjin also had the Beiyang Women's Medical School (later renamed Beiyang Women's Medical College), established in 1908 and affiliated with Beiyang Women's Hospital, which specialized in nursing education. There were also several Christian girls' schools, all of which created conditions for cultivating new women with gender equality awareness and liberated thinking.

Tianjin's relaxed and open urban social atmosphere provided a favorable environment for women's education and career development. At the same time, the social environment characterized by stark wealth disparities and the increasingly serious national crisis awakened a group of progressive young female intellectuals who embarked on the path of revolutionary activism. Deng Yingchao's (1904–1992) revolutionary career began in Tianjin. In 1915, at the age of only 12, Deng entered the Zhili First Women's Normal School. That year, Chang Poling acted as the acting principal of the Zhili First Women's Normal School in Tianjin, and Ma Qianli also went there as the school supervisor to carry out administrative duties. Due to Ma Qianli's advocacy, progressive ideas were spread among the female teachers, and the school was filled with a spirit of freedom and progress. Deng Yingchao began absorbing new knowledge here, seeking the truth of saving the country and the people, and gradually grew into a leader of student movements. In 1919, during the May Fourth Movement, the Zhili First Women's Normal School became the core of the women's movement in Tianjin and even across the country. On May 25th, Liu Qingyang, Guo Longzhen, Deng Yingchao, and others established Tianjin's first women's patriotic organization, the "Tianjin Patriotic Women's Association," with the aim of "promoting domestic products and arousing patriotic feelings among women." The Patriotic Women's Association paid particular attention to women's issues, such as gender equality, women's liberation, and opposing arranged marriages. They conducted education and patriotic publicity among the general public, especially women, through various forms such as organizing lectures, running women's schools, and publishing periodicals in an easy-to-understand and popular manner. Later, the Patriotic Women's Association merged with the Tianjin Student Union to form the "Juewu She" (Awakening Society). From the outset, the Juewu She explicitly advocated gender equality. After a struggle with the reactionary

从土洋结合的生活方式到第一次地方选举

长久以来，只有东亚和中东才有大城市，自 16 世纪起，城市才在西方成长起来并逐渐超过东方。国外学者认为，由于中国人对待城市的态度不同于西方人，才导致了东西方城市发展程度的差异。虽然，东西方的城市都是建立在流通和交换的基础之上，但是之后的城市发展轨道却截然不同。欧洲城市化进程的背后，代表着一种生活方式向另一种生活方式的转化，这个过程同时造就了市民阶层，他们主导着城市的文明进程。

封建社会的中国没有截然的城乡对立，中国文明的独特之处在于其"农"字是不含鄙视之意的，在中国，城市并不代表着比乡村更高的文明水平。中国人的价值标准使城市中没有形成市民阶层和上流社会，城市人也没有代表和支配中国人生活的基调：无论在服装式样、饮食方式、交通工具或是日常生活的其他显见的方面，都没有显示出应有的区分。由于缺少市民阶层，中国的城市没有市政厅，官吏是代表中央政府在进行统治而不是自治的。城里人并不以身为城市人为荣，相反，他们崇尚在经商或从政成功之后退隐乡村的生活方式。陶渊明隐居乡野"采菊东篱下，悠然见南山"的田园生活，几乎是所有高尚士绅的理想生活境界。中国的城市，不像欧洲那样分为高级住宅区和贫民窟，而是穷人富人杂处一起，但是每一位有钱的官员或者富商都有自己的私人庭院，因而中国人对建造城市公共建筑、公共园林缺乏兴趣。总之，在近代，中国与欧洲的城市在市政建设方面的明显差异，既受到工业化发展程度的影响，也受到不同文化价值观的影响。

近代天津租界的发展，吸引了大量中国人来到租界居住。20 世纪初，天津的八国租界里总共居住着 9433 户、61712 名中国人，甚至超过了外国人口的总和。房地产商们兴建了大量里弄式建筑以供市民居住，而有钱的中国人则纷纷设计建造自己的房子，借以体现他们的权势和财富。例如，清末宫廷的大太监小德张在天津修建了一座宏伟的宅邸，外观上它是殖民地外廊式建筑，围在高高的中式院墙中，内部有宽阔的内厅；屋内的雕花门是中式的，门上的玻璃

government for six months, the intellectuals in the Juewu She realized that it was difficult to accomplish the task of transforming old China and saving China from peril solely through individual and small group efforts. It was only by transforming various groups that true unity could be achieved. In 1922, two years after graduating, Deng Yingchao returned to Tianjin and taught at Daren Girls' School while also engaging in the women's movement in Tianjin. In 1924, Deng Yingchao joined the Chinese Socialist Youth League in Tianjin and served as a special branch publicity officer. In March 1925, Deng Yingchao formally joined the Communist Party of China, becoming a steadfast revolutionary.[1]

In addition to participating in social work, another important sign of women's liberation is the renewal of attitudes towards love, marriage, and family. Free love, tolerant divorce, and women's remarriage have become social trends. In 1913, the *Ta Kung Pao* reported: "In modern court cases, there are many cases of divorce by both men and women."[2] In the autumn of 1931, a sensational divorce case occurred in Tianjin, "unprecedented in the past and unparalleled in the future." Puyi, the last emperor, left the Forbidden City in Beijing with his empress and concubines to reside in Tianjin. Under the influence of new ideas, "Imperial Concubine" Wenxiu resolutely left home, and hired a lawyer to sue Puyi for divorce, ultimately succeeding in the divorce and obtaining "alimony." In the 1920s and 1930s, the "fashion" of Tianjin women ranked among the forefront nationwide. Many women who received modern education not only became more fashionable and westernized in their attire, but their thoughts also became more open, individualistic, and inclined towards personal independence and freedom. The changes and developments within this group reflect the diversity, openness, and inclusiveness of Tianjin's social and cultural transformation during the modern era.

From the Combination of Eastern and Western Lifestyles to the First Local Elections

For a long time, only East Asia and the Middle East had large cities. It wasn't until the 16th century that cities began to grow in the West and gradually surpass the East. Foreign scholars believe that the difference in the development of urban areas between East and West is due to the different attitudes of Chinese people toward cities compared to Westerners. Although both Eastern and Western cities are built on the foundation of circulation and

---

① Jin Feng. *Biography of Deng Yingchao*. People's Publishing House, 1993.

② *Ta Kung Pao* on September 15, 1913.

庆王府花园。刘悦摄于 2020 年
The garden of Prince Qing's Mansion. Taken by Liu Yue in 2020

则全部在比利时订造，玻璃上的图案既有中式的山水，又有欧洲花卉水粉画；庭院中有假山、中式凉亭，还有西式喷泉……总之，这是真正的中西合璧式住宅。在租界里，类似的建筑物还有很多。建筑作为人们生活居住的空间场所，代表了其拥有者的审美品位和文化观念。在建筑学家看来，这种中西合璧的折衷主义建筑形式，是"暴发户"们将所有自己中意的建筑装饰符号熔于一炉，而对于这些符号的内在联系并不了解也不在意。在历史学家看来，这种土洋结合、洋为中用的建筑风格其实并不只是简单的"文化挪用"，它代表的是一种文化变迁和社会变迁，是将人类社会权力和文化积淀融合，用建筑这种形式具象地展示出来，是对西方文明的接受。

迁入租界的中国人很快接受了西方的生活方式、生产方式及风

exchange, their subsequent trajectories of urban development are markedly different. The urbanization process in Europe represents a transformation of lifestyle from one way of life to another, a process that simultaneously gave rise to the middle class, who led the civilization process in cities.

In feudal China, there was no stark urban-rural divide. The uniqueness of Chinese civilization lies in the fact that the character "nóng" (meaning "agriculture") does not carry any derogatory connotation. In China, cities do not necessarily represent a higher level of civilization compared to rural areas. Chinese values did not give rise to a distinct urban middle class or upper class, nor did urban dwellers dominate or set the tone for Chinese life. There were no visible distinctions in clothing, dietary habits, modes of transportation, or other aspects of daily life between urban and rural dwellers. Due to the absence of a civic middle class, Chinese cities lacked municipal halls, and officials represented the central government's rule rather than local autonomy. Urban dwellers did not take pride in being city residents; instead, they admired the lifestyle of retiring to the countryside after achieving success in commerce or politics. The pastoral life depicted by Tao Yuanming, "picking chrysanthemums by the eastern fence, leisurely watching the southern mountains," was almost the ideal life for all noble gentlemen. Chinese cities were not divided into upscale residential areas and slums like in Europe; rather, rich and poor mingled together. However, every wealthy official or merchant had their own private courtyard, leading to a lack of interest among Chinese people in constructing public buildings and parks in cities. In summary, the significant differences in urban development between China and Europe in modern times were influenced both by the level of industrialization and by different cultural values.

The development of the modern Tianjin concessions attracted a large number of Chinese people to live in the concessions. In the early 20th century, there were a total of 9,433 households and 61,712 Chinese residents living in the eight foreign concessions in Tianjin, even outnumbering the total number of foreigners. Real estate developers built many alley-style buildings for citizens to live in, while wealthy Chinese people designed and built their own houses to showcase their power and wealth. For example, Xiao Dezhang, a eunuch of the late Qing dynasty, built a magnificent mansion in Tianjin. Its exterior was colonial-style, surrounded by tall Chinese-style courtyard walls, and the interior had spacious halls. The carved doors inside the house were Chinese-style, while the glass on the doors was all custom-made in Belgium, featuring both Chinese landscapes and European floral watercolor paintings. There were rockeries and Chinese-style pavilion in the courtyard, as well as Western-style fountain... In short, this was a true blend of Chinese and Western architecture.

俗习惯，并将这些新鲜事物传播到中国社会，促进了中国社会的现代化进程。除了自来水、下水道、电灯、电话、马车、汽车等物质文明，还包括按钟点作息制度、星期制度、教育制度、市政管理制度、选举制度等制度文明，都对天津、上海、汉口、青岛等近代通商口岸的城市发展和社会演进产生了"极其广泛而复杂的影响"。[1]

19世纪末20世纪初，中国近代第一所大学、第一所工业技术学校、第一所西医医院、第一所女子师范学校、第一个市政机构、第一座机器铸币厂、第一家电报局、第一家机械化农场……诸多中国现代化进程中的"第一"纷纷在天津出现，天津在近代邮政和铁路、新式教育和职业教育、市政机构和司法等领域引领风气之先，且成为北方乃至全国清末新政之示范。这不能不说是侨民和租界所带来的西方现代文明对中国的现代化所产生的影响由表及里、由物质层面向制度层面逐渐转化的深刻体现。

作为近代民主化进程中的第一次高潮，袁世凯在天津进行了中国第一次地方选举。1905年，清王朝试行君主立宪，由直隶总督袁世凯在天津先行试办地方自治。为了推行地方自治，袁世凯派员赴日考察日本自治情形，并积极培训自治人员，派出宣讲员并出版报纸宣讲自治利益。同时，他还设立自治研究所，成立天津自治局，制定试办自治章程。1906年3月开始进行初选，1907年6月进行复选，然后成立议会。这是中国第一次创行投票选举的情形，也是普选制度的首次试行。[2]

可以说，天津的地方自治无论从机构设置、选举办法还是自治内容上，都是对各租界董事会章程的模仿。经选民选举产生的议事会是议决机关，董事会是行政机关，后者由前者选举产生并受其监督。议事会与董事会既相互独立又相互制约，体现了近代的分权原则。议员由选民自由选举，议决问题取决于投票多寡。两会均采取合议制形式。议事会每季一次，允许旁听，"会议非有议员半数以上到

---

① 刘海岩等编，《八国联军占领实录：天津临时政府会议纪要》，天津社会科学院出版社，2004年，序。

② 沈怀玉，《清末地方自治之萌芽》，《台湾"中研院"近代史研究所集刊》（9），台湾"中研院"近代史研究所，1980年7月，第308页。

In the concessions, there were many similar buildings. As places where people lived, buildings represented the aesthetic tastes and cultural concepts of their owners. In the eyes of architects, this kind of eclectic architecture blending Chinese and Western styles was a result of the nouveau riche combining all their favorite architectural decorative symbols without understanding or caring about the inherent connections between these symbols. In the eyes of historians, this combination of Chinese and Western styles, this adaptation of Western elements to Chinese use, was not just a simple "cultural appropriation". It represented a cultural and social transformation, a fusion of human social power and cultural heritage, manifested in the form of architecture, and an acceptance of Western civilization.

The Chinese who moved into the concessions quickly embraced Western lifestyles, modes of production, and customs, and disseminated these novelties to Chinese society, promoting the modernization process in China. In addition to material civilization such as running water, sewage systems, electric lights, telephones, horse-drawn carriages, automobiles, and others, institutional civilizations including the clock-based work schedule, the weekly system, educational systems, municipal management systems, electoral systems, and others had "extremely broad and complex influences" on the development of cities and social evolution in modern treaty ports such as Tianjin, Shanghai, Hankou, Qingdao, and others.[1]

At the end of the 19th century and the beginning of the 20th century, many "firsts" in China's modernization process appeared in Tianjin: the first modern university, the first industrial technical school, the first Western medicine hospital, the first women's normal school, the first municipal institution, the first mechanized coin mint, the first telegraph office, the first mechanized farm, and so on. Tianjin led the way in fields such as modern postal and railway services, modern and vocational education, municipal institutions, and judiciary, becoming a model for the New Policies of the late Qing Dynasty, not only in the northern region but also across the country. This profound transformation from the influence of Western modern civilization brought by expatriates and concessions has gradually shifted from the material level to the institutional level, which is a significant manifestation of China's modernization.

As the first climax in the process of modern democratization, Yuan Shikai conducted China's first local elections in Tianjin. In 1905, during the

---

① Liu Haiyan, et al (eds.). *Record of the Eight-Nation Alliance's Occupation: Minutes of the Tianjin Provisional Government Meeting*. Tianjin Academy of Social Sciences Press, 2004, Preface.

天津咨议局
Tianjin Provincial Assembly

会，不得议决"，"凡议事可否，以到会议员过半数之所决为准"，凡关涉正副议长、议员及其亲属的事项，该员不得与议。董事会每月一次，"非董事会职员全数三分之二以上到会，不得议决"，议事会成员也到会，但无表决权，其他规定同议事会。①从内容上来看，天津的地方自治内容主要是关于城镇的建设和发展。自治章程中设定的七大类经办事项中，多涉及城市的管理和建设，诸如建筑公用房屋、修缮清洁道路和疏通沟渠等工程，开办路灯、电车、电灯、自来水等公共营业，以及建立医院、医学堂、公园、工艺厂、工业学堂、救火会等，这些内容与天津各租界工部局董事会的日常行政内容是基本一致的，体现了浓厚的民主精神。

天津地方自治在全国创办最早且颇为成功，成为全国地方自治的表率。这不能不说是天津对外开放之后引进西方文明所造成的重要影响。首先，由侨民引入的资本主义生产方式给天津带来了工业化和城市化，其结果必然导致社会结构发生转型。城市中出现了新

①　高旺，《清末地方自治运动及其对近代中国政治发展的影响》，《天津社会科学》，2001 年 3 月，第 107—109 页。

Qing Dynasty's attempt at constitutional monarchy, Yuan Shikai, the Viceroy of Zhili Province, took the initiative to trial local autonomy in Tianjin. To promote local autonomy, Yuan Shikai sent representatives to Japan to study Japanese autonomy practices, actively trained autonomous personnel, dispatched propagandists, and published newspapers to promote the benefits of autonomy. At the same time, he established an Institute of Autonomy, set up the Tianjin Local Autonomy Bureau, and formulated trial autonomy regulations. The preliminary elections began in March 1906, followed by final elections in June 1907, and then the establishment of a parliament. This was the first instance of voting elections in China and also the first trial of a universal suffrage system.[1]

It can be said that Tianjin's local autonomy, whether in terms of institutional setup, election methods, or the content of autonomy, is an imitation of the charters of various concession boards. The council elected by voters is the deliberative body, while the board of directors is the executive body, the latter being elected by the former and subject to its supervision. The council and the board of directors are both independent and mutually restrictive, reflecting the modern principle of separation of powers. Members of the council are freely elected by voters, and decisions are based on the number of votes cast. Both bodies operate on a deliberative system. The council meets quarterly and allows for attendance by observers. "No decision shall be made unless more than half of the members are present," and "decisions shall be made based on the majority of members present." Regarding matters involving the chairman, vice chairman, members, and their relatives, the member in question shall not participate in the discussion. The board of directors meets monthly, and "no decision shall be made unless two-thirds or more of the board members are present." Council members also attend but do not have voting rights, with other provisions similar to those of the council.[2] In terms of content, Tianjin's local autonomy mainly concerns the construction and development of urban areas. Among the seven major categories of matters stipulated in the autonomy charter, many involve urban management and construction, such as building public housing, repairing and cleaning roads, and dredging ditches. Additionally, establishing public utilities such as streetlights, trams, electric lights, and running water, as

①　Shen Huaiyu. *The Rudiment of Local Self-Governance in the Late Qing Dynasty*. Institute of Modern History, Academia of Taiwan. *Collected Papers of the Institute of Modern History, Academia of Taiwan* (9), July 1980, p.308.

②　Gao Wang. *The Local Self-Governance Movement in the Late Qing Dynasty and Its Impact on the Political Development of Modern China*. *Tianjin Social Sciences*, March 2001, pp.107-109.

式学堂培养出来的近代知识分子，包括记者、编辑、医生、律师、教师等，还有大批城市工商业者，以及有一技之长的自由职业者，他们共同构成了市民阶层。新兴的市民阶层逐渐产生了较为一致的利益和心理认同感，为地方自治的发展奠定了阶级基础。其次，租界的社区建设给天津的城市化树立了榜样，由此也产生了处于国家与社会之间、公民参与公共事务的公共领域。这为地方自治提供了自治的范围和内容。第三，西方侨民社区建设是最直接的展示，它把西方先进的物质文明以及民主制度具体而直观地展现在天津的华人地方官员和精英阶层面前。在工业化和城市化的进程中逐渐产生的本地精英，特别是长期驻在天津的直隶总督，亲眼见到西方社区建设和地方自治的优越性，潜移默化地影响了他们对西方民主制度的认识和态度，当适宜的机会出现时，就会付诸实践。天津地方自治，不仅是对近代租界自治制度的照抄照搬和对临时政府自治法令的被迫接受，更是在民族意识觉醒之后的一种自发行动，体现了天津民众在学习西方的过程中，从被动到主动、从强制到自觉的转变。正是这种制度变迁和文化变迁，使天津地方文化成为近代中国历史上最为耀眼的城市之光。

well as establishing hospitals, medical schools, parks, workshops, industrial schools, and fire departments, are consistent with the daily administrative contents of the various municipal councils in Tianjin. This reflects a strong spirit of democracy.

Tianjin's local autonomy was among the earliest and most successful in the country, serving as a model for local autonomy nationwide. This can be attributed to the significant impact of the introduction of Western civilization to Tianjin after its opening to the outside world. Firstly, the introduction of capitalist modes of production by expatriates brought industrialization and urbanization to Tianjin, inevitably leading to a transformation of social structure. Modern intellectuals emerged from new-style schools in the city, including journalists, editors, doctors, lawyers, teachers, and many urban industrialists and merchants, as well as skilled professionals, collectively forming a bourgeois class. This emerging bourgeois class gradually developed a more unified set of interests and psychological identity, laying the class foundation for the development of local autonomy. Secondly, the community development in concessions served as a model for urbanization in Tianjin, leading to the emergence of a public domain between the state and society, where citizens participated in public affairs. This provided the scope and content for local autonomy. Thirdly, Western expatriate community development was the most direct demonstration, presenting advanced Western material civilization and democratic systems concretely and intuitively to Tianjin's Chinese local officials and elites. The local elites that gradually emerged during industrialization and urbanization, especially the long-term governors of Zhili Province stationed in Tianjin, witnessed firsthand the superiority of Western community development and local autonomy. This subtle influence affected their understanding and attitude towards Western democratic systems, which they would put into practice when appropriate opportunities arose. Tianjin's local autonomy not only involved the direct adoption of the autonomy system of the modern concessions and the forced acceptance of provisional government autonomy regulations but also represented a spontaneous action after the awakening of national consciousness. It reflected a shift in Tianjin people from passive to active and from coerced to voluntary during the process of learning from the West. It is precisely this institutional and cultural change that has made Tianjin's local culture the most dazzling light in modern Chinese history among cities.

海河中的轮船和帆船。摄于 20 世纪初。图片来源：德国"东亚之友"协会提供
The steamships and sailboats in the Hai River. Taken in the early 20th century. Source: StuDeo

天津港夜景。张建勇摄
Nightview of Tianjin Port. Taken by Zhang Jianyong

在本书的编纂与出版过程中，天津社会科学发展研究中心的多位同仁凭借其卓越的专业能力和热情，承担了繁重且关键的任务。安红女士负责美术设计与排版工作，她严谨的态度和经典的审美赋予本书别具一格的视觉魅力。唐倩、姜雨晨、牌梦迪三位女士参与了全书的中英文校对工作，并提供了许多宝贵建议，极大地提升了书稿质量。在此，我们向上述同仁表达最诚挚的感谢。正是他们的辛勤付出与不懈努力，确保了本书的顺利完成，并为其增光添彩。

During the compilation and publication of this book, several colleagues from Tianjin Social Science Development Research Center, with their outstanding professional skills and enthusiasm, undertook the heavy and crucial tasks involved. Ms. An Hong was responsible for the art design and layout. Her meticulous approach and classic aesthetic endowed the book with a distinctive visual appeal. Ms. Tang Qian, Ms. Jiang Yuchen, and Ms. Pai Mengdi contributed to the bilingual proofreading of the entire manuscript and offered many valuable suggestions, greatly enhancing the quality of the book. Here, we express our sincere gratitude to these colleagues. It is their hard work and relentless efforts that ensured the successful completion of this book and added brilliance to it.

· 档案、汇编类 ·

1.《明太宗实录》卷三六。

2.《明神宗实录》卷三五四，卷三五六。

3.《筹办夷务始末》同治朝，卷七六。

4. 中国史学会主编，《鸦片战争》，神州国光社，1954 年。

5. 中国近代经济史资料丛刊编辑委员会主编，《中国海关与中日战争》，中华书局，1983 年。

6. 中国第一历史档案馆、福建师范大学历史系编，《清末教案》，中华书局，2006 年。

7. 中国史学会主编，中国近代史资料丛刊《义和团》，上海人民出版社，1957 年。

8. 中国社会科学院近代史研究所《近代史资料》编辑组编，《义和团史料》，中国社会科学出版社，1982 年。

9. 中国史学会主编，《中日战争》，新知识出版社，1956 年。

10. 陈霞飞主编，《中国海关密档——赫德、金登干函电汇编（1874—1907）》，中华书局，第一卷，1990 年；第二卷，1900 年；第六卷，1995 年。

11. 中国近代经济史资料丛刊编辑委员会主编，《中国海关与邮政》，中华书局，1983 年。

12. 天津海关译编委员会编译，《津海关史要览》，中国海关出版社，2004 年。

13. 吴弘明编译，《津海关贸易年报（1865~1946）》，天津社会科学院出版社，2006 年。

14. 天津市地方史志编修委员会总编辑室编，《二十世纪初的天津概况》，内部发行，1986 年。

15. 刘海岩等编，《八国联军占领实录：天津临时政府会议纪要》，天津社会科学院出版社，2004 年。

16. 天津市地方史志编修委员会编著，《天津通志·港口志》，天津社会科学院出版社，1999 年。

17. 天津市地方史志编修委员会编著，《天津通志·附志·租界》，天津社会科学院出版社，1996 年。

18. 天津市地方史志编修委员会编著，《天津通志·旧志点校卷》，南开大学出版社，2001 年。

19. 天津市档案馆编，《近代以来天津城市化进程实录》，天津人民出版社，2005 年。

20. 宓汝成编，《中国近代铁路史资料（1863—1911）》，中华书局，1963 年。

21. 熊性美、阎光华主编，《开滦煤矿矿权史料》，南开大学出版社，2004 年。

22. 天津市档案馆等编，《天津商会档案汇编（1903—1911）》，天津人民出版社，1989 年。

23. 天津市档案馆等编，《天津商会档案汇编（1912—1928）》，天津人民出版社，1992 年。

24. 北京市地方志编纂委员会，《北京志·市政卷·铁路运输志》，北京出版社，2004 年。

25. 中国社会科学院近代史研究所翻译室，《近代来华外国人名辞典》，中国社会科学出版社，1981 年。

26. 熊志勇、苏浩、陈涛编，《中国近现代外交史资料选辑》，世界知识出版社，2012 年。

27. 天津历史博物馆、南开大学历史系《五四运动在天津》编辑组编，《五四运动在天津——历史资料选辑》，天津人民出版社，1979 年。

28. 张侠等编，《清末海军史料》，海洋出版社，1982年。

29. 中国人民政治协商会议天津市委员会文史资料研究委员会编，《沦陷时期的天津》，内部发行，1992年。

30. 天津市地方史志编修委员会编著，《中国天津通鉴》，中国青年出版社，2005年。

31. 中国第一历史档案馆、天津大学，《中国近代第一所大学——北洋大学（天津大学）历史档案珍藏图录》，天津大学出版社，2005年。

32. 张允侯等编，《留法勤工俭学运动》，上海人民出版社，1980年。

33. 李文海主编，《民国时期社会调查丛编（二编）城市（劳工）生活卷》，福建教育出版社，2014年。

34. 沈怀玉，《清末地方自治之萌芽》，《中央研究院近代史研究所集刊》（9），中央研究院近代史研究所，1980年7月。

35. 美国达特茅斯学院馆藏"丁家立档案"。

36. 比利时外交部档案馆藏"天津比利时租界档案"。

37. 比利时根特大学档案馆"内恩斯档案"。

·文集、日记、回忆录类·

1. 夏东元编，《郑观应集》，上海人民出版社，1982年。

2. 《湘乡曾氏文献》第7册，台湾学生书局，1965年。

3. 《曾文正公奏稿》第二十九卷，传忠书局，光绪二年刊本。

4. 顾廷龙、戴逸主编，《李鸿章全集》，安徽教育出版社，2008年。

5. 北京市档案馆编，《那桐日记》，新华出版社，2006年。

6. 方豪编录，《英敛之先生日记遗稿》，文海出版社，1974年。

7. 中国社会科学院近代史研究所译，《顾维钧回忆录》第1分册，中华书局，1983年。

8. 南开大学历史系编，《天津义和团调查》，天津古籍出版社，1990年。

9. 天津社会科学院历史研究所编，《八国联军在天津》，齐鲁书社，1980年。

10. 北京市政协文史资料研究委员会、天津市政协文史资料研究委员会编，《京津蒙难记——八国联军侵华纪实》，中国文史出版社，1990年。

11. 中国人民政治协商会议全国委员会文史资料研究委员会编，《辛亥革命回忆录·第八集》，中国文史出版社，2012年。

12. 中国人民政治协商会议天津市委员会、南开区委员会文史资料委员会合编，《天津老城忆旧》，天津人民出版社，1997年。

13. 张焘，《津门杂记》，天津古籍出版社，1986年。

14. （意）马可·波罗著，冯承钧译，《马可波罗行纪》，上海书店出版社，2006年。

15. （英）马戛尔尼著，刘半农译，《1793乾隆英使觐见记》，天津人民出版社，2006年。

16. （英）司当东著，叶笃义译，《英使谒见乾隆纪实》，三联书店（香港）有限公司，1994年。

17. （俄）德米特里·扬契维茨基著，许崇信等译，《八国联军目击记》，福建人民出版社，1983年。

18. （日）曾根俊虎著，范建明译，《北中国纪行：清国漫游志》，中华书局，2007年。

19. Constantin von Hanneken, *Briefe aus China: 1879—1886; als deutscher Offizier im Reich der Mitte*, Köln: Böhlau Verlag GmbH & Cie, 1998.

20. H. Shabas, *The Chinese Carpet Industry*.

·报刊类·

1. 《向导》1924年9月3日。

2. 《新青年》1918年11月15日，第五卷第五号。

3. 《大公报》1913年、1927年、1933年。

4. 《益世报》1916年、1919年、1928年、1935年。

5. 《申报》1918年、1919年、1939年。

6. 《益世报》（北京）1916年。

7. 《东方杂志》第32卷第16号，1935年8月16日。

8. *Tientsin Hong-List*, published by the N. C. Advertising Co., printed by the Tientsin Press, 1928.

9. *North China Star*, 1919年。

·专著、译著类·

1. 《马克思恩格斯全集》（第2卷），人民出版社，1957年。

2. 《李大钊文集》（上），人民出版社，1984年。

3. 《张太雷文集》，人民出版社，2013年。

4. 梁启超，《饮冰室合集》，中华书局，1936年。

5. 蒋廷黻，《中国近代史》，中国华侨出版社，2015年。

6. 蒋国珍，《中国新闻发达史》，世界书局，1927年。

7. 严景耀，《中国的犯罪问题与社会变迁的关系》，北京大学出版社，1986年。

8. 陈旭麓，《近代中国社会的新陈代谢》，上海人民出版社，1992年。

9. 王觉非主编，《近代英国史》，南京大学出版社，1997年。

10. 刘祚昌、王觉非主编，《世界史·近代史编》，高等教育出版社，2001年。

11. 来新夏主编，《天津近代史》，南开大学出版社，1987年。

12. 罗澍伟主编，《近代天津城市史》，中国社会科学出版社，1993年。

13. 杨大辛，《津门古今杂谭》，天津人民出版社，2015年。

14. 天津市政协文史资料研究委员会编，《天津的洋行与买办》，天津人民出版社，1987年。

15. 李竞能主编，《天津人口史》，南开大学出版社，1990年。

16. 姚洪卓主编，《近代天津对外贸易（1861~1948年）》，天津社会科学院出版社，1993年。

17. 张大民主编，《天津近代教育史》，天津人民出版社，1993年。

18. 尚克强、刘海岩主编，《天津租界社会研究》，天津人民出版社，1996年。

19. 天津市政协文史资料委员会编，《近代天津十二大报人》，天津人民出版社，2001年。

20. 宋美云，《近代天津商会》，天津社会科学院出版社，2002年。

21. 刘海岩，《空间与社会：近代天津城市的演变》，天津社会科学院出版社，2003年。

22. 张仲编著，《天津早年的衣食住行》，天津古籍出版社，2004年。

23. 江沛、王先明主编，《近代华北区域社会史研究》，天津古籍出版社，2005年。

24. 王述祖、航鹰编著，《近代中国看天津：百项中国第一》，天津人民出版社，2007年。

25. 朱慧颖，《天津公共卫生建设研究：1900~1937》，天津古籍出版社，2015年。

26. 张利民、刘凤华，《抗战时期日本对天津的经济统制与掠夺》，社会科学文献出版社，2016年。

27. 郭登浩、周俊旗主编，《日本占领天津时期罪行实录》，社会科学文献出版社，2016年。

28. 万鲁建，《近代天津日本租界研究》，天津社会科学院出版社，2022年。

29. 李秉新、徐俊元、石玉新主编，《侵华日军暴行总录》，河北人民出版社，1995年。

30. 王立新，《美国传教士与晚清中国现代化》，天津人民出版社，1997年。

31. 王受之，《世界现代建筑史》，中国建筑工业出版社，1999年。

32. 李育民，《中国废约史》，中华书局，2005年。

33. 陈学恂、田正平编，《留学教育》，上海教育出版社，2007年。

34. 陈存仁，《银元时代生活史》，广西师范大学出版社，2007年。

35. 张鸣，《北洋裂变：军阀与五四》，广西师范大学出版社，2010年。

36. 李玉贞，《国民党与共产国际（1919—1927）》，人民出版社，2012年。

37. 张畅、刘悦，《李鸿章的洋顾问：德璀琳与汉纳根》，台北传记文学出版社，2012年。

38. 傅光明，《凌叔华：古韵精魂》，大象出版社，2004年。

39. 金凤，《邓颖超传》，人民出版社，1993年。

40. 王忠和，《吕碧城传》，百花文艺出版社，2010年。

41. 丁言模，《张太雷传》，上海辞书出版社，2011年。

42. 李良玉、吴修申主编，《倪嗣冲与北洋军阀》，黄山书社，2012年。

43. 郑毓秀，《不寻常的玫瑰枝：郑毓秀自述》，中国法制出版社，2018年。

44. （美）马士著，张汇文等译，《中华帝国对外关系史》，上海书店出版社，2006年。

45. （英）雷穆森著，许逸凡等译，《天津租界史（插图本）》，天津人民出版社，2009年。

46. （美）威罗贝著，王绍坊译，《外人在华特权和利益》，生活·读书·新知三联书店，1957年。

47. （英）菲利浦·约瑟夫著，胡滨译，《列强对华外交（1894—1900）：对华政治经济关系的研究》，商务印书馆，1959年。

48. （美）费正清等编，中国社会科学院历史研究所编译室译，《剑桥中国晚清史.1800—1911》，中国社会科学出版社，1985年。

49. （英）魏尔特著，陈敉才等译，《赫德与中国海关》，厦门大学出版社，1993年。

50. （美）保罗·福塞尔著，梁丽真等译，《格调：社会等级与生活品味》，中国社会科学出版社，1998年。

51. （法）费尔南·布罗代尔著，顾良等译，《十五至十八世纪的物质文明、经济与资本主义》，生活·读书·新知三联书店，2002年。

52. （美）魏斐德著，芮传明译，《上海歹土——战时恐怖活动与城市犯罪，1937—1941》，上海古籍出版社，2003年。

53. （比）比利时驻华大使馆、《使馆商社贸易快讯》杂志社编，《走进比利时》，世界在线外交传媒集团，2004年。

54. （加）卜正民、格力高利·布鲁主编，古伟瀛等译，《中国与历史资本主义：汉学知识的系谱学》，新星出版社，2005年。

55. （德）马克斯·韦伯著，王容芬译，《世界宗教的经济伦理·儒教与道教》，广西师范大学出版社，2008 年。

56. （美）特拉维斯·黑尼斯三世、弗兰克·萨奈罗著，周辉荣译，《鸦片战争》，生活·读书·新知三联书店，2005 年。

57. （美）刘易斯·芒福德著，宋俊岭等译，《城市文化》，中国建筑工业出版社，2009 年。

58. （美）史瀚波著，池桢译，《乱世中的信任：民国时期天津的货币、银行及国家 – 社会关系》，上海辞书出版社，2016 年。

59. （美）齐锡生著，杨云若、萧延中译，《中国的军阀政治（1916—1928）》，中国人民大学出版社，2010 年。

60. （美）阿尔弗雷德·考尼比斯著，刘悦译，《扛龙旗的美国大兵：美国第十五步兵团在中国 1912~1938》，作家出版社，2011 年。

61. （美）德龄著，顾秋心译，《清宫二年记》，中国人民大学出版社，2012 年。

62. （美）周策纵著，陈永明等译，《"五四"运动史》，世界图书出版公司，2016 年。

63. （比）约翰·麦特勒等著，刘悦等译，《比利时—中国：昔日之路（1870—1930）》，社会科学文献出版社，2021 年。

64. Austin Coates, *China Races*, Cambridge: Oxford University Press, 1983.

65. Roderick Floud, *Labour Marker Evolution, The Economic History of Britain Since 1700*, Cambridge University Press, 1994.

· 文章类 ·

1. 列岛编，《鸦片战争史论文专集》，生活·读书·新知三联书店，1958 年。

2. 黄逸平编，《中国近代经济史论文选集（二）》，上海师范大学历史系，1979 年。

3. 刘正刚，《清代以来广东人在天津的经济活动》，《中国经济史研究》2002 年第 3 期。

4. 刘莉萍，《社会变迁中的天津会馆》，《聊城大学学报》（社会科学版）2008 年第 4 期。

5. 来新夏，《天津早期民族近代工业发展简况及黄金时期资本来源的特点》，天津市政协文史资料未刊稿。

6. 王素香、李丽敏，《解放前天津历年水灾概况》，《天津档案史料》，1966 年创刊号。

7. 张畅，《近代西方侨民来华原因剖析》，《天津师范大学学报（社会科学版）》，2007 年第 5 期。

8. 姚涵、潘乐，《十月革命"一声炮响"怎样传入中国》，《解放日报》，2021 年 6 月 29 日。

9. 涂小元等，《辛亥革命后天津兵变发生的缘起及影响》，《天津史志》，1998 年第 4 期。

10. 郭立珍，《近代天津居民饮食消费变动及影响探究——以英敛之日记为中心》，《历史教学》，2011 年第 3 期。

11. 杨丽娜、孙世圃，《浅论天津近代服饰变革及其在我国服装发展演变中的重要影响》，《中国轻工教育》，2009 年第 1 期。

12. （法）多米尼克·马亚尔、曲辰，《第一次世界大战期间在法国的中国劳工》，《国际观察》，2009 年第 2 期。

13. （比）Dominiek Dendooven & Piet Chielens, *La Cinq Premiere Continents Guerre au Front Mondiale*, (Editions Racine, 2008)。

14. 高旺，《清末地方自治运动及其对近代中国政治发展的影响》，《天津社会科学》，2001 年第 3 期。

· 网上资料 ·

1. "The Queen's rejoin the China Station: 1930". https://www.queensroyalsurreys. org.uk/1661to1966/hongkong_china/hkc08_1.shtml.

2. "中国北方外国人的"圣经"：《京津泰晤士报》（*Peking & Tientsin Times*）"。http://www.022tj.net/tianjinwei/article.php?itemid–12–type–news.html.

3. 天津档案方志网。https://www.tjdag.gov.cn/zh_tjdag/jytj/jgsl/jgfq/details/ 1594032502517.html.